BUILDING CONSTRUCTION ILLUSTRATED

BUILDING CONSTRUCTION ILLUSTRATED

SECOND EDITION

FRANCIS D.K. CHING
WITH CASSANDRA ADAMS

VNR **VAN NOSTRAND REINHOLD**
New York

I⊤P™ A division of International Thomson Publishing, Inc.
The ITP logo is a trademark under license

Printed in the United States of America

For more information, contact:

Van Nostrand Reinhold
115 Fifth Avenue
New York, NY 10003

Chapman & Hall GmbH
Pappelallee 3
69469 Weinheim
Germany

Chapman & Hall
2-6 Boundary Row
London
SE1 8HN
United Kingdom

International Thomson Publishing Asia
221 Henderson Road #05-10
Henderson Building
Singapore 0315

Thomas Nelson Australia
102 Dodds Street
South Melbourne, 3205
Victoria, Australia

International Thomson Publishing Japan
Hirakawacho Kyowa Building, 3F
2-2-1 Hirakawacho
Chiyoda-ku, 102 Tokyo
Japan

Nelson Canada
1120 Birchmount Road
Scarborough, Ontario
Canada M1K 5G4

International Thomson Editores
Campos Eliseos 385, Piso 7
Col. Polanco
11560 Mexico D.F. Mexico

97 98 99 00 01 EDW 15 14 13 12 11 10

Library of Congress Cataloging-in-Publication Data
Ching, Francis D.K., 1943–
    Building construction illustrated / Francis D.K. Ching;
with Cassandra Adams.—2nd ed.
        p.   cm.
    Includes bibliographical references and index.
    ISBN 0-442-23498-8 (pbk.)
    ISBN 0-442-00895-3 (cloth)
    1. Building.   2. House construction.
I. Adams, Cassandra.   II. Title.
TH146.C52   1991
690—dc20

PREFACE

The original edition of this illustrated guide to building construction introduced the student of architecture and interested lay people to the basic principles of how buildings are built. It provided an overview of the major systems of a building, how each is constructed, and how each is influenced by its relationship to other systems. While this second edition retains this perspective, it updates information where appropriate, and includes coverage of basic structural steel, reinforced concrete, and curtain wall systems. It presents as clearly as possible the material and structural choices available to the designer, and how these choices affect a building's form and dimensions, and its relationship to its site. Since this visual imagery is implicitly a very important element in the presentation of the material, information in this second edition continues to be conveyed primarily through graphic illustrations.

This handbook is organized according to a building's major components and systems. It begins with a look at the building site and the factors that influence a building's location, organization, and orientation. Following this is a description of a building's major systems, how they relate to each other, and the structural forces a building must be designed and constructed to resist. Each succeeding chapter then describes a major building system according to type of building material, structural geometry, and how each component interfaces with adjoining systems. The last chapter and the appendix provide reference information on building materials and space planning. The bibliography lists sources which, if one is interested in pursuing a subject further, can provide more in-depth information.

It would be nearly impossible to cover all building materials and construction techniques, but the information presented here should be applicable to most residential and light construction situations encountered today. Construction techniques continue to change with the development of new building materials, products, and standards. What does not change are the fundamental principles which underlie the design and construction of a building. This illustrated guide focuses on these principles, which should provide a useful context for the application of new information in the preliminary planning and design of a building.

Each building element, component, or system is described in terms of its end use. The specific form, quality, capability, and availability of an element or component will vary with manufacturer and locale. It is therefore important to always follow the manufacturer's recommendations in the use of a material and to pay careful attention to the building code requirements in effect for a building's use and location. It is the user's responsibility to judge the appropriateness of the information contained in this book and how it is to be used. Seek the expert advice of a professional when needed. On the following page is an outline of the basic considerations which may be applied to almost any building material, component, or system to measure its appropriateness for a given design or construction situation.

The information in this book can be categorized according to the following factors:

MATERIALS............ • Structural properties (see STRUCTURE below)
                                 • Physical properties of..... ○ Weight and density
                                                       ○ Thermal expansion and conductivity
   ○ Permeability to water vapor
   ○ Fire resistance
   ○ Acoustical value
     • Form, dimensional characteristics, and visual properties
     • Durability — resistance to ○ Physical wear and abrasion
   ○ The effects of sun, wind, and rain
   ○ Corrosion caused by moisture or chemical action
     • Finish and maintenance requirements
     • Method of manufacture and supply

STRUCTURE............ • Form and geometry: linear, planar, or volumetric
     • Forces to be resolved..... ○ Compressive, tensile, shear
   ○ Vertical (downward or uplift), lateral, or angled
   ○ Concentrated or uniformly distributed
   ○ Static dead and live loads; dynamic wind and
     seismic forces
     • Strength, stiffness, and elasticity of the materials used
     • Types of connections required
   ○ Pinned, rigid, or roller joints
   ○ Butt, lap, or interlocking connections
     • Foundation, bearing, and support requirements
     • Structural requirements for cantilevers, suspended construction, and openings

CONSTRUCTION......... • Number and sizes of the pieces to be assembled
     • Modular constraints, if any
     • Method of fastening required
   ○ Mechanical (nails, screws, bolts, rivets, clips)
   ○ Welded
   ○ Adhesive
     • Equipment, tools, and workmanship required
     • Place of assembly: on-site or at the factory
     • Standardization of parts and prefabrication where advantageous
     • Work coordination, erection time, and labor requirements

THE CONSTRUCTION
ASSEMBLY............. • Control of the flow of Heat ○ Thermal conductivity and reflectivity
   ○ Thermal expansion characteristics
     Air ○ Ventilation and infiltration
     Water ○ Permeability to water vapor
   ○ Waterproofing requirements
   ○ Ice and snow protection
     • Fire resistance and acoustical rating
     • Construction thickness or depth
     • Accommodation of mechanical and electrical equipment and systems

GENERAL FACTORS..... • Fitness for use and purpose
     • Safety, comfort, and health requirements
     • Compliance with applicable building codes
     • Initial and life costs

CONTENTS

THE BUILDING SITE 1

In planning the design and construction of a building, we should carefully consider the environmental forces which the physical context for the building—its site—presents. A site's geographic location, topography, plant materials, climate, and orientation to the sun and prevailing winds all influence decisions at a very early stage in the design process. These environmental forces can help shape a building's form, articulate its enclosure, establish its relationship to the ground plane, and suggest the way its interior spaces are laid out.

In addition to environmental forces, there may exist the regulatory forces of zoning ordinances. These regulations may prescribe acceptable uses for a building site as well as limit the size and shape of the building mass and where it may be located on the site.

Included in this chapter are site improvements which modify a building site for access and use, define the boundaries of exterior spaces, and relate the building to the surrounding ground plane. These construction details typically are closely related to the design of the building itself and can be seen to be logical extensions of the way the building is constructed.

GEOGRAPHIC FACTORS:

SOIL

The soil type affects:
- the type and size of a building's foundation system
- the drainage of ground and surface water
- the types of plant material able to grow on a site

TOPOGRAPHY

Land forms and ground slopes affect:
- the building foundation type
- the building form and its relationship to the ground plane
- site drainage
- the site's micro-climate: wind, temperature, solar radiation

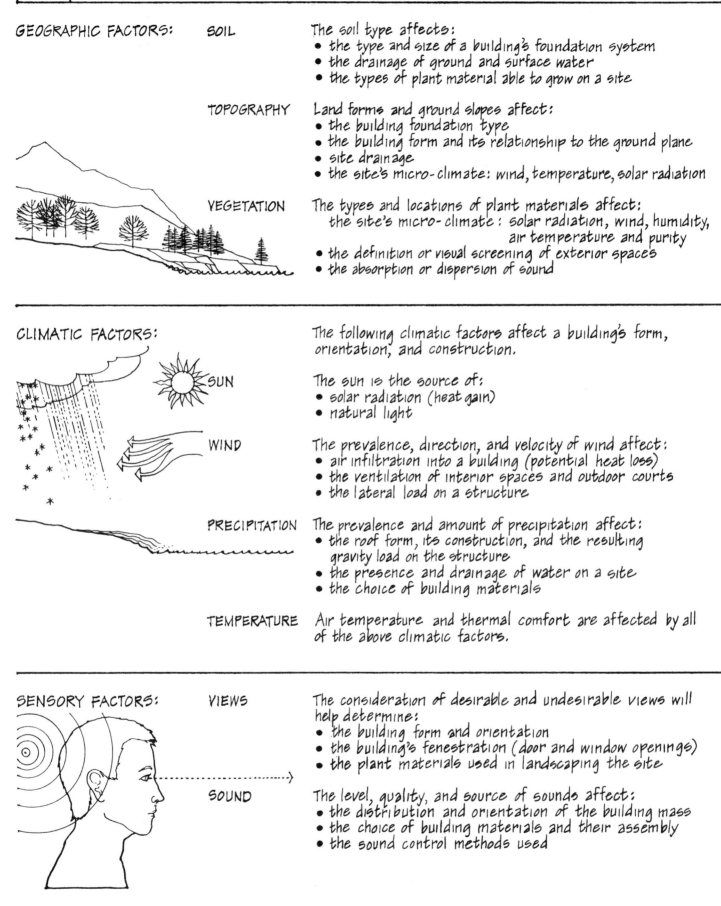

VEGETATION

The types and locations of plant materials affect:
  the site's micro-climate: solar radiation, wind, humidity, air temperature and purity
- the definition or visual screening of exterior spaces
- the absorption or dispersion of sound

CLIMATIC FACTORS:

The following climatic factors affect a building's form, orientation, and construction.

SUN

The sun is the source of:
- solar radiation (heat gain)
- natural light

WIND

The prevalence, direction, and velocity of wind affect:
- air infiltration into a building (potential heat loss)
- the ventilation of interior spaces and outdoor courts
- the lateral load on a structure

PRECIPITATION

The prevalence and amount of precipitation affect:
- the roof form, its construction, and the resulting gravity load on the structure
- the presence and drainage of water on a site
- the choice of building materials

TEMPERATURE

Air temperature and thermal comfort are affected by all of the above climatic factors.

SENSORY FACTORS:

VIEWS

The consideration of desirable and undesirable views will help determine:
- the building form and orientation
- the building's fenestration (door and window openings)
- the plant materials used in landscaping the site

SOUND

The level, quality, and source of sounds affect:
- the distribution and orientation of the building mass
- the choice of building materials and their assembly
- the sound control methods used

Zoning ordinances govern the use and bulk of buildings and structures within a municipality or land use district. These ordinances typically regulate:

ZONING ORDINANCES REGULATE

- the types of activities which may occur on a given piece of land

LAND USE

- how much of the land can be covered by a building
- how far a building must be set back from each of the property lines
- how tall the building structure can be
- the total floor area that can be constructed

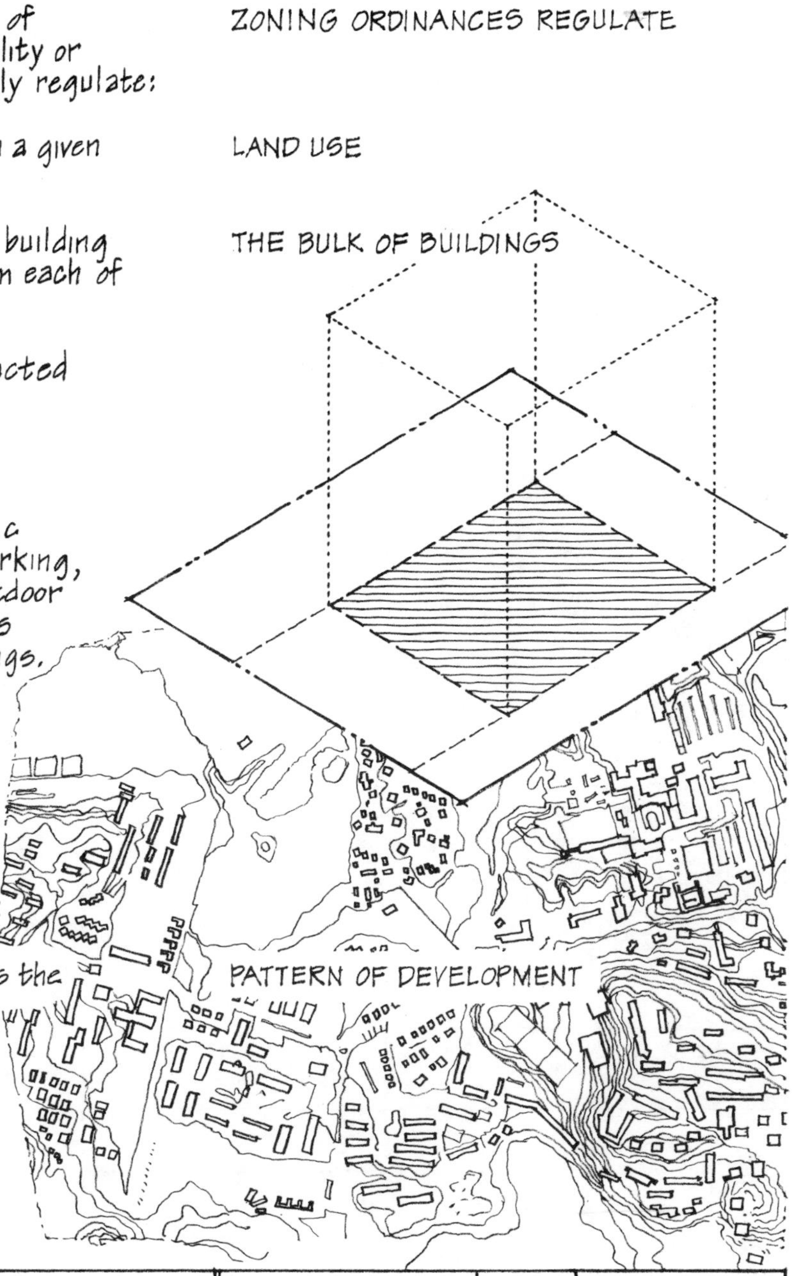

THE BULK OF BUILDINGS

A zoning ordinance may also contain specific requirements for access and off-street parking, accessory structures such as fences and outdoor decks, and the projections from a building's facades such as balconies and roof overhangs.

The cumulative effect of zoning ordinances is the management of the density and pattern of development within various land use zones.

PATTERN OF DEVELOPMENT

Other regulatory instruments exist which affect the way buildings are sited and constructed. These statutes — commonly referred to as the building code — establish the relationship between:

- the type of occupancy a building houses
- the fire-resistance rating of its structure and construction
- the allowable height and floor areas of the building, and its separation from neighboring structures

See Appendix for more information on building codes.

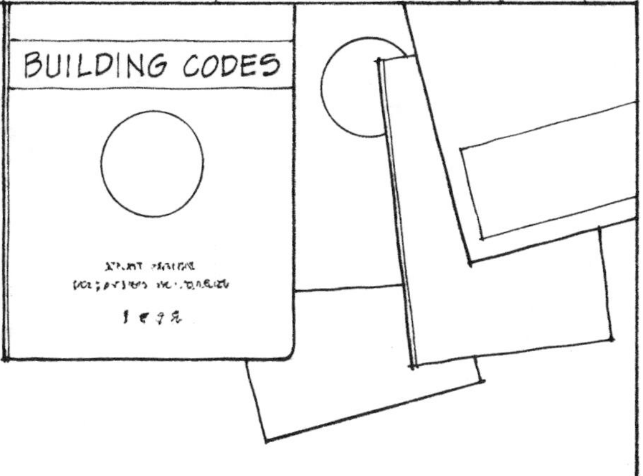

BUILDING CODES

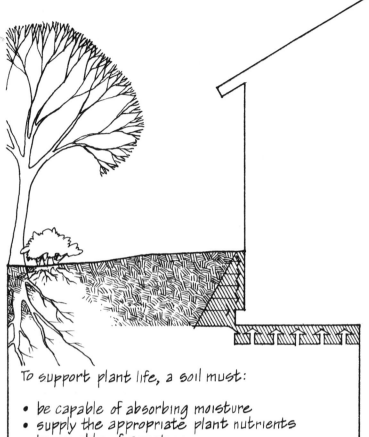

To support plant life, a soil must:

• be capable of absorbing moisture
• supply the appropriate plant nutrients
• be capable of aeration
• be free of concentrated salts

Practically all buildings rely on soil for their ultimate support. The integrity of a building structure therefore depends ultimately on the type of soil underlying the foundation and the soil's strength under loading.

There are two broad classes of soils— coarse-grained and fine-grained soils. Coarse-grained soils include gravels and sands which consist of relatively large particles. The individual particles of fine-grained soils are much smaller and often cannot be seen by the eye. The soil underlying a building site may actually consist of superimposed layers, each of which contains a mix of soil types.

A soil's stability and strength under loading depends largely on its resistance to shear, which is a function of both its internal friction and its cohesiveness. Coarse-grained soils with a relatively low percentage of void spaces are more stable as a foundation material than silt or clay. Clay soils, in particular, tend to be unstable since they shrink and swell considerably with changes in moisture content.

SOIL CLASSIFICATION		Sieve Size	Particle Size (mm)
Coarse-grained soils	Cobbles	> 3"	> 60.
	Coarse gravel	> 3/4"	> 19.
	Fine gravel	> Nº 4	> 5.5
	Coarse sand	> Nº 10	> 2.0
	Medium sand	> Nº 40	> 0.6
	Fine sand	> Nº 200	> 0.08
Fine-grained soils	Fines (silt and clay)	< Nº 200	< 0.08

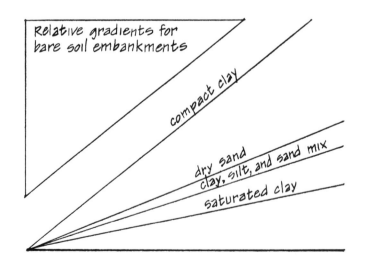

Relative gradients for bare soil embankments

compact clay

dry sand
clay, silt, and sand mix

saturated clay

On sloping sites, and during the excavation of a flat site, a soil's potential for lateral displacement should be considered. The natural angle of repose for dry, granular soils tend to be shallower than for more cohesive soils like compacted clay.

The usual measure of a soil's strength is its bearing capacity in pounds per square foot. A foundation system must distribute a building's loads in such a way that the resultant unit load on the soil does not exceed the soil's bearing capacity and is uniform under all portions of the structure. While high bearing capacity soils present few problems, low bearing capacity soils may dictate the type of foundation and load distribution pattern for a building, which in turn affects the building's form. Unstable soils usually render a site unbuildable unless an elaborately engineered and expensive foundation system is put in place.

The table below outlines, for reference only, the relative strengths of various soil types. Refer to the local building code for the allowable bearing capacities of general classes of soils. Most soils are in fact a combination of different soil types. The stratification, composition, and density of the soil bed, variations in particle size, and the presence or absence of water are all important factors in determining a soil's bearing capacity. When designing a sizable structure or when there are unusual load conditions, it is advisable to have a soils engineer test borings taken from the actual site.

- In cold weather, the freezing and subsequent thawing of soil can cause ground heaving, which places stress on a building's foundation and structure. The extent of this frost action depends on the site's geographic region and the soil type. Fine-grained soils are more susceptible to frost action than coarse-grained soils. In any case, a building's footings should always be placed well below the site's frost line.

- A soil's permeability should also be taken into account to ensure that surface and ground water can be properly channeled away from the building structure. Proper drainage is required to avoid deterioration of a soil's bearing capacity and to minimize the possibility of water leaking into a building's interior. Coarse-grained soils are more permeable and drain better than fine-grained soils. Fine silts and clays also have greater capillarity which can cause water to migrate upward above a site's water table.

SOIL TYPE	Presumed Bearing Capacity (tons/ft.²)	(kg/m²)	Susceptibility to Frost Action	Drainage (permeability)
Compact, partially cemented gravel; well-graded with little or no fines	10	97 650	none	excellent
Compact gravel; gravel and sand mixtures	6	58 590	none	excellent
Coarse, compact sand; loose gravel; hard, dry clay	4	39 060	slight	fair to good
Coarse, loose sand and gravel mixtures; fine, compact sand	3	29 295	slight	fair to good
Fine, loose sand; dry, stiff clay	2	19 530	high	fair to poor
Soft clay; soft, broken shale	1.5	14 648	high	poor
Organic soils	Unsuitable as a foundation material; can be highly unstable due to bacterial decomposition and changes in moisture content			

All of the following factors
affect variations in local climate:

- ground elevation
- land forms
- site orientation and slope
- types of ground cover
- large bodies of water

- temperature in the atmosphere decreases
  with altitude—approximately 1°F for every
  400 feet in elevation (1°F = 0.5556 °C)

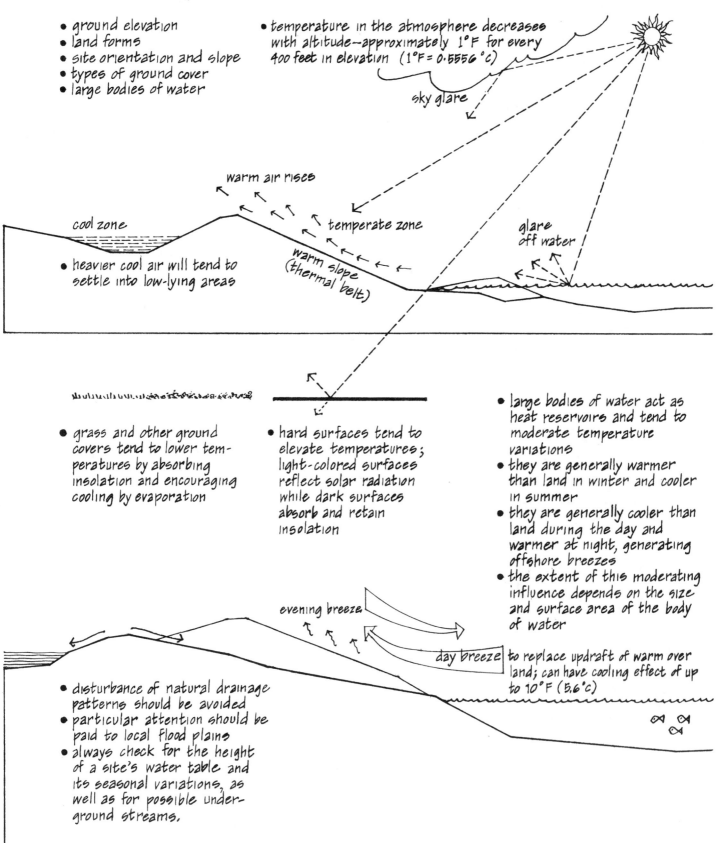

sky glare

warm air rises

cool zone

temperate zone

glare
off water

- heavier cool air will tend to
  settle into low-lying areas

warm slope
(thermal belt)

- grass and other ground
  covers tend to lower temperatures by absorbing
  insolation and encouraging
  cooling by evaporation

- hard surfaces tend to
  elevate temperatures;
  light-colored surfaces
  reflect solar radiation
  while dark surfaces
  absorb and retain
  insolation

- large bodies of water act as
  heat reservoirs and tend to
  moderate temperature
  variations
- they are generally warmer
  than land in winter and cooler
  in summer
- they are generally cooler than
  land during the day and
  warmer at night, generating
  offshore breezes
- the extent of this moderating
  influence depends on the size
  and surface area of the body
  of water

evening breeze

day breeze to replace updraft of warm over
land; can have cooling effect of up
to 10°F (5.6°C)

- disturbance of natural drainage
  patterns should be avoided
- particular attention should be
  paid to local flood plains
- always check for the height
  of a site's water table and
  its seasonal variations, as
  well as for possible underground streams.

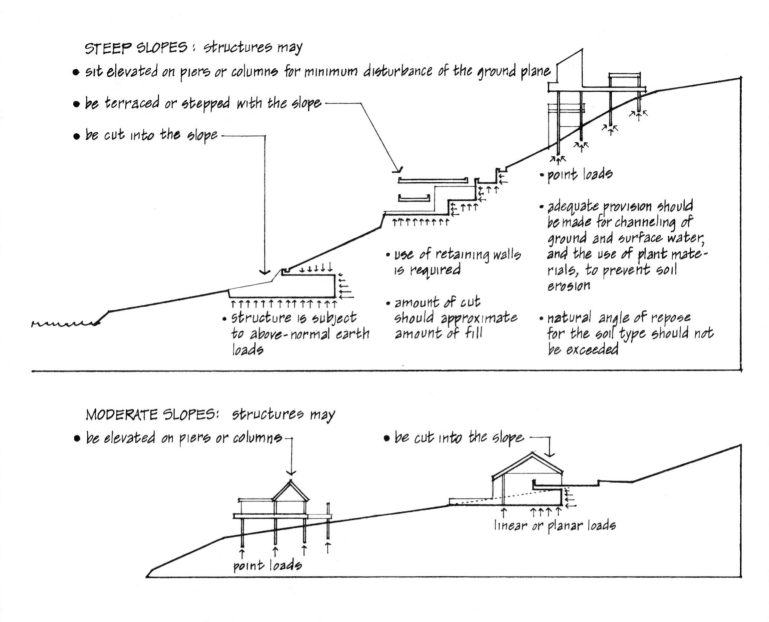

STEEP SLOPES: structures may

- sit elevated on piers or columns for minimum disturbance of the ground plane
- be terraced or stepped with the slope
- be cut into the slope

- point loads

- adequate provision should be made for channeling of ground and surface water, and the use of plant materials, to prevent soil erosion

- use of retaining walls is required

- amount of cut should approximate amount of fill

- natural angle of repose for the soil type should not be exceeded

- structure is subject to above-normal earth loads

MODERATE SLOPES: structures may

- be elevated on piers or columns
- be cut into the slope

linear or planar loads

point loads

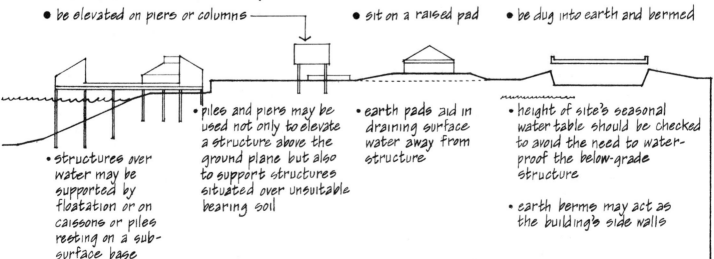

FLAT SLOPES: structures may

- be elevated on piers or columns
- sit on a raised pad
- be dug into earth and bermed

- structures over water may be supported by floatation or on caissons or piles resting on a sub-surface base

- piles and piers may be used not only to elevate a structure above the ground plane but also to support structures situated over unsuitable bearing soil

- earth pads aid in draining surface water away from structure

- height of site's seasonal water table should be checked to avoid the need to waterproof the below-grade structure

- earth berms may act as the building's side walls

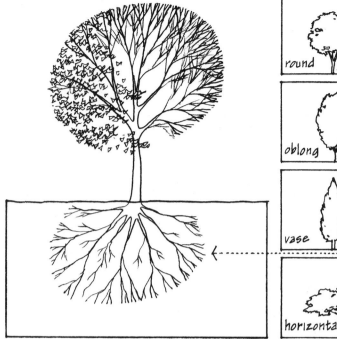

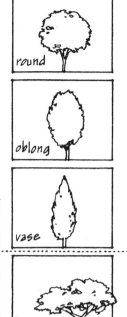

round

oblong

vase

horizontal

Factors to consider in the selection and use of trees in landscaping include:

- form, density, texture, and color of the foliage
- potential growth height and spread
- speed or rate of growth
- size and depth of the root structure
- requirements for soil, water, sunlight, air and temperature

- the root systems of trees planted too close to a building may disturb the foundation system
- similarly, a tree's root structure may interfere with underground utility lines

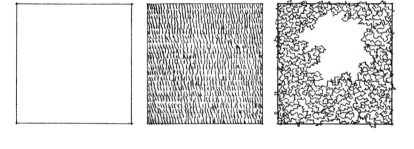

- the manner in which trees and other plant life adapt their forms to climate provides clues to the ways buildings might do the same

Grass and other ground covers:

- can reduce air temperatures by absorbing insolation and encouraging cooling by evaporation
- aid in stabilizing soil and preventing erosion
- increase a soil's permeability to air and water

- Vines can reduce the heat transmission through a sunlit wall by providing shade and cooling the immediate environment by evaporation

Trees affect the immediate environment of a building by:

- providing shade
  the amount of shade depends on the tree's
    - orientation to the sun
    - proximity to the building
    - shape, spread, and height
    - density and branch structure

    - deciduous trees provide shade and glare protection during the summer, and let solar radiation (as well as glare) through during the winter
    - evergreens provide shade throughout the year and help reduce snow glare during the winter

- reducing sky, ground, and snow glare

- providing wind protection
    - foliage reduces wind-blown dust
    - evergreens can form effective windbreaks during the winter and reduce a building's heat losses

- intercepting precipitation and filtering the air

- aiding in soil stabilization, increasing its permeability to water and air, and preventing erosion

- defining space and directing views

- providing visual screening and privacy

- attenuating airborne sounds

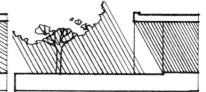

- trees shade a building most effectively from the southeast and the southwest when the morning and late afternoon sun has a low altitude and casts long shadows
- south-facing overhangs provide more efficient shading during the midday period when the sun is high and casts short shadows

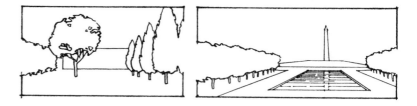

A partially penetrable windbreak can actually extend leeward shadow

H = height of trees

2-5H — windward if trees are dense
10-15H — leeward wind shadow

- the approximate area of protection indicated above varies with the height and density of the trees, and with wind velocity
- the protection provided is primarily a reduction in wind velocity producing an area of relative calm

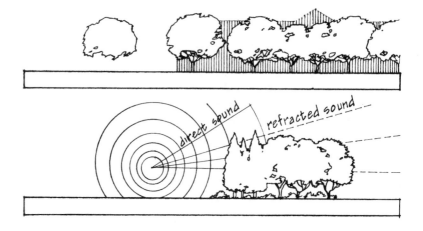

direct sound
refracted sound

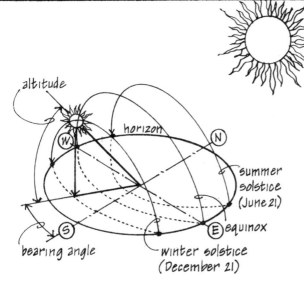

altitude

horizon

W

N

summer solstice (June 21)

S

E equinox

bearing angle

winter solstice (December 21)

A building's location, orientation, and form should take advantage of the sun's thermal, hygienic, and psychological benefits. The sun's radiation, however, may not always be beneficial, depending on the building site's climate. In determining a building's form and orientation, the objective should be to maintain a balance between underheated periods when solar radiation is beneficial and overheated periods when radiation should be avoided. The long face of a building should normally face south if possible. East and west exposures are generally warmer in summer and cooler in winter than southern exposures.

The sun's path through the sky varies with the seasons and a site's latitude. Its altitude and bearing angle range should be determined before calculating solar heat gain and shading requirements for a specific site.

The table below pertains primarily to isolated buildings. The information presented should be considered along with other contextual and programmatic requirements.

OPTIMUM SHAPE	LOCATION	GENERAL OBJECTIVES	ORIENTATION
low temperatures encourage minimizing of a building's surface area		COOL REGIONS • increase solar radiation absorption • reduce radiation, conduction, and evaporation heat loss • provide wind protection	
temperate climate allows for elongation along the east-west axis		TEMPERATE REGIONS • balance solar heat gain with shade protection on a seasonal basis • encourage air movement in hot weather; protect from wind in cold weather	
closed forms; building mass enclosing cool air ponds desirable		HOT-ARID REGIONS • reduce solar radiation and conduction heat gain • promote cooling by evaporation using water and plantings • provide shade	
form may be freely elongated along east-west axis to minimize east and west exposure		HOT-HUMID REGIONS • reduce solar heat gain • utilize wind to promote cooling by evaporation • provide shade	

Shading devices shield a building's exterior surfaces and interior spaces from solar radiation. Their effectiveness depends on their form and orientation relative to the sun's angles. Exterior shading devices are more efficient than those located within a building's spaces since they intercept the sun's radiation before it can reach the building's surfaces.

Below are illustrated basic types of solar shading devices. Their orientation, form, materials, and construction may vary to suit specific situations. Their visual qualities (pattern, texture, rhythm, and the shadows they cast) contribute much to a building's appearance.

Since a building's exterior walls and roof are its primary sheltering elements against solar radiation, the materials used in their construction should be considered in terms of their reflectivity and thermal conductivity. A material's reflectivity depends on its color and texture. Light colors and shiny surfaces tend to reflect more radiation than dark, textured ones. Effective insulating materials usually incorporate some form of captured dead air space. Massive materials such as masonry absorb and store heat for a period of time, thus delaying heat transmission.

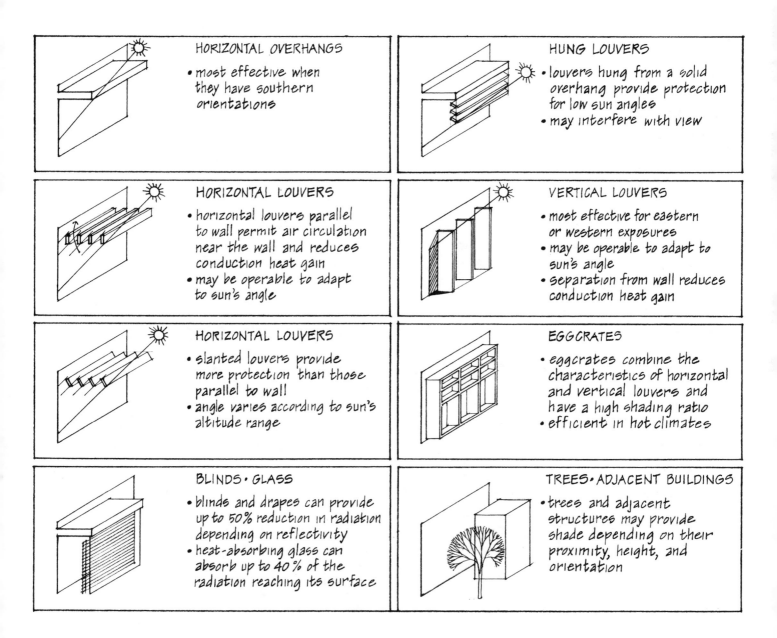

HORIZONTAL OVERHANGS
- most effective when they have southern orientations

HUNG LOUVERS
- louvers hung from a solid overhang provide protection for low sun angles
- may interfere with view

HORIZONTAL LOUVERS
- horizontal louvers parallel to wall permit air circulation near the wall and reduces conduction heat gain
- may be operable to adapt to sun's angle

VERTICAL LOUVERS
- most effective for eastern or western exposures
- may be operable to adapt to sun's angle
- separation from wall reduces conduction heat gain

HORIZONTAL LOUVERS
- slanted louvers provide more protection than those parallel to wall
- angle varies according to sun's altitude range

EGGCRATES
- eggcrates combine the characteristics of horizontal and vertical louvers and have a high shading ratio
- efficient in hot climates

BLINDS · GLASS
- blinds and drapes can provide up to 50% reduction in radiation depending on reflectivity
- heat-absorbing glass can absorb up to 40% of the radiation reaching its surface

TREES · ADJACENT BUILDINGS
- trees and adjacent structures may provide shade depending on their proximity, height, and orientation

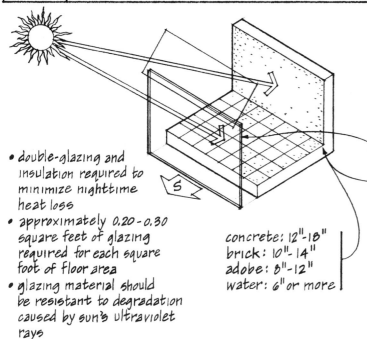

Passive solar design refers to using the sun's energy to heat a building's interior spaces through nonmechanical means. Passive solar systems rely on the natural heat transfer processes of conduction, convection, and radiation for the collection, storage, distribution, and control of solar energy. There are two basic elements in every passive solar system:

① south-facing glass or transparent plastic for solar collection
② thermal mass for heat collection, storage, and distribution, oriented to receive maximum solar exposure

The thermal mass allows the sun's heat to be absorbed and retained until it is needed, and also helps to reduce internal temperature fluctuations.

Based on the relationship between the sun, the interior space, and the heat collection system, there are three ways in which passive solar heating can be accomplished: direct gain, indirect gain, and isolated gain.

- double-glazing and insulation required to minimize nighttime heat loss
- approximately 0.20 - 0.30 square feet of glazing required for each square foot of floor area
- glazing material should be resistant to degradation caused by sun's ultraviolet rays

concrete: 12"-18"
brick: 10"-14"
adobe: 8"-12"
water: 6" or more

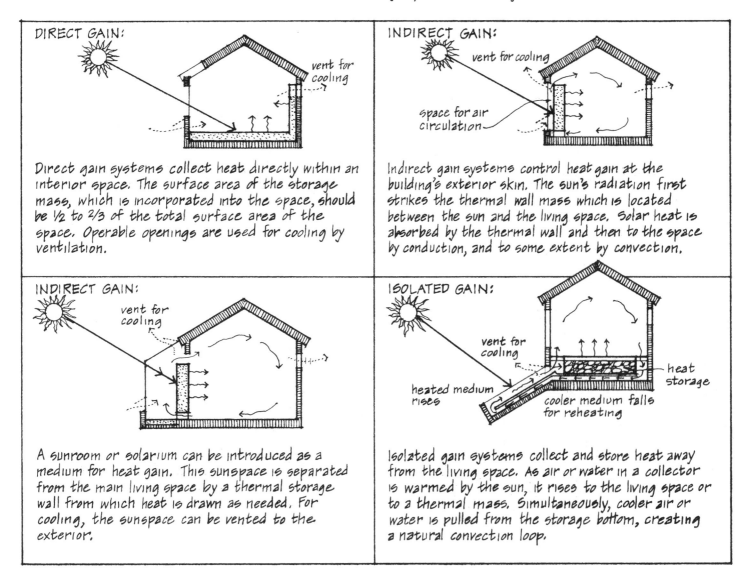

DIRECT GAIN:

vent for cooling

Direct gain systems collect heat directly within an interior space. The surface area of the storage mass, which is incorporated into the space, should be ½ to ⅔ of the total surface area of the space. Operable openings are used for cooling by ventilation.

INDIRECT GAIN:

vent for cooling

space for air circulation

Indirect gain systems control heat gain at the building's exterior skin. The sun's radiation first strikes the thermal wall mass which is located between the sun and the living space. Solar heat is absorbed by the thermal wall and then to the space by conduction, and to some extent by convection.

INDIRECT GAIN:

vent for cooling

A sunroom or solarium can be introduced as a medium for heat gain. This sunspace is separated from the main living space by a thermal storage wall from which heat is drawn as needed. For cooling, the sunspace can be vented to the exterior.

ISOLATED GAIN:

vent for cooling

heated medium rises

cooler medium falls for reheating

heat storage

Isolated gain systems collect and store heat away from the living space. As air or water in a collector is warmed by the sun, it rises to the living space or to a thermal mass. Simultaneously, cooler air or water is pulled from the storage bottom, creating a natural convection loop.

DAYLIGHTING

The sun's radiation provides not only heat but also light for a building's interior spaces. This daylight has psychological benefit as well as practical utility. While intense, the sun's light will vary with the time of day, from season to season, and from place to place. It can be diffused by cloud cover, haze, and precipitation, and reflected from the ground and other surrounding surfaces. The quantity and quality of daylighting in a space are determined primarily by the size and orientation of its window openings.

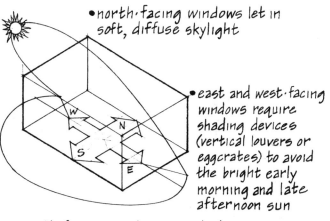

- north-facing windows let in soft, diffuse skylight
- east and west-facing windows require shading devices (vertical louvers or eggcrates) to avoid the bright early morning and late afternoon sun
- south-facing windows are ideal sources for daylight if horizontal shading devices can control excessive solar radiation and glare

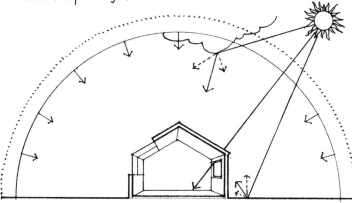

The level of illumination provided by daylight falls off as it penetrates an interior space. Generally, the larger and higher a window is, the more daylight will enter a room. A useful rule of thumb is that daylighting can be effective for task illumination up to a depth of twice the height of a window.

The ceiling and back wall of a space are more effective than the side walls or the floor in the reflection and distribution of daylight. Light-colored surfaces reflect and distribute light more efficiently but large areas of shiny surfaces can cause glare.

Excessive brightness ratios can lead to glare and impairment of visual performance. There are two types of glare. Direct glare is caused by the excessive contrast between light in our normal field of vision and the subject of a visual task. Indirect glare is caused by a task surface reflecting a light source into our eyes. Glare can be controlled by the use of shading devices, the proper orientation of task surfaces, and allowing daylight to enter a space from at least two directions.

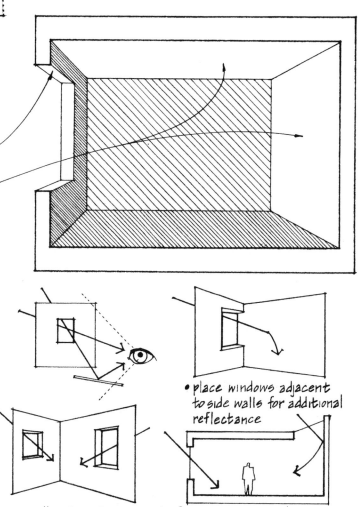

- place windows adjacent to side walls for additional reflectance
- allow light to penetrate from at least two directions

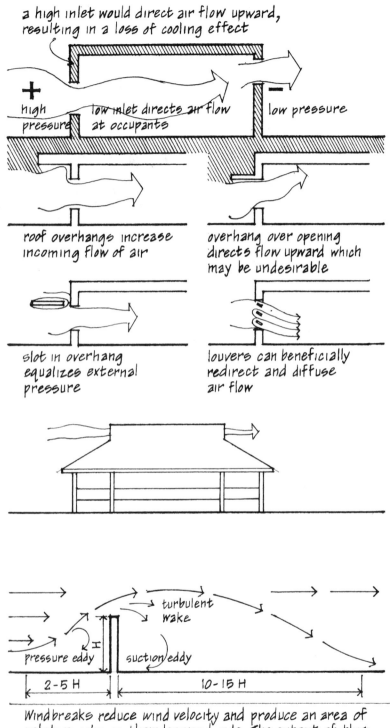

a high inlet would direct air flow upward, resulting in a loss of cooling effect

+ high pressure

low inlet directs air flow at occupants

− low pressure

roof overhangs increase incoming flow of air

overhang over opening directs flow upward which may be undesirable

slot in overhang equalizes external pressure

louvers can beneficially redirect and diffuse air flow

turbulent wake

pressure eddy   suction eddy

2-5 H   10-15 H

Windbreaks reduce wind velocity and produce an area of relative calm on their leeward side. The extent of this wind shadow depends on a windbreak's height, density, depth, and orientation to the wind.

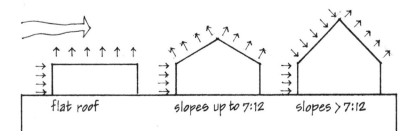

flat roof   slopes up to 7:12   slopes > 7:12

Wind prevalence, velocity, temperature, and direction are important site considerations in all climatic regions. In evaluating the wind's potential effect on a building, its seasonal and daily variations should be carefully considered.

Wind-induced ventilation of interior spaces aids in the air exchange necessary for health and odor removal. In hot weather, and especially in humid climates, ventilation is beneficial for convective or evaporative cooling.

Natural ventilation in buildings is generated by differences in air pressure as well as temperature. The resulting air flow patterns are affected more by building geometry than by air speed.

- position of outlet has little effect on air flow pattern, but should be high to let rising warm air escape
- outlet should be as large or larger than inlet for maximum air flow
- interior partitions and large furnishings may adversely alter air flow patterns

The ventilation of concealed roof and crawl spaces is required to remove moisture and control condensation. In hot weather, attic ventilation can also reduce overhead radiant heat gain.

A building should be buffered against cold winds to reduce air infiltration into its interior and lower heat loss. A windbreak may be in the form of an earth beam, a garden wall, or dense trees.

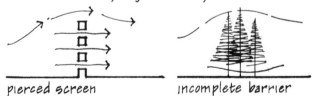

pierced screen   incomplete barrier

A partially penetrable windscreen creates less pressure differential, resulting in a larger wind shadow to the lee side of the screen.

Wind creates pressure on the windward side of a building and suction on its other three sides. Wind also produces suction on flat roofs, on the leeward side of sloping roofs, and even on the windward side of roofs with a pitch less than 7:12.

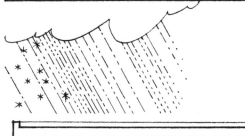

- flat roofs require either interior roof drains or scuppers along their perimeter
- water-cooled roofs used in hot-dry climates must support above normal roof loads
- in cold climates, flat roofs are subject to heavy snow loads; layer of snow can act as additional insulation

- moderately pitched roofs easily shed rain but may hold snow

- steeply pitched roofs have fast runoff of rain water, and if the angle of the slope is greater than 60°, can also slough off snow

- overhangs protect a building's exterior walls from the weathering effects of sun and rain

- dampproofing or waterproofing is required for below-grade spaces when ground water is present
- ground water should be drained away from a structure's foundation to a natural outfall, dry well, or storm drainage system

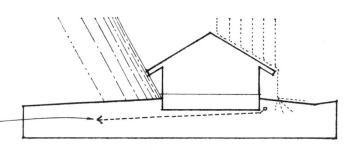

- natural surface drainage patterns are least disturbed by lifting a structure off the ground plane with piers

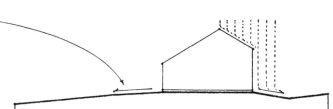

- always slope the ground plane away from a building to avoid water leakage problems
- to prevent soil erosion, planted ground covers should be provided for swales with grades over 3% and for ground slopes with grades over 33%

- minimum grade for planted ground cover areas: 2% (3% recommended)

- minimum grade for paved areas: 0.5% (1% recommended)

- bodies of water can moderate temperature variations and temper their immediate environment
- in hot-dry climates, even small bodies of water are desirable, both psychologically and physically, for their evaporative cooling effect
- protection from reflected glare should be provided

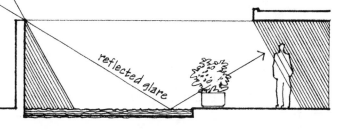

reflected glare

A building's window openings should be positioned not only to satisfy natural light and ventilation requirements but also to frame desirable views. Depending on a site's context, these views may be close or distant in nature. Even when desirable views are nonexistent, a pleasant outlook can often be created within a building site.

A window may be created within a wall in a number of ways, depending on the nature of the view and the way it is framed in the wall's construction. It is important to note that the size and location of windows also affects a room's spatial quality, daylighting, and potential heat loss or gain.

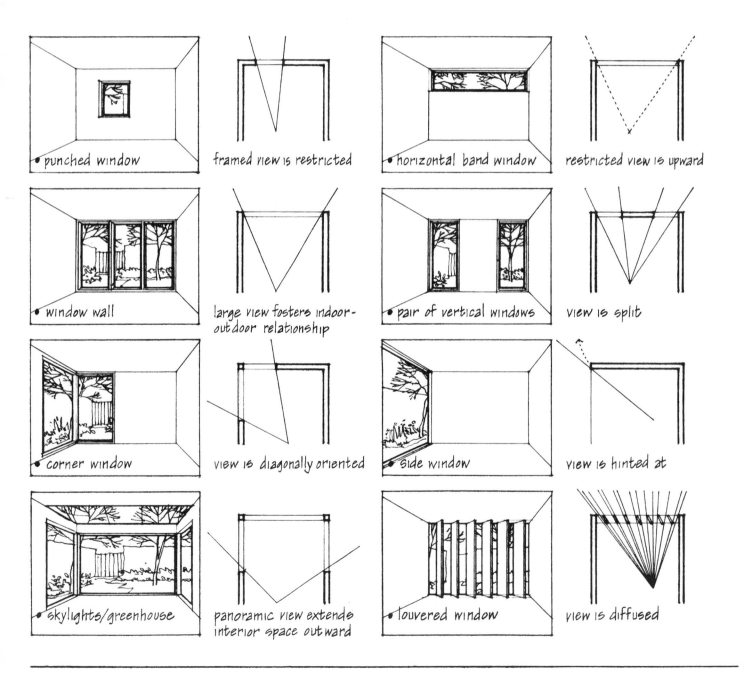

• punched window — framed view is restricted

• horizontal band window — restricted view is upward

• window wall — large view fosters indoor-outdoor relationship

• pair of vertical windows — view is split

• corner window — view is diagonally oriented

• side window — view is hinted at

• skylights/greenhouse — panoramic view extends interior space outward

• louvered window — view is diffused

Sound requires a source and a path. Undesirable exterior sounds or noise are caused by vehicular traffic, aircraft, and other machinery. The sound energy they generate travels through the air outward from the source in all directions in a continuously expanding wave. This sound energy, however, lessens in intensity as it disperses over a wide area. To reduce the impact of exterior noise, therefore, the first consideration should be distance — locating a building as far from the noise source as possible. When a site's constraints do not make this possible, then the interior spaces of a building may be screened from the noise source by:

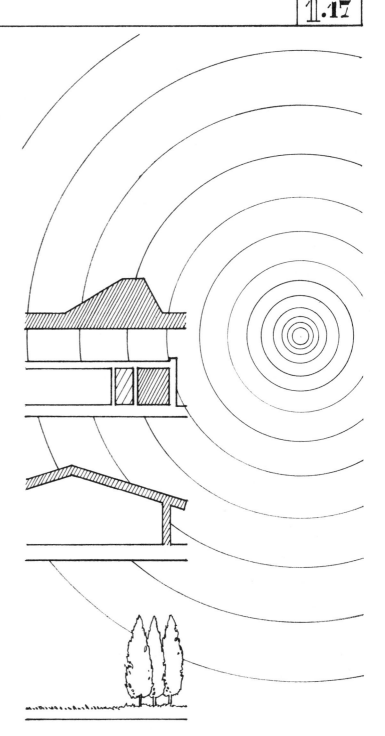

- physical mass such as earth berms

- building zones where noise can be tolerated: eg. mechanical, service, and utility areas

- the construction of exterior walls and roof, which are a building's primary barriers against exterior noise; door and window openings are the weak spots in these barriers and should, if possible, be oriented away from undesirable noise sources

- dense plantings of trees and shrubs, which can be effective in diffusing or scattering sound
- grass or ground covers, which are more absorptive than the hard, reflective surfaces of pavement

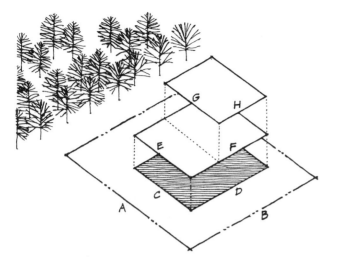

Within a municipality or land-use district, zoning ordinances are generally intended to manage growth, regulate land-use patterns, control building density, direct development to areas with adequate services and amenities, protect environmentally sensitive areas, and conserve open space.

For any single building site, a zoning ordinance will regulate both the types of activity that may occur on it and the bulk of the building(s) constructed to house such activities. A special type of zoning ordinance is the Planned Unit Development, which allows a fairly large tract of land to be developed as a single entity for added flexibility in the placement, grouping, size, and use of structures.

$$\% \text{ allowable lot coverage} = \frac{C \times D}{A \times B}$$

$$\% \text{ allowable total floor area} = \frac{(C \times D) + (E \times F) + (G \times H)}{A \times B}$$

It is important to understand how a zoning ordinance might constrain the allowable size and shape of a building. The bulk of a building is regulated directly by specifying:

$$\% \text{ allowable width or depth} = \frac{C}{A} \text{ or } \frac{D}{B}$$

- how much of the land can be covered by a building structure and the total floor area that may be constructed, expressed as percentages of the lot area

- the maximum width and depth a building may have, expressed as percentages of the site's dimensions

- how tall the building structure can be

The size and shape of a building are also controlled indirectly by specifying how far a building must be set back from each of the property lines.
In addition, existing easements and right-of-ways may further limit the buildable area of a site.

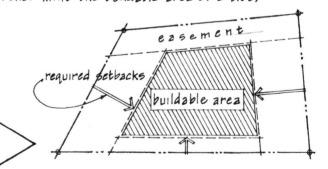

All of the above requirements, together with any restrictions on type and density of use, define a three-dimensional envelope beyond which a building's volume may not extend. Check the applicable zoning ordinance for specific requirements.

Exclusions to the general requirements of a zoning ordinance may exist in the form of exceptions or allowances. Exceptions to the normal setback requirements are typically made for:

- projections of architectural features such as roof overhangs, cornices, bay windows, and balconies
- accessory structures such as low-level decks, fences, and detached carports
- precedents set by existing, neighboring structures

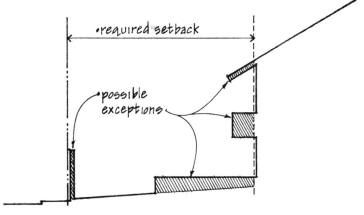

Exceptions are often made for sloping sites, or for sites adjacent to public open spaces.

- sloping roofs, chimneys, and other roof projections may be allowed to extend beyond the normal height limitation
- the height limit may be directly related to the slope of a site
- a reduction in the setback requirements may be made for sloping sites or for sites fronting on open space

In order to provide for adequate light, air, and space, and to enhance the streetscape and pedestrian environment, requirement may exist for:

- open space accessible to the public
- additional setbacks if a structure rises above a certain height
- modulation of a building's facades
- vehicular access and parking

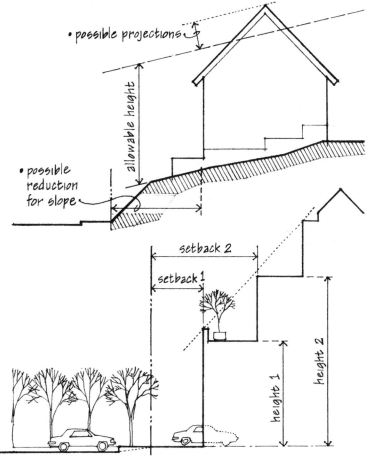

Zoning ordinances may also contain requirements that apply only to specific use categories as well as procedures for requesting a variance from the regulations.

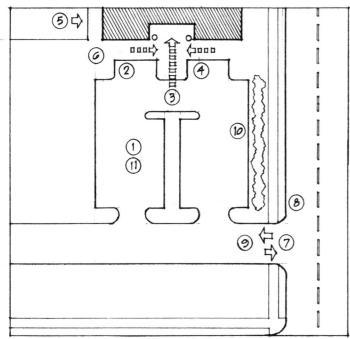

Providing for vehicular access and parking are important aspects of site planning which influence both the location of a building on its site and the orientation of its entrances. Outlined on these pages are some fundamental criteria for estimating the space required for roadways and surface parking. Any planning of vehicular access and parking must take into consideration the safe and convenient movement of pedestrians about a site and from parking to building entrances.

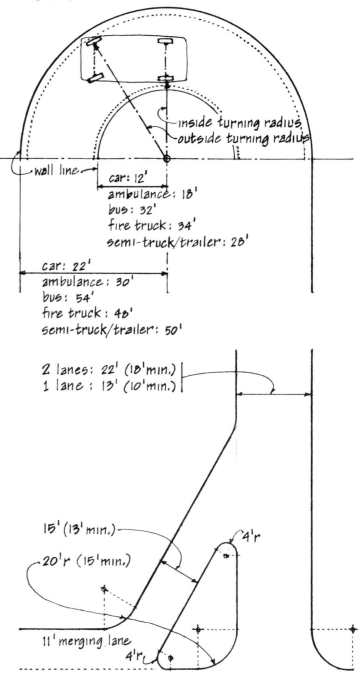

PLANNING CONSIDERATIONS:

1. number of parking spaces required by zoning ordinance is based on type of occupancy; may be related to number of living units or to floor area of building
2. number, size, and location of spaces for the handicapped; curb cuts and ramps for wheelchair access
3. pedestrian access to building entrances from parking areas
4. loading zones for buses and other public transportation vehicles
5. separation of service and truck loading areas
6. access for emergency vehicles such as fire trucks
7. allowable width and location of curb cuts, and distance from public street intersections
8. clear sight lines for vehicles entering public roadway
9. control of access to parking areas
10. space for landscaping; screening of parking areas may be required by zoning ordinance
11. drainage of parking surfaces; space for snow removal

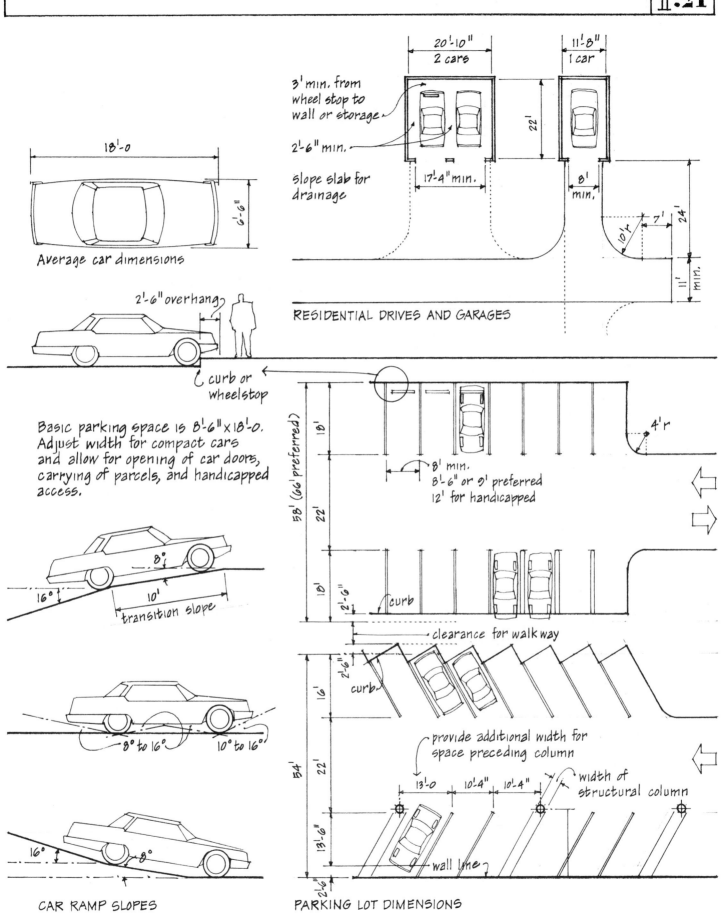

Average car dimensions

18'-0
6'-6"

2'-6" overhang

Basic parking space is 8'-6" × 18'-0. Adjust width for compact cars and allow for opening of car doors, carrying of parcels, and handicapped access.

8°
16°
10'
transition slope

8° to 16°
10° to 16°

16°
8°

CAR RAMP SLOPES

3' min. from wheel stop to wall or storage
2'-6" min.
slope slab for drainage

20'-10"
2 cars

11'-8"
1 car

22'
17'-4" min.
8' min.
24'
10'r
7'
11' min.

RESIDENTIAL DRIVES AND GARAGES

curb or wheelstop

58' (66' preferred)
10'
22'
10'
2'-6"
curb

8' min.
8'-6" or 9' preferred
12' for handicapped

4'r

clearance for walkway

2'-6"
curb

16'
54'
22'
13'-6"
2'-6"

provide additional width for space preceding column

13'-0
10'-4"
10'-4"

width of structural column

wall line

PARKING LOT DIMENSIONS

Paving provides a wearing surface for pedestrian or vehicular traffic on a site. It is a composite structure whose thickness and construction are directly related to the type and intensity of traffic and loads to be carried, and the bearing capacity and permeability of the subgrade.

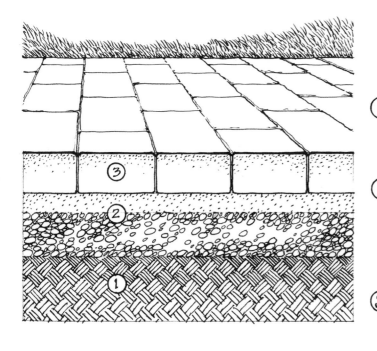

① The subgrade, which must ultimately carry the pavement load, should be undisturbed soil or compacted fill. Since it also receives moisture from infiltration, it should be sloped to drain.

② The base is a foundation of well-graded aggregate that transfers the pavement load to the subgrade. It also prevents the upward migration of capillary water. Heavy-duty loads may require an additional layer— a subbase of coarser aggregate such as crushed stone.

③ The pavement receives the traffic wear, protects the base, and transfers its load to the base structure. There are two types of pavement: flexible and rigid. Flexible pavements, such as bituminous concrete or unit pavers on a sand setting bed, are somewhat resilient and distribute loads to the subgrade in a radiating manner. Rigid pavements, such as reinforced concrete slabs or paving units mortared over a concrete slab, distribute their loads internally and transfer them to the subgrade over a broad area. Rigid pavements generally do not require as thick a base as flexible pavements.

Flexible pavements require wood, steel, stone, masonry, or concrete edging to restrain the horizontal movement of the paving material. Rigid pavements require reinforcement and an extension of the base material along their edges.

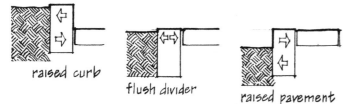

raised curb   flush divider   raised pavement

EDGE CONDITIONS

SLOPE FOR DRAINAGE

0.5% min.; 1% preferred;
highly textured pavements may require a steeper (2%) slope for drainage.

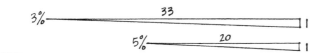

3% —————33—————| 1

5% ———20———| 1

SLOPES: 0%-3% preferred; 5% maximum

8% ——12.5——| 1

RAMPS: 5% - 8%; use only where climatic conditions permit

Additional notes:
● Pavement color and texture are important aesthetic considerations which also affect the pavement's absorption or reflection of heat and light.
● Provide traction for ramps and pavements in areas subject to icy conditions.
● Avoid surface irregularities for wheelchair traffic.
● Provide tactile warning strips for the visually impaired at grade changes and hazardous vehicular areas.

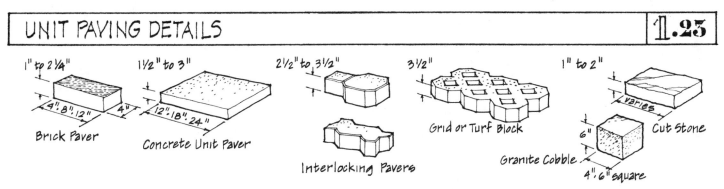

Brick Paver — 1" to 2 1/4", 4", 8", 12", 4"

Concrete Unit Paver — 1 1/2" to 3", 12", 18", 24"

Interlocking Pavers — 2 1/2" to 3 1/2"

Grid or Turf Block — 3 1/2"

Cut Stone — 1" to 2", varies

Granite Cobble — 6", 4", 6" square

PAVING MATERIALS: Consult local supplier for availability of shapes, sizes, colors, textures, absorption properties, compressive strength, and installation recommendations.

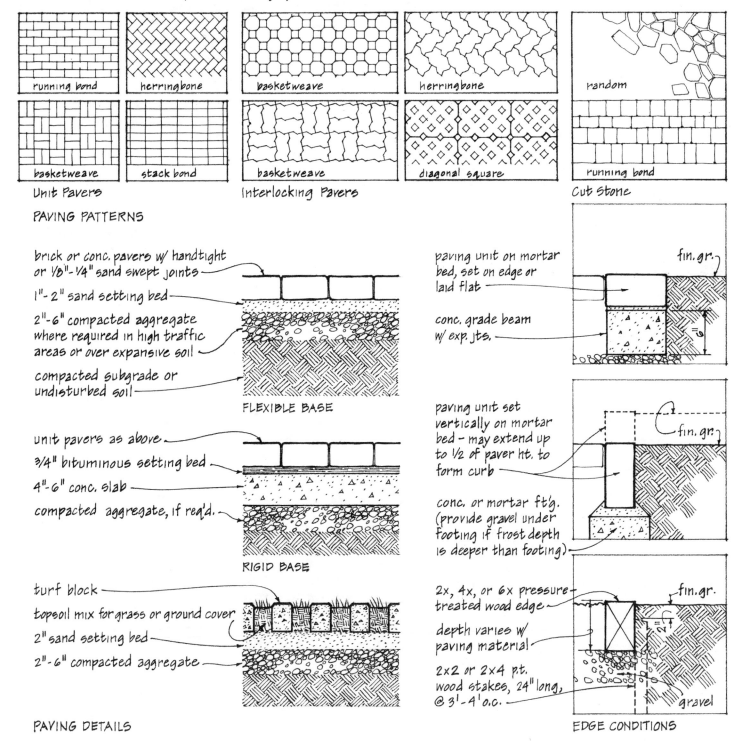

Unit Pavers — running bond, herringbone, basketweave, stack bond

Interlocking Pavers — basketweave, basketweave, herringbone, diagonal square

Cut Stone — random, running bond

PAVING PATTERNS

brick or conc. pavers w/ handtight or 1/8"-1/4" sand swept joints

1"- 2" sand setting bed

2"-6" compacted aggregate where required in high traffic areas or over expansive soil

compacted subgrade or undisturbed soil

FLEXIBLE BASE

unit pavers as above

3/4" bituminous setting bed

4"-6" conc. slab

compacted aggregate, if req'd.

RIGID BASE

turf block

topsoil mix for grass or ground cover

2" sand setting bed

2"-6" compacted aggregate

PAVING DETAILS

paving unit on mortar bed, set on edge or laid flat

conc. grade beam w/ exp. jts.

fin. gr.

paving unit set vertically on mortar bed - may extend up to 1/2 of paver ht. to form curb

conc. or mortar ft'g. (provide gravel under footing if frost depth is deeper than footing)

fin. gr.

2x, 4x, or 6x pressure treated wood edge

depth varies w/ paving material

2x2 or 2x4 p.t. wood stakes, 24" long, @ 3'-4' o.c.

fin. gr.

gravel

EDGE CONDITIONS

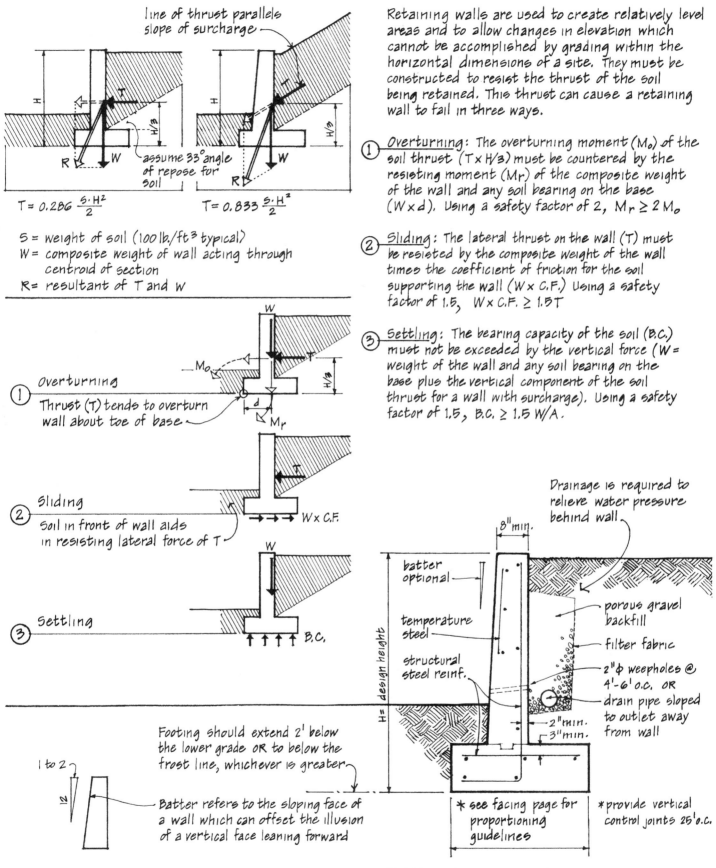

line of thrust parallels slope of surcharge

assume 33° angle of repose for soil

$$T = 0.286 \frac{S \cdot H^2}{2}$$

$$T = 0.833 \frac{S \cdot H^2}{2}$$

S = weight of soil (100 lb./ft³ typical)
W = composite weight of wall acting through centroid of section
R = resultant of T and W

Retaining walls are used to create relatively level areas and to allow changes in elevation which cannot be accomplished by grading within the horizontal dimensions of a site. They must be constructed to resist the thrust of the soil being retained. This thrust can cause a retaining wall to fail in three ways.

① Overturning: The overturning moment (M_o) of the soil thrust ($T \times H/3$) must be countered by the resisting moment (M_r) of the composite weight of the wall and any soil bearing on the base ($W \times d$). Using a safety factor of 2, $M_r \geq 2 M_o$

② Sliding: The lateral thrust on the wall (T) must be resisted by the composite weight of the wall times the coefficient of friction for the soil supporting the wall ($W \times C.F.$). Using a safety factor of 1.5, $W \times C.F. \geq 1.5 T$

③ Settling: The bearing capacity of the soil (B.C.) must not be exceeded by the vertical force (W = weight of the wall and any soil bearing on the base plus the vertical component of the soil thrust for a wall with surcharge). Using a safety factor of 1.5, $B.C. \geq 1.5 W/A$.

① Overturning
Thrust (T) tends to overturn wall about toe of base

② Sliding
Soil in front of wall aids in resisting lateral force of T

③ Settling

$W \times C.F.$

B.C.

Drainage is required to relieve water pressure behind wall

8" min.

batter optional

temperature steel

structural steel reinf.

H = design height

porous gravel backfill

filter fabric

2"⌀ weepholes @ 4'-6' o.c. OR drain pipe sloped to outlet away from wall

2" min.
3" min.

Footing should extend 2' below the lower grade OR to below the frost line, whichever is greater

1 to 2
12

Batter refers to the sloping face of a wall which can offset the illusion of a vertical face leaning forward

* see facing page for proportioning guidelines

* provide vertical control joints 25' o.c.

REINFORCED CONCRETE RETAINING WALL

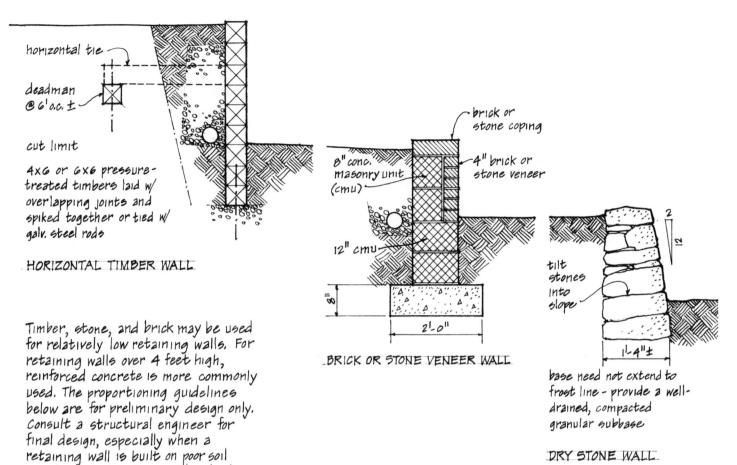

horizontal tie

deadman @ 6' o.c. ±

cut limit

4x6 or 6x6 pressure-treated timbers laid w/ overlapping joints and spiked together or tied w/ galv. steel rods

HORIZONTAL TIMBER WALL

Timber, stone, and brick may be used for relatively low retaining walls. For retaining walls over 4 feet high, reinforced concrete is more commonly used. The proportioning guidelines below are for preliminary design only. Consult a structural engineer for final design, especially when a retaining wall is built on poor soil or subject to surcharge or live loads.

brick or stone coping

8" conc. masonry unit (cmu)

4" brick or stone veneer

12" cmu

8"

2'-0"

BRICK OR STONE VENEER WALL

2
12

tilt stones into slope

1'-4"±

base need not extend to frost line - provide a well-drained, compacted granular subbase

DRY STONE WALL

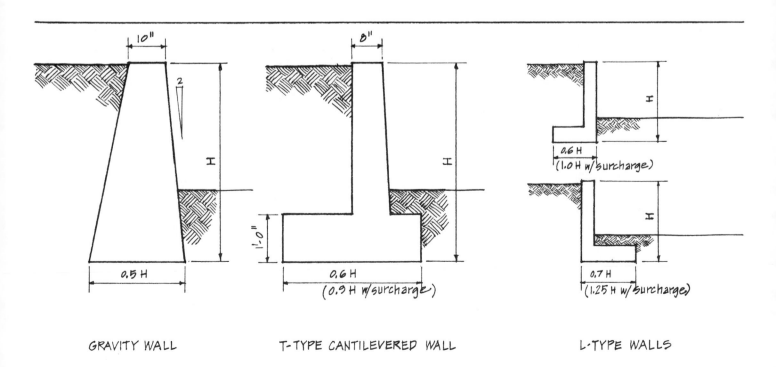

10"

2

H

0.5 H

GRAVITY WALL

8"

H

1'-0"

0.6 H
(0.9 H w/surcharge)

T-TYPE CANTILEVERED WALL

H

0.6 H
(1.0 H w/surcharge)

H

0.7 H
(1.25 H w/surcharge)

L-TYPE WALLS

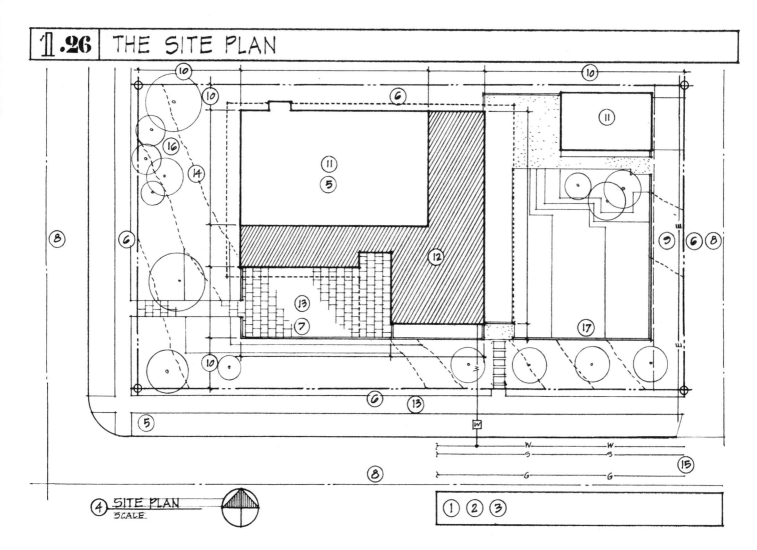

The site plan illustrates the existing natural and built features of a site and describes proposed construction in relation to the existing features. Usually based on an engineer's land survey, the site plan is essential for studying the influence of environmental and regulatory factors on the planning, siting, and massing of a building. A site plan should include the following items:

1. Name and address of property owner
2. Address of property, if different from owner's address
3. Legal description of property
4. North arrow and scale of drawing
5. Bench marks which establish the reference points for the location and elevations of new construction

6. Description of the site's boundaries: dimensions of property lines and their bearing relative to north, angles of corners, radii of curves
7. Project limits, if different from site boundaries
8. Identification of adjacent streets, alleys, and other public right-of-ways
9. Location and dimensions of any easements that cross the site or other pertinent legal features
10. Dimensions of setbacks required by the zoning ordinance

11. Location and size of existing structures and a description of any demolition required by the new construction
12. Location, shape, and size of structures proposed for construction, including roof overhangs and other projections
13. Location and dimensions of existing and proposed paved drives, parking areas, and walkways
14. Existing ground elevations and contour lines, and, where regrading is necessary, new contour lines
15. Location of existing utility lines (electric, gas, water, sewer) and proposed hookup points
16. Existing plant materials to remain and those to be moved
17. Proposed landscaping features, such as fencing and plantings
18. Existing water features, such as drainage swales, creeks, or shorelines

19. References to other drawings and details

THE BUILDING ☐2

This chapter begins by outlining the major types of drawing which we use to develop and communicate design ideas. The subject of this discussion then serves to illustrate a building as the embodiment of a number of necessarily related, coordinated, and integrated systems. This series of illustrations provides a context for the following chapters, each of which takes a major building component, illustrates its construction in various materials, and describes how it relates to other components. Included in this chapter is a brief introduction to a building's structure, the system which both figuratively and physically holds all of the other building systems together.

Architectural drawings make up the graphic language of building design and construction. In the design process, drawings are used to visualize possibilities, study alternatives, and present design ideas about the form and spaces of a building. For the execution of a design, construction or "working" drawings are necessary to accurately describe the constituent parts of a building, articulate their relationships, and reveal how they go together.

Construction drawings consist primarily of plan, section, and elevation views, which are orthographic projections onto a perpendicular drawing surface. These are also called multiview drawings since a series of related views is required to understand the three-dimensional form of a design and its constituent parts. The main advantage of this type of drawing, and the reason why it is used in building construction, is that building elements are seen in true size (to scale), shape, and orientation when viewed from a perpendicular aspect. Orthographic drawing's main disadvantage is its inherent ambiguity in the definition of depth or the third dimension. For this reason, reliance on conventions and symbols is necessary for the description and understanding of what is drawn.

Orthographic plans, sections, and elevations are used not only to portray whole building forms but also to describe the form and construction of a building's components, such as in wall sections, window details, and cabinet drawings. See 2.5.

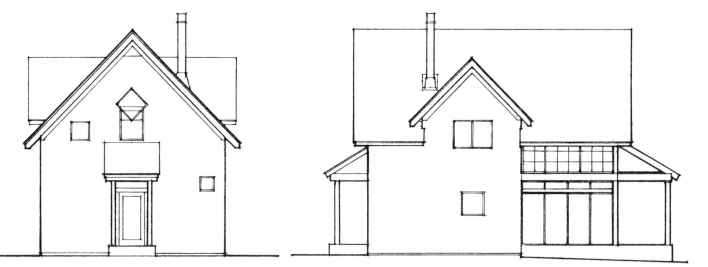

NORTH ELEVATION

WEST ELEVATION

The site plan is a view looking down at a building from above, illustrating its location and orientation on a plot of land and providing information about the site's topography, landscaping, utilities, and sitework. See 1.26.

The floor plan is also a view looking down, but after a horizontal plane is cut through a building about 4 feet above the floor plane and the top section removed. It illustrates the horizontal dimensions of a building's spaces, as well as the thickness and construction of the vertical walls and columns that define these spaces.

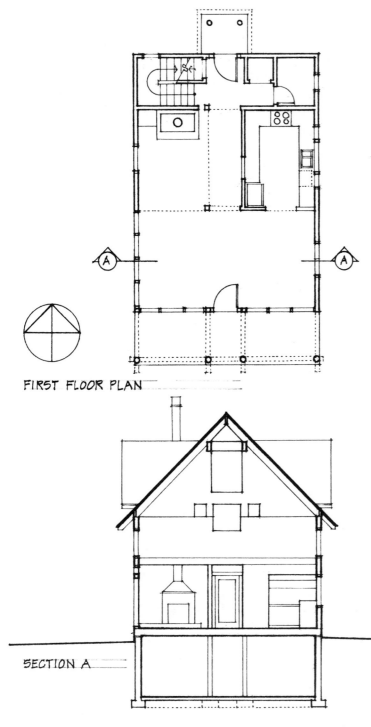

FIRST FLOOR PLAN

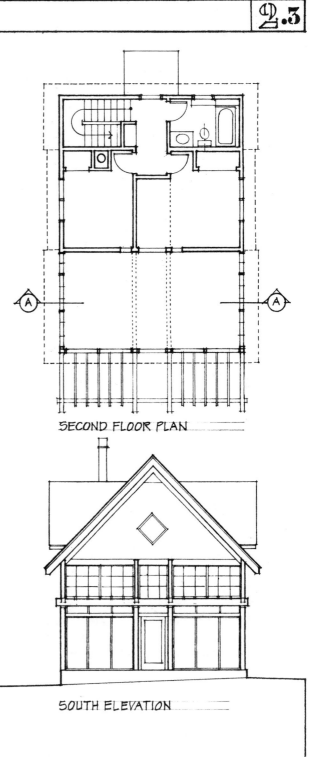

SECOND FLOOR PLAN

SECTION A

SOUTH ELEVATION

The building section is a horizontal view after a vertical plane is cut through a building and the front portion removed. It reveals the vertical and, in one direction, the horizontal dimensions of a building's spaces. While it illustrates primarily the thickness and construction of floors, roofs, and walls, it may also include exterior and interior elevations seen beyond the plane of the cut.

Building elevations are horizontal views of a building's exterior, usually taken from a point of view perpendicular to the principal vertical surfaces. They illustrate the size, shape, and materials of the exterior surfaces as well as the size, proportion, and nature of the door and window openings within them.

Plan oblique views are projected from an orthographic view of a horizontal floor or ground plane, which is oriented at some angle to the horizontal (45°/45°; 60°/30°; 30°/60°). The orientation we use determines how much we see of each plane.

Elevation obliques are similar but projected from an elevation. Depth is usually foreshortened depending on the angle of projection.

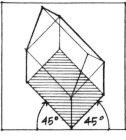

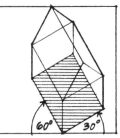

Isometric views are projected along x-, y-, and z-axes which are 120° apart on the picture plane. If verticals remain vertical, then the x- and y-axes are each drawn 30° to the horizontal. Isometrics are not subject to the distortion of oblique views, give a truer image of relative proportions, and are drawn from a slightly lower angle of view.

All drawing is convention utilizing varying degrees of abstraction. The type of drawing that comes closest to communicating three-dimensional form as we naturally perceive it is an accurately drawn perspective. Its pictorial value, however, cannot be taken advantage of in construction drawings since elements within the perspective are foreshortened and cannot be scaled. A type of drawing that combines the pictorial value of a perspective and the scalability of orthographic drawings is the paraline drawing. For this reason, whenever possible, graphic information in this book is presented via paraline drawings.

On this page are paraline views of the building drawn orthographically on the previous two pages. In a paraline drawing, parallel lines remain parallel and dimensions along the x-, y-, and z-axes can be drawn to scale. Note that forms in a paraline drawing are always seen from above or below.

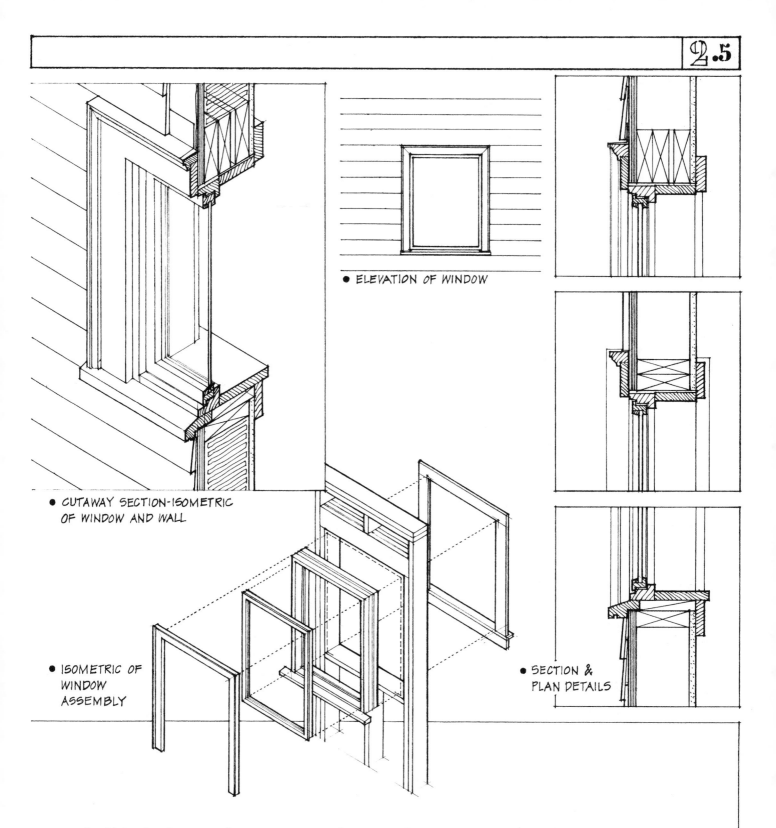

● ELEVATION OF WINDOW

● CUTAWAY SECTION-ISOMETRIC
OF WINDOW AND WALL

● ISOMETRIC OF
WINDOW
ASSEMBLY

● SECTION &
PLAN DETAILS

We should be familiar with the various types of
drawing conventions. Construction drawings
consist primarily of plan, section, and elevation
views. These orthographic drawings clearly
illustrate the shape of elements when perpendicular to our line of sight and reveal their
horizontal and vertical dimensions and
relationships.

Paraline views can also be effective in
describing—in a three-dimensional way—
the parts of a building, how these elements
relate to each other, and how they are
assembled in construction. The choice of which
drawing type to use will depend ultimately on
the nature of what we want to illustrate.

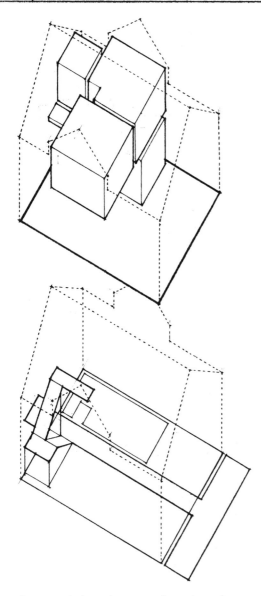

Architecture and building construction are not necessarily one and the same. An understanding of how the various elements, components, and systems of a building come together — and how they must be compatible and integrated with one another — is necessary during both the design and construction of a building. This understanding, however, enables one to build architecture but does not guarantee it. A working knowledge of building construction is only one of several critical factors in the execution of architecture.

When we speak of architecture as the art of building, we should consider conceptual systems of order in addition to the physical ones of construction.

- the definition, scale, proportion, and organization of a building's interior spaces

- the functional zoning of a building's spaces according to purpose and use

- horizontal and vertical paths of movement through a building's interior

- the physical imagery of a building: form, space, light, color, texture, and pattern

- context: the building as an integrated component within the natural and built environment

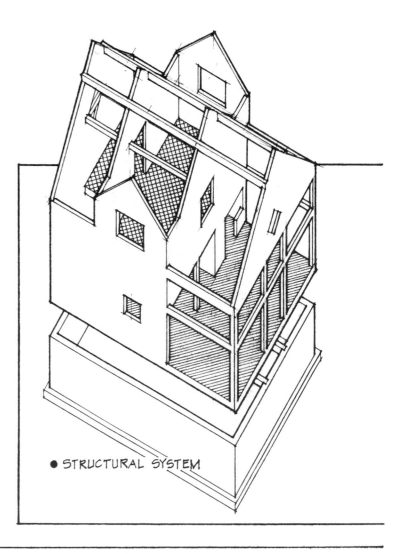

- STRUCTURAL SYSTEM

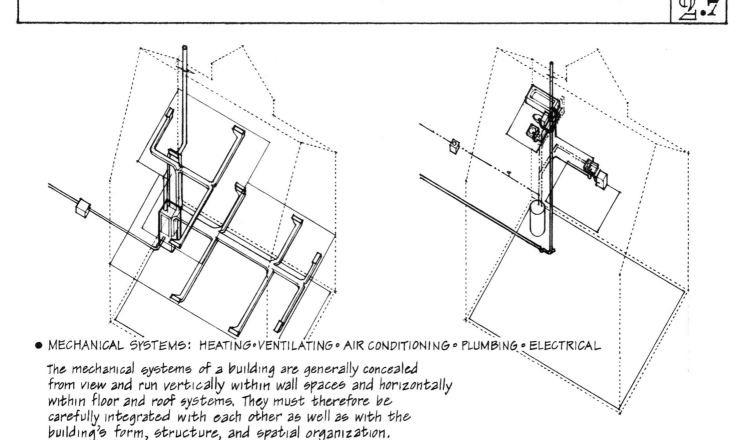

● MECHANICAL SYSTEMS: HEATING ● VENTILATING ● AIR CONDITIONING ● PLUMBING ● ELECTRICAL

The mechanical systems of a building are generally concealed from view and run vertically within wall spaces and horizontally within floor and roof systems. They must therefore be carefully integrated with each other as well as with the building's form, structure, and spatial organization.

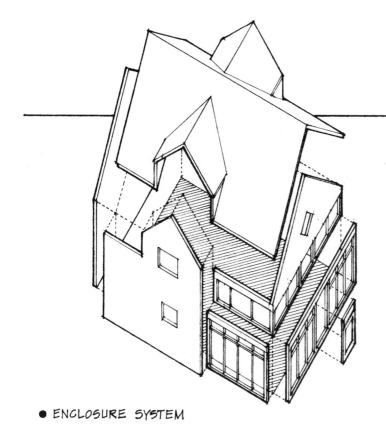

● ENCLOSURE SYSTEM

Of primary interest to us in this book are the physical elements that define, organize, and reinforce the perceptual and conceptual ordering of a building. On the following page we will begin to break a building down into these constituent elements which will then be elaborated on in succeeding chapters. The focus of the remainder of this chapter will be a building's structural system — the configuration of structural elements that literally and figuratively holds all of the other building systems together.

A building can generally be broken down into the following physical systems:

◇ STRUCTURAL SYSTEM
◇ EXTERIOR ENVELOPE
◇ INTERIOR SUBDIVISIONS OF SPACE

Each of these, in turn, can be seen to be made up of linear and planar assemblies.

○ Planar Assemblies
 • horizontal or sloping roof planes
 • horizontal floor planes
 • vertical wall planes

○ Linear Assemblies
 • horizontal beams
 • vertical columns

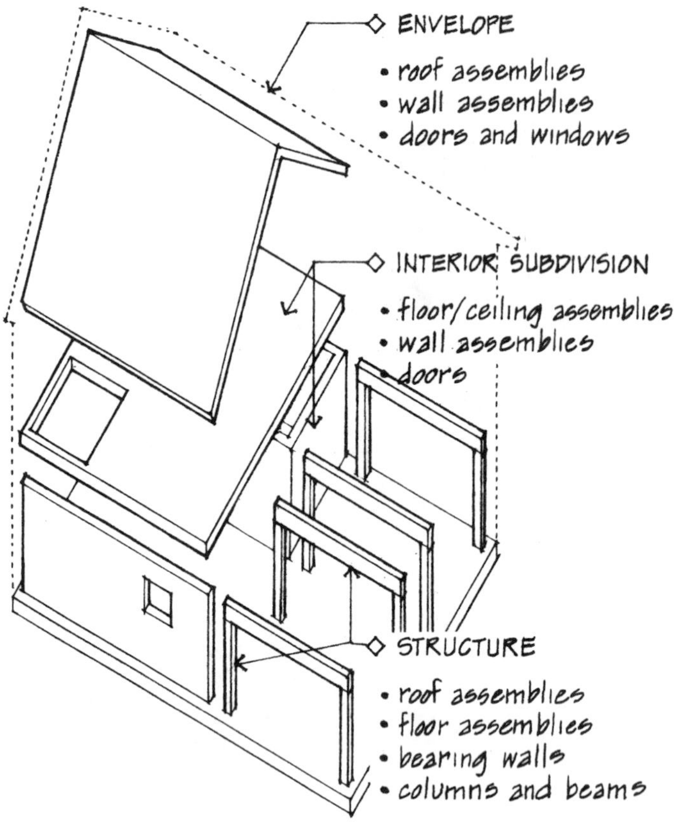

These elements and assemblies can come together in a number of ways, depending on the nature of the materials used, the method for transferring and resolving the forces acting on a building, and the desired physical form. Presented below are the basic types of connections used in building construction.

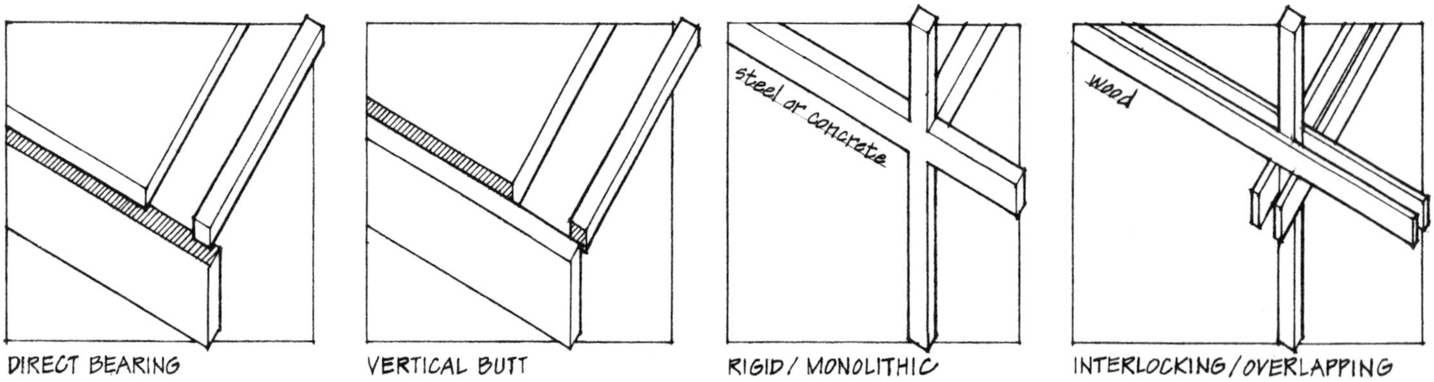

◇ ENVELOPE
 • roof assemblies
 • wall assemblies
 • doors and windows

◇ INTERIOR SUBDIVISION
 • floor/ceiling assemblies
 • wall assemblies
 • doors

◇ STRUCTURE
 • roof assemblies
 • floor assemblies
 • bearing walls
 • columns and beams

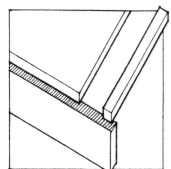

DIRECT BEARING

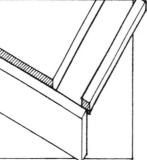

VERTICAL BUTT

RIGID / MONOLITHIC

steel or concrete

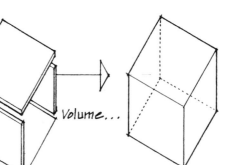

INTERLOCKING / OVERLAPPING

wood

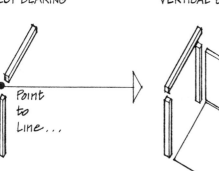

Point to Line...

Plane...

Volume...

A useful way of seeing the forms of building elements in a comparative manner is to categorize them according to the geometric elements of point, line, plane, and volume. These elements are joined together in construction to form a building's various components and subsystems. The drawing on the facing page illustrates these subsystems and serves as a visual index to the organization of this book.

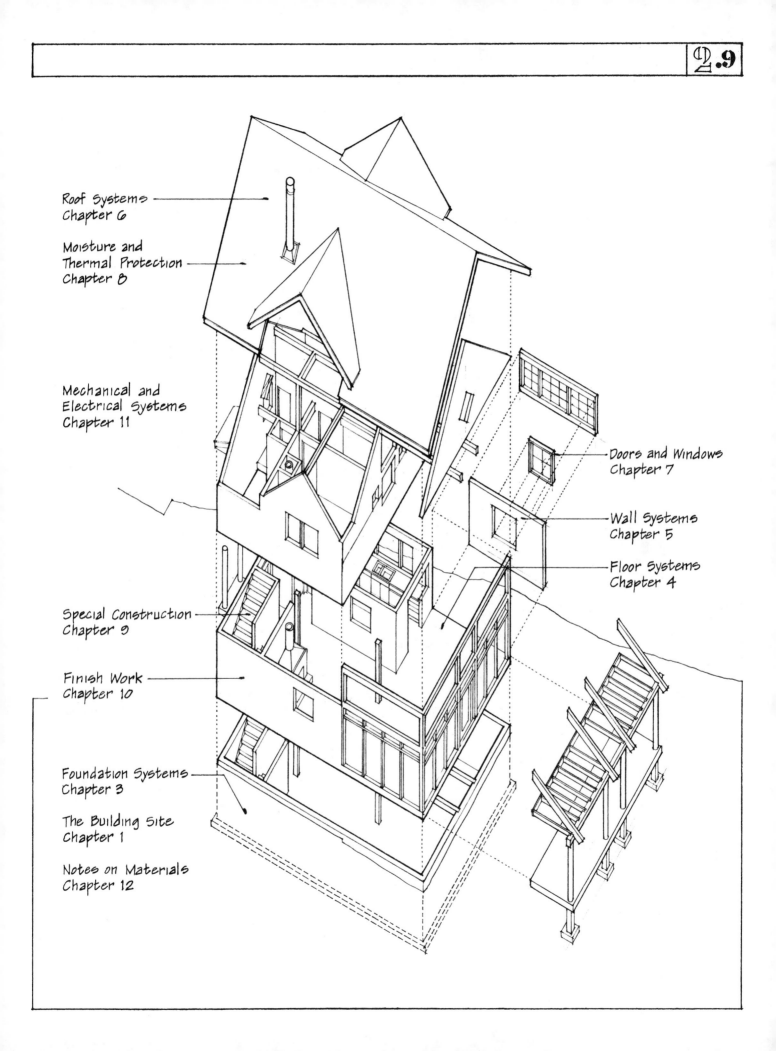

Roof Systems
Chapter 6

Moisture and
Thermal Protection
Chapter 8

Mechanical and
Electrical Systems
Chapter 11

Doors and Windows
Chapter 7

Wall Systems
Chapter 5

Floor Systems
Chapter 4

Special Construction
Chapter 9

Finish Work
Chapter 10

Foundation Systems
Chapter 3

The Building Site
Chapter 1

Notes on Materials
Chapter 12

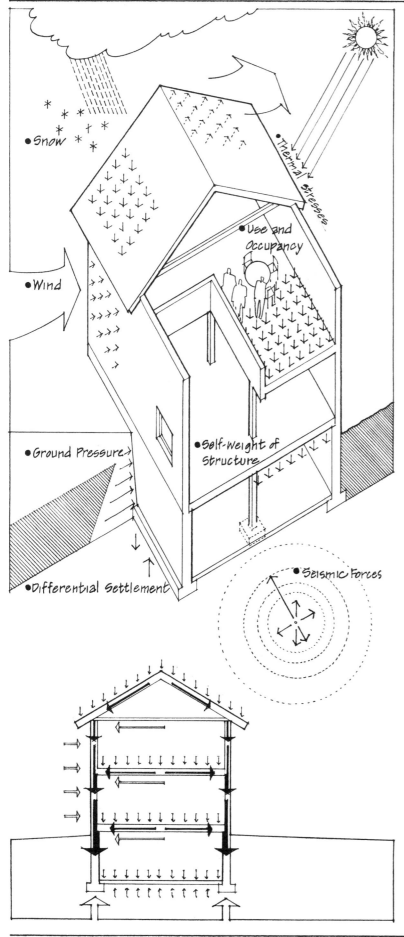

- Snow
- Thermal Stresses
- Use and Occupancy
- Wind
- Self-weight of Structure
- Ground Pressure
- Differential Settlement
- Seismic Forces

In enclosing space for habitation, a building's structure must be able to support two types of loads—static and dynamic.

STATIC LOADS are assumed to be constant in nature and are of two kinds:

- Dead loads are relatively fixed and include the weight of the building structure itself as well as the weights of any permanent elements within the building, such as mechanical equipment.

- Live loads are movable loads which may not be present all of the time. They include the weights of a building's occupants and furnishings, as well as snow loads on roofs.

DYNAMIC LOADS can be applied to a structure suddenly and vary in magnitude and location.

- Wind loads can produce pressure or suction on a building's walls and roof planes, depending on their geometry and orientation. The dynamic effects of wind on tall buildings are especially important.

- Seismic forces result from sudden movements in the earth's crust. They are multidirectional in nature and propagated in the form of waves. These cause the earth's surface and any buildings resting on it to vibrate because of the tendency of a building's mass to remain at rest.

While a building's dead loads are relatively fixed in character, static live and dynamic wind and seismic loads can vary in magnitude, duration, and point of application. A building's structure must nevertheless be designed for these possibilities. Building codes typically provide equivalent distributed or concentrated loads for design purposes. These are based on the net effect of the maximum expected combination of forces. (See Appendix for weights of common building materials and typical occupancy and environmental loads.)

The following is a brief introduction to the way a structural system must resolve the forces acting on a building and channel them to the ground. For more complete information on the structural analysis of buildings, see Bibliography.

STRUCTURAL FORCES

In the structural analysis of buildings, we are concerned with the magnitude, direction, and point of application of forces, and their resolution to produce a state of equilibrium. Three conditions are necessary for a structural system to be in equilibrium:

1. The sum (Σ) of all vertical forces = 0
2. Σ of all horizontal forces = 0
3. Σ of all moments of all forces about any point = 0.

Therefore, as each structural element is loaded, its supporting elements must react with equal but opposite forces.

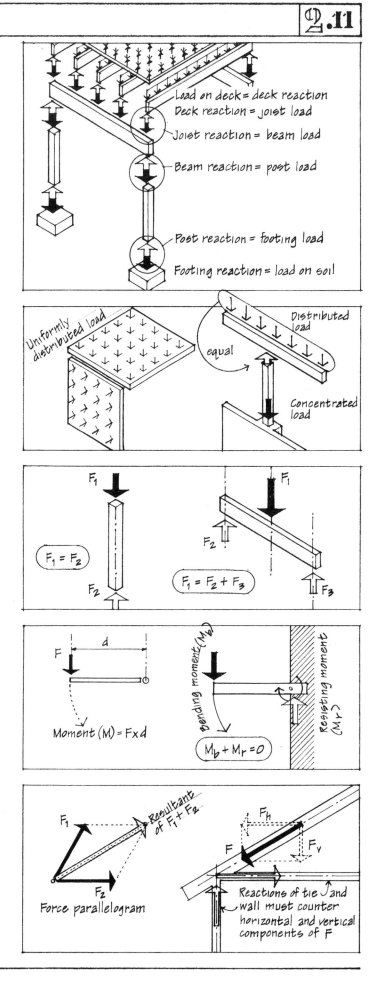

Load on deck = deck reaction
Deck reaction = joist load
Joist reaction = beam load
Beam reaction = post load
Post reaction = footing load
Footing reaction = load on soil

Forces can be assumed to be applied in a uniformly distributed manner, as in the case of a live load on a floor or a wind load on a wall. A force can also be a concentrated load, as when a beam bears on a post or a column bears on its footing.

Uniformly distributed load

Distributed load

equal

Concentrated load

Forces may be parallel and colinear, as when a column supports a vertical load from above. They can also be parallel but not meet, as when a beam supports a load at its midspan. These parallel, nonconcurrent forces will tend to cause a rigid structural element to bend and deflect, which must be resisted by the material's internal strength.

$F_1 = F_2$

$F_1 = F_2 + F_3$

Any force will tend to cause a body to move in the direction of its line of action. The force can also cause the body to rotate if it does not pass through the body's center of gravity. This rotational effect of a force is called a moment. For each moment created by the forces acting on a structural element there must be an equal but opposite resisting moment.

Moment (M) = F × d

Bending moment (M_b)

Resisting moment (M_r)

$M_b + M_r = 0$

A number of concurrent forces, acting through a common point, can be resolved into a single resultant which is equivalent to the several forces. In a similar manner, an inclined force can be resolved into vertical and horizontal components.

Resultant of $F_1 + F_2$

Force parallelogram

F_h

F_v

Reactions of tie and wall must counter horizontal and vertical components of F

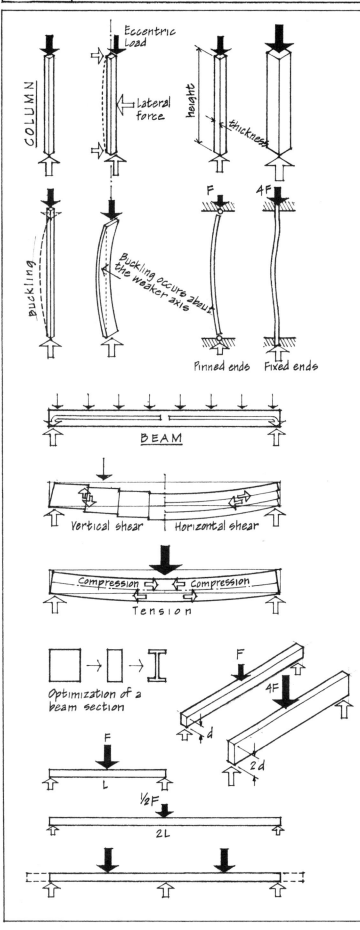

Structural elements can be classified according to their geometry, rigidity, and how they respond to the forces applied to them. External loads create internal stresses within structural elements.

The two basic types of rigid, linear structural elements are the column and beam. A column transmits compressive forces vertically along its shaft. If the load is centered, the column will simply compress. If, however, the load is off center or applied laterally, the column will experience curvature.

The load carrying capacity of a column varies inversely with its length. The thicker a column is relative to its height, the more it can carry and the better it will withstand eccentric or lateral loading. This height-to-thickness ratio is known as a column's slenderness ratio. Tall, slender columns are especially susceptible to buckling.

A beam transfers its load laterally along its length to its supports. Due to the nonconcurrent pattern of forces, a beam is subject to bending. This results in a combination of compressive and tensile stresses which are greatest along the beam's top and bottom edges. In bending, a beam also becomes subject to horizontal and vertical shear stresses.

As a general rule, the strength of a beam will increase according to the square of its increase in depth, while its stiffness will increase according to the cube of its increase in depth. Similarly, if a beam's length is doubled, the bending stress will double and it will be able to carry only half of its original load. Its deflection under loading will also increase according to the cube of its increase in length.

Cantilevering a beam beyond its end supports can reduce its maximum internal bending moment. Spanning a beam continuously over three or more supports can also reduce the design moment and make the structure more rigid.

A truss consists of short, straight, rigid members assembled into a triangulated pattern. This triangulation is what makes a truss a rigid structural unit. While a truss as a whole is subject to bending, the individual members are subject only to compression or tension.

When a beam is supported by two columns, the assembly defines an invisible plane and qualifies the space around it. The typical column-and-beam assembly is not capable of resisting lateral forces unless it is braced. If the joints between the columns and beam are made rigid, then the assembly is called a frame. A rigid frame has a greater measure of lateral stability in the direction of its plane and both columns and beam are subject to bending.

If we fill in the plane defined by two columns and a beam, it acts as a long, thin column in transmitting compressive forces to the ground. This wall, if constructed of reinforced concrete, is capable of resisting lateral forces. If of unit masonry, however, the bearing wall is capable of carrying only in-plane loads. Stresses in a bearing wall have to flow around any door and window openings within the plane.

A planar structural element, such as a reinforced concrete slab, can span horizontally and transfer its loads to its supports by bending. A one-way slab acts as a wide, flat beam spanning between two supports. A two-way slab, supported along four sides, is more versatile since it provides more paths along which stresses may travel to the supporting elements.

Long, narrow planar elements can be joined along their edges to form folded plates. These act as beams but are capable of spanning fairly long distances.

Also capable of long spans is the space frame. While it acts as a planar structural unit, it consists of short, rigid linear members assembled into a three-dimensional triangulated pattern.

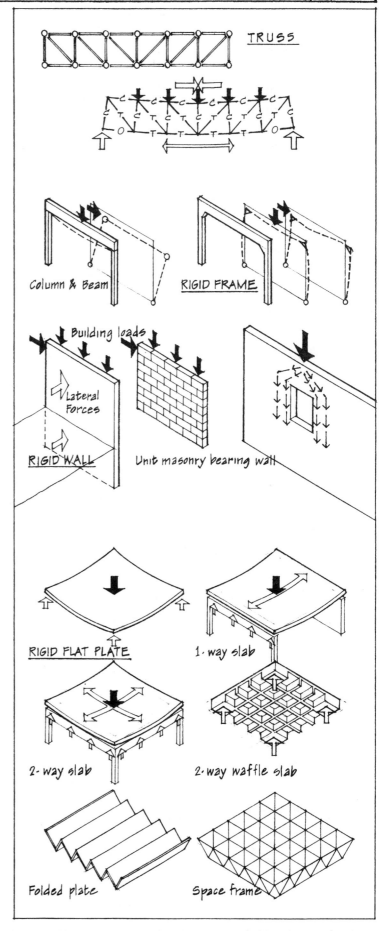

TRUSS

Column & Beam   RIGID FRAME

RIGID WALL   Unit masonry bearing wall

Building loads

Lateral Forces

RIGID FLAT PLATE   1. way slab

2. way slab   2. way waffle slab

Folded plate   Space frame

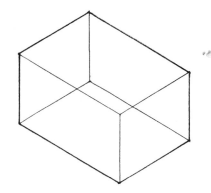

With the primary structural elements of column, beam, slab, and load-bearing wall, it is possible to form a basic structural unit capable of defining and enclosing a volume of space for habitation. This structural unit, whether used alone or in a repetitive manner, is the basic building block for a building's structural system.

On these two pages are described basic types of structural units. The vertical supports may be load-bearing walls, a framework of columns and beams, or simply columns supporting a two-way reinforced concrete flat plate.

The horizontal spanning element can be a one- or two-way rigid plate of reinforced concrete. An alternative system consists of a hierarchical arrangement of decking supported by one-way joists, beams, and girders.

Linear columns and beams form a three-dimensional skeletal framework with a potential for openness. Load-bearing walls supporting a one-way slab form a planar system which imparts a directional quality to the space defined. Horizontal slabs supported by columns free up the location of walls and define horizontal layers of space.

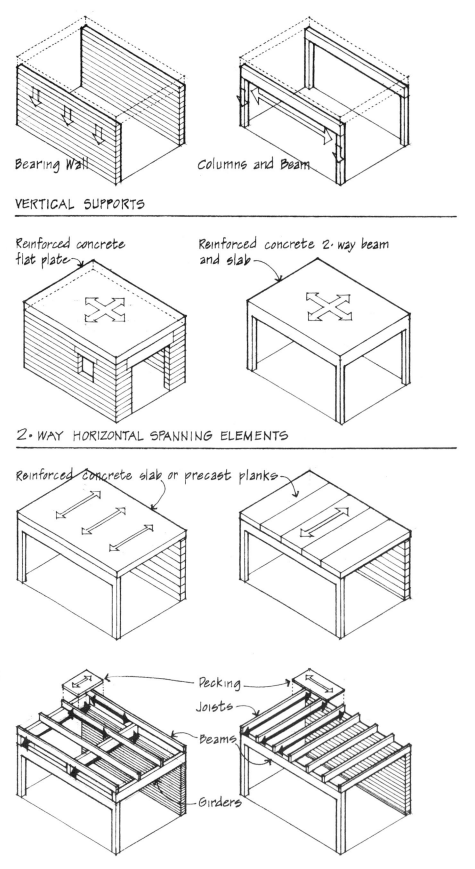

Bearing Wall   Columns and Beam

VERTICAL SUPPORTS

Reinforced concrete flat plate   Reinforced concrete 2-way beam and slab

2·WAY HORIZONTAL SPANNING ELEMENTS

Reinforced concrete slab or precast planks

Decking
Joists
Beams
Girders

1·WAY HORIZONTAL SPANNING ELEMENTS

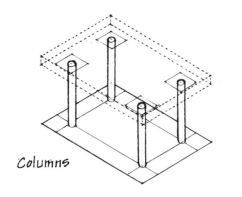

Columns

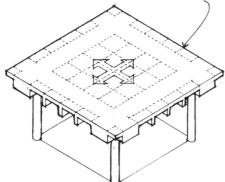

Reinforced concrete waffle slab

The spanning capability of horizontal elements determines the spacing of their vertical supports. This fundamental relationship between the span and spacing of structural elements influences the dimensions and scale of the spaces defined by a building's structural system. The dimensions and proportion of the system's structural units, in turn, should be related to the programmatic requirements of the building's spaces.

A fundamental distinction between one-way and two-way spanning systems lies in the proportion of the structural bay each can efficiently span. One-way systems are generally preferred when the structural bay is rectangular—i.e., the ratio of the long to the short dimensions is greater than 1.5—or when the structural grid forms a linear pattern. Two-way systems, on the other hand, are more effective for square bays or when the structural grid extends equally in two directions.

Representative SPAN RANGES of different systems in feet	10	20	30	40	50	60	70	80	90	100
1° WAY SPANNING SYSTEMS — Timber — Planks	▨									
Joists	▨									
Laminated Beams		▨	▨	▨	▨	▨	▨	▨		
Trusses		▨	▨	▨	▨	▨	▨	▨	▨	▨
Steel — Decking	▨									
Wide-flange Beams		▨	▨	▨	▨	▨				
Open-web trusses		▨	▨	▨	▨	▨	▨	▨	▨	▨ ⇨
Reinforced Concrete — Slabs	▨									
Pan Joists		▨	▨	▨	▨	▨				
Precast Planks		▨	▨	▨	▨					
Precast Tees		▨	▨	▨	▨	▨	▨	▨	▨	▨ ⇨
2° WAY — Reinforced Concrete — Flat Plate	▨									
2° way Beam and Slab		▨	▨							
Waffle Slab		▨	▨	▨	▨	▨				

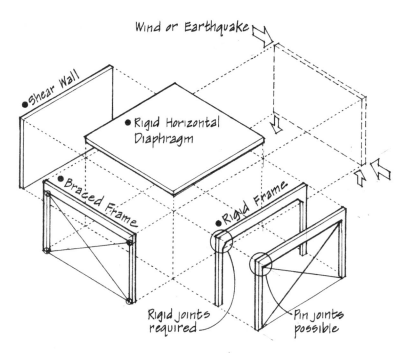

A building's structural elements must be configured to form a stable structure under any possible load conditions. Therefore, while a structural system is designed primarily to carry vertical gravity loads, it must also be able to withstand lateral wind or earthquake forces. There are three basic mechanisms for ensuring lateral stability.

- **Diagonal Bracing** (timber or steel)
  Bracing a frame with diagonal members

- **Rigid Frame** (steel or reinforced concrete)
  Developing a frame with rigid joints capable of resisting changes in angular relationships

- **Shear Wall** (wood, concrete, or masonry)
  Using a rigid planar element capable of resisting shape changes

Any of these systems may be used to stabilize a structure or they may be used in combination. Of the three, a rigid frame tends to be the least efficient. However, rigid frames can be useful when diagonally braced frames or shear walls form barriers which cause functional problems.

Stabilizing elements are required to resist lateral forces in all directions.

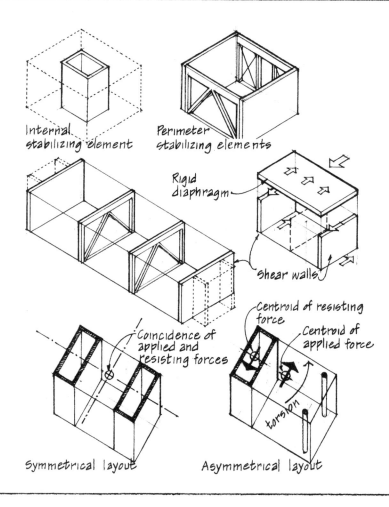

Lateral stabilizing elements may be placed within a building or along its perimeter, and combined in various ways. In all cases, however, a number of stabilizing elements must be used to resist lateral forces in all directions.

Rigid horizontal diaphragms, acting as flat, deep beams, span between shear walls. These are necessary to transfer lateral loads from non-load-bearing walls to the load-carrying shear walls.

Lateral loads tend to be more critical in the short direction of rectangular buildings and the more efficient mechanisms (shear walls or braced frames) are used in this direction. In the long direction, either similar elements or a rigid frame can be used.

The arrangement of lateral stabilizing elements is important to the stability of a structure as a whole. An asymmetrical layout, where the centroid of the applied force is not coincident with the centroid of the resisting mass, can cause torsional effects. A symmetrical arrangement of lateral stabilizing element is therefore always desirable. This principle is especially important for tall buildings.

Tall buildings are particularly susceptible to the effects of lateral loads. Under lateral loading, they can be seen to act as vertical cantilevers. The overturning moment must be countered by the internal resisting moment of the structure. The wider a tall building is, the greater is its resistance to bending.

A rigid frame is the least efficient way to achieve lateral stability and is appropriate only for low- to medium-rise structures. As the height of a building increases, it becomes necessary to supplement a rigid frame with additional bracing mechanisms, such as a rigid core or diagonal bracing. A stiffer tube structure capable of resisting all lateral forces can be developed by using closely spaced columns rigidly connected to horizontal spandrel beams. For extremely tall structures, major diagonal bracing elements can be superimposed over a rigid frame or tube structure.

Earthquakes can produce dynamic and complex movements of the ground on which a building rests. While these motions are three-dimensional in nature, from a structural design viewpoint, horizontal ground movements are the most important. Seismic forces are therefore considered to be primarily lateral in character.

When designing for seismic loads, it is always desirable to use simple geometric forms with a symmetrical layout of building mass, load distribution, and lateral stabilizing elements.

Linear L, T, and H plan shapes should be broken into shorter segments with seismic joints. These allow adjacent sections of a building to move freely and independently of each other.

In resisting seismic and other lateral forces, asymmetrical layouts such as these — can result in undesirable torsional effects.

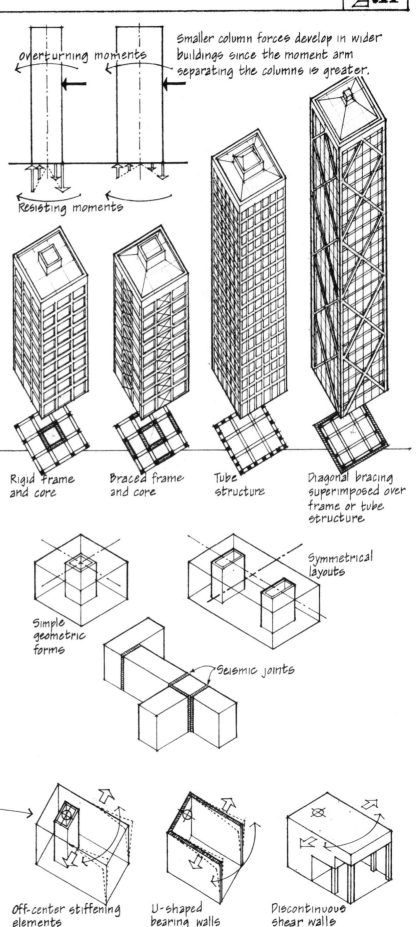

overturning moments

Smaller column forces develop in wider buildings since the moment arm separating the columns is greater.

Resisting moments

Rigid frame and core

Braced frame and core

Tube structure

Diagonal bracing superimposed over frame or tube structure

Simple geometric forms

Symmetrical layouts

Seismic joints

Off-center stiffening elements

U-shaped bearing walls

Discontinuous shear walls

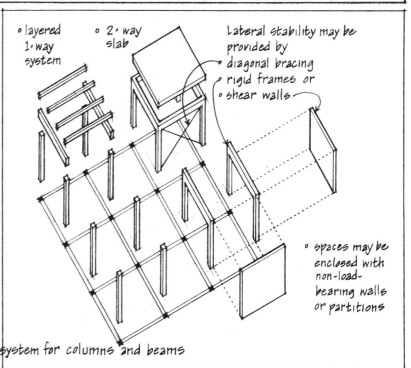

○ layered
1·way
system

○ 2·way
slab

Lateral stability may be
provided by
○ diagonal bracing
○ rigid frames or
○ shear walls

○ spaces may be
enclosed with
non-load-
bearing walls
or partitions

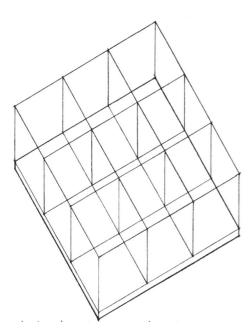

• Idealized 3·dimensional grid as the organizing system for columns and beams

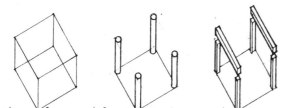

Volume of space defined by 4 columns and 2 beams

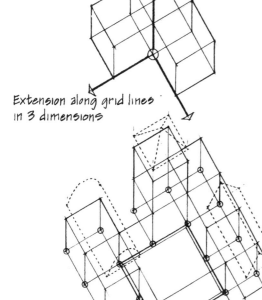

Extension along grid lines
in 3 dimensions

The primary linear structural elements—columns and beams—
form a skeletal type of structural system. In plan, the
critical points of this linear framework are those at which
building loads are carried vertically to the ground along
column lines. This gives rise to the use of a grid where the
grid lines represent the horizontal continuity of beams
and the intersections of the grid lines represent the
locations of columns. The inherent geometric order of a
grid can be used in the design process to initiate and
reinforce a building's functional and spatial organization.

To the left are diagrams which illustrate how a single
module of space is defined by four columns supporting two
beams. This basic building block can logically be extended
vertically along column lines and horizontally along beam
lines to form a variety of building shapes. The basic
grid can also be altered to accommodate special needs
such as large spaces or unusual site conditions.

The use of a regular column grid implies the development
of a series of repetitive spaces. However, since the walls
necessary for the enclosure of interior spaces need not be
load-bearing, they can be freely manipulated to define a
variety of spatial configurations.

There should be a functional fit between the vertical support pattern of a structural system and the spatial and functional organization of a building. The dimensions and proportions of a structural grid also tell us something about the type of system used to span horizontally between column supports. Two-way systems can efficiently span square bays while one-way systems are generally preferred when spanning linear and rectangular grids. If exposed to view, the directional quality of the horizontal system transfers itself to the interior spaces being spanned.

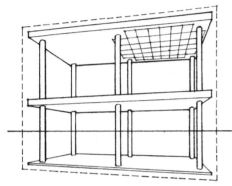

A double grid can be offset to develop interstitial spaces. These intervening spaces can be used to define patterns of movement, mediate between a series of larger spaces, or to house mechanical services.

Non-uniform or irregular grids can be used to reflect the functional or hierarchical ordering of a building's spaces. It is also possible to combine different grid patterns in a single structure. One pattern can be a subset of a larger pattern and be related at column locations. When the two patterns cannot be conveniently aligned, a third element, such as a bearing wall, a mediating space, or a finer-grained spanning system, can be used.

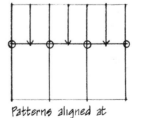

Patterns aligned at column points

Random intersection along a bearing line

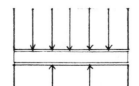

Patterns separated by a mediating space

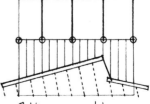

Patterns joined by a third spanning system

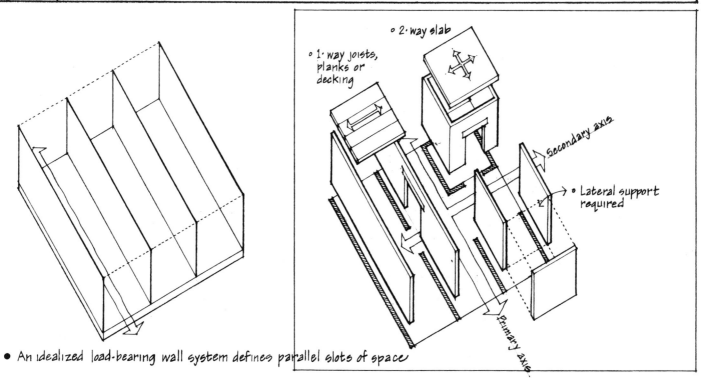

- ° 2·way slab
- ° 1·way joists, planks or decking
- Secondary axis
- ° Lateral support required
- Primary axis

- An idealized load-bearing wall system defines parallel slots of space

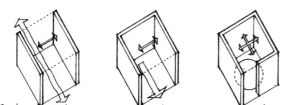

Bi-directional space...Directional space...Introverted space

Extension in 3 dimensions

The major planar structural elements are the vertical load-bearing wall and the horizontal slab. These rigid elements can be combined to form a structural system that is capable of enclosing space as well as supporting building loads.

A planar structural system typically consists of a parallel series of load-bearing walls. Two such walls naturally define an axial, bi-directional space. Closing one end with a shear wall results in a space oriented towards the open end. Closing the other end as well creates an introverted space capable of being spanned with a two-way system.

Secondary axes can be developed perpendicular to the primary axis with openings within the load-bearing walls. Care should be taken that these openings do not weaken the wall's integrity, strength, and rigidity.

Load-bearing walls are most effective in resisting forces along their planes, and most vulnerable to forces perpendicular to their planes. The stability of a load-bearing wall system therefore depends on the support of perpendicular shear wall planes as well as the rigidity, stiffness, and mass of the walls themselves.

To the left are diagrams which illustrate the variations in form possible through the manipulation of the length, height, spacing, and orientation of load-bearing walls.

The parallel nature of a load-bearing wall pattern fits well with one-way spanning systems. Since load-bearing walls are most effective when carrying distributed loads, they typically support a series of joists, planks, or a one-way slab. Any system using widely spaced beams creates concentrated loads which require reinforcement or thickening at the beam support locations.

A common plan configuration is a series of load-bearing walls which define and separate a number of repetitive spaces. Openings are possible at either end of the spaces if lateral stability can be achieved with transverse frames or shear walls.

More complex plan configurations are possible since sets of parallel load-bearing walls can be arranged perpendicular to each other. Because of the planar nature of load-bearing walls, there should be a correspondence between their spacing and the functional requirements of the defined spaces. The location and orientation of load-bearing walls, however, should also be determined by the requirements for lateral stability.

Load-bearing walls may be thick enough that voids within their construction can be used as service spaces. Even double walls organized along a tartan grid can be seen to be similar in nature to thick load-bearing walls.

In order to transfer lateral wind or earthquake forces to load-bearing walls that serve as shear planes, floor planes must be designed as rigid horizontal diaphragms. Since these act as thin, deep beams, they should be carefully designed. Plan shapes not suitable as normal beam shapes should be avoided.

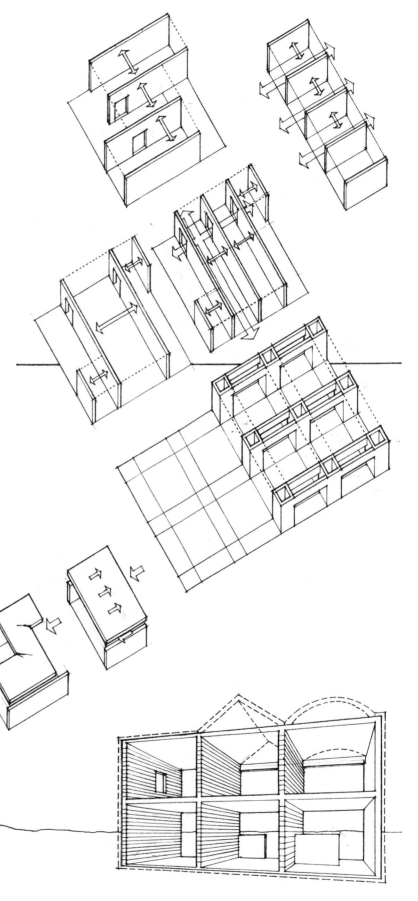

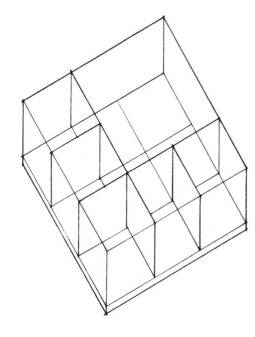

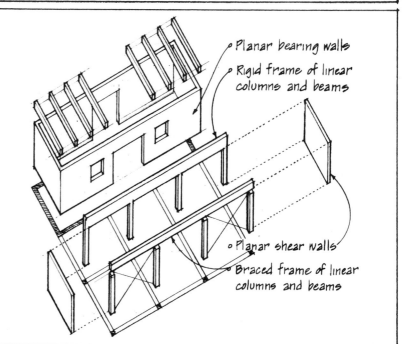

- Planar bearing walls
- Rigid frame of linear columns and beams
- Planar shear walls
- Braced frame of linear columns and beams

- Planar slab
- Planar planks
- Planar decking over linear beams
- Planar decking over linear joists

Combining both linear and planar structural elements, it is possible to form a composite structural system. Composite structural systems allow a building to be more flexible in responding to the programmatic requirements of its spaces and the context of its site. Even when a building utilizes a single primary type of structural system, the secondary and tertiary systems consist of both linear and planar elements.

A grid can again be used to coordinate a building's structural, spatial, and functional systems, and to organize how the structural system collects and channels its loads to the ground.

The manner in which forces are transferred from one structural element to the next and how a structural system performs as a whole depend to a great extent on the types of joints and connections used. On the following page are described the basic types of connections used in building construction.

Structural elements can be joined to each other in three ways. Butt joints allow one of the elements to be continuous and usually require a third mediating element to make the connection. Over-lapping joints allow all of the connected elements to bypass each other and be continuous across the joint. The structural elements can also be molded or shaped to form the connection.

The connectors used to join the structural elements can be in the form of a point, line, or surface. While line and surface types of connectors resist rotation, point connectors do not unless distributed across a large surface area.

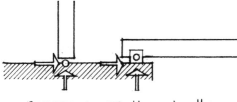

PINNED JOINTS theoretically allow rotation but no translation in any direction.

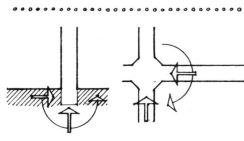

FIXED or RIGID JOINTS resist moments and forces in any direction and therefore do not allow any rotation or translation to occur.

ROLLER JOINTS allow rotation but resist translation in one direction only. They are not as commonly used as pinned or fixed connections but the principle behind roller joints can be seen to apply to joints that allow expansion and contraction of a structural element to occur.

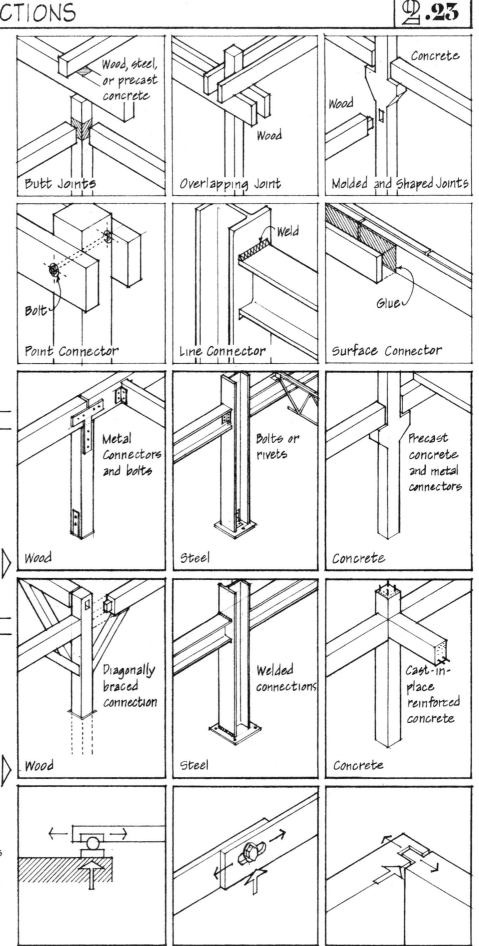

Butt Joints — Wood, steel, or precast concrete

Overlapping Joint — Wood

Molded and Shaped Joints — Concrete, Wood

Point Connector — Bolt

Line Connector — Weld

Surface Connector — Glue

Wood — Metal Connectors and bolts

Steel — Bolts or rivets

Concrete — Precast concrete and metal connectors

Wood — Diagonally braced connection

Steel — Welded connections

Concrete — Cast-in-place reinforced concrete

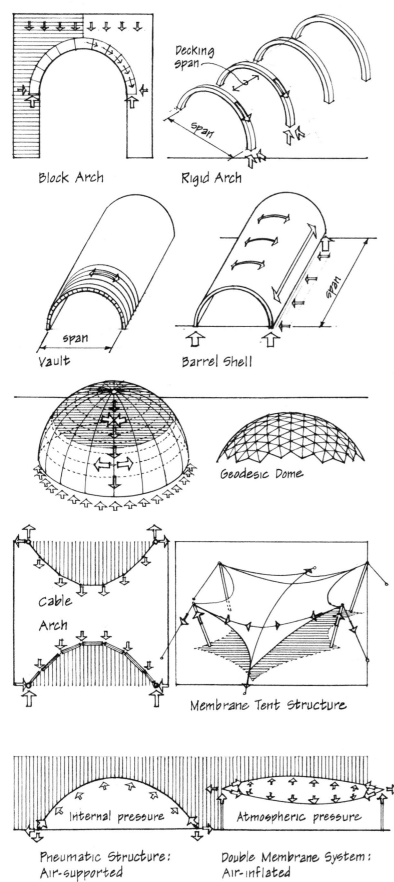

Block Arch

Rigid Arch

Decking span

span

span

Vault

span

Barrel Shell

Geodesic Dome

Cable

Arch

Membrane Tent Structure

Internal pressure

Atmospheric pressure

Pneumatic Structure:
Air-supported

Double Membrane System:
Air-inflated

Columns, beams, and slabs are the most common structural elements because of the rectilinear building geometry they are capable of generating. There are, however, other means of spanning and enclosing space. These are generally form-active elements which make efficient use of their material for the distances spanned because of their geometry and shape. While beyond the scope of this book, they are briefly described below.

An ARCH is a curved structural element that spans between two points. A block arch is capable of carrying only in-plane forces which cause the segments to compress uniformly. A rigid arch, on the other hand, consists of a continuous piece of a curved rigid material such as steel or concrete.

A VAULT is a singly curved structural plane that spans transversely, like a continuous block arch. A CYLINDRICAL SHELL is similar in form but spans longitudinally like a beam with the curve perpendicular to the span.

A DOME is a spherical surface structure that can be made of stacked blocks, a continuous rigid material like reinforced concrete, or of short, rigid linear elements as in the case of a geodesic dome. A dome is similar to a rotated arch except that circumferential forces are developed which are compressive near the crown and tensile in the lower portion.

CABLES are flexible structural elements which must be used purely in tension. When subject to concentrated loads, a cable's shape consists of straight-line segments. Under a uniformly distributed load, it will take on the shape of an inverted arch. A NET is a three-dimensional surface made up of a series of crossed curved cables.

MEMBRANES are also flexible structural elements. The thin sheet material may be suspended or stretched between posts, or be supported by air pressure.

FOUNDATION SYSTEMS

The foundation system for a building— its substructure—is the critical link in the transmission of building loads down to the ground. Bearing directly on the soil, the foundation system must distribute vertical loads so that settlement of a building is either negligible or uniform under all parts of a building. It must also anchor the building's superstructure against uplifting and racking due to wind or earthquake forces. The most critical factor in determining the foundation system of a building is the type and bearing capacity of the soil to which the building loads are distributed.

Foundation systems are presented in three categories according to the geometric analogies of point, line, and plane. Each type of foundation system described in this chapter can support certain wall and floor systems. Just as the type of foundation system used is regulated by the soil and topography of the building site, the choice also affects the potential form of the superstructure.

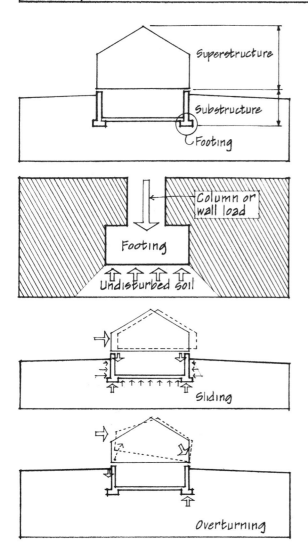

The foundation system is that part of a building's substructure which transmits the building's loads down to the supporting soil. These loads include the dead load of the building's weight and the live load of its occupants and contents. A foundation system may also have to resist ground pressure as well as anchor the building's superstructure against uplift or racking due to lateral wind or earthquake forces.

TYPES OF FOUNDATION SYSTEMS

A foundation system typically consists of columns, piers, or walls which rest on footings. These footings are the widened parts of the foundation which rest directly on the soil. They are spread in order to distribute their loads over a wide enough area that the soil's bearing capacity is not exceeded.

Footings should always rest on undisturbed soil. When this is not possible, concrete or a specially engineered and compacted fill should be used to make up the extra depth. Avoid bearing on unstable or organic soils, wet clays, or on ground with poor drainage.

When the soil underlying a foundation system is not adequate to support the building's loads, column-like piles are used to penetrate down to a more suitable bearing stratum of rock or dense sands and gravels. Piles can also be supported by the frictional resistance developed between the pile surfaces and the surrounding soil.

Spread footings are usually of plain or reinforced concrete while piles may be of wood, steel, plain concrete, or reinforced concrete. These basic types of foundation systems are discussed further on 3.4 and 3.5.

FOOTING SIZE

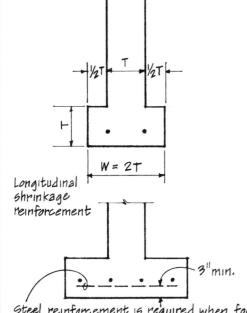

Since footings for residential and other light construction transmit relatively light loads, their size can usually be estimated by the following when they bear on stable soil.

For foundation walls: Width (W) = 2 x thickness of foundation wall
Thickness (T) = thickness of foundation wall

For columns and piers: A = P/S, where
A = horizontal bearing surface of footing
P = column load in pounds
S = soil bearing capacity in lbs./S.F.

When bearing on poor soil or designing for heavy loads or sloping sites, soil samples should be tested and an engineering analysis made to determine the type and size of foundation system that is required. Consult a structural engineer.

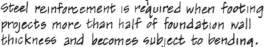

Steel reinforcement is required when footing projects more than half of foundation wall thickness and becomes subject to bending.

BUILDING SETTLEMENT

As a building bears down on the supporting soil, some settlement is to be expected. A properly designed and constructed foundation system should minimize this settlement or make it negligible. Whatever settlement does occur should be equal under all parts of a building. This is accomplished by laying out and proportioning the foundation supports so that they transmit an equal load per unit area to the soil. Uneven or differential settlement can cause a building to shift out of plumb and cracks to occur in its foundation, structure, or finishes. If extreme, differential settlement can result in the failure of a building's structural integrity.

Settlement is due primarily to a reduction in the volume of voids in the soil. This reduction is slight and occurs rather quickly as loads are applied on dense, granular soils. On clays, settlement can be greater since clay has a relatively large percentage of voids. Consolidation of clay can also be continuous over a long period of time since any water present cannot pass through the clay easily. Though not as common, the lateral displacement of soil in embankments or adjacent to excavations can also cause settlement to occur.

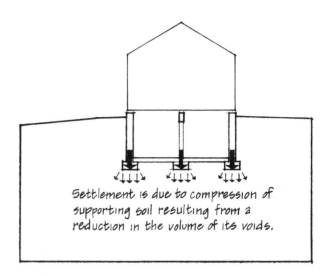

Settlement is due to compression of supporting soil resulting from a reduction in the volume of its voids.

WATER

Ground water can place pressure on and penetrate foundation walls and ground slabs below grade, especially if they lie below a site's water table. Foundation walls enclosing basement spaces should be waterproofed and a perimeter drainage system used to collect and divert water away from the foundation. In cohesive soils, ground water can also rise through capillary action and penetrate a building's ground slab or crawl space. Capillarity can be controlled with a combination of granular base materials and vapor barriers.

Surface water should be drained away from a building using protective slopes: 3% minimum for grassy or planted areas and 1% for paved surfaces.

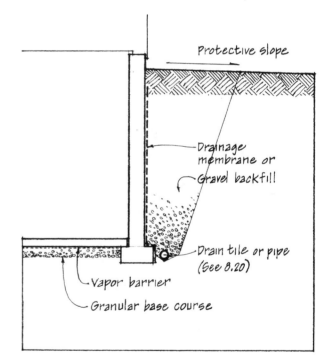

Protective slope

Drainage membrane or Gravel backfill

Drain tile or pipe (see 8.20)

Vapor barrier

Granular base course

FROST

Since water expands upon freezing, ground heaving can occur as soil moisture freezes in cold weather. To minimize the effect of this frost action on a foundation, footings should be placed below the deepest frost penetration expected at the building site. Since this frostline varies from region to region, its depth should be verified when a specific site is selected. In addition, footings should not be placed on frozen ground. As the frozen soil thaws under the pressure of the building load, excess water can cause the soil to lose much of its bearing capacity.

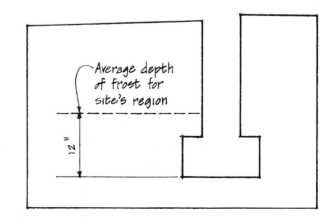

Average depth of frost for site's region

12"

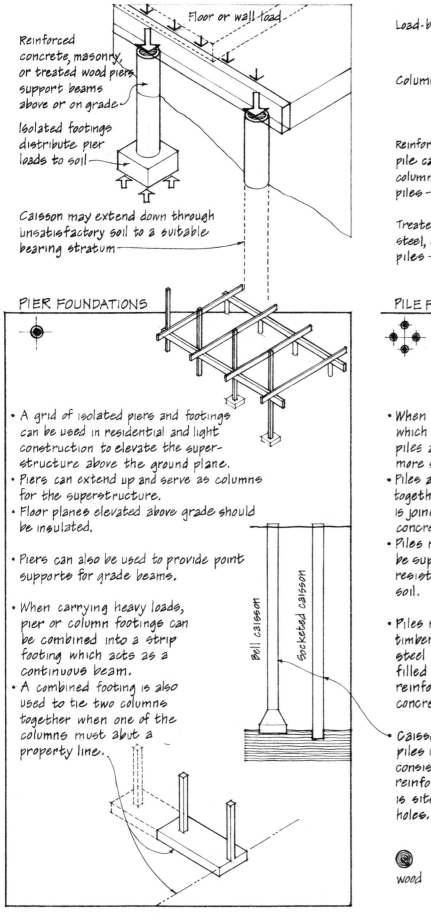

Floor or wall load

Reinforced concrete, masonry, or treated wood piers support beams above or on grade

Isolated footings distribute pier loads to soil

Caisson may extend down through unsatisfactory soil to a suitable bearing stratum

PIER FOUNDATIONS

- A grid of isolated piers and footings can be used in residential and light construction to elevate the super-structure above the ground plane.
- Piers can extend up and serve as columns for the superstructure.
- Floor planes elevated above grade should be insulated.

- Piers can also be used to provide point supports for grade beams.

- When carrying heavy loads, pier or column footings can be combined into a strip footing which acts as a continuous beam.
- A combined footing is also used to tie two columns together when one of the columns must abut a property line.

Bell caisson

Socketed caisson

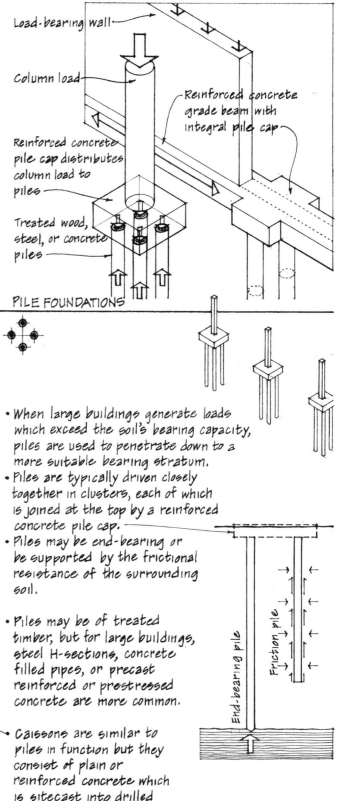

Load-bearing wall

Column load

Reinforced concrete grade beam with integral pile cap

Reinforced concrete pile cap distributes column load to piles

Treated wood, steel, or concrete piles

PILE FOUNDATIONS

- When large buildings generate loads which exceed the soil's bearing capacity, piles are used to penetrate down to a more suitable bearing stratum.
- Piles are typically driven closely together in clusters, each of which is joined at the top by a reinforced concrete pile cap.
- Piles may be end-bearing or be supported by the frictional resistance of the surrounding soil.

- Piles may be of treated timber, but for large buildings, steel H-sections, concrete filled pipes, or precast reinforced or prestressed concrete are more common.

- Caissons are similar to piles in function but they consist of plain or reinforced concrete which is sitecast into drilled holes.

End-bearing pile

Friction pile

wood steel concrete

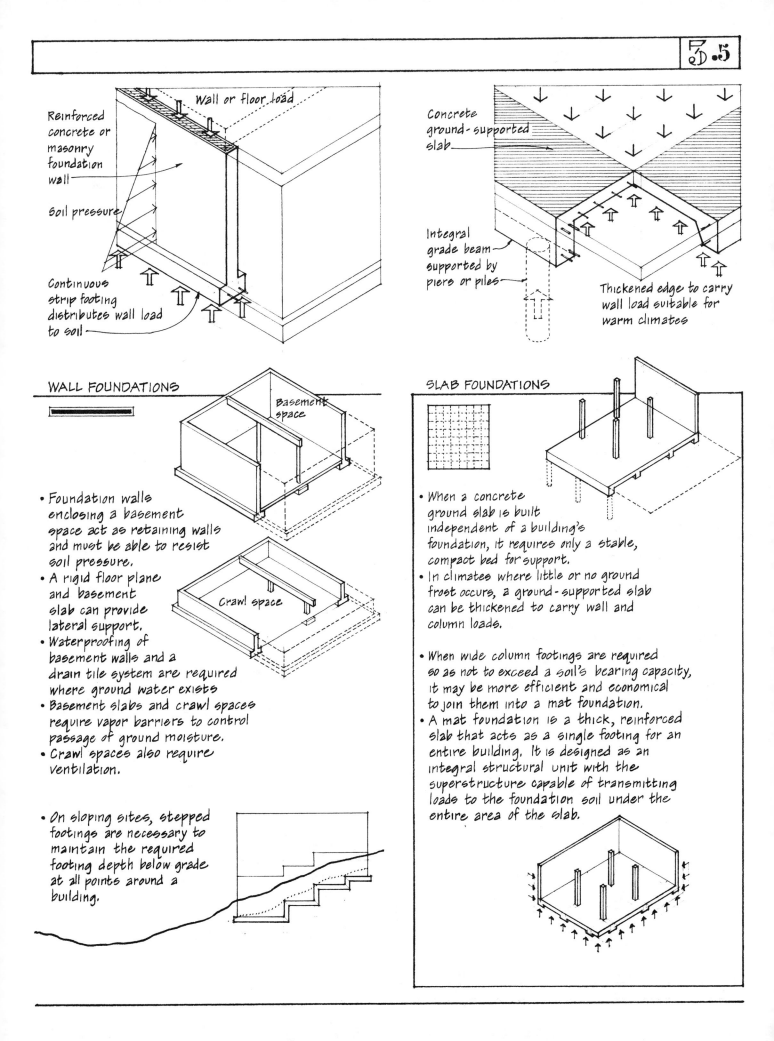

Reinforced concrete or masonry foundation wall

Wall or floor load

Soil pressure

Continuous strip footing distributes wall load to soil

Concrete ground-supported slab

Integral grade beam supported by piers or piles

Thickened edge to carry wall load suitable for warm climates

WALL FOUNDATIONS

Basement space

Crawl space

- Foundation walls enclosing a basement space act as retaining walls and must be able to resist soil pressure.
- A rigid floor plane and basement slab can provide lateral support.
- Waterproofing of basement walls and a drain tile system are required where ground water exists
- Basement slabs and crawl spaces require vapor barriers to control passage of ground moisture.
- Crawl spaces also require ventilation.

- On sloping sites, stepped footings are necessary to maintain the required footing depth below grade at all points around a building.

SLAB FOUNDATIONS

- When a concrete ground slab is built independent of a building's foundation, it requires only a stable, compact bed for support.
- In climates where little or no ground frost occurs, a ground-supported slab can be thickened to carry wall and column loads.

- When wide column footings are required so as not to exceed a soil's bearing capacity, it may be more efficient and economical to join them into a mat foundation.
- A mat foundation is a thick, reinforced slab that acts as a single footing for an entire building. It is designed as an integral structural unit with the superstructure capable of transmitting loads to the foundation soil under the entire area of the slab.

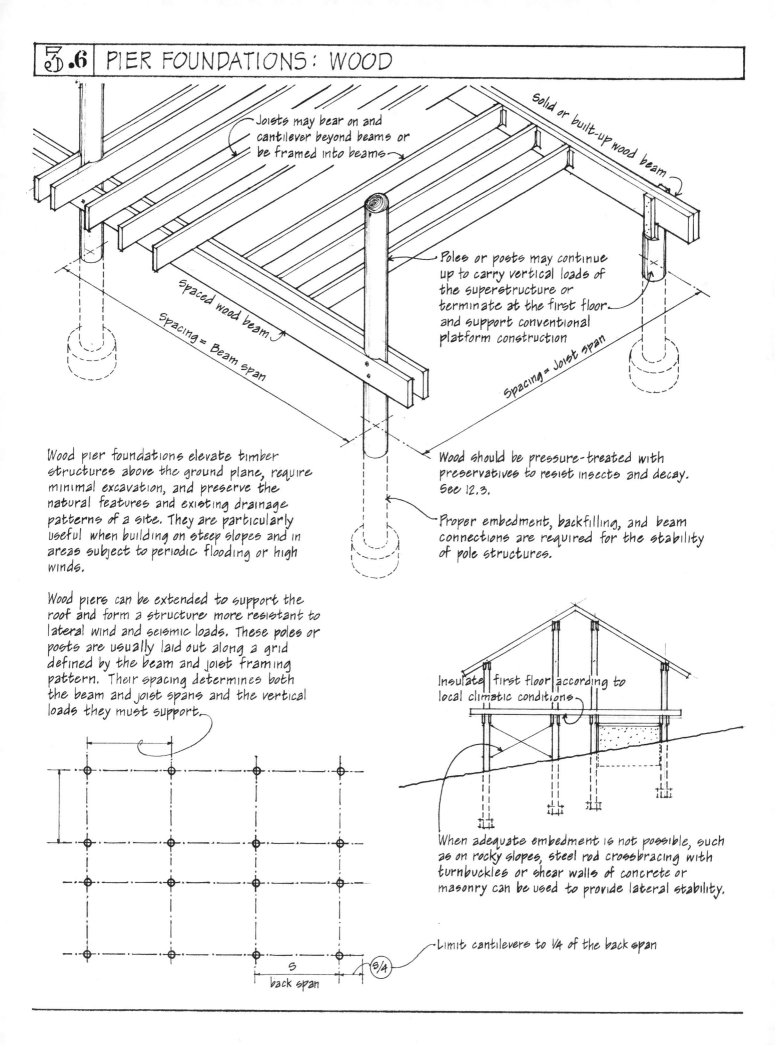

Joists may bear on and cantilever beyond beams or be framed into beams

Solid or built-up wood beam

Poles or posts may continue up to carry vertical loads of the superstructure or terminate at the first floor and support conventional platform construction

Spaced wood beam

Spacing = Beam span

Spacing = Joist span

Wood pier foundations elevate timber structures above the ground plane, require minimal excavation, and preserve the natural features and existing drainage patterns of a site. They are particularly useful when building on steep slopes and in areas subject to periodic flooding or high winds.

Wood should be pressure-treated with preservatives to resist insects and decay. See 12.3.

Proper embedment, backfilling, and beam connections are required for the stability of pole structures.

Wood piers can be extended to support the roof and form a structure more resistant to lateral wind and seismic loads. These poles or posts are usually laid out along a grid defined by the beam and joist framing pattern. Their spacing determines both the beam and joist spans and the vertical loads they must support.

Insulate first floor according to local climatic conditions

When adequate embedment is not possible, such as on rocky slopes, steel rod crossbracing with turnbuckles or shear walls of concrete or masonry can be used to provide lateral stability.

s
back span

(3/4)

Limit cantilevers to 1/4 of the back span

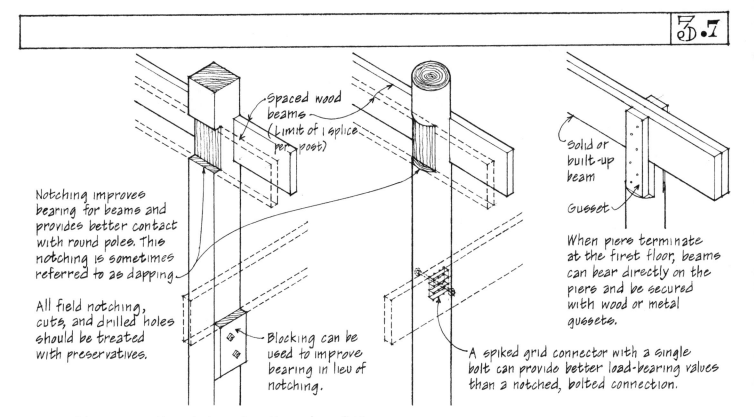

Notching improves bearing for beams and provides better contact with round poles. This notching is sometimes referred to as dapping.

All field notching, cuts, and drilled holes should be treated with preservatives.

Spaced wood beams (Limit of 1 splice per post)

Blocking can be used to improve bearing in lieu of notching.

Solid or built-up beam

Gusset

When piers terminate at the first floor, beams can bear directly on the piers and be secured with wood or metal gussets.

A spiked grid connector with a single bolt can provide better load-bearing values than a notched, bolted connection.

Spaced beams are through-bolted to the sides of the supporting posts or poles, which can then continue up to serve as the load-bearing frame for the superstructure.

CONNECTIONS

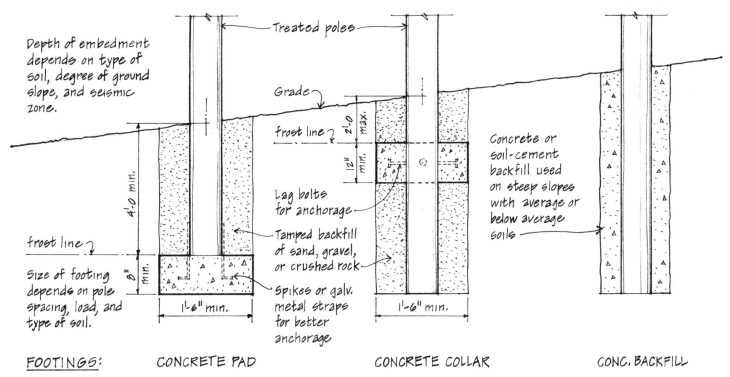

Depth of embedment depends on type of soil, degree of ground slope, and seismic zone.

Treated poles

Grade

frost line

2'-0 max.

12" min.

4'-0 min.

Lag bolts for anchorage

Tamped backfill of sand, gravel, or crushed rock

frost line

8" min.

Size of footing depends on pole spacing, load, and type of soil.

1'-6" min.

Spikes or galv. metal straps for better anchorage

Concrete or soil-cement backfill used on steep slopes with average or below average soils

1'-6" min.

FOOTINGS: CONCRETE PAD   CONCRETE COLLAR   CONC. BACKFILL

Poles are set in holes dug by hand or by a power auger. Concrete pads or collars increase the poles' contact with the soil and distribute their loads over a larger area.

Poles can also be driven as end- or friction-bearing piles. When used in this manner, consult an engineer.

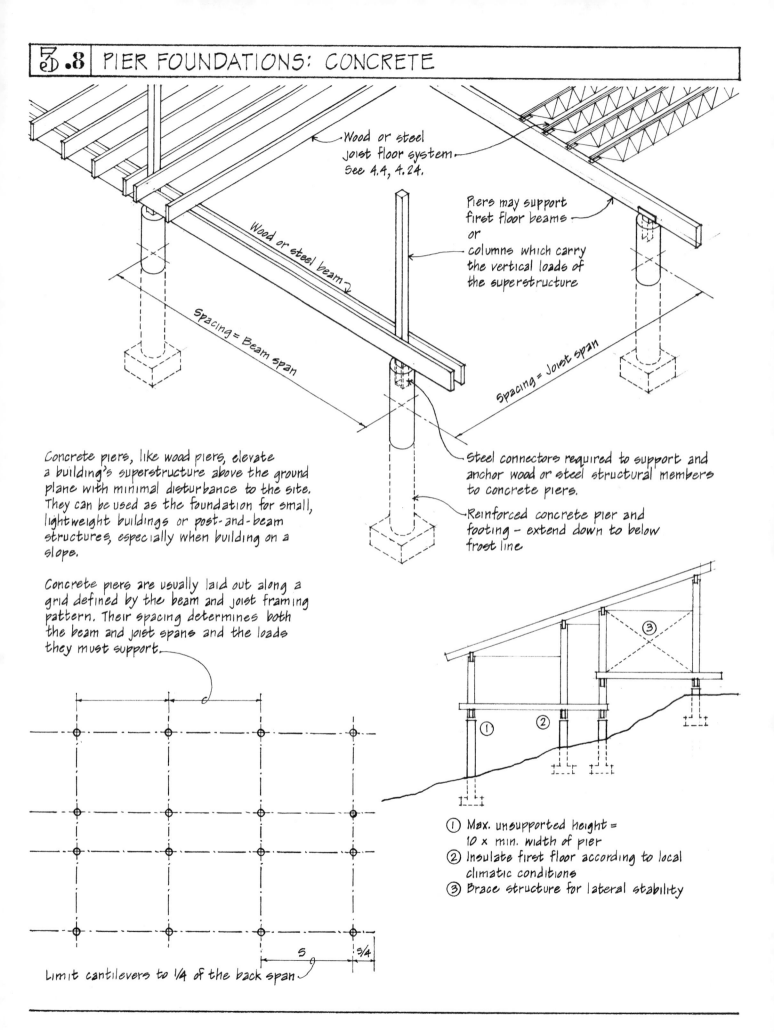

Wood or steel joist floor system. See 4.4, 4.24.

Piers may support first floor beams or columns which carry the vertical loads of the superstructure

Wood or steel beam

Spacing = Beam span

Spacing = Joist span

Concrete piers, like wood piers, elevate a building's superstructure above the ground plane with minimal disturbance to the site. They can be used as the foundation for small, lightweight buildings or post-and-beam structures, especially when building on a slope.

Concrete piers are usually laid out along a grid defined by the beam and joist framing pattern. Their spacing determines both the beam and joist spans and the loads they must support.

Steel connectors required to support and anchor wood or steel structural members to concrete piers.

Reinforced concrete pier and footing - extend down to below frost line

① Max. unsupported height = 10 × min. width of pier

② Insulate first floor according to local climatic conditions

③ Brace structure for lateral stability

5
———
9/4

Limit cantilevers to 1/4 of the back span

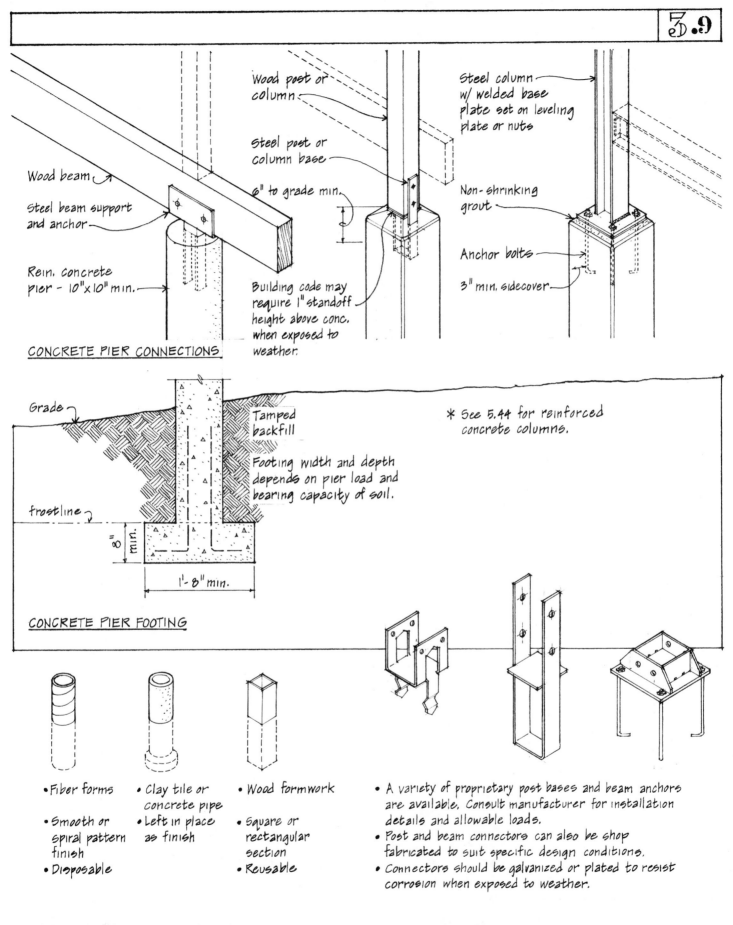

Wood post or column

Steel post or column base

6" to grade min.

Wood beam

Steel beam support and anchor

Rein. concrete pier - 10"x10" min.

Building code may require 1" standoff height above conc. when exposed to weather.

Steel column w/ welded base plate set on leveling plate or nuts

Non-shrinking grout

Anchor bolts

3" min. sidecover.

CONCRETE PIER CONNECTIONS

Grade

Tamped backfill

Footing width and depth depends on pier load and bearing capacity of soil.

* See 5.44 for reinforced concrete columns.

frostline

8" min.

1'- 8" min.

CONCRETE PIER FOOTING

• Fiber forms
• Smooth or spiral pattern finish
• Disposable

• Clay tile or concrete pipe
• Left in place as finish

• Wood formwork
• Square or rectangular section
• Reusable

• A variety of proprietary post bases and beam anchors are available. Consult manufacturer for installation details and allowable loads.
• Post and beam connectors can also be shop fabricated to suit specific design conditions.
• Connectors should be galvanized or plated to resist corrosion when exposed to weather.

CONCRETE PIER FORMWORK   STEEL CONNECTORS

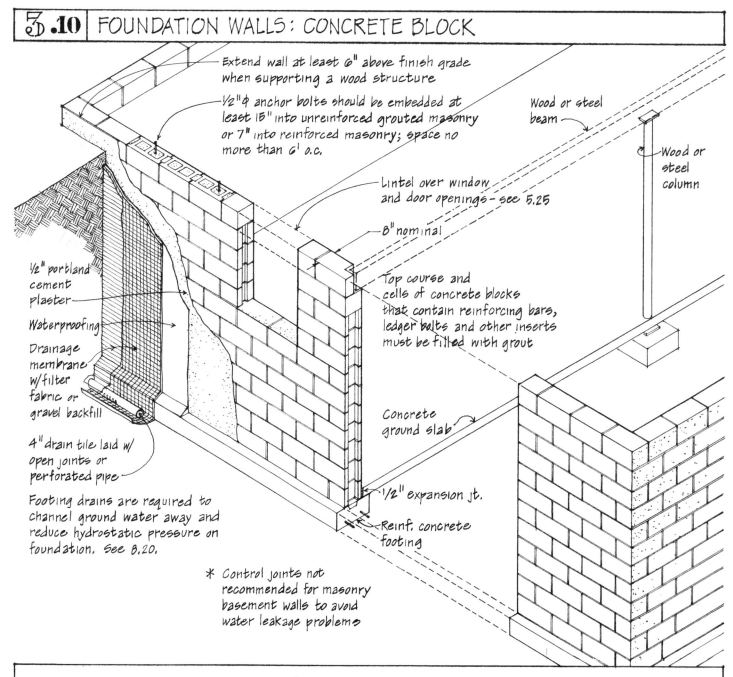

Extend wall at least 6" above finish grade when supporting a wood structure

1/2"⌀ anchor bolts should be embedded at least 15" into unreinforced grouted masonry or 7" into reinforced masonry; space no more than 6' o.c.

Wood or steel beam

Wood or steel column

Lintel over window and door openings - see 5.25

8" nominal

1/2" portland cement plaster

Waterproofing

Drainage membrane w/filter fabric or gravel backfill

Top course and cells of concrete blocks that contain reinforcing bars, ledger bolts and other inserts must be filled with grout

Concrete ground slab

4" drain tile laid w/ open joints or perforated pipe

Footing drains are required to channel ground water away and reduce hydrostatic pressure on foundation. See 8.20.

1/2" expansion jt.

Reinf. concrete footing

* Control joints not recommended for masonry basement walls to avoid water leakage problems

FOUNDATION WALL SYSTEMS • Thickness and reinforcement of foundation wall, and the size of its footing are determined by:

1. Building load and distribution pattern
2. Type and bearing capacity of soil
3. Lateral loading from soil and ground water
4. Lateral bracing provided by basement ground slab and first floor system.

• Presence of ground water requires waterproofing of foundation walls and installation of footing drains.
• Provide rough openings for windows and doors as well as pipe sleeves for water, sewer, gas, oil and electrical lines.
• Type of floor and wall systems being supported will determine the top edge condition.

The form and support pattern of the foundation wall system should respond to the form of the super-structure as well as to the building site's soil and topographic conditions.

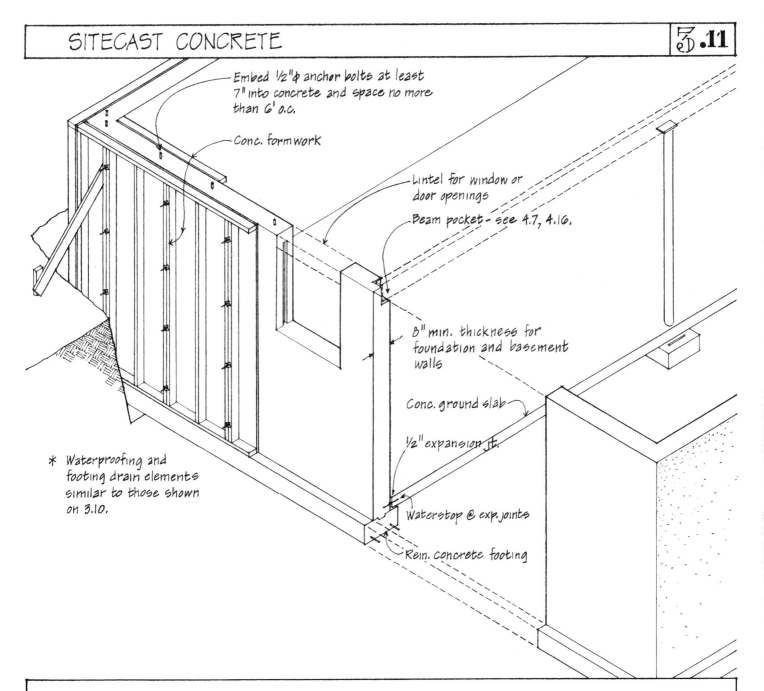

Embed ½"⌀ anchor bolts at least 7" into concrete and space no more than 6' o.c.

Conc. formwork

Lintel for window or door openings

Beam pocket – see 4.7, 4.16.

8" min. thickness for foundation and basement walls

Conc. ground slab

½" expansion jt.

Waterstop @ exp. joints

Rein. concrete footing

* Waterproofing and footing drain elements similar to those shown on 3.10.

CONCRETE BLOCK FOUNDATION WALLS

- No formwork required; utilize easily handled small units; less erection time than for sitecast concrete walls
- Since concrete block is a modular material, all major dimensions (lengths, heights, offsets, wall openings) should be modular to minimize cutting of block.
- Concrete block walls are susceptible to differential settlement and cracking.
- See 5.22, 5.31.

SITECAST CONCRETE FOUNDATION WALLS

- Formwork and access to place concrete required
- Generally stronger but more expensive than concrete block foundations
- Modular dimensioning not necessary unless required by superstructure above

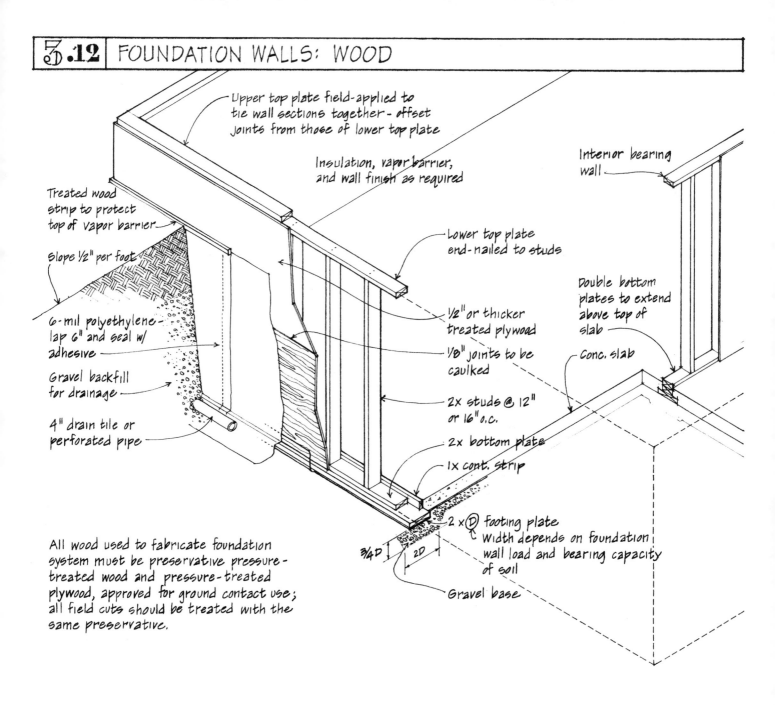

Upper top plate field-applied to tie wall sections together - offset joints from those of lower top plate

Insulation, vapor barrier, and wall finish as required

Interior bearing wall

Treated wood strip to protect top of vapor barrier

Slope ½" per foot

6-mil polyethylene - lap 6" and seal w/ adhesive

Gravel backfill for drainage

4" drain tile or perforated pipe

Lower top plate end-nailed to studs

½" or thicker treated plywood

⅛" joints to be caulked

2x studs @ 12" or 16" o.c.

2x bottom plate

1x cont. strip

2 x (D) footing plate
Width depends on foundation wall load and bearing capacity of soil

Gravel base

Double bottom plates to extend above top of slab

Conc. slab

¾D   2D

All wood used to fabricate foundation system must be preservative pressure-treated wood and pressure-treated plywood, approved for ground contact use; all field cuts should be treated with the same preservative.

WOOD FOUNDATION WALLS

- Wood foundation systems can be used for both basement and crawl space construction.
- Foundation wall sections may be factory fabricated or built on site; offers reduced erection time.
- Foundation walls supporting a first floor beam should be designed to carry the beam's concentrated load, and distribute it so that the allowable bearing capacity of the gravel base and soil is not exceeded.
- A sump may be required to ensure foundation drainage.

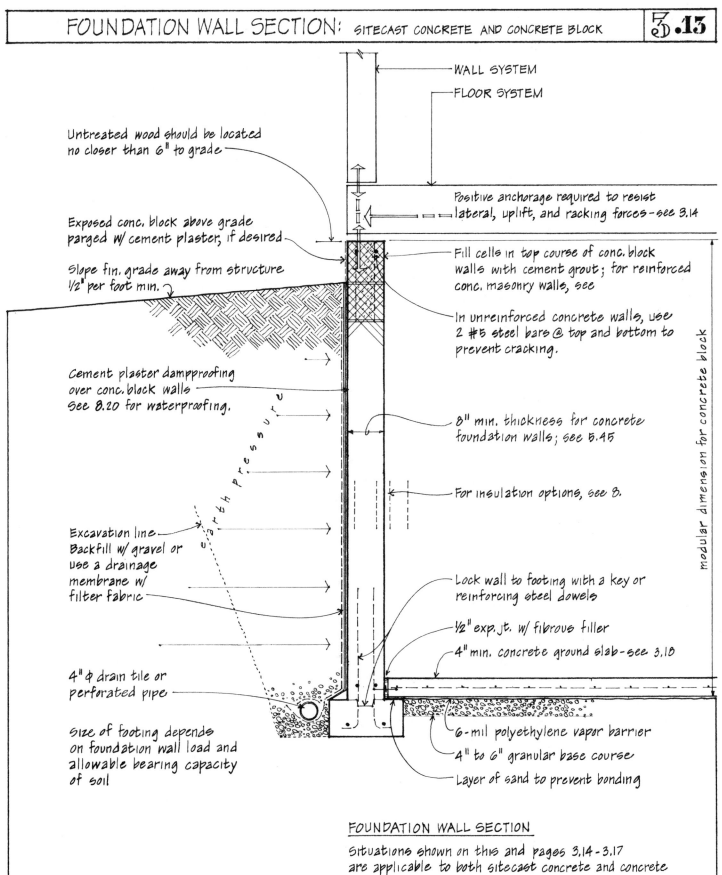

WALL SYSTEM

FLOOR SYSTEM

Untreated wood should be located no closer than 6" to grade

Positive anchorage required to resist lateral, uplift, and racking forces—see 3.14

Exposed conc. block above grade parged w/ cement plaster, if desired

Fill cells in top course of conc. block walls with cement grout; for reinforced conc. masonry walls, see

Slope fin. grade away from structure ½" per foot min.

In unreinforced concrete walls, use 2 #5 steel bars @ top and bottom to prevent cracking.

Cement plaster dampproofing over conc. block walls See 8.20 for waterproofing.

8" min. thickness for concrete foundation walls; see 5.45

earth pressure

For insulation options, see 8.

Excavation line Backfill w/ gravel or use a drainage membrane w/ filter fabric

Lock wall to footing with a key or reinforcing steel dowels

½" exp. jt. w/ fibrous filler

4" min. concrete ground slab—see 3.18

4" ⌀ drain tile or perforated pipe

6-mil polyethylene vapor barrier

4" to 6" granular base course

Size of footing depends on foundation wall load and allowable bearing capacity of soil

Layer of sand to prevent bonding

modular dimension for concrete block

FOUNDATION WALL SECTION

Situations shown on this and pages 3.14 - 3.17 are applicable to both sitecast concrete and concrete block walls.

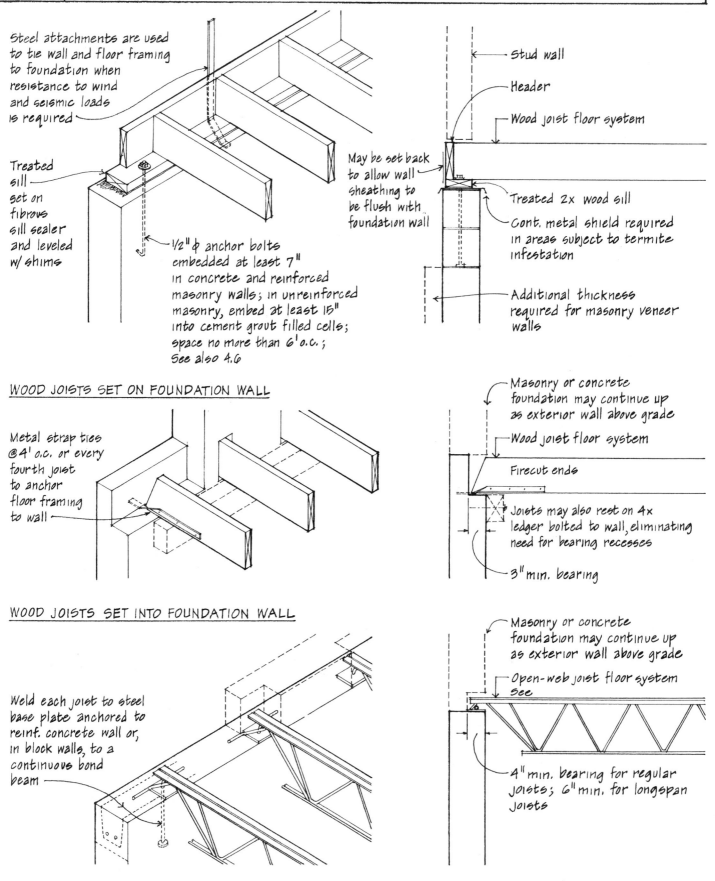

Steel attachments are used to tie wall and floor framing to foundation when resistance to wind and seismic loads is required

Treated sill set on fibrous sill sealer and leveled w/ shims

½" ⌀ anchor bolts embedded at least 7" in concrete and reinforced masonry walls; in unreinforced masonry, embed at least 15" into cement grout filled cells; space no more than 6' o.c.; see also 4.6

Stud wall

Header

Wood joist floor system

May be set back to allow wall sheathing to be flush with foundation wall

Treated 2x wood sill

Cont. metal shield required in areas subject to termite infestation

Additional thickness required for masonry veneer walls

WOOD JOISTS SET ON FOUNDATION WALL

Metal strap ties @4' o.c. or every fourth joist to anchor floor framing to wall

Masonry or concrete foundation may continue up as exterior wall above grade

Wood joist floor system

Firecut ends

Joists may also rest on 4x ledger bolted to wall, eliminating need for bearing recesses

3" min. bearing

WOOD JOISTS SET INTO FOUNDATION WALL

Weld each joist to steel base plate anchored to reinf. concrete wall or, in block walls, to a continuous bond beam

Masonry or concrete foundation may continue up as exterior wall above grade

Open-web joist floor system see

4" min. bearing for regular joists; 6" min. for longspan joists

OPEN-WEB STEEL JOISTS SET ON OR INTO FOUNDATION WALL

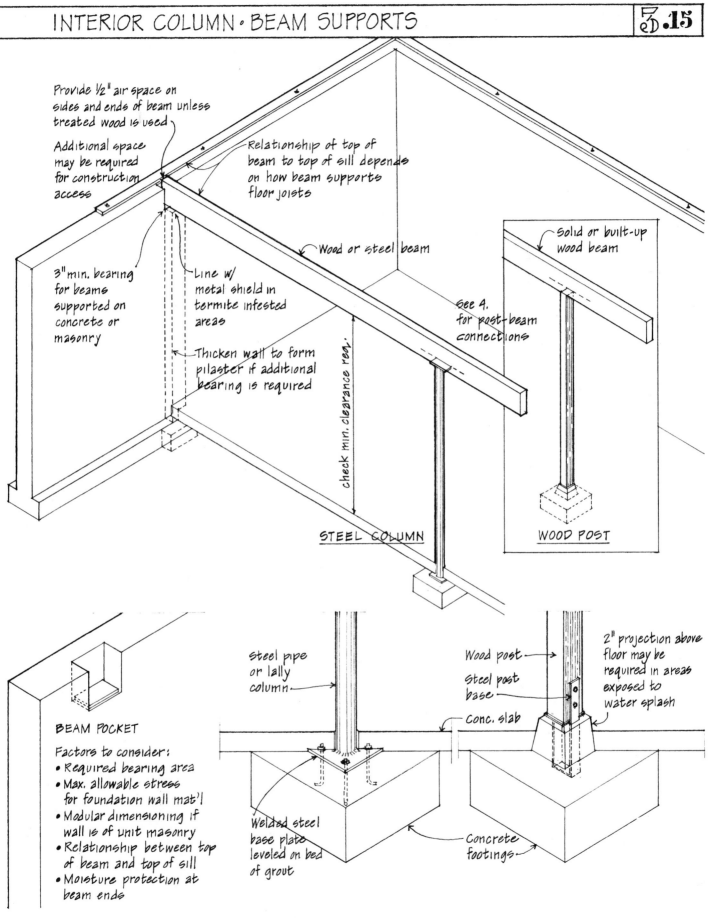

Provide ½" air space on sides and ends of beam unless treated wood is used

Additional space may be required for construction access

Relationship of top of beam to top of sill depends on how beam supports floor joists

Wood or steel beam

Solid or built-up wood beam

3" min. bearing for beams supported on concrete or masonry

Line w/ metal shield in termite infested areas

See 4. for post-beam connections

Thicken wall to form pilaster if additional bearing is required

check min. clearance reqd.

STEEL COLUMN

WOOD POST

BEAM POCKET

Factors to consider:
- Required bearing area
- Max. allowable stress for foundation wall mat'l
- Modular dimensioning if wall is of unit masonry
- Relationship between top of beam and top of sill
- Moisture protection at beam ends

Steel pipe or lally column

Welded steel base plate leveled on bed of grout

Wood post

Steel post base

Conc. slab

2" projection above floor may be required in areas exposed to water splash

Concrete footings

COLUMN BASE FOOTINGS

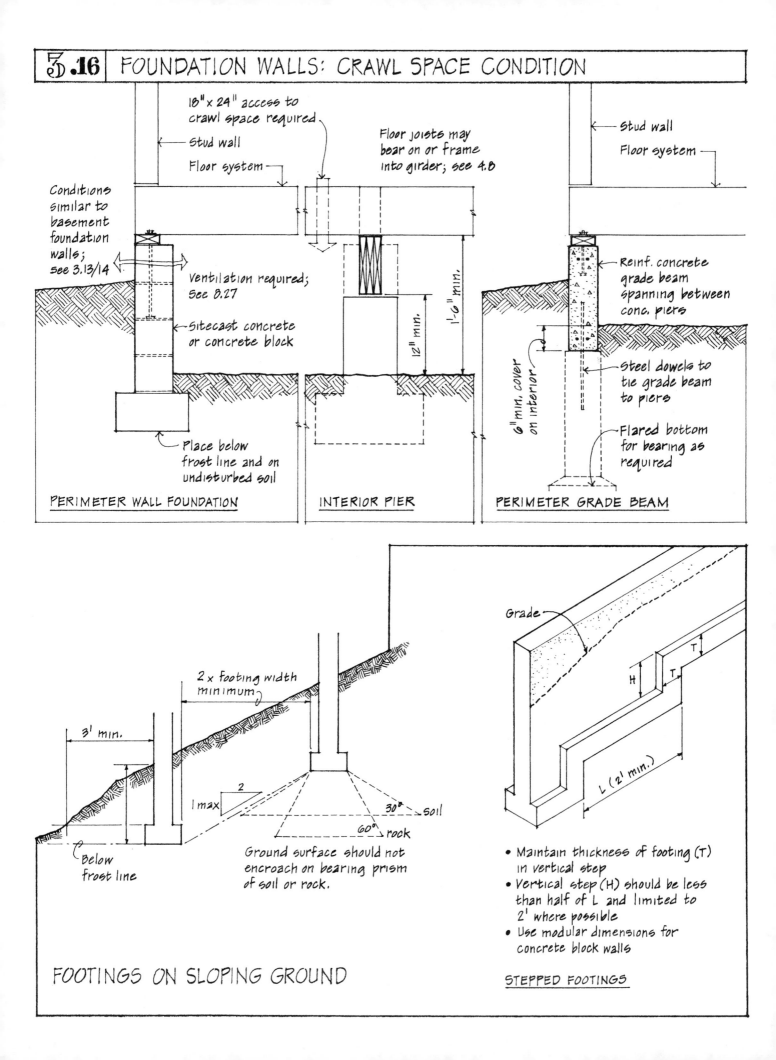

18" x 24" access to crawl space required

Stud wall

Floor system

Floor joists may bear on or frame into girder; see 4.8

Stud wall

Floor system

Conditions similar to basement foundation walls; see 3.13/14

Ventilation required; see 8.27

Sitecast concrete or concrete block

12" min.

1'-6" min.

Reinf. concrete grade beam spanning between conc. piers

6" min. cover on interior

Steel dowels to tie grade beam to piers

Flared bottom for bearing as required

Place below frost line and on undisturbed soil

PERIMETER WALL FOUNDATION

INTERIOR PIER

PERIMETER GRADE BEAM

2 x Footing width minimum

3' min.

Below frost line

1 max / 2

30° soil

60° rock

Ground surface should not encroach on bearing prism of soil or rock.

FOOTINGS ON SLOPING GROUND

Grade

T

H

T

L (2' min.)

- Maintain thickness of footing (T) in vertical step
- Vertical step (H) should be less than half of L and limited to 2' where possible
- Use modular dimensions for concrete block walls

STEPPED FOOTINGS

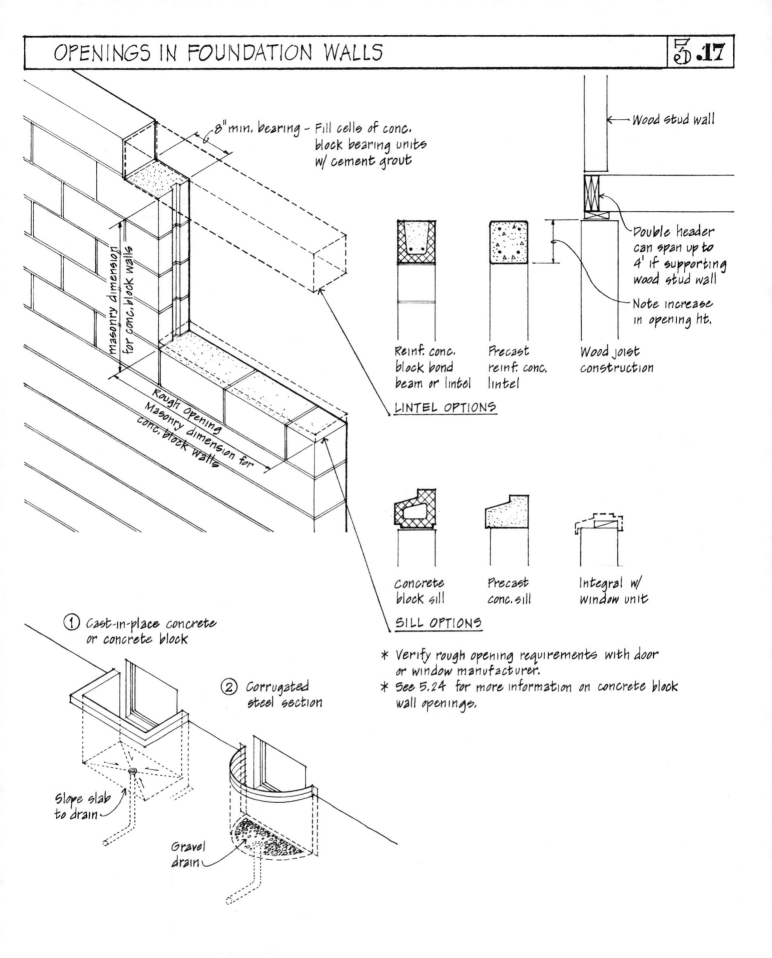

8" min. bearing - Fill cells of conc. block bearing units w/ cement grout

Wood stud wall

Double header can span up to 4' if supporting wood stud wall

Note increase in opening ht.

Masonry dimension for conc. block walls

Rough Opening Masonry dimension for conc. block walls

Reinf. conc. block bond beam or lintel

Precast reinf. conc. lintel

Wood joist construction

LINTEL OPTIONS

Concrete block sill

Precast conc. sill

Integral w/ window unit

SILL OPTIONS

* Verify rough opening requirements with door or window manufacturer.
* See 5.24 for more information on concrete block wall openings.

① Cast-in-place concrete or concrete block

② Corrugated steel section

Slope slab to drain

Gravel drain

BASEMENT WINDOW AREAWAYS

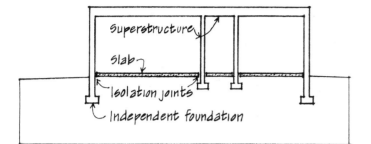

- 4" min. slab thickness
- Should rest on stable, compacted soil with no organic matter
- Does not carry any superstructure loads
- Reinforced with steel mesh fabric which controls thermal stresses, shrinkage cracking, and slight differential movement in the soil bed

GROUND-SUPPORTED SLAB

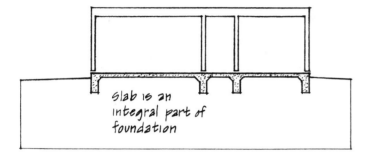

- Used over problem soils
- Structural reinforcement enables slab to act as a monolithic unit with foundation
- Superstructure loads are distributed over entire slab area
- Requires engineering analysis and design

STRUCTURALLY-REINFORCED SLAB

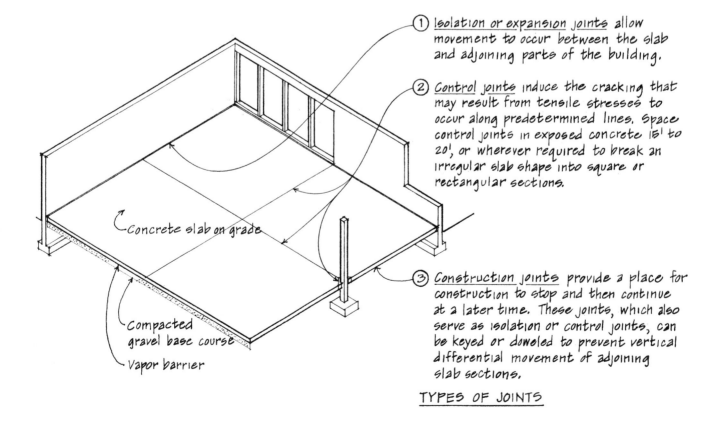

① Isolation or expansion joints allow movement to occur between the slab and adjoining parts of the building.

② Control joints induce the cracking that may result from tensile stresses to occur along predetermined lines. Space control joints in exposed concrete 15' to 20', or wherever required to break an irregular slab shape into square or rectangular sections.

③ Construction joints provide a place for construction to stop and then continue at a later time. These joints, which also serve as isolation or control joints, can be keyed or doweled to prevent vertical differential movement of adjoining slab sections.

TYPES OF JOINTS

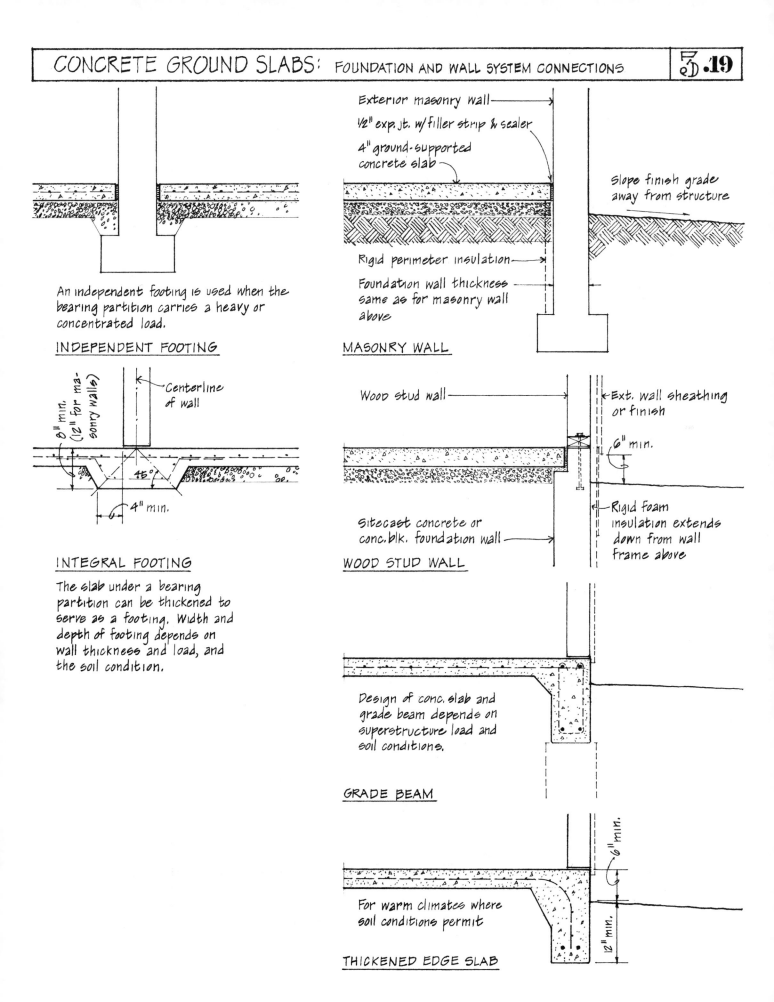

An independent footing is used when the bearing partition carries a heavy or concentrated load.

INDEPENDENT FOOTING

MASONRY WALL

Exterior masonry wall

½" exp. jt. w/ filler strip & sealer

4" ground-supported concrete slab

Slope finish grade away from structure

Rigid perimeter insulation

Foundation wall thickness same as for masonry wall above

Centerline of wall

8" min. (12" for masonry walls)

45°

4" min.

6"

INTEGRAL FOOTING

The slab under a bearing partition can be thickened to serve as a footing. Width and depth of footing depends on wall thickness and load, and the soil condition.

WOOD STUD WALL

Wood stud wall

Ext. wall sheathing or finish

6" min.

Sitecast concrete or conc. blk. foundation wall

Rigid foam insulation extends down from wall frame above

GRADE BEAM

Design of conc. slab and grade beam depends on superstructure load and soil conditions.

THICKENED EDGE SLAB

6" min.

12" min.

For warm climates where soil conditions permit

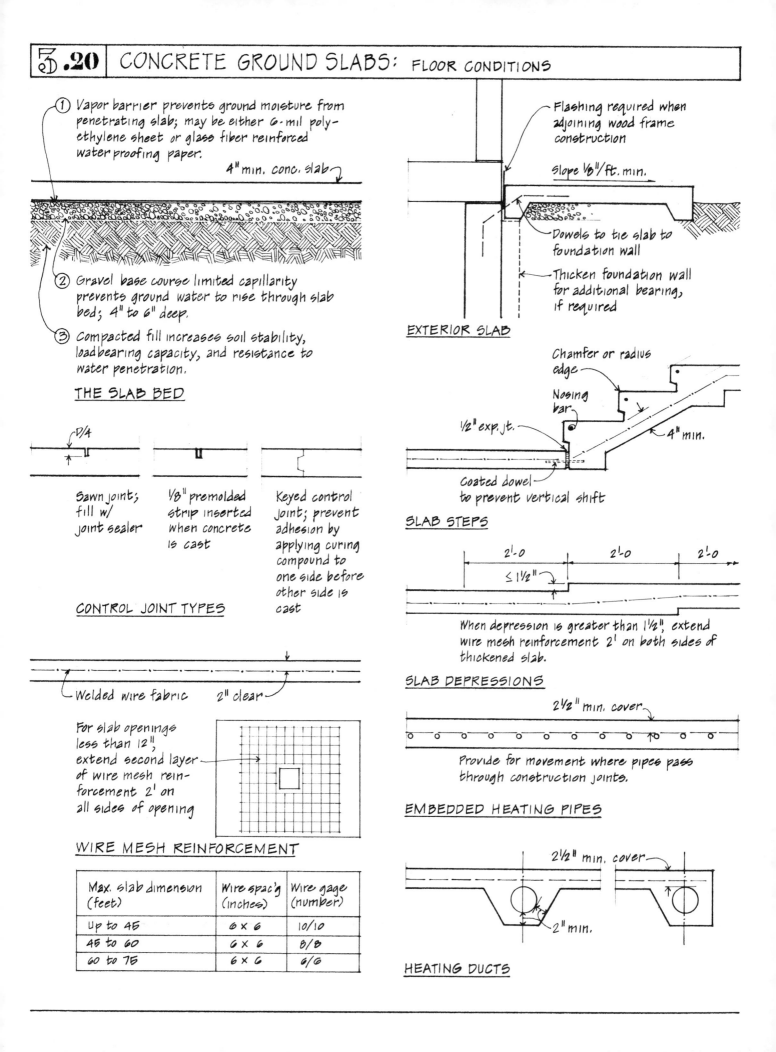

① Vapor barrier prevents ground moisture from penetrating slab; may be either 6-mil polyethylene sheet or glass fiber reinforced water proofing paper.

4" min. conc. slab

② Gravel base course limited capillarity prevents ground water to rise through slab bed; 4" to 6" deep.

③ Compacted fill increases soil stability, loadbearing capacity, and resistance to water penetration.

THE SLAB BED

D/4

Sawn joint; fill w/ joint sealer

1/8" premolded strip inserted when concrete is cast

Keyed control joint; prevent adhesion by applying curing compound to one side before other side is cast

CONTROL JOINT TYPES

Welded wire fabric   2" clear

For slab openings less than 12", extend second layer of wire mesh reinforcement 2' on all sides of opening

WIRE MESH REINFORCEMENT

Max. slab dimension (feet)	Wire spac'g (inches)	Wire gage (number)
Up to 45	6 × 6	10/10
45 to 60	6 × 6	8/8
60 to 75	6 × 6	6/6

Flashing required when adjoining wood frame construction

Slope 1/8"/ft. min.

Dowels to tie slab to foundation wall

Thicken foundation wall for additional bearing, if required

EXTERIOR SLAB

Chamfer or radius edge

Nosing bar

1/2" exp. jt.

4" min.

Coated dowel to prevent vertical shift

SLAB STEPS

2'-0   2'-0   2'-0

≤ 1 1/2"

When depression is greater than 1 1/2", extend wire mesh reinforcement 2' on both sides of thickened slab.

SLAB DEPRESSIONS

2 1/2" min. cover

Provide for movement where pipes pass through construction joints.

EMBEDDED HEATING PIPES

2 1/2" min. cover

2" min.

HEATING DUCTS

FLOOR SYSTEMS

Floor systems are a building's primary horizontal planes which must support both live loads—people, furnishings, and movable equipment—and dead loads—the weight of the floor construction itself. Floor systems must transfer their loads horizontally across space to either beams and columns or to bearing walls. Rigid wall planes can also serve as horizontal diaphragms which act as thin, wide beams spanning between shear wall planes.

A floor system may be composed of a series of linear beams and joists overlaid with a plane of sheathing or decking, or it may consist of a nearly homogeneous slab of reinforced concrete. The depth of a floor system is directly related to the size and proportion of the structural bays it must span and the strength of the materials used. The size and placement of any cantilevers and openings within the floor plane should also be considered in the layout of a floor system's structural supports. A floor system's edge conditions and connections to supporting foundation and wall systems affect both a building's structural integrity and its physical appearance.

Since it must safely support moving loads, a floor system should be relatively stiff while maintaining its elasticity. Due to the detrimental effects that excessive deflection and vibration would have on finish flooring and ceiling materials, as well as concern for human comfort, deflection rather than bending becomes the critical controlling factor.

The depth of the floor construction and the cavities within it should be considered if it is necessary to accommodate runs of mechanical or electrical lines within the floor system. For floor systems between living spaces stacked one above another, an additional factor to consider is the blockage of both airborne and structure-borne sound.

Except for exterior decks, a building's floor systems are normally not exposed to weather. Since they all must support traffic, however, durability, resistance to wear, and maintenance requirements are factors to consider in the selection of a floor finish and the system required to support it.

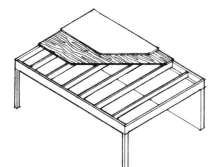
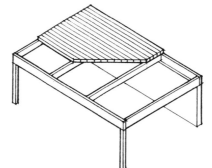

Wood joist floor system

- Relatively short spans for subflooring, underlayment, and applied ceiling
- Flexible in form and shape

Wood plank and beam system

- If underside of construction is left exposed, it is more difficult to run concealed mechanical and electrical lines, and the system is less resistant to sound transmission
- Concentrated loads and floor openings may require additional framing

Wood joist system

- Relatively small joist members closely spaced
- Joists supported by either beams or walls

Wood plank and beam

- Larger beams spaced further apart and spanned with structural planking or decking
- Beams supported by girders, posts, or walls

WOOD

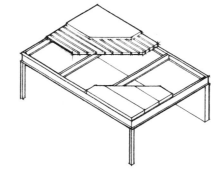

Steel joist floor system

- Relatively short spans for decking
- Underside of structure may be left exposed, or have a ceiling applied
- Limited cantilever potential

Steel beam and decking system

- Typically an integral part of a steel skeleton frame system
- Concentrated loads and floor openings may require additional framing

Steel joist system

- Lightgage or open-web joists closely spaced
- Joists supported by beams or walls

STEEL

Steel beam and decking

- Heavier beams spaced further apart and spanned with steel decking or precast concrete planks
- Beams supported by girders, columns, or walls

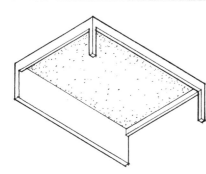

- Precast or cast-in-place
- Concrete floor systems are classified according to the type of span and the resulting form:
  - One-way and two-way slabs
  - One-way joist slab
  - Two-way waffle slab
  - Two-way flat slab
  - Two-way flat plate
- Factors in system choice include the type and magnitude of load conditions, the desired floor depth, and the desired size and proportion of the structural bays

CONCRETE

Subfloor and underlayment
for finish flooring ⟶

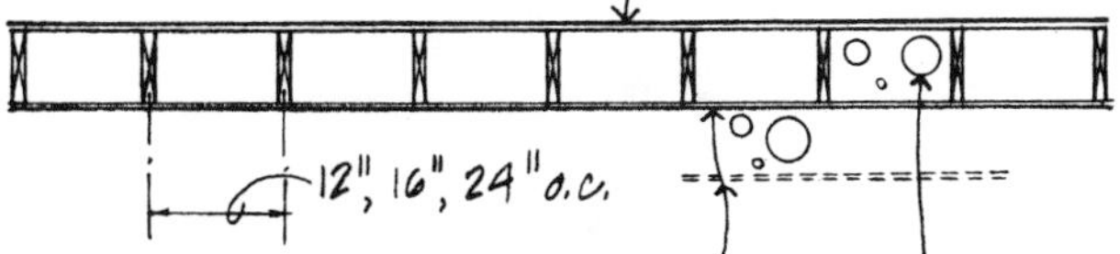

Finish wood flooring over decking;
resilient tile and similar flooring require
underlayment; decking may be left
exposed in rough construction ⟶

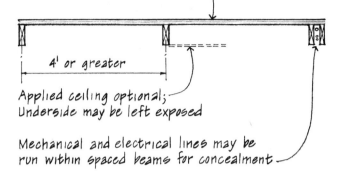

⊢—12", 16", 24" o.c.

4' or greater

Ceiling applied directly
to underside of joists or
suspended from joists

Applied ceiling optional;
Underside may be left exposed

Mechanical and electrical lines
normally run parallel to joists; may
run perpendicular to and penetrate
joists under certain conditions

Mechanical and electrical lines may be
run within spaced beams for concealment ⟶

WOOD JOIST SYSTEM

WOOD PLANK AND BEAM SYSTEM

Concrete fill or slab over
steel floor decking ⟶

Precast conc. planks, or conc. fill or slab
over steel floor decking ⟶

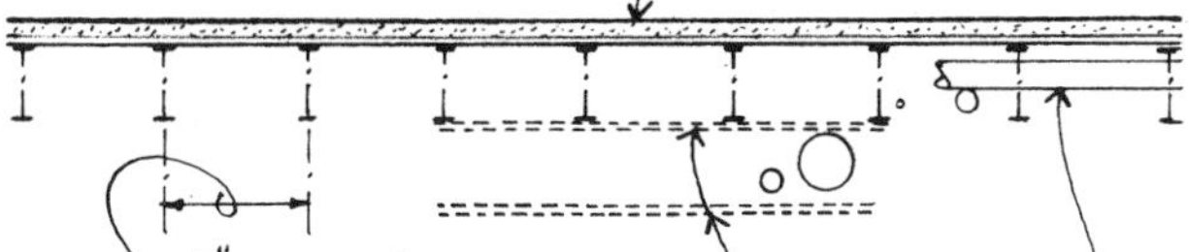

24" or greater,
depending on floor
load and spanning
capability of deck

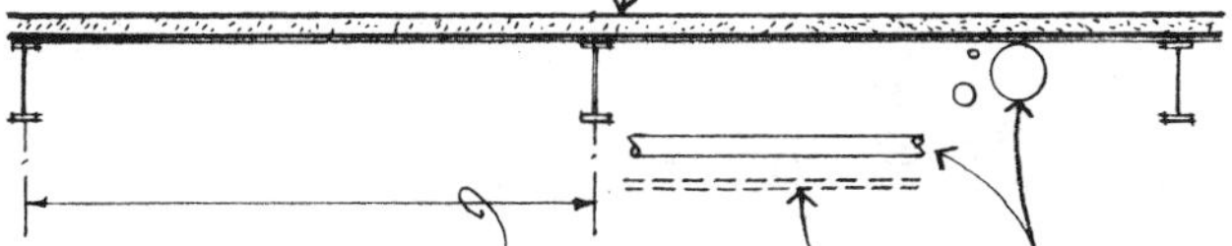

Beam size and spacing
related to floor load,
beam span, and spanning
capability of deck

Underside of structure may
be left exposed, or a ceiling may
be hung from joists

Underside of structure may be left
exposed, or a ceiling may be suspended
from deck

Mechanical and electrical lines may run
parallel or perpendicular to open-web joists

Mechanical and electrical lines run parallel to
beams, or perpendicular to and beneath beams;
may penetrate beams under certain conditions

STEEL JOIST SYSTEM

STEEL BEAM AND DECKING

✳ See 4.32 - 4.33 for overview of concrete floor systems.

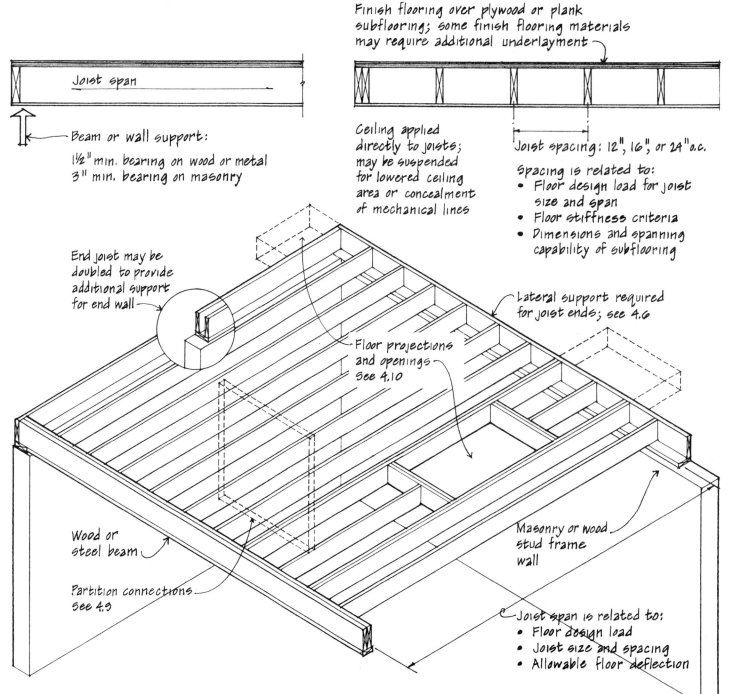

Finish flooring over plywood or plank subflooring; some finish flooring materials may require additional underlayment

Joist span

Beam or wall support:

1½" min. bearing on wood or metal
3" min. bearing on masonry

Ceiling applied directly to joists; may be suspended for lowered ceiling area or concealment of mechanical lines

Joist spacing: 12", 16", or 24" o.c.

Spacing is related to:
- Floor design load for joist size and span
- Floor stiffness criteria
- Dimensions and spanning capability of subflooring

End joist may be doubled to provide additional support for end wall

Lateral support required for joist ends; see 4.6

Floor projections and openings See 4.10

Wood or steel beam

Masonry or wood stud frame wall

Partition connections see 4.9

Joist span is related to:
- Floor design load
- Joist size and spacing
- Allowable floor deflection

WOOD JOIST FLOOR SYSTEM

- Most typical wood floor system
- Flexible in form and shape because of the workability of the material, the relatively small pieces, and the various means of fastening available
- Fire-resistance rating depends on finish floor and ceiling materials

The joist span table below is for preliminary sizing of members only. It assumes that joists have simple spans. A rule of thumb for estimating joist spans: Span = 24 × joist depth.

SIZE nominal	SPACING center to center	SPAN AS LIMITED BY DEFLECTION *			SPAN AS LIMITED BY BENDING			
		E = 1,200,000 psi			F_b = 1200 psi		F_b = 1400 psi	
		Live load in lbs. per S.F.	40	60	40	60	40	60
2 × 6	12"		9'-8"	8'-7"	10'-11"	9'-5"	11'-9"	10'-2"
	16"		8'-10"	7'-10"	9'-6"	8'-2"	10'-3"	8'-10"
	24"		7'-9"	6-10"	7-10"	6'-8"	8'-5"	7'-3"
2 × 8	12		12-10	11-5	14-5	12-6	15-7	13-6
	16		11-8	10-5	12-7	10-10	13-7	11-9
	24		10-3	9-2	10-4	8-11	11-2	9-8
2 × 10	12		16-1	14-5	18-2	15-8	19-7	17-0
	16		14-9	13-2	15-10	13-8	17-2	14-9
	24		13-0	11-6	13-1	11-3	14-2	12-2
2 × 12	12		19-5	17-4	21-10	18-11	23-7	20-5
	16		17-9	15-10	19-1	16-6	20-8	17-10
	24		15-8	13-11	15-9	13-7	17-0	14-8
2 × 14	12		22-7	20-3	25-5	22-1	27-6	23-10
	16		20-9	18-7	22-4	19-3	24-1	20-10
	24		18-4	16-4	18-5	15-11	19-11	17-2

* Joist deflection not to exceed 1/360th of span; stiffness of joist system under stress is more critical than its strength.
- Generally, if the overall construction depth is acceptable, deeper joists spaced further apart are more desirable for stiffness than shallow joists spaced more closely together.
- E = modulus of elasticity; F_b = allowable unit stress in extreme fiber bending; both vary according to species and of grade of lumber used.

BRIDGING

Bridging consists of wood or metal crossbracing or full-depth blocking between each joist at 8' intervals. Bridging may be required by some building codes if the joist depth is 6 or more times its thickness. However, it is usually not necessary if the joist ends are supported laterally and their top compression edges are restrained by the subflooring.

CUTS IN JOISTS

To allow plumbing and electrical lines to pass through floor joists, cuts may be made according to the following guidelines:

2" min. to joist edge

Max. diameter = 1/3 joist depth

1/6 of joist depth maximum and not within middle third of span

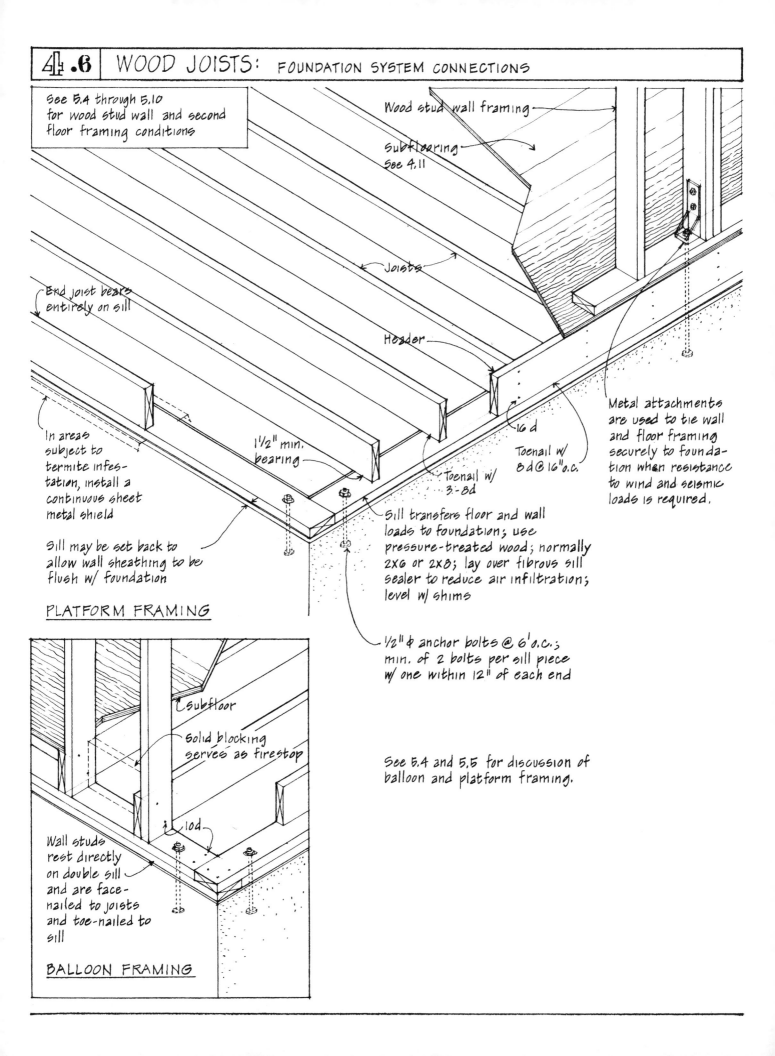

See 5.4 through 5.10 for wood stud wall and second floor framing conditions

Wood stud wall framing

Subflooring See 4.11

Joists

Header

End joist bears entirely on sill

In areas subject to termite infestation, install a continuous sheet metal shield

1½" min. bearing

16 d

Toenail w/ 8d @ 16"o.c.

Toenail w/ 3 - 8d

Metal attachments are used to tie wall and floor framing securely to foundation when resistance to wind and seismic loads is required.

Sill may be set back to allow wall sheathing to be flush w/ foundation

Sill transfers floor and wall loads to foundation; use pressure-treated wood; normally 2x6 or 2x8; lay over fibrous sill sealer to reduce air infiltration; level w/ shims

PLATFORM FRAMING

½" ⌀ anchor bolts @ 6' o.c.; min. of 2 bolts per sill piece w/ one within 12" of each end

Subfloor

Solid blocking serves as firestop

See 5.4 and 5.5 for discussion of balloon and platform framing.

10d

Wall studs rest directly on double sill and are face-nailed to joists and toe-nailed to sill

BALLOON FRAMING

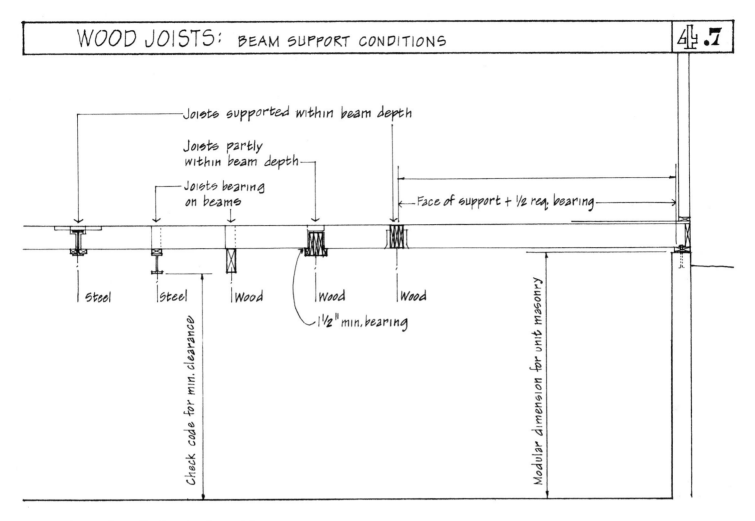

Joists supported within beam depth

Joists partly within beam depth

Joists bearing on beams

Face of support + ½ req. bearing

Steel Steel Wood Wood Wood

1½" min. bearing

Check code for min. clearance

Modular dimension for unit masonry

* See 4.13 for types of wood beams and beam span table

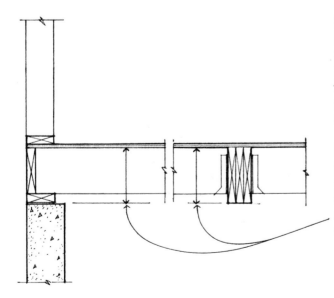

Wood joists may be supported by wood or steel beams. In either case, the height of the beam and its supports should be coordinated with both the perimeter sill condition and how the beam supports the floor joists.
See next page for details of joist-beam connections.

Wood is most susceptible to shrinkage perpendicular to its grain. For this reason, the total depth of wood construction for both the sill condition and the joist-beam connection should be equalized to avoid subsidence of the floor plane.

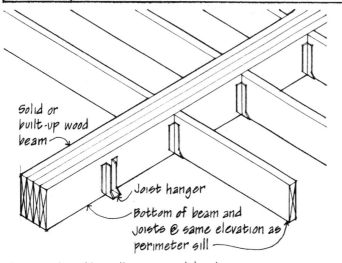

Solid or built-up wood beam

Joist hanger

Bottom of beam and joists @ same elevation as perimeter sill

*Use only with well-seasoned lumber

TOP OF JOISTS FLUSH W/ BEAM

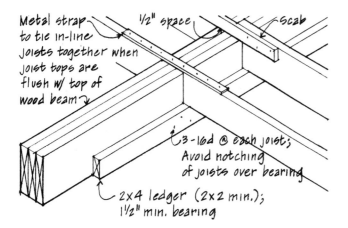

Metal strap to tie in-line joists together when joist tops are flush w/ top of wood beam

½" space

Scab

3-16d @ each joist; Avoid notching of joists over bearing

2x4 ledger (2x2 min.); 1½" min. bearing

LEDGER BEARING

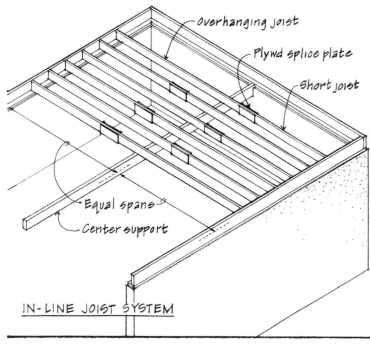

Overhanging joist

Plywd splice plate

Short joist

Equal spans

Center support

IN-LINE JOIST SYSTEM

Scab ties joists together, maintains horizontal continuity of floor structure, and supports subfloor

½" space to allow for joist shrinkage

8d

Nailing plate bolted to bottom flange; of same thickness as perimeter sill to equalize shrinkage

Steel beam

LEDGER BEARING

In-line joists w/ scab or metal tie strap

4" min. lap

1½" min. bearing

16d

Toenail w/ 8d

Wood sill of same thickness as perimeter sill; bolted w/ threaded rod welded to top flange

STEEL BEAM BEARING

The in-line joist system allows the use of one size smaller joists that would normally be used in conventional framing. When used with studs and rafters spaced 24" o.c., in-line joists also make efficient use of 48" wide sheathing materials. These material savings, however, may be offset by increased labor costs.

The system consists of uneven length joists, the longer ones overhanging the center support ¼ to ⅓ of the simple span, at a point where the bending moment approaches zero. The shorter joists are connected to the overhanging joists with shear-resisting metal connectors or plywood splice plates. The overhanging and short joists alternate sides and form joists continuous over two spans.

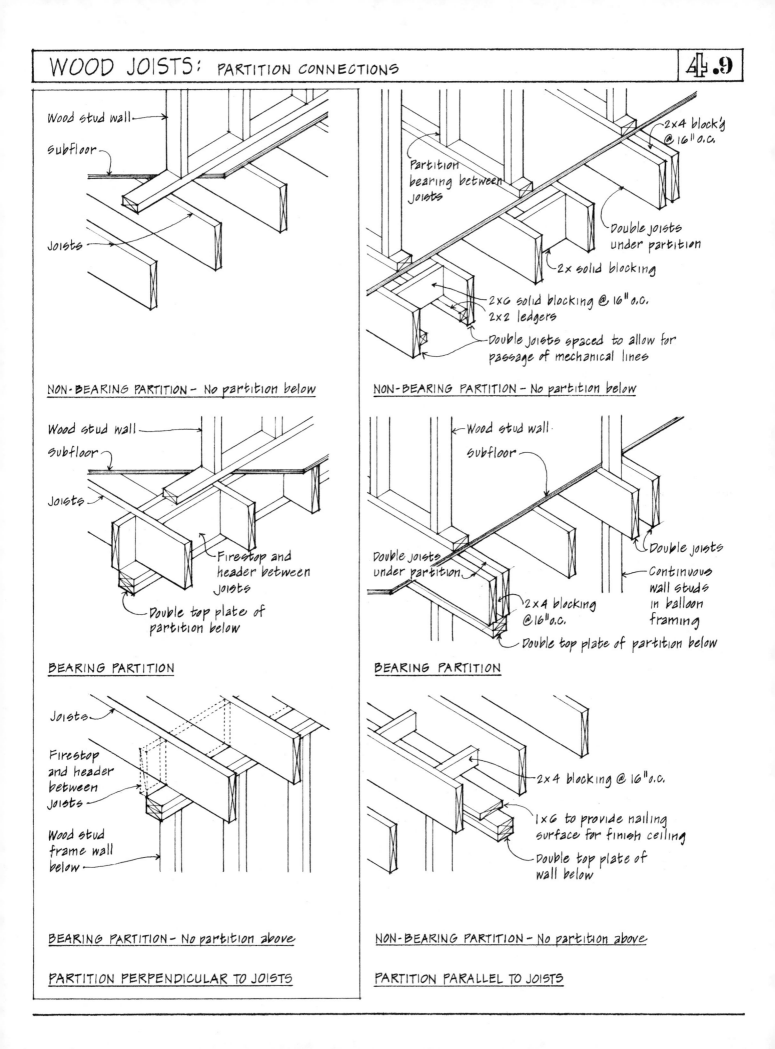

Wood stud wall

Subfloor

Joists

NON-BEARING PARTITION – No partition below

Partition bearing between joists

2×4 block'g @ 16" o.c.

Double joists under partition

2× solid blocking

2×6 solid blocking @ 16" o.c.
2×2 ledgers

Double joists spaced to allow for passage of mechanical lines

NON-BEARING PARTITION – No partition below

Wood stud wall

Subfloor

Joists

Firestop and header between joists

Double top plate of partition below

BEARING PARTITION

Wood stud wall

Subfloor

Double joists under partition

Double joists

Continuous wall studs in balloon framing

2×4 blocking @ 16" o.c.

Double top plate of partition below

BEARING PARTITION

Joists

Firestop and header between joists

Wood stud frame wall below

2×4 blocking @ 16" o.c.

1×6 to provide nailing surface for finish ceiling

Double top plate of wall below

BEARING PARTITION – No partition above

PARTITION PERPENDICULAR TO JOISTS

NON-BEARING PARTITION – No partition above

PARTITION PARALLEL TO JOISTS

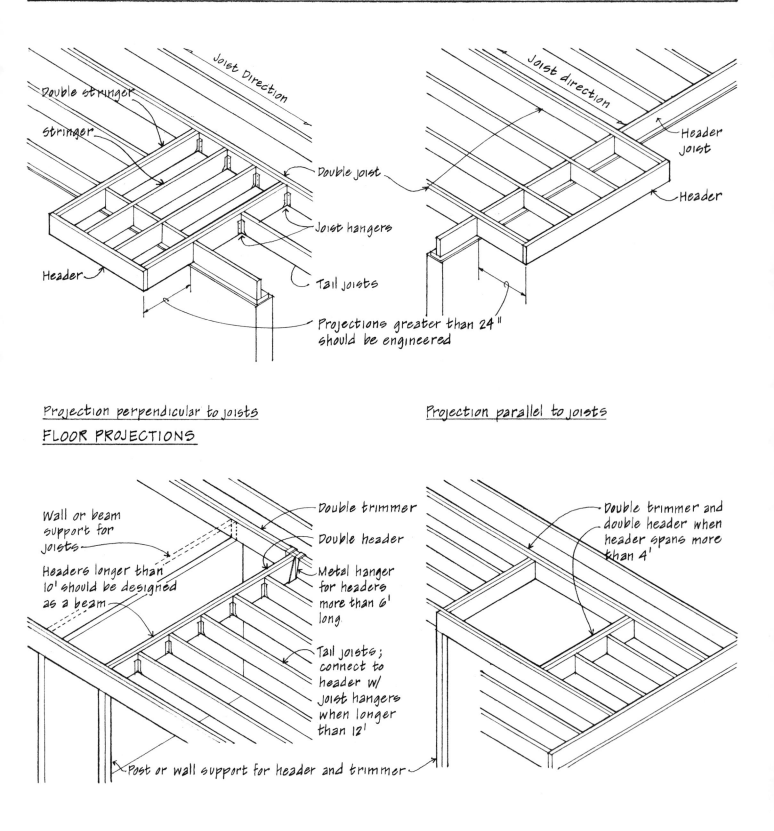

Joist Direction

Double stringer

Stringer

Double joist

Joist hangers

Header

Tail joists

Projections greater than 24" should be engineered

Joist direction

Header Joist

Header

Projection perpendicular to joists

Projection parallel to joists

FLOOR PROJECTIONS

Wall or beam support for joists

Headers longer than 10' should be designed as a beam

Double trimmer

Double header

Metal hanger for headers more than 6' long

Tail joists; connect to header w/ joist hangers when longer than 12'

Post or wall support for header and trimmer

Double trimmer and double header when header spans more than 4'

Length perpendicular to joists

Length parallel to joists

FLOOR OPENINGS

Subflooring is the structural material that spans across floor joists, serves as a working platform during construction, and provides a base for the finish flooring. The joist and subfloor assembly can also be used as a diaphragm to resist horizontal forces if constructed according to approved standards. Consult the building code.

SUBFLOOR	THICKNESS (inch)	PANEL INDEX	SPAN (inches)
BOARDS			
1x4, 1x6	3/4	–	16
PANEL SUBFLOOR			
For rated	5/8	32/16	16
sheathing &	1/2·5/8	36/16	16
Structural I	5/8·3/4·7/8	42/20	20
& II grades	3/4·7/8	48/24	24
UNDERLAYMENT			
Underlayment	1/4	Over panel subfloor	
or C-C plugged (ext.) grades	3/8	Over board subfloor	
COMBINED SUBFLOOR-UNDERLAYMENT			
For APA rated	5/8	16	16
Sturd-i-floor	5/8·3/4	20	20
grades	3/4·7/8·1	24	24
2-4-1	1⅛	48	48

Span rating is part of gradestamp found on back of panel; Span = max. joist spacing

Underlayment required before application of resilient flooring, carpet, or other non-structural flooring

Typically plywood, although other non-veneer panel materials such as oriented strand board (OSB), waferboard, and particleboard can be used if manufactured according to approved standards. Consult American Plywood Association (APA).

May be 24" if 25/32" wood strip flooring is laid perpendicular to joists

Underlayment provides impact load resistance and a smooth surface for the direct application of non-structural flooring materials; may be applied as a separate layer over board or panel subflooring, or be combined in a single thickness with the subfloor panel; when floor is subject to unusual moisture conditions, use panels with exterior glue (Exposure 1). or Exterior plywood.

6d ring shank nails for thicknesses through 3/4" (8d for panels 7/8"and thicker); nail @ 6"o.c. along edges and 10"o.c. along intermediate supports (6"o.c. for 2-4-1 panels)

Support ends of board subflooring unless end-matched boards are used and each piece rests on at least 2 joists.

PANEL SUBFLOOR AND UNDERLAYMENT

Indicated spans assume panels are laid continuously over 2 or more spans with their long dimension perpendicular to the joists.

Stagger end joints.

Space joints ⅛" unless otherwise recommended by panel manufacturer; space butt joints in underlayment 1/32".

Provide blocking under edges or use tongue-and-groove panel edges; not required if underlayment joints are offset from subfloor joints.

GLUED FLOOR SYSTEM

Gluing combined subfloor-underlayment panels to the floor joists enables the panels to act together with the joists to form integral T-beam units. This application system lessens floor creep and squeaking, and may increase floor stiffness and, in some cases, the allowable spans for the joists. These benefits, of course, are contingent on the quality of the application.

Panels are secured with power-driven fasteners or with 6d deformed shank nails @ 12"o.c. (6"o.c. for 2-4-1 panels). Consult APA for detail recommendations.

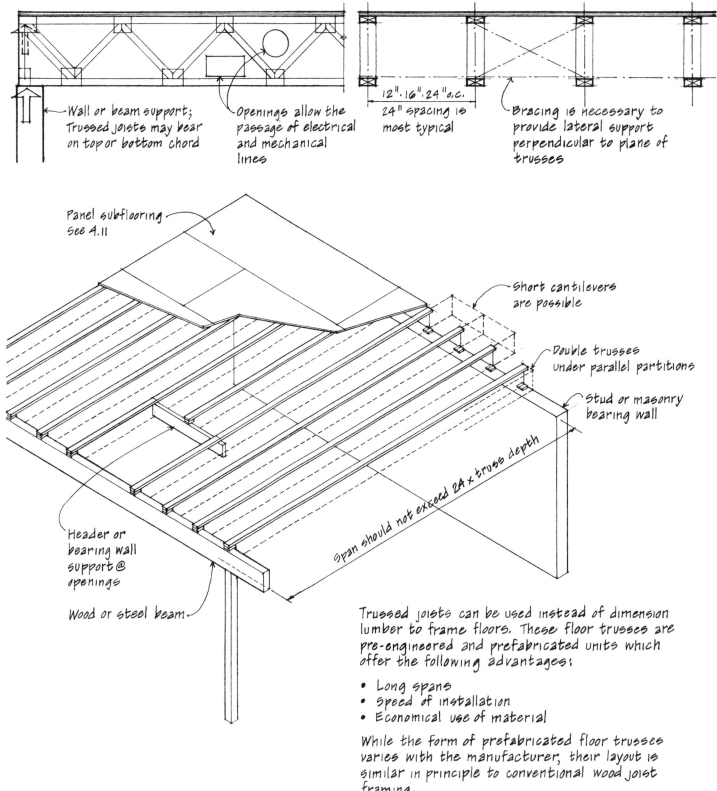

Wall or beam support; Trussed joists may bear on top or bottom chord

Openings allow the passage of electrical and mechanical lines

12".16".24" o.c. 24" spacing is most typical

Bracing is necessary to provide lateral support perpendicular to plane of trusses

Panel subflooring see 4.11

Short cantilevers are possible

Double trusses under parallel partitions

Stud or masonry bearing wall

Span should not exceed 24 x truss depth

Header or bearing wall support @ openings

Wood or steel beam

Trussed joists can be used instead of dimension lumber to frame floors. These floor trusses are pre-engineered and prefabricated units which offer the following advantages:

• Long spans
• Speed of installation
• Economical use of material

While the form of prefabricated floor trusses varies with the manufacturer, their layout is similar in principle to conventional wood joist framing.

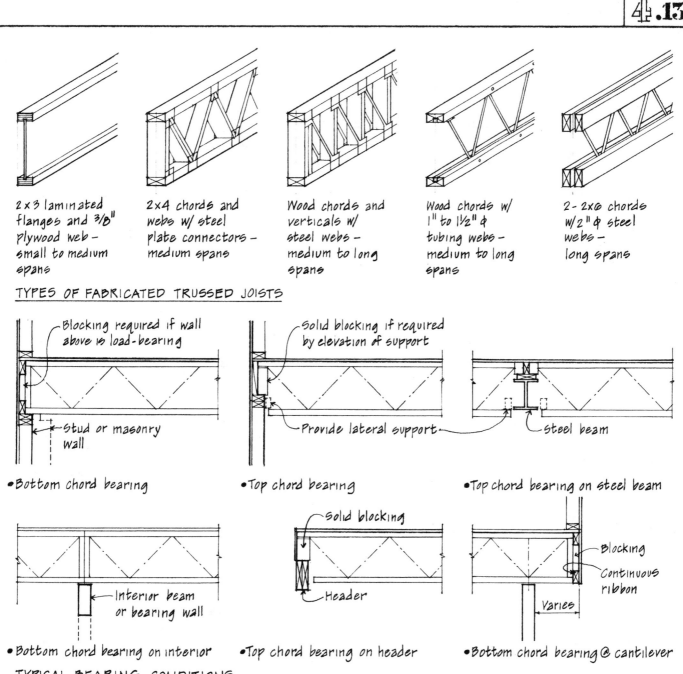

2 x 3 laminated flanges and 3/8" plywood web — small to medium spans

2 x 4 chords and webs w/ steel plate connectors — medium spans

Wood chords and verticals w/ steel webs — medium to long spans

Wood chords w/ 1" to 1½" ⌀ tubing webs — medium to long spans

2 - 2x6 chords w/2" ⌀ steel webs — long spans

TYPES OF FABRICATED TRUSSED JOISTS

Blocking required if wall above is load-bearing

Stud or masonry wall

- Bottom chord bearing

Solid blocking if required by elevation of support

Provide lateral support

- Top chord bearing

steel beam

- Top chord bearing on steel beam

Interior beam or bearing wall

- Bottom chord bearing on interior

Solid blocking

Header

- Top chord bearing on header

Blocking

Continuous ribbon

Varies

- Bottom chord bearing @ cantilever

TYPICAL BEARING CONDITIONS

The floor truss span table to the right is to be used for preliminary design only. Spans should not exceed 24 × truss depth.

Consult manufacturer for sizes, spacing, allowable spans, bearing conditions, and truss specifications.

Live load	55 lbs. per S.F.			80 lbs. per S.F.		
Spacing	12" o.c.	16" o.c.	24" o.c.	12" o.c.	16" o.c.	24" o.c.
Depth						
12"	23'-4"	21'-0	17'-0	19'-0	17'-4"	15'-0
14"	26-4	22-8	18-8	21-4	19-4	16-6
16"	28-6	24-8	20-0	23-6	21-4	17-8
18"	30-6	26-4	21-6	25-8	23-4	19-0
20"	32-4	27-8	22-8	27-8	24-8	20-4
24"	35-0	30-8	25-0	31-6	27-4	22-0

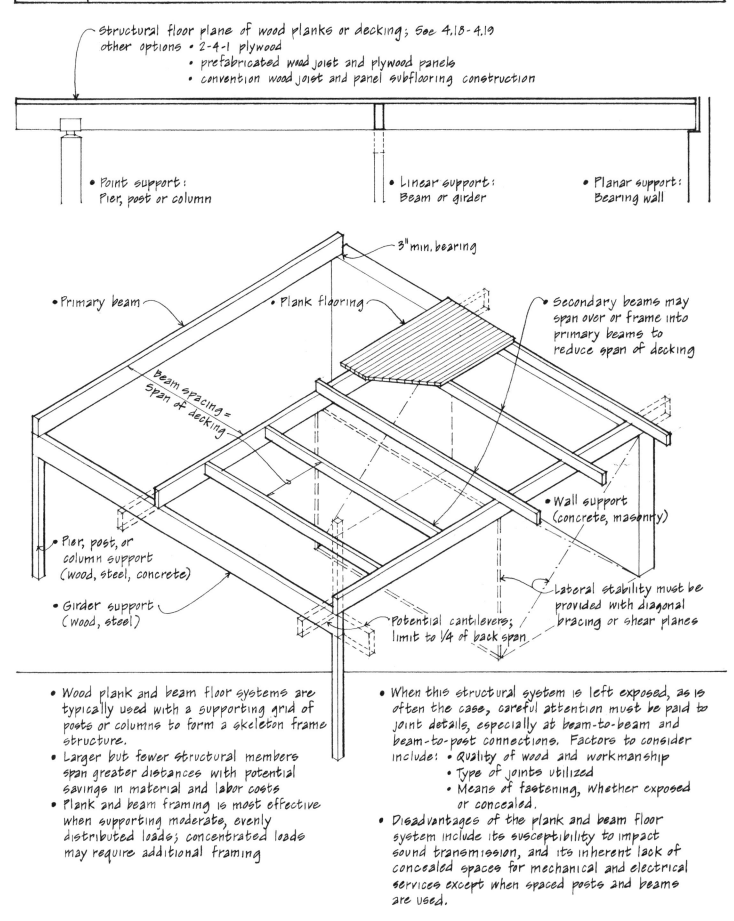

Structural floor plane of wood planks or decking; See 4.18 - 4.19
other options • 2-4-1 plywood
• prefabricated wood joist and plywood panels
• convention wood joist and panel subflooring construction

• Point support:
Pier, post or column

• Linear support:
Beam or girder

• Planar support:
Bearing wall

3" min. bearing

• Primary beam

• Plank flooring

• Secondary beams may span over or frame into primary beams to reduce span of decking

Beam spacing = Span of decking

• Wall support (concrete, masonry)

• Pier, post, or column support (wood, steel, concrete)

• Girder support (wood, steel)

Lateral stability must be provided with diagonal bracing or shear planes

Potential cantilevers; limit to 1/4 of back span

• Wood plank and beam floor systems are typically used with a supporting grid of posts or columns to form a skeleton frame structure.
• Larger but fewer structural members span greater distances with potential savings in material and labor costs
• Plank and beam framing is most effective when supporting moderate, evenly distributed loads; concentrated loads may require additional framing

• When this structural system is left exposed, as is often the case, careful attention must be paid to joint details, especially at beam-to-beam and beam-to-post connections. Factors to consider include: • Quality of wood and workmanship
• Type of joints utilized
• Means of fastening, whether exposed or concealed.
• Disadvantages of the plank and beam floor system include its susceptibility to impact sound transmission, and its inherent lack of concealed spaces for mechanical and electrical services except when spaced posts and beams are used.

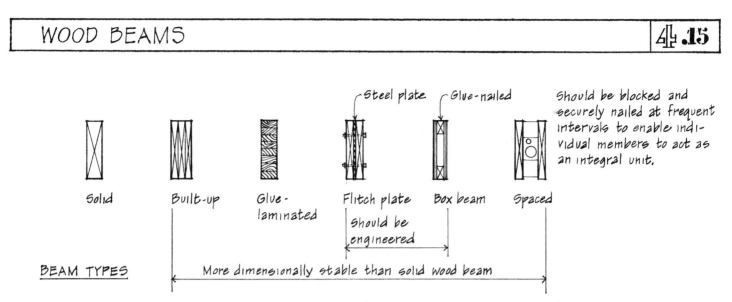

Steel plate — Glue-nailed

Should be blocked and securely nailed at frequent intervals to enable individual members to act as an integral unit.

Solid   Built-up   Glue-laminated   Flitch plate   Box beam   Spaced

Should be engineered

BEAM TYPES   More dimensionally stable than solid wood beam

The following span tables for common types of wood beams are for preliminary sizing only. In the selection of a wood beam, the following must be considered: the species and grade of lumber used, its modulus of elasticity, and the allowable bending and shear stress values. In addition, attention must be paid to the precise loading condition, the types of connections used, and the allowable deflection. See Bibliography for sources of more detailed span and load tables.

SOLID AND BUILT-UP WOOD BEAMS			GLUE-LAMINATED BEAMS		
SPAN Feet	SPACING Feet	SIZE Nominal in inches	SPAN Feet	SPACING Feet	SIZE Actual in inches
10	4	2 · 2 × 8	12	6	3 1/8 × 9
	6	2 · 2 × 10		8	3 1/8 × 10 1/2
	8	4 × 10		10	3 1/8 × 10 1/2
				12	3 1/8 × 12
12	4	3 × 10	16	6	3 1/8 × 13 1/2
	6	2 · 2 × 12		8	3 1/8 × 15
	8	4 × 12		10	3 1/8 × 15
				12	3 1/8 × 15
14	4	4 × 10	20	6	3 1/8 × 16 1/2
	6	6 × 10		8	5 1/8 × 15
	8	3 · 2 × 12		10	5 1/8 × 18
				12	5 1/8 × 18
16	6	3 · 2 × 12	24	6	5 1/8 × 16 1/2
	8	4 · 2 × 12		8	5 1/8 × 18
				10	5 1/8 × 21
				12	5 1/8 × 22 1/2
18	6	6 × 12	28	6	5 1/8 × 19 1/2
	8	8 × 12		8	5 1/8 × 21
				10	5 1/8 × 24
				12	5 1/8 × 25 1/2
20	6	2 · 3 × 14	32	6	5 1/8 × 21
	8	2 · 4 × 14		8	5 1/8 × 24
				10	5 1/8 × 27
				12	6 3/4 × 27

These tables assume the following:

Total live load = 40 lbs. per S.F.
Allowable deflection = 1/360 of span
Extreme fiber stress in bending (Fb) = 1200 psi
    (2400 psi for glu-lam) →
Modulus of Elasticity (E) = 1.4 × 10⁶ psi
    (1.8 × 10⁶ psi for glu-lam) →

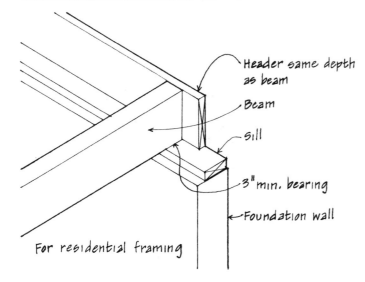

Header same depth as beam

Beam

Sill

3" min. bearing

Foundation wall

For residential framing

FOUNDATION WALL SUPPORT

½" min. clearance on end and sides; more space may be required for construction access

steel clip angles and base plate on bed of dryset grout

Anchor bolts

Optional prefabricated beam seat

To resist both uplift and horizontal forces

MASONRY OR CONCRETE WALL SUPPORT

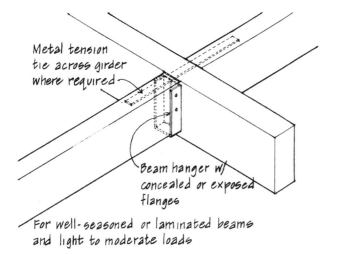

Metal tension tie across girder where required

Beam hanger w/ concealed or exposed flanges

For well-seasoned or laminated beams and light to moderate loads

GIRDER SUPPORT

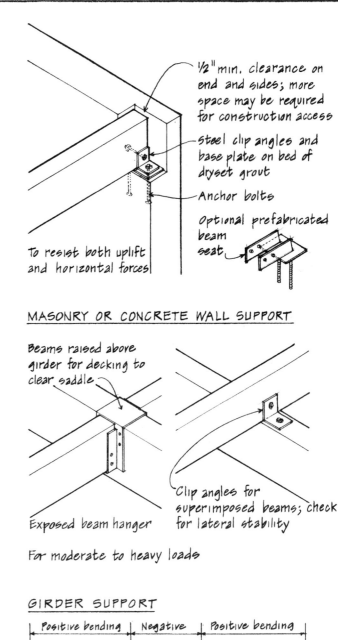

Beams raised above girder for decking to clear saddle

Exposed beam hanger

Clip angles for superimposed beams; check for lateral stability

For moderate to heavy loads

GIRDER SUPPORT

Positive bending | Negative | Positive bending

Splice

A variety of metal attachments are manufactured for wood-to-wood, wood-to-metal, and wood-to-masonry connections. These include joist and beam hangers, post bases and caps, framing angles and anchors, and floor ties and holddowns. Consult manufacturer for specific sizes, configurations, allowable loads, and fastening requirements. Depending on the magnitude of the loads being resisted or transferred, the connectors may be nailed or bolted.

Continuous spans produce more uniform stresses than simple spans, resulting in more efficient use of material. Any splices should occur at points of minimum bending stress, approximately 1/4 to 1/3 of the span on either side of an interior support.

Supported beam

Cantilevered beam

Wedges

STEEL SPLICE CONNECTOR   MORTISE SPLICE

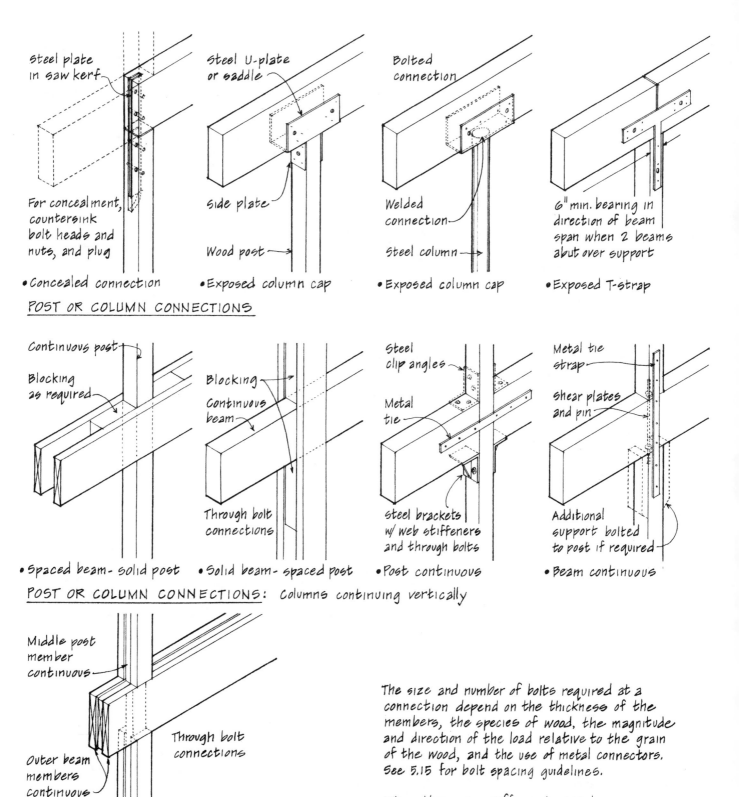

steel plate in saw kerf

For concealment, countersink bolt heads and nuts, and plug

• Concealed connection

steel U-plate or saddle

side plate

Wood post

• Exposed column cap

Bolted connection

Welded connection

Steel column

• Exposed column cap

6" min. bearing in direction of beam span when 2 beams abut over support

• Exposed T-strap

POST OR COLUMN CONNECTIONS

Continuous post

Blocking as required

• Spaced beam- solid post

Blocking

Continuous beam

Through bolt connections

• Solid beam- spaced post

Steel clip angles

Metal tie

steel brackets w/ web stiffeners and through bolts

• Post continuous

Metal tie strap

shear plates and pin

Additional support bolted to post if required

• Beam continuous

POST OR COLUMN CONNECTIONS: Columns continuing vertically

Middle post member continuous

Outer beam members continuous

Through bolt connections

INTERLOCKING POST AND BEAM

The size and number of bolts required at a connection depend on the thickness of the members, the species of wood, the magnitude and direction of the load relative to the grain of the wood, and the use of metal connectors. See 5.15 for bolt spacing guidelines.

When there is insufficient area to accommodate the required number of bolts, shear plate or split ring connectors, which can develop greater stresses per unit bearing, can be used.

- Non-bearing partitions perpendicular to floor planking have their load distributed evenly across the planks

Sole plate

Beam must be framed into posts or other beams for support

Wood stud frame wall

- Partitions parallel to floor planking may be supported by beams either below or above the planking

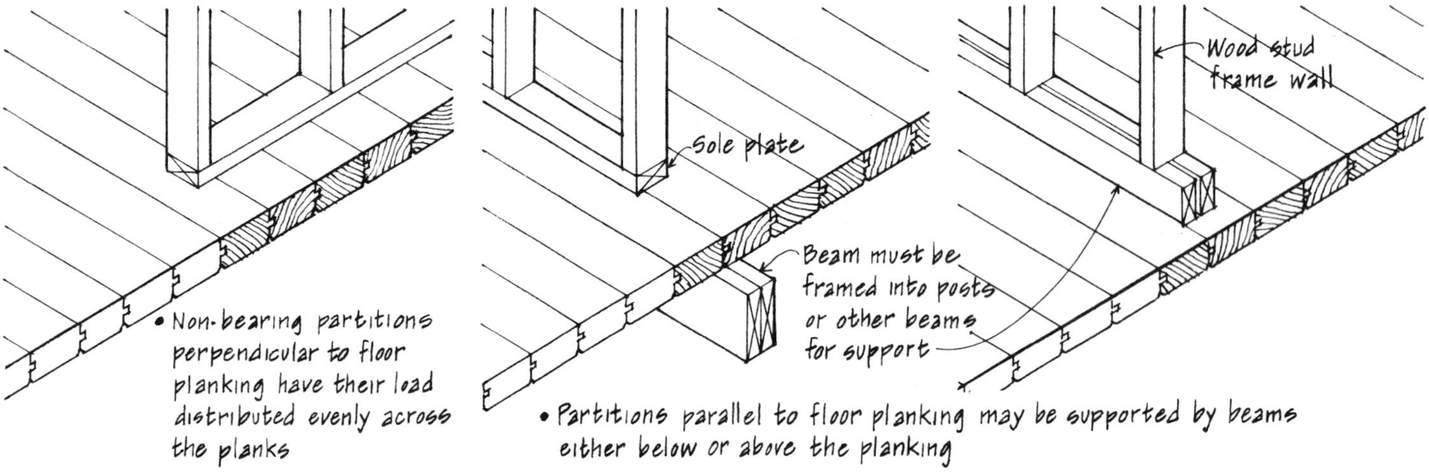

NON-BEARING PARTITIONS OVER WOOD PLANK FLOOR

In the plank and beam framing system, the beam grid layout should be carefully integrated with the required placement of interior partitions for both structural and visual reasons. Normally, most partitions in this system are non-bearing and may be placed as shown above. If bearing partitions are required, however, they should continue down to a foundation wall or be placed over floor beams large enough to carry the additional load.

FLOOR SYSTEMS SPANNING BETWEEN BEAMS

Other than the conventional wood joist and panel subfloor system, the following can be utilized:

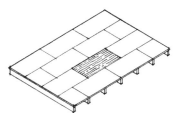

2-4-1 Plywood
(combined subfloor-underlayment)

- 1⅛" thick
- Can span up to 4'
- Tongue and groove edges
- Laid continuously over 2 spans with face plies perpendicular to beams and end joints staggered
- No overhang possible
- See 4.11

Prefabricated panels

- Plywood sheathing over nominal 2" framing which acts as floor joists
- Glue-nailed or bonded with adhesives under heat and pressure to form stressed skin panels
- Insulation, vapor barrier, and interior finish may be applied at one time
- Limited overhang possible

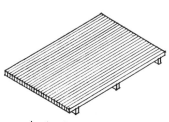

Wood planking

- See facing page
- Limited overhang possible
- Openings and concentrated loads require additional framing
- Wood strip flooring laid at right angles to planking
- Underlayment required for resilient and thinset tile flooring

Solid
Nominal 2×6, 2×8

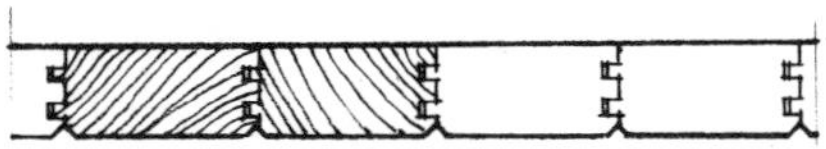

Solid
Nominal 3×6, 4×6

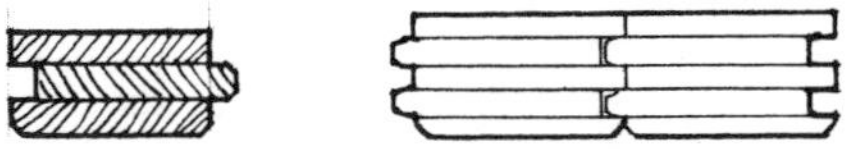

Laminated
Nominal 3×6,8,10; 4×6,8; 5×6,8

TYPES OF WOOD DECKING

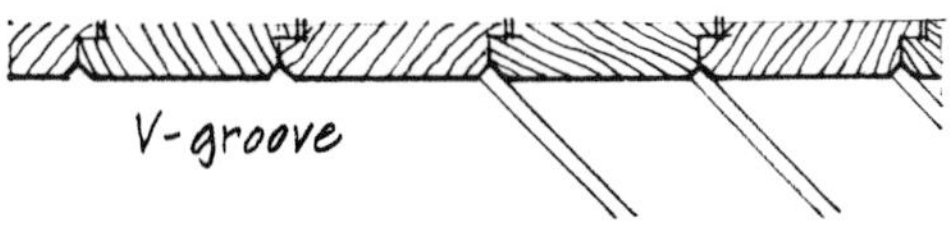

V-groove

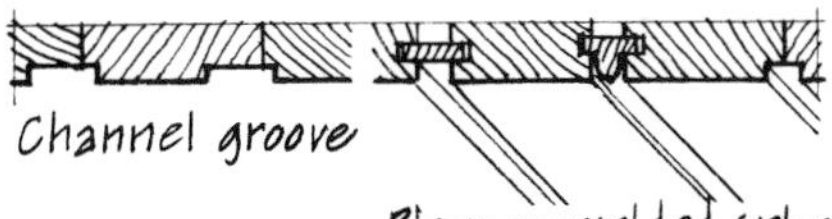

Channel groove

Plain or molded spline

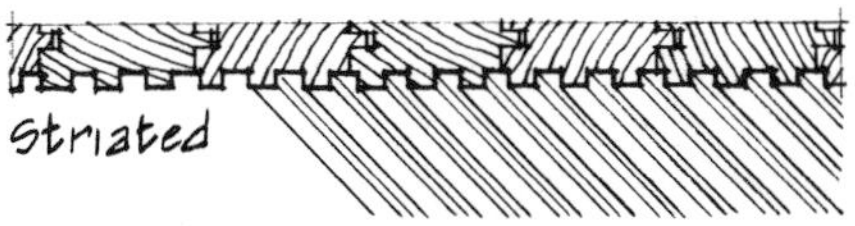

Striated

SURFACE PATTERNS for exposed plank ceilings

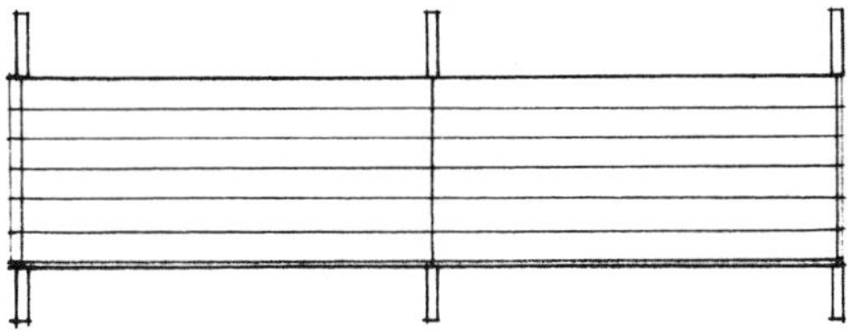

Simple span

Planks simply supported at each
end have the most deflection for
a given load.

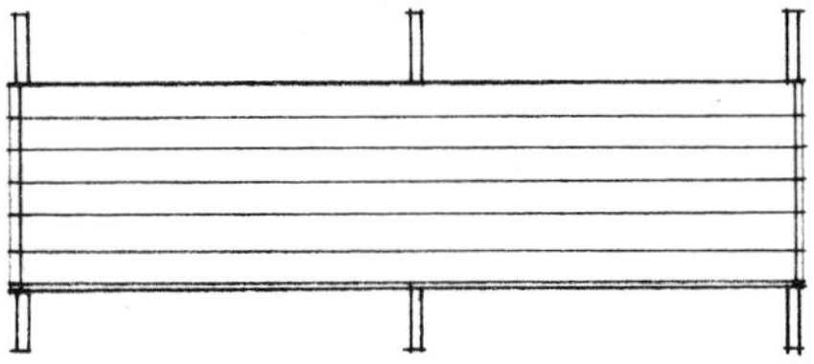

TYPES OF DECKING SPANS

Double span

Structurally, the most efficient
use of material of a given length.

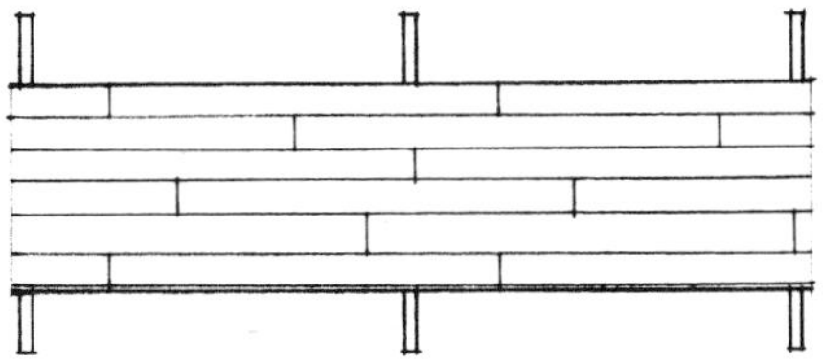

Continuous span over 4 or more
supports; use of random lengths
reduces waste; layout must be
carefully controlled.

- Distance between end joints
  in adjacent courses must be
  at least 2'
- Joints in the same general
  line must rest on at least
  one support
- Joints in non-adjacent rows
  must be separated by 12" or
  2 rows of planks
- Only one joint should occur
  in each course between
  supports
- Each plank must rest on at
  least one support
- In end spans, one-third of
  the planks should be free
  of joints.

TOTAL ALLOWABLE UNIFORMLY DISTRIBUTED LOADS *			
Nominal deck thickness in inches	Span feet	Simple span lbs. per S.F.	Controlled random layup lbs. per S.F.
2	6	46	
	8	20	25
3	8	62	106
	10	32	54
	12	18	31
3 (superthick)	10	53	90
	12	31	52
	14	19	33
4	12	44	74
	14	28	47
	16	19	31
5	14	51	86
	16	34	58
	18	24	41
	20	18	30

* This table is to be used for
  preliminary sizing only.
  Consult manufacturer's
  literature.

The above assumes: Fiber stress in bending (F_b) = 1500 psi
Modulus of elasticity (E) = 1.3×10^6 psi
Allowable deflection = 1/240 of decking span

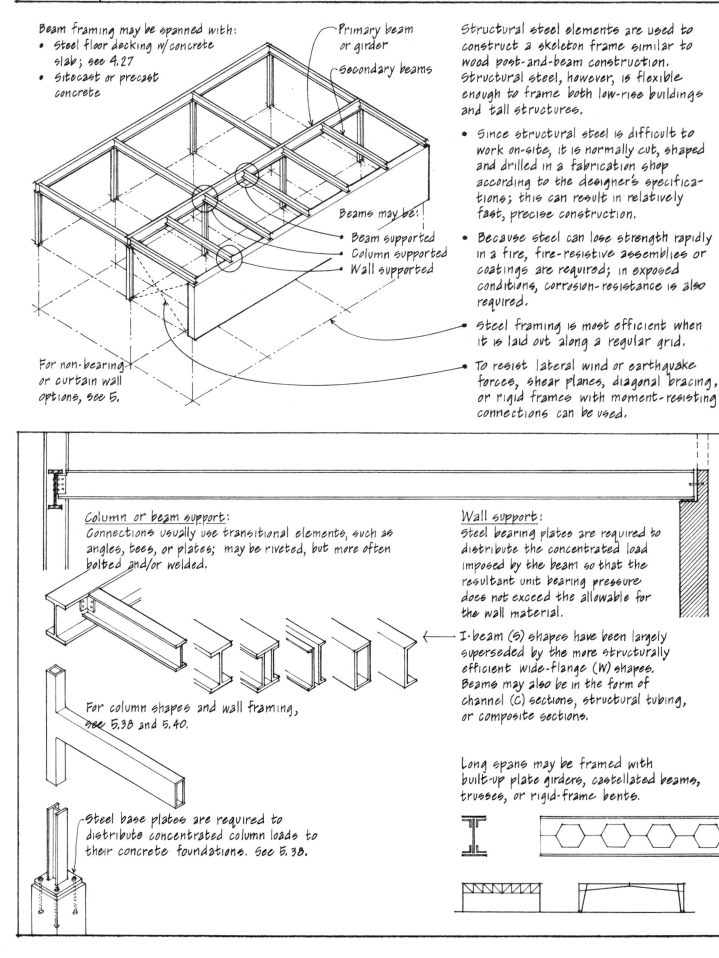

Beam framing may be spanned with:
- Steel floor decking w/concrete slab; see 4.27
- Sitecast or precast concrete

Primary beam or girder

Secondary beams

Beams may be:
- Beam supported
- Column supported
- Wall supported

For non-bearing or curtain wall options, see 5.

Structural steel elements are used to construct a skeleton frame similar to wood post-and-beam construction. Structural steel, however, is flexible enough to frame both low-rise buildings and tall structures.

- Since structural steel is difficult to work on-site, it is normally cut, shaped and drilled in a fabrication shop according to the designer's specifications; this can result in relatively fast, precise construction.

- Because steel can lose strength rapidly in a fire, fire-resistive assemblies or coatings are required; in exposed conditions, corrosion-resistance is also required.

- Steel framing is most efficient when it is laid out along a regular grid.

- To resist lateral wind or earthquake forces, shear planes, diagonal bracing, or rigid frames with moment-resisting connections can be used.

Column or beam support:
Connections usually use transitional elements, such as angles, tees, or plates; may be riveted, but more often bolted and/or welded.

For column shapes and wall framing, see 5.38 and 5.40.

Steel base plates are required to distribute concentrated column loads to their concrete foundations. See 5.38.

Wall support:
Steel bearing plates are required to distribute the concentrated load imposed by the beam so that the resultant unit bearing pressure does not exceed the allowable for the wall material.

I-beam (S) shapes have been largely superseded by the more structurally efficient wide-flange (W) shapes. Beams may also be in the form of channel (C) sections, structural tubing, or composite sections.

Long spans may be framed with built-up plate girders, castellated beams, trusses, or rigid-frame bents.

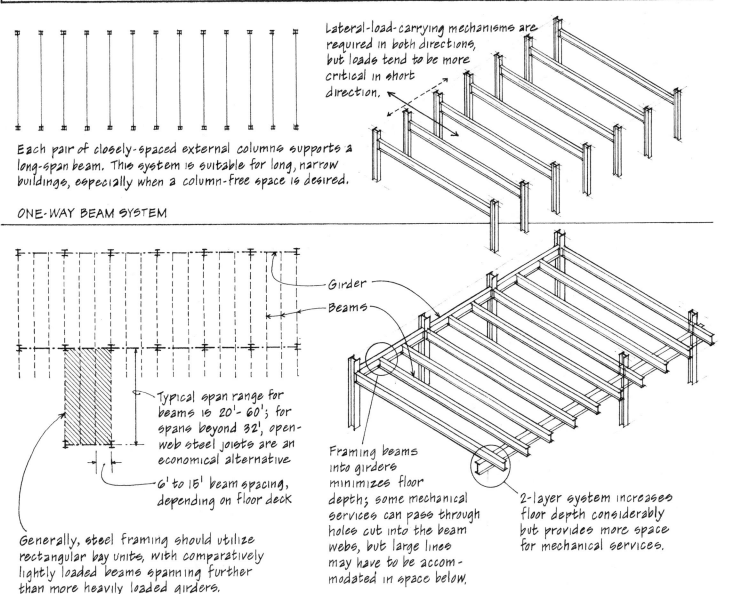

Lateral-load-carrying mechanisms are required in both directions, but loads tend to be more critical in short direction.

Each pair of closely-spaced external columns supports a long-span beam. This system is suitable for long, narrow buildings, especially when a column-free space is desired.

ONE-WAY BEAM SYSTEM

Girder

Beams

Typical span range for beams is 20'- 60'; for spans beyond 32', open-web steel joists are an economical alternative

6' to 15' beam spacing, depending on floor deck

Generally, steel framing should utilize rectangular bay units, with comparatively lightly loaded beams spanning further than more heavily loaded girders.

Framing beams into girders minimizes floor depth; some mechanical services can pass through holes cut into the beam webs, but large lines may have to be accommodated in space below.

2-layer system increases floor depth considerably but provides more space for mechanical services.

TWO-WAY BEAM SYSTEM

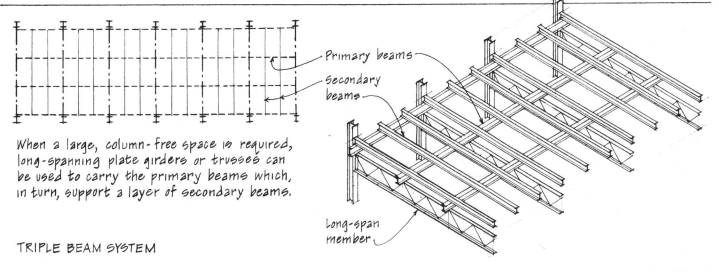

Primary beams

Secondary beams

When a large, column-free space is required, long-spanning plate girders or trusses can be used to carry the primary beams which, in turn, support a layer of secondary beams.

Long-span member

TRIPLE BEAM SYSTEM

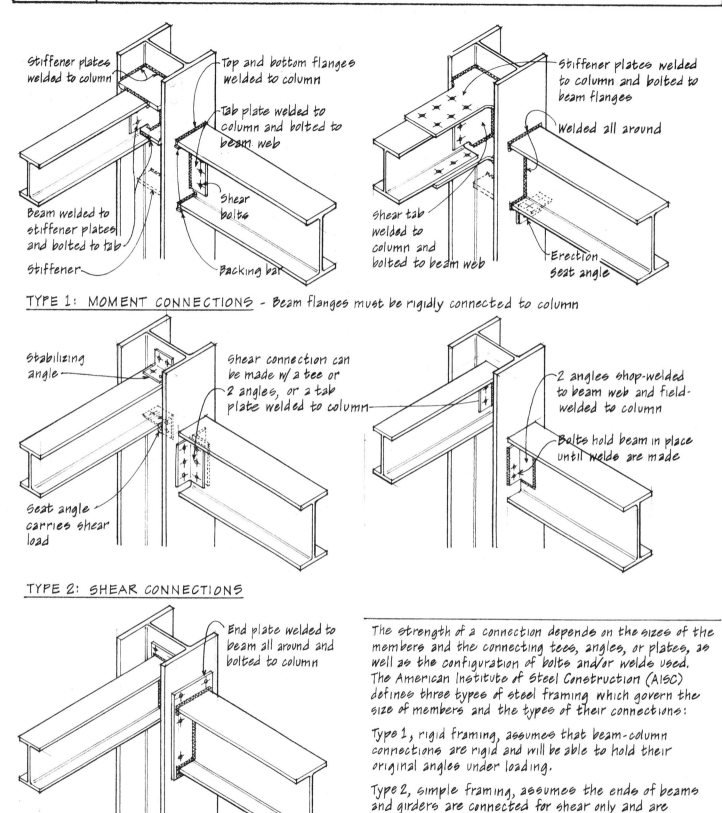

Stiffener plates welded to column

Top and bottom flanges welded to column

Tab plate welded to column and bolted to beam web

Shear bolts

Beam welded to stiffener plates and bolted to tab

Stiffener

Backing bar

Stiffener plates welded to column and bolted to beam flanges

Welded all around

Shear tab welded to column and bolted to beam web

Erection seat angle

TYPE 1: MOMENT CONNECTIONS - Beam flanges must be rigidly connected to column

Stabilizing angle

Shear connection can be made w/ a tee or 2 angles, or a tab plate welded to column

Seat angle carries shear load

2 angles shop-welded to beam web and field-welded to column

Bolts hold beam in place until welds are made

TYPE 2: SHEAR CONNECTIONS

End plate welded to beam all around and bolted to column

TYPE 3: SEMI-RIGID CONNECTION

The strength of a connection depends on the sizes of the members and the connecting tees, angles, or plates, as well as the configuration of bolts and/or welds used. The American Institute of Steel Construction (AISC) defines three types of steel framing which govern the size of members and the types of their connections:

Type 1, rigid framing, assumes that beam-column connections are rigid and will be able to hold their original angles under loading.

Type 2, simple framing, assumes the ends of beams and girders are connected for shear only and are free to rotate under gravity loads.

Type 3, semi-rigid framing, assumes beam and girder connections possess a limited but known moment-resisting capacity.

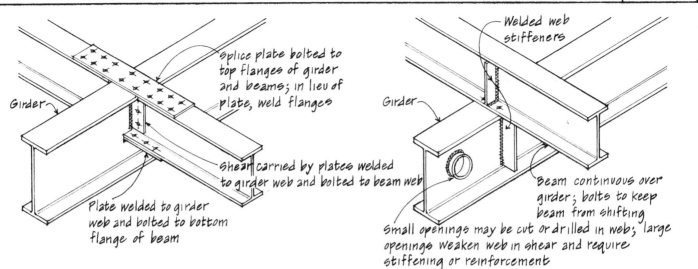

Splice plate bolted to top flanges of girder and beams; in lieu of plate, weld flanges

Girder

Shear carried by plates welded to girder web and bolted to beam web

Plate welded to girder web and bolted to bottom flange of beam

Welded web stiffeners

Girder

Beam continuous over girder; bolts to keep beam from shifting

Small openings may be cut or drilled in web; large openings weaken web in shear and require stiffening or reinforcement

MOMENT CONNECTIONS - Continuity in beam flanges is required

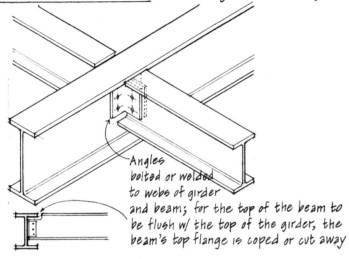

Angles bolted or welded to webs of girder and beam; for the top of the beam to be flush w/ the top of the girder, the beam's top flange is coped or cut away

SHEAR CONNECTION

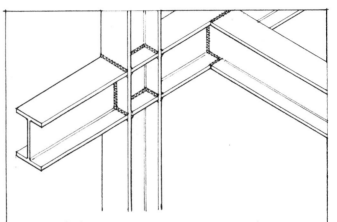

All-welded connections are aesthetically pleasing, especially when ground smooth, but they can be very expensive to fabricate.

There are many ways in which steel connections can be made, using different types of connectors and various combinations of bolts and welds. Refer the AISC Manual of Steel Construction for steel section properties and dimensions, allowable load tables for beams and columns, and requirements for welded and bolted connections.

In addition to strength and degree of rigidity, connections should be evaluated for economy of fabrication and erection, and for visual appearance if the structure is exposed to view.

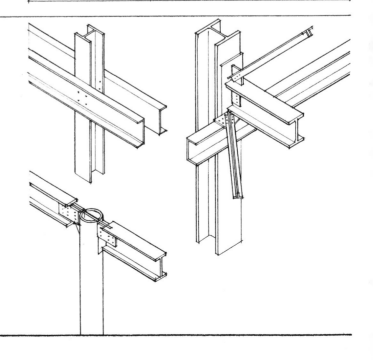

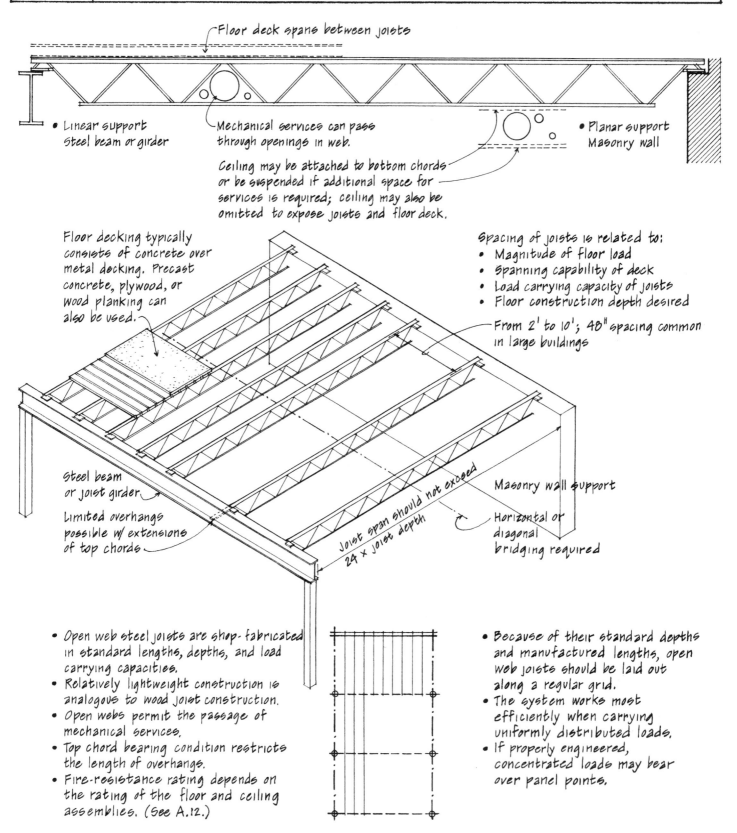

Floor deck spans between joists

• Linear support
Steel beam or girder

Mechanical services can pass through openings in web.

• Planar support
Masonry wall

Ceiling may be attached to bottom chords or be suspended if additional space for services is required; ceiling may also be omitted to expose joists and floor deck.

Floor decking typically consists of concrete over metal decking. Precast concrete, plywood, or wood planking can also be used.

Spacing of joists is related to:
• Magnitude of floor load
• Spanning capability of deck
• Load carrying capacity of joists
• Floor construction depth desired

From 2' to 10'; 48" spacing common in large buildings

Steel beam or joist girder

Limited overhangs possible w/ extensions of top chords

Joist span should not exceed 24 x joist depth

Masonry wall support

Horizontal or diagonal bridging required

• Open web steel joists are shop-fabricated in standard lengths, depths, and load carrying capacities.
• Relatively lightweight construction is analogous to wood joist construction.
• Open webs permit the passage of mechanical services.
• Top chord bearing condition restricts the length of overhangs.
• Fire-resistance rating depends on the rating of the floor and ceiling assemblies. (See A.12.)

• Because of their standard depths and manufactured lengths, open web joists should be laid out along a regular grid.
• The system works most efficiently when carrying uniformly distributed loads.
• If properly engineered, concentrated loads may bear over panel points.

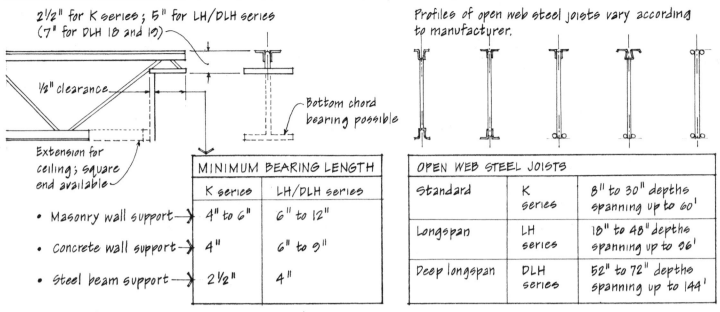

2½" for K series; 5" for LH/DLH series
(7" for DLH 18 and 19)

½" clearance

Bottom chord bearing possible

Extension for ceiling; square end available

Profiles of open web steel joists vary according to manufacturer.

MINIMUM BEARING LENGTH		
	K series	LH/DLH series
• Masonry wall support →	4" to 6"	6" to 12"
• Concrete wall support →	4"	6" to 9"
• Steel beam support →	2½"	4"

OPEN WEB STEEL JOISTS		
Standard	K series	8" to 30" depths spanning up to 60'
Longspan	LH series	18" to 48" depths spanning up to 96'
Deep longspan	DLH series	52" to 72" depths spanning up to 144'

Horizontal or diagonal bridging is required to prevent lateral movement of joist chords. Spacing of bridging, from 10' to 20' o.c., depends on the joist span and chord size.

The following table is to be used for preliminary sizing of joists only. Consult the Steel Joist Institute for specifications and complete load tables for all joist types.

ALLOWABLE UNIFORMLY DISTRIBUTED LOAD (lbs. per S.F.)												
Joist series	Joist designation	Span in feet										
		12	16	20	24	28	32	36	42	48	54	60
K	8 K 1	442	245									
	10 K 1	550	312	200								
	12 K 3	550	475	302	208							
	14 K 4		550	428	295	216						
	16 K 5		550	550	384	280	214					
	18 K 6			550	472	345	264	208				
	20 K 7			550	550	430	328	260				
	22 K 9				550	550	435	344	252			
	24 K 9				550	550	478	376	275	210		
	26 K 10					550	548	486	356	272		
	28 K 10					550	548	486	384	294	232	
	30 K 11						548	486	416	362	284	230
	30 K 12						548	486	416	364	324	262
LH	18 LH 5					580	448	354				
	20 LH 6					722	560	444				
	24 LH 7							588	446	342		
	28 LH 9								638	500	400	
	32 LH 10										450	389
	㉚ LH 11											450

Joist depth in inches

Joist Type

Chord

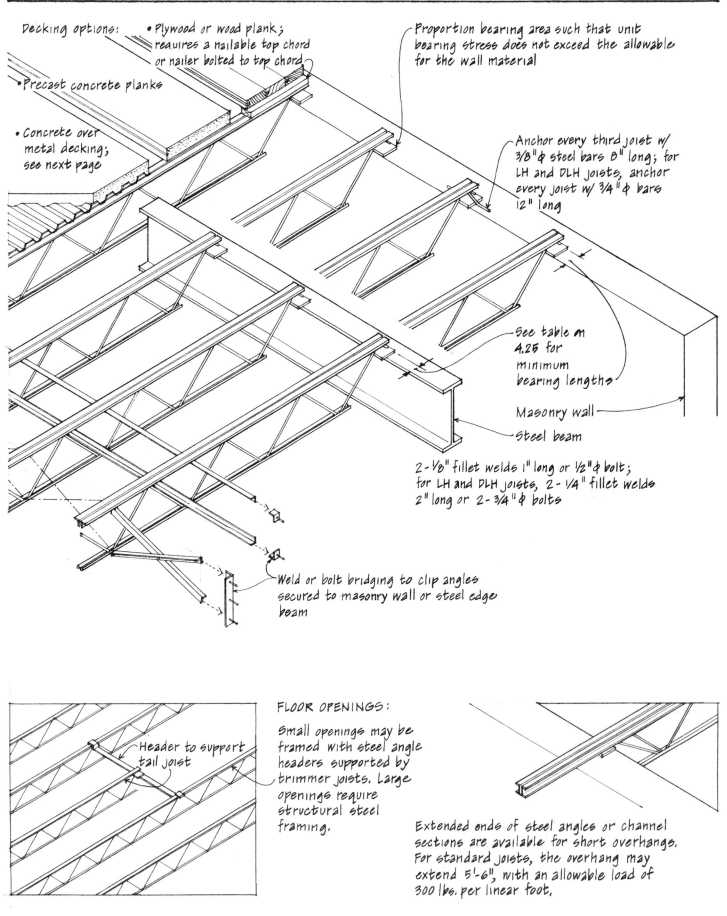

Decking options:
- Plywood or wood plank; requires a nailable top chord or nailer bolted to top chord
- Precast concrete planks
- Concrete over metal decking; see next page

Proportion bearing area such that unit bearing stress does not exceed the allowable for the wall material

Anchor every third joist w/ 3/8"∅ steel bars 8" long; for LH and DLH joists, anchor every joist w/ 3/4"∅ bars 12" long

See table on 4.25 for minimum bearing lengths

Masonry wall

Steel beam

2 - 1/8" fillet welds 1" long or 1/2"∅ bolt; for LH and DLH joists, 2 - 1/4" fillet welds 2" long or 2 - 3/4"∅ bolts

Weld or bolt bridging to clip angles secured to masonry wall or steel edge beam

Header to support tail joist

FLOOR OPENINGS:

Small openings may be framed with steel angle headers supported by trimmer joists. Large openings require structural steel framing.

Extended ends of steel angles or channel sections are available for short overhangs. For standard joists, the overhang may extend 5'-6", with an allowable load of 300 lbs. per linear foot.

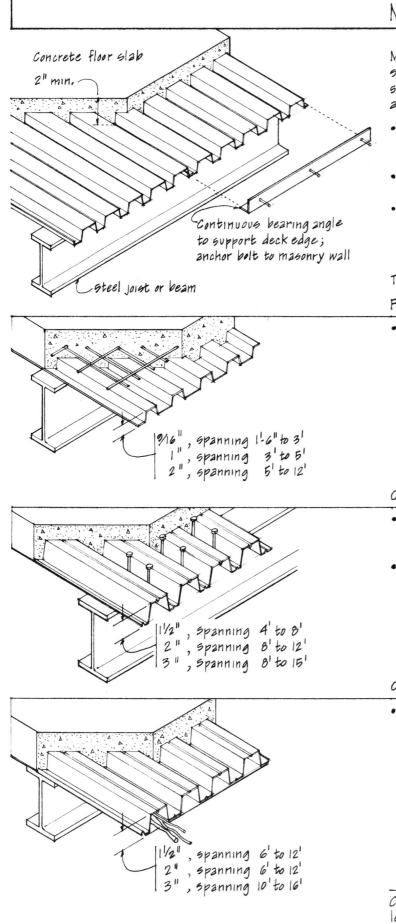

Concrete floor slab
2" min.

Continuous bearing angle
to support deck edge;
anchor bolt to masonry wall

steel joist or beam

$\frac{9}{16}$", spanning 1'-6" to 3'
1", spanning 3' to 5'
2", spanning 5' to 12'

1½", spanning 4' to 8'
2", spanning 8' to 12'
3", spanning 8' to 15'

1½", spanning 6' to 12'
2", spanning 6' to 12'
3", spanning 10' to 16'

Metal decking is corrugated to increase its
stiffness and spanning capability. The floor deck
serves as a working platform during construction
and as formwork for concrete.

- The decking panels are generally secured by
  puddle-welding through the decking to the
  supporting steel joists or beams.
- The panels are fastened to each other along
  their sides with screws or welds.
- If the deck is to serve as a lateral diaphragm,
  its perimeter must be welded to steel supports;
  in addition, more stringent requirements for
  support and side lap fastening may apply.

There are three types of metal decking:

FORM DECKING

- The decking serves as permanent formwork
  for a reinforced concrete slab; it supports
  the concrete until the slab can support
  itself and its live load.

COMPOSITE DECKING

- The decking serves as tensile reinforcement
  for the concrete slab to which it is bonded with
  embossed rib patterns.
- Composite action between the concrete slab
  and the floor beams can be achieved by
  welding shear studs through the decking to
  the supporting below.

CELLULAR DECKING

- Cellular decking is manufactured by welding
  a corrugated sheet to a flat one. The spaces
  created can be used as raceways for
  electrical and communications wiring;
  special cutouts are available for floor outlets.

Consult the manufacturer for patterns, widths,
lengths, gages, finishes, and allowable spans.

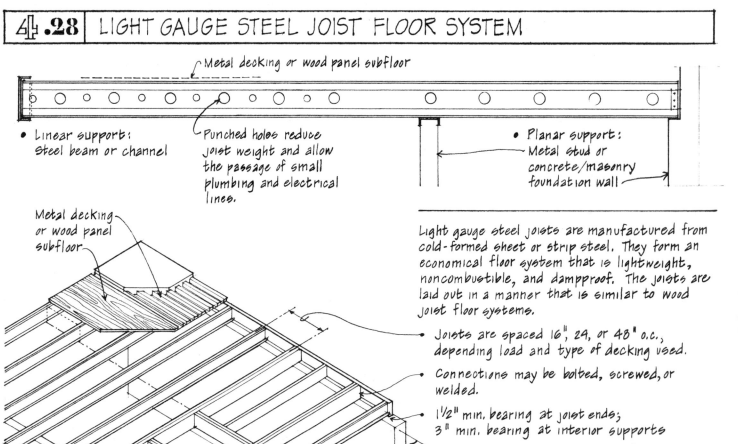

Metal decking or wood panel subfloor

- Linear support: Steel beam or channel

Punched holes reduce joist weight and allow the passage of small plumbing and electrical lines.

- Planar support: Metal stud or concrete/masonry foundation wall

Metal decking or wood panel subfloor

Light gauge steel joists are manufactured from cold-formed sheet or strip steel. They form an economical floor system that is lightweight, noncombustible, and dampproof. The joists are laid out in a manner that is similar to wood joist floor systems.

- Joists are spaced 16", 24, or 48" o.c., depending load and type of decking used.

- Connections may be bolted, screwed, or welded.

- 1½" min. bearing at joist ends; 3" min. bearing at interior supports

- Strap bridging at 5' to 8' o.c, depending on joist span

Overhangs and floor openings are framed in a manner similar to wood joist floors.

Web stiffeners are required where concentrated loads might cripple joist webs, such as at joist ends, or over interior supports.

LIGHT GAUGE JOISTS

Nailable joist   "C" joist   Joist closure

Depths: 6, 8, 9, 10, 12 inches - nominal
Flange widths: 1⅝", 1¾", 1⅞", 2", 2½"
Gauges: 14 through 22

The following table is to be used for preliminary sizing only. Consult manufacturers' literature to confirm joist sizes, framing details, and allowable spans and loads.

ALLOWABLE UNIFORM LOADS (lbs. per S.F.)

JOIST SIZE	SPACING	SPAN in feet					JOIST SIZE	SPACING	SPAN in feet				
		10	12	14	16	18			.14	16	18	20	22
8"	16"	233	135	85	57	53	10"	16"	186	125	87	64	48
	24"	156	90	57	38	34		24"	124	83	58	43	32
	48"	78	45	28	19	17		48"	62	42	29	21	16
9"	16"			114	76	54	12"	16"				163	123
	24"			76	51	36		24"				100	82
	48"			38	26	18		48"				54	41

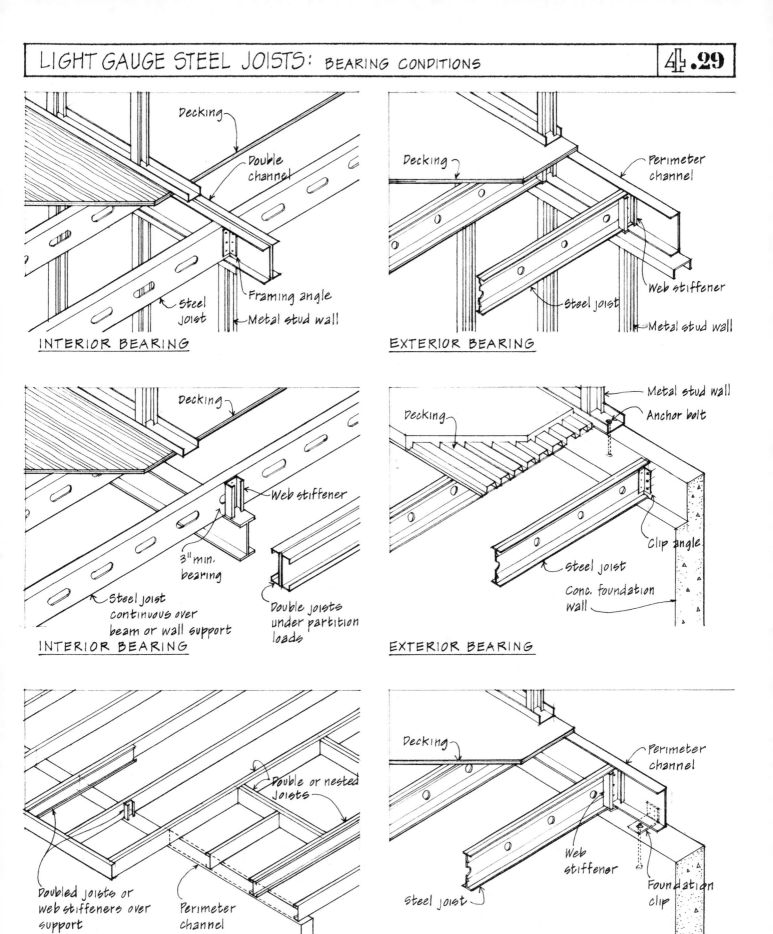

INTERIOR BEARING

Decking
Double channel
Steel Joist
Framing angle
Metal stud wall

EXTERIOR BEARING

Decking
Perimeter channel
Web stiffener
Steel joist
Metal stud wall

INTERIOR BEARING

Decking
Web stiffener
3" min. bearing
Steel joist continuous over beam or wall support
Double joists under partition loads

EXTERIOR BEARING

Decking
Metal stud wall
Anchor bolt
Clip angle
steel joist
Conc. foundation wall

FLOOR PROJECTIONS AND OPENINGS

Double or nested joists
Doubled joists or web stiffeners over support
Perimeter channel

EXTERIOR BEARING

Decking
Perimeter channel
Web stiffener
steel joist
Foundation clip

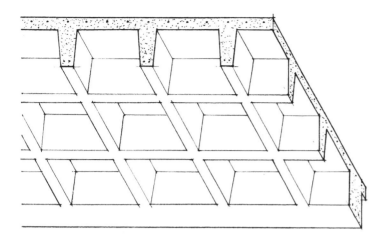

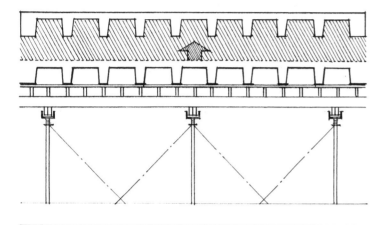

Reinforced concrete can be cast into almost any shape. Its flexibility of form is limited only by the formwork and steel reinforcement required, and the method used for its placement or casting. It may be formed into either linear or planar elements and configured into skeletal frame, bearing wall, or shell structures.

Concrete must be shaped and supported by formwork until it cures and can support itself. This formwork is often designed as a separate structural system because of the considerable weight and fluid pressure the concrete can exert on it.

The contact surfaces of forms are coated with a parting compound (oil, wax, or plastic) to aid in their removal. From a design standpoint, the shape of a concrete section must allow for the easy removal of the formwork. Use tapered sections where the formwork might otherwise be trapped by the surrounding concrete. Sharp external corners are usually bevelled or rounded to avoid chipping and ragged edges.

For economy, standard forms should be used in a repetitive manner. When possible, use columns and beams of a constant size and vary the amount of steel required.

STEEL REINFORCEMENT

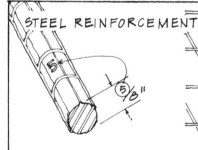

Since concrete is relatively weak in tension, steel reinforcement is required to handle tensile stresses in structural concrete members. Steel reinforcement is also required to tie vertical and horizontal elements, reinforce the edges around openings, minimize shrinkage cracking, and control thermal expansion and contraction.

REINFORCING BARS are hot-rolled steel sections that have ribs for better bonding to the concrete. The bar number refers to its diameter in eighths of an inch. e.g., A #5 bar is 5/8" in diameter.

For cross-sectional area tables, see 12.9

WELDED WIRE FABRIC consists of cold-drawn wires arranged in a grid and welded at their points of intersection. The fabric is typically used to provide temperature reinforcement for slabs but the heavier gauges can also be used to reinforce concrete walls. The fabric is designated by the wire spacing and its gauge or cross-sectional area.

Reinforcing steel must be protected by the surrounding concrete against fire and corrosion. Minimum requirements for cover and spacing are specified by the American Concrete Institute (ACI) <u>Building Code Requirements for Reinforced Concrete</u> according to the concrete's exposure, and the size of the coarse aggregate and steel used. These requirements are noted on the following drawings where appropriate. See also 12.9.

Reinforcement should be designed by a qualified structural engineer.

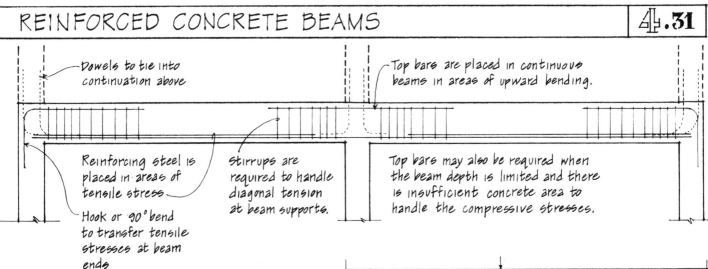

Dowels to tie into continuation above

Top bars are placed in continuous beams in areas of upward bending.

Reinforcing steel is placed in areas of tensile stress

Stirrups are required to handle diagonal tension at beam supports.

Top bars may also be required when the beam depth is limited and there is insufficient concrete area to handle the compressive stresses.

Hook or 90° bend to transfer tensile stresses at beam ends

Sitecast concrete beams are almost always formed and cast along with the slab they support. Since a portion of the slab acts as a part of the beam, the depth of the beam is measured to the top of the slab. A rule of thumb for estimating a beam's depth is:

* Beam span in feet = Beam depth in inches.

Continuity between columns, beams, slabs, and walls is desirable to minimize bending moments at these junctures. Since continuity is easily attainable in concrete construction, structures continuous over 3 or more spans are usually the most efficient.

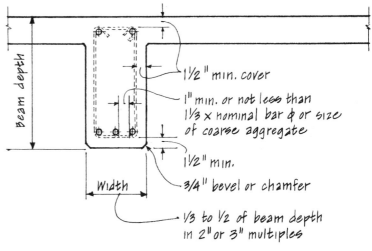

1½" min. cover

1" min. or not less than 1⅓ × nominal bar ∅ or size of coarse aggregate

1½" min.

3/4" bevel or chamfer

1/3 to 1/2 of beam depth in 2" or 3" multiples

When loaded to its full load-carrying capacity, a conventionally reinforced concrete beam is susceptible to cracking under tension in its lower zone. Prestressing the beam reduces tension cracks by placing its entire cross-section into compression. This is achieved by stretching the reinforcing steel to a high tension, anchoring it at the beam ends, and then releasing it. Prestressing reduces beam deflection and allows the use of shallower beams and longer spans.

There are two types of prestressing techniques. Pretensioning is accomplished in a precasting plant. Post-tensioning is usually performed at the building site, especially when the structural units are too large to transport from factory to site.

PRESTRESSED CONCRETE BEAMS

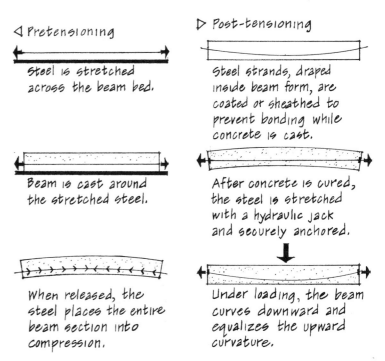

◁ Pretensioning

Steel is stretched across the beam bed.

Beam is cast around the stretched steel.

When released, the steel places the entire beam section into compression.

▷ Post-tensioning

Steel strands, draped inside beam form, are coated or sheathed to prevent bonding while concrete is cast.

After concrete is cured, the steel is stretched with a hydraulic jack and securely anchored.

Under loading, the beam curves downward and equalizes the upward curvature.

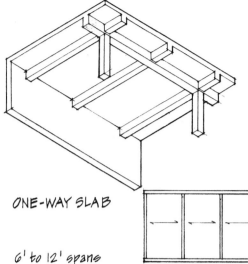

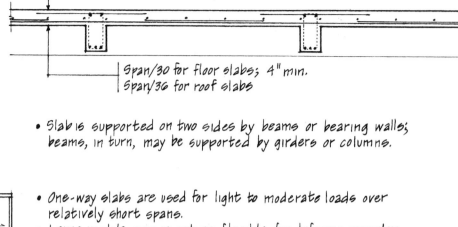

Span/30 for floor slabs; 4" min.
Span/36 for roof slabs

- Slab is supported on two sides by beams or bearing walls; beams, in turn, may be supported by girders or columns.

ONE-WAY SLAB

6' to 12' spans

- One-way slabs are used for light to moderate loads over relatively short spans.
- Large module size is not as flexible for defining irregular bays as smaller modules of waffle slab.

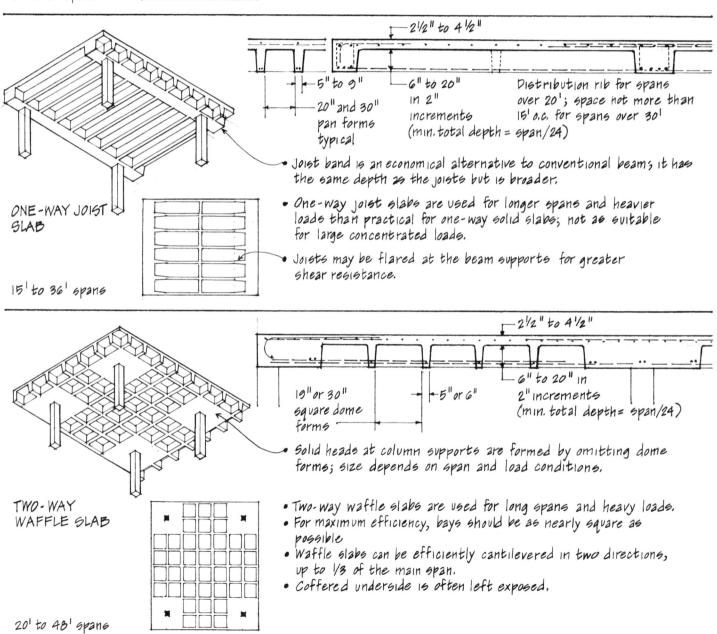

2½" to 4½"

5" to 9"

20" and 30" pan forms typical

6" to 20" in 2" increments

Distribution rib for spans over 20'; space not more than 15' o.c. for spans over 30' (min. total depth = span/24)

- Joist band is an economical alternative to conventional beams; it has the same depth as the joists but is broader.

ONE-WAY JOIST SLAB

15' to 36' spans

- One-way joist slabs are used for longer spans and heavier loads than practical for one-way solid slabs; not as suitable for large concentrated loads.
- Joists may be flared at the beam supports for greater shear resistance.

2½" to 4½"

19" or 30" square dome forms

5" or 6"

6" to 20" in 2" increments (min. total depth = span/24)

- Solid heads at column supports are formed by omitting dome forms; size depends on span and load conditions.

TWO-WAY WAFFLE SLAB

20' to 48' spans

- Two-way waffle slabs are used for long spans and heavy loads.
- For maximum efficiency, bays should be as nearly square as possible.
- Waffle slabs can be efficiently cantilevered in two directions, up to 1/3 of the main span.
- Coffered underside is often left exposed.

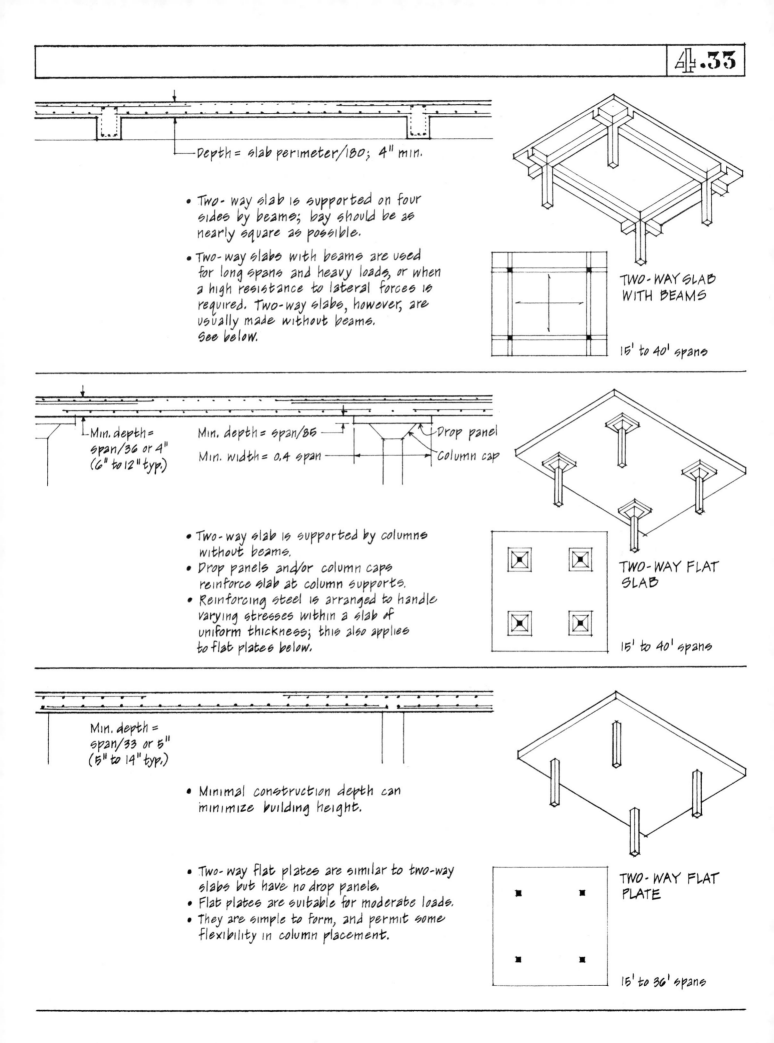

—Depth = slab perimeter/180; 4" min.

- Two-way slab is supported on four sides by beams; bay should be as nearly square as possible.
- Two-way slabs with beams are used for long spans and heavy loads, or when a high resistance to lateral forces is required. Two-way slabs, however, are usually made without beams. See below.

TWO-WAY SLAB WITH BEAMS

15' to 40' spans

—Min. depth = span/36 or 4" (6" to 12" typ.)

Min. depth = span/35

Min. width = 0.4 span

Drop panel

Column cap

- Two-way slab is supported by columns without beams.
- Drop panels and/or column caps reinforce slab at column supports.
- Reinforcing steel is arranged to handle varying stresses within a slab of uniform thickness; this also applies to flat plates below.

TWO-WAY FLAT SLAB

15' to 40' spans

Min. depth = span/33 or 5" (5" to 14" typ.)

- Minimal construction depth can minimize building height.

- Two-way flat plates are similar to two-way slabs but have no drop panels.
- Flat plates are suitable for moderate loads.
- They are simple to form, and permit some flexibility in column placement.

TWO-WAY FLAT PLATE

15' to 36' spans

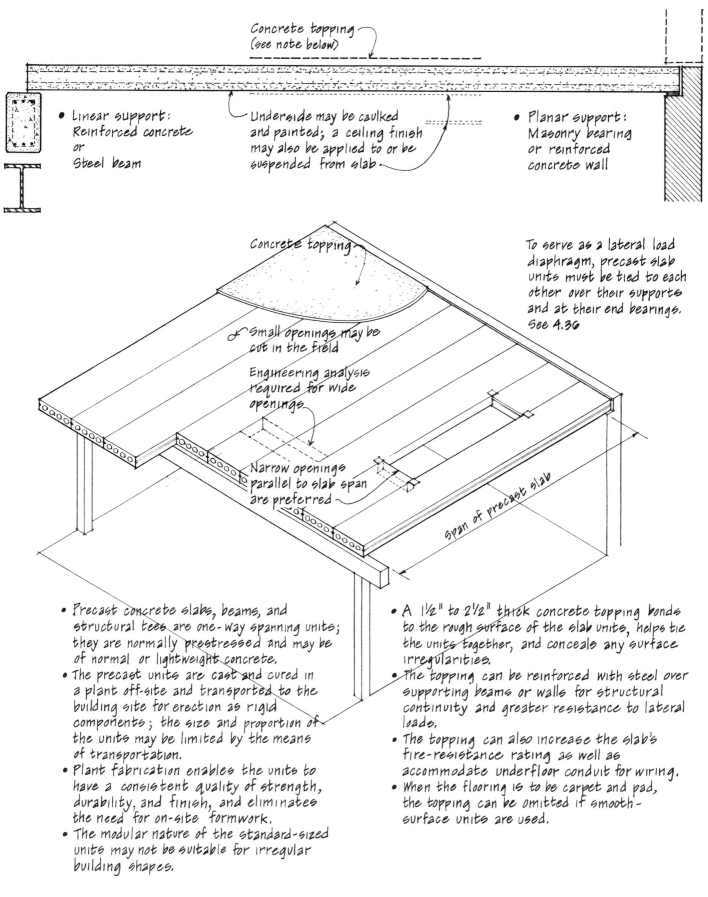

Concrete topping
(see note below)

• Linear support:
Reinforced concrete
or
Steel beam

Underside may be caulked
and painted; a ceiling finish
may also be applied to or be
suspended from slab.

• Planar support:
Masonry bearing
or reinforced
concrete wall

Concrete topping

To serve as a lateral load
diaphragm, precast slab
units must be tied to each
other over their supports
and at their end bearings.
See 4.36

Small openings may be
cut in the field

Engineering analysis
required for wide
openings

Narrow openings
parallel to slab span
are preferred

Span of precast slab

• Precast concrete slabs, beams, and
structural tees are one-way spanning units;
they are normally prestressed and may be
of normal or lightweight concrete.
• The precast units are cast and cured in
a plant off-site and transported to the
building site for erection as rigid
components; the size and proportion of
the units may be limited by the means
of transportation.
• Plant fabrication enables the units to
have a consistent quality of strength,
durability, and finish, and eliminates
the need for on-site formwork.
• The modular nature of the standard-sized
units may not be suitable for irregular
building shapes.

• A 1½" to 2½" thick concrete topping bonds
to the rough surface of the slab units, helps tie
the units together, and conceals any surface
irregularities.
• The topping can be reinforced with steel over
supporting beams or walls for structural
continuity and greater resistance to lateral
loads.
• The topping can also increase the slab's
fire-resistance rating as well as
accommodate underfloor conduit for wiring.
• When the flooring is to be carpet and pad,
the topping can be omitted if smooth-
surface units are used.

The table below illustrates the basic types of precast concrete structural units. The span ranges indicated are to be used for preliminary sizing only. Consult manufacturer for availability of sizes, exact dimensions, connection details, and span-load tables.

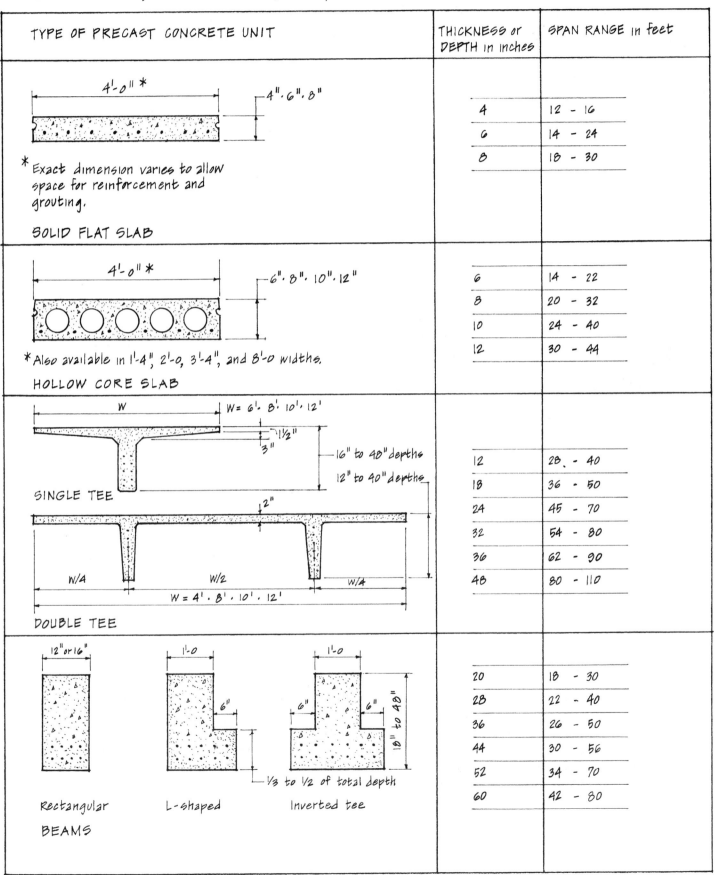

TYPE OF PRECAST CONCRETE UNIT	THICKNESS or DEPTH in inches	SPAN RANGE in feet
SOLID FLAT SLAB	4	12 - 16
	6	14 - 24
	8	18 - 30
HOLLOW CORE SLAB	6	14 - 22
	8	20 - 32
	10	24 - 40
	12	30 - 44
SINGLE TEE / DOUBLE TEE	12	28 - 40
	18	36 - 50
	24	45 - 70
	32	54 - 80
	36	62 - 90
	48	80 - 110
BEAMS	20	18 - 30
	28	22 - 40
	36	26 - 50
	44	30 - 56
	52	34 - 70
	60	42 - 80

Solid flat slab: 4'-0" *, 4". 6". 8"
* Exact dimension varies to allow space for reinforcement and grouting.

Hollow core slab: 4'-0" *, 6". 8". 10". 12"
* Also available in 1'-4", 2'-0, 3'-4", and 8'-0 widths.

Single tee: W, W= 6'. 8'. 10'. 12', 1½", 3", 16" to 48" depths
Double tee: 2", 12" to 40" depths, W/4, W/2, W/4, W = 4'. 8'. 10'. 12'

Beams: Rectangular 12" or 16"; L-shaped 1'-0, 6"; Inverted tee 1'-0, 6", 6", 18" to 48", ⅓ to ½ of total depth

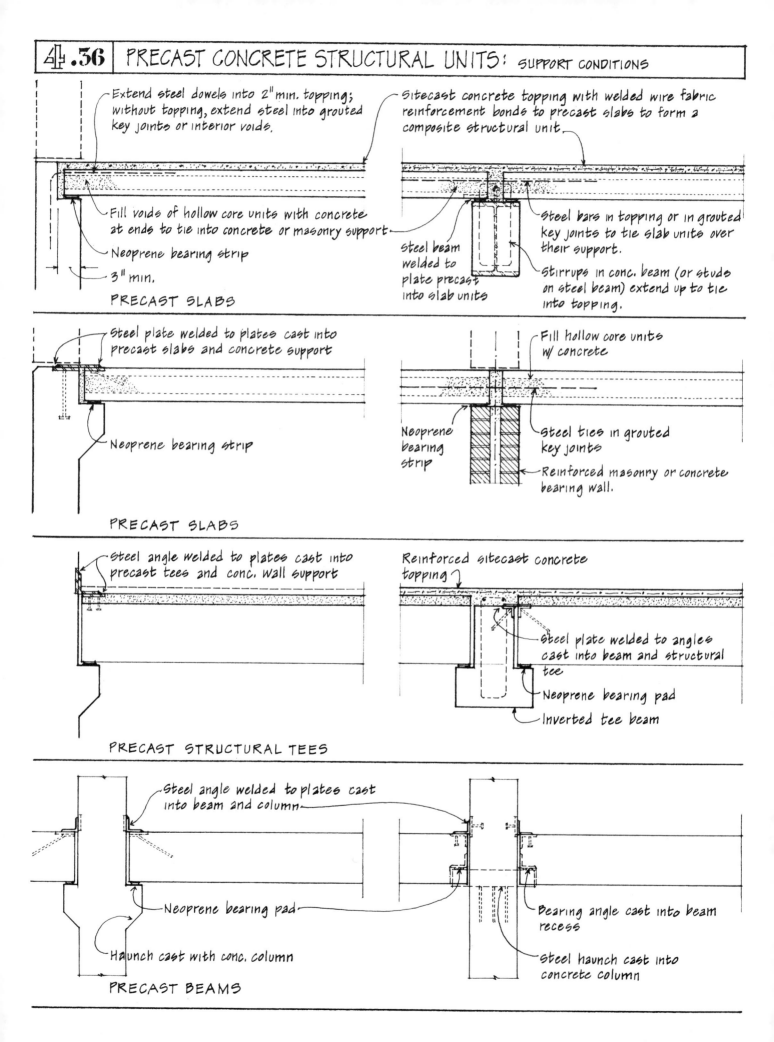

Extend steel dowels into 2" min. topping; without topping, extend steel into grouted key joints or interior voids.

Sitecast concrete topping with welded wire fabric reinforcement bonds to precast slabs to form a composite structural unit

Fill voids of hollow core units with concrete at ends to tie into concrete or masonry support

Neoprene bearing strip

3" min.

steel beam welded to plate precast into slab units

Steel bars in topping or in grouted key joints to tie slab units over their support.

Stirrups in conc. beam (or studs on steel beam) extend up to tie into topping.

PRECAST SLABS

Steel plate welded to plates cast into precast slabs and concrete support

Fill hollow core units w/ concrete

Neoprene bearing strip

Neoprene bearing strip

Steel ties in grouted key joints

Reinforced masonry or concrete bearing wall.

PRECAST SLABS

Steel angle welded to plates cast into precast tees and conc. wall support

Reinforced sitecast concrete topping

Steel plate welded to angles cast into beam and structural tee

Neoprene bearing pad

Inverted tee beam

PRECAST STRUCTURAL TEES

Steel angle welded to plates cast into beam and column

Neoprene bearing pad

Haunch cast with conc. column

Bearing angle cast into beam recess

Steel haunch cast into concrete column

PRECAST BEAMS

WALL SYSTEMS $\boxed{5}$

Wall systems are the vertical planes of a building which define and enclose its interior spaces. They may be bearing walls of homogeneous or composite construction, or they may be constructed of linear columns and beams with nonstructural panels filling in between them. How these walls and columns support floor and roof systems above, and how they are supported in turn by wall and foundation systems below, are determined by the structural compatibility of these systems and the type of materials and connections used. If rigid, walls can also serve as shear planes which are designed to resist lateral wind and earthquake forces.

Exterior walls serve as a protective shield against the weather for a building's interior spaces. Their construction should control the passage of heat and cold, air, moisture, and water vapor. The exterior skin, which may either be applied to or be integral with the wall structure, should be durable and resistant to the weathering effects of sun, wind, and rain.

The interior walls which subdivide the space within a building may be either nonstructural or load-bearing. Their construction should be able to support the desired finish materials, provide the required degree of acoustical separation, and accommodate when necessary runs of mechanical and electrical lines.

The size and location of door and window openings in walls are determined by the requirements for natural light, ventilation, view, and physical access. These openings must be constructed so that any vertical loads are distributed around the openings and not transferred to the door and window units themselves.

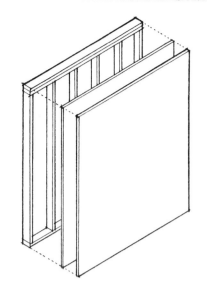

WOOD STUD WALLS

- Walls are normally 2x4s, but may be 2x6s or larger to accommodate more thermal insulation or rise more than 14 feet.
- Studs are spaced 16" or 24" o.c.; this spacing is related to the width and length of common sheathing materials.
- Studs carry vertical loads while the wall sheathing or diagonal bracing help to make the frame rigid.
- Thermal insulation, vapor barriers, and small mechanical services can be accommodated within the stud wall frame.
- Stud frames can accept a variety of interior or exterior wall finishes; some finishes require a nail-base sheathing.
- The fire-resistance rating of the wall assembly depends on its finish materials.
- Stud wall frames may be fabricated on-site or panelized off-site.
- Stud walls are flexible in form due to the workability of relatively small pieces and the various means of fastening available.

METAL STUD WALLS

- Metal stud walls are similar in structure to wood stud walls.
- Connections may be screwed or welded.

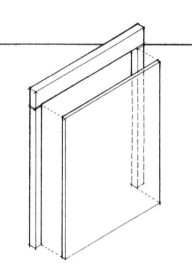

WOOD POST AND BEAM FRAMING

- Post and beam system uses fewer but larger structural members than stud framing.
- Frame requires diagonal bracing, shear planes, or rigid connections for lateral stability.
- Detailing of connections is critical for structural and visual reasons. Frame may be left exposed.
- Non-bearing infill panels enclose space and, on exterior walls, serve as a weather barrier.
- It may be difficult to accommodate mechanical and electrical services within the structural framework.
- Posts are usually laid out along a grid to support plank and beam floor and roof structures.

STEEL AND REINFORCED CONCRETE FRAMES

- Steel and concrete frames are similar in form to wood post and beam structures.
- Stronger materials can span greater distances and carry heavier loads; rigid connections are feasible.
- Structural frame can support a variety of curtain wall systems.

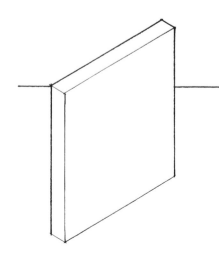

MASONRY AND CONCRETE BEARING WALLS

- Masonry and concrete bearing walls rely on their mass for their load carrying capability; while strong in compression, they may require reinforcing to handle any tensile stresses.
- Their height-to-width ratio, provisions for lateral stability, and proper placement of expansion joints are critical.
- Wall surface may be left exposed; materials have good fire-resistance.
- Mechanical and electrical services may be integrated into wall.
- Thermal insulation may be contained in wall cavity or be applied to wall surface.

FACTORS IN WALL DESIGN AND CONSTRUCTION

Strength in:
- Supporting vertical loads from floor, wall, and roof structures above
- Resisting lateral wind and seismic forces and lateral loads from supported floor and roof structures.

Connection to foundation, floor, and roof systems:
- Floor and roof systems may bear on the wall system so that their edges are exposed and cantilevers are made possible.
- Floor and roof systems may frame into the wall system which is continuous for the height of the building.

Wall finish desired:
- Compatibility between base material of wall and desired wall finish
- Visual characteristics of color, texture, pattern, and jointing.

Door and window openings:
- Structural and/or modular limitations on size, proportion, and location
- Effect on daylighting and potential for heat loss or gain.

Weathertightness and the control of:
- Heat flow
- Air infiltration
- Moisture and water vapor flow
- Sound transmission.

Expansion and contraction:
- Type and location of expansion joints, if required.

Accommodation of mechanical and electrical services and outlets.

Fire-resistance rating desired or required by the building code.

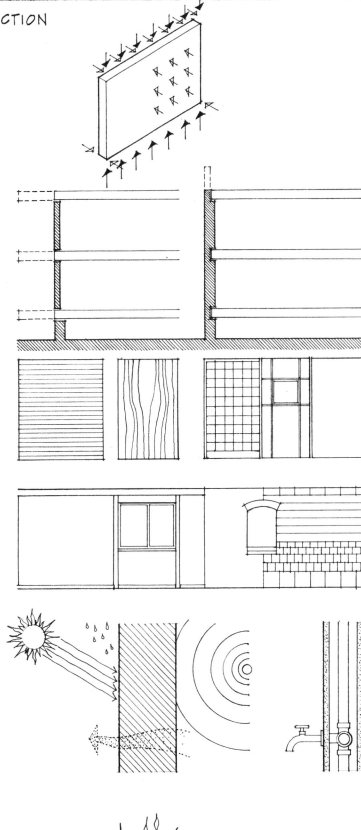

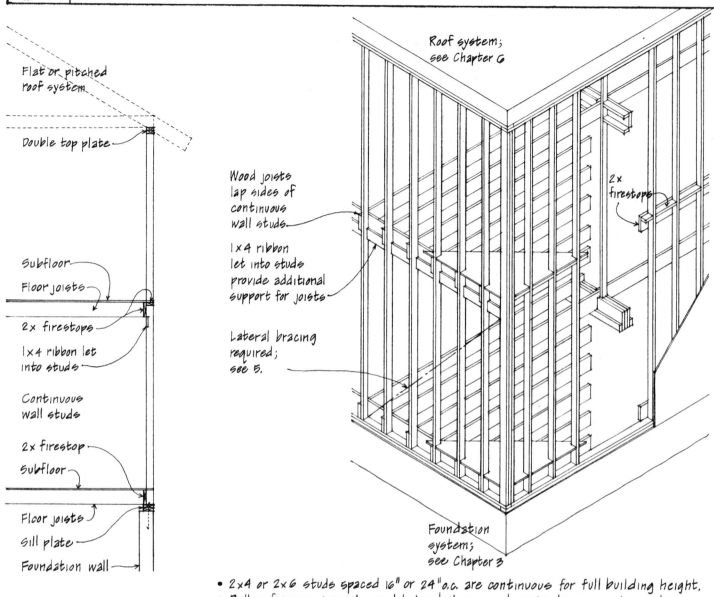

Flat or pitched roof system

Double top plate

Wood joists lap sides of continuous wall studs

1×4 ribbon let into studs provide additional support for joists

Lateral bracing required; see 5.

Subfloor

Floor joists

2× firestops

1×4 ribbon let into studs

Continuous wall studs

2× firestop

Subfloor

Floor joists

Sill plate

Foundation wall

Roof system; see Chapter 6

2× firestops

Foundation system; see Chapter 3

- 2x4 or 2x6 studs spaced 16" or 24" o.c. are continuous for full building height.
- Balloon framing is rarely used today but minimal vertical movement may be desirable for brick veneer and stucco finishes.
- First floor joists bear on a foundation sill plate while second floor joists lap the studs and rest on a continuous ribbon let into the studs.
- Concealed spaces in frames require 2x firestops to prevent drafts between stories and between a top story and the roof.

WALL STUD SIZES for both balloon and platform framing	Max. unsupported height	Maximum spacing
2 X 4 studs	14'	16" o.c., except when supporting only a ceiling and roof, 2x4 studs not more than 10' high may be spaced 24" o.c.
2 X 6 studs	20'	24" o.c., except when supporting 2 stories and a roof, space 2x6 studs not more than 16" o.c.

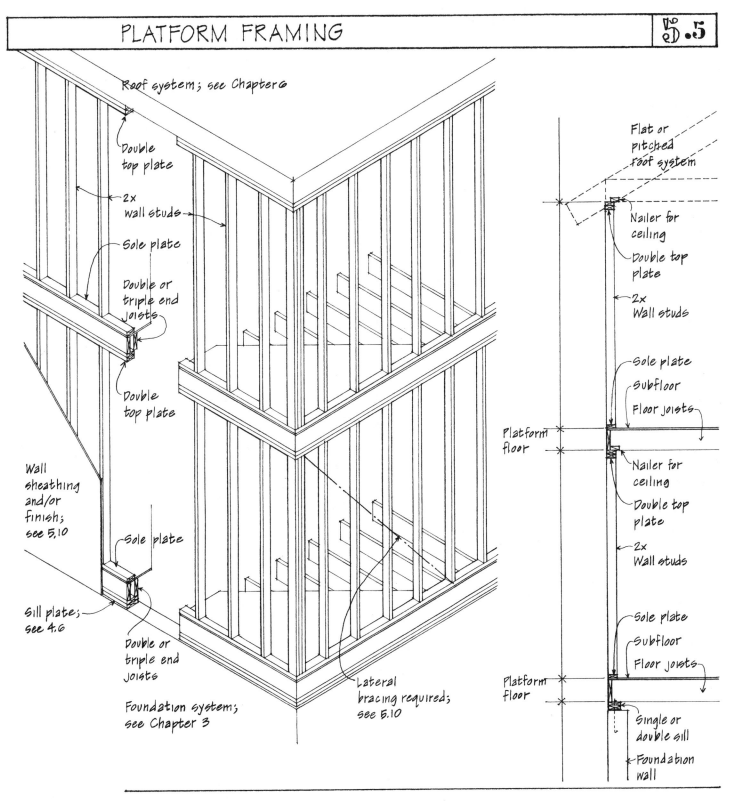

Roof system; see Chapter 6

Double top plate

2x wall studs

Sole plate

Double or triple end Joists

Double top plate

Wall sheathing and/or finish; see 5.10

Sole plate

Sill plate; see 4.6

Double or triple end Joists

Foundation system; see Chapter 3

Lateral bracing required; see 5.10

Flat or pitched Roof system

Nailer for ceiling

Double top plate

2x Wall studs

Sole plate
Subfloor
Floor Joists

Platform floor

Nailer for ceiling

Double top plate

2x Wall studs

Sole plate
Subfloor
Floor Joists

Platform floor

Single or double sill

Foundation wall

- 2x4 or 2x6 story height studs are spaced 16" or 24" o.c.
- Floor joists rest on foundation sill plate or top plate of stud wall below.
- Subfloor extends to outer edge of wall frame and serves as a work platform.
- Although vertical shrinkage is greater than in balloon framing, it is equalized between floors.
- Stud walls are adaptable to off-site fabrication as panels and tilt-up construction.
- Concealed spaces within frame require 2x firestops to prevent drafts between stories and between a top story and the roof.

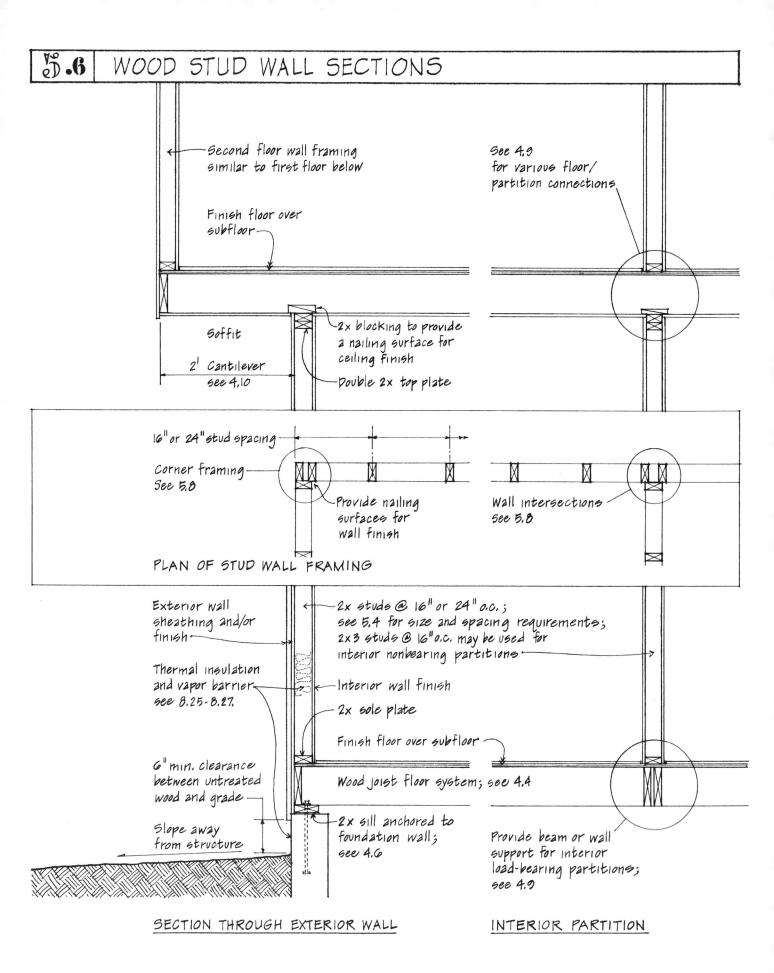

Second floor wall framing similar to first floor below

See 4.9 for various floor/ partition connections

Finish floor over subfloor

Soffit

2' Cantilever see 4.10

2x blocking to provide a nailing surface for ceiling finish

Double 2x top plate

16" or 24" stud spacing

Corner framing See 5.8

Provide nailing surfaces for wall finish

Wall intersections see 5.8

PLAN OF STUD WALL FRAMING

Exterior wall sheathing and/or finish

2x studs @ 16" or 24" o.c.; see 5.4 for size and spacing requirements; 2x3 studs @ 16" o.c. may be used for interior nonbearing partitions

Thermal insulation and vapor barrier see 8.25-8.27.

Interior wall finish

2x sole plate

Finish floor over subfloor

6" min. clearance between untreated wood and grade

Wood joist floor system; see 4.4

Slope away from structure

2x sill anchored to foundation wall; see 4.6

Provide beam or wall support for interior load-bearing partitions; see 4.9

SECTION THROUGH EXTERIOR WALL

INTERIOR PARTITION

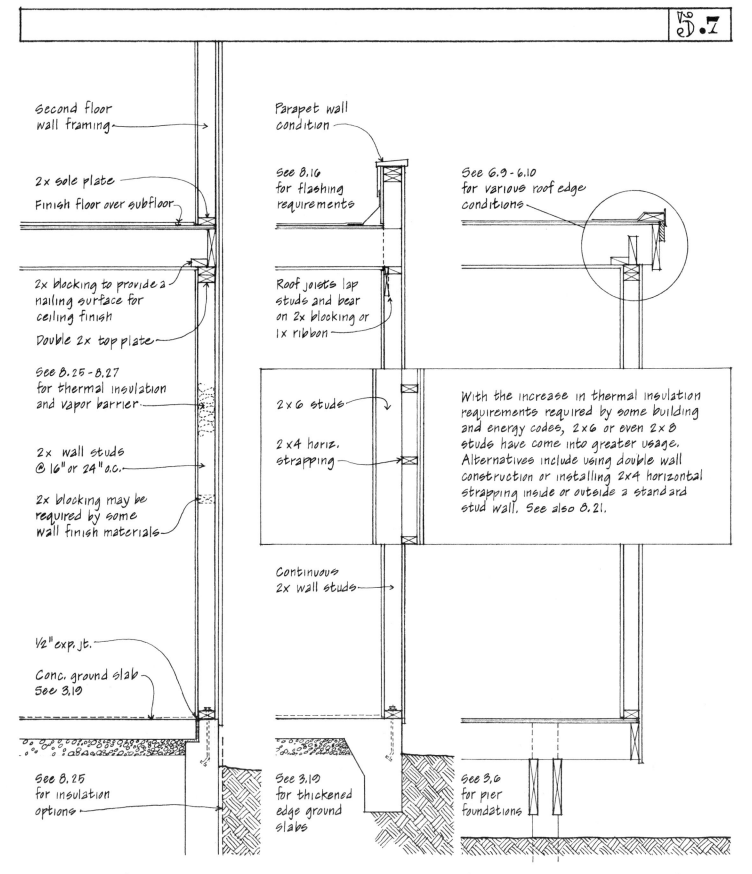

Second floor wall framing

2x sole plate

Finish floor over subfloor

2x blocking to provide a nailing surface for ceiling finish

Double 2x top plate

See 8.25 - 8.27 for thermal insulation and vapor barrier.

2x wall studs @ 16" or 24" o.c.

2x blocking may be required by some wall finish materials

½" exp. jt.

Conc. ground slab See 3.19

See 8.25 for insulation options

Parapet wall condition

See 8.16 for flashing requirements

Roof joists lap studs and bear on 2x blocking or 1x ribbon

2x6 studs

2x4 horiz. strapping

Continuous 2x wall studs

See 3.19 for thickened edge ground slabs

See 6.9 - 6.10 for various roof edge conditions

With the increase in thermal insulation requirements required by some building and energy codes, 2x6 or even 2x8 studs have come into greater usage. Alternatives include using double wall construction or installing 2x4 horizontal strapping inside or outside a standard stud wall. See also 8.21.

See 3.6 for pier foundations

NOTE: The wall sections on this and the preceding page are not intended to be complete. They exclude specific wall, floor and ceiling finishes, trim, insulation, and vapor barriers. Instead, they attempt to illustrate the ways wood stud walls connect to various foundation, floor, and roof systems. Wood stud walls are typically used with wood joist and rafter systems.

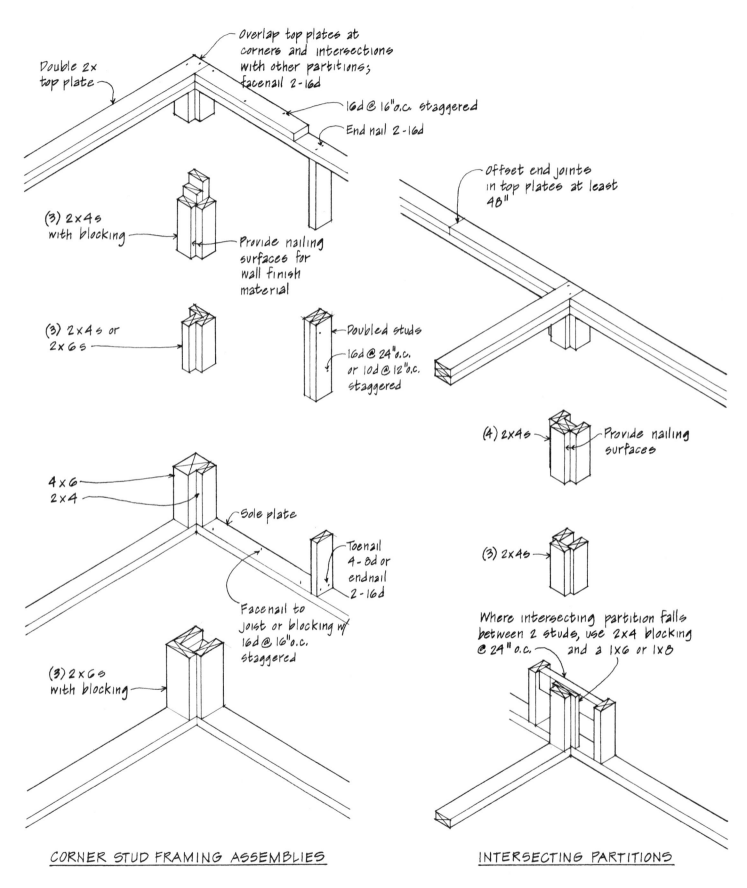

Double 2x top plate

Overlap top plates at corners and intersections with other partitions; facenail 2-16d

16d @ 16"o.c. staggered

End nail 2-16d

(3) 2x4s with blocking

Provide nailing surfaces for wall finish material

(3) 2x4s or 2x6s

Doubled studs

16d @ 24"o.c. or 10d @ 12"o.c. staggered

offset end joints in top plates at least 48"

(4) 2x4s — Provide nailing surfaces

4x6
2x4

Sole plate

(3) 2x4s

Toenail 4-8d or endnail 2-16d

Facenail to joist or blocking w/ 16d @ 16"o.c. staggered

(3) 2x6s with blocking

Where intersecting partition falls between 2 studs, use 2x4 blocking @ 24"o.c. and a 1x6 or 1x8

CORNER STUD FRAMING ASSEMBLIES

INTERSECTING PARTITIONS

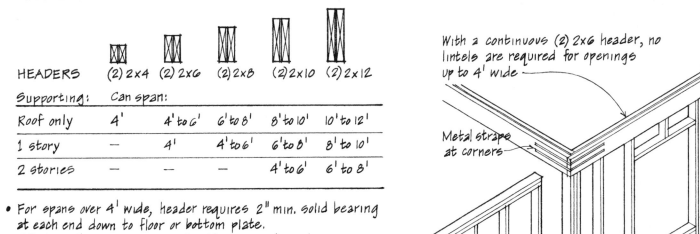

HEADERS	(2) 2x4	(2) 2x6	(2) 2x8	(2) 2x10	(2) 2x12
Supporting:	Can span:				
Roof only	4'	4' to 6'	6' to 8'	8' to 10'	10' to 12'
1 story	—	4'	4' to 6'	6' to 8'	8' to 10'
2 stories	—	—	—	4' to 6'	6' to 8'

- For spans over 4' wide, header requires 2" min. solid bearing at each end down to floor or bottom plate.
- ½" plywood spacers are used with 2x members to match 2x4 or 2x6 stud width.
- For unusual load conditions, header should be engineered as a beam.

With a continuous (2) 2x6 header, no lintels are required for openings up to 4' wide

Metal straps at corners

Oversized header can be used to eliminate short cripples

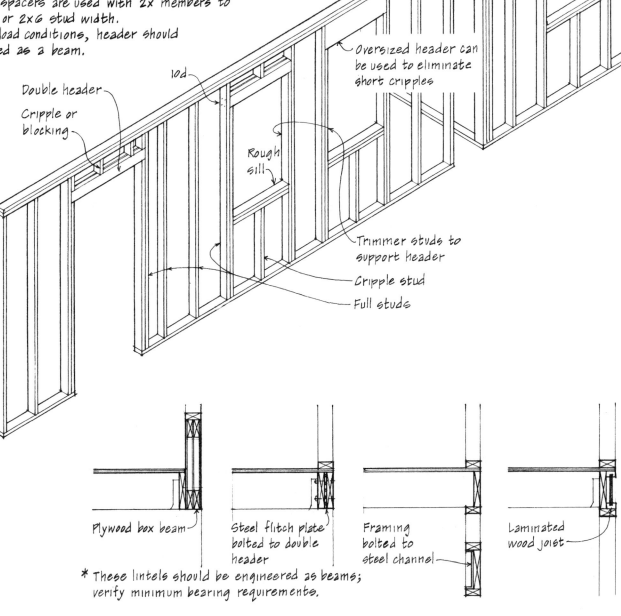

Double header

Cripple or blocking

10d

Rough sill

Trimmer studs to support header

Cripple stud

Full studs

Plywood box beam

Steel flitch plate bolted to double header

Framing bolted to steel channel

Laminated wood joist

* These lintels should be engineered as beams; verify minimum bearing requirements.

LINTEL OPTIONS FOR WIDE OPENINGS

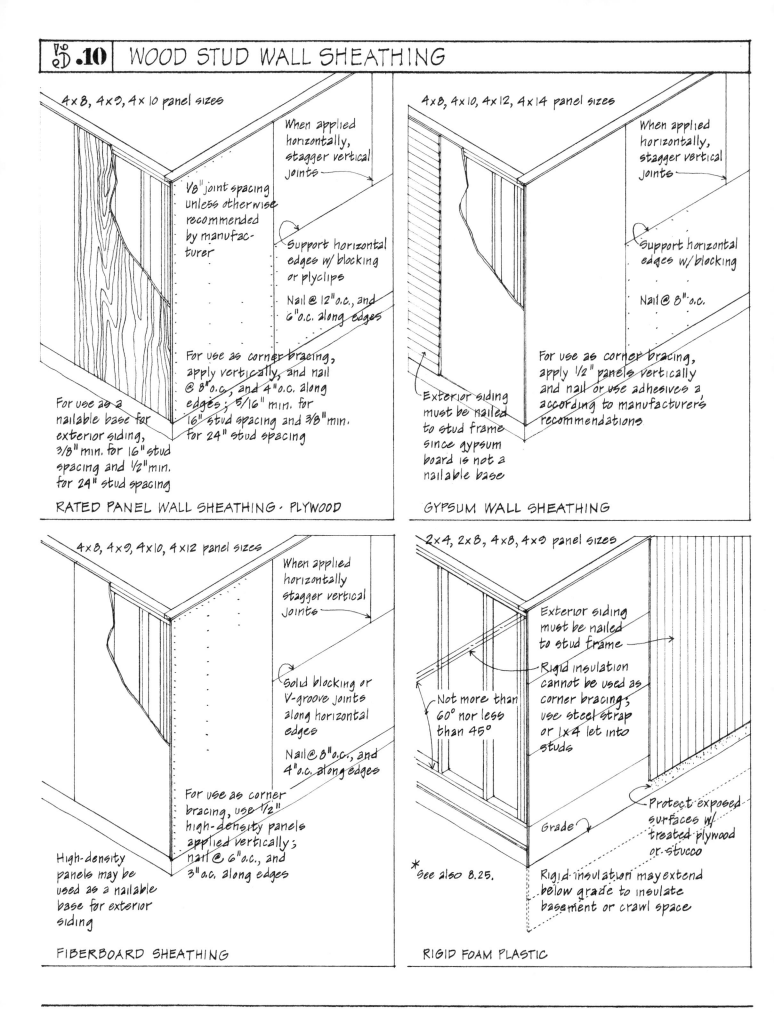

RATED PANEL WALL SHEATHING · PLYWOOD

4x8, 4x9, 4x10 panel sizes

When applied horizontally, stagger vertical joints

⅛" joint spacing unless otherwise recommended by manufacturer

Support horizontal edges w/ blocking or plyclips

Nail @ 12" o.c., and 6" o.c. along edges

For use as corner bracing, apply vertically, and nail @ 8" o.c., and 4" o.c. along edges; 5/16" min. for 16" stud spacing and 3/8" min. for 24" stud spacing

For use as a nailable base for exterior siding, 3/8" min. for 16" stud spacing and 1/2" min. for 24" stud spacing

GYPSUM WALL SHEATHING

4x8, 4x10, 4x12, 4x14 panel sizes

When applied horizontally, stagger vertical joints

Support horizontal edges w/ blocking

Nail @ 8" o.c.

For use as corner bracing, apply 1/2" panels vertically and nail or use adhesives according to manufacturer's recommendations

Exterior siding must be nailed to stud frame since gypsum board is not a nailable base

FIBERBOARD SHEATHING

4x8, 4x9, 4x10, 4x12 panel sizes

When applied horizontally stagger vertical joints

Solid blocking or V-groove joints along horizontal edges

Nail @ 8" o.c., and 4" o.c. along edges

For use as corner bracing, use 1/2" high-density panels applied vertically; nail @ 6" o.c., and 3" o.c. along edges

High-density panels may be used as a nailable base for exterior siding

RIGID FOAM PLASTIC

2x4, 2x8, 4x8, 4x9 panel sizes

Exterior siding must be nailed to stud frame

Rigid insulation cannot be used as corner bracing; use steel strap or 1x4 let into studs

Not more than 60° nor less than 45°

Grade

Protect exposed surfaces w/ treated plywood or stucco

* See also 8.25.

Rigid insulation may extend below grade to insulate basement or crawl space

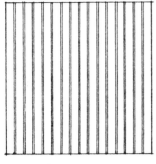

Plywood siding   Board and batten   Diagonal board siding   Vertical board siding

Wood shingles   Stucco   Bevel lap siding   Brick veneer

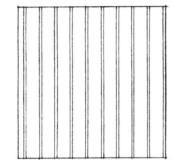

Vinyl or aluminum siding   Metal siding

Illustrated on this page are some common finish materials which can be used with wood stud wall framing. Refer to the pages noted for wall section details.

Some factors to consider in the selection of a wall finish material are:

- Stud spacing required
- Sheathing or backing requirements
- Color, texture, pattern, and scale desired
- Standard widths and heights of panel sidings
- Detailing of corners and vertical and horizontal joints.
- Integration of door and window openings into wall pattern
- Durability, maintenance requirements, and weathering characteristics
- Heat conductivity, reflectance, and porosity of the material
- Expansion joints, if required

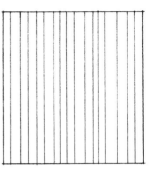

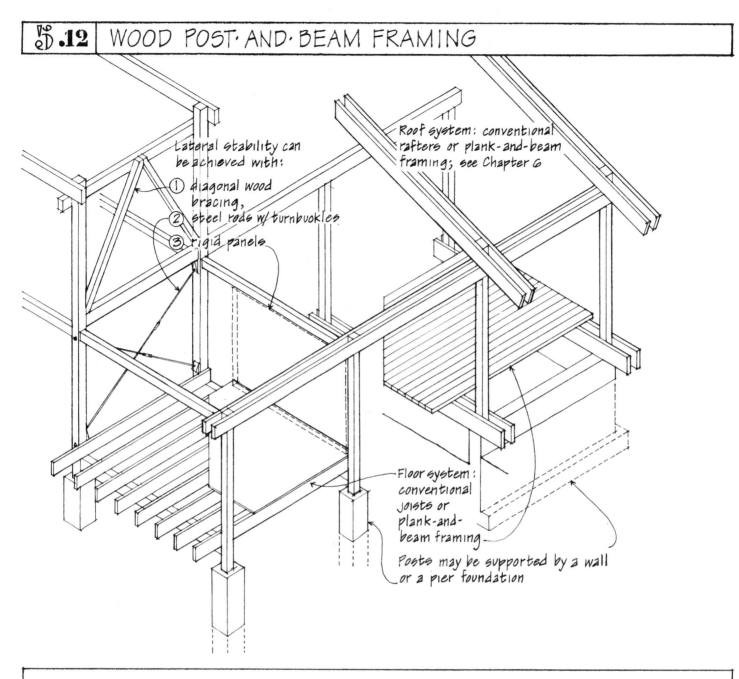

Lateral stability can be achieved with:
① diagonal wood bracing,
② steel rods w/ turnbuckles
③ rigid panels

Roof system: conventional rafters or plank-and-beam framing; see Chapter 6

Floor system: conventional joists or plank-and-beam framing

Posts may be supported by a wall or a pier foundation

- The beams supporting the floor and roof systems transmit their loads to posts which are supported by the foundation system.
- Together with plank-and-beam floor and roof systems, the post-and-beam wall system forms a three-dimensional grid of spaces which may be expanded vertically or horizontally.
- The skeleton frame of posts and beams is often left exposed to form a visible framework within which wall panels, doors, and windows are integrated.
- When the post-and-beam frame is left exposed, the type of wood used, the careful detailing of the post-and-beam connections, and the quality of workmanship are important factors.

- Column spacing is directly related to the desired bay size and the spanning capability of the beams and floor systems used.

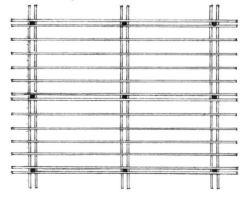

- To qualify as heavy timber or mill constructions, members must have a certain thickness. See A.13.

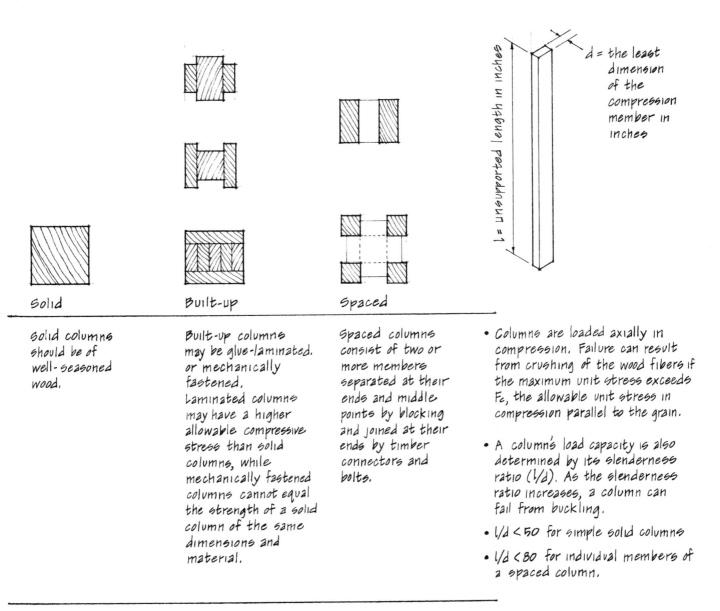

Solid   Built-up   Spaced

d = the least dimension of the compression member in inches

l = unsupported length in inches

Solid columns should be of well-seasoned wood.

Built-up columns may be glue-laminated. or mechanically fastened. Laminated columns may have a higher allowable compressive stress than solid columns, while mechanically fastened columns cannot equal the strength of a solid column of the same dimensions and material.

Spaced columns consist of two or more members separated at their ends and middle points by blocking and joined at their ends by timber connectors and bolts.

- Columns are loaded axially in compression. Failure can result from crushing of the wood fibers if the maximum unit stress exceeds F_c, the allowable unit stress in compression parallel to the grain.

- A column's load capacity is also determined by its slenderness ratio (l/d). As the slenderness ratio increases, a column can fail from buckling.

- $l/d < 50$ for simple solid columns

- $l/d < 80$ for individual members of a spaced column.

The following table is to be used only for the preliminary sizing of solid wood columns.

ALLOWABLE AXIAL LOADS FOR SOLID WOOD COLUMNS (in pounds)										
Length in feet	Nominal size and resulting P/A *									
	4 x 4	P/A (psi)	4 x 6	P/A (psi)	6 x 6	P/A (psi)	6 x 8	P/A (psi)	8 x 8	P/A (psi)
8	5860	478	9210	478	35,760	1182	47,140	1182	116,285	2208
10	3750	306	5890	306	22,872	756	30,150	756	74,425	1414
12	2605	212	4095	212	15,880	525	20,942	525	51,686	982
14					11,665	386	15,380	386	37,975	721
16					8,935	295	11,776	295	29,071	552
18							9,308	233	22,972	436
20									18,606	353

* The above assumes the modulus of elasticity (E) = 1.2×10^6 psi. P/A should not exceed F_c, the allowable unit stress in compression parallel to grain, for the wood used.

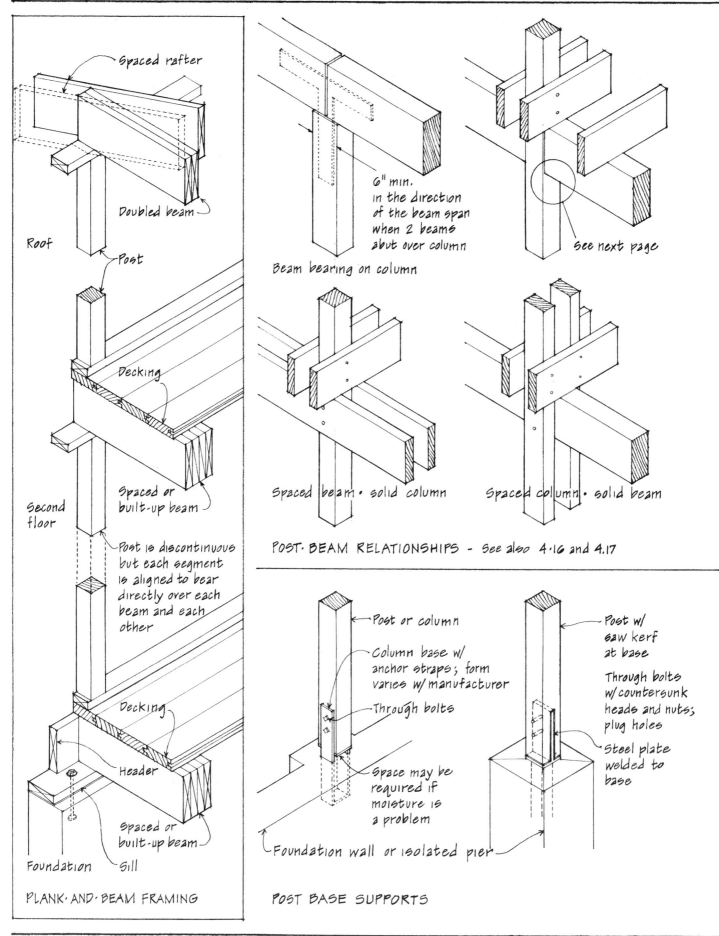

Spaced rafter

Doubled beam

Roof

Post

Decking

Spaced or built-up beam

Second floor

Post is discontinuous but each segment is aligned to bear directly over each beam and each other

Decking

Header

Spaced or built-up beam

Foundation   Sill

PLANK·AND·BEAM FRAMING

6" min. in the direction of the beam span when 2 beams abut over column

Beam bearing on column

see next page

Spaced beam · solid column

Spaced column · solid beam

POST·BEAM RELATIONSHIPS - see also 4.16 and 4.17

Post or column

Column base w/ anchor straps; form varies w/ manufacturer

Through bolts

Space may be required if moisture is a problem

Foundation wall or isolated pier

Post w/ saw kerf at base

Through bolts w/ countersunk heads and nuts; plug holes

Steel plate welded to base

POST BASE SUPPORTS

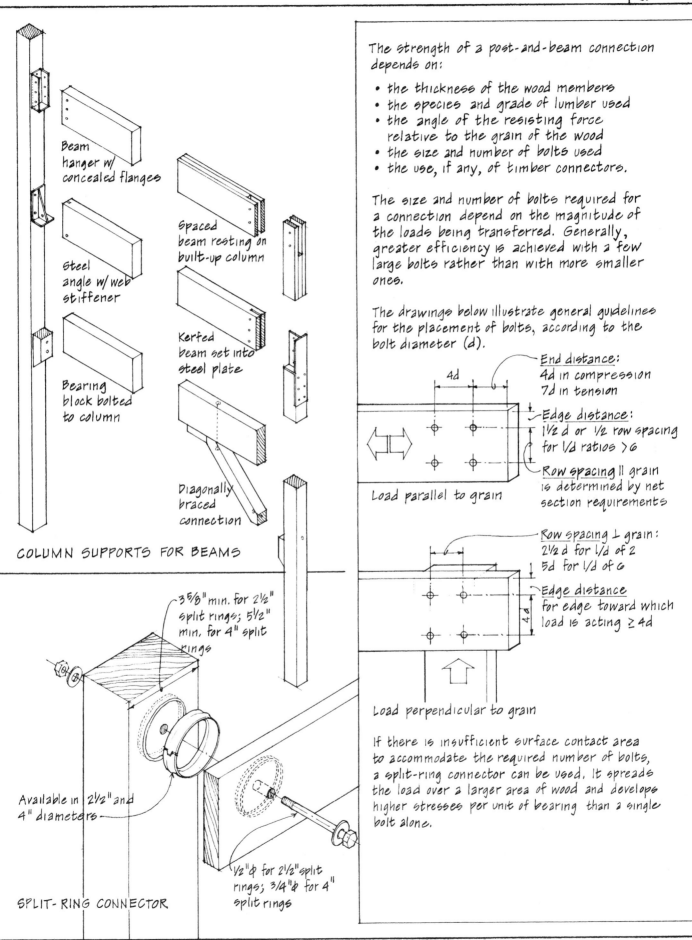

Beam hanger w/ concealed flanges

Steel angle w/ web stiffener

Bearing block bolted to column

Spaced beam resting on built-up column

Kerfed beam set into steel plate

Diagonally braced connection

COLUMN SUPPORTS FOR BEAMS

The strength of a post-and-beam connection depends on:

- the thickness of the wood members
- the species and grade of lumber used
- the angle of the resisting force relative to the grain of the wood
- the size and number of bolts used
- the use, if any, of timber connectors.

The size and number of bolts required for a connection depend on the magnitude of the loads being transferred. Generally, greater efficiency is achieved with a few large bolts rather than with more smaller ones.

The drawings below illustrate general guidelines for the placement of bolts, according to the bolt diameter (d).

4d

End distance:
4d in compression
7d in tension

Edge distance:
1½ d or ½ row spacing for l/d ratios > 6

Row spacing ‖ grain is determined by net section requirements

Load parallel to grain

Row spacing ⊥ grain:
2½ d for l/d of 2
5d for l/d of 6

Edge distance for edge toward which load is acting ≥ 4d

4d

Load perpendicular to grain

If there is insufficient surface contact area to accommodate the required number of bolts, a split-ring connector can be used. It spreads the load over a larger area of wood and develops higher stresses per unit of bearing than a single bolt alone.

3⅝" min. for 2½" split rings; 5½" min. for 4" split rings

Available in 2½" and 4" diameters

½" ⌀ for 2½" split rings; ¾" ⌀ for 4" split rings

SPLIT-RING CONNECTOR

These generalized sections illustrate various foundation, floor, and roof system connections to post and beam walls. Note that beams are integral parts of both wall and floor or roof systems. The type of floor and roof systems used and how they are supported by the wood posts or columns affect the construction depth of the floor and roof planes and the overall height of the structure.

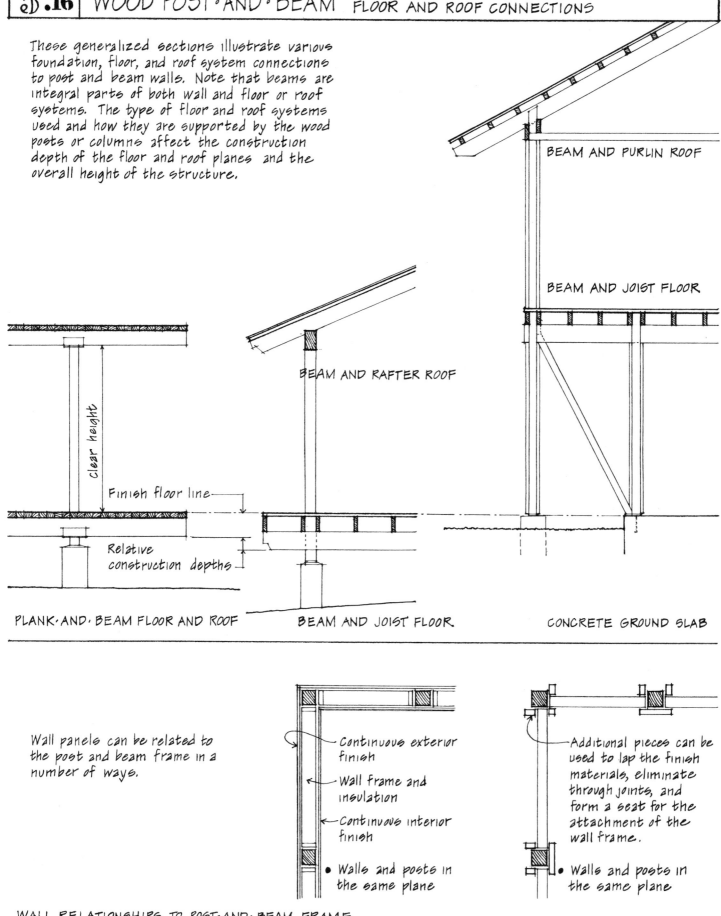

BEAM AND PURLIN ROOF

BEAM AND JOIST FLOOR

BEAM AND RAFTER ROOF

clear height

Finish floor line

Relative construction depths

PLANK·AND·BEAM FLOOR AND ROOF

BEAM AND JOIST FLOOR

CONCRETE GROUND SLAB

Wall panels can be related to the post and beam frame in a number of ways.

— Continuous exterior finish

— Wall Frame and insulation

— Continuous interior finish

• Walls and posts in the same plane

— Additional pieces can be used to lap the finish materials, eliminate through joints, and form a seat for the attachment of the wall frame.

• Walls and posts in the same plane

WALL RELATIONSHIPS TO POST·AND·BEAM FRAME

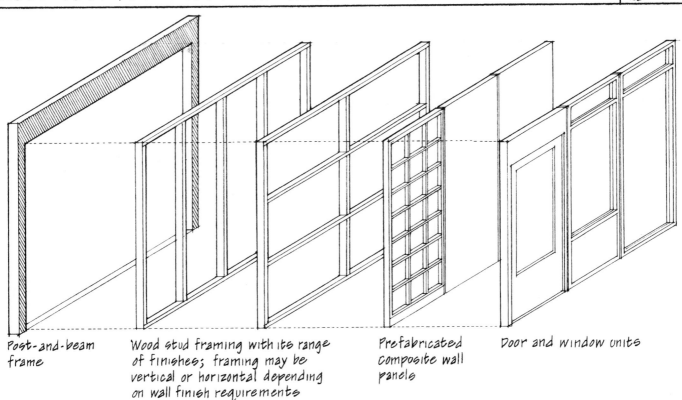

Post-and-beam frame

Wood stud framing with its range of finishes; framing may be vertical or horizontal depending on wall finish requirements

Prefabricated composite wall panels

Door and window units

The pattern created by the wall panels should be regulated by the grid established by the post-and-beam framework. Additional factors to consider include:

- The connections between the wall panels and the structural frame must be able to transfer dead, wind, and possibly, bracing loads.
- The tolerances required for the installation of the wall panels must be built into the joint details.
- The joint details should also provide for a weathertight seal through the use of offsets, flashing, or caulking.

- Allowance should be made for movement of exposed wood due to changes in moisture content, and, when joining dissimilar materials, for different rates of thermal expansion and contraction.

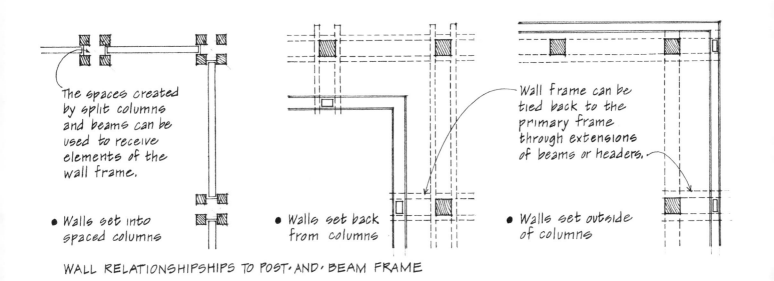

The spaces created by split columns and beams can be used to receive elements of the wall frame.

Wall frame can be tied back to the primary frame through extensions of beams or headers.

- Walls set into spaced columns
- Walls set back from columns
- Walls set outside of columns

WALL RELATIONSHIPSHIPS TO POST·AND·BEAM FRAME

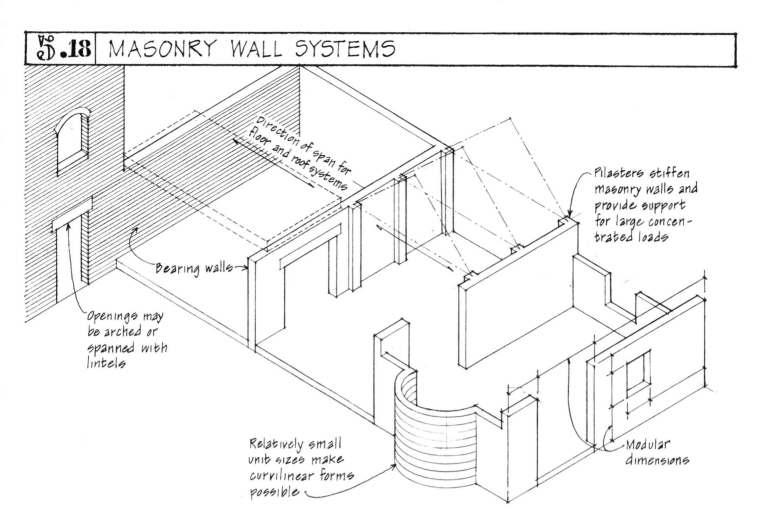

Direction of span for floor and roof systems

Pilasters stiffen masonry walls and provide support for large concentrated loads

Bearing walls

Openings may be arched or spanned with lintels

Relatively small unit sizes make curvilinear forms possible

Modular dimensions

Masonry walls consist of modular building blocks bonded together with mortar to form walls which are structurally most efficient in compression.

The most common types of masonry units are:
• Brick, a heat-hardened clay unit
• Concrete block, a chemically-hardened unit

Other types of masonry units include structural clay tile, structural glass block, and natural or cast stone.

• Masonry bearing walls are typically arranged in parallel sets to support wood, steel, or concrete spanning systems.
• Masonry walls provide strong spatial definition and enclosure, weather protection, and an integral and durable wall finish with a single material
• Differential movements in masonry walls due to changes in temperature or moisture content, or to stress concentrations, require the use of expansion and control joints.
• Water penetration through porous masonry materials must be controlled through the use of tooled joints, cavity spaces, flashing, and caulking.
• For fire-resistance ratings of masonry walls, see A.13.

To minimize cutting and for appearance, the major dimensions of masonry walls should be based on the size of the modular units used.

Grid lines @ 8" o.c. for standard concrete block

2⅔" units	3⅕" units	4" units
Standard modular, Norman, SCR brick	Engineer, Norwegian, 6" Norwegian	Economy, Jumbo utility, 6" and 8" Jumbo

Relative Course Heights (Nominal)

• For lengths, use multiples of 4", 8", or 12"
• Wall thicknesses vary with type wall; see 5.20

• For thermal insulation, see 8.25.

MINIMUM THICKNESS OF MASONRY WALLS

Type of masonry (see 5.20 - 5.22)	Max. ratio of UL or UH to T*	Min. thickness (nominal)
Bearing walls:		
Stone masonry	14	16"
Cavity wall masonry	18	8"
Hollow unit masonry	18	8"
Solid masonry	20	8"
Grouted masonry	20	6"
Reinf. masonry	25	6"
Nonbearing walls:		
Ext. unreinforced	20	See note
Ext. reinforced	30	below
Int. unreinforced	36	2"
Int. reinforced	48	2"

Exterior nonbearing walls may be 4" less than required for bearing walls, but not less than 8" thick, except where 6" walls are permitted in residences.

* UL = Unsupported length between cross walls, piers, or attached columns

UH = Unsupported height between floors or between floor and roof.

Sufficient bonding or anchorage is required to transfer loads from masonry wall to its supports

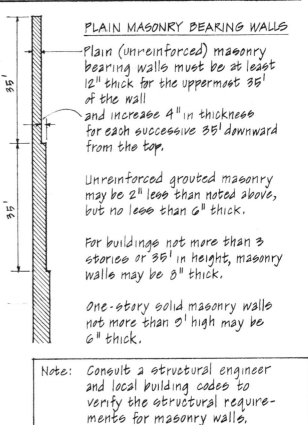

PLAIN MASONRY BEARING WALLS

Plain (unreinforced) masonry bearing walls must be at least 12" thick for the uppermost 35' of the wall and increase 4" in thickness for each successive 35' downward from the top.

Unreinforced grouted masonry may be 2" less than noted above, but no less than 6" thick.

For buildings not more than 3 stories or 35' in height, masonry walls may be 8" thick.

One-story solid masonry walls not more than 9' high may be 6" thick.

Note: Consult a structural engineer and local building codes to verify the structural requirements for masonry walls.

ALLOWABLE COMPRESSIVE STRESSES IN UNREINFORCED MASONRY WALLS (psi)

Material	Type M	Type S	Type N
Solid brick			
4500+ psi	250	225	200
2500-4500 psi	175	160	140
Solid concrete units			
Grade N	175	160	140
Grade S	125	115	100
Grouted masonry			
4500+ psi	350	275	Not permitted
2500-4500 psi	275	215	
Cavity walls			
Solid units	140	130	110
Hollow units	70	60	50
Hollow units	170	150	140
Natural stone	140	120	100

MORTAR is used to join masonry units together, bond reinforcing steel to the masonry, and seal the masonry wall against wind and rain penetration. It consists of Portland or masonry cement, hydrated lime, aggregate, and water.

Type M - A high-strength mortar for masonry walls below grade, and walls subject to high lateral or compressive loads or to severe frost action.

Type S - A medium-high-strength mortar for walls where bond and flexural strength are more important than high compressive strength.

Type N - A medium-strength mortar for general use above grade.

Type O - A low-strength mortar for interior nonbearing partitions.

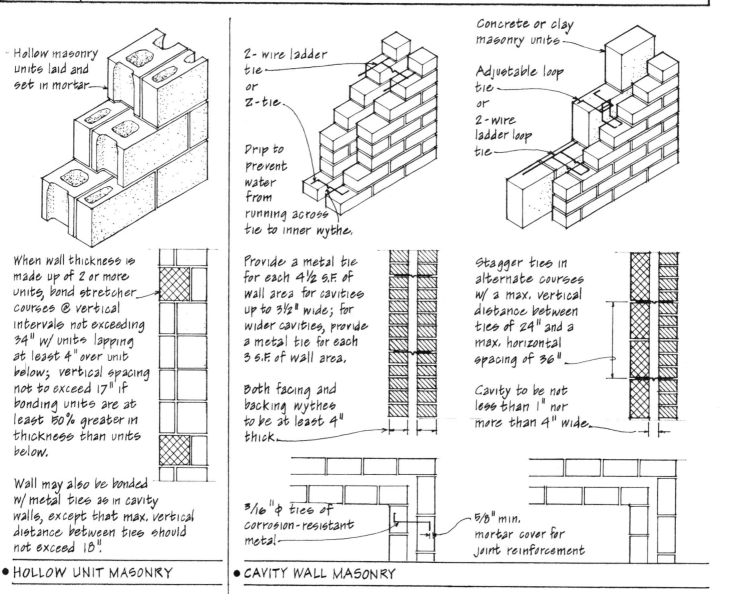

Hollow masonry units laid and set in mortar

2-wire ladder tie or Z-tie

Drip to prevent water from running across tie to inner wythe.

Concrete or clay masonry units

Adjustable loop tie or 2-wire ladder loop tie

When wall thickness is made up of 2 or more units, bond stretcher courses @ vertical intervals not exceeding 34" w/ units lapping at least 4" over unit below; vertical spacing not to exceed 17" if bonding units are at least 50% greater in thickness than units below.

Wall may also be bonded w/ metal ties as in cavity walls, except that max. vertical distance between ties should not exceed 18".

Provide a metal tie for each 4½ S.F. of wall area for cavities up to 3½" wide; for wider cavities, provide a metal tie for each 3 S.F. of wall area.

Both facing and backing wythes to be at least 4" thick.

3/16"ϕ ties of corrosion-resistant metal

Stagger ties in alternate courses w/ a max. vertical distance between ties of 24" and a max. horizontal spacing of 36".

Cavity to be not less than 1" nor more than 4" wide.

5/8" min. mortar cover for joint reinforcement

● HOLLOW UNIT MASONRY

Hollow unit masonry walls consist of hollow clay or concrete masonry units laid and set in mortar. When the wall thickness is made up of two or more units, the stretcher courses must be bonded with masonry headers or metal ties. When bonded with metal ties, the wall must conform to the thickness and height requirements of cavity walls.

● CAVITY WALL MASONRY

Cavity wall masonry is made up of a facing and a backing wythe of brick, structural clay tile, or concrete masonry units. The two wythes are completely separated by an air space except for the metal ties which are required for bonding.

When computing the ratio of unsupported height or length to thickness, the value for thickness is equal to the sum of the nominal thicknesses of the inner and outer wythes.

Cavity walls have two advantages over other types of masonry walls:

① The cavity enhances the insulation value of the wall and permits the installation of additional thermal insulation material.

② The air space acts as a barrier against water penetration if the cavity is kept clear, and if adequate weep holes and flashing are provided.

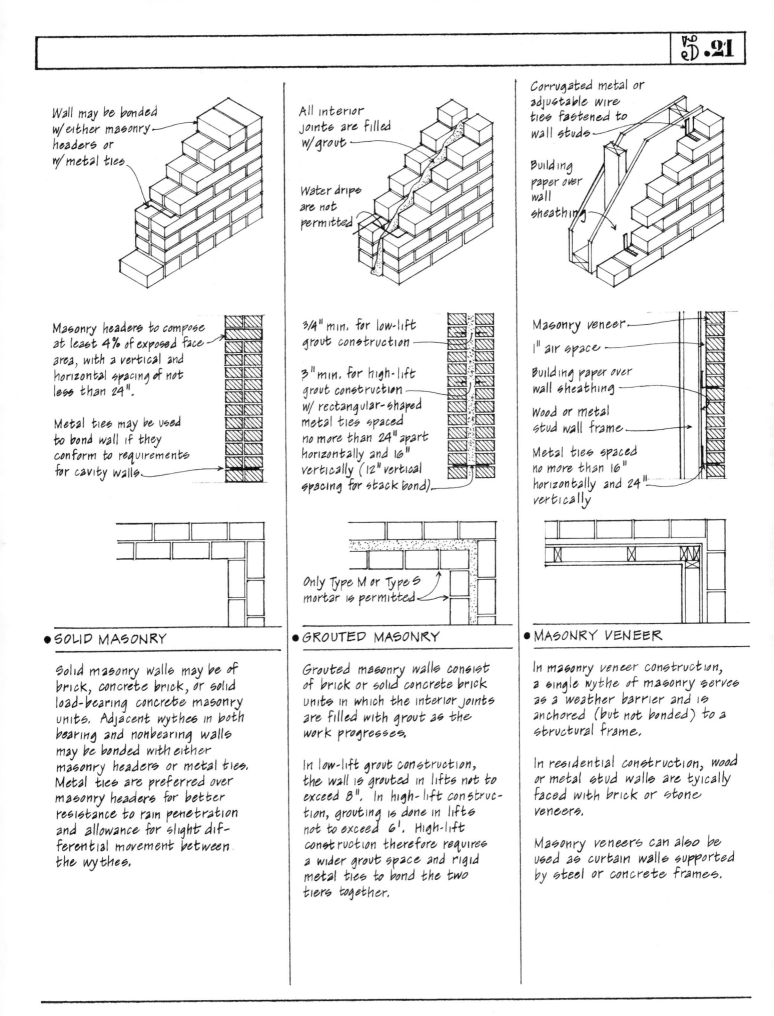

Wall may be bonded w/ either masonry headers or w/ metal ties

All interior joints are filled w/ grout

Water drips are not permitted

Corrugated metal or adjustable wire ties fastened to wall studs

Building paper over wall sheathing

Masonry headers to compose at least 4% of exposed face area, with a vertical and horizontal spacing of not less than 24".

Metal ties may be used to bond wall if they conform to requirements for cavity walls.

3/4" min. for low-lift grout construction

3" min. for high-lift grout construction w/ rectangular-shaped metal ties spaced no more than 24" apart horizontally and 16" vertically (12" vertical spacing for stack bond)

Masonry veneer

1" air space

Building paper over wall sheathing

Wood or metal stud wall frame

Metal ties spaced no more than 16" horizontally and 24" vertically

Only Type M or Type S mortar is permitted

• SOLID MASONRY

Solid masonry walls may be of brick, concrete brick, or solid load-bearing concrete masonry units. Adjacent wythes in both bearing and nonbearing walls may be bonded with either masonry headers or metal ties. Metal ties are preferred over masonry headers for better resistance to rain penetration and allowance for slight differential movement between the wythes.

• GROUTED MASONRY

Grouted masonry walls consist of brick or solid concrete brick units in which the interior joints are filled with grout as the work progresses.

In low-lift grout construction, the wall is grouted in lifts not to exceed 8". In high-lift construction, grouting is done in lifts not to exceed 6'. High-lift construction therefore requires a wider grout space and rigid metal ties to bond the two tiers together.

• MASONRY VENEER

In masonry veneer construction, a single wythe of masonry serves as a weather barrier and is anchored (but not bonded) to a structural frame.

In residential construction, wood or metal stud walls are typically faced with brick or stone veneers.

Masonry veneers can also be used as curtain walls supported by steel or concrete frames.

Reinforcing steel bars embedded in grout

Metal tie

1/4" min. mortar or grout cover between reinforcement and masonry; #2 bars may be placed in 1/2" horizontal joints

5/8" min. mortar cover for horizontal joint reinforcement

Portland cement grout

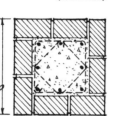

Least dimension of reinforced masonry columns to be 12" with an unsupported length of 20 x least dimension

REINFORCED GROUTED MASONRY

Reinforced grouted masonry should conform to the requirements for plain grouted masonry. See 5.21.

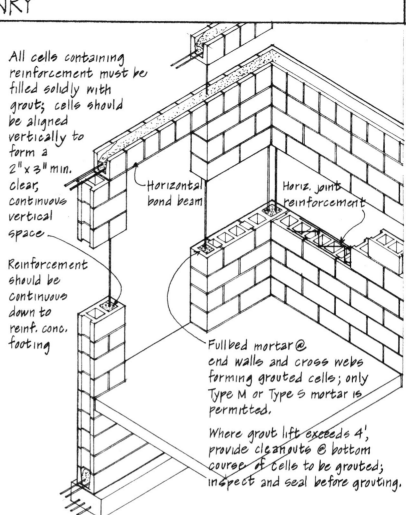

All cells containing reinforcement must be filled solidly with grout; cells should be aligned vertically to form a 2" x 3" min. clear, continuous vertical space

Reinforcement should be continuous down to reinf. conc. footing

Horizontal bond beam

Horiz. joint reinforcement

Full bed mortar @ end walls and cross webs forming grouted cells; only Type M or Type S mortar is permitted.

Where grout lift exceeds 4', provide cleanouts @ bottom course of cells to be grouted; inspect and seal before grouting.

REINFORCED HOLLOW UNIT MASONRY

Reinforced hollow unit masonry consists of hollow masonry units in which certain cells contain reinforcing steel fully embedded in concrete or portland cement grout.

General Notes:

Load-bearing masonry walls may be plain (unreinforced), partially reinforced, or reinforced. Reinforced masonry walls are similar to reinforced concrete walls. They use standard deformed reinforcing steel bars, fully embedded in grout, for increased resistance to buckling and lateral wind and seismic loads. It is essential that a strong bond develop between the reinforcing steel, grout, and masonry units.

Consult a structural engineer and local building code requirements for the design of reinforced masonry walls.

Provide horizontal reinforcement:
• at top of parapet walls,
• at structurally connected floors and roofs,
• at top of wall openings,
• in the top of footings.

Reinforcement to be 3/8" ⌀ min., with a maximum spacing of 4' o.c.

The sum of vertical and horizontal reinforcement to be at least 0.002 x the gross cross-sectional area of the wall.

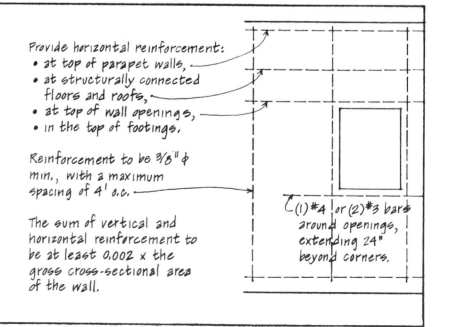

(1) #4 or (2) #3 bars around openings, extending 24" beyond corners.

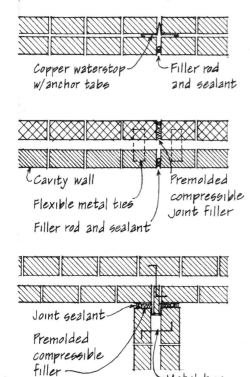

Copper waterstop w/anchor tabs

Filler rod and sealant

Cavity wall

Flexible metal ties

Filler rod and sealant

Premolded compressible Joint Filler

Joint sealant

Premolded compressible filler

Metal ties

* For expansion joint sizes, see 8.26

Expansion joints should be weathertight and allow movement in the plane of the wall.

EXPANSION JOINTS

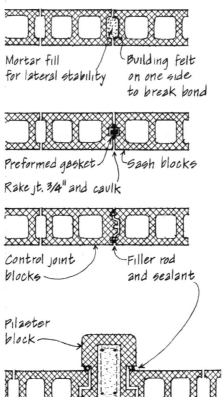

Mortar fill for lateral stability

Building felt on one side to break bond

Preformed gasket

Sash blocks

Rake jt. 3/4" and caulk

Control joint blocks

Filler rod and sealant

Pilaster block

Control joints should be weathertight and provide lateral stability across the joint.

CONTROL JOINTS

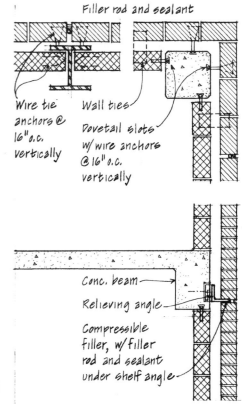

Filler rod and sealant

Wire tie anchors @ 16" o.c. vertically

Wall ties

Dovetail slots w/ wire anchors @ 16" o.c. vertically

Conc. beam

Relieving angle

Compressible filler, w/ filler rod and sealant under shelf angle

Vertical and horizontal control joints are required between steel or concrete frames and supported masonry walls or panels.

Masonry materials expand and contract with changes in temperature and moisture content. Expansion joints allow this movement to occur in a masonry wall by providing a complete separation through the structure. They should generally be located at 125' intervals along unbroken wall lengths, and at offsets and corners of U, L, and T shaped buildings.

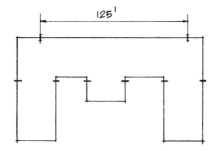

A concrete masonry wall is subject to shrinkage as it dries after construction. Shrinkage cracking can be controlled by using Type 1 moisture-controlled concrete masonry units, reinforcing horizontal joints, and properly placing control joints.

Control joints are also used to control cracking where points of weakness or stress concentration are expected:

① at changes in wall height or thickness
② at columns, pilasters, and wall intersections
③ near corners
④ both sides of openings >6'
⑤ one side of openings <6'

Control Joint Spacing w/ Type 1 units	Vertical Spacing of Joint Reinforcement	
	16"	8"
Wall length (L) between control jts.	50'	60'
L/H ratio	3	4

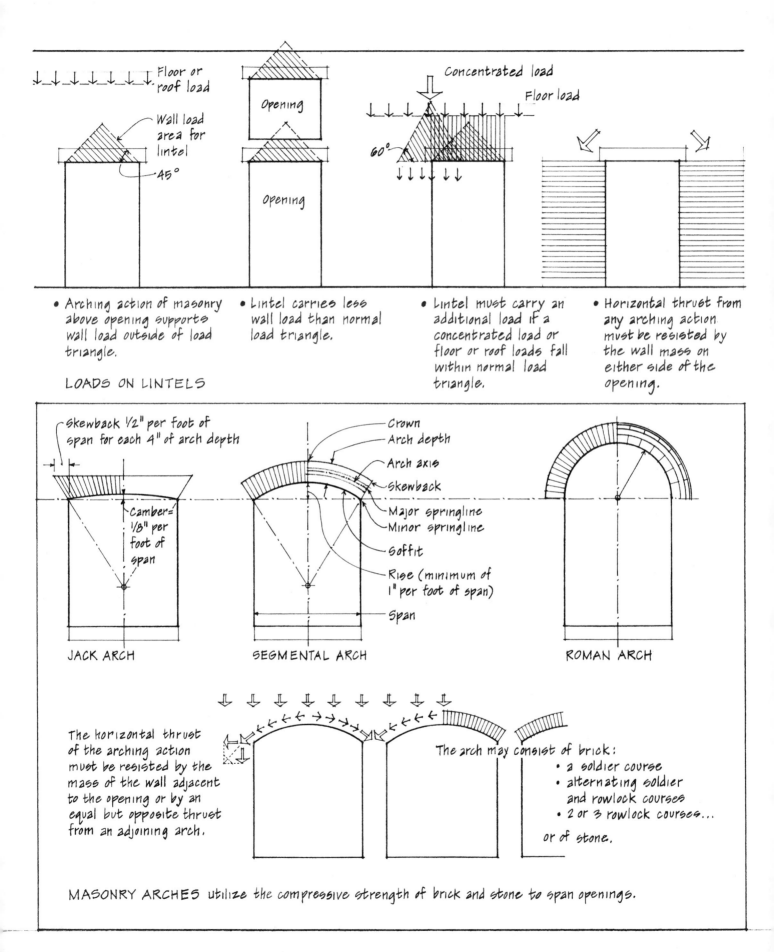

Floor or roof load

Wall load area for lintel

45°

Opening

Opening

Concentrated load

Floor load

60°

- Arching action of masonry above opening supports wall load outside of load triangle.

- Lintel carries less wall load than normal load triangle.

- Lintel must carry an additional load if a concentrated load or floor or roof loads fall within normal load triangle.

- Horizontal thrust from any arching action must be resisted by the wall mass on either side of the opening.

LOADS ON LINTELS

Skewback ½" per foot of span for each 4" of arch depth

Camber = ⅛" per foot of span

Crown
Arch depth
Arch axis
Skewback
Major springline
Minor springline
Soffit
Rise (minimum of 1" per foot of span)
Span

JACK ARCH

SEGMENTAL ARCH

ROMAN ARCH

The horizontal thrust of the arching action must be resisted by the mass of the wall adjacent to the opening or by an equal but opposite thrust from an adjoining arch.

The arch may consist of brick:
- a soldier course
- alternating soldier and rowlock courses
- 2 or 3 rowlock courses...

or of stone.

MASONRY ARCHES utilize the compressive strength of brick and stone to span openings.

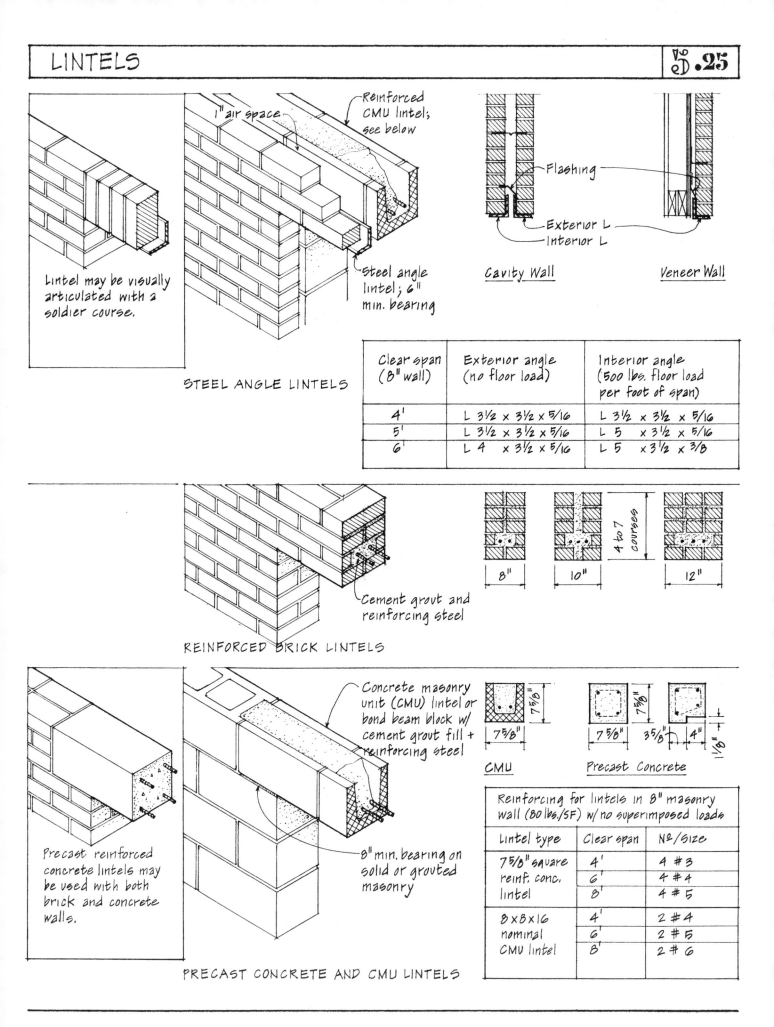

Lintel may be visually articulated with a soldier course.

1" air space

Reinforced CMU lintel; see below

Steel angle lintel; 6" min. bearing

STEEL ANGLE LINTELS

Flashing

Exterior L

Interior L

Cavity Wall

Veneer Wall

Clear span (8" wall)	Exterior angle (no floor load)	Interior angle (500 lbs. floor load per foot of span)
4'	L 3½ x 3½ x 5/16	L 3½ x 3½ x 5/16
5'	L 3½ x 3½ x 5/16	L 5 x 3½ x 5/16
6'	L 4 x 3½ x 5/16	L 5 x 3½ x 3/8

Cement grout and reinforcing steel

REINFORCED BRICK LINTELS

4 to 7 courses

8"

10"

12"

Concrete masonry unit (CMU) lintel or bond beam block w/ cement grout fill + reinforcing steel

7 5/8"

7 5/8"

CMU

Precast Concrete

7 5/8"

3 5/8"

4"

1/8"

Precast reinforced concrete lintels may be used with both brick and concrete walls.

8" min. bearing on solid or grouted masonry

Reinforcing for lintels in 8" masonry wall (80 lbs./SF) w/ no superimposed loads		
Lintel type	Clear span	No./size
7 5/8" square reinf. conc. lintel	4'	4 #3
	6'	4 #4
	8'	4 #5
8 x 8 x 16 nominal CMU lintel	4'	2 #4
	6'	2 #5
	8'	2 #6

PRECAST CONCRETE AND CMU LINTELS

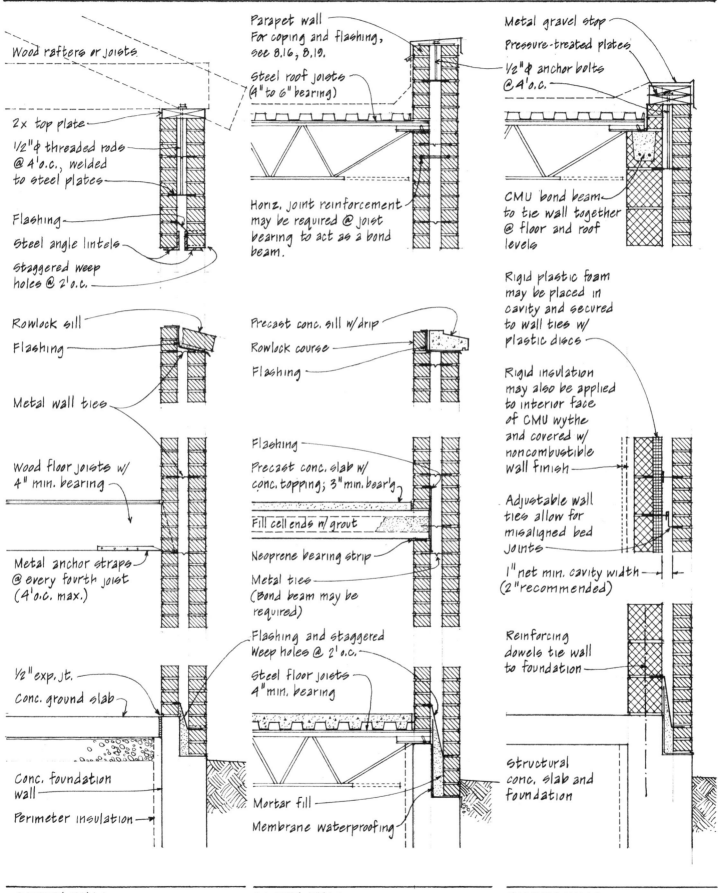

Wood rafters or joists

2x top plate

1/2"ø threaded rods @ 4' o.c., welded to steel plates

Flashing

Steel angle lintels

Staggered weep holes @ 2' o.c.

Rowlock sill

Flashing

Metal wall ties

Wood floor joists w/ 4" min. bearing

Metal anchor straps @ every fourth joist (4' o.c. max.)

1/2" exp. jt.

Conc. ground slab

Conc. foundation wall

Perimeter insulation

Parapet wall
For coping and flashing, see 8.16, 8.19.

Steel roof joists (4" to 6" bearing)

Horiz. joint reinforcement may be required @ joist bearing to act as a bond beam.

Precast conc. sill w/drip

Rowlock course

Flashing

Flashing

Precast conc. slab w/ conc. topping; 3" min. bear'g

Fill cell ends w/ grout

Neoprene bearing strip

Metal ties
(Bond beam may be required)

Flashing and staggered weep holes @ 2' o.c.

Steel floor joists 4" min. bearing

Mortar fill

Membrane waterproofing

Metal gravel stop

Pressure-treated plates

1/2"ø anchor bolts @ 4' o.c.

CMU bond beam to tie wall together @ floor and roof levels

Rigid plastic foam may be placed in cavity and secured to wall ties w/ plastic discs

Rigid insulation may also be applied to interior face of CMU wythe and covered w/ noncombustible wall finish

Adjustable wall ties allow for misaligned bed joints

1" net min. cavity width (2" recommended)

Reinforcing dowels tie wall to foundation

Structural conc. slab and foundation

CAVITY WALL   CAVITY WALL   CAVITY WALL

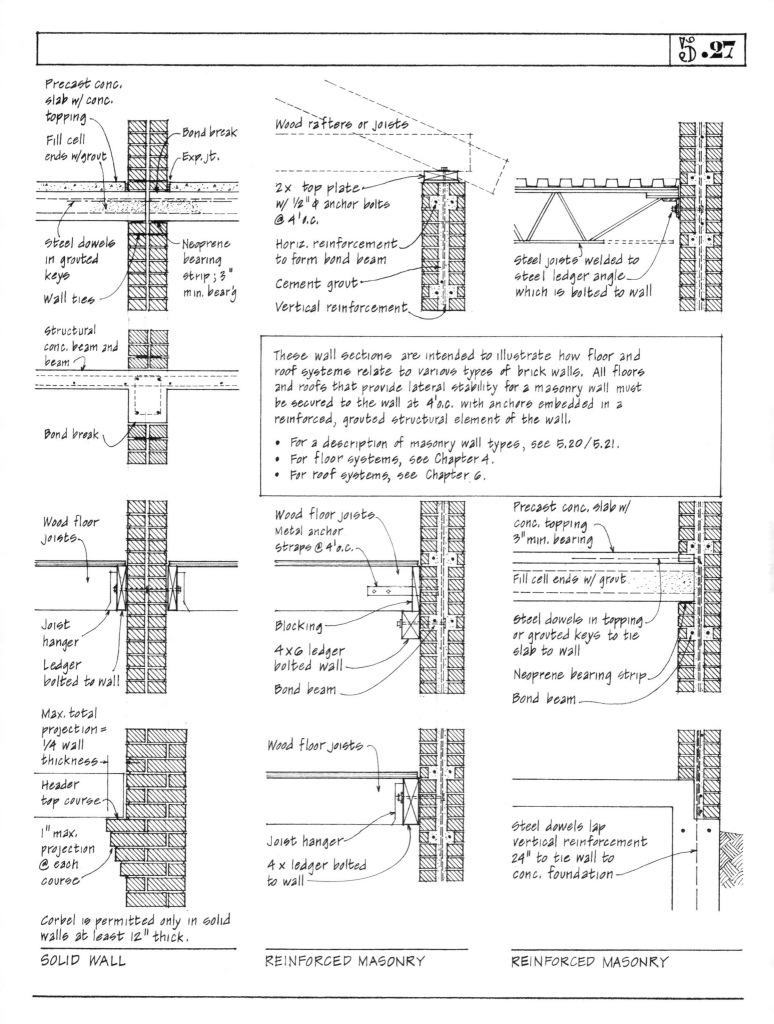

Precast conc. slab w/ conc. topping

Fill cell ends w/ grout

Bond break

Exp. jt.

steel dowels in grouted keys

Wall ties

Neoprene bearing strip; 3" min. bear'g

Structural conc. beam and beam

Bond break

Wood floor joists

Joist hanger

Ledger bolted to wall

Max. total projection = ¼ wall thickness

Header top course

1" max. projection @ each course

Corbel is permitted only in solid walls at least 12" thick.

SOLID WALL

Wood rafters or joists

2x top plate w/ ½"⌀ anchor bolts @ 4' o.c.

Horiz. reinforcement to form bond beam

Cement grout

Vertical reinforcement

These wall sections are intended to illustrate how floor and roof systems relate to various types of brick walls. All floors and roofs that provide lateral stability for a masonry wall must be secured to the wall at 4' o.c. with anchors embedded in a reinforced, grouted structural element of the wall.

- For a description of masonry wall types, see 5.20/5.21.
- For floor systems, see Chapter 4.
- For roof systems, see Chapter 6.

Wood floor joists Metal anchor straps @ 4' o.c.

Blocking

4x6 ledger bolted wall

Bond beam

Wood floor joists

Joist hanger

4 x ledger bolted to wall

REINFORCED MASONRY

Steel joists welded to steel ledger angle which is bolted to wall

Precast conc. slab w/ conc. topping 3" min. bearing

Fill cell ends w/ grout

Steel dowels in topping or grouted keys to tie slab to wall

Neoprene bearing strip

Bond beam

Steel dowels lap vertical reinforcement 24" to tie wall to conc. foundation

REINFORCED MASONRY

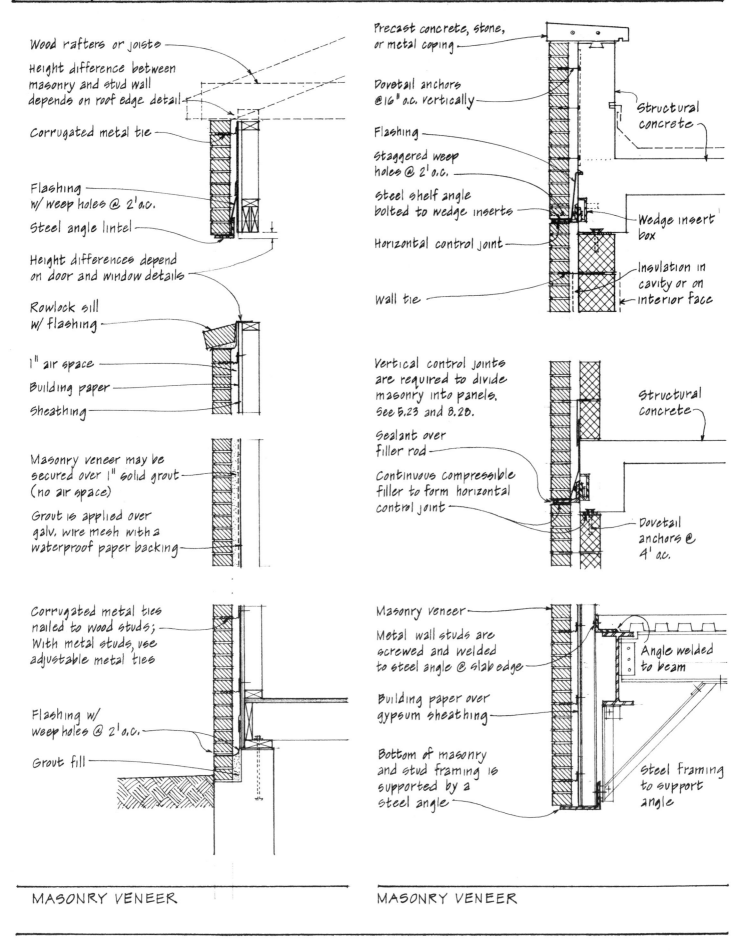

Wood rafters or joists

Height difference between masonry and stud wall depends on roof edge detail

Corrugated metal tie

Flashing w/ weep holes @ 2' o.c.

Steel angle lintel

Height differences depend on door and window details

Rowlock sill w/ flashing

1" air space

Building paper

Sheathing

Masonry veneer may be secured over 1" solid grout (no air space)

Grout is applied over galv. wire mesh with a waterproof paper backing

Corrugated metal ties nailed to wood studs; With metal studs, use adjustable metal ties

Flashing w/ weep holes @ 2' o.c.

Grout fill

Precast concrete, stone, or metal coping

Dovetail anchors @ 16" o.c. vertically

Flashing

Staggered weep holes @ 2' o.c.

Steel shelf angle bolted to wedge inserts

Horizontal control joint

Wall tie

Structural concrete

Wedge insert box

Insulation in cavity or on interior face

Vertical control joints are required to divide masonry into panels. See 5.23 and 8.28.

Sealant over filler rod

Continuous compressible filler to form horizontal control joint

Structural concrete

Dovetail anchors @ 4' o.c.

Masonry veneer

Metal wall studs are screwed and welded to steel angle @ slab edge

Building paper over gypsum sheathing

Bottom of masonry and stud framing is supported by a steel angle

Angle welded to beam

Steel framing to support angle

MASONRY VENEER   MASONRY VENEER

Running Bond
This is the simplest pattern which is used in cavity and veneer walls.

Common Bond
This is similar to running bond except for a header course at every 5th, 6th, or 7th course.

Stack Bond
Since units do not overlap, longitudinal reinforcement is required in unreinforced walls @ 16" o.c. vertically.

Flemish Bond
Each course consists of alternating headers and stretchers.

Common Bond
Every sixth course is composed of Flemish headers.

English Bond
Pattern consists of alternating stretcher and header courses.

BRICK BOND PATTERNS

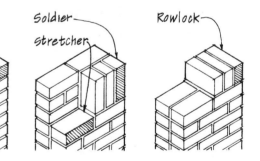

Bed joint are typically 3/8" thick. They should not be less than 1/4" nor more than 5/8" in thickness.

Wythe
Collar Joint
Course
Head Joint
Bed Joint

Header
Blind header

Soldier
Stretcher

Rowlock

Raked   Flush   Struck   Weathered   Vee   Concave
Troweled   Tooled

TYPES OF MORTAR JOINTS

Tooling compresses the mortar and forces it tightly against the mortar. Tooled joints provide maximum protection against water penetration and are recommended in areas subject to high winds or heavy rains.

In troweled joints, the mortar is cut or struck off with a trowel. The most effective of these is the weathered joint since it sheds water.

Raked joints are for interior use only.

- For mortar types, see 5.10 and 12.6
- For description of brick, see 12.6

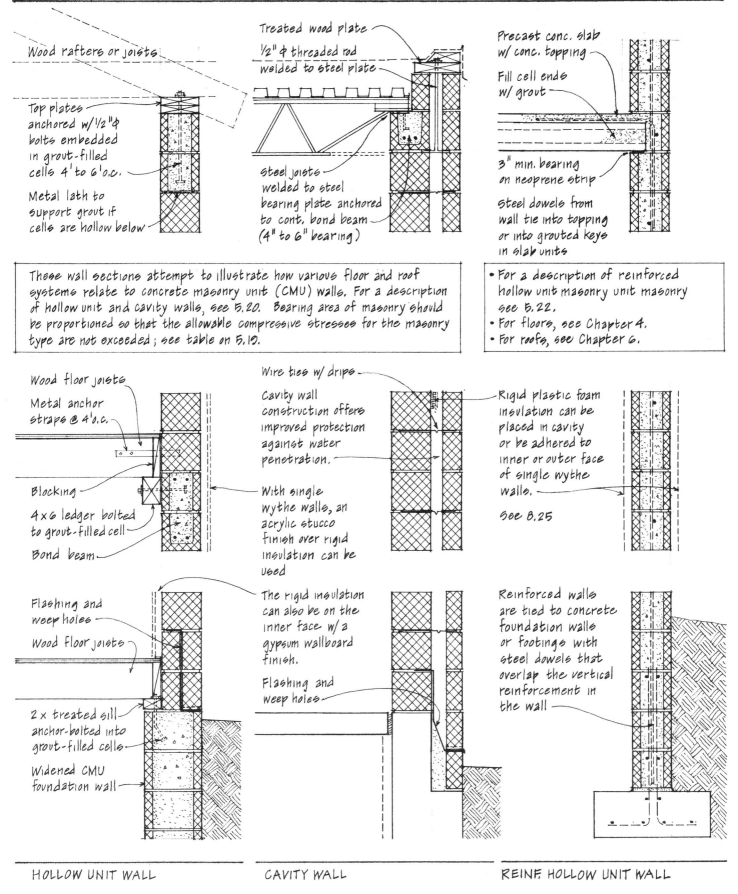

Wood rafters or joists

Top plates anchored w/ ½"∅ bolts embedded in grout-filled cells 4' to 6' o.c.

Metal lath to support grout if cells are hollow below

Treated wood plate

½"∅ threaded rod welded to steel plate

steel joists welded to steel bearing plate anchored to cont. bond beam (4" to 6" bearing)

Precast conc. slab w/ conc. topping

Fill cell ends w/ grout

3" min. bearing on neoprene strip

Steel dowels from wall tie into topping or into grouted keys in slab units

These wall sections attempt to illustrate how various floor and roof systems relate to concrete masonry unit (CMU) walls. For a description of hollow unit and cavity walls, see 5.20. Bearing area of masonry should be proportioned so that the allowable compressive stresses for the masonry type are not exceeded; see table on 5.10.

- For a description of reinforced hollow unit masonry unit masonry see 5.22.
- For floors, see Chapter 4.
- For roofs, see Chapter 6.

Wood floor joists

Metal anchor straps @ 4' o.c.

Blocking

4 x 6 ledger bolted to grout-filled cell

Bond beam

Wire ties w/ drips

Cavity wall construction offers improved protection against water penetration.

With single wythe walls, an acrylic stucco finish over rigid insulation can be used

The rigid insulation can also be on the inner face w/ a gypsum wallboard finish.

Flashing and weep holes

Rigid plastic foam insulation can be placed in cavity or be adhered to inner or outer face of single wythe walls.

See 8.25

Flashing and weep holes

Wood floor joists

2 x treated sill anchor-bolted into grout-filled cells

Widened CMU foundation wall

Flashing and weep holes

Reinforced walls are tied to concrete foundation walls or footings with steel dowels that overlap the vertical reinforcement in the wall

HOLLOW UNIT WALL   CAVITY WALL   REINF. HOLLOW UNIT WALL

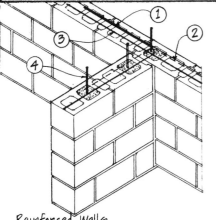

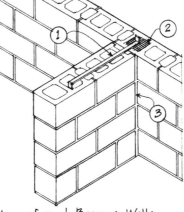

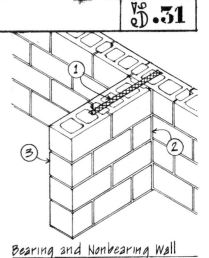

Reinforced Walls

1. Lap splice bars 40 bar diameters or 24"
2. Turn every other bar in opposite direction
3. Horizontal or bond beam reinforcement
4. Vertical reinforcement in fully grouted cells

Unreinforced Bearing Walls

1. 1½" x ¼" x 30" metal strap anchor w/ends bent up 2"; space verti- cally @ 4' o.c. maximum
2. Metal lath to support grout in cell above
3. Control joint

Bearing and Nonbearing Wall

1. Metal lath @ 16" o.c. vertically
2. Control joint - rake and caulk
3. Nonbearing wall

WALL INTERSECTIONS

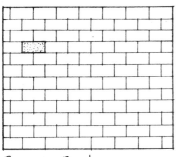

Running Bond

Stack Bond
Requires horizontal joint reinforcement @ 16" o.c. vertically

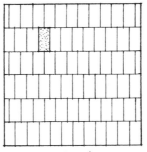

Running Bond

Coursed Ashlar
Alternating courses of 4" and 8" units

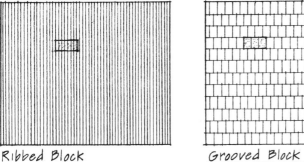

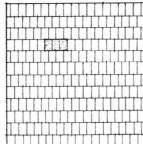

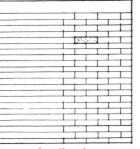

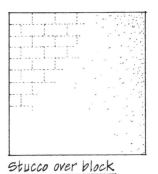

Ribbed Block
With ribbed and grooved block, the color of the mortar should match the color of the block.

Grooved Block

Concrete Brick

Stucco over block

CONCRETE MASONRY BOND PATTERNS

• For mortar joints, see 5.29
• For description of concrete masonry units, see 12.7

Structural facing tile is a clay masonry product glazed on one or both faces. These tiles are generally used for interior partitions or the inner wythe of exterior cavity walls, especially when the durable and easily cleaned surfaces of their glazed faces are desired.

There are two shape groups of structural facing tile:

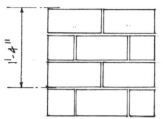

6T shapes have nominal 5⅓" x 12" faces

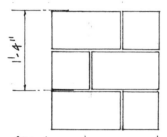

8W shapes have nominal 8" x 16" faces.

In each shape group, there are several types of units:

- Stretchers
- Corners and jambs
- Sills and caps
- Cove bases

Consult manufacturer for specific types, sizes, colors, and nomenclature.

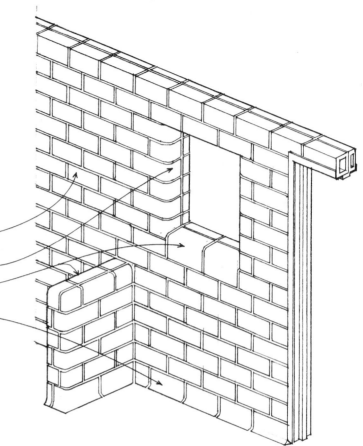

(Nominal dimensions include the thickness of the mortar joints.)

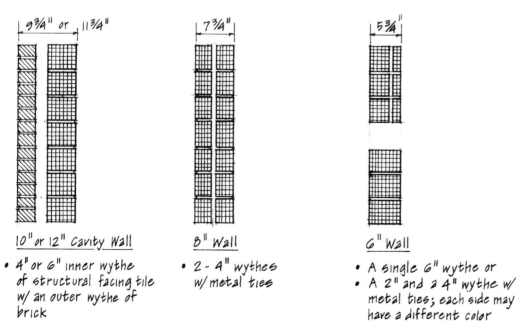

10" or 12" Cavity Wall	8" Wall	6" Wall	4" Wall
9¾" or 11¾"	7¾"	5¾"	3¾"

10" or 12" Cavity Wall
- 4" or 6" inner wythe of structural facing tile w/ an outer wythe of brick

8" Wall
- 2 - 4" wythes w/ metal ties

6" Wall
- A single 6" wythe or
- A 2" and a 4" wythe w/ metal ties; each side may have a different color

4" Wall
- A single 4" wythe or
- 2 - 2" wythes w/ metal ties

WALL SECTIONS : For hollow unit and cavity wall requirements, see 5.20 and 5.21.

Glass block may be used in non-loadbearing exterior and interior walls, and in conventionally framed window openings. The glass block units are laid in Type S mortar with joints at least 1/4" but not more than 3/8" thick. Typically, a wall panel is mortared at the sill support and provided with expansion joints at the head and jamb to allow for movement and settling.

Various surface textures are available as well as inserts and coatings to control heat gain, glare, and brightness.

Square units:
6" x 6"
8" x 8"
12" x 12"

Rectangular units:
4" x 8"
6" x 8"

4" for hollow units
3" for solid units

NOMINAL DIMENSIONS
Includes the thickness of 1/4" mortar joints

Exterior wall panels may not exceed 144 S.F. in unsupported wall area nor 15' in any dimension.

Interior wall panels may not exceed 250 S.F. in unsupported wall area nor 25' in any dimension.

Vertical stiffeners and horizontal shelves can break larger wall areas into the required panel sizes.

Curved wall panels should have expansion joints at each change of direction.

3/16" inside jt.
5/8" outside jt.

Minimum radii:
6" glass block - 4'
8" glass block - 6'
12" glass block - 8'

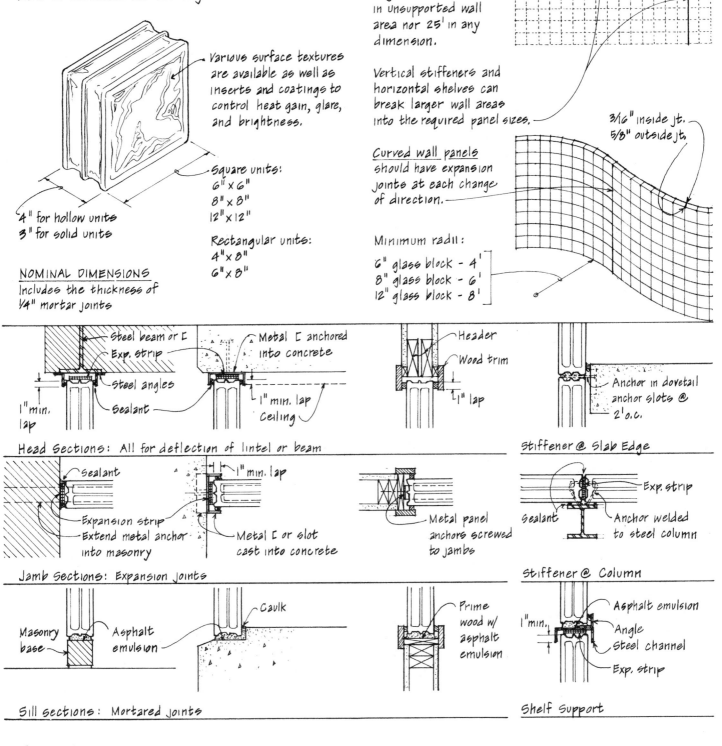

Steel beam or C
Exp. strip
Steel angles
Sealant
1" min. lap

Metal C anchored into concrete
1" min. lap Ceiling

Header
Wood trim
1" lap

Anchor in dovetail anchor slots @ 2' o.c.

Head Sections: All for deflection of lintel or beam

Stiffener @ Slab Edge

Sealant
Expansion strip
Extend metal anchor into masonry

1" min. lap
Metal C or slot cast into concrete

Metal panel anchors screwed to jambs

Exp. strip
Sealant
Anchor welded to steel column

Jamb Sections: Expansion Joints

Stiffener @ Column

Masonry base
Asphalt emulsion

Caulk

Prime wood w/ asphalt emulsion

1" min.
Asphalt emulsion
Angle
Steel channel
Exp. strip

Sill sections: Mortared Joints

Shelf Support

GLASS BLOCK DETAILS

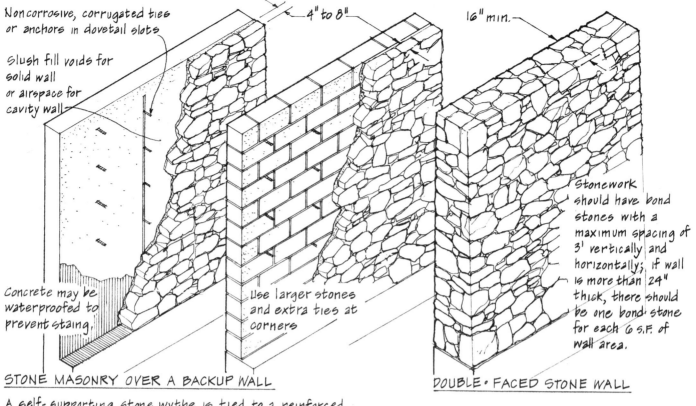

Noncorrosive, corrugated ties or anchors in dovetail slots

Slush fill voids for solid wall or airspace for cavity wall

4" to 8"

16" min.

Concrete may be waterproofed to prevent staining.

Use larger stones and extra ties at corners

Stonework should have bond stones with a maximum spacing of 3' vertically and horizontally; if wall is more than 24" thick, there should be one bond stone for each 6 s.f. of wall area.

STONE MASONRY OVER A BACKUP WALL

A self-supporting stone wythe is tied to a reinforced concrete or CMU wall.

DOUBLE-FACED STONE WALL

Natural stone may be bonded with mortar and laid up as a double-faced loadbearing wall or used as veneer tied to a concrete or masonry backup wall. The stone should be protected from staining by using nonstaining cement mortar, especially with porous and light colored stones. Only non-corrosive ties, anchors, and flashings should be used. Copper, brass, and bronze may stain under certain conditions.

Stone masonry may be laid up in various patterns as illustrated below.

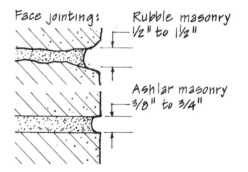

Face jointing: Rubble masonry 1/2" to 1 1/2"

Ashlar masonry 3/8" to 3/4"

RANDOM RUBBLE

- There is no apparent coursing.
- Bed joints are approximately horizontal for stability and appearance; pointing is kept back of face to emphasize natural shapes of stone.

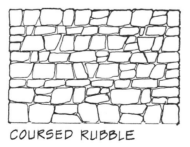

COURSED RUBBLE

- Bed joints are approximately continuous and horizontal.

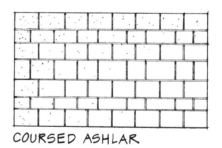

COURSED ASHLAR

- Stone is cut and dressed to design dimensions in the mill.
- Cut stone is laid in a running bond pattern with varying course heights.

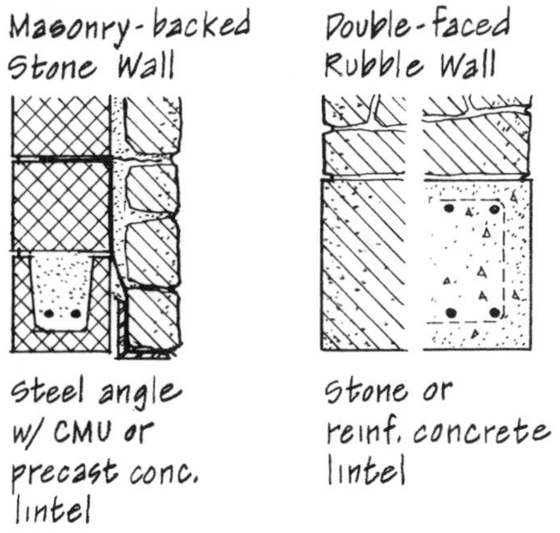

Masonry-backed
Stone Wall

Double-faced
Rubble Wall

Steel angle
w/ CMU or
precast conc.
lintel

Stone or
reinf. concrete
lintel

LINTELS

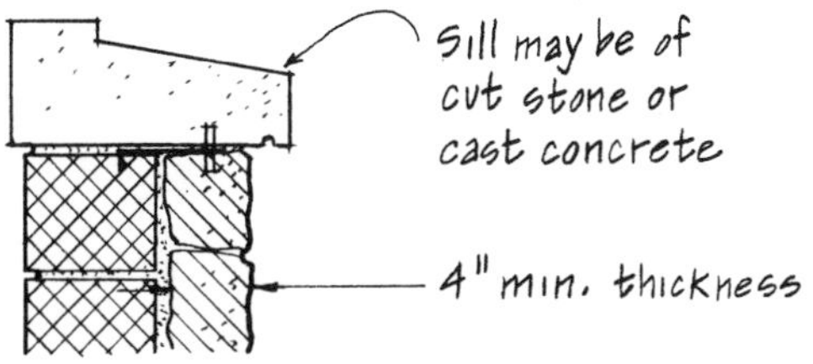

Sill may be of
cut stone or
cast concrete

4" min. thickness

SILL

Stone masonry wall details for:
• foundation supports
• floor and roof system connections
• lateral bracing
• flashing
are similar to those of clay and
concrete unit masonry. See 5.26-5.27
and 5.30. Differences will result,
however, from the uneven coursing
of ashlar masonry, the irregular
shapes and sizes of stone rubble,
and the varying physical properties
of the different types of stone
which may be used in a wall's
construction. See 12.14.

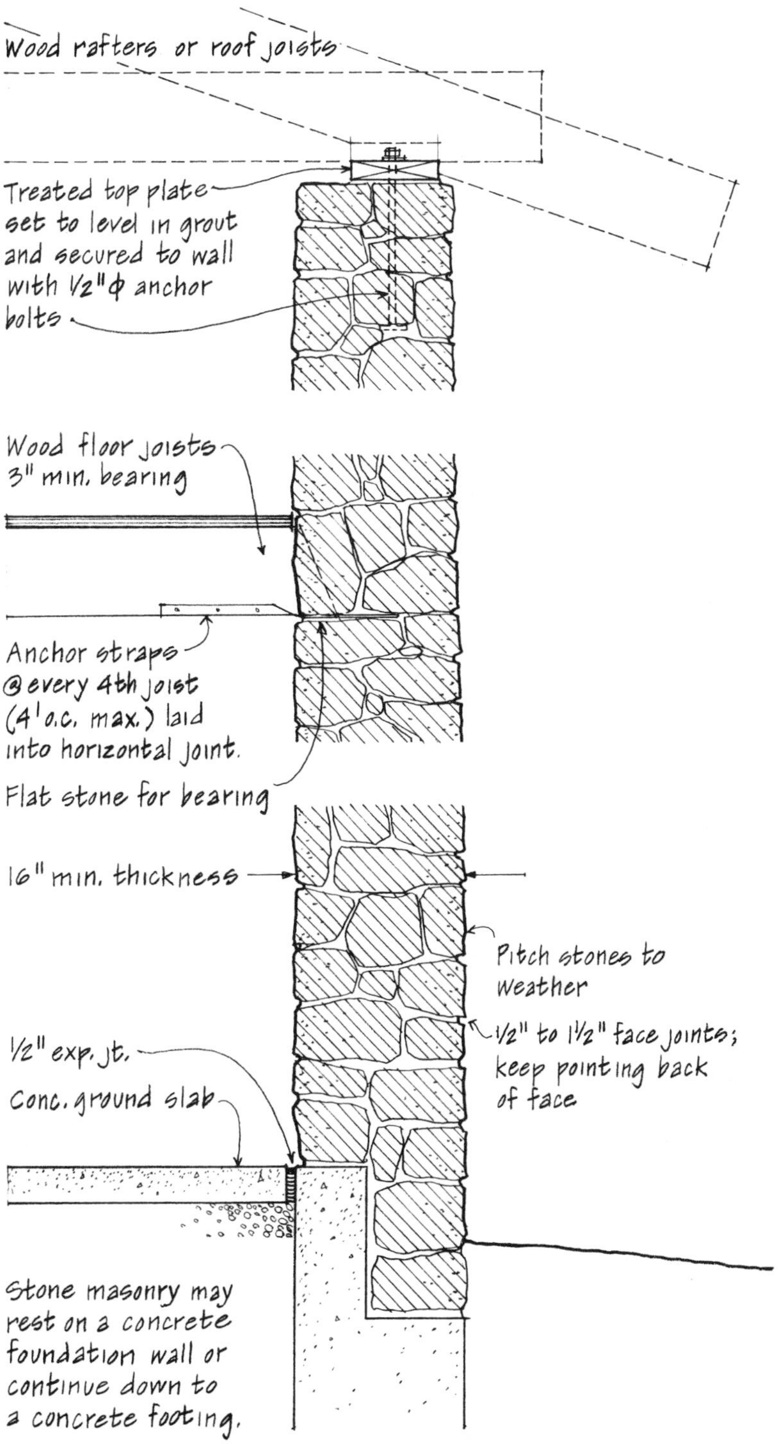

Wood rafters or roof joists

Treated top plate
set to level in grout
and secured to wall
with 1/2"⌀ anchor
bolts.

Wood floor joists
3" min. bearing

Anchor straps
@ every 4th joist
(4' o.c. max.) laid
into horizontal joint.

Flat stone for bearing

16" min. thickness

Pitch stones to
weather

1/2" to 1 1/2" face joints;
keep pointing back
of face

1/2" exp. jt.

Conc. ground slab

Stone masonry may
rest on a concrete
foundation wall or
continue down to
a concrete footing.

EXAMPLE OF A DOUBLE-FACED RUBBLE
WALL SECTION

This type of wall is usually limited to three
stories in height.

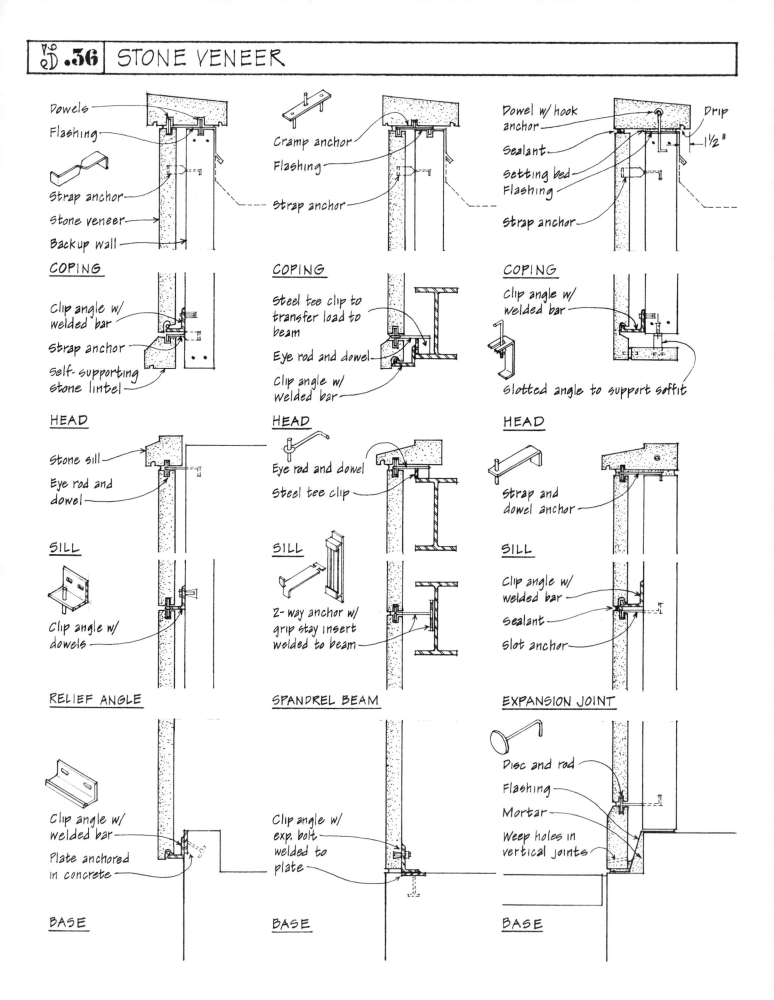

COPING

Dowels
Flashing
Strap anchor
Stone veneer
Backup wall

Cramp anchor
Flashing
Strap anchor

Dowel w/ hook anchor
Sealant
Setting bed
Flashing
Strap anchor
Drip
1½"

HEAD

Clip angle w/ welded bar
Strap anchor
Self-supporting stone lintel

Steel tee clip to transfer load to beam
Eye rod and dowel
Clip angle w/ welded bar

Clip angle w/ welded bar
Slotted angle to support soffit

SILL

Stone sill
Eye rod and dowel

Eye rod and dowel
Steel tee clip

Strap and dowel anchor

RELIEF ANGLE

Clip angle w/ dowels

2-way anchor w/ grip stay insert welded to beam

Clip angle w/ welded bar
Sealant
Slot anchor

SPANDREL BEAM

Clip angle w/ welded bar
Plate anchored in concrete

Clip angle w/ exp. bolt welded to plate

EXPANSION JOINT

Disc and rod
Flashing
Mortar
Weep holes in vertical joints

BASE

On the facing page are illustrated generalized conditions for fastening stone veneer to a concrete or masonry backup wall or to a structural steel frame. While stone veneer may vary from thin (1½"-2½") panels to thicker (3"-4") facing, the connecting relationships remain similar. The required anchorages should be carefully engineered and take into account the following:

• The stone's strength values
• Gravity and lateral loads
• Expected thermal movement

Some anchors must carry the weight of the stonework and transfer the load to a major structural element. Others only restrain the stonework from lateral movement. Still others must offer shear resistance.

All connecting hardware should be of stainless steel to resist corrosion and prevent staining of the stonework. Adequate tolerances must be built in to allow for proper fitting and shimming, if necessary.

For accurate assembly and economy in on-site labor costs, stone veneer may be preassembled into panels in the shop. The stone units may be attached to a steel frame or to a precast concrete panel.

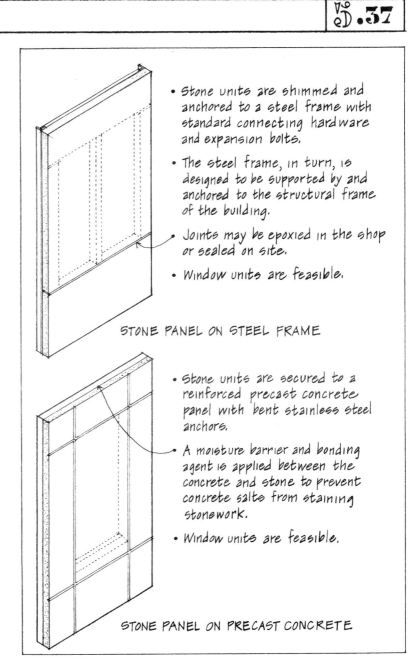

• Stone units are shimmed and anchored to a steel frame with standard connecting hardware and expansion bolts.

• The steel frame, in turn, is designed to be supported by and anchored to the structural frame of the building.

• Joints may be epoxied in the shop or sealed on site.

• Window units are feasible.

STONE PANEL ON STEEL FRAME

• Stone units are secured to a reinforced precast concrete panel with bent stainless steel anchors.

• A moisture barrier and bonding agent is applied between the concrete and stone to prevent concrete salts from staining stonework.

• Window units are feasible.

STONE PANEL ON PRECAST CONCRETE

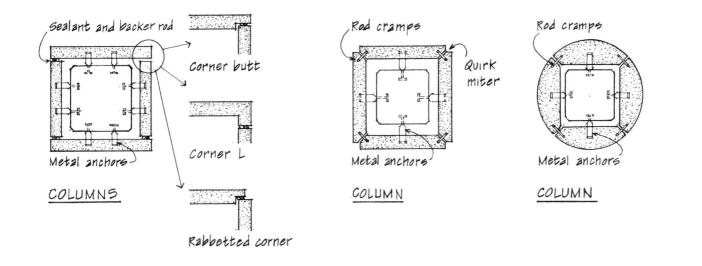

Sealant and backer rod

Corner butt

Corner L

Metal anchors

COLUMNS

Rabbetted corner

Rod cramps

Quirk miter

Metal anchors

COLUMN

Rod cramps

Metal anchors

COLUMN

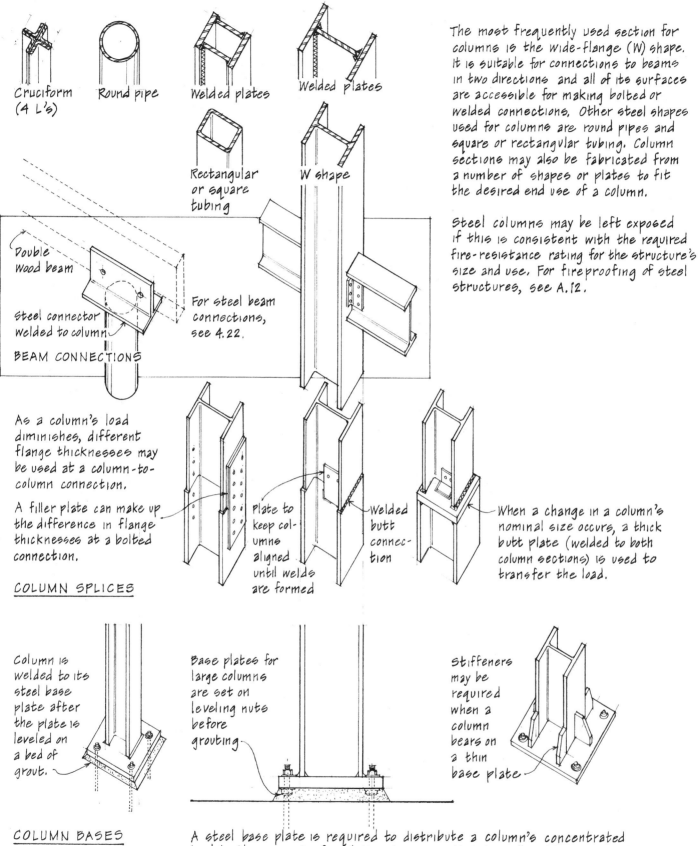

Cruciform (4 L's)

Round pipe

Welded plates

Welded plates

Rectangular or square tubing

W shape

The most frequently used section for columns is the wide-flange (W) shape. It is suitable for connections to beams in two directions and all of its surfaces are accessible for making bolted or welded connections. Other steel shapes used for columns are round pipes and square or rectangular tubing. Column sections may also be fabricated from a number of shapes or plates to fit the desired end use of a column.

Steel columns may be left exposed if this is consistent with the required fire-resistance rating for the structure's size and use. For fireproofing of steel structures, see A.12.

Double wood beam

steel connector welded to column

For steel beam connections, see 4.22.

BEAM CONNECTIONS

As a column's load diminishes, different flange thicknesses may be used at a column-to-column connection.

A filler plate can make up the difference in flange thicknesses at a bolted connection.

Plate to keep columns aligned until welds are formed

Welded butt connection

When a change in a column's nominal size occurs, a thick butt plate (welded to both column sections) is used to transfer the load.

COLUMN SPLICES

Column is welded to its steel base plate after the plate is leveled on a bed of grout.

Base plates for large columns are set on leveling nuts before grouting.

Stiffeners may be required when a column bears on a thin base plate.

COLUMN BASES

A steel base plate is required to distribute a column's concentrated load to the concrete foundation to ensure that the allowable stresses in the concrete are not exceeded.

The allowable load on a steel column depends on its cross-sectional area and its slenderness ratio (L/r), where (L) is the unsupported length of the column in inches and (r) is the least radius of gyration for the column's cross section. The table below should be used for preliminary sizing only.

ALLOWABLE CONCENTRIC LOADS ON COLUMNS IN KIPS. 1 KIP = 1000 lbs.

Round Pipes and Rectangular Tubing	Wall thickness (in.)	Unsupported length in feet								
		8	10	12	14	16	18	20	22	24
○ 3" (3½"OD)	0.216	34	28	22	16	12	10			
	0.300	45	37	28	21	16	12			
	0.600	77	60	43	32	24				
3½" (4"OD)	0.226	44	38	32	25	19	15	12	10	
	0.318	59	51	43	33	25	20	16		
4" (4½"OD)	0.237	54	49	43	36	29	23	19	15	13
	0.337	75	67	59	49	39	31	25	21	17
	0.674	133	118	100	81	62	49	40	33	
5" (5 9/16"OD)	0.258	78	73	68	61	55	47	39	32	27
	0.375	111	103	95	86	76	65	54	44	37
	0.750	202	187	170	151	130	108	87	72	61
6" (6⅝"OD)	0.280	106	111	95	89	82	75	67	59	51
	0.432	159	151	142	132	122	111	99	86	73
	0.864	292	275	257	237	216	193	168	142	119
▢ 3" x 3"	0.250	44	32	23	17					
4" x 4"	0.250	73	64	54	42					
5" x 5"	0.250	103	95	86	76	65	53			
6" x 6"	0.250	132	124	116	107	98	87	76	64	
▯ 2" x 4"	0.250	25	16	11						
3" x 4"	0.250	54	42	29	22	17	13			
3" x 6"	0.250	74	59	43						
4" x 6"	0.250	96	86	74	60					
4" x 8"	0.250	119	107	93	78	61				
W-Shapes	Wt. (lbs.) per foot									
W4	13	51	39	27	20	15				
W5	16	74	64	52	39	30	24	19		
W6	15	75	67	58	48	38	30	24	20	17
	20	100	91	80	68	54	43	35	29	24
	25	126	114	101	86	70	55	45	37	31
W8	24	123	113	101	88	73	59	47	39	33
	28	144	132	118	103	86	69	56	46	39
	31	169	159	148	136	123	110	95	79	66
	35	191	180	168	155	141	125	109	91	76

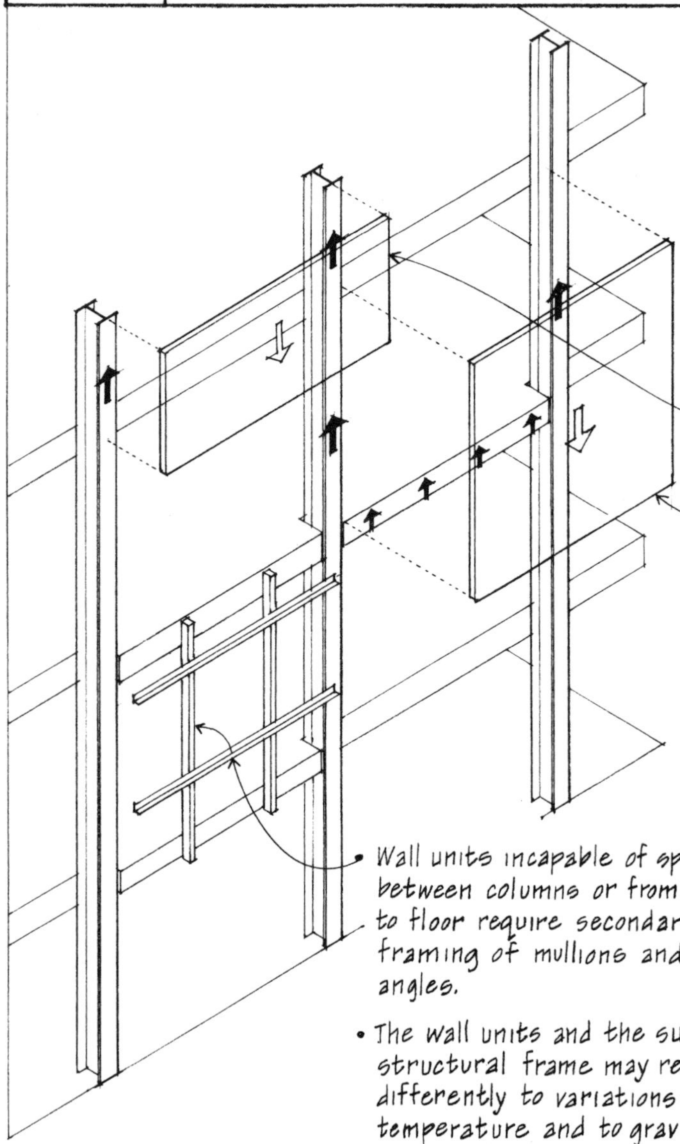

Since the columns in a steel frame structure carry the loads, the exterior walls are non-loadbearing. They can therefore be relatively thin, lightweight claddings of:

- Metal and glass (7.28)
- Precast concrete (5.48)
- Masonry (5.28)
- Cut stone (5.36)

These walls may be supported by:

- The columns alone
- The columns as well as by spandrel beams or the edges of floor slabs

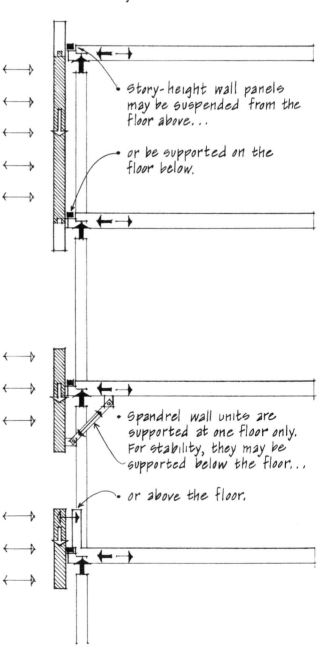

- Story-height wall panels may be suspended from the floor above...

- or be supported on the floor below.

- Spandrel wall units are supported at one floor only. For stability, they may be supported below the floor...

- or above the floor.

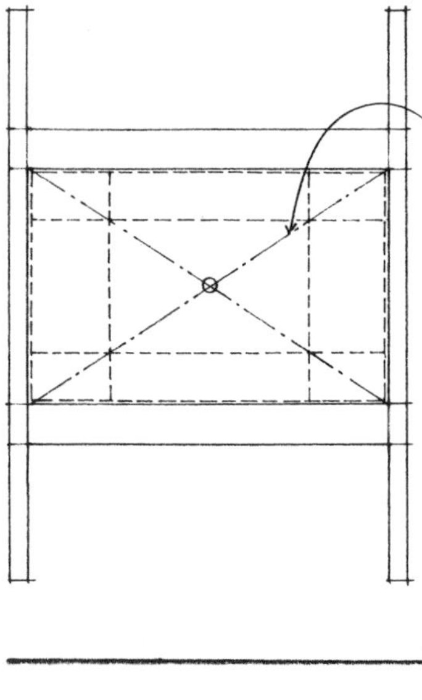

- Wall units incapable of spanning between columns or from floor to floor require secondary framing of mullions and shelf angles.

- The wall units and the supporting structural frame may respond differently to variations in temperature and to gravity or wind loads. Connection details should allow for the differential movement between the wall and structural frame, as well as between the wall units themselves.

- The wall may be subject to both wind pressure and suction.

- If diagonals are used to brace the structural frame, they will affect the design of the wall units.

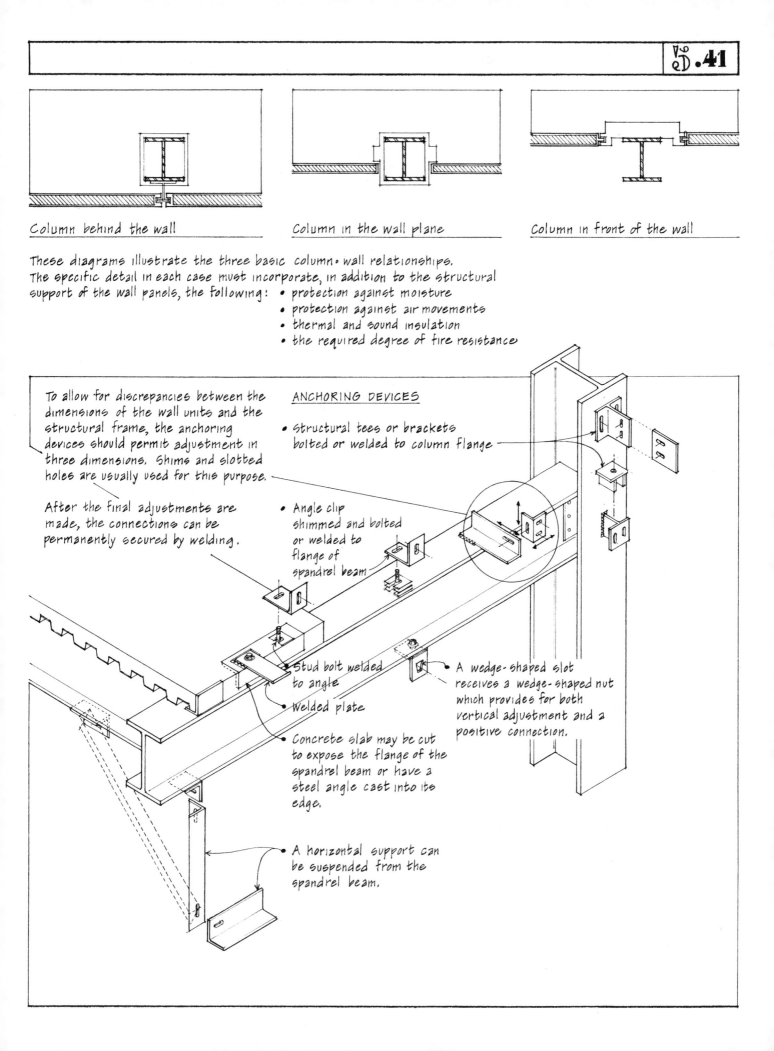

Column behind the wall

Column in the wall plane

Column in front of the wall

These diagrams illustrate the three basic column-wall relationships. The specific detail in each case must incorporate, in addition to the structural support of the wall panels, the following:
- protection against moisture
- protection against air movements
- thermal and sound insulation
- the required degree of fire resistance

To allow for discrepancies between the dimensions of the wall units and the structural frame, the anchoring devices should permit adjustment in three dimensions. Shims and slotted holes are usually used for this purpose.

After the final adjustments are made, the connections can be permanently secured by welding.

ANCHORING DEVICES

- Structural tees or brackets bolted or welded to column flange

- Angle clip shimmed and bolted or welded to flange of spandrel beam

- Stud bolt welded to angle
- Welded plate

- Concrete slab may be cut to expose the flange of the spandrel beam or have a steel angle cast into its edge.

- A wedge-shaped slot receives a wedge-shaped nut which provides for both vertical adjustment and a positive connection.

- A horizontal support can be suspended from the spandrel beam.

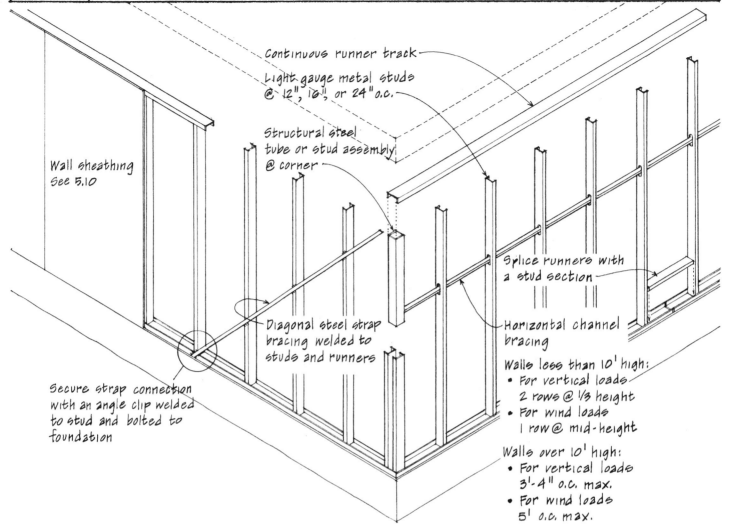

Continuous runner track

Light gauge metal studs @ 12", 16", or 24" o.c.

Structural steel tube or stud assembly @ corner

Wall sheathing See 5.10

Diagonal steel strap bracing welded to studs and runners

Secure strap connection with an angle clip welded to stud and bolted to foundation

Splice runners with a stud section

Horizontal channel bracing

Walls less than 10' high:
- For vertical loads 2 rows @ 1/3 height
- For wind loads 1 row @ mid-height

Walls over 10' high:
- For vertical loads 3'-4" o.c. max.
- For wind loads 5' o.c. max.

Light gauge steel stud framing systems are similar in form and layout to wood stud wall systems and accept the same range of finishes. See 5.11. They may be used as non-loadbearing partitions or as bearing walls supporting light gauge steel joists.

Connections may be made with screws or welds.

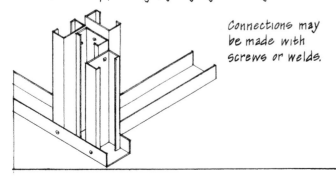

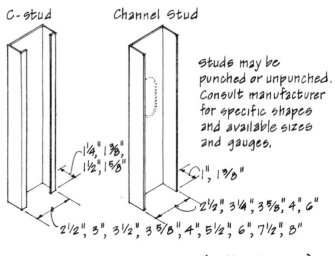

C-stud

Channel Stud

Studs may be punched or unpunched. Consult manufacturer for specific shapes and available sizes and gauges.

1¼", 1⅜", 1½", 1⅝"

2½", 3", 3½", 3⅝", 4", 5½", 6", 7½", 8"

1", 1⅜"

2½", 3¼", 3⅝", 4", 6"

LIGHT GAUGE STEEL STUDS (14 through 22 ga.)

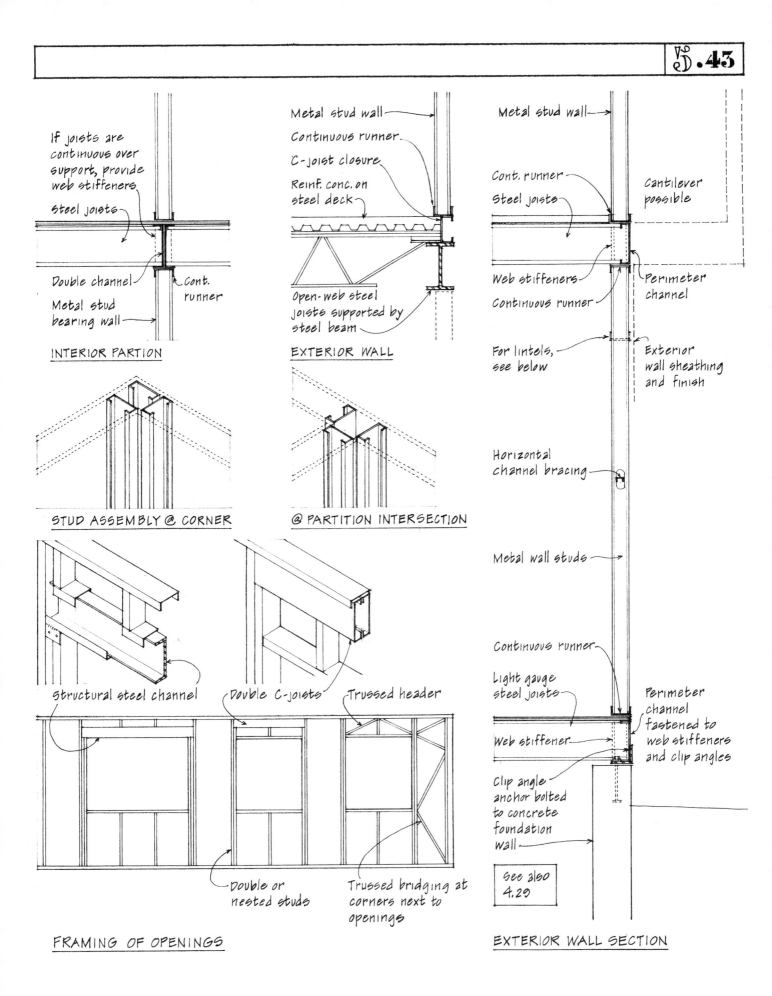

If joists are continuous over support, provide web stiffeners

steel joists

Double channel

Cont. runner

Metal stud bearing wall

INTERIOR PARTION

Metal stud wall

Continuous runner.

C-joist closure

Reinf. conc. on steel deck

Open-web steel joists supported by steel beam

EXTERIOR WALL

STUD ASSEMBLY @ CORNER

@ PARTITION INTERSECTION

Structural steel channel

Double C-joists

Trussed header

Double or nested studs

Trussed bridging at corners next to openings

FRAMING OF OPENINGS

Metal stud wall

Cont. runner

Steel joists

Cantilever possible

Web stiffeners

Perimeter channel

Continuous runner

For lintels, see below

Exterior wall sheathing and finish

Horizontal channel bracing

Metal wall studs

Continuous runner

Light gauge steel joists

Web stiffener

Perimeter channel fastened to web stiffeners and clip angles

Clip angle anchor bolted to concrete foundation wall

See also 4.29

EXTERIOR WALL SECTION

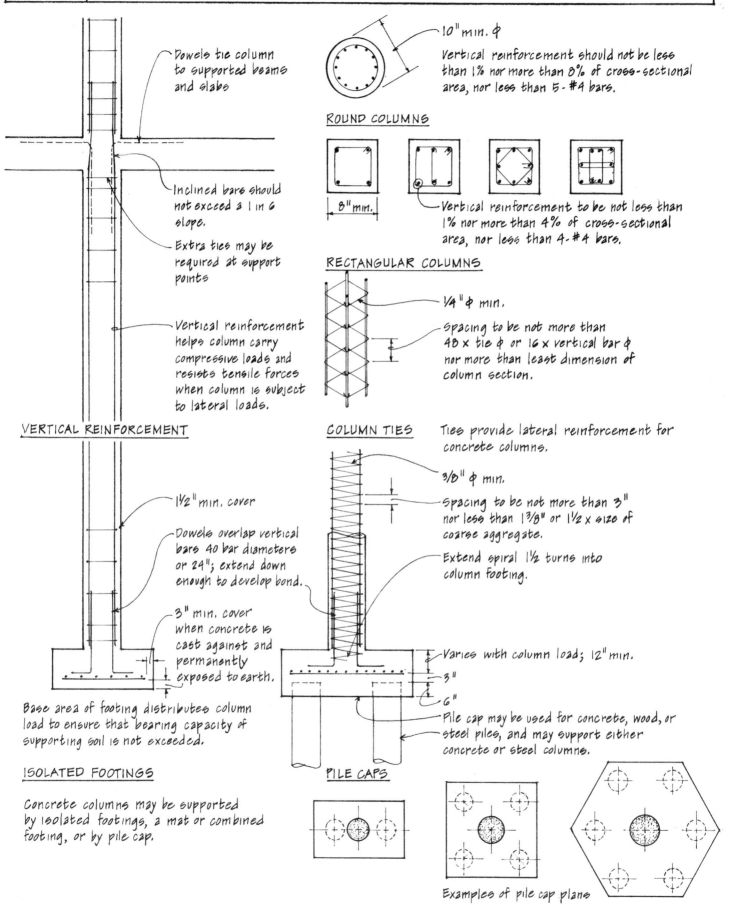

Dowels tie column to supported beams and slabs

Inclined bars should not exceed a 1 in 6 slope.

Extra ties may be required at support points

Vertical reinforcement helps column carry compressive loads and resists tensile forces when column is subject to lateral loads.

VERTICAL REINFORCEMENT

1½" min. cover

Dowels overlap vertical bars 40 bar diameters or 24"; extend down enough to develop bond.

3" min. cover when concrete is cast against and permanently exposed to earth.

Base area of footing distributes column load to ensure that bearing capacity of supporting soil is not exceeded.

ISOLATED FOOTINGS

Concrete columns may be supported by isolated footings, a mat or combined footing, or by pile cap.

10" min. φ

Vertical reinforcement should not be less than 1% nor more than 8% of cross-sectional area, nor less than 5 - #4 bars.

ROUND COLUMNS

8" min.

Vertical reinforcement to be not less than 1% nor more than 4% of cross-sectional area, nor less than 4 - #4 bars.

RECTANGULAR COLUMNS

¼" φ min.

Spacing to be not more than 48 x tie φ or 16 x vertical bar φ nor more than least dimension of column section.

COLUMN TIES

Ties provide lateral reinforcement for concrete columns.

⅜" φ min.

Spacing to be not more than 3" nor less than 1⅜" or 1½ x size of coarse aggregate.

Extend spiral 1½ turns into column footing.

Varies with column load; 12" min.

3"

6"

Pile cap may be used for concrete, wood, or steel piles, and may support either concrete or steel columns.

PILE CAPS

Examples of pile cap plans

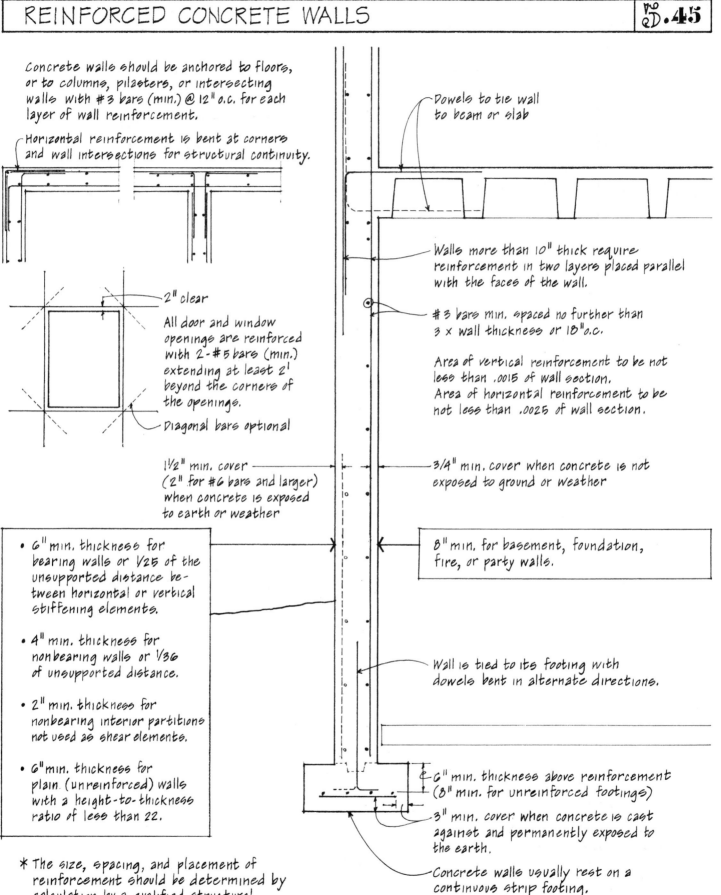

Concrete walls should be anchored to floors, or to columns, pilasters, or intersecting walls with #3 bars (min.) @ 12" o.c. for each layer of wall reinforcement.

Horizontal reinforcement is bent at corners and wall intersections for structural continuity.

Dowels to tie wall to beam or slab

2" clear

All door and window openings are reinforced with 2 - #5 bars (min.) extending at least 2' beyond the corners of the openings.

Diagonal bars optional

Walls more than 10" thick require reinforcement in two layers placed parallel with the faces of the wall.

#3 bars min. spaced no further than 3 x wall thickness or 18" o.c.

Area of vertical reinforcement to be not less than .0015 of wall section.
Area of horizontal reinforcement to be not less than .0025 of wall section.

1½" min. cover (2" for #6 bars and larger) when concrete is exposed to earth or weather

3/4" min. cover when concrete is not exposed to ground or weather

• 6" min. thickness for bearing walls or 1/25 of the unsupported distance between horizontal or vertical stiffening elements.

• 4" min. thickness for nonbearing walls or 1/30 of unsupported distance.

• 2" min. thickness for nonbearing interior partitions not used as shear elements.

• 6" min. thickness for plain (unreinforced) walls with a height-to-thickness ratio of less than 22.

8" min. for basement, foundation, fire, or party walls.

Wall is tied to its footing with dowels bent in alternate directions.

6" min. thickness above reinforcement (8" min. for unreinforced footings)

3" min. cover when concrete is cast against and permanently exposed to the earth.

Concrete walls usually rest on a continuous strip footing.

* The size, spacing, and placement of reinforcement should be determined by calculation by a qualified structural engineer.

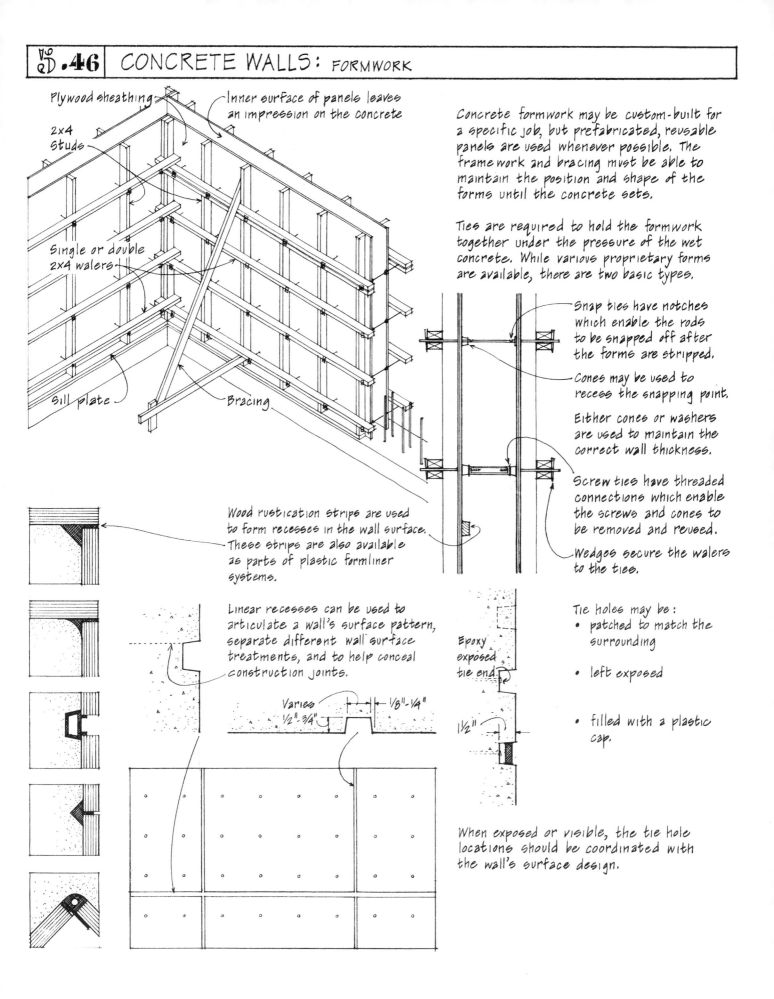

Plywood sheathing

2x4 Studs

Inner surface of panels leaves an impression on the concrete

Single or double 2x4 walers

Sill plate

Bracing

Concrete formwork may be custom-built for a specific job, but prefabricated, reusable panels are used whenever possible. The framework and bracing must be able to maintain the position and shape of the forms until the concrete sets.

Ties are required to hold the formwork together under the pressure of the wet concrete. While various proprietary forms are available, there are two basic types.

Snap ties have notches which enable the rods to be snapped off after the forms are stripped.

Cones may be used to recess the snapping point.

Either cones or washers are used to maintain the correct wall thickness.

Screw ties have threaded connections which enable the screws and cones to be removed and reused.

Wedges secure the walers to the ties.

Wood rustication strips are used to form recesses in the wall surface. These strips are also available as parts of plastic formliner systems.

Linear recesses can be used to articulate a wall's surface pattern, separate different wall surface treatments, and to help conceal construction joints.

Varies 1/2"-3/4"   1/8"-1/4"

Epoxy exposed tie end

1/2"

Tie holes may be:
- patched to match the surrounding
- left exposed
- filled with a plastic cap.

When exposed or visible, the tie hole locations should be coordinated with the wall's surface design.

Various surface patterns and textures can be produced by:

- **Selection of the concrete ingredients**

  The color of concrete can be controlled with the use of colored cement and aggregates.

  The aggregate can be exposed by scrubbing or hosing after the initial set of the concrete to remove the surface layer of cement paste. Chemicals can be sprayed on the forms to help retard the setting of the cement paste.

- **The impressions left by the forms**

  Plywood forms can be smooth or be sandblasted or wirebrushed to accentuate the grain pattern.

  Sheathing lumber can be used to produce a board texture.

  Metal or plastic formliners can produce a variety of textures and patterns.

- **Treatment after the concrete is set.**

  Concrete can be painted or dyed after it has set. The surface can be sandblasted, rubbed, or ground smooth.

  Both smooth and textured surfaces can be bush or jack-hammered to produce coarser textures.

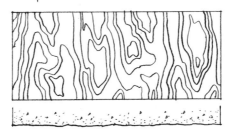
Sandblasted plywood

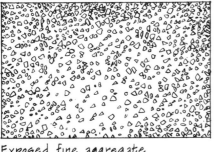
Exposed fine aggregate

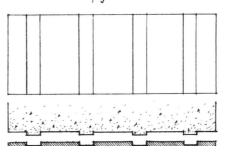
Board and batten pattern

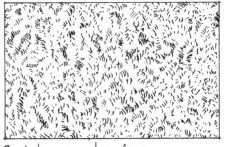
Bush hammered surface

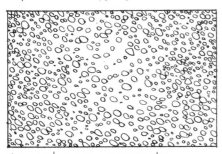
Exposed coarse aggregate

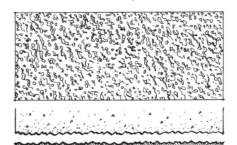
Aggregate textured formliner

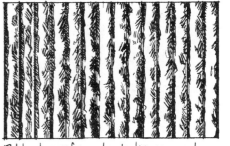
Ribbed surface bush hammered

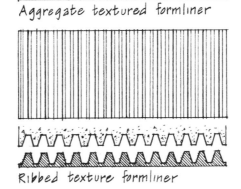
Ribbed texture formliner

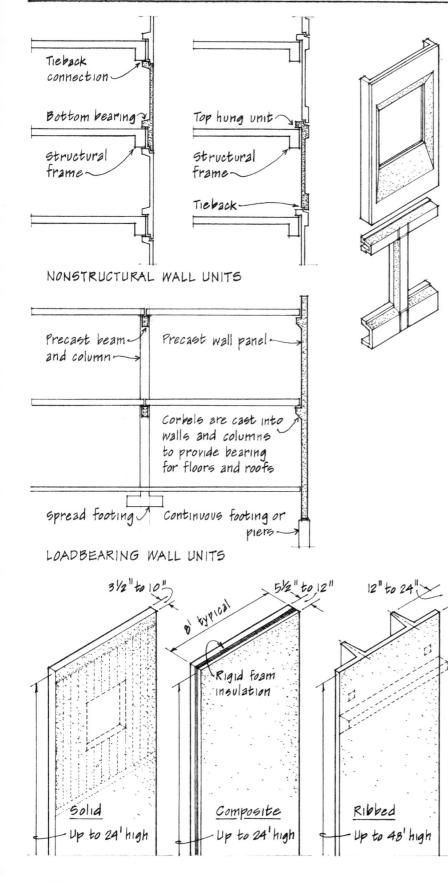

Tieback connection

Bottom bearing

Structural frame

Top hung unit

Structural frame

Tieback

NONSTRUCTURAL WALL UNITS

Precast beam and column

Precast wall panel

Corbels are cast into walls and columns to provide bearing for floors and roofs

spread footing

Continuous footing or piers

LOADBEARING WALL UNITS

3½" to 10"

8' typical

5½" to 12"

Rigid foam insulation

12" to 24"

Solid — Up to 24' high

Composite — Up to 24' high

Ribbed — Up to 48' high

PRECAST CONCRETE WALL PANELS

Precast concrete wall units may be used as nonbearing facing panels or as load-bearing structural elements. Nonbearing wall units are supported by a structural steel or concrete frame, and may be either top hung or bottom bearing. They are connected to the supporting frame with dowels grouted in position or with clip angles and bolts. Where there is a possibility of corrosion and staining, use stainless steel devices.

Instead of conventionally reinforced concrete, glass fiber reinforced concrete (GFRC) can be used to produce much thinner and lighter veneer panels.

Precast structural units can form bearing walls which are capable of supporting floor and roof systems of sitecast concrete, precast concrete, steel, or wood. Precast concrete columns, beams and slabs can be used with the walls to form an entirely precast structural system.

Structural precast concrete wall units may be of solid, composite, or ribbed construction. They may be prestressed or post-tensioned for greater structural efficiency, reduced panel thicknesses, and longer spans.

Window and door openings, corbels, and anchoring devices can be cast into the wall units, along with a variety of surface textures and patterns.

For preliminary sizing, the following sizes of precast columns can support the total floor and roof areas indicated.

10" x 10"

2000 S.F.

12" x 12"

2750 S.F.

16" x 16"

4500 S.F.

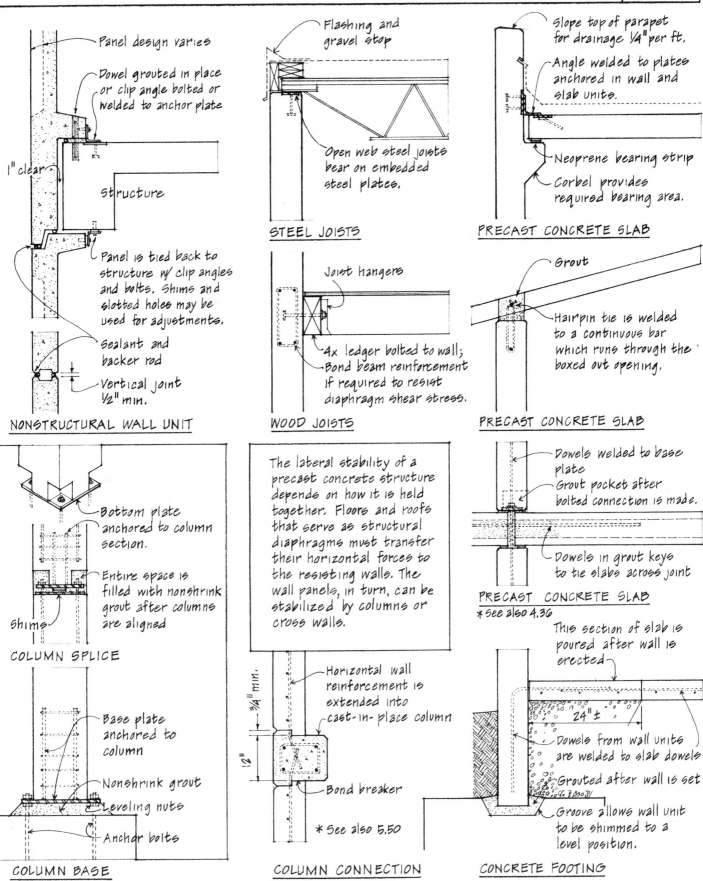

Panel design varies

Dowel grouted in place or clip angle bolted or welded to anchor plate

1" clear

Structure

Panel is tied back to structure w/ clip angles and bolts. Shims and slotted holes may be used for adjustments.

Sealant and backer rod

Vertical joint ½" min.

NONSTRUCTURAL WALL UNIT

Flashing and gravel stop

Open web steel joists bear on embedded steel plates.

STEEL JOISTS

Joist hangers

4x ledger bolted to wall; Bond beam reinforcement if required to resist diaphragm shear stress.

WOOD JOISTS

Slope top of parapet for drainage ¼" per ft.

Angle welded to plates anchored in wall and slab units.

Neoprene bearing strip

Corbel provides required bearing area.

PRECAST CONCRETE SLAB

Grout

Hairpin tie is welded to a continuous bar which runs through the boxed out opening.

PRECAST CONCRETE SLAB

Bottom plate anchored to column section.

Entire space is filled with nonshrink grout after columns are aligned

Shims

COLUMN SPLICE

The lateral stability of a precast concrete structure depends on how it is held together. Floors and roofs that serve as structural diaphragms must transfer their horizontal forces to the resisting walls. The wall panels, in turn, can be stabilized by columns or cross walls.

Dowels welded to base plate

Grout pocket after bolted connection is made.

Dowels in grout keys to tie slabs across joint

PRECAST CONCRETE SLAB
*see also 4.36

Base plate anchored to column

Nonshrink grout

Leveling nuts

Anchor bolts

COLUMN BASE

¾" min.

12"

Horizontal wall reinforcement is extended into cast-in-place column

Bond breaker

*See also 5.50

COLUMN CONNECTION

This section of slab is poured after wall is erected

24" ±

Dowels from wall units are welded to slab dowels

Grouted after wall is set

Groove allows wall unit to be shimmed to a level position.

CONCRETE FOOTING

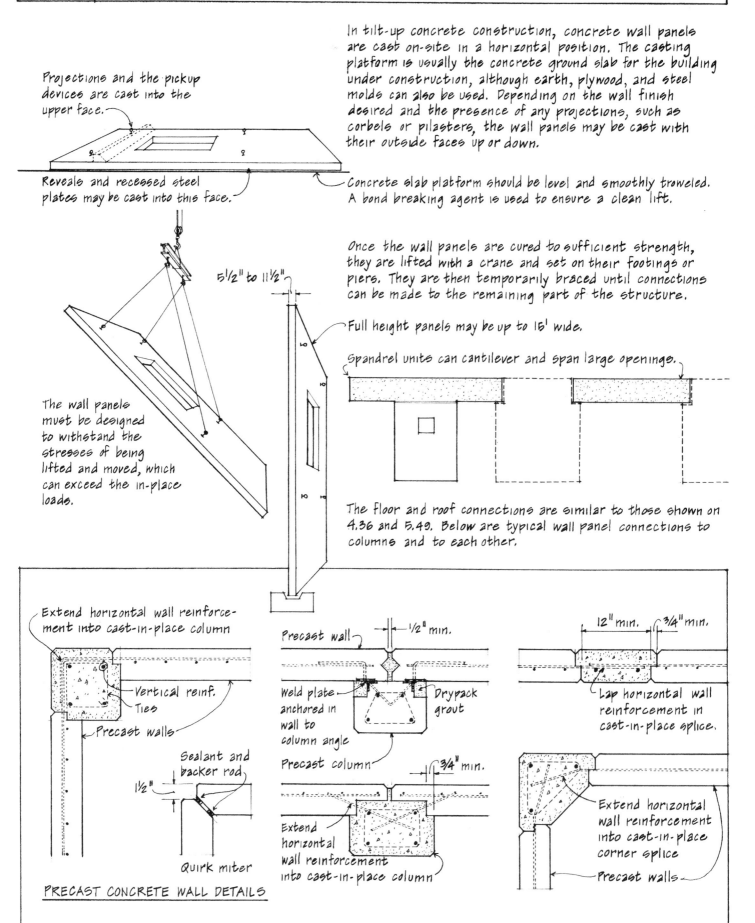

In tilt-up concrete construction, concrete wall panels are cast on-site in a horizontal position. The casting platform is usually the concrete ground slab for the building under construction, although earth, plywood, and steel molds can also be used. Depending on the wall finish desired and the presence of any projections, such as corbels or pilasters, the wall panels may be cast with their outside faces up or down.

Projections and the pickup devices are cast into the upper face.

Reveals and recessed steel plates may be cast into this face.

Concrete slab platform should be level and smoothly troweled. A bond breaking agent is used to ensure a clean lift.

Once the wall panels are cured to sufficient strength, they are lifted with a crane and set on their footings or piers. They are then temporarily braced until connections can be made to the remaining part of the structure.

5½" to 11½"

Full height panels may be up to 15' wide.

Spandrel units can cantilever and span large openings.

The wall panels must be designed to withstand the stresses of being lifted and moved, which can exceed the in-place loads.

The floor and roof connections are similar to those shown on 4.36 and 5.49. Below are typical wall panel connections to columns and to each other.

Extend horizontal wall reinforcement into cast-in-place column

Vertical reinf.
Ties
Precast walls

Sealant and backer rod

1½"

Quirk miter

PRECAST CONCRETE WALL DETAILS

Precast wall
½" min.
Weld plate anchored in wall to column angle
Drypack grout
Precast column

¾" min.
Extend horizontal wall reinforcement into cast-in-place column

12" min.   ¾" min.
Lap horizontal wall reinforcement in cast-in-place splice.

Extend horizontal wall reinforcement into cast-in-place corner splice
Precast walls

ROOF SYSTEMS $\boxed{6}$

The roof system functions as the primary sheltering element for the interior spaces of a building. Its form and construction should control the flow of water as well as the passage of water, air, heat and cold. Like floor systems, a roof must be structured to span across space and carry both its own weight and live loads such as wind and snow. The gravity loads for a building begin with the roof system. Its structural layout must therefore correspond to that of the wall and column systems through which its loads are transferred down to the foundation system.

Depending on the type of construction required by the building code, the roof structure and the roofing material itself may have to be fire-resistant. In addition, the depth of the roof system may have to accommodate mechanical and electrical equipment. Because of its varied functional tasks spread over a large area, the roof system is potentially the most expensive system of a building. Economy of erection and maintenance, durability, and thermal insulation value should all be considered in the choice of a roof system and its materials.

The form of a roof system—whether flat or sloped, gabled or hipped—has a vital impact on a building's visual image. How a roof form is structured, in turn, affects the choice of roofing material, the interior ceiling system, and the layout of a building's interior spaces. Long roof spans would open up a more flexible interior space while shorter roof spans might suggest more rigidly defined spaces.

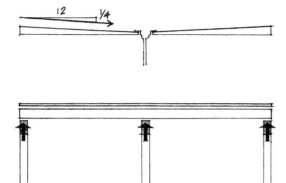

- Minimum recommended slope: 1/4" per foot.
- Slope may be achieved by sloping the structural members or by tapering the roof deck or rigid insulation.
- Slope usually leads to interior drains; perimeter scuppers can be used as overflow drains.

- Flat roofs can efficiently cover a building of any horizontal dimension, and can be designed to serve as outdoor space.

- Roof structure may consist of:
  - Joists and sheathing
  - Beams and decking
  - Flat trusses
  - Concrete slabs

FLAT ROOFS

- Flat roofs require continuous membrane roofing.

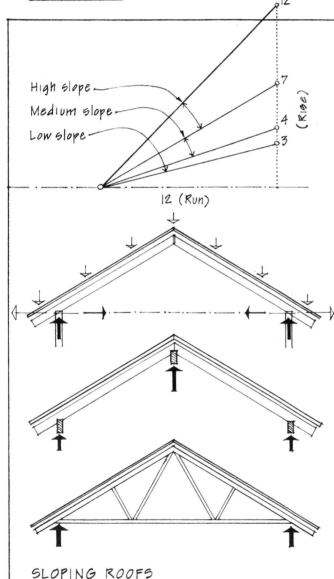

- Sloping roofs may be categorized into
  Medium to high slope – 4:12 to 12:12
  Low slope – up to 3:12

- Sloping roofs shed water easily to eave gutters.

- Roof height and area increase with its horizontal dimension.
- Space under the roof may be usable.

- Sloping roofs may have a structure of:
  - Rafters and sheathing
  - Beams, purlins, and decking
  - Trusses

- Medium and high slope roofs may be covered with shingles, tiles, or sheet materials.

- Low slope roofs require roll or continuous membrane roofing; some shingle and sheet materials may be used on 3-in-12 pitches.

- The roof slope also affects the design loads and the requirements for underlayment and eave flashing.

- Sloping roof planes may be combined to form a variety of roof forms. See 6.6 - 6.7.

SLOPING ROOFS

- Roof structure must be designed to carry:
  - Dead loads: Roof structure, deck, insulation, roofing, and any equipment located on top of or suspended from roof
  - Live loads: Accumulated rain, snow and ice, and traffic, if any
  - Wind loads: Pressure or suction from wind. (See 1.14)

- The type of roofing required for the roof slope:
  - Shingles, tiles, sheet, or membrane. (See Chapter 8)

- The degree of protection required against:
  - Surface water from the outside
  - Water vapor diffusion from the inside
  - Moist air flow
  - Heat flow and solar radiation

- The drainage pattern of the roof form:
  - The location of roof drains, scuppers, gutters, and downspouts. (See 8.14)

- Flashing requirements: (See 8.15-8.18)
  - Along ridges, hips, and valleys
  - Along eaves, rakes, and intersection with vertical surfaces
  - Around roof openings.

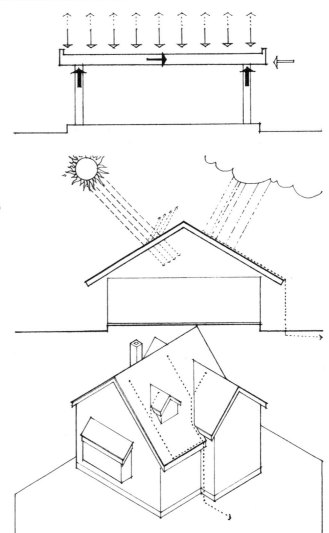

- The effect of the roof support pattern on interior spaces:
  - Point or linear supports (columns or bearing walls)
  - Length of roof spans
  - Bay sizes and proportions
  - The roof form, if its underside is exposed
  - The types of ceilings that may be supported.

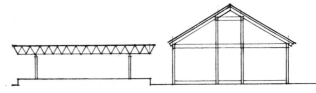

- The effect of the roof form on the building:
  - Flat or sloped roof forms
  - Single or multiple forms
  - Roof edge conditions
    - Concealed behind a parapet
    - Exposed and flush with or overhanging the wall planes.

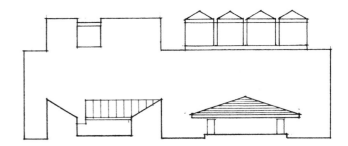

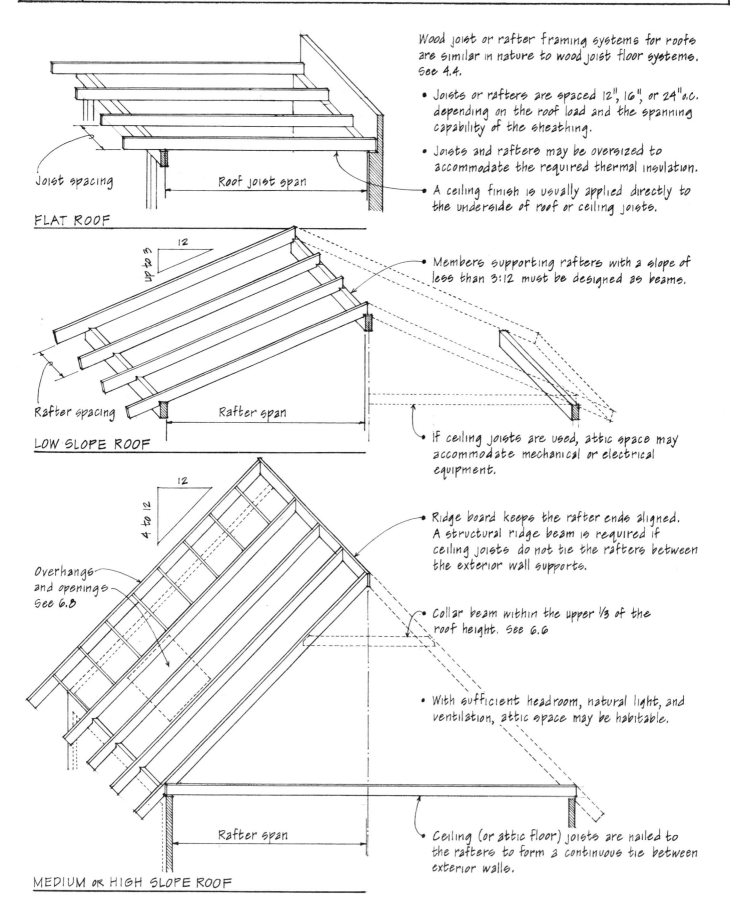

Wood joist or rafter framing systems for roofs are similar in nature to wood joist floor systems. See 4.4.

• Joists or rafters are spaced 12", 16", or 24" o.c. depending on the roof load and the spanning capability of the sheathing.

• Joists and rafters may be oversized to accommodate the required thermal insulation.

• A ceiling finish is usually applied directly to the underside of roof or ceiling joists.

Joist spacing

Roof joist span

FLAT ROOF

12
up to 3

• Members supporting rafters with a slope of less than 3:12 must be designed as beams.

Rafter spacing

Rafter span

LOW SLOPE ROOF

• If ceiling joists are used, attic space may accommodate mechanical or electrical equipment.

12
4 to 12

Overhangs and openings See 6.8

• Ridge board keeps the rafter ends aligned. A structural ridge beam is required if ceiling joists do not tie the rafters between the exterior wall supports.

• Collar beam within the upper ⅓ of the roof height. See 6.6

• With sufficient headroom, natural light, and ventilation, attic space may be habitable.

Rafter span

MEDIUM OR HIGH SLOPE ROOF

• Ceiling (or attic floor) joists are nailed to the rafters to form a continuous tie between exterior walls.

The rafter span table below is for preliminary sizing of members only. It assumes that the rafters have simple spans.

SIZE nominal	SPACING center to center	SPAN AS LIMITED BY DEFLECTION*		SPAN AS LIMITED BY BENDING			
		E = 1,200,000 psi	1,400,000 psi	Fb = 1000 psi	1200 psi	1400 psi	1600 psi
		Live Load: 20 lbs. per S.F.					
2 x 4	12"	6'-9"	7'-2"	8'-1"	8'-10"	9'-6"	10'-2"
	16"	6-2	6-6	7-0	7-8	8-3	8-10
	24"	5-5	5-9	5-9	6-4	6-10	7-3
2 x 6	12	10-5	11-0	12-4	13-6	14-7	15-7
	16	9-7	10-1	10-9	11-10	12-9	13-8
	24	8-5	8-10	8-11	9-9	10-6	11-3
2 x 8	12	13-10	14-7	16-3	17-10	19-3	20-7
	16	12-8	13-4	14-3	15-7	16-10	18-0
	24	11-2	11-9	11-9	12-11	13-11	14-11
2 x 10	12	17-5	18-4	20-4	22-4	24-1	25-9
	16	15-11	16-9	17-10	19-7	21-2	22-7
	24	14-1	14-10	14-10	16-3	17-6	18-9
2 x 12	12	20-11	22-0	24-4	26-8	28-10	30-10
	16	19-2	20-2	21-5	23-6	25-5	27-2
	24	16-11	17-10	17-10	19-6	21-1	22-6
2 x 14	12	24-4	25-7	28-4	31-0	-	-
	16	22-5	23-7	25-0	27-4	29-6	-
	24	19-10	20-10	20-9	22-9	24-7	26-4
		Live Load: 30 lbs. per S.F.					
2 x 6	12"	9-8	10-2	11-0	12-0	13-0	13-10
	16"	8-10	9-3	9-7	10-6	11-4	12-1
	24"	7-9	8-2	7-10	8-7	9-4	9-11
2 x 8	12	12-10	13-6	14-6	15-10	17-0	18-4
	16	11-8	12-4	12-8	13-10	15-2	16-0
	24	10-3	10-10	10-5	11-5	12-4	13-2
2 x 10	12	16-1	17-0	18-2	19-11	21-6	23-0
	16	14-9	15-6	15-11	17-5	18-10	20-2
	24	13-0	13-8	13-2	14-5	15-7	16-8
2 x 12	12	19-5	20-5	21-10	23-11	25-10	27-7
	16	17-9	18-9	19-2	21-0	22-8	24-3
	24	15-8	16-6	15-10	17-4	18-9	20-0
2 x 14	12	22-7	23-10	25-5	27-10	30-0	-
	16	20-9	21-10	22-4	24-5	26-5	28-3
	24	18-4	19-4	18-6	20-3	21-11	23-5

* Maximum allowable deflection = 1/360 of span.
- E = modulus of elasticity; Fb = allowable unit stress in bending; both vary according to the species and grade of lumber used.
- Rafters are often oversized to accommodate required thermal insulation.

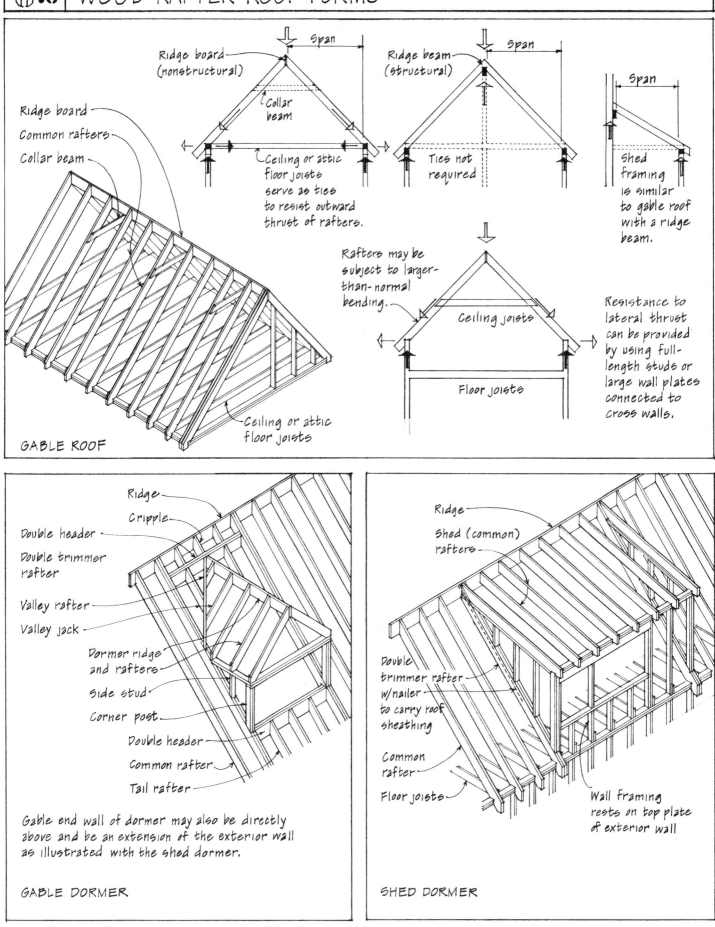

Ridge board
(nonstructural)

Ridge beam
(structural)

Span

Span

Span

Collar
beam

Ridge board
Common rafters
Collar beam

Ceiling or attic
Floor joists
serve as ties
to resist outward
thrust of rafters.

Ties not
required

Shed
framing
is similar
to gable roof
with a ridge
beam.

Rafters may be
subject to larger-
than-normal
bending.

Ceiling joists

Resistance to
lateral thrust
can be provided
by using full-
length studs or
large wall plates
connected to
cross walls.

Floor joists

Ceiling or attic
Floor joists

GABLE ROOF

Ridge

Cripple

Double header

Double trimmer
rafter

Valley rafter

Valley jack

Dormer ridge
and rafters

Side stud

Corner post

Double header

Common rafter

Tail rafter

Gable end wall of dormer may also be directly
above and be an extension of the exterior wall
as illustrated with the shed dormer.

GABLE DORMER

Ridge

Shed (common)
rafters

Double
trimmer rafter
w/ nailer
to carry roof
sheathing

Common
rafter

Floor joists

Wall framing
rests on top plate
of exterior wall

SHED DORMER

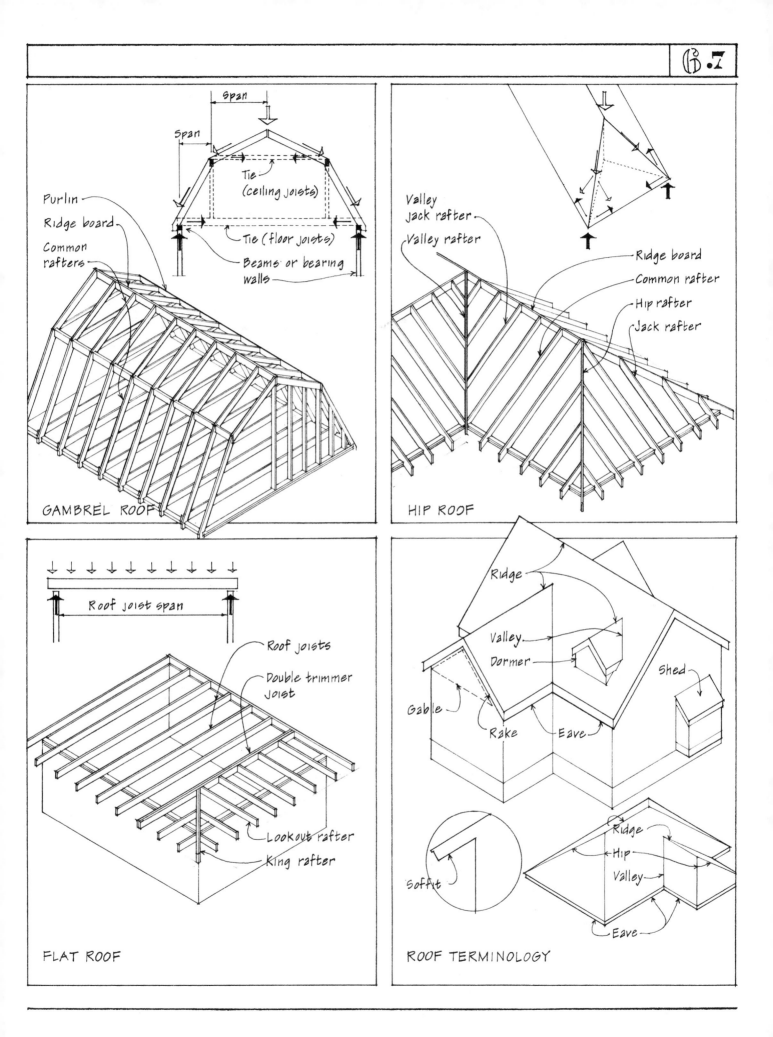

Span

Span

Tie
(ceiling joists)

Tie (floor joists)

Beams or bearing
walls

Purlin

Ridge board

Common
rafters

GAMBREL ROOF

Valley
Jack rafter

Valley rafter

Ridge board

Common rafter

Hip rafter

Jack rafter

HIP ROOF

Roof joist span

Roof joists

Double trimmer
joist

Lookout rafter

King rafter

FLAT ROOF

Ridge

Valley

Dormer

Gable

Rake

Eave

Shed

Soffit

Ridge

Hip

Valley

Eave

ROOF TERMINOLOGY

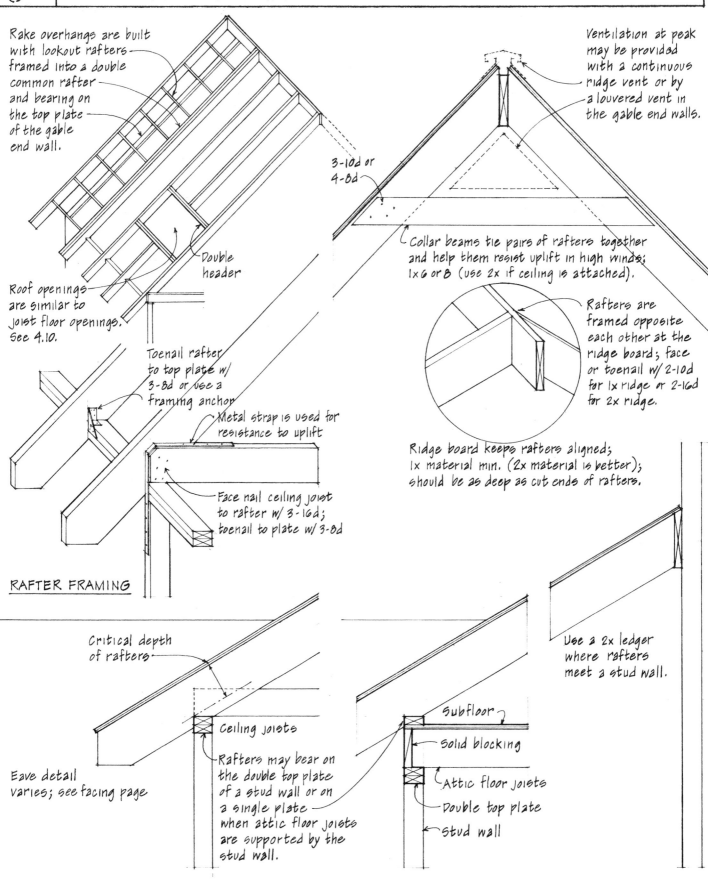

Rake overhangs are built with lookout rafters framed into a double common rafter and bearing on the top plate of the gable end wall.

Roof openings are similar to joist floor openings. See 4.10.

Double header

3-10d or 4-8d

Toenail rafter to top plate w/ 3-8d or use a framing anchor

Metal strap is used for resistance to uplift

Face nail ceiling joist to rafter w/ 3-16d; toenail to plate w/ 3-8d

Ventilation at peak may be provided with a continuous ridge vent or by a louvered vent in the gable end walls.

Collar beams tie pairs of rafters together and help them resist uplift in high winds; 1x6 or 8 (use 2x if ceiling is attached).

Rafters are framed opposite each other at the ridge board; face or toenail w/ 2-10d for 1x ridge or 2-16d for 2x ridge.

Ridge board keeps rafters aligned; 1x material min. (2x material is better); should be as deep as cut ends of rafters.

RAFTER FRAMING

Critical depth of rafters

Eave detail varies; see facing page

Ceiling joists

Rafters may bear on the double top plate of a stud wall or on a single plate when attic floor joists are supported by the stud wall.

Use a 2x ledger where rafters meet a stud wall.

Subfloor

Solid blocking

Attic floor joists

Double top plate

Stud wall

RAFTER SUPPORT CONDITIONS

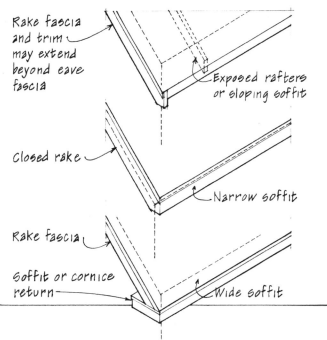

Rake fascia and trim may extend beyond eave fascia

Exposed rafters or sloping soffit

Closed rake

Narrow soffit

Rake fascia

Soffit or cornice return

Wide soffit

It is important to consider how the roof eave detail turns the corner and meets the rake detail.

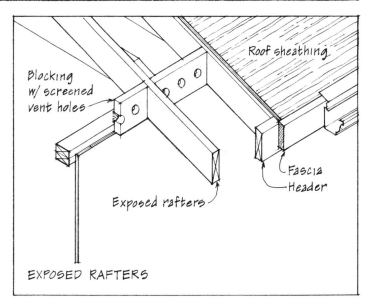

Blocking w/ screened vent holes

Roof sheathing

Exposed rafters

Fascia

Header

EXPOSED RAFTERS

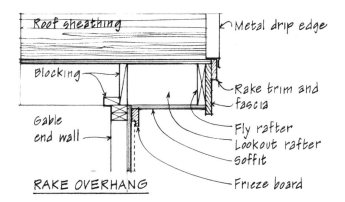

Roof sheathing

Metal drip edge

Blocking

Rake trim and fascia

Gable end wall

Fly rafter
Lookout rafter
Soffit
Frieze board

RAKE OVERHANG

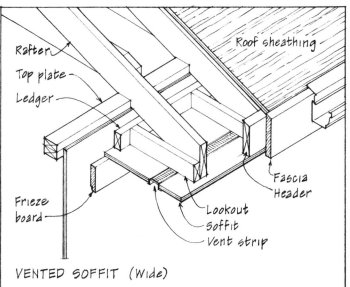

Rafter

Top plate

Ledger

Roof sheathing

Frieze board

Fascia
Header

Lookout
Soffit
Vent strip

VENTED SOFFIT (Wide)

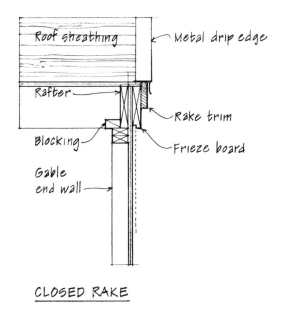

Roof sheathing

Metal drip edge

Rafter

Rake trim

Blocking

Frieze board

Gable end wall

CLOSED RAKE

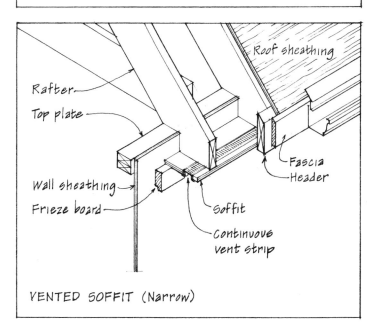

Rafter

Roof sheathing

Top plate

Wall sheathing
Frieze board

Fascia
Header

Soffit

Continuous vent strip

VENTED SOFFIT (Narrow)

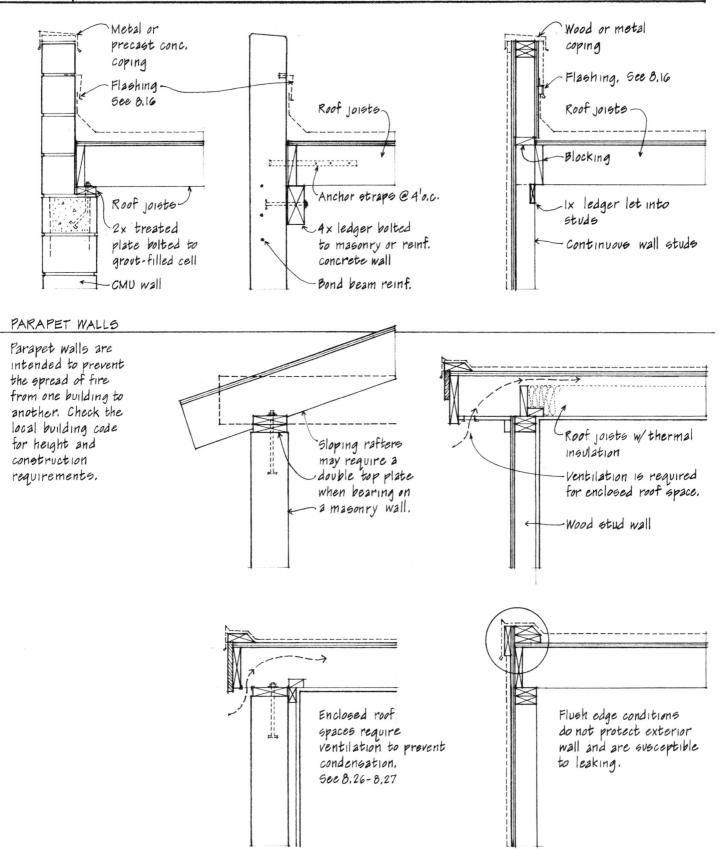

Metal or precast conc. coping

Flashing See 8.16

Roof joists

2x treated plate bolted to grout-filled cell

CMU wall

Roof joists

Anchor straps @ 4'o.c.

4x ledger bolted to masonry or reinf. concrete wall

Bond beam reinf.

Wood or metal coping

Flashing. See 8.16

Roof joists

Blocking

1x ledger let into studs

Continuous wall studs

PARAPET WALLS

Parapet walls are intended to prevent the spread of fire from one building to another. Check the local building code for height and construction requirements.

Sloping rafters may require a double top plate when bearing on a masonry wall.

Roof joists w/ thermal insulation

Ventilation is required for enclosed roof space.

Wood stud wall

Enclosed roof spaces require ventilation to prevent condensation. See 8.26-8.27

Flush edge conditions do not protect exterior wall and are susceptible to leaking.

FLAT ROOF JOISTS

PANEL ROOF SHEATHING

Panel Identification Index	Panel thickness (in.)	Maximum Span (in.)		Total Live Load (lbs/S.F.)
		w/ edge support	w/o edge support	
12/0	5/16	12		150
16/0	5/16, 3/8	16		75
20/0	5/16, 3/8	20		65
24/0	3/8	24	16	50
24/0	1/2	24	24	50
32/16	1/2, 5/8	32	28	40
40/20	5/8, 3/4, 7/8	40	32	35
(48)/24	3/4, 7/8	(48)	36	35

A panel's span rating can be determined from its identifying grade stamp

Sheathing over wood rafters typically consists of performance-rated plywood or nonveneered panels. These panels may be exterior grade plywood, or Exposure 1 (exterior glue) or Exposure 2 (intermediate glue) panels.

Panel sheathing enhances the stiffness of the roof framing and provides a solid base for the application of various roofing materials. Sheathing and underlayment requirements should be in accordance with the recommendations of the roofing manufacturer.

In damp climates not subject to blizzard conditions, spaced sheathing of 1x4 or 1x6 boards may be used with wood shingle or shake roofing. See 8.8-8.9.

The table above assumes that the panels are laid continuously over two or more spans with their long dimension perpendicular to the supports.

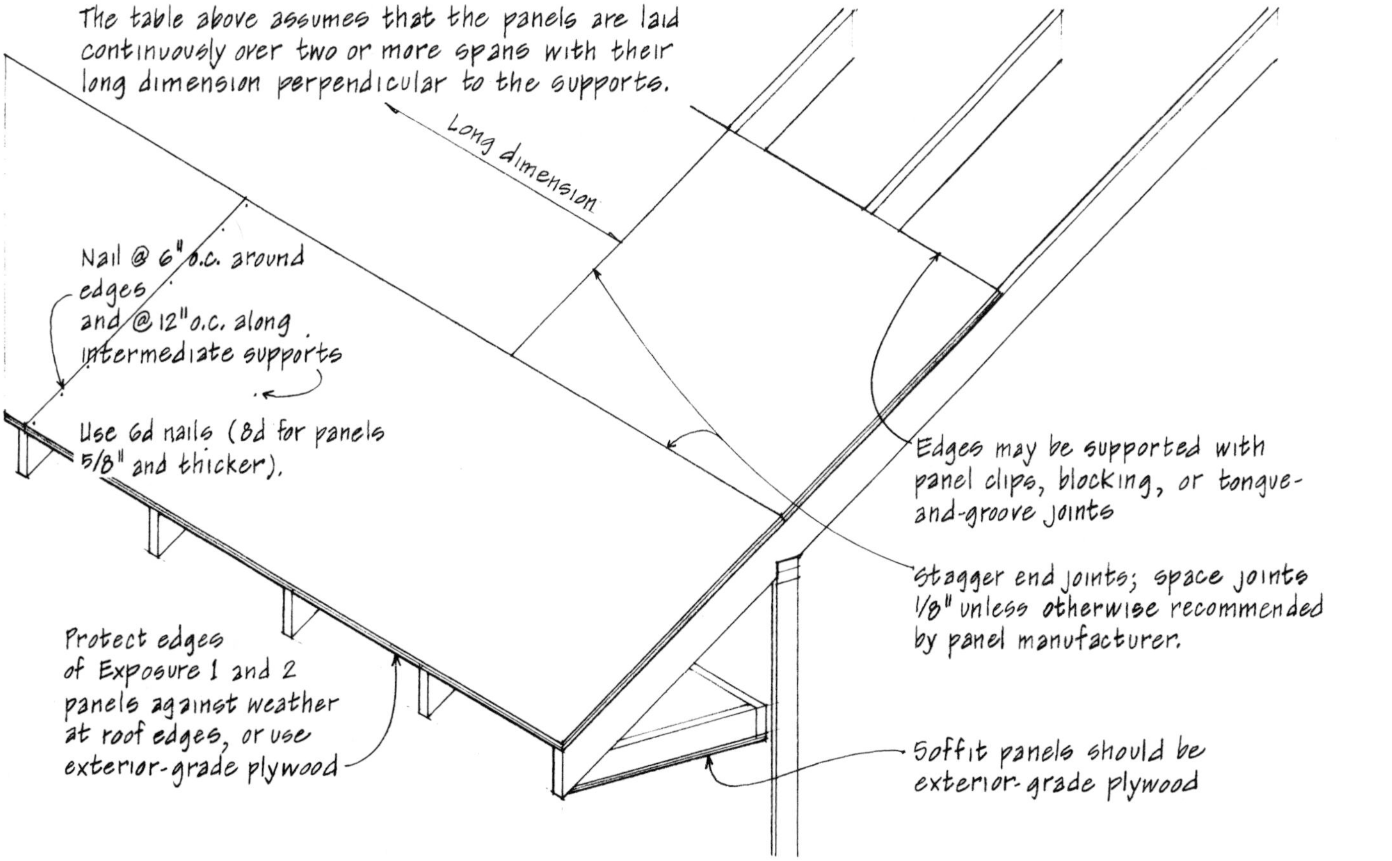

Long dimension

Nail @ 6" o.c. around edges and @ 12" o.c. along intermediate supports

Use 6d nails (8d for panels 5/8" and thicker).

Protect edges of Exposure 1 and 2 panels against weather at roof edges, or use exterior-grade plywood

Edges may be supported with panel clips, blocking, or tongue-and-groove joints

Stagger end joints; space joints 1/8" unless otherwise recommended by panel manufacturer.

Soffit panels should be exterior-grade plywood

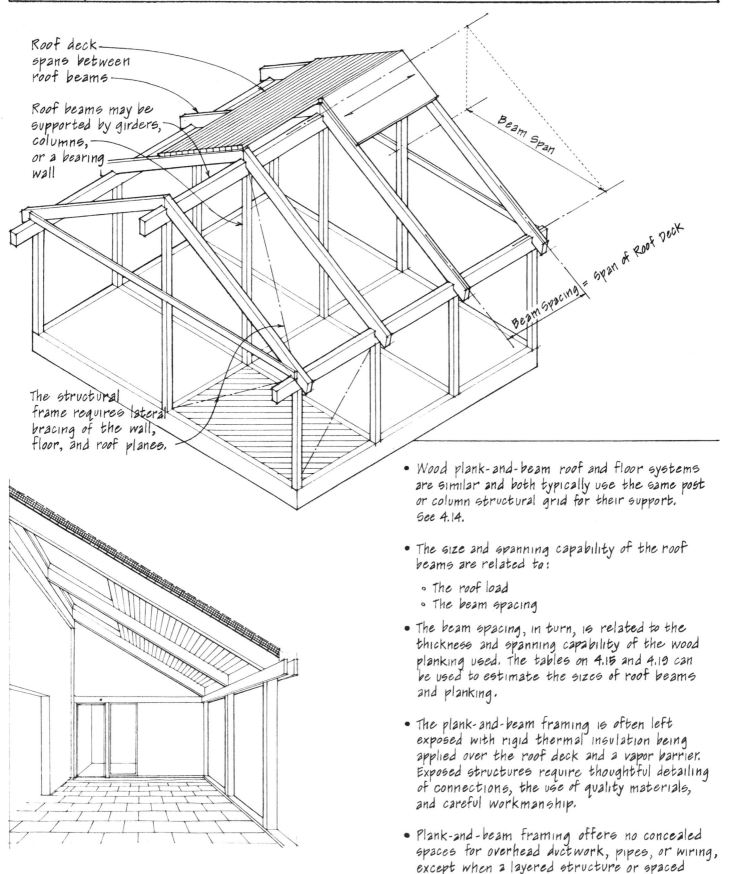

Roof deck spans between roof beams

Roof beams may be supported by girders, columns, or a bearing wall

The structural frame requires lateral bracing of the wall, floor, and roof planes.

Beam Span

Beam Spacing = Span of Roof Deck

- Wood plank-and-beam roof and floor systems are similar and both typically use the same post or column structural grid for their support. See 4.14.

- The size and spanning capability of the roof beams are related to:
  - The roof load
  - The beam spacing

- The beam spacing, in turn, is related to the thickness and spanning capability of the wood planking used. The tables on 4.15 and 4.19 can be used to estimate the sizes of roof beams and planking.

- The plank-and-beam framing is often left exposed with rigid thermal insulation being applied over the roof deck and a vapor barrier. Exposed structures require thoughtful detailing of connections, the use of quality materials, and careful workmanship.

- Plank-and-beam framing offers no concealed spaces for overhead ductwork, pipes, or wiring, except when a layered structure or spaced structural members are used.

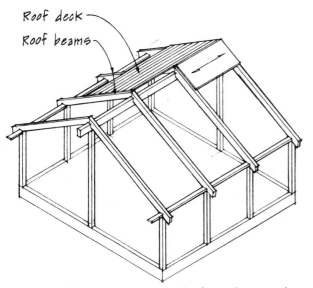

Roof deck
Roof beams

The roof beams are spaced 6' to 8' o.c. and spanned with solid or glue-laminated wood planks. The beams may be supported by girders, columns, or a masonry or concrete bearing wall.

ROOF BEAMS PARALLEL WITH THE SLOPE

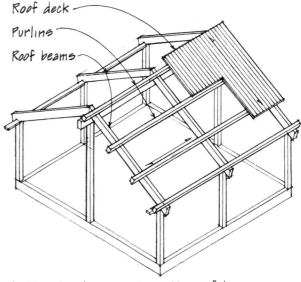

Roof deck
Purlins
Roof beams

In this two-layer system, the roof beams may be spaced further apart and support a series of purlins. These purlins, in turn, are spanned with wood planks or a rigid, sheet roofing material.

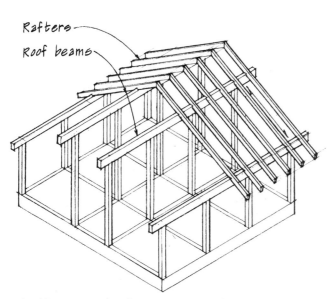

Rafters
Roof beams

In this example of a two-layer structure, the roof beams support a conventional system of wood rafters.

ROOF BEAMS PERPENDICULAR TO SLOPE

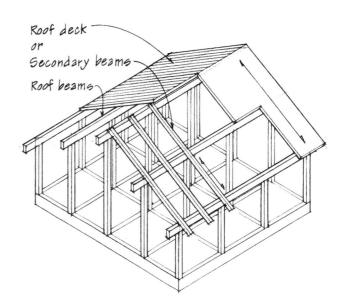

Roof deck
or
Secondary beams
Roof beams

The roof beams may be spaced close enough to be spanned with wood planks. Spaced further apart, the beams can support a series of secondary beams parallel with the slope.

Illustrated above are alternatives for the framing of a plank-and-beam roof structure. They differ in the direction and spacing of the roof beams, the elements used to span the beams, and the overall depth of the construction.

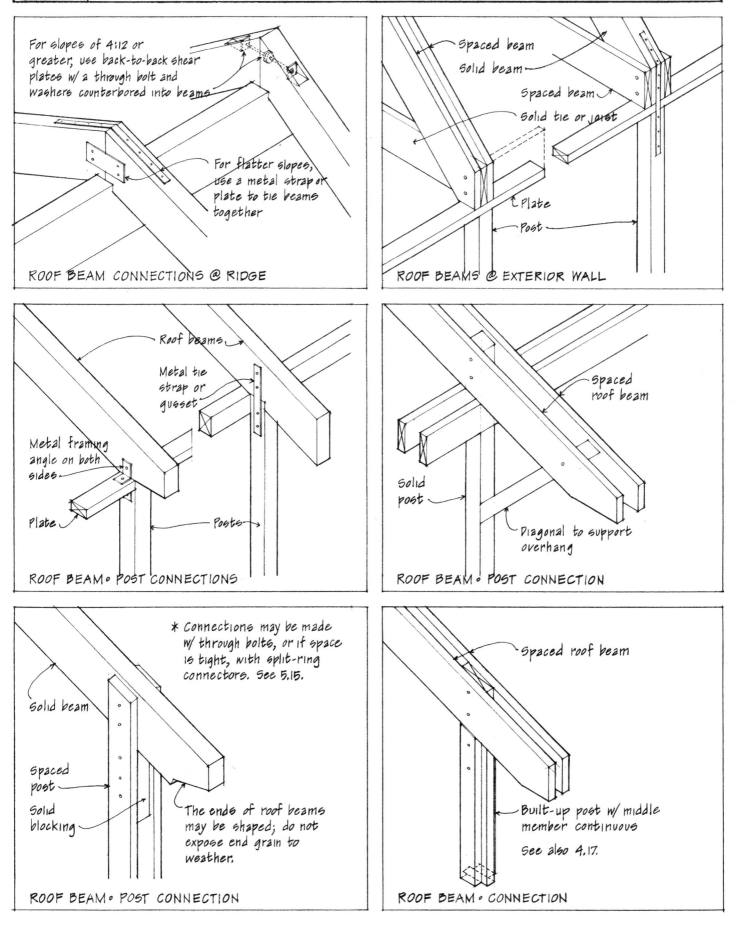

For slopes of 4:12 or greater, use back-to-back shear plates w/ a through bolt and washers counterbored into beams

For flatter slopes, use a metal strap or plate to tie beams together

ROOF BEAM CONNECTIONS @ RIDGE

Spaced beam
Solid beam
Spaced beam
Solid tie or joist
Plate
Post

ROOF BEAMS @ EXTERIOR WALL

Roof beams

Metal tie strap or gusset

Metal framing angle on both sides

Plate

Posts

ROOF BEAM·POST CONNECTIONS

Spaced roof beam

Solid post

Diagonal to support overhang

ROOF BEAM·POST CONNECTION

Solid beam

Spaced post

Solid blocking

* Connections may be made w/ through bolts, or if space is tight, with split-ring connectors. See 5.15.

The ends of roof beams may be shaped; do not expose end grain to weather.

ROOF BEAM·POST CONNECTION

Spaced roof beam

Built-up post w/ middle member continuous

See also 4.17.

ROOF BEAM·CONNECTION

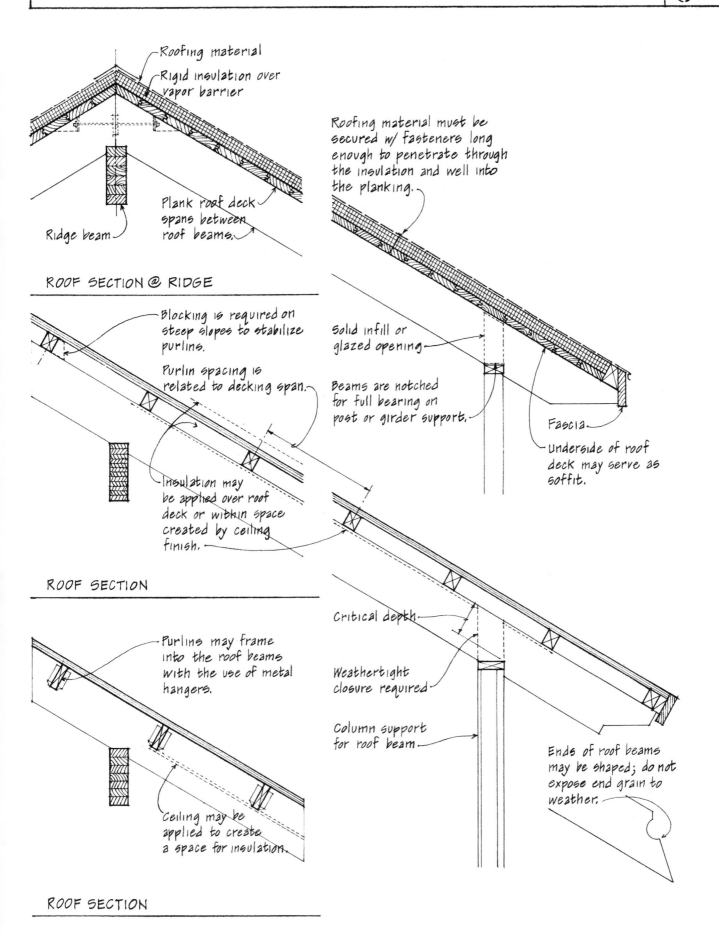

Roofing material

Rigid insulation over vapor barrier

Ridge beam

Plank roof deck spans between roof beams.

Roofing material must be secured w/ fasteners long enough to penetrate through the insulation and well into the planking.

ROOF SECTION @ RIDGE

Blocking is required on steep slopes to stabilize purlins.

Purlin spacing is related to decking span.

Insulation may be applied over roof deck or within space created by ceiling finish.

Solid infill or glazed opening

Beams are notched for full bearing on post or girder support.

Fascia

Underside of roof deck may serve as soffit.

ROOF SECTION

Purlins may frame into the roof beams with the use of metal hangers.

Ceiling may be applied to create a space for insulation.

Critical depth

Weathertight closure required

Column support for roof beam

Ends of roof beams may be shaped; do not expose end grain to weather.

ROOF SECTION

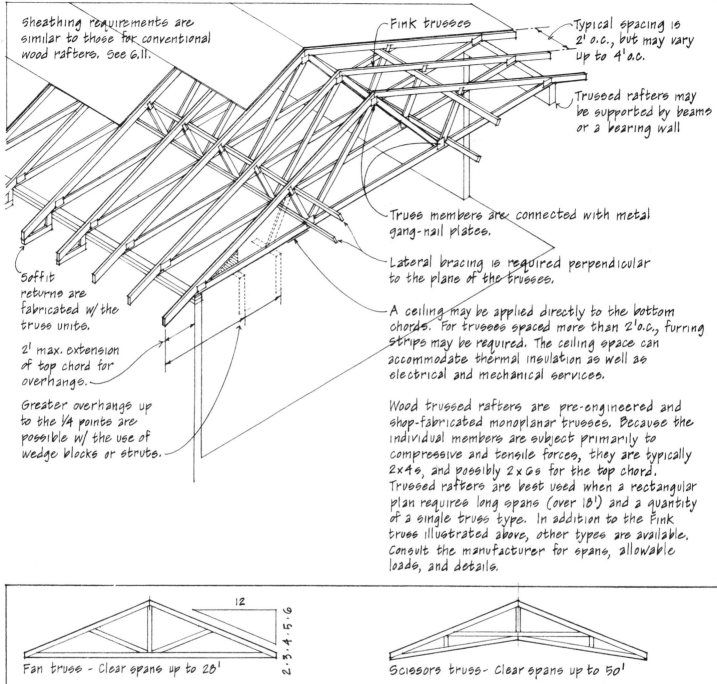

Sheathing requirements are similar to those for conventional wood rafters. See 6.11.

Fink trusses

Typical spacing is 2' o.c., but may vary up to 4' o.c.

Trussed rafters may be supported by beams or a bearing wall

Soffit returns are fabricated w/ the truss units.

2' max. extension of top chord for overhangs.

Greater overhangs up to the ¼ points are possible w/ the use of wedge blocks or struts.

Truss members are connected with metal gang-nail plates.

Lateral bracing is required perpendicular to the plane of the trusses.

A ceiling may be applied directly to the bottom chords. For trusses spaced more than 2'o.c., furring strips may be required. The ceiling space can accommodate thermal insulation as well as electrical and mechanical services.

Wood trussed rafters are pre-engineered and shop-fabricated monoplanar trusses. Because the individual members are subject primarily to compressive and tensile forces, they are typically 2x4s, and possibly 2x6s for the top chord. Trussed rafters are best used when a rectangular plan requires long spans (over 18') and a quantity of a single truss type. In addition to the Fink truss illustrated above, other types are available. Consult the manufacturer for spans, allowable loads, and details.

12

2·3·4·5·6

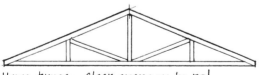

Fan truss - Clear spans up to 28'

Scissors truss- Clear spans up to 50'

Howe truss - Clear spans up to 50'

6-panel Howe truss- Clear spans up to 70'

Monopitch truss- Clear spans up to 40'

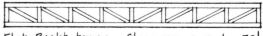

Flat Pratt truss- Clear spans up to 70'

TRUSS TYPES

Member sizes and joint details are determined by engineering calculations based on truss type, load pattern, span, and type of wood used.

Members are 2x or 3x material; wide faces offer more area for fastenings.

Trusses usually do not exceed 5 members in thickness

5½" min.

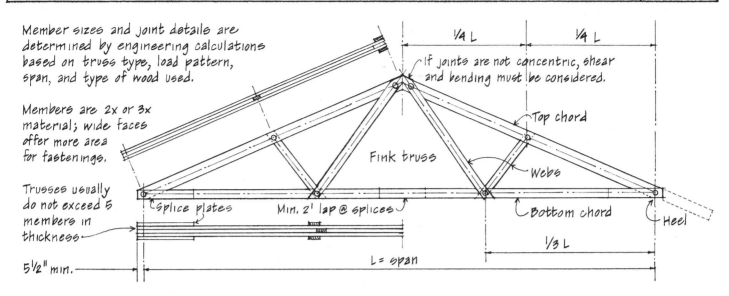

¼ L   ¼ L

If joints are not concentric, shear and bending must be considered.

Top chord

Fink truss

Webs

Splice plates   Min. 2' lap @ splices   Bottom chord   Heel

⅓ L

L = span

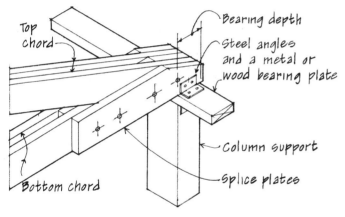

Top chord

Bottom chord

Bearing depth

Steel angles and a metal or wood bearing plate

Column support

Splice plates

HEEL JOINT

In contrast to monoplanar trussed rafters, heavier wood trusses can be made up of multiple members which are joined at the panel points with split-ring connectors. These wood trusses are capable of carrying greater loads than trussed rafters and are spaced further apart. When spanned simply with wood plank sheathing, the trusses can be spaced up to 8' or more, depending on the sheathing thickness. When purlins are used to frame between the trusses, the truss spacing may be increased up to 20'.

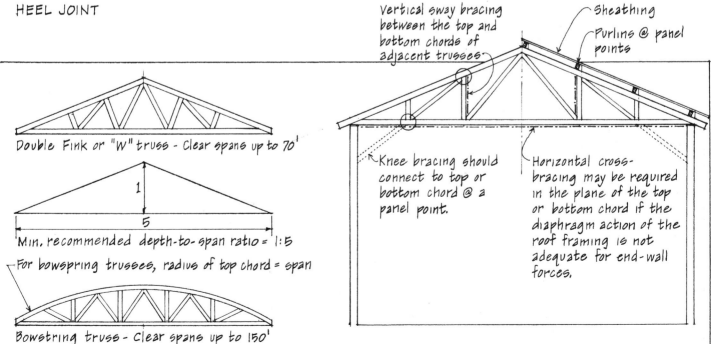

Double Fink or "W" truss - Clear spans up to 70'

1
5

Min. recommended depth-to-span ratio = 1:5

For bowspring trusses, radius of top chord = span

Bowstring truss - Clear spans up to 150'

Vertical sway bracing between the top and bottom chords of adjacent trusses

Sheathing

Purlins @ panel points

Knee bracing should connect to top or bottom chord @ a panel point.

Horizontal cross-bracing may be required in the plane of the top or bottom chord if the diaphragm action of the roof framing is not adequate for end-wall forces.

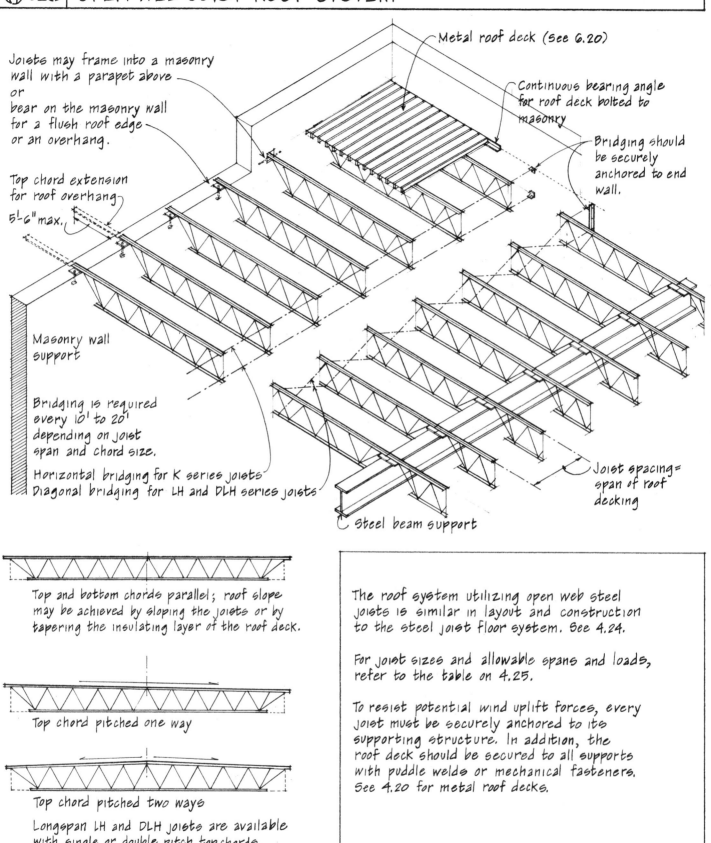

Metal roof deck (see 6.20)

Joists may frame into a masonry wall with a parapet above
or
bear on the masonry wall for a flush roof edge or an overhang.

Continuous bearing angle for roof deck bolted to masonry

Bridging should be securely anchored to end wall.

Top chord extension for roof overhang

5'-6" max.

Masonry wall support

Bridging is required every 10' to 20' depending on joist span and chord size.

Horizontal bridging for K series joists
Diagonal bridging for LH and DLH series joists

Steel beam support

Joist spacing = span of roof decking

Top and bottom chords parallel; roof slope may be achieved by sloping the joists or by tapering the insulating layer of the roof deck.

Top chord pitched one way

Top chord pitched two ways

Longspan LH and DLH joists are available with single or double pitch top chords. Standard slope is 1/8" per foot.

The roof system utilizing open web steel joists is similar in layout and construction to the steel joist floor system. See 4.24.

For joist sizes and allowable spans and loads, refer to the table on 4.25.

To resist potential wind uplift forces, every joist must be securely anchored to its supporting structure. In addition, the roof deck should be secured to all supports with puddle welds or mechanical fasteners. See 4.20 for metal roof decks.

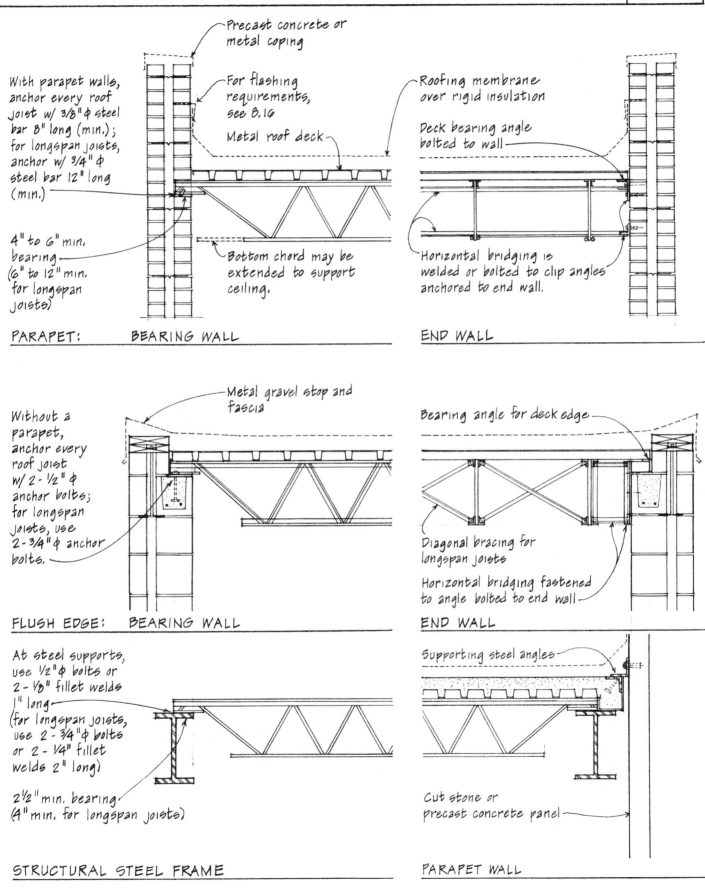

PARAPET: BEARING WALL

With parapet walls, anchor every roof joist w/ 3/8" φ steel bar 8" long (min.); for longspan joists, anchor w/ 3/4" φ steel bar 12" long (min.)

4" to 6" min. bearing (6" to 12" min. for longspan joists)

Precast concrete or metal coping

For flashing requirements, see 8.16

Metal roof deck

Bottom chord may be extended to support ceiling.

END WALL

Roofing membrane over rigid insulation

Deck bearing angle bolted to wall

Horizontal bridging is welded or bolted to clip angles anchored to end wall.

FLUSH EDGE: BEARING WALL

Without a parapet, anchor every roof joist w/ 2 - 1/2" φ anchor bolts; for longspan joists, use 2 - 3/4" φ anchor bolts.

Metal gravel stop and fascia

END WALL

Bearing angle for deck edge

Diagonal bracing for longspan joists

Horizontal bridging fastened to angle bolted to end wall

STRUCTURAL STEEL FRAME

At steel supports, use 1/2" φ bolts or 2 - 1/8" fillet welds 1" long (for longspan joists, use 2 - 3/4" φ bolts or 2 - 1/4" fillet welds 2" long)

2 1/2" min. bearing (4" min. for longspan joists)

PARAPET WALL

Supporting steel angles

Cut stone or precast concrete panel

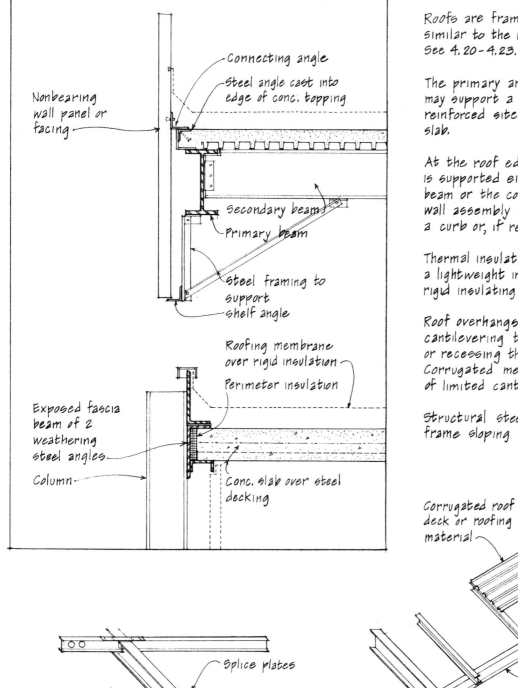

Connecting angle

Steel angle cast into edge of conc. topping

Nonbearing wall panel or facing

Secondary beam

Primary beam

steel framing to support shelf angle

Roofing membrane over rigid insulation

Perimeter insulation

Exposed fascia beam of 2 weathering steel angles

Column

Conc. slab over steel decking

Splice plates

Web stiffeners

Cantilevered beams may be framed within the depth of the primary beam or be continuous over the main beam support.

Ends of beams may be tapered or lightened with cutouts.

Corrugated roof deck or roofing material

Purlins span between roof beams; purlin spacing is related to the span of the roof deck or roofing material.

Roofs are framed with structural steel similar to the way steel floors are framed. See 4.20 - 4.23.

The primary and secondary roof beams may support a metal roof deck or a reinforced sitecast or precast concrete slab.

At the roof edge, a spandrel wall unit is supported either by the steel edge beam or the concrete roof slab. The wall assembly may extend up to form a curb or, if required, a parapet.

Thermal insulation may be provided with a lightweight insulating concrete fill or rigid insulating boards.

Roof overhangs may be achieved by cantilevering the secondary roof beams or recessing the exterior wall construction. Corrugated metal decking is also capable of limited cantilevers beyond its support.

Structural steel can also be used to frame sloping roofs.

Corrugated metal roof decking may span across open web steel joists or more widely spaced steel beams. The decking panels are puddle welded or mechanically fastened to the supporting steel. Side laps between panels are fastened with screws or welds. If the deck is to serve as a diaphragm, its perimeter must be welded to steel supports.

Metal roof decking may have a sitecast concrete topping or be covered with rigid board insulation before the application of the roofing membrane. To provide maximum surface area for the effective adhesion of rigid insulation, the top flange should be wide and flat. If the decking has stiffening grooves, the insulation layer may have to be mechanically fastened.

Metal decking has low-vapor permeance but, because of the many discontinuities between the panels, it is not airtight. If an air barrier is required to prevent the migration of moisture into the roofing assembly, a concrete topping can be used. When lightweight insulating concrete fill is used, the decking may have perforated vents for the release of latent moisture and vapor pressure.

Acoustic roof decks have a filler of glass fiber or other acoustic insulating material.

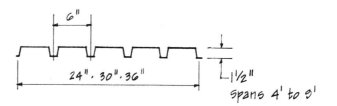

RIBBED ROOF DECKING

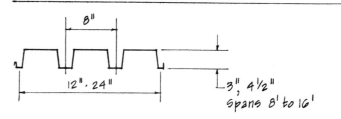

RIBBED ROOF DECK

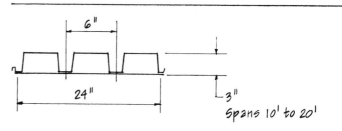

CELLULAR ROOF DECK

* Decking profiles vary with the manufacturer. Consult manufacturer for available profiles, lengths, gauges, allowable spans, and details for installation.

CEMENTITIOUS ROOF PLANK

Cementitious roof panels consist of wood fibers which are chemically processed and bonded under pressure with portland cement. These structural planks can be used to span wood or steel roof framing. They have thermal and acoustic insulation value and may be used in fire-resistant construction. They can serve as roof sheathing or as permanent formwork for a concrete slab, and their undersides may be left exposed as a finish ceiling.

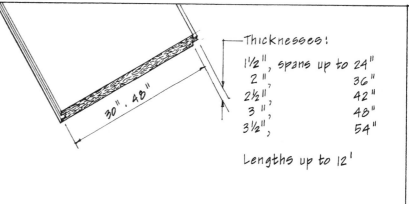

SPACE FRAMES

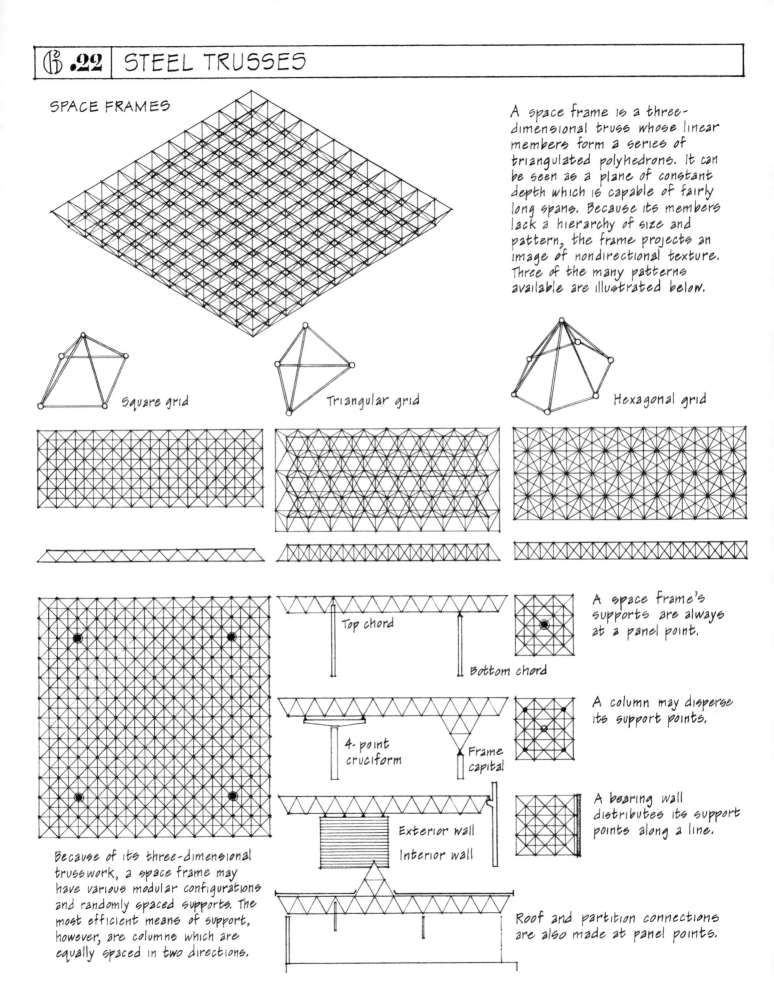

A space frame is a three-dimensional truss whose linear members form a series of triangulated polyhedrons. It can be seen as a plane of constant depth which is capable of fairly long spans. Because its members lack a hierarchy of size and pattern, the frame projects an image of nondirectional texture. Three of the many patterns available are illustrated below.

Square grid

Triangular grid

Hexagonal grid

Top chord

Bottom chord

A space frame's supports are always at a panel point.

4-point cruciform

Frame capital

A column may disperse its support points.

Exterior wall

Interior wall

A bearing wall distributes its support points along a line.

Because of its three-dimensional trusswork, a space frame may have various modular configurations and randomly spaced supports. The most efficient means of support, however, are columns which are equally spaced in two directions.

Roof and partition connections are also made at panel points.

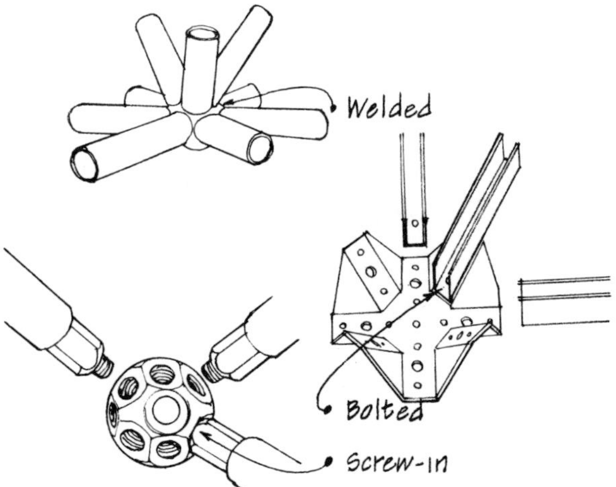

Welded

Bolted

Screw-in

Chord members of space frames may be structural pipe, tubing, channel, tee, or W-shapes.

The complex connection between the large number of members may be welded, bolted, or of the screw-in type. Consult manufacturer for details, module size, and allowable spans.

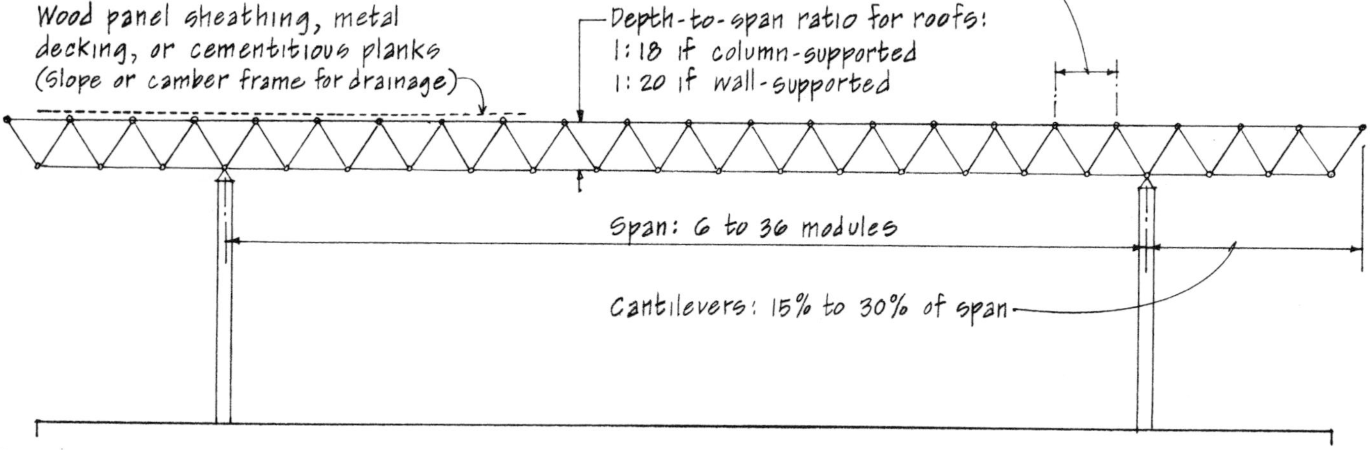

Typical modules: 4', 5', 8', 12'

Depth-to-span ratio for roofs:
1:18 if column-supported
1:20 if wall-supported

Wood panel sheathing, metal decking, or cementitious planks (Slope or camber frame for drainage)

Span: 6 to 36 modules

Cantilevers: 15% to 30% of span

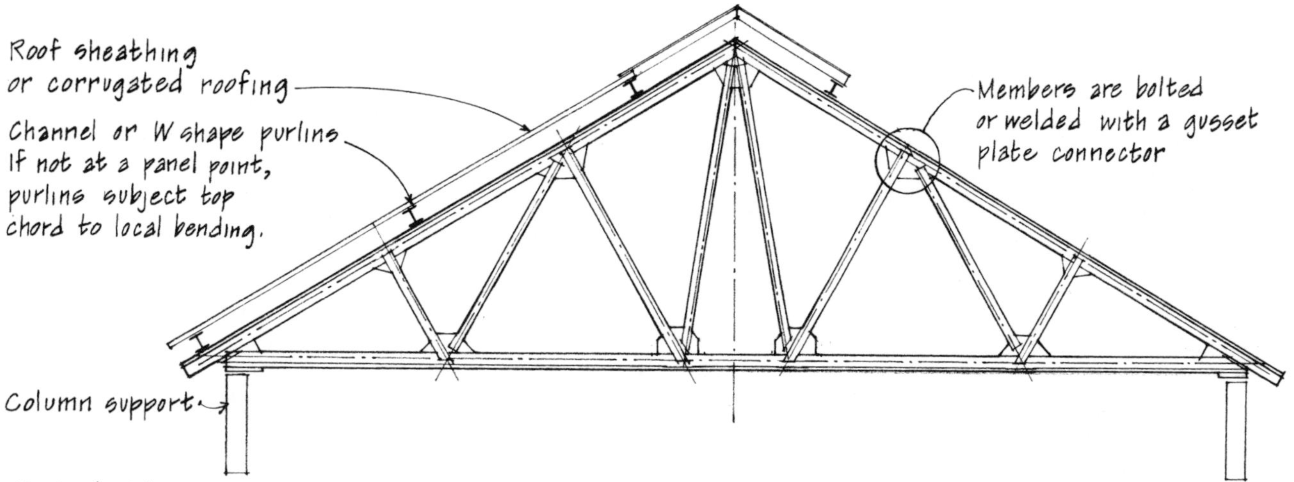

Roof sheathing or corrugated roofing

Channel or W shape purlins If not at a panel point, purlins subject top chord to local bending.

Members are bolted or welded with a gusset plate connector

Column support

Illustrated here is a Belgian truss. See 6.16 - 6.17 for other truss configurations. It is generally best to use truss type in which the longer web members are loaded in tension.

Plane roof trusses may be fabricated with structural steel angle and tee shapes. Because of the members' slenderness, connections usually require the use of gusset plates.

PLANE STEEL TRUSSES

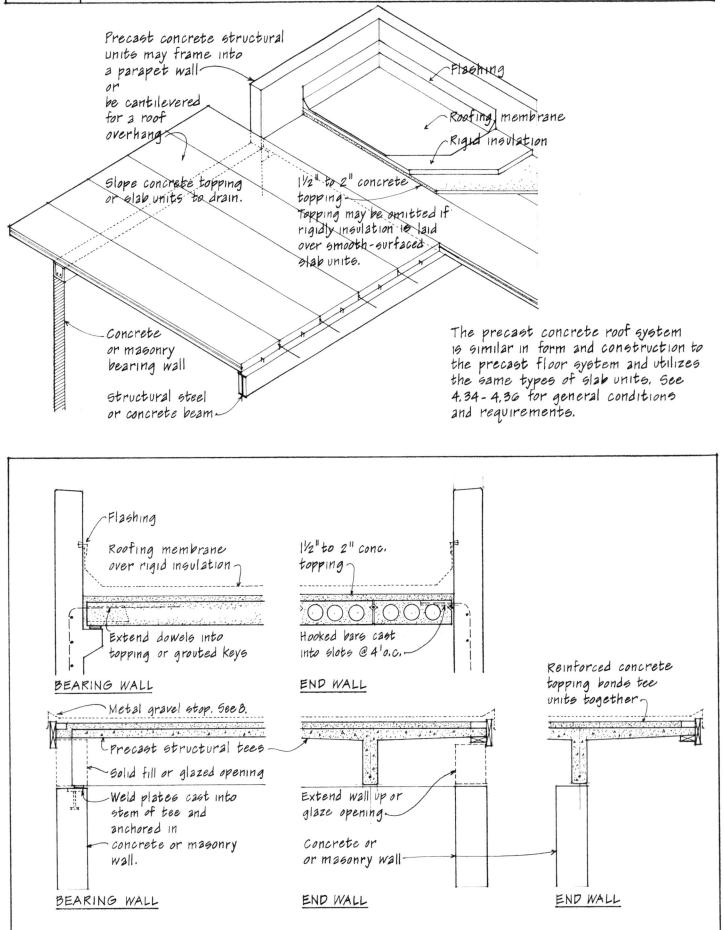

Precast concrete structural units may frame into a parapet wall
or
be cantilevered for a roof overhang

Flashing

Roofing membrane

Rigid insulation

Slope concrete topping or slab units to drain.

1½" to 2" concrete topping.
Topping may be omitted if rigidly insulation is laid over smooth-surfaced slab units.

Concrete or masonry bearing wall

Structural steel or concrete beam

The precast concrete roof system is similar in form and construction to the precast floor system and utilizes the same types of slab units. See 4.34 - 4.36 for general conditions and requirements.

Flashing

Roofing membrane over rigid insulation

1½" to 2" conc. topping

Extend dowels into topping or grouted keys

Hooked bars cast into slots @ 4' o.c.

Reinforced concrete topping bonds tee units together

BEARING WALL

END WALL

Metal gravel stop. See 8.

Precast structural tees

Solid fill or glazed opening

Weld plates cast into stem of tee and anchored in concrete or masonry wall.

Extend wall up or glaze opening.

Concrete or or masonry wall

BEARING WALL

END WALL

END WALL

Reinforced concrete roof slabs are formed and sitecast in the same way as the concrete floor systems illustrated on 4.32 and 4.33.

Roof slabs are normally roofed with a membrane type of roofing as shown in the cross-section. See 8.2 - 8.5 for details.

A parapet may be cast with the slab.

Slope top of slab for roof drainage. (1/4" per foot min. recommended)

The roof slab may be supported by a reinforced concrete beam or wall, or by a reinforced masonry wall.

Slab may be cantilevered beyond support for a roof overhang.

Top cover
Roofing membrane
Thermal insulation
Vapor barrier
Concrete roof slab

The edge of a concrete roof slab may be treated in three different ways.

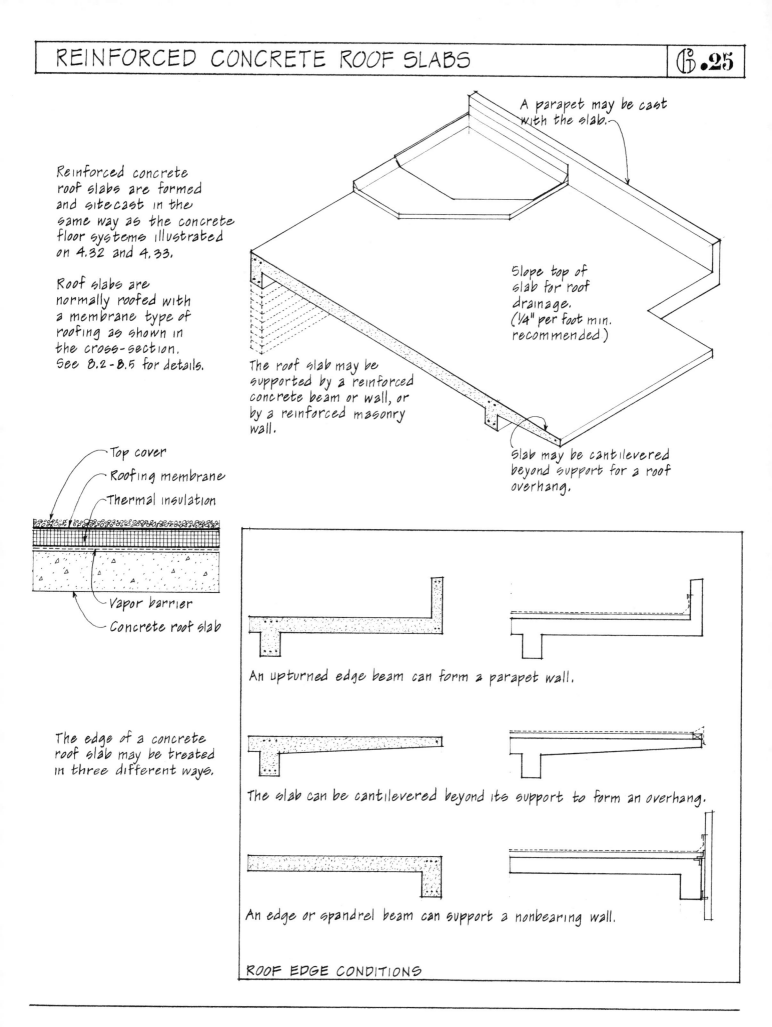

An upturned edge beam can form a parapet wall.

The slab can be cantilevered beyond its support to form an overhang.

An edge or spandrel beam can support a nonbearing wall.

ROOF EDGE CONDITIONS

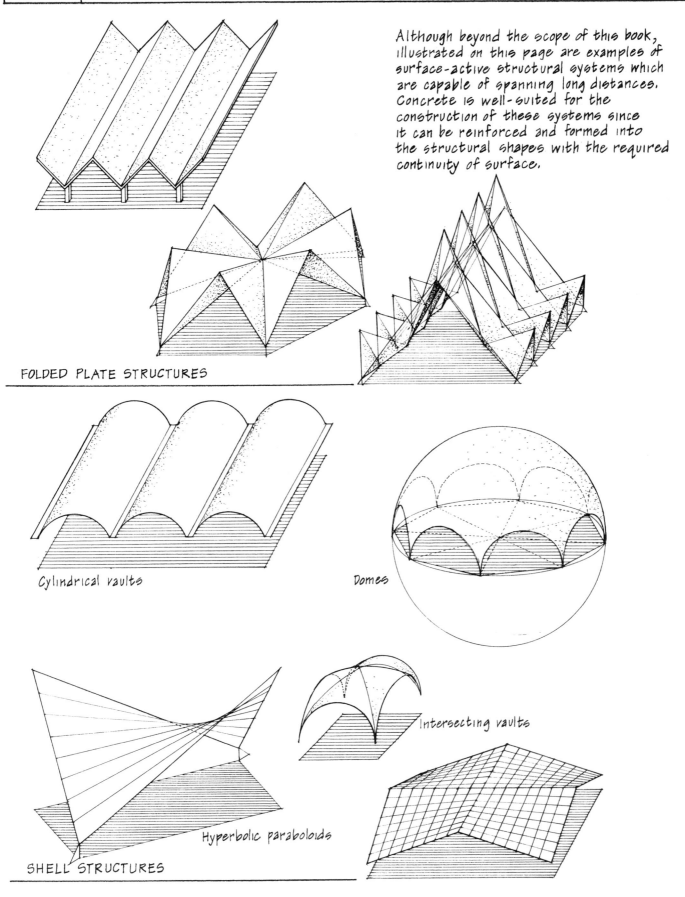

Although beyond the scope of this book, illustrated on this page are examples of surface-active structural systems which are capable of spanning long distances. Concrete is well-suited for the construction of these systems since it can be reinforced and formed into the structural shapes with the required continuity of surface.

FOLDED PLATE STRUCTURES

Cylindrical vaults

Domes

SHELL STRUCTURES

Hyperbolic paraboloids

Intersecting vaults

DOORS & WINDOWS

Doors and doorways provide access into a building's interior from the exterior and passage between interior spaces. Exterior doors should provide weathertight seals when closed and maintain the approximate insulation value of the building's exterior walls. At the same time, doorways should be large enough to move through easily and accommodate the moving of furnishings and equipment. Ease of operation, requirements for privacy and security, and any need for light, ventilation, and view should also be considered in a door's performance.

Interior doors provide for passage, visual privacy, and sound control between interior spaces. Doors into closets and storage spaces are primarily for visual screening although ventilation may also be a requirement.

There are many types and sizes of windows, the choice of which affects not only the physical appearance of a building, but also the natural lighting, ventilation, view potential, and spatial quality of the building's interior. As with exterior doors, windows should provide a weathertight seal when closed, have insulation value, and resist the formation of condensation on their interior surfaces.

Since door and window units are normally factory-built, manufacturers may have standard sizes and corresponding rough-opening requirements for the various door and window types. The size and location of doors and windows should be carefully planned so that adequate rough openings with properly sized lintels can be built into the building's wall systems.

From an exterior point of view, doors and windows are important compositional elements in a building's facades. The manner in which they break up a building's wall surfaces affects the massing, visual weight, scale, and articulation of the building form.

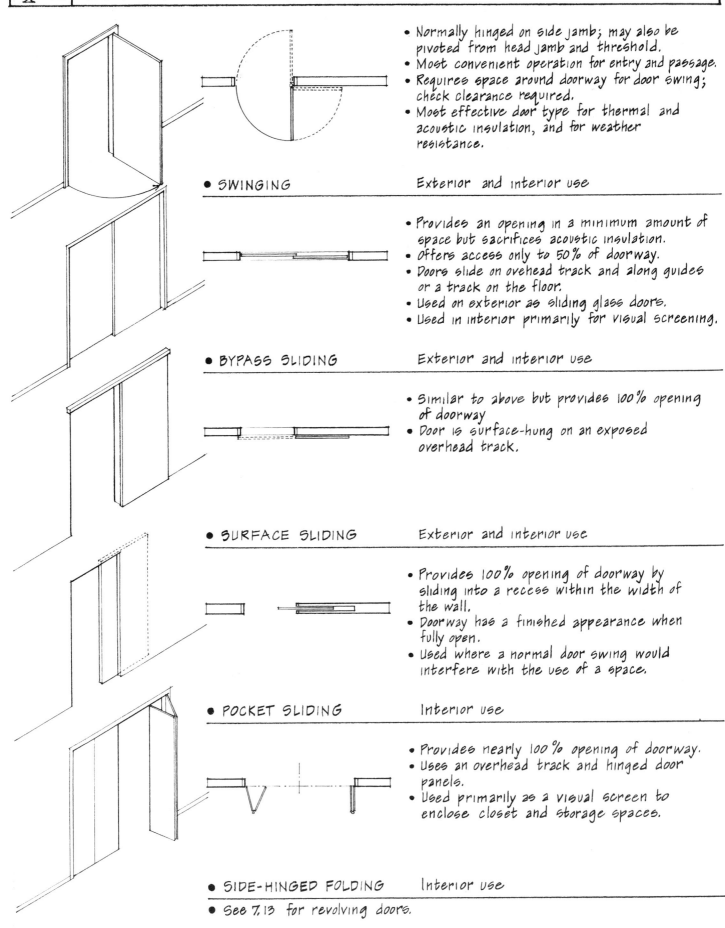

- Normally hinged on side jamb; may also be pivoted from head jamb and threshold.
- Most convenient operation for entry and passage.
- Requires space around doorway for door swing; check clearance required.
- Most effective door type for thermal and acoustic insulation, and for weather resistance.

● SWINGING   Exterior and interior use

- Provides an opening in a minimum amount of space but sacrifices acoustic insulation.
- Offers access only to 50% of doorway.
- Doors slide on overhead track and along guides or a track on the floor.
- Used on exterior as sliding glass doors.
- Used in interior primarily for visual screening.

● BYPASS SLIDING   Exterior and interior use

- Similar to above but provides 100% opening of doorway
- Door is surface-hung on an exposed overhead track.

● SURFACE SLIDING   Exterior and interior use

- Provides 100% opening of doorway by sliding into a recess within the width of the wall.
- Doorway has a finished appearance when fully open.
- Used where a normal door swing would interfere with the use of a space.

● POCKET SLIDING   Interior use

- Provides nearly 100% opening of doorway.
- Uses an overhead track and hinged door panels.
- Used primarily as a visual screen to enclose closet and storage spaces.

● SIDE-HINGED FOLDING   Interior use

● See 7.13 for revolving doors.

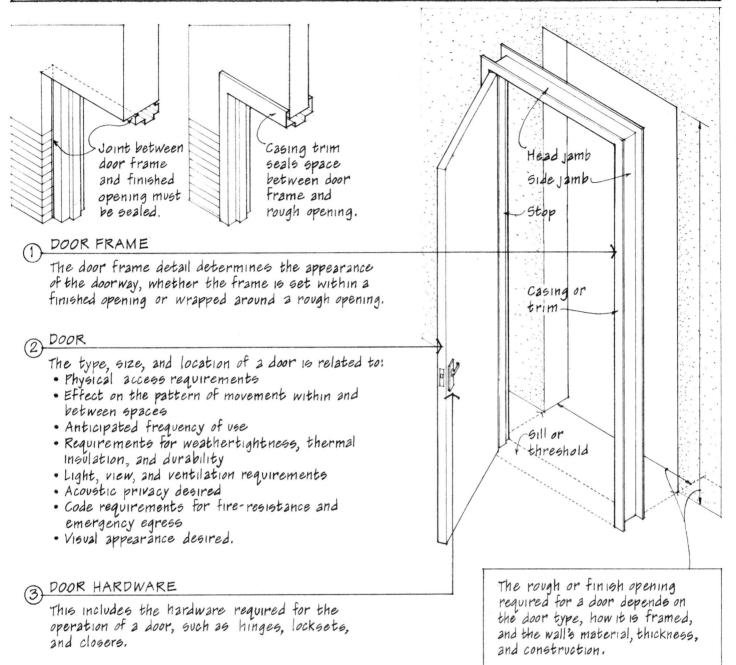

Joint between door frame and finished opening must be sealed.

Casing trim seals space between door frame and rough opening.

Head jamb

Side jamb

Stop

Casing or trim

Sill or threshold

① DOOR FRAME

The door frame detail determines the appearance of the doorway, whether the frame is set within a finished opening or wrapped around a rough opening.

② DOOR

The type, size, and location of a door is related to:

- Physical access requirements
- Effect on the pattern of movement within and between spaces
- Anticipated frequency of use
- Requirements for weathertightness, thermal insulation, and durability
- Light, view, and ventilation requirements
- Acoustic privacy desired
- Code requirements for fire-resistance and emergency egress
- Visual appearance desired.

③ DOOR HARDWARE

This includes the hardware required for the operation of a door, such as hinges, locksets, and closers.

The rough or finish opening required for a door depends on the door type, how it is framed, and the wall's material, thickness, and construction.

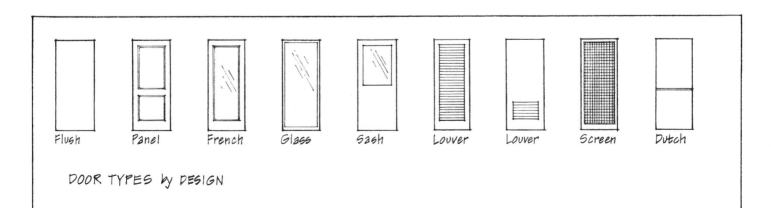

| Flush | Panel | French | Glass | Sash | Louver | Louver | Screen | Dutch |

DOOR TYPES by DESIGN

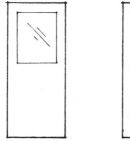

Flush   With glass inserts   With louvered insert

- Openings should be less than 40% of door area and no closer than 5" to any edge.
- Height of openings in hollow core doors should be less than half the door height.

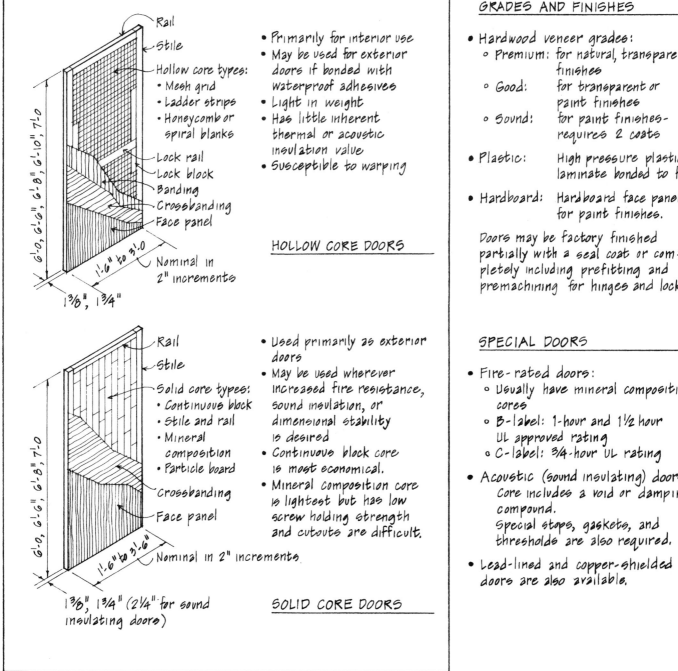

Rail
Stile
Hollow core types:
- Mesh grid
- Ladder strips
- Honeycomb or spiral blanks
Lock rail
Lock block
Banding
Crossbanding
Face panel

6'-0, 6'-6", 6'-8", 6'-10", 7'-0
1'-6" to 3'-0
Nominal in 2" increments
1⅜", 1¾"

- Primarily for interior use
- May be used for exterior doors if bonded with waterproof adhesives
- Light in weight
- Has little inherent thermal or acoustic insulation value
- Susceptible to warping

HOLLOW CORE DOORS

Rail
Stile
Solid core types:
- Continuous block
- Stile and rail
- Mineral composition
- Particle board
Crossbanding
Face panel

6'-0, 6'-6", 6'-8", 7'-0
1'-6" to 3'-6"
Nominal in 2" increments
1⅜", 1¾" (2¼" for sound insulating doors)

- Used primarily as exterior doors
- May be used wherever increased fire resistance, sound insulation, or dimensional stability is desired
- Continuous block core is most economical.
- Mineral composition core is lightest but has low screw holding strength and cutouts are difficult.

SOLID CORE DOORS

GRADES AND FINISHES

- Hardwood veneer grades:
  - Premium: for natural, transparent finishes
  - Good: for transparent or paint finishes
  - Sound: for paint finishes- requires 2 coats
- Plastic: High pressure plastic laminate bonded to face
- Hardboard: Hardboard face panels for paint finishes.

Doors may be factory finished partially with a seal coat or completely including prefitting and premachining for hinges and locksets.

SPECIAL DOORS

- Fire-rated doors:
  - Usually have mineral composition cores
  - B-label: 1-hour and 1½ hour UL approved rating
  - C-label: ¾-hour UL rating
- Acoustic (sound insulating) doors: Core includes a void or damping compound. Special stops, gaskets, and thresholds are also required.
- Lead-lined and copper-shielded doors are also available.

Panel

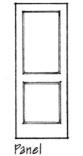

Panel

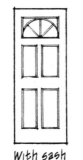

Panel

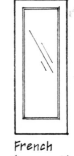

With sash

Louvered

French (casement)

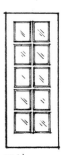

With divided lights

Panel doors consist of a framework of vertical (stile) and horizontal (rail) members which hold solid wood or plywood panels, glass lights, or louvers in place. The stiles and rails may be solid softwood or veneered hardwood.

GRADES AND FINISHES

○ Premium (select) grade: for natural clear or stained finishes
○ Standard grade: for paint finishes only

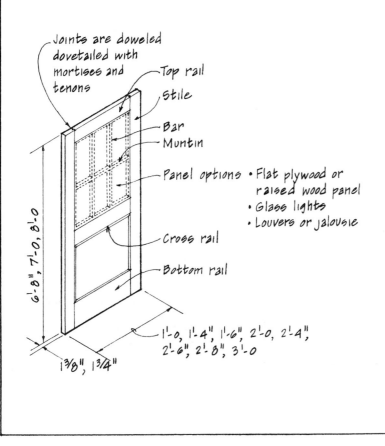

Joints are doweled dovetailed with mortises and tenons

Top rail

Stile

Bar

Muntin

Panel options • Flat plywood or raised wood panel
• Glass lights
• Louvers or jalousie

Cross rail

Bottom rail

6'-8", 7'-0, 8'-0

1'-0, 1'-4", 1'-6", 2'-0, 2'-4", 2'-6", 2'-8", 3'-0

1³⁄₈", 1³⁄₄"

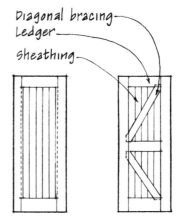

Diagonal bracing
Ledger
Sheathing

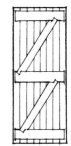

Batten doors

Batten doors consist of vertical boards (sheathing) nailed at right angles to cross strips (ledgers). Diagonal bracing is nailed between and notched into the ledgers.

• Used primarily for economy in rough construction
• Usually site fabricated
• Tongue-and-groove sheathing is recommended for weathertightness.
• Subject to expansion and contraction with changes in moisture content.

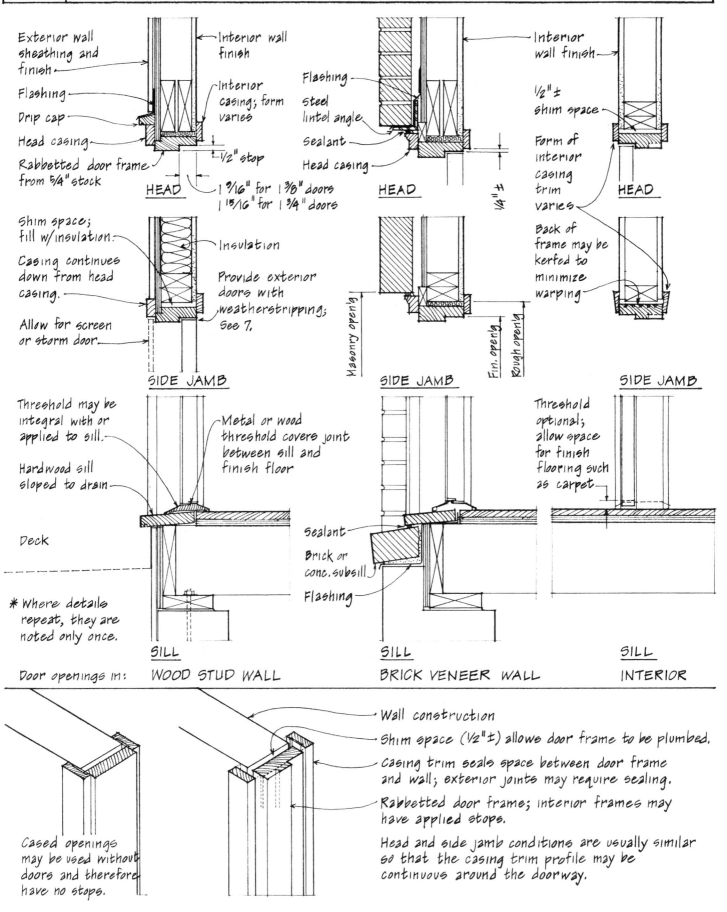

Exterior wall sheathing and finish

Flashing

Drip cap

Head casing

Rabbetted door frame from 5/4" stock

Interior wall finish

Interior casing; form varies

1/2" stop

1 9/16" for 1 3/8" doors
1 15/16" for 1 3/4" doors

HEAD

Flashing

steel lintel angle

Sealant

Head casing

Interior wall finish

1/2"± shim space

Form of interior casing trim varies

Back of frame may be kerfed to minimize warping

HEAD

Shim space; fill w/insulation

Casing continues down from head casing.

Allow for screen or storm door

Insulation

Provide exterior doors with weatherstripping; See 7.

SIDE JAMB

Masonry open'g

Fin. open'g
Rough open'g

SIDE JAMB

SIDE JAMB

Threshold may be integral with or applied to sill.

Hardwood sill sloped to drain

Deck

Metal or wood threshold covers joint between sill and finish floor

Sealant

Brick or conc. subsill

Flashing

Threshold optional; allow space for finish flooring such as carpet

* Where details repeat, they are noted only once.

Door openings in: **WOOD STUD WALL**   **BRICK VENEER WALL**   **INTERIOR**

SILL   **SILL**   **SILL**

Wall construction

Shim space (1/2"±) allows door frame to be plumbed.

Casing trim seals space between door frame and wall; exterior joints may require sealing.

Rabbetted door frame; interior frames may have applied stops.

Head and side jamb conditions are usually similar so that the casing trim profile may be continuous around the doorway.

Cased openings may be used without doors and therefore have no stops.

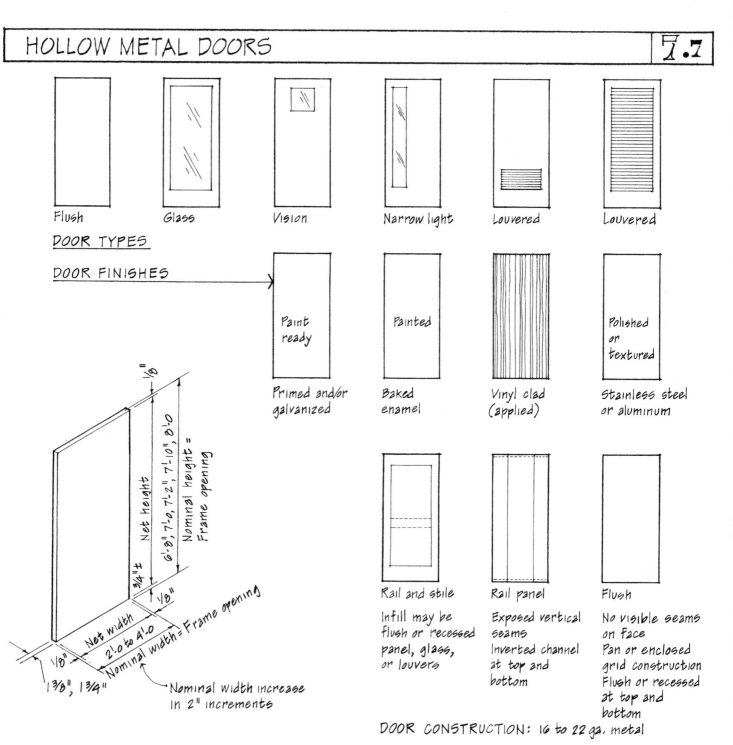

DOOR TYPES

Flush   Glass   Vision   Narrow light   Louvered   Louvered

DOOR FINISHES

Paint ready — Primed and/or galvanized

Painted — Baked enamel

Vinyl clad (applied)

Polished or textured — Stainless steel or aluminum

Rail and stile
- Infill may be flush or recessed panel, glass, or louvers

Rail panel
- Exposed vertical seams
- Inverted channel at top and bottom

Flush
- No visible seams on face
- Pan or enclosed grid construction
- Flush or recessed at top and bottom

DOOR CONSTRUCTION: 16 to 22 ga. metal

Nominal height = Frame opening

6'-8", 7'-0, 7'-2", 7'-10", 8'-0

Net height

¾"±

⅛"

⅛"

Net width

2'-0 to 4'-0

Nominal width = Frame opening

1⅜", 1¾"

Nominal width increase in 2" increments

FIRE DOORS: Fire door assemblies (door, frame, and hardware) are required to protect openings in fire-rated walls. See A.11.

UL label	Rating	Glazing permitted *
A	3 hour	No glass permitted
B	1½ hour	100 sq. in. per leaf
C	¾ hour	1296 sq. in. per leaf; 54" max. dimension
D	1½ hour	No glass permitted
E	¾ hour	720 sq. in. per light; 54" max. dimension

* ¼" wire glass

General requirements

- Maximum door size: 4' x 10'
- Door frame and hardware must have a rating similar to that of door.
- Door must be self-latching and be equipped with closers.
- Louvers with fusible links are permitted for B and C label doors; max. area = 576 sq. in.
- No glass and louver combinations are permitted.

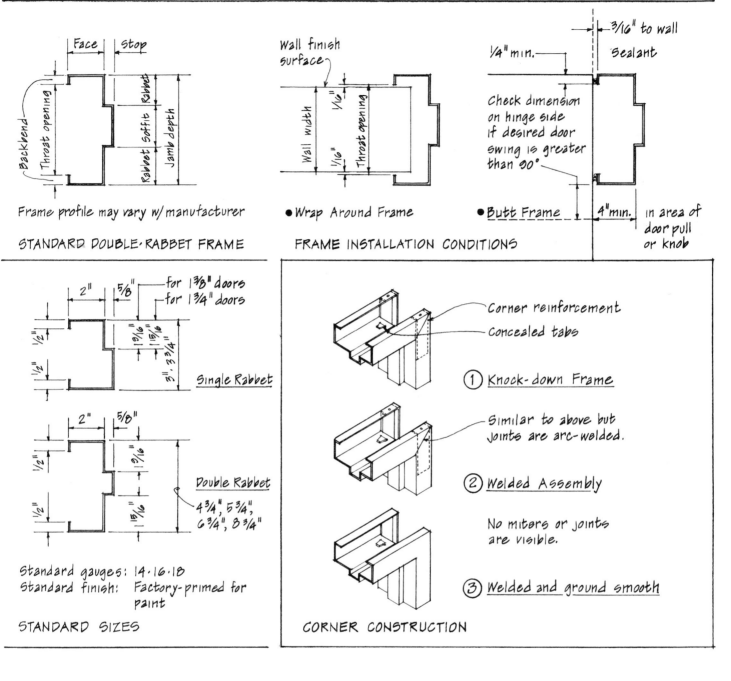

STANDARD DOUBLE-RABBET FRAME

Face / Stop / Backbend / Throat opening / Rabbet Soffit Rabbet / Jamb depth

Frame profile may vary w/ manufacturer

FRAME INSTALLATION CONDITIONS

Wall finish surface / Wall width / 1/16" / Throat opening

• Wrap Around Frame

3/16" to wall / Sealant / 1/4" min.

Check dimension on hinge side if desired door swing is greater than 90°

• Butt Frame / 4" min. / in area of door pull or knob

STANDARD SIZES

2" / 5/8" / for 1 3/8" doors / for 1 3/4" doors / 1/2" / 1/2" / 13/16" / 15/16" / 3", 3 3/4"

Single Rabbet

2" / 5/8" / 1/2" / 1/2" / 13/16" / 15/16"

Double Rabbet
4 3/4", 5 3/4", 6 3/4", 8 3/4"

Standard gauges: 14·16·18
Standard finish: Factory-primed for paint

CORNER CONSTRUCTION

Corner reinforcement
Concealed tabs

① Knock-down Frame

Similar to above but joints are arc-welded.

② Welded Assembly

No miters or joints are visible.

③ Welded and ground smooth

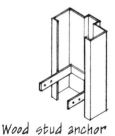

Wood stud anchor

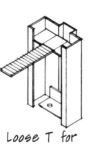

Loose T for masonry

UL approved masonry anchor

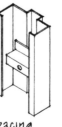

Spacing bracket anchor for existing walls

Steel stud anchor

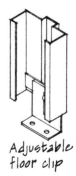

Adjustable floor clip

ANCHOR TYPES (Minimum of 3 required per jamb)

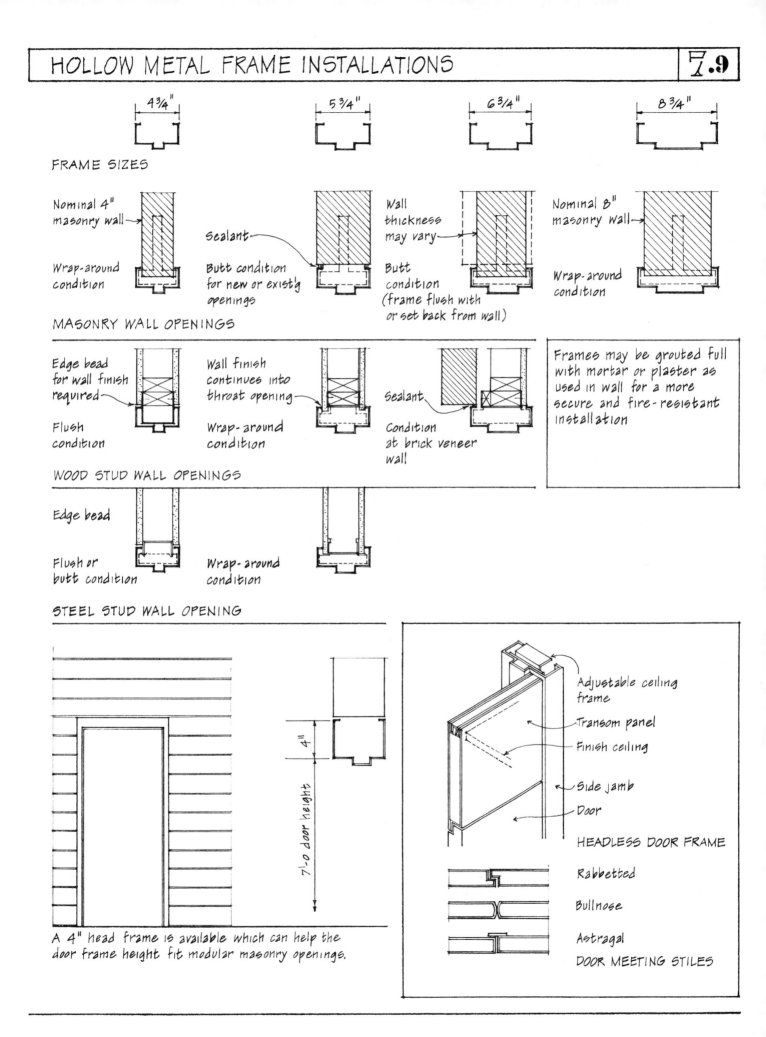

4 3/4"   5 3/4"   6 3/4"   8 3/4"

FRAME SIZES

Nominal 4" masonry wall →

Wrap-around condition

Sealant

Butt condition for new or exist'g openings

Wall thickness may vary →

Butt condition (frame flush with or set back from wall)

Nominal 8" masonry wall →

Wrap-around condition

MASONRY WALL OPENINGS

Edge bead for wall finish required →

Flush condition

Wall finish continues into throat opening →

Wrap-around condition

Sealant

Condition at brick veneer wall

Frames may be grouted full with mortar or plaster as used in wall for a more secure and fire-resistant installation

WOOD STUD WALL OPENINGS

Edge bead

Flush or butt condition

Wrap-around condition

STEEL STUD WALL OPENING

4"

7'-0 door height

A 4" head frame is available which can help the door frame height fit modular masonry openings.

Adjustable ceiling frame

Transom panel

Finish ceiling

Side jamb

Door

HEADLESS DOOR FRAME

Rabbetted

Bullnose

Astragal

DOOR MEETING STILES

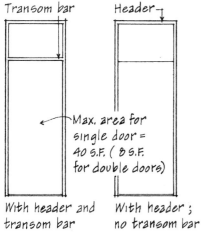

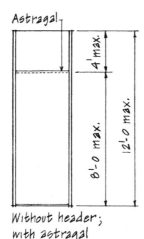

Transom bar   Header   Astragal

Max. area for single door = 40 S.F. (8 S.F. for double doors)

4' max.

8'-0 max.

12'-0 max.

With header and transom bar   With header; no transom bar   Without header; with astragal

TRANSOM PANEL CONDITIONS

Transom panels continue the door plane up to the finish ceiling. They may have an A or B label fire-resistance rating.

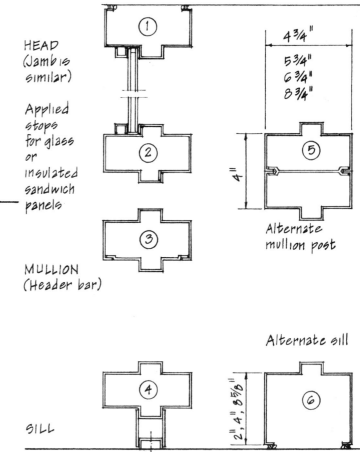

Headless frame

Transom panel may be fixed or removable, and may be:
① Solid, similar to door construction
② Glass
③ Louvers.

Astragal

Transom bar is similar in size and profile to standard frame.

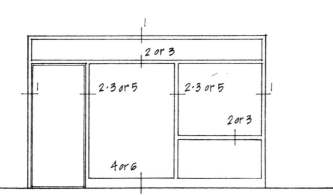

2 or 3

2·3 or 5   2·3 or 5

2 or 3

4 or 6

The framing members are similar in size, profile, and finish to standard hollow metal door frames. They may be used to frame sidelights, borrowed lights, and transoms.

- Primarily a stick system which can be arranged in various ways.
- The types of fastenings, joints, and anchorages used vary with the system manufacturer.

HOLLOW METAL FRAMES FOR WINDOW WALLS

HEAD (Jamb is similar)

Applied stops for glass or insulated sandwich panels

①   ②   ③

MULLION (Header bar)

4 3/4"
5 3/4"
6 3/4"
8 3/4"

4"

⑤

Alternate mullion post

Alternate sill

④

SILL

2", 4", 8 5/8"

⑥

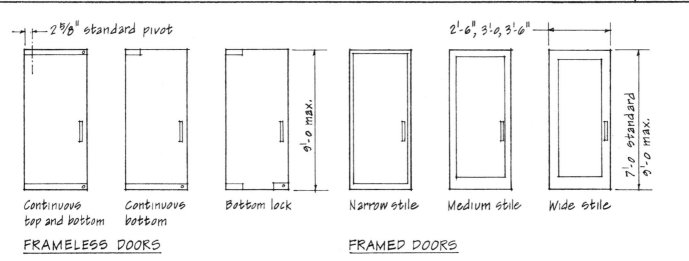

Continuous top and bottom

Continuous bottom

Bottom lock

FRAMELESS DOORS

Narrow stile

Medium stile

Wide stile

FRAMED DOORS

- Consult local codes for safety requirements.
- Consult manufacturer for sizes, glazing options, and frame requirements.
- Frameless doors are difficult to weatherstrip effectively.

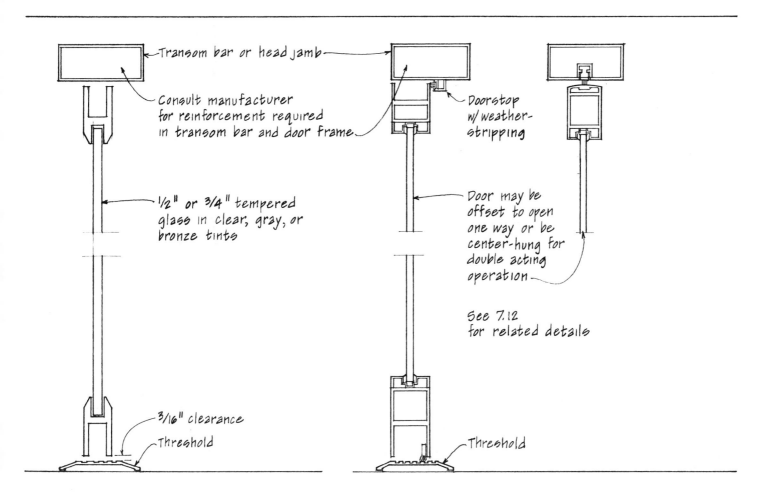

Transom bar or head jamb

Consult manufacturer for reinforcement required in transom bar and door frame.

Doorstop w/ weatherstripping

1/2" or 3/4" tempered glass in clear, gray, or bronze tints

Door may be offset to open one way or be center-hung for double acting operation

See 7.12 for related details

3/16" clearance

Threshold

Threshold

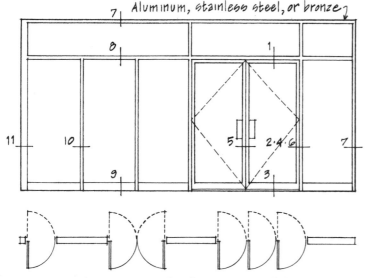

Aluminum, stainless steel, or bronze

Door may be single or double acting, and be arranged in various ways.

Size and spacing of mullions are related to the glass thickness and the wind load on the wall plane. Limit the deflection normal to the wall plane to 1/200 of each component's clear span; limit the deflection of glass supports to 1/300 of the support distance.

Consult manufacturer for frame sizes, profiles, and installation details. Consult applicable code for safety glazing requirements.

All glass wall systems should be engineered. The thickness of the glass mullions is related to the width and height of the glass panels and the wind load on the wall plane. Consult glass manufacturer for sizing recommendations.

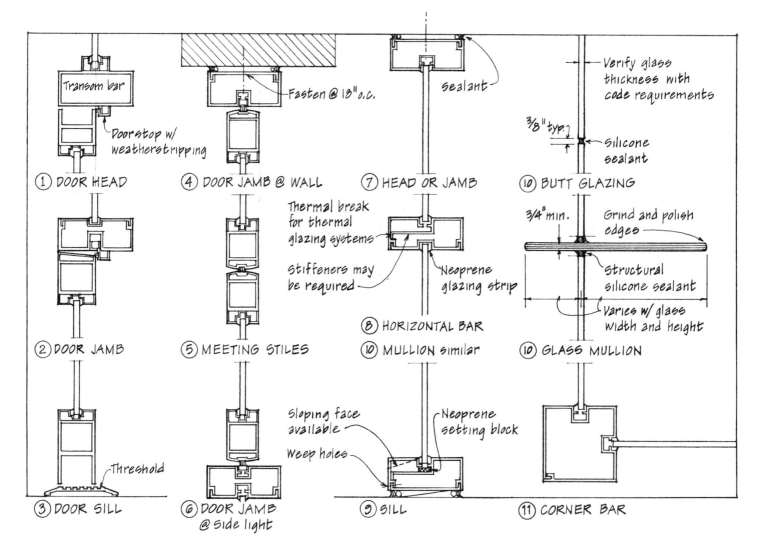

Transom bar

Doorstop w/ weatherstripping

Fasten @ 18" o.c.

sealant

Verify glass thickness with code requirements

3/8" typ.

Silicone sealant

① DOOR HEAD   ④ DOOR JAMB @ WALL   ⑦ HEAD OR JAMB   ⑩ BUTT GLAZING

Thermal break for thermal glazing systems

Stiffeners may be required

Neoprene glazing strip

3/4" min.

Grind and polish edges

Structural silicone sealant

Varies w/ glass width and height

② DOOR JAMB   ⑤ MEETING STILES   ⑧ HORIZONTAL BAR

⑩ MULLION similar   ⑩ GLASS MULLION

Sloping face available

Weep holes

Neoprene setting block

Threshold

③ DOOR SILL   ⑥ DOOR JAMB @ side light   ⑨ SILL   ⑪ CORNER BAR

Revolving doors provide a continuous weatherseal, eliminate drafts, and hold heating and cooling losses to a minimum while accommodating a moderate flow of traffic.

- Can handle approximately 2000 persons per hour.

- Normally used in commercial and institutional buildings.

- 6'-6" diameter for general use; for large traffic areas, use 7'-0 diameter or greater.

- Heating and/or cooling source may be integral with or adjacent to enclosure.

- Optional speed control automatically aligns doors at quarter points when not in use and turns wings 3/4 of a revolution at walking speed when activated by slight pressure.

- Door wings are collapsible in panic situations.

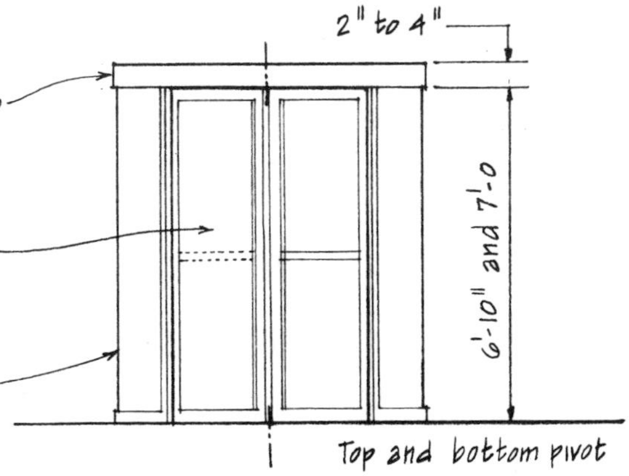

- Some codes may credit revolving doors with satisfying 50% of the legal exit requirements. Other codes do not credit revolving doors and require adjacent hinged doors for use as emergency exits.

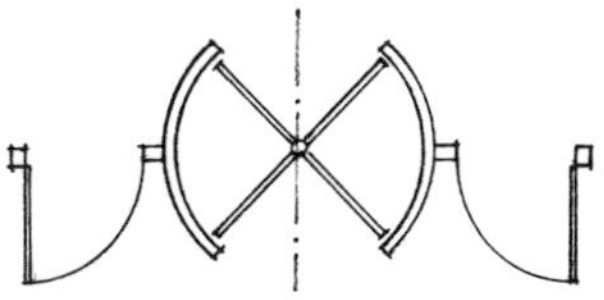

Deck includes provision for ceiling lights; may be glazed with tempered glass

Doors of tempered glass with aluminum, stainless steel, or bronze frames

Enclosure may be metal or glass (tempered, wire, or laminated).

2" to 4"

6'-10" and 7'-0

Top and bottom pivot

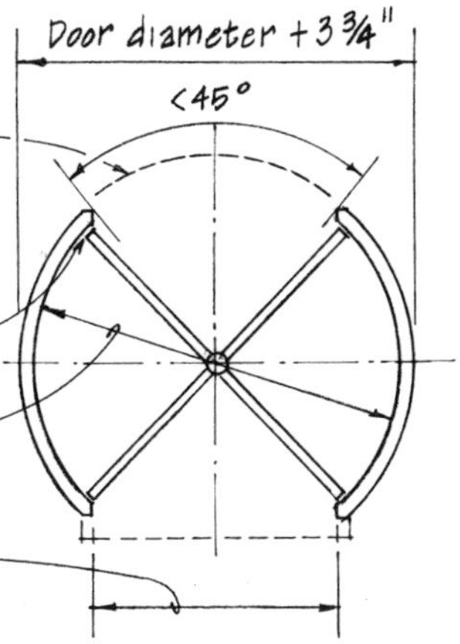

Door diameter + 3¾"

< 45°

Line of soffit may be curved or straight.

Weatherseal is provided by rubber and felt tip sweep at door stiles, and at top and bottom rails.

Door diameter

Door diameter	Opening
6'-6"	4'-5"
6'-8"	4'-6"
6'-10"	4'-8"
7'-0	4'-9"
7'-2"	4'-11"
7'-4"	5'-0

Enclosure flanked by hinged doors

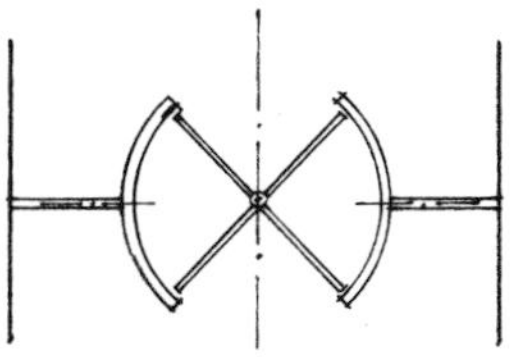

Side lights centered on enclosure

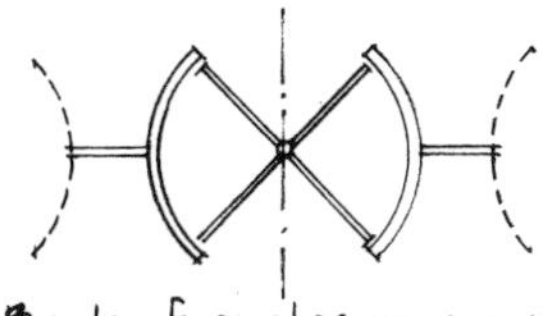

Bank of enclosures with side lights between

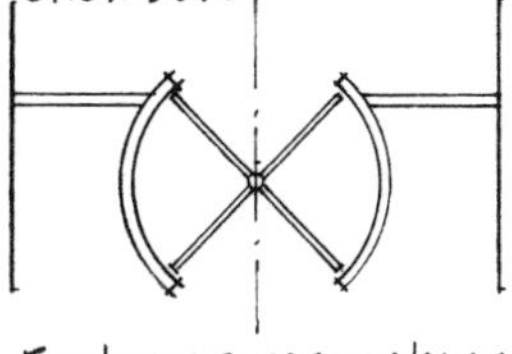

Enclosure projecting from side lights

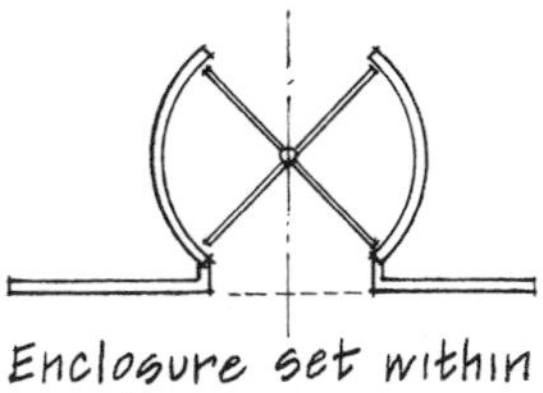

Enclosure set within a wall plane

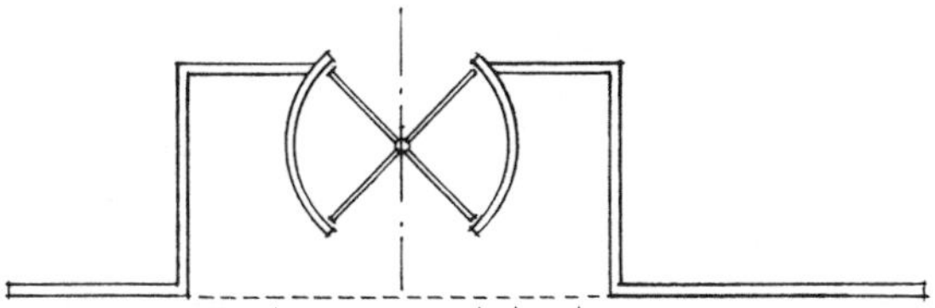

Enclosure set back within a wall recess

REVOLVING DOOR LAYOUTS

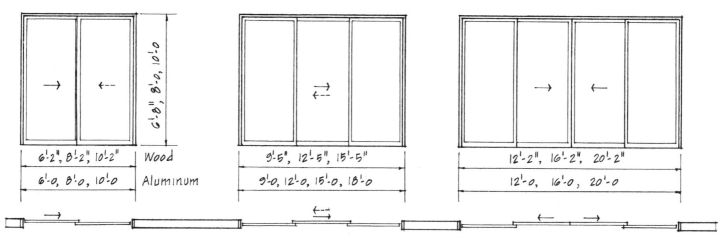

Wood
6'-2", 8'-2", 10'-2"

Aluminum
6'-0, 8'-0, 10'-0

6'-8", 8'-0, 10'-0

9'-5", 12'-5", 15'-5"

9'-0, 12'-0, 15'-0, 18'-0

12'-2", 16'-2", 20'-2"

12'-0, 16'-0, 20'-0

Above dimensions are nominal stock sizes; consult manufacturer for rough or masonry openings required. As a guide, add 1" to nominal width for rough openings, and 3" for masonry openings.

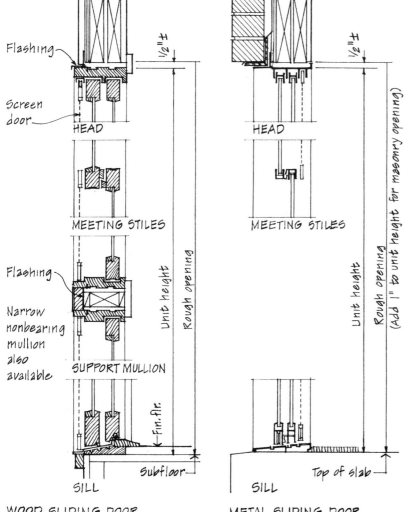

Flashing

Screen door

HEAD

MEETING STILES

Flashing

Narrow nonbearing mullion also available

SUPPORT MULLION

Unit height

Rough opening

Fin. flr.

Subfloor

SILL

HEAD

MEETING STILES

Unit height

Rough opening

(Add 1" to unit height for masonry opening)

Top of slab

SILL

WOOD SLIDING DOOR
in wood frame

METAL SLIDING DOOR
in brick veneer wall

(Hatched sections are normally supplied by manufacturer.)

Residential sliding glass doors are available with wood, aluminum, or steel frames. Wood frames may be treated with preservative, primed for painting, or clad in aluminum or vinyl. Metal frames are available in a variety of finishes, with thermal breaks and integral windproof mounting fins.

For safety, all glazing should be of tempered glass. For energy conservation, units are available with insulating glass.

Sliding glass doors are manufactured as standard units complete with operating hardware and weatherstripping. Screen and operating door panels may be on the interior or exterior.

Consult manufacturer for stock sizes, required rough or masonry openings, glazing options, and installation details.

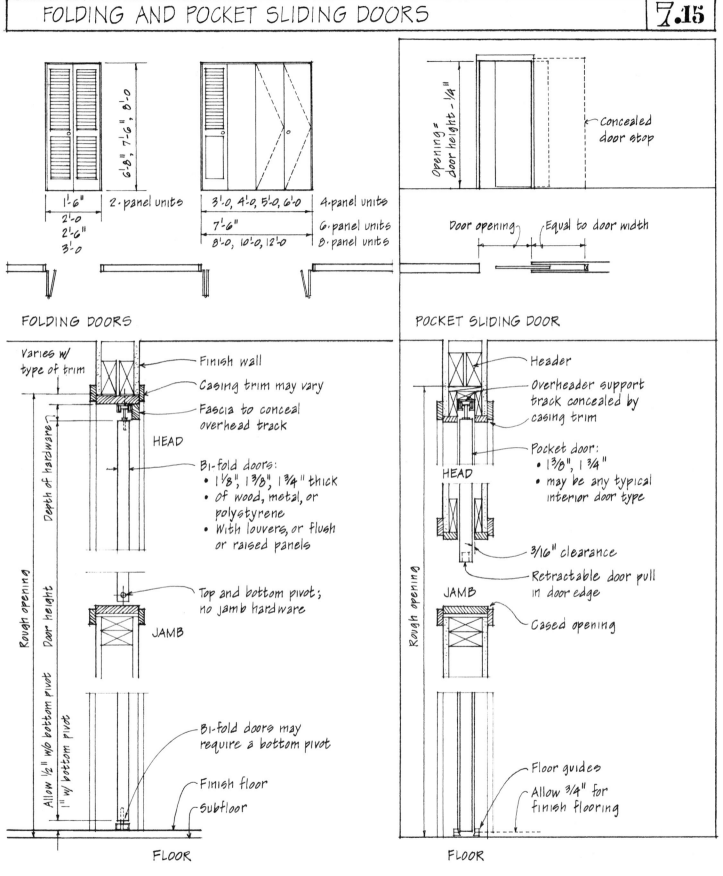

FOLDING DOORS

2-panel units

1'-6"
2'-0
2'-6"
3'-0

6'-8", 7'-6", 8'-0

4-panel units — 3'-0, 4'-0, 5'-0, 6'-0
6-panel units — 7'-6"
8-panel units — 8'-0, 10'-0, 12'-0

POCKET SLIDING DOOR

Opening = door height - 1/4"

Concealed door stop

Door opening — Equal to door width

Varies w/ type of trim — Finish wall

Casing trim may vary

Fascia to conceal overhead track

HEAD

Bi-fold doors:
- 1⅛", 1⅜", 1¾" thick
- of wood, metal, or polystyrene
- With louvers, or flush or raised panels

Depth of hardware

Rough opening

Door height

Top and bottom pivot; no jamb hardware

JAMB

Allow ½" w/o bottom pivot
1" w/ bottom pivot

Bi-fold doors may require a bottom pivot

Finish floor
Subfloor

FLOOR

Header

Overheader support track concealed by casing trim

HEAD

Pocket door:
- 1⅜", 1¾"
- may be any typical interior door type

3/16" clearance

Retractable door pull in door edge

JAMB

Cased opening

Rough opening

Floor guides
Allow ¾" for finish flooring

FLOOR

Generalized conditions for wood frame construction are illustrated. Details for hollow metal doors and frames are similar. Consult hardware manufacturer for installation details.

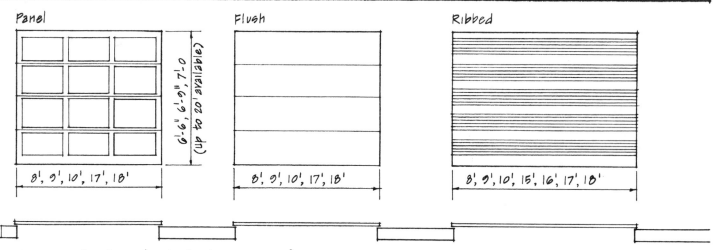

Panel

Flush

Ribbed

6'-6", 6'-9", 7'-0 (up to 20 available)

8', 9', 10', 17', 18'

8', 9', 10', 17', 18'

8', 9', 10', 15', 16', 17', 18'

Doors may be of wood, steel, aluminum, or fiberglass. Glazing in panel design may be located as desired. In addition to the sizes indicated above, commercial overhead doors can be up to 20' high and 30' wide. Consult manufacturer for details.

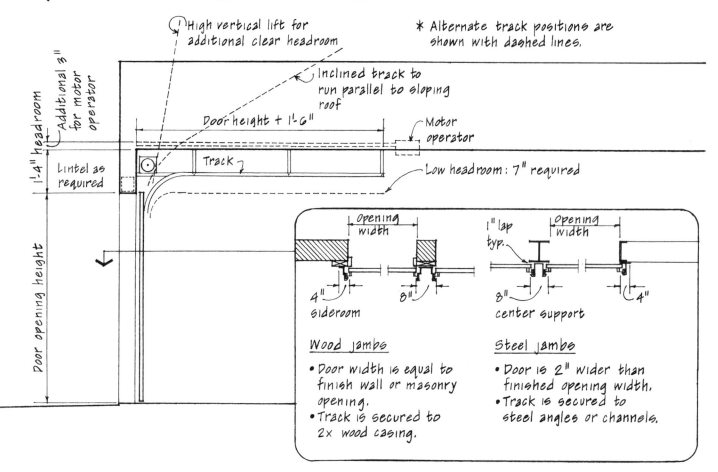

† High vertical lift for additional clear headroom

* Alternate track positions are shown with dashed lines.

Additional 3" for motor operator

Inclined track to run parallel to sloping roof

Door height + 1'-6"

Motor operator

1'-4" headroom

Lintel as required

Track

Low headroom: 7" required

Door opening height

opening width

opening width

1" lap typ.

4" sideroom

8"

8" center support

4"

Wood jambs

- Door width is equal to finish wall or masonry opening.
- Track is secured to 2x wood casing.

Steel jambs

- Door is 2" wider than finished opening width.
- Track is secured to steel angles or channels.

Overhead doors may be operated manually, or by a chain hoist or electric motor. Chain hoist and motor operations may require additional head, side, and back room.

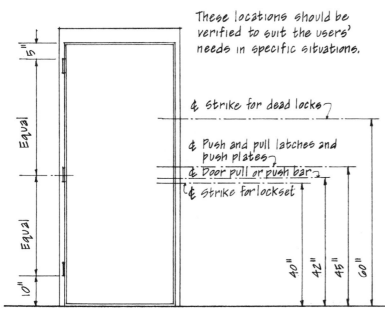

These locations should be verified to suit the users' needs in specific situations.

℄ Strike for dead locks

℄ Push and pull latches and push plates

℄ Door pull or push bar

℄ Strike for lockset

40" 42" 45" 60"

RECOMMENDED DOOR HARDWARE LOCATIONS

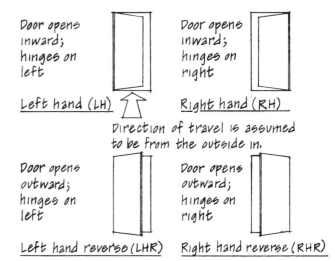

Door opens inward; hinges on left

Door opens inward; hinges on right

Left hand (LH)   **Right hand (RH)**

Direction of travel is assumed to be from the outside in.

Door opens outward; hinges on left

Door opens outward; hinges on right

Left hand reverse (LHR)   **Right hand reverse (RHR)**

The above door hand conventions are used in specifying door hardware such as locksets and closers.

DOOR HAND CONVENTIONS

HARDWARE FINISHES

BHMA Code	U.S. Nº	Finish
600	USP	Primed for painting (steel)
603	US2G	Zinc plated (steel)
605	US3	Bright brass, clear coated
606	US4	Satin brass, clear coated
611	US9	Bright bronze, clear coated
612	US10	Satin bronze, clear coated
613	US10B	Oxidized satin bronze, oil rubbed
618	US14	Bright nickel plated, clear coated (brass)
619	US15	Satin nickel plated, clear coated (brass)
622	US19	Flat black coated (brass, bronze)
623	US20	Light oxidized bright bronze
624	US20A	Dark oxidized statuary bronze
625	US26	Bright chromium plated (brass, bronze)
626	US26D	Satin chromium plated (brass, bronze)
628	US28	Satin aluminum, clear anodized
629	US32	Bright stainless steel
630	US32D	Satin stainless steel
684	–	Black chrome, bright (brass, bronze)
685	–	Black chrome, satin (brass, bronze)

Builders' Hardware Manufacturers Association (BHMA) codes are given with the nearest U.S. equivalent.

FINISH DOOR HARDWARE includes:

- Locksets ○ Locks, latches, bolts,
            ○ Cylinder and stop works
            ○ Operating trim
- Hinges
- Closers
- Panic hardware
- Push and pull bars and plates
- Kick plates
- Stops and holders
- Thresholds
- Weatherstripping
- Door tracks and guides

SELECTION FACTORS:

- Function and ease of operation
- Recessed or surface-mounted installation
- Material, finish, texture, and color
- Durability in terms of:
    ○ Anticipated frequency of use
    ○ Possible exposure to weather or corrosive conditions.

BASE MATERIALS include brass, bronze, steel, stainless steel, and aluminum.

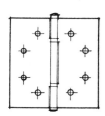

Template

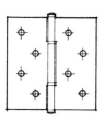

Non-template (for wood doors)

Butt <u>hinges</u> are normally used with wood and hollow metal doors and frames. They are mortised into the door edge and jamb so that only the knuckle is visible when the door is closed.

The pin in the knuckle may be removable (loose) or fixed (non-rising). Self-locking pins which cannot be removed when the door is closed are also available for security.

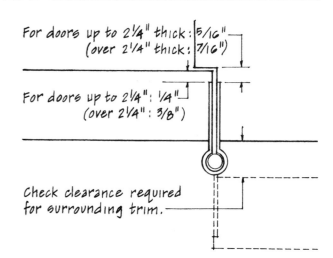

For doors up to $2\frac{1}{4}$" thick: $5/16$"
(over $2\frac{1}{4}$" thick: $7/16$")

For doors up to $2\frac{1}{4}$": $1/4$"
(over $2\frac{1}{4}$": $3/8$")

Check clearance required for surrounding trim.

HINGE SIZES

Width is determined by door thickness and clearance required.
Height is determined by door width and thickness.

Door thickness	Door width	Clearance required	Hinge height	Hinge width
$3/4$" to $7/8$" (cabinet)	to 24"		$2\frac{1}{2}$"	
$7/8$" to $1\frac{1}{8}$" (screen)	to 36"		3"	
$1\frac{3}{8}$"	to 36"	$1\frac{1}{4}$"	$3\frac{1}{2}$" - 4"	$3\frac{1}{2}$"
$1\frac{3}{4}$"	to 36"	1"	4"	4"
	36" to 48"	$1\frac{1}{2}$"	$4\frac{1}{2}$"	$4\frac{1}{2}$"
$2\frac{1}{4}$"	to 42"	1"	5"	5"
	over 42"	2"	6"	6"

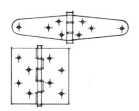

Surface hinges

• Used where mortising of door or jamb is not possible

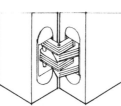

Invisible hinge

• Hinge is completely concealed when door is closed

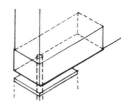

Floor hinge

• Used with mortise pivot at door head for double-acting door; may be provided with a closer mechanism

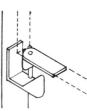

Gravity type pivot

• Used with double-acting swing doors (eg. cafe door)

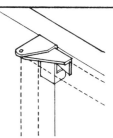

Pivot hinge

• Used primarily with cabinet doors

SPECIAL-PURPOSE HINGES

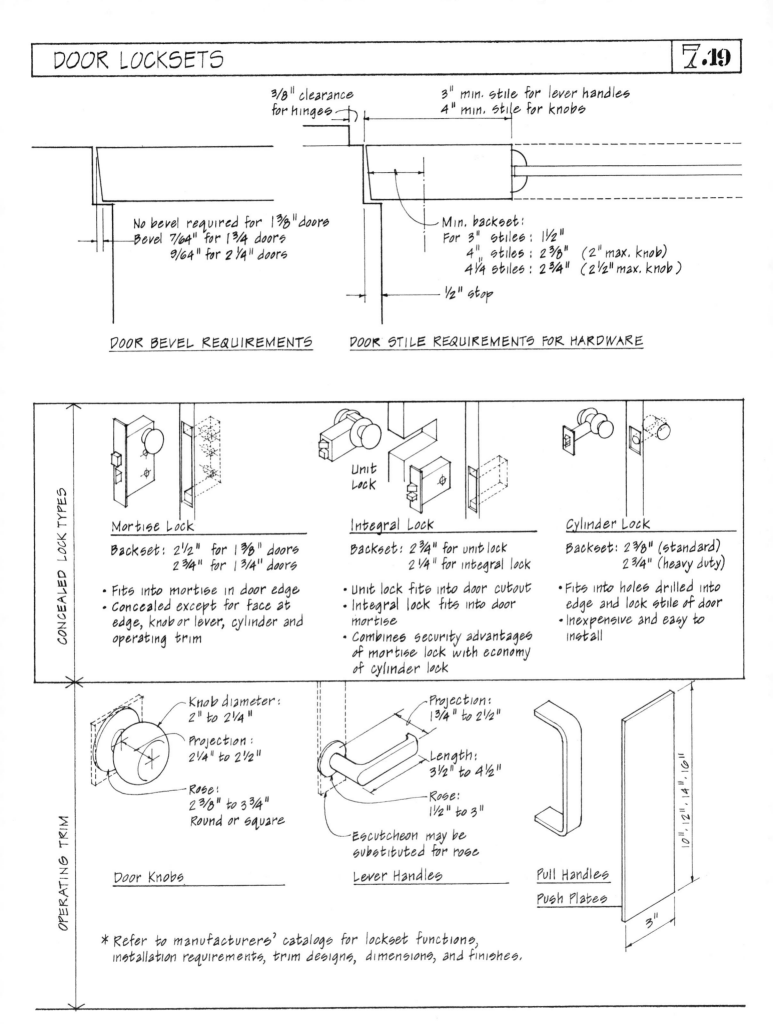

3/8" clearance for hinges

3" min. stile for lever handles
4" min. stile for knobs

No bevel required for 1 3/8" doors
Bevel 7/64" for 1 3/4 doors
9/64" for 2 1/4" doors

Min. backset:
For 3" stiles: 1 1/2"
4" stiles: 2 3/8" (2" max. knob)
4 1/4" stiles: 2 3/4" (2 1/2" max. knob)

1/2" stop

DOOR BEVEL REQUIREMENTS

DOOR STILE REQUIREMENTS FOR HARDWARE

CONCEALED LOCK TYPES

Unit Lock

Mortise Lock

Backset: 2 1/2" for 1 3/8" doors
2 3/4" for 1 3/4" doors

• Fits into mortise in door edge
• Concealed except for face at edge, knob or lever, cylinder and operating trim

Integral Lock

Backset: 2 3/4" for unit lock
2 1/4" for integral lock

• Unit lock fits into door cutout
• Integral lock fits into door mortise
• Combines security advantages of mortise lock with economy of cylinder lock

Cylinder Lock

Backset: 2 3/8" (standard)
2 3/4" (heavy duty)

• Fits into holes drilled into edge and lock stile of door
• Inexpensive and easy to install

OPERATING TRIM

Knob diameter: 2" to 2 1/4"

Projection: 2 1/4" to 2 1/2"

Rose: 2 3/8" to 3 3/4"
Round or square

Door Knobs

Projection: 1 3/4" to 2 1/2"

Length: 3 1/2" to 4 1/2"

Rose: 1 1/2" to 3"

Escutcheon may be substituted for rose

Lever Handles

10", 12", 14", 16"

3"

Pull Handles

Push Plates

* Refer to manufacturers' catalogs for lockset functions, installation requirements, trim designs, dimensions, and finishes.

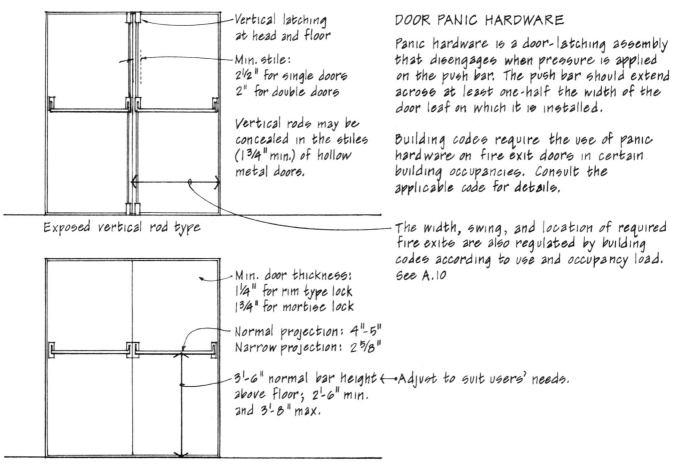

Vertical latching at head and floor

Min. stile:
2½" for single doors
2" for double doors

Vertical rods may be concealed in the stiles (1¾" min.) of hollow metal doors.

Exposed vertical rod type

Min. door thickness:
1¼" for rim type lock
1¾" for mortise lock

Normal projection: 4"–5"
Narrow projection: 2⅝"

3'-6" normal bar height ← Adjust to suit users' needs.
above floor; 2'-6" min.
and 3'-8" max.

Concealed type with lateral latching

DOOR PANIC HARDWARE

Panic hardware is a door-latching assembly that disengages when pressure is applied on the push bar. The push bar should extend across at least one-half the width of the door leaf on which it is installed.

Building codes require the use of panic hardware on fire exit doors in certain building occupancies. Consult the applicable code for details.

The width, swing, and location of required fire exits are also regulated by building codes according to use and occupancy load. See A.10

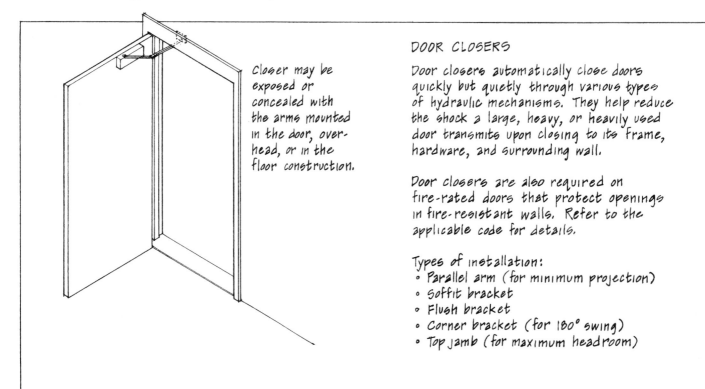

Closer may be exposed or concealed with the arms mounted in the door, overhead, or in the floor construction.

DOOR CLOSERS

Door closers automatically close doors quickly but quietly through various types of hydraulic mechanisms. They help reduce the shock a large, heavy, or heavily used door transmits upon closing to its frame, hardware, and surrounding wall.

Door closers are also required on fire-rated doors that protect openings in fire-resistant walls. Refer to the applicable code for details.

Types of installation:
∘ Parallel arm (for minimum projection)
∘ Soffit bracket
∘ Flush bracket
∘ Corner bracket (for 180° swing)
∘ Top jamb (for maximum headroom)

Thresholds conceal the joints between flooring materials at doorways and serve as a weather barrier at exterior sills.

- Thresholds have recessed undersides to fit snugly against the flooring or sill.
- When installed at exterior sills, joint sealant is used for a tight seal.
- Metal thresholds may be cast or covered with abrasive material to provide a non-slip surface.

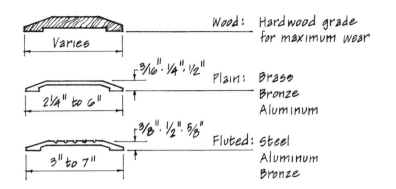

Wood: Hardwood grade for maximum wear

Varies

Plain: Brass
Bronze
Aluminum

3/16", 1/4", 1/2"
2 1/4" to 6"

Fluted: Steel
Aluminum
Bronze

3/8", 1/2", 5/8"
3" to 7"

Weatherstripping of exterior doors reduces air infiltration and the resulting heating and cooling loss. It can also prevent dust and wind-blown rain from penetrating a building's interior.

- Weatherstripping may be fastened to the door edge or face, or to the door frame and threshold.

- The weatherstripping material should be durable under extended use, non-corrosive, and replaceable.

- Basic types of weatherstripping include:
  ○ Metal spring-tensioned strip of aluminum, bronze, or stainless or galvanized steel
  ○ Vinyl or neoprene gaskets
  ○ Sponge plastic or rubber strips
  ○ Woven pile strips

- Weatherstripping is often supplied by the manufacturer of:
  ○ Sliding glass doors
  ○ Glass entrance doors
  ○ Revolving doors
  ○ Garage and overhead doors

1/2" max. for handicapped access

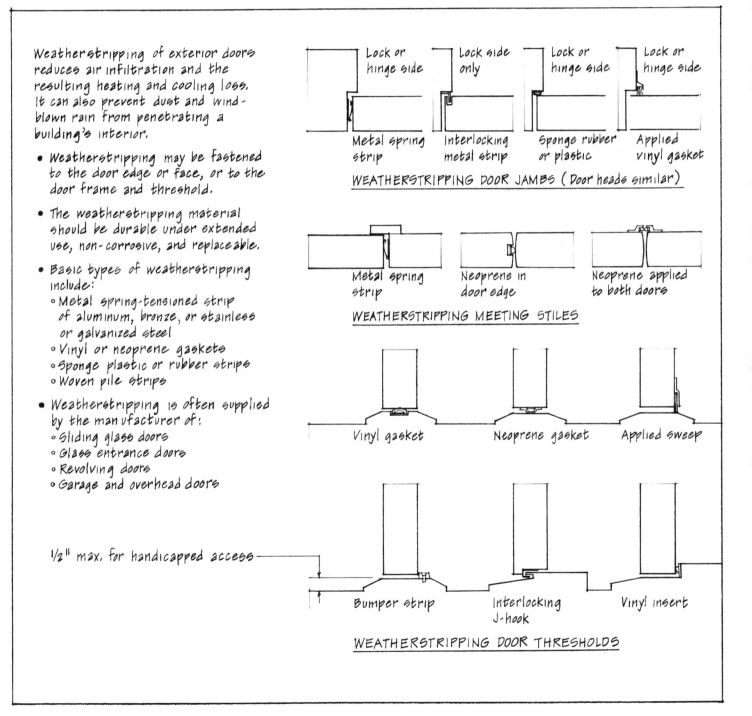

Lock or hinge side — Metal spring strip

Lock side only — Interlocking metal strip

Lock or hinge side — Sponge rubber or plastic

Lock or hinge side — Applied vinyl gasket

WEATHERSTRIPPING DOOR JAMBS (Door heads similar)

Metal spring strip

Neoprene in door edge

Neoprene applied to both doors

WEATHERSTRIPPING MEETING STILES

Vinyl gasket

Neoprene gasket

Applied sweep

Bumper strip

Interlocking J-hook

Vinyl insert

WEATHERSTRIPPING DOOR THRESHOLDS

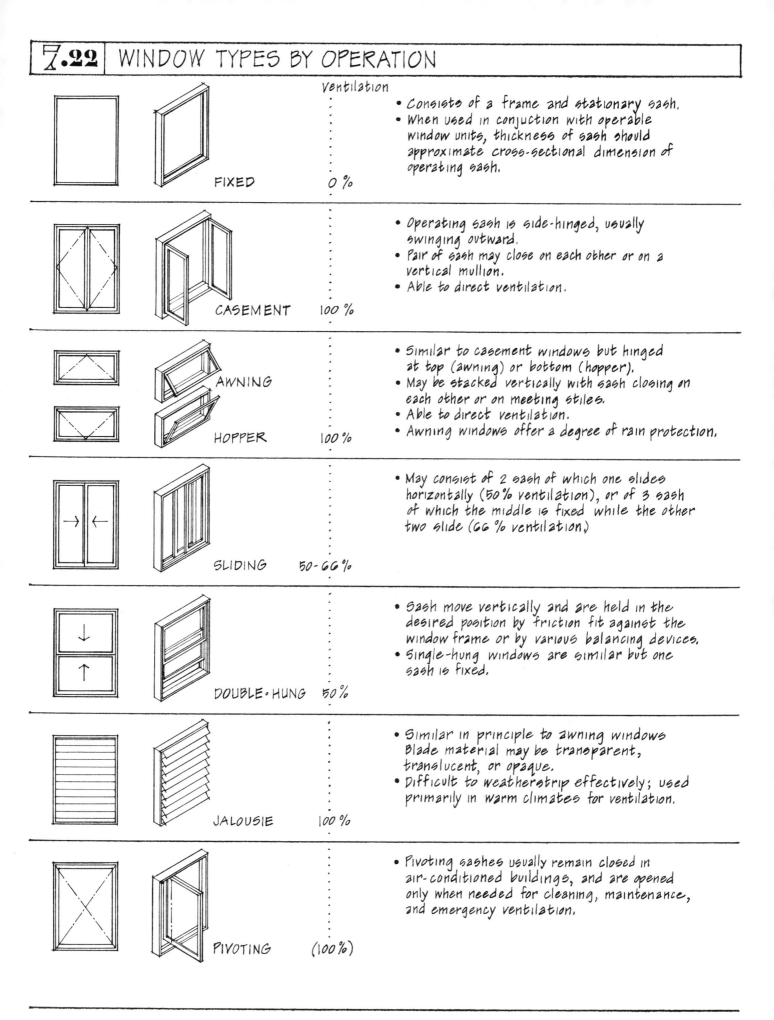

Ventilation

FIXED — 0 %

- Consists of a frame and stationary sash.
- When used in conjuction with operable window units, thickness of sash should approximate cross-sectional dimension of operating sash.

CASEMENT — 100 %

- Operating sash is side-hinged, usually swinging outward.
- Pair of sash may close on each other or on a vertical mullion.
- Able to direct ventilation.

AWNING

HOPPER — 100 %

- Similar to casement windows but hinged at top (awning) or bottom (hopper).
- May be stacked vertically with sash closing on each other or on meeting stiles.
- Able to direct ventilation.
- Awning windows offer a degree of rain protection.

SLIDING — 50-66 %

- May consist of 2 sash of which one slides horizontally (50% ventilation), or of 3 sash of which the middle is fixed while the other two slide (66 % ventilation.)

DOUBLE-HUNG — 50 %

- Sash move vertically and are held in the desired position by friction fit against the window frame or by various balancing devices.
- Single-hung windows are similar but one sash is fixed.

JALOUSIE — 100 %

- Similar in principle to awning windows. Blade material may be transparent, translucent, or opaque.
- Difficult to weatherstrip effectively; used primarily in warm climates for ventilation.

PIVOTING — (100%)

- Pivoting sashes usually remain closed in air-conditioned buildings, and are opened only when needed for cleaning, maintenance, and emergency ventilation.

WINDOW FRAMES

Wood window frames: See 7.24
- Kiln-dried, clear, straight grain
- Factory-treated with water-repellant preservative
- Primed for painting or clad with vinyl or aluminum

Metal window frames: See 7.26
- Aluminum in a variety of anodized finishes
- Steel may be galvanized and/or bonderized and primed.

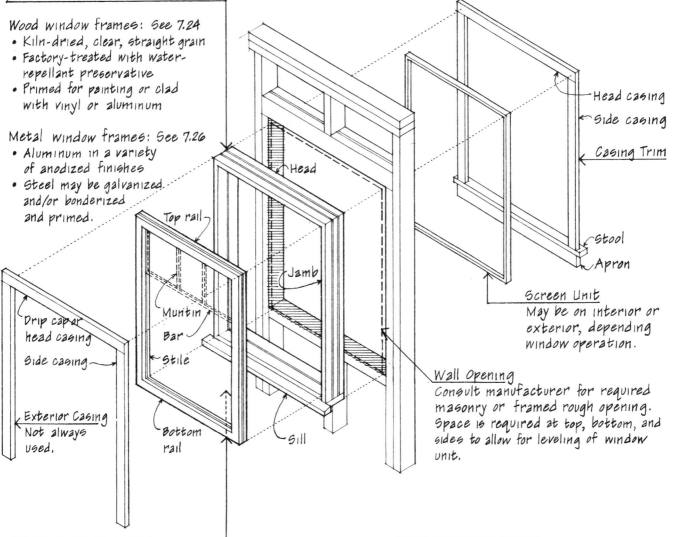

Head casing
Side casing
Casing Trim
Stool
Apron

Head
Jamb
Top rail
Muntin
Bar
Stile
Bottom rail
Sill

Drip cap or head casing
Side casing
Exterior Casing
Not always used.

Screen Unit
May be on interior or exterior, depending window operation.

Wall Opening
Consult manufacturer for required masonry or framed rough opening. Space is required at top, bottom, and sides to allow for leveling of window unit.

SASH AND GLAZING

The sash frames the glass and forms the operating part of a window unit. Its section profile varies with material, manufacturer, and type of operation.

Single glazing offers little resistance to heat flow. For a reasonable thermal resistance value (R), double glazing or a separate storm is required. Using glass with a reflective coating or triple glazing is an option if a higher R-value is required.

Just as important as a window's insulating value is its weathertightness. Operating sash should have continuous weatherstripping. The joint between the window frame and the surrounding wall should be sealed, and have a windbreak built into the detail.

CODE REQUIREMENTS

In selecting a window unit, review the building code requirements for:

- Natural light and ventilation of habitable spaces.
- Resistance to wind loads
- Thermal insulation value of the window assembly
- Clear opening of any window that serves as an emergency exit for a residential sleeping space.

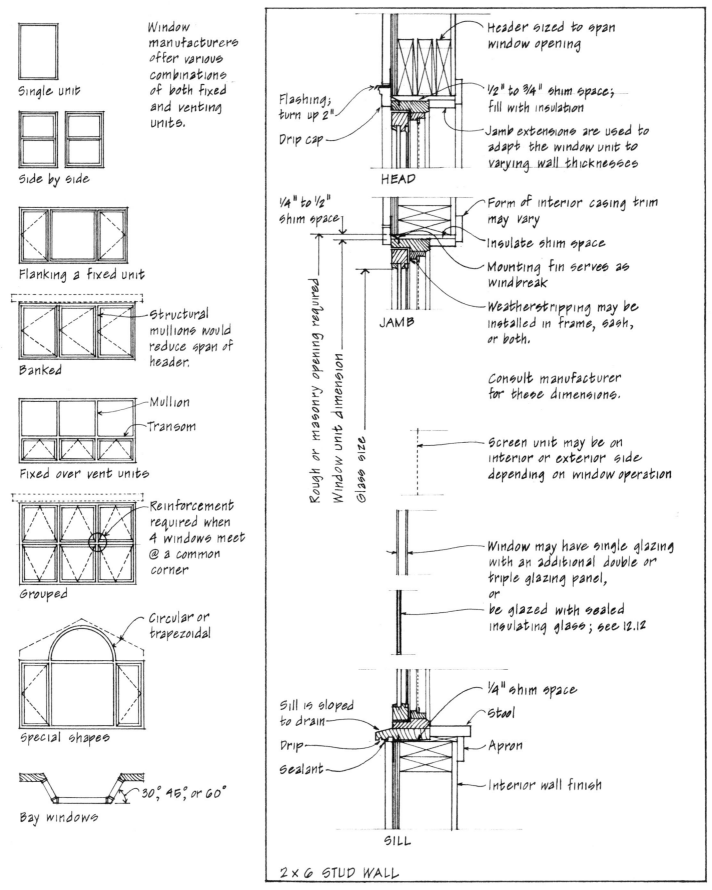

Single unit

Side by side

Flanking a fixed unit

Window manufacturers offer various combinations of both fixed and venting units.

Banked
Structural mullions would reduce span of header.

Fixed over vent units
Mullion
Transom

Grouped
Reinforcement required when 4 windows meet @ a common corner

Special shapes
Circular or trapezoidal

Bay windows
30°, 45°, or 60°

HEAD
Header sized to span window opening
Flashing; turn up 2"
Drip cap
½" to ¾" shim space; fill with insulation
Jamb extensions are used to adapt the window unit to varying wall thicknesses

JAMB
¼" to ½" shim space
Form of interior casing trim may vary
Insulate shim space
Mounting fin serves as windbreak
Weatherstripping may be installed in frame, sash, or both.

Rough or masonry opening required
Window unit dimension
Glass size

Consult manufacturer for these dimensions.

Screen unit may be on interior or exterior side depending on window operation

Window may have single glazing with an additional double or triple glazing panel,
or
be glazed with sealed insulating glass; see 12.12

SILL
Sill is sloped to drain
Drip
Sealant
¼" shim space
Stool
Apron
Interior wall finish

2 x 6 STUD WALL

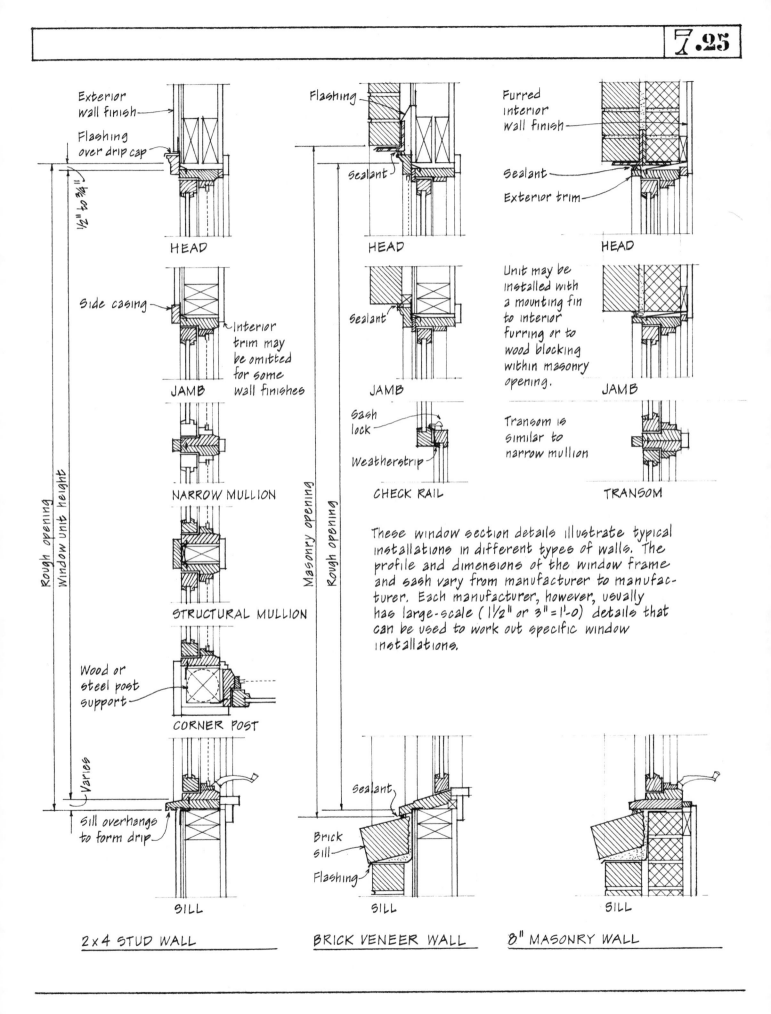

2 x 4 STUD WALL

Exterior wall finish

Flashing over drip cap

1/2" to 3/4"

HEAD

Side casing

Interior trim may be omitted for some wall finishes

JAMB

NARROW MULLION

STRUCTURAL MULLION

Wood or steel post support

CORNER POST

Rough opening

Window unit height

Varies

Sill overhangs to form drip

SILL

BRICK VENEER WALL

Flashing

Sealant

HEAD

Sealant

JAMB

Sash lock

Weatherstrip

CHECK RAIL

Masonry opening

Rough opening

Sealant

Brick sill

Flashing

SILL

8" MASONRY WALL

Furred interior wall finish

Sealant

Exterior trim

HEAD

Unit may be installed with a mounting fin to interior furring or to wood blocking within masonry opening.

JAMB

Transom is similar to narrow mullion

TRANSOM

These window section details illustrate typical installations in different types of walls. The profile and dimensions of the window frame and sash vary from manufacturer to manufacturer. Each manufacturer, however, usually has large-scale (1½" or 3" = 1'-0) details that can be used to work out specific window installations.

SILL

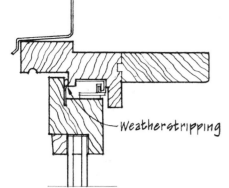

WOOD FRAMES

Wood is a fairly good thermal insulator. The size of the sash section depends on the type and thickness used.

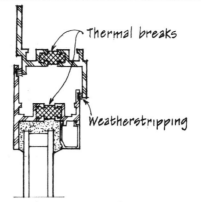

Thermal breaks

Weatherstripping

ALUMINUM FRAMES

Aluminum frames should have a plastic or synthetic rubber thermal break to interrupt the flow of heat from the warm to the cool side.

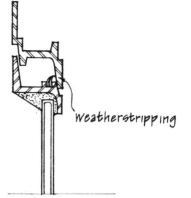

Weatherstripping

STEEL FRAMES

Steel frame and sash sections are more rigid than aluminum sections and are usually thinner in profile.

Rain drips are required for windows that are flush with the exterior wall and for transom bars or horizontal mullions.

Metal window frames usually have fins that serve as a windbreak for the joint between the window unit and the wall. The fins may also be used for attaching the frame to the supporting structure.

The head, jamb, and sill sections are usually similar in profile. Head and sill sections, however, may have integral rain drips.

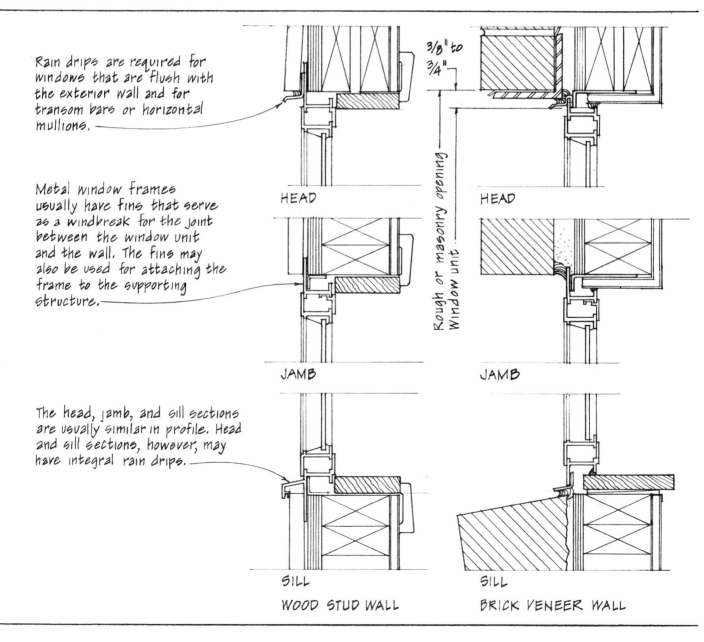

HEAD

JAMB

SILL

WOOD STUD WALL

3/8" to 3/4"

Rough or masonry opening

Window unit

HEAD

JAMB

SILL

BRICK VENEER WALL

Shown on this and the preceding page are generalized conditions for the installation of metal windows in different types of walls. Since the frame and sash sections vary greatly from one manufacturer to the next, refer to the manufacturer's literature for:

- Large-scale details of frame and sash
- Methods of attachment
- Rough or masonry openings required
- Alloy, weight, and thickness of sections
- Finishes available
- Glazing method and options
- Thermal performance of window assembly

Some manufacturers offer stock sizes while others only do custom work.

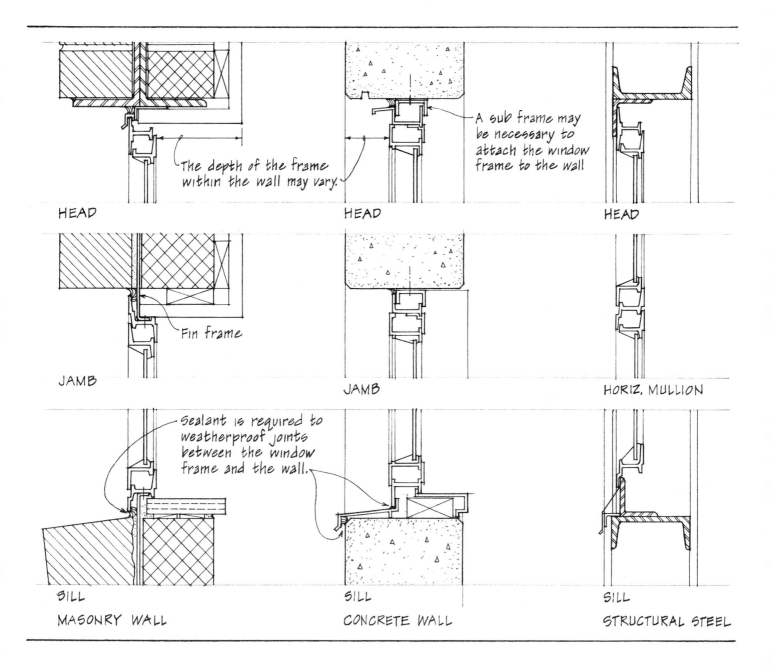

The depth of the frame within the wall may vary.

A sub frame may be necessary to attach the window frame to the wall

HEAD   HEAD   HEAD

Fin frame

JAMB   JAMB   HORIZ. MULLION

Sealant is required to weatherproof joints between the window frame and the wall.

SILL   SILL   SILL

MASONRY WALL   CONCRETE WALL   STRUCTURAL STEEL

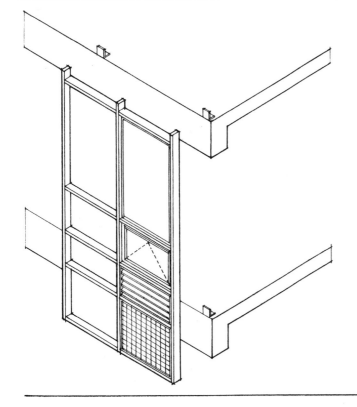

A curtain wall is a nonbearing exterior enclosure which is supported by a building's structural steel or concrete frame. The wall may consist of preassembled panels or a metal framework which can hold either glass or opaque units. See 7.30 for an outline of these curtain wall types and materials.

While simple in theory, curtain wall construction is complex and requires careful development, testing, and erection. Close coordination is also required between the architect, engineer, contractor, and a fabricator who is experienced in curtain wall construction.

For more detailed information, refer to the _Aluminum Curtain Wall Design Guide Manual_, published by the American Architectural Manufacturers Association, Des Plaines, Illinois.

For accessibility, top anchorages are best.

Angle cast into slab edge

Embedded unistrut channel

Malleable cast iron insert that accepts an askew head bolt for vertical adjustment

Steel deck

Slab edge angle

3-way adjustability is desirable for the connections to compensate for the tolerances permitted in the building frame.

Shim plates for leveling.

Angles with slotted holes for adjustment; they may be welded later if a fixed connection is required.

Some connections between the curtain wall and the building structure are fixed to resist loads applied from any direction. Others are movable and are designed to resist only lateral wind loads. These movable joints accommodate the differential movement between the wall and building frame. Differential movement can occur because of the building frame deflecting under loading or the curtain wall reacting to thermal stresses and changes in temperature.

ANCHORAGES

As with other exterior walls, a curtain wall must be able to withstand the following elements:

WATER . . . . Rain can collect on the wall surface and be wind-driven under pressure through the smallest openings. Water vapor that condenses and collects within the wall must be drained to the outside.

WIND . . . . Wind can create both positive and negative pressure on a wall, depending on its direction and the shape and height of the building. The wall must be able to transfer any wind loads to the building frame without deflecting too much. Wind-induced movement of the wall should be anticipated in the design of its joints and connections.

SUN . . . . Brightness and glare should be controlled with shading devices or the use of reflective or tinted glass. The sun's ultraviolet rays can also cause deterioration of joint and glazing materials and fading of interior furnishings.

TEMPERATURE . Daily and seasonal variations cause expansion and contraction of a wall's material, especially metals. Joints and sealants must be able to withstand the movement caused by thermal stresses. Heat flow should be controlled by insulating opaque panels, using insulating glass, and incorporating thermal breaks into metal frames.

LOADS . . . . Any deflection or deformation of the building frame under loading should not be transferred to the wall. Seismic forces require the use of energy-absorbing connections.

FIRE . . . . A firestopping material must be installed at each floor within column covers and between the wall and the floor edge. Building codes also specify the fire resistance requirements for the wall itself.

Pressure differential between inside and outside can cause water to leak through even the smallest openings in wall joints. Pressure-equalization design can significantly reduce this cause of water leakage. It requires three elements to be present:

① An exterior rain screen that deters water penetration.

② A confined air space that must be connected to the exterior so that its pressure is maintained equal to the outside pressure.

③ A continuous interior air and vapor barrier that seals the air space.

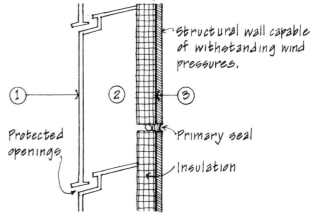

Structural wall capable of withstanding wind pressures.

Protected openings

Primary seal

Insulation

Air space should be segmented into relatively small areas with few openings, and be able to drain any water that enters to the outside.

DIAGRAM

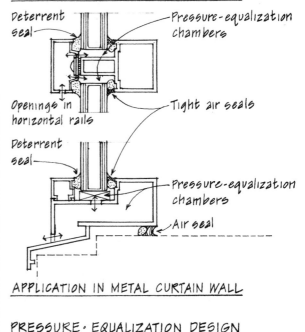

Deterrent seal

Pressure-equalization chambers

Openings in horizontal rails

Tight air seals

Deterrent seal

Pressure-equalization chambers

Air seal

APPLICATION IN METAL CURTAIN WALL

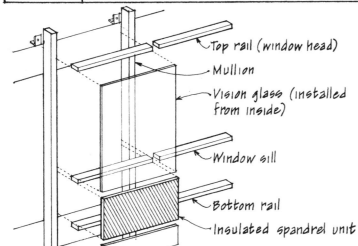

- Top rail (window head)
- Mullion
- Vision glass (installed from inside)
- Window sill
- Bottom rail
- Insulated spandrel unit

Curtain walls can first be categorized according to their method of assembly.

○ STICK SYSTEM

The stick system is assembled piece by piece. It offers relatively low shipping and handling costs and can be adjusted more readily than the other systems to on-site conditions.

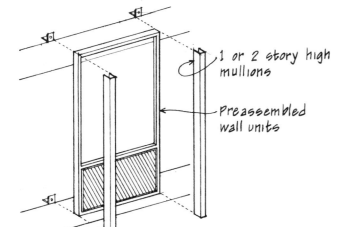

- 1 or 2 story high mullions
- Preassembled wall units

○ UNIT AND MULLION SYSTEM

In this system, mullions are installed first. Pre-assembled panel units are then lowered into place behind the mullions. The panel units may be full-story height, pre-glazed or unglazed, or may be separate vision glass and spandrel units. Shipping bulk is greater than with the stick system, but less field labor and erection time is required.

○ PANEL SYSTEM

Panel systems consist entirely of large wall units, which may be either pre-assembled framed units or homogeneous panels. The wall units may be one, two, or three stories in height, and may be preglazed or glazed after installation. Panel systems offer controlled shop assembly and rapid erection, but are bulky to ship and handle.

Wall panels:

Preassembled frame unit

Brick- 5.28
Stone- 5.36
Precast concrete- 5.48

Curtain systems can also be classified according to whether they are:

- Custom-designed specifically for a project.
- Assembled with parts and details which are standardized by the manufacturer.
- Composed of preformed sheet metal panels, typically for industrial-type buildings.

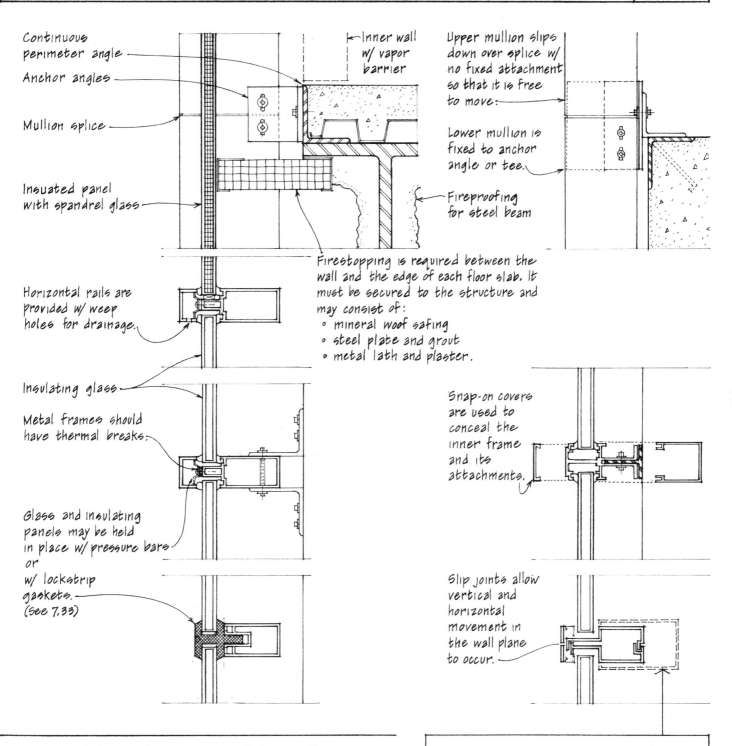

Continuous perimeter angle

Anchor angles

Mullion splice

Insulated panel with spandrel glass

Inner wall w/ vapor barrier

Upper mullion slips down over splice w/ no fixed attachment so that it is free to move.

Lower mullion is fixed to anchor angle or tee.

Fireproofing for steel beam

Firestopping is required between the wall and the edge of each floor slab. It must be secured to the structure and may consist of:
- mineral wool safing
- steel plate and grout
- metal lath and plaster.

Horizontal rails are provided w/ weep holes for drainage.

Insulating glass

Metal frames should have thermal breaks.

Snap-on covers are used to conceal the inner frame and its attachments.

Glass and insulating panels may be held in place w/ pressure bars or w/ lockstrip gaskets. (see 7.33)

Slip joints allow vertical and horizontal movement in the wall plane to occur.

These metal and glass curtain wall details illustrate typical conditions only. When using standard fabricated wall systems, there is no need for extensive detailing except when components are modified. Things to note include:
- Overall wall pattern
- Type of glazing
- Type, size, and location of any operable windows
- Type and finish of infill panels
- Perimeter, corner, and anchorage conditions.

The required size, strength, and stiffness of the frame are determined by the loads the frame must carry — primarily lateral wind loads and relatively light vertical loads. Consult the manufacturer for the structural capacity of the wall's glazing and framing.

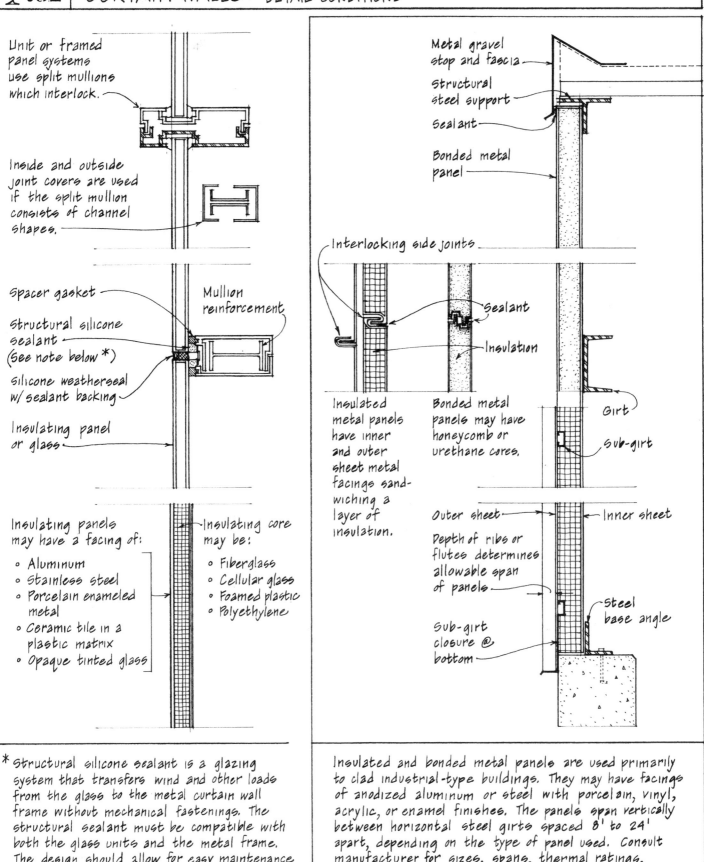

Unit or framed panel systems use split mullions which interlock.

Inside and outside joint covers are used if the split mullion consists of channel shapes.

Spacer gasket

Structural silicone sealant (See note below *)

silicone weatherseal w/ sealant backing

Insulating panel or glass

Mullion reinforcement

Insulating panels may have a facing of:

- Aluminum
- Stainless steel
- Porcelain enameled metal
- Ceramic tile in a plastic matrix
- Opaque tinted glass

Insulating core may be:

- Fiberglass
- Cellular glass
- Foamed plastic
- Polyethylene

Metal gravel stop and fascia

Structural steel support

Sealant

Bonded metal panel

Interlocking side joints

Sealant

Insulation

Insulated metal panels have inner and outer sheet metal facings sandwiching a layer of insulation.

Bonded metal panels may have honeycomb or urethane cores.

Girt

Sub-girt

Outer sheet

Inner sheet

Depth of ribs or flutes determines allowable span of panels

Steel base angle

Sub-girt closure @ bottom

* Structural silicone sealant is a glazing system that transfers wind and other loads from the glass to the metal curtain wall frame without mechanical fastenings. The structural sealant must be compatible with both the glass units and the metal frame. The design should allow for easy maintenance and replacement of broken glass units. Factory-glazing is preferred for better quality control. Consult manufacturer for details.

Insulated and bonded metal panels are used primarily to clad industrial-type buildings. They may have facings of anodized aluminum or steel with porcelain, vinyl, acrylic, or enamel finishes. The panels span vertically between horizontal steel girts spaced 8' to 24' apart, depending on the type of panel used. Consult manufacturer for sizes, spans, thermal ratings, and installation details.

The glazing system should allow the glass unit to float in its opening and be cushioned with a resilient glazing material.
There should be no direct contact between the glass and the perimeter frame.
The perimeter frame itself must support the glass against wind pressure or suction, and be strong enough that structural movements and thermal stresses are not transferred to the glass.

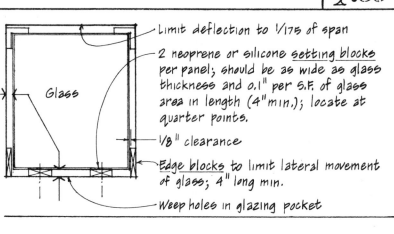

- Limit deflection to 1/175 of span
- 2 neoprene or silicone setting blocks per panel; should be as wide as glass thickness and 0.1" per S.F. of glass area in length (4" min.); locate at quarter points.
- 1/8" clearance
- Edge blocks to limit lateral movement of glass; 4" long min.
- Weep holes in glazing pocket

GLAZING MATERIALS

Small lights may be glazed using glazier's points and a glazing compound, or for wood frames, a wood stop. Large lights (more than 6 S.F. in area) may be glazed with:

① Preformed butyl or polyisobutylene tape
② Compression gaskets of neoprene or silicone
③ Liquid high-range sealant of silicone or polyurethane

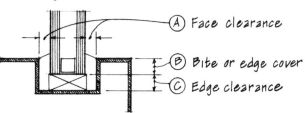

Ⓐ Face clearance
Ⓑ Bite or edge cover
Ⓒ Edge clearance

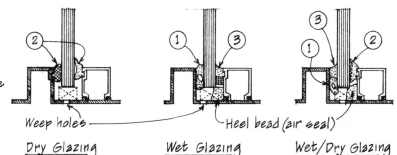

Weep holes

Heel bead (air seal)

Dry Glazing   Wet Glazing   Wet/Dry Glazing

BITE, EDGE, AND FACE CLEARANCES

Glass Type		Ⓐ	Ⓑ	Ⓒ
Sheet glass	SS	1/16"	1/4"	1/8"
	DS	1/8"	1/4"	1/8"
Plate glass	1/4"	1/8"	3/8"	1/4"
	3/8"	3/16"	7/16"	5/16"
	1/2"	1/4"	7/16"	3/8"
Insulating glass	1/2"	1/8"	1/2"	1/8"
	5/8"	1/8"	1/2"	1/8"
	3/4"	3/16"	1/2"	1/4"
	1"	3/16"	1/2"	1/4"

Heat-strengthened and tempered glass may require additional face clearance.

LOCKSTRIP GASKETS

Structural gaskets are preformed of neoprene or other elastomeric material. They require smooth contact surfaces and a frame or opening with exacting dimensional tolerances and true plane alignment. The glass must be supported on at least two sides by the frame or a supported gasket.

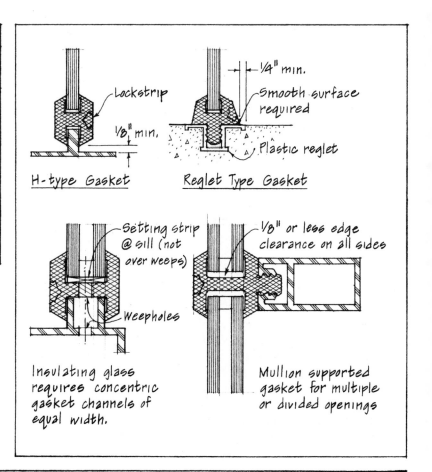

Lockstrip

1/8" min.

1/4" min.

Smooth surface required

Plastic reglet

H-type Gasket   Reglet Type Gasket

Setting strip @ sill (not over weeps)

Weepholes

1/8" or less edge clearance on all sides

Insulating glass requires concentric gasket channels of equal width.

Mullion supported gasket for multiple or divided openings

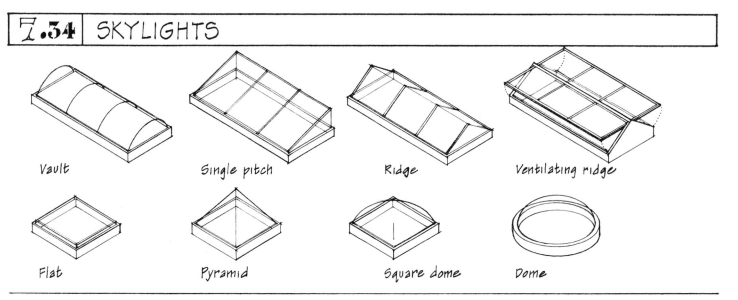

Vault   Single pitch   Ridge   Ventilating ridge

Flat   Pyramid   Square dome   Dome

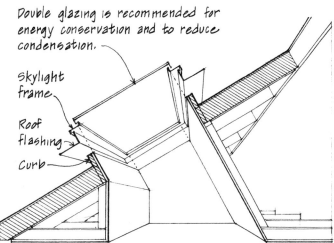

Double glazing is recommended for energy conservation and to reduce condensation.

Skylight frame

Roof flashing

Curb

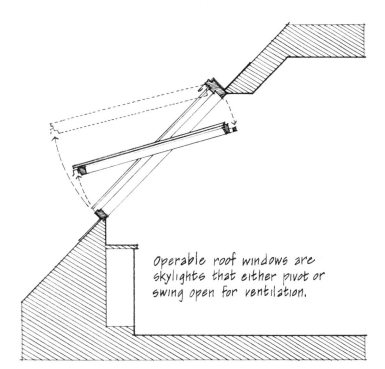

Operable roof windows are skylights that either pivot or swing open for ventilation.

Skylights provide daylight for interior spaces from above. This daylighting can be in place of or in addition to normal daylighting from windows. Careful consideration should be paid to the control of brightness and glare, which may require the use of louvers, shades, or reflector panels. Horizontal and south-facing skylights also increase solar heat gain in the winter, but in the summer, shading may again be required to prevent excessive heat gain.

Skylights require a framed roof opening with a curb at least 4" high. This curb may be job-built or be an integral part of the skylight unit. The skylight unit itself must be able to carry the normal roof loads.

Skylights are available as preassembled units, complete with a wood or metal frame, glazing, and flashing, in stock sizes and shapes. (See illustration above.)

The glazing may be of plastic (acrylic or polycarbonate) or of glass. Building codes usually require the use of wire, laminated, or tempered glass, and limit the spacing of their supports to:

∘ Flat wired glass - 25"
∘ Corrugated wire glass - 60"
∘ Laminated glass - 48"
∘ Tempered glass - 72"

The minimum slope for flat or corrugated plastic skylights is 4:12. Plastic domes should rise at least 10% of the span or at least 5".

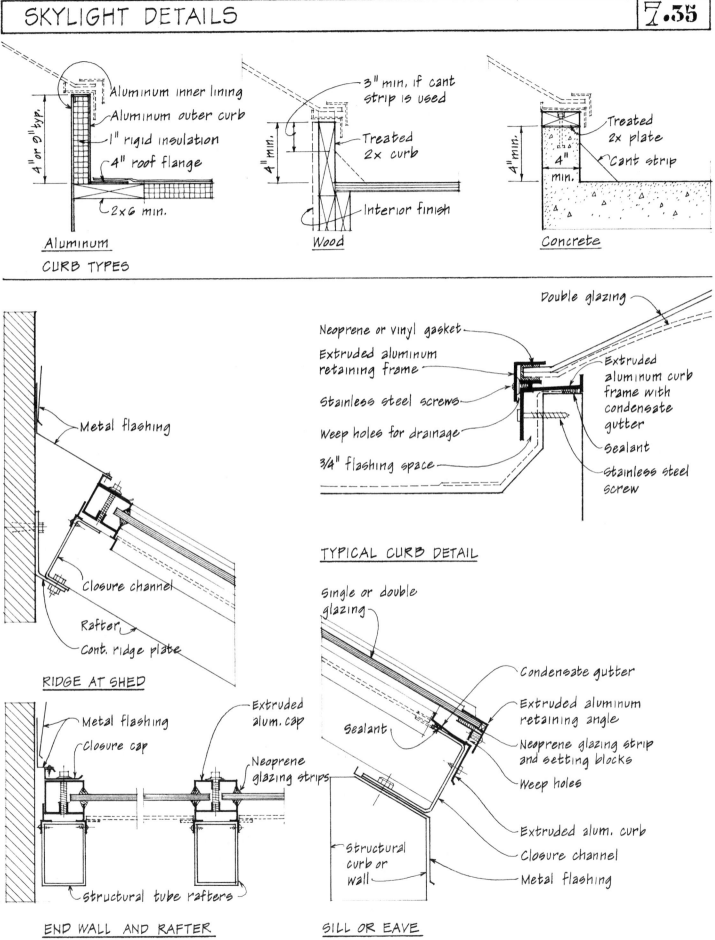

CURB TYPES

Aluminum
- Aluminum inner lining
- Aluminum outer curb
- 1" rigid insulation
- 4" roof flange
- 4" or 9" typ.
- 2x6 min.

Wood
- 3" min. if cant strip is used
- 4" min.
- Treated 2x curb
- Interior finish

Concrete
- Treated 2x plate
- Cant strip
- 4" min.
- 4" min.

RIDGE AT SHED
- Metal flashing
- Closure channel
- Rafter
- Cont. ridge plate

TYPICAL CURB DETAIL
- Double glazing
- Neoprene or vinyl gasket
- Extruded aluminum retaining frame
- Stainless steel screws
- Weep holes for drainage
- 3/4" flashing space
- Extruded aluminum curb frame with condensate gutter
- Sealant
- Stainless steel screw

END WALL AND RAFTER
- Metal flashing
- Closure cap
- Extruded alum. cap
- Neoprene glazing strips
- Structural tube rafters

SILL OR EAVE
- Single or double glazing
- Sealant
- Condensate gutter
- Extruded aluminum retaining angle
- Neoprene glazing strip and setting blocks
- Weep holes
- Structural curb or wall
- Extruded alum. curb
- Closure channel
- Metal flashing

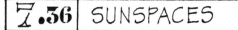

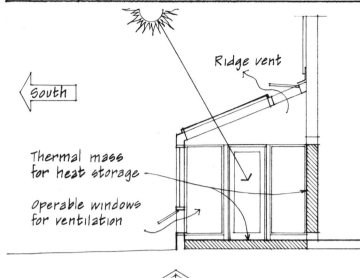

Ridge vent

South

Thermal mass for heat storage

Operable windows for ventilation

A sunspace can be a solarium adjoining another living space or be an attached greenhouse. It is often used in passive solar design in conjunction with a thermal mass of masonry, rock, or concrete to store the solar heat gain. Because of the possibility of overheating, provision should be made for shading and ventilation with operable windows and, if necessary, an exhaust fan.

Sunspaces and greenhouses are available as manufactured systems with wood or metal frames, complete with glazing, flashing, and accessories such as shades, blinds, and exhaust fans. A sunspace can also be constructed with standard window, door, and skylight units supported by a stud and rafter or a post and beam structural frame.

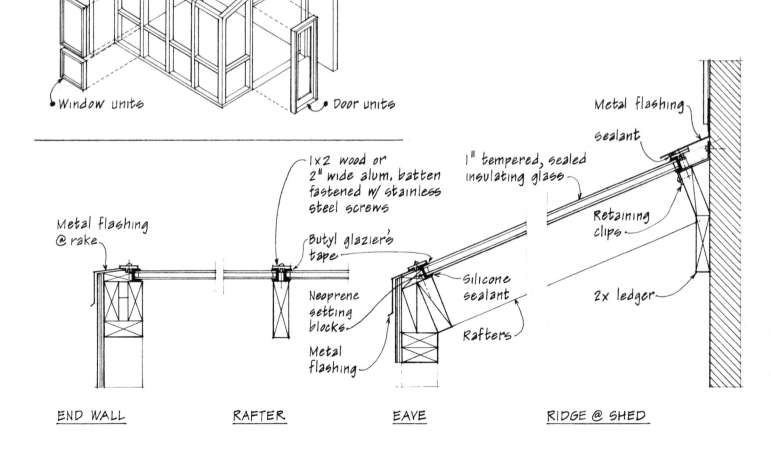

• Skylight units

Structural Frame

• Window units

• Door units

Metal flashing @ rake

1×2 wood or 2" wide alum. batten fastened w/ stainless steel screws

Butyl glazier's tape

Neoprene setting blocks

Metal flashing

1" tempered, sealed insulating glass

Metal flashing

sealant

Retaining clips

2x ledger

Silicone sealant

Rafters

END WALL   RAFTER   EAVE   RIDGE @ SHED

MOISTURE & THERMAL PROTECTION

Roofing materials provide the water-resistant covering for a roof system. They range in form from virtually continuous, impervious membranes to fabrics of overlapping or interlocking pieces of material. The type of finish roofing that may be used depends on the form of the roof structure, the roof pitch, and the appearance desired. While a sloping roof easily sheds water, a flat roof must depend on a continuous water-proof membrane to contain the water while it drains or evaporates. A flat roof (and any well-insulated sloped roof capable of retaining snow) should therefore be designed to support a greater live load than a moderately or high-pitched roof. Additional factors to consider in the selection of a roofing material include installation and maintenance requirements, durability, degree of wind and fire resistance required, and the roofing's color, texture, and pattern.

Flashing is required along roof edges, where roofs change slope or abut vertical planes, and where roofs are penetrated by chimneys, vent pipes, and skylights. Flashing materials must be installed to prevent leakage of water into the roof construction and eventually the interior of a building. Exterior walls must also be flashed where leakage might occur— at door and window openings and along joints where materials meet in the wall plane.

A waterproof membrane, fabric, or coating must be applied to those floors and walls below grade where water may be present in sufficient quantity or under sufficient pressure to cause leakage into a building's interior.

Moisture is normally present in a building's interior in the form of water vapor. When this water vapor reaches a surface cooled by heat loss to the cold outside air, condensation may occur. This condensation may be visible, as on an uninsulated window pane, or it can collect in concealed roof, wall, or floor spaces. Means of combating condensation include the correct place-ment of insulation and vapor barriers, and the ventilation of concealed spaces such as attics and crawl spaces.

Building materials expand and contract due to variations within the normal temperature range, as well as exposure to solar radiation and wind. To allow for this movement and help relieve the stresses caused by a material's expansion and contraction, expansion joints should be flexible, weathertight, durable, and correctly placed to be effective.

Potential heat loss or gain through a building's exterior enclosure is an important factor when estimating the amount of mechanical equipment and energy required to maintain the desired level of environmental comfort in a building's interior. The proper selection of building materials, the correct construction and insulation of a building's enclosure, and the orientation of a building on its site are the basic means of controlling heat loss and gain.

CONVENTIONAL FLAT ROOFING SYSTEM

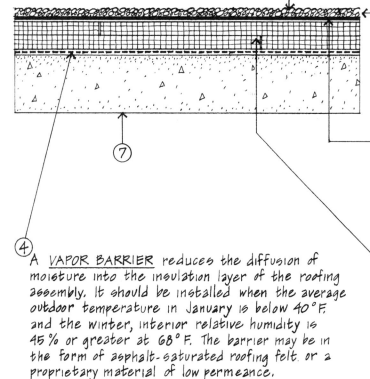

(1) The WEAR COURSE protects the roofing from mechanical abrasion. It may be provided by built-up roofing aggregate, ballast aggregate, or plaza deck pavers.

(2) The DRAINAGE LAYER permits the free flow of water to the roof drains. It may consist of the aggregate layer in a built-up roofing system, the ballast layer in a loose-laid single-ply roofing system, the surface of a fully adhered single-ply roof, or the drainage fabric or space under the pavers in a plaza deck system.

(3) The ROOFING MEMBRANE is the waterproofing layer of the roof. It should be sloped 1/4" per foot to transport stormwater to the roof drains. Two major membrane systems are:

- Built-up roofing systems
- Single-ply roofing systems

(4) A VAPOR BARRIER reduces the diffusion of moisture into the insulation layer of the roofing assembly. It should be installed when the average outdoor temperature in January is below 40° F. and the winter, interior relative humidity is 45 % or greater at 68° F. The barrier may be in the form of asphalt-saturated roofing felt or a proprietary material of low permeance.

When a vapor barrier is present, the insulation layer may have to be vented to allow vapor pressure to escape from between the vapor barrier and the roofing membrane.

(5) THERMAL INSULATION provides the required resistance to heat flow through the roof assembly. It is usually installed under the roofing membrane in the form of a lightweight concrete fill or rigid insulation panels. Rigid insulation should be installed in at least two staggered layers to minimize heat loss through the joints. The first layer should be mechanically fastened to resist wind uplift; the upper layers are fully adhered with hot steep asphalt. When rigid plastic foam insulation (polyurethane, polystyrene, or polyisocyanurate) is used, the top layer should be perlite or gypsum board to provide a stable underlayment for the roofing membrane and to comply with code requirements.

Thermal insulation can, in some cases, be placed under the roof deck or over the roofing membrane. See drawing to the left. In this inverted system, the insulation layer protects the roofing membrane from sunlight and temperature extremes, but not from almost continual dampness. Moisture-resistant polystyrene is required for the insulating layer.

PROTECTED MEMBRANE SYSTEM

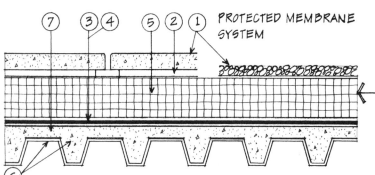

(6) An AIR BARRIER can help prevent moist indoor air from penetrating the roof assembly. It must be airtight and rigid enough to withstand wind pressure as well as pressure from below.

Both vapor and air barriers should be continuous, sealed at all roof penetrations, and tied into the wall assembly around the perimeter of the roof.

(7) The ROOF DECK must be stiff enough to maintain the desired slope under expected loading conditions, and be smooth, clean, and dry enough for the rigid insulation or roofing membrane to adhere properly. See table on next page for roof deck types. Large roof areas may require expansion joints or area dividers. For these and other FLASHING DETAILS, see 8.15.

Roof deck
(See table below)

Vapor barrier
(if required)

Thermal insulation
in at least two
staggered layers

Base sheet
of glass fiber (2" lap)
organic base felt (4" lap)

Plysheets
of fiberglass, asphalt saturated
felt, or coal tar saturated felt
placed with hot steep asphalt
or coal tar bitumen.

Wear course of
gravel, slag, or white
marble chips aids in
stiffening membrane and
resisting wind blowoff.

Surfacing bitumen
of coal tar or
asphalt

1/4 : 12

Min. recommended slope

3:12

Max. slope for aggregate surfaces

6 to 9:12

Max. slope for smooth surface roofs

For slopes over 1:12,
lay plies parallel to
slope and back nail
to prevent slippage;
provide non-nailable
decks with treated
wood nailers for back
nailing.

Felt overlap for 2 ply roofing: 19"
3 ply roofing: 24 2/3"
4 ply roofing: 27 1/2"

TYPES OF ROOF DECKS OR SUBSTRATES	Consult roofing manufacturer for: ○ Approved types of deck, insulation, and fastenings ○ Installation details, and vapor barrier/venting requirements ○ Underwriters' Laboratories (UL) Fire-Hazard Classification of the roofing assembly.
Steel Deck	22 gauge min.; code may require overlayment of perlite or gypsum bd.
Wood	Min. 1" nominal thickness; of well-seasoned lumber; tongue and grooved or splined; cover knotholes and large cracks with sheet metal.
Plywood	Min. 1/2" thick; face plies perpendicular to supports spaced no more than 24" o.c.; tongue and groove joints or blocking under joints.
Structural Wood-Fiber Deck	Must be dense enough to hold mechanical fasteners.
Poured Concrete	Should be well-cured, dry, frost-free, smooth, and sloped to drain.
Precast Concrete	All joints should be grouted; any unevenness between units must be leveled with a vented topping or fill.
Lightweight Insulating Concrete . . .	Must be fully cured and air dried; consult manufacturer for acceptability.

Single-ply roofing may be applied in sheet or liquid form. Sheet materials used for single-ply roofing include:

- EPDM (ethylene propylene diene monomer), an elastomeric material.
- PVC (polyvinyl chloride), a thermoplastic material.
- CSPE (chlorosulfonated polyethylene), a synthetic rubber.
- Neoprene (polychloroprene), a synthetic rubber
- Polymer-modified bitumens, a composite material.

These materials are thin (0.03 to 0.10 inches in thickness), flexible, and strong. They vary in their resistance to flame propagation, oils, chemicals, ultraviolet rays, pollutants, and abrasion. Some are reinforced with glass fiber or polyester; others have coatings for greater heat-reflectance or resistance to flame spread. Consult the roofing manufacturer for:

- Material specifications
- Approved types of roof deck, insulation, and fastenings
- Installation and flashing details
- Underwriters' Laboratories (UL) Fire-Hazard Classification of the roof assembly.

The details on this and the following page refer to EPDM roofing. Details for other single-ply membranes are similar in principle.

There are three generic systems for the application of EPDM roofing:

1. Fully adhered system
2. Mechanically fastened system
3. Loose laid, ballasted system

On large domed, vaulted, or complex roof forms, the roofing membrane may be rolled or sprayed on in liquid form. Materials used for liquid-applied membranes include silicone, neoprene, butyl rubber, and polyurethane. Consult manufacturer for details.

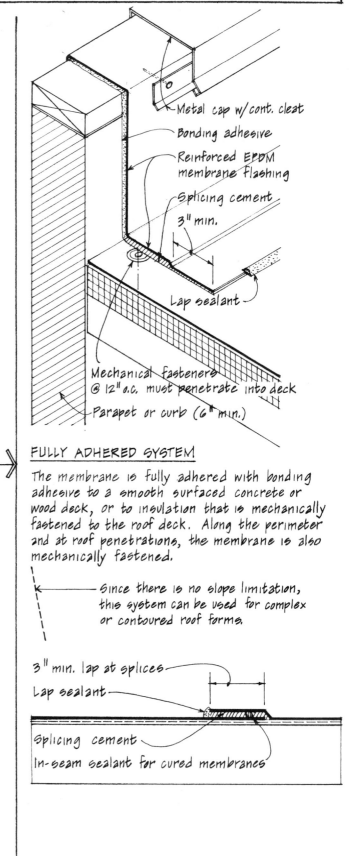

Metal cap w/cont. cleat
Bonding adhesive
Reinforced EPDM membrane flashing
Splicing cement
3" min.
Lap sealant
Mechanical fasteners @ 12" o.c. must penetrate into deck
Parapet or curb (6" min.)

FULLY ADHERED SYSTEM

The membrane is fully adhered with bonding adhesive to a smooth surfaced concrete or wood deck, or to insulation that is mechanically fastened to the roof deck. Along the perimeter and at roof penetrations, the membrane is also mechanically fastened.

— Since there is no slope limitation, this system can be used for complex or contoured roof forms.

3" min. lap at splices
Lap sealant
Splicing cement
In-seam sealant for cured membranes

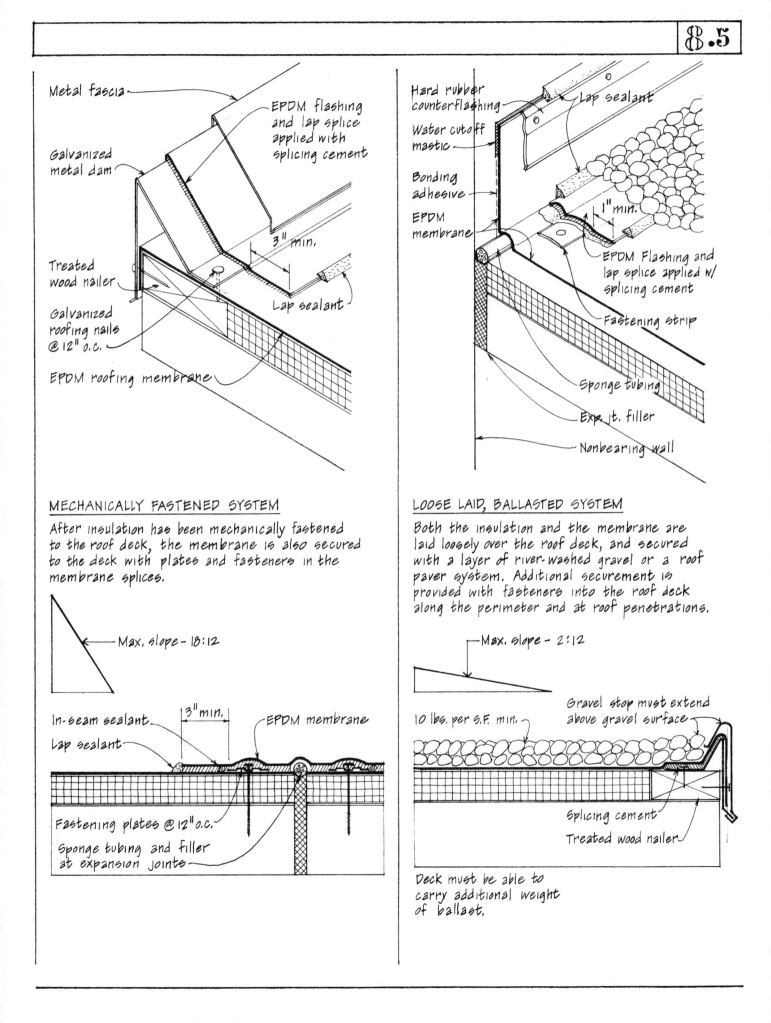

MECHANICALLY FASTENED SYSTEM

After insulation has been mechanically fastened to the roof deck, the membrane is also secured to the deck with plates and fasteners in the membrane splices.

Max. slope - 18:12

In-seam sealant
Lap sealant
EPDM membrane
3" min.

Fastening plates @ 12" o.c.
Sponge tubing and filler at expansion joints

LOOSE LAID, BALLASTED SYSTEM

Both the insulation and the membrane are laid loosely over the roof deck, and secured with a layer of river-washed gravel or a roof paver system. Additional securement is provided with fasteners into the roof deck along the perimeter and at roof penetrations.

Max. slope - 2:12

10 lbs. per S.F. min.
Gravel stop must extend above gravel surface
Splicing cement
Treated wood nailer

Deck must be able to carry additional weight of ballast.

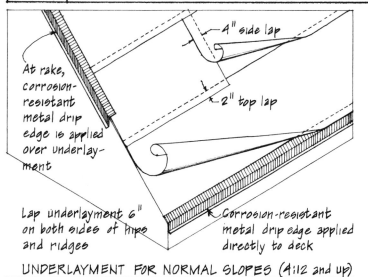

At rake, corrosion-resistant metal drip edge is applied over underlayment

4" side lap

2" top lap

Lap underlayment 6" on both sides of hips and ridges

Corrosion-resistant metal drip edge applied directly to deck

UNDERLAYMENT FOR NORMAL SLOPES (4:12 and up)

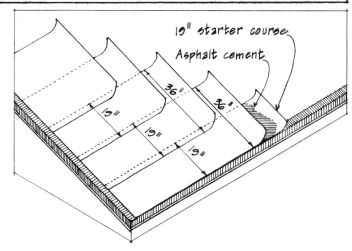

19" starter course

Asphalt cement

36"

19"

UNDERLAYMENT FOR LOW SLOPE ROOFS (3:12-4:12)

Underlayment protects the roof sheathing from moisture absorption until the shingles are applied. Once the roofing is applied, the underlayment provides the sheathing with additional protection from wind-driven rain. The underlayment material should have low vapor resistance so that moisture does not accumulate between the underlayment and the roof sheathing. Only enough nails are used to hold the underlayment in place until the roofing shingles are applied.

Drip edges of corrosion-resistant metal protect the roof edge and allow water to drip free of the roof edge. They may be omitted on wood shingle and shake roofs since the shingles themselves form drips by projecting beyond the roof edge.

EAVE FLASHING is recommended whenever there is a possibility that ice might form along the eave and cause water to back up under the roofing shingles.

On normal slope roofs, eave flashing consists of 50 lb. smooth roll roofing extending up the roof to a point 24" inside the interior wall line.

On low slope roofs, an additional course of underlayment is cemented in place, and extended to a point 36" inside the interior wall line.

Eave Flashing

24"

(36" for low slope roofs)

UNDERLAYMENT AND SHEATHING FOR SHINGLE ROOFS						
Roofing Type	Sheathing	Underlayment	Normal Slope		Low Slope	
Fiberglass shingles	Solid	15 lb. asphalt saturated felt	4:12 and up	Single layer	3:12 to 4:12	Double layer
Asphalt shingles	Solid	15 lb. asphalt saturated felt	4:12 and up	Single layer	2:12 to 4:12	Double layer
Wood shakes	Spaced	30 lb. asphalt saturated felt (interlayment)	4:12 and up	Underlayment starter course; interlayment over entire roof	Not recommended	
	Solid	30 lb. asphalt saturated felt (interlayment)	4:12 and up	Underlayment starter course; interlayment over entire roof	3:12 to 4:12	Single layer underlayment and interlayment over entire roof
Wood shingles	Spaced	Not required	5:12 and up	Not required	3:12 to 5:12	Reduce weather exposure
	Solid (to minimize air infiltration)	15 lb. asphalt saturated felt	5:12 and up	Not required but may be desirable to protect sheathing	3:12 to 5:12	Not required but may be desirable to protect sheathing

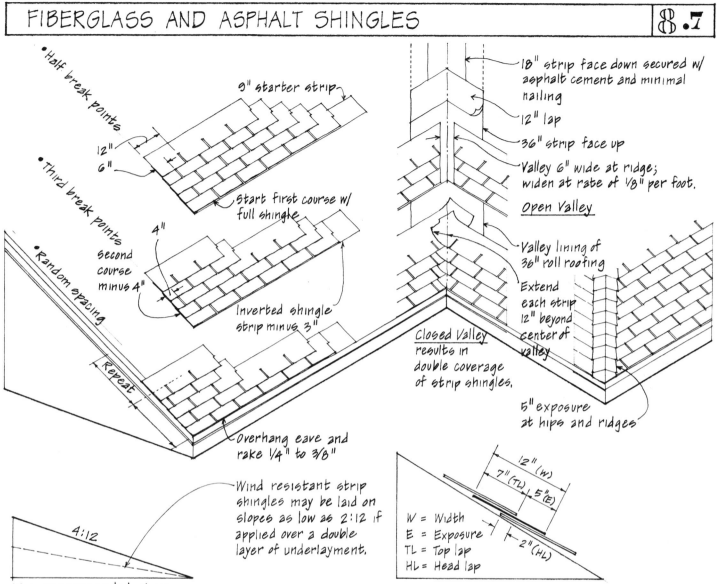

- Half break points

9" starter strip

12"

6"

Start first course w/ full shingle

4"

Third break points

second course minus 4"

Inverted shingle strip minus 3"

- Random spacing

Repeat

Overhang eave and rake 1/4" to 3/8"

18" strip face down secured w/ asphalt cement and minimal nailing

12" lap

36" strip face up

Valley 6" wide at ridge; widen at rate of 1/8" per foot.

Open Valley

Valley lining of 36" roll roofing

Extend each strip 12" beyond center of valley

Closed Valley results in double coverage of strip shingles.

5" exposure at hips and ridges

Wind resistant strip shingles may be laid on slopes as low as 2:12 if applied over a double layer of underlayment.

12" (W)
7" (TL)
5" (E)
2" (HL)

W = Width
E = Exposure
TL = Top lap
HL = Head lap

4:12

Min. recommended slope

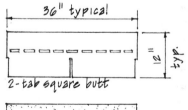

36" typical

12" typ.

2-tab square butt

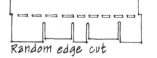

3-tab square butt

Random edge cut

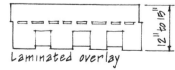

12" to 15"

Laminated overlay

Fiberglass and asphalt shingles are similar in size, appearance, and application. Fiberglass shingles have an inorganic base that gives them excellent fire resistance (UL Class A). Asphalt shingles, having an organic felt base, possess only a moderate resistance to fire (UL Class C).

Most shingles have self-sealing adhesive or locking tabs that make them wind resistant. Wind resistance is important when shingles are used on low slope roofs and in areas subject to high winds.

Shingles vary in weight from 205 to 380 lbs. per square. (One square = 100 S.F.)

Consult the roofing manufacturer for sizes, patterns, colors, and installation details.

Spaced 1x4 or 1x6 sheathing provides ventilation for the shingles. Board spacing is equal to the shingle exposure. See table below. Solid sheathing sheathing may be desirable in areas subject to blizzard conditions.

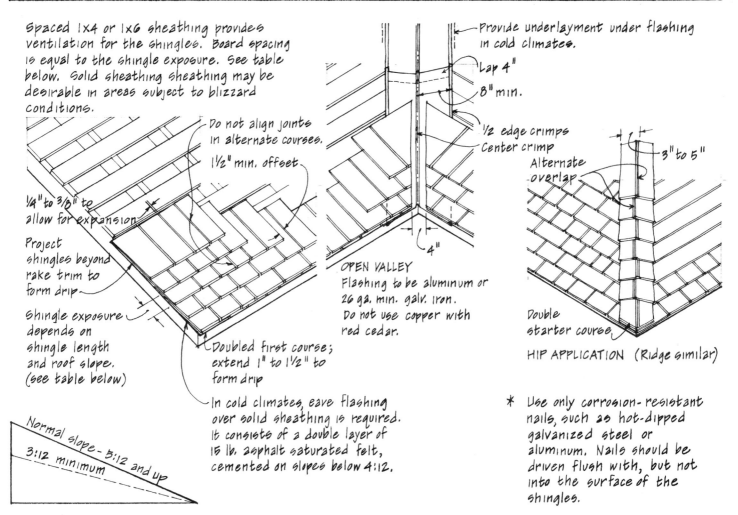

Do not align joints in alternate courses.

1½" min. offset

¼" to ⅜" to allow for expansion

Project shingles beyond rake trim to form drip

Shingle exposure depends on shingle length and roof slope. (see table below)

Doubled first course; extend 1" to 1½" to form drip

In cold climates, eave flashing over solid sheathing is required. It consists of a double layer of 15 lb. asphalt saturated felt, cemented on slopes below 4:12.

Provide underlayment under flashing in cold climates.

Lap 4"

8" min.

½ edge crimps
Center crimp

4"

OPEN VALLEY
Flashing to be aluminum or 26 ga. min. galv. iron. Do not use copper with red cedar.

3" to 5"

Alternate overlap

Double starter course

HIP APPLICATION (Ridge similar)

* Use only corrosion-resistant nails, such as hot-dipped galvanized steel or aluminum. Nails should be driven flush with, but not into the surface of the shingles.

Normal slope - 5:12 and up
3:12 minimum

MAXIMUM RECOMMENDED EXPOSURE

Shingle grade and length		Roof slope:	
		4:12 and up	3:12 to 4:12
Nº 1	16"	5"	3¾"
	18"	5½"	4¼"
	24"	7½"	5¾"
Nº 2	16"	4"	3½"
	18"	4½"	4"
	24"	6½"	5½"
Nº 3	16"	3½"	3"
	18"	4"	3½"
	24"	5½"	5"
Wood Shakes	18"	7½"	Not recommended
	24"	10"	

For wall siding applications of wood shingles and shakes, see 10.25.

Wood shingles and shakes are normally of red cedar, although white cedar and redwood shingles may be available. Red cedar has a fine, even grain and is naturally resistant to water, rot, and sunlight.

Red cedar shingles are available in 16", 18", and 24" lengths, and in the following grades:

Nº 1 Premium Grade.... 100% heartwood, 100% clear
(Blue Label)   100% edge grain

Nº 2 Intermediate Grade.. 10" clear on 16" shingles
(Red Label)   11" clear on 18" shingles
                                          16" clear on 24" shingles
                                          Some flat grain permitted

Nº 3 Utility Grade....... 6" clear on 16" and 18" shingles
(Black Label)   10" clear on 24" shingles

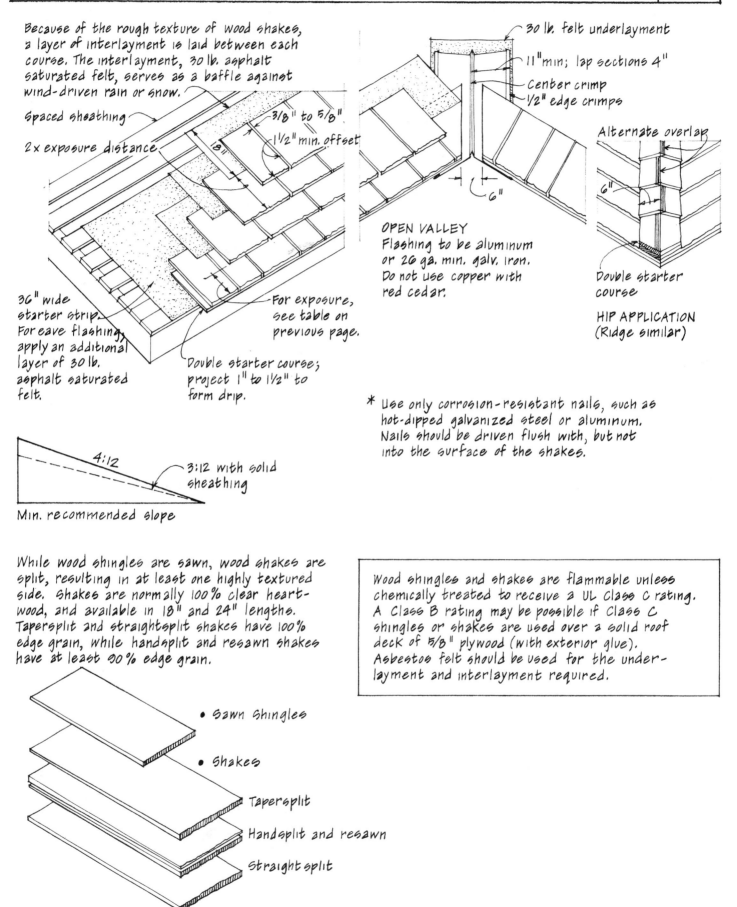

Because of the rough texture of wood shakes, a layer of interlayment is laid between each course. The interlayment, 30 lb. asphalt saturated felt, serves as a baffle against wind-driven rain or snow.

Spaced sheathing

2 x exposure distance

3/8" to 5/8"

1 1/2" min. offset

36" wide starter strip. For eave flashing, apply an additional layer of 30 lb. asphalt saturated felt.

For exposure, see table on previous page.

Double starter course; project 1" to 1 1/2" to form drip.

4:12

3:12 with solid sheathing

Min. recommended slope

30 lb. felt underlayment

11" min; lap sections 4"

Center crimp

1/2" edge crimps

Alternate overlap

6"

OPEN VALLEY
Flashing to be aluminum or 26 ga. min. galv. iron. Do not use copper with red cedar.

6"

Double starter course

HIP APPLICATION
(Ridge similar)

* Use only corrosion-resistant nails, such as hot-dipped galvanized steel or aluminum. Nails should be driven flush with, but not into the surface of the shakes.

While wood shingles are sawn, wood shakes are split, resulting in at least one highly textured side. Shakes are normally 100% clear heart-wood, and available in 18" and 24" lengths. Tapersplit and straightsplit shakes have 100% edge grain, while handsplit and resawn shakes have at least 90% edge grain.

• Sawn Shingles

• Shakes

Tapersplit

Handsplit and resawn

Straight split

Wood shingles and shakes are flammable unless chemically treated to receive a UL Class C rating. A Class B rating may be possible if Class C shingles or shakes are used over a solid roof deck of 5/8" plywood (with exterior glue). Asbestos felt should be used for the under-layment and interlayment required.

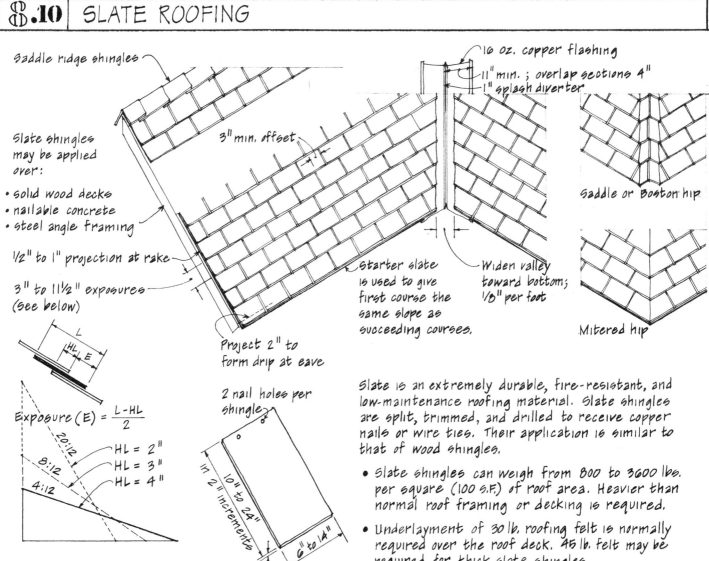

Saddle ridge shingles

Slate shingles may be applied over:

- solid wood decks
- nailable concrete
- steel angle framing

1/2" to 1" projection at rake

3" to 11½" exposures (see below)

3" min. offset

$$\text{Exposure } (E) = \frac{L - HL}{2}$$

20:12 — HL = 2"
8:12 — HL = 3"
4:12 — HL = 4"

Project 2" to form drip at eave

2 nail holes per shingle

In 2" increments 10" to 24"

6" to 14"

3/16" to 1"

Starter slate is used to give first course the same slope as succeeding courses.

16 oz. copper flashing

11" min. ; overlap sections 4"
1" splash diverter

Widen valley toward bottom; 1/8" per foot

Saddle or Boston hip

Mitered hip

Slate is an extremely durable, fire-resistant, and low-maintenance roofing material. Slate shingles are split, trimmed, and drilled to receive copper nails or wire ties. Their application is similar to that of wood shingles.

- Slate shingles can weigh from 800 to 3600 lbs. per square (100 S.F.) of roof area. Heavier than normal roof framing or decking is required.
- Underlayment of 30 lb. roofing felt is normally required over the roof deck. 45 lb. felt may be required for thick slate shingles.

ASBESTOS-CEMENT SHINGLES

Asbestos-cement shingles are highly fire-resistant and have a texture resembling that of slate or wood shakes. In addition to the rectangular shingle shape of slate, other shapes have been developed to decrease the amount of material required to cover a given area. These include diamond, hexagonal, and Dutch lap shingles.

The individual shingles are predrilled for nailing. Because the shingles have only a small overlap, storm anchors or clips are used to hold the exposed edges of the shingles down. To simplify the application of the shingles, eave starter strips, hip and ridge shingles, and ridge rolls are available.

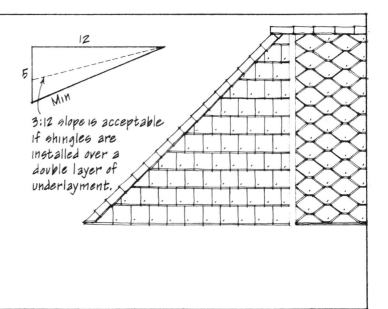

12
5
Min

3:12 slope is acceptable if shingles are installed over a double layer of underlayment.

Tile roofing consists of clay or concrete units which overlap or interlock to create a strong textural pattern. Like slate, roofing tiles are fire resistant, durable, and require little maintenance. They are also heavy and require roof framing that is strong enough to carry the weight of the tiles.

Roofing tiles are normally installed over a solid plywood deck with an underlayment of 30 lb. or 45 lb. roofing felt. Special tile units are used at ridges, hips, rakes, and eaves.

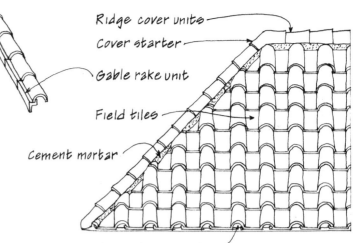

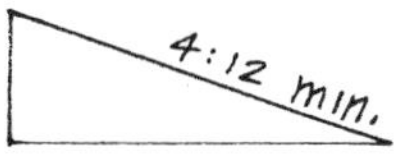

Ridge cover units
Cover starter
Gable rake unit
Field tiles
Cement mortar
Eave closure unit

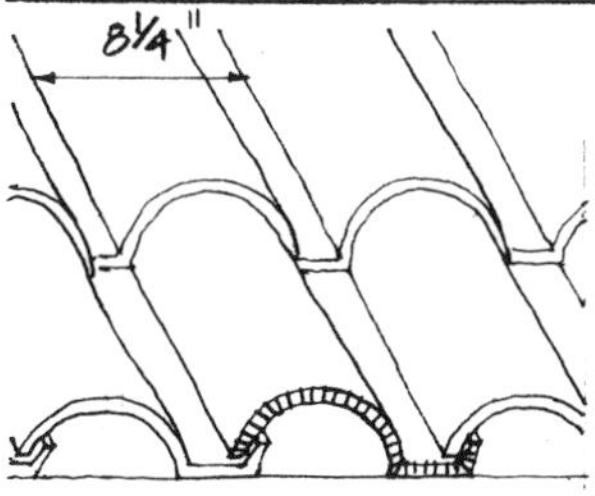

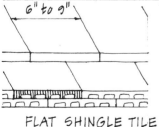

SPANISH

8¼"

4:12 min.

Length: 13¼"
Weight: 850 - 900 lbs./square
Exposure: 10½"

MISSION

9" to 12"

4:12 min.

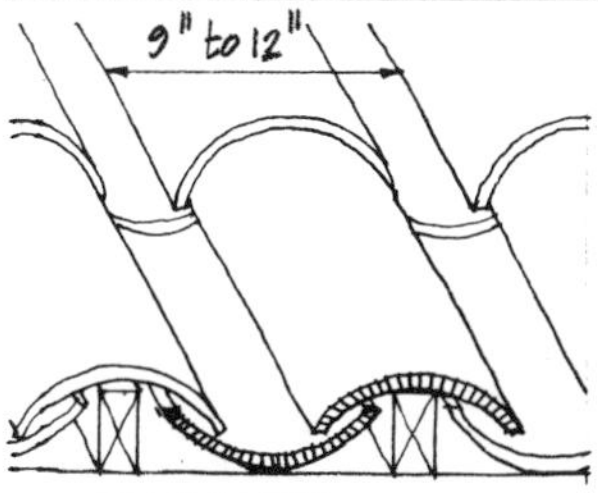

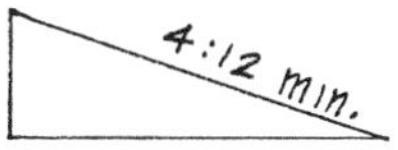

Length: 14" to 18"
Weight: 1250 lbs./square
Exposure: 11" to 15"

GREEK

12"

4:12 min.

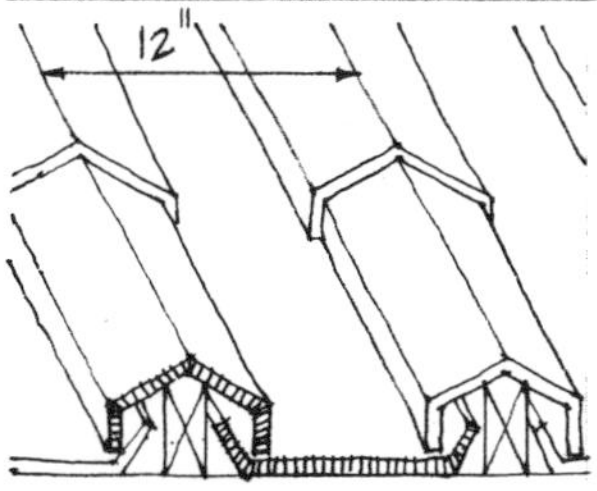

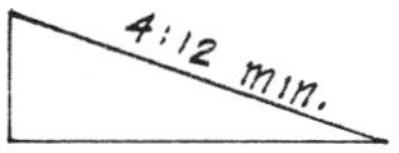

Length: 12¾"
Weight: 1250 lbs./square
Exposure: 10"

FLAT SHINGLE TILE

6" to 9"

3:12 min.

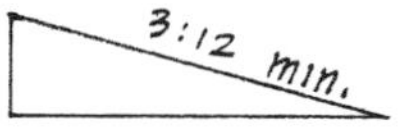

Length: 12" to 15"
Weight: 800 - 1200 lbs./square
Exposure: 9" to 12"

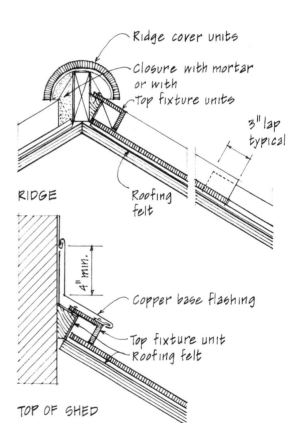

Ridge cover units
Closure with mortar or with
Top fixture units
3" lap typical
RIDGE
Roofing felt

4" min.

Copper base flashing
Top fixture unit
Roofing felt

TOP OF SHED

Confirm sizes, weights, and installation details with tile manufacturer.

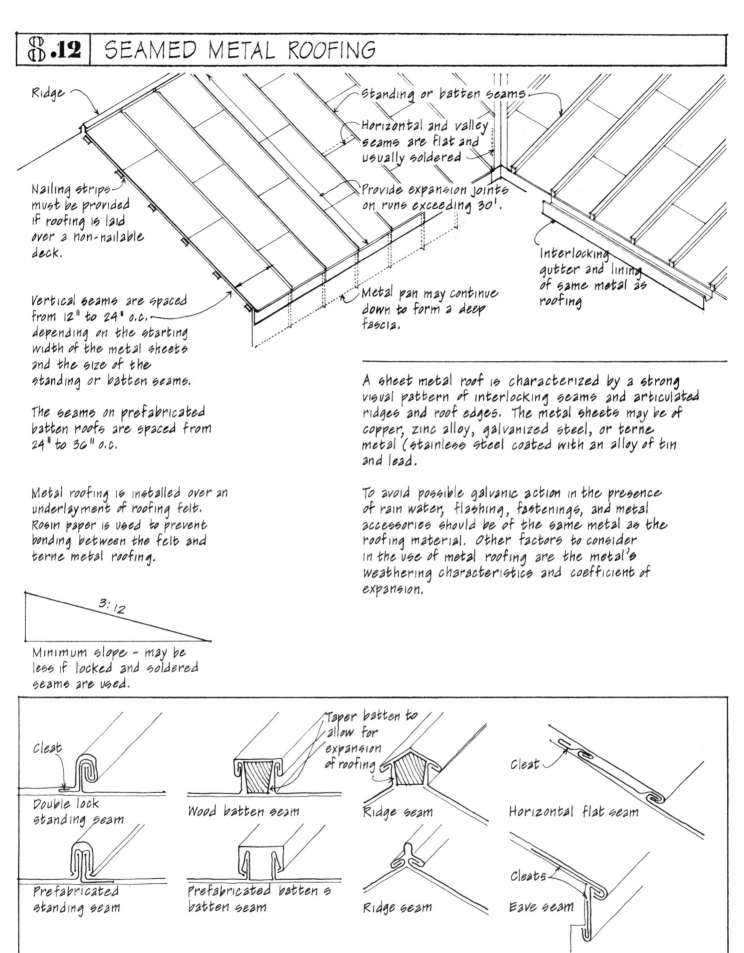

Ridge

Nailing strips must be provided if roofing is laid over a non-nailable deck.

Vertical seams are spaced from 12" to 24" o.c. depending on the starting width of the metal sheets and the size of the standing or batten seams.

The seams on prefabricated batten roofs are spaced from 24" to 36" o.c.

Metal roofing is installed over an underlayment of roofing felt. Rosin paper is used to prevent bonding between the felt and terne metal roofing.

Standing or batten seams

Horizontal and valley seams are flat and usually soldered

Provide expansion joints on runs exceeding 30'.

Metal pan may continue down to form a deep fascia.

Interlocking gutter and lining of same metal as roofing

A sheet metal roof is characterized by a strong visual pattern of interlocking seams and articulated ridges and roof edges. The metal sheets may be of copper, zinc alloy, galvanized steel, or terne metal (stainless steel coated with an alloy of tin and lead.

To avoid possible galvanic action in the presence of rain water, flashing, fastenings, and metal accessories should be of the same metal as the roofing material. Other factors to consider in the use of metal roofing are the metal's weathering characteristics and coefficient of expansion.

3:12

Minimum slope - may be less if locked and soldered seams are used.

Cleat

Double lock standing seam

Prefabricated standing seam

Taper batten to allow for expansion of roofing

Wood batten seam

Prefabricated batten s batten seam

Ridge seam

Ridge seam

Cleat

Horizontal flat seam

Cleats

Eave seam

EXAMPES OF SEAM TYPES

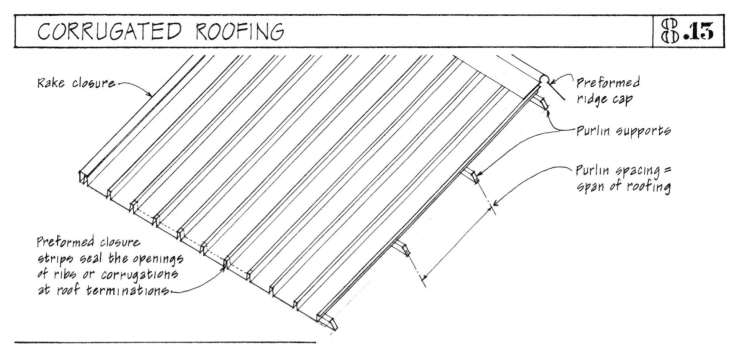

Rake closure

Preformed ridge cap

Purlin supports

Purlin spacing = span of roofing

Preformed closure strips seal the openings of ribs or corrugations at roof terminations

Corrugated or ribbed roofing panels are self-supporting and span between roof beams or purlins running across the slope. The roofing panels may be of:

○ Aluminum, natural mill or enameled
○ Galvanized steel
○ Asbestos cement
○ Fiberglass or reinforced plastic
○ Corrugated structural glass

Consult manufacturer for material specifications, panel sizes and weights, finishes, allowable spans, and installation details.

3:12 min. slope

Many corrugation and rib patterns are available.

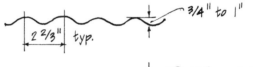
2 2/3" typ.   3/4" to 1"

1 1/8" to 2 1/4"

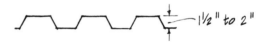
1 1/2" to 2"

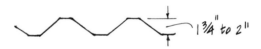
1 3/4" to 2"

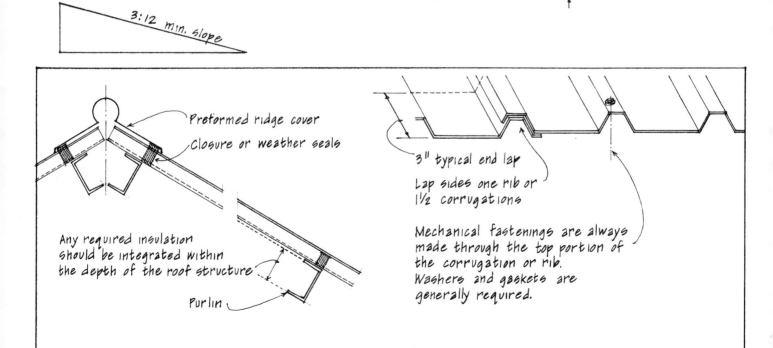

Preformed ridge cover

Closure or weather seals

Any required insulation should be integrated within the depth of the roof structure

Purlin

3" typical end lap

Lap sides one rib or 1 1/2 corrugations

Mechanical fastenings are always made through the top portion of the corrugation or rib. Washers and gaskets are generally required.

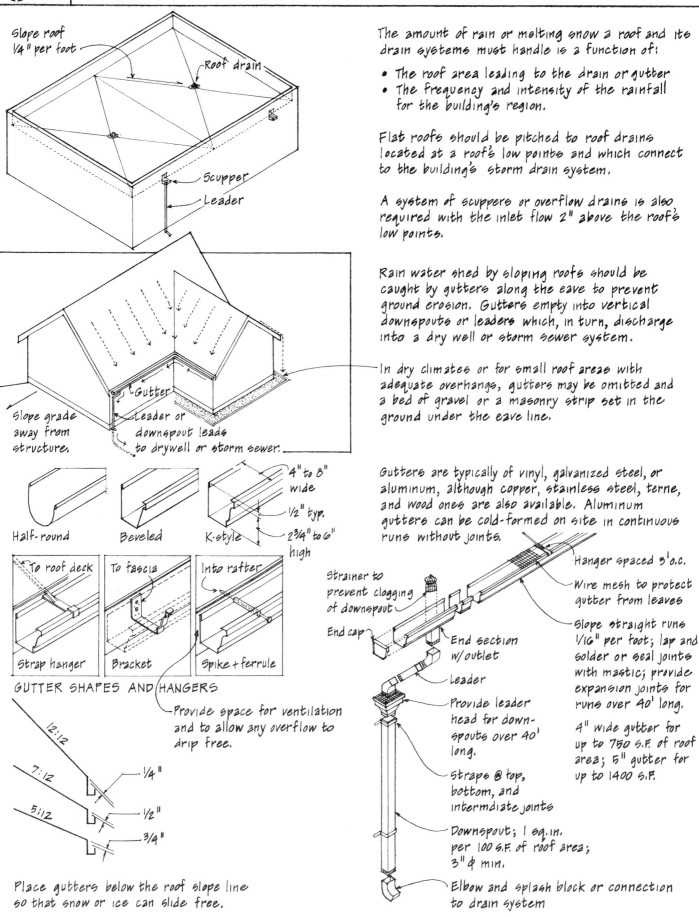

Slope roof 1/4" per foot

Roof drain

Scupper

Leader

The amount of rain or melting snow a roof and its drain systems must handle is a function of:

- The roof area leading to the drain or gutter
- The frequency and intensity of the rainfall for the building's region.

Flat roofs should be pitched to roof drains located at a roof's low points and which connect to the building's storm drain system.

A system of scuppers or overflow drains is also required with the inlet flow 2" above the roof's low points.

Rain water shed by sloping roofs should be caught by gutters along the eave to prevent ground erosion. Gutters empty into vertical downspouts or leaders which, in turn, discharge into a dry well or storm sewer system.

In dry climates or for small roof areas with adequate overhangs, gutters may be omitted and a bed of gravel or a masonry strip set in the ground under the eave line.

Slope grade away from structure.

Gutter

Leader or downspout leads to drywell or storm sewer.

Half-round   Beveled   K-style

4" to 8" wide
1/2" typ.
2 3/4" to 6" high

Gutters are typically of vinyl, galvanized steel, or aluminum, although copper, stainless steel, terne, and wood ones are also available. Aluminum gutters can be cold-formed on site in continuous runs without joints.

To roof deck   To fascia   Into rafter

Strap hanger   Bracket   Spike + ferrule

GUTTER SHAPES AND HANGERS

Provide space for ventilation and to allow any overflow to drip free.

12:12
7:12
5:12
1/4"
1/2"
3/4"

Place gutters below the roof slope line so that snow or ice can slide free.

Strainer to prevent clogging of downspout

End cap

Hanger spaced 3' o.c.

Wire mesh to protect gutter from leaves

Slope straight runs 1/16" per foot; lap and solder or seal joints with mastic; provide expansion joints for runs over 40' long.

End section w/outlet

Leader

Provide leader head for downspouts over 40' long.

Straps @ top, bottom, and intermediate joints

Downspout; 1 sq. in. per 100 s.f. of roof area; 3" ⌀ min.

Elbow and splash block or connection to drain system

4" wide gutter for up to 750 s.f. of roof area; 5" gutter for up to 1400 s.f.

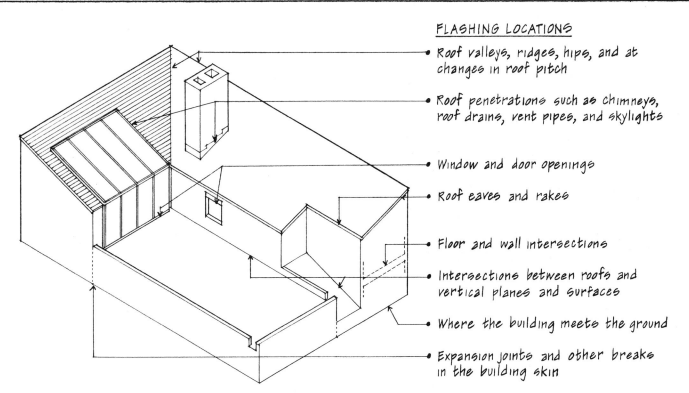

FLASHING LOCATIONS

- Roof valleys, ridges, hips, and at changes in roof pitch
- Roof penetrations such as chimneys, roof drains, vent pipes, and skylights
- Window and door openings
- Roof eaves and rakes
- Floor and wall intersections
- Intersections between roofs and vertical planes and surfaces
- Where the building meets the ground
- Expansion joints and other breaks in the building skin

Flashing refers to the thin, impervious materials used to prevent water from entering the joints of a building. Flashing generally operates on the principle that, for water to penetrate a joint, it must work itself upward against the force of gravity, or, in the case of wind driven rain, it would have to follow a tortuous path during which the driving force is dissipated. (See also 7.29 for discussion of pressure-equalization design.)

Flashing may be exposed or concealed. Exposed flashing is usually of sheet metal: aluminum
copper
Metal flashing should be provided with expansion joints on long runs to prevent deformation of the flashing. Metal flashing also should not stain or be stained by adjacent materials, or react chemically with them.

painted galv. steel
stainless steel
zinc alloy
terne metal
copper-clad lead

Flashing concealed within a building's construction may be of metal or a waterproof membrane such as bituminous fabric or plastic sheet material.

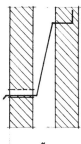

Water must work against gravity at upturned edges.

Sloping surfaces use gravity to lead water to the outside.

Interlocking seams form a labyrinth which inhibits the passage of water.

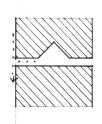

While drips and cavities are not flashing, they help stop water from penetrating through surface tension and capillary action.

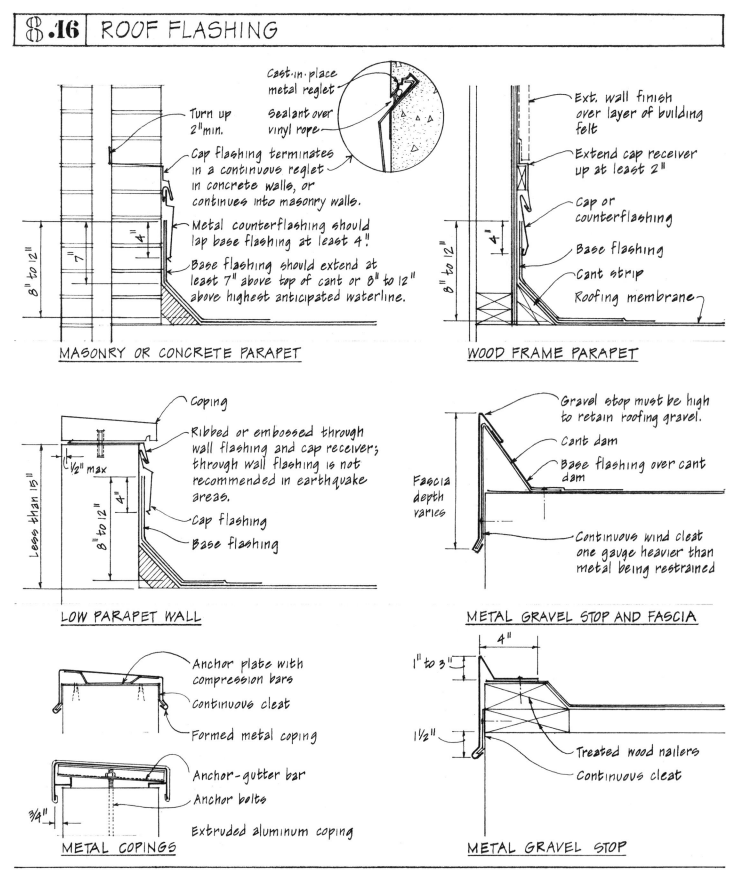

MASONRY OR CONCRETE PARAPET

Cast-in-place metal reglet

Turn up 2" min.

Sealant over vinyl rope

Cap flashing terminates in a continuous reglet in concrete walls, or continues into masonry walls.

Metal counterflashing should lap base flashing at least 4".

Base flashing should extend at least 7" above top of cant or 8" to 12" above highest anticipated waterline.

7"

4"

8" to 12"

WOOD FRAME PARAPET

Ext. wall finish over layer of building felt

Extend cap receiver up at least 2"

Cap or counterflashing

Base flashing

Cant strip

Roofing membrane

4"

8" to 12"

LOW PARAPET WALL

Coping

Ribbed or embossed through wall flashing and cap receiver; through wall flashing is not recommended in earthquake areas.

Cap flashing

Base flashing

Less than 15"

1/2" max

4"

8" to 12"

METAL GRAVEL STOP AND FASCIA

Gravel stop must be high to retain roofing gravel.

Cant dam

Base flashing over cant dam

Fascia depth varies

Continuous wind cleat one gauge heavier than metal being restrained

METAL COPINGS

Anchor plate with compression bars

Continuous cleat

Formed metal coping

Anchor-gutter bar

Anchor bolts

Extruded aluminum coping

3/4"

METAL GRAVEL STOP

4"

1" to 3"

1 1/2"

Treated wood nailers

Continuous cleat

The flashing details on this and the following pages illustrate general conditions and can be adapted for use with various building materials and assemblies.

Consult manufacturer's literature for details of flashing and roofing accessories.

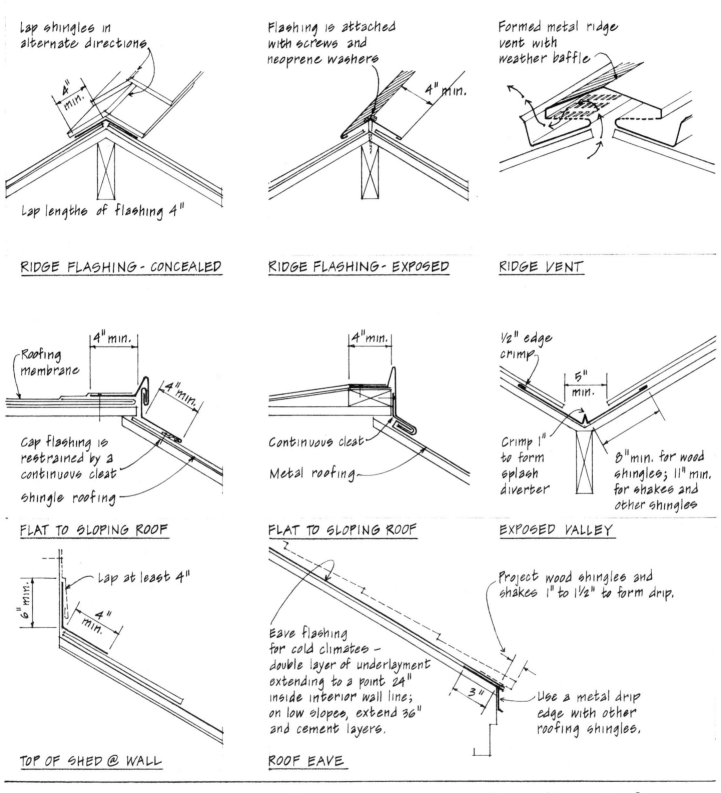

Lap shingles in alternate directions

4" min.

Lap lengths of flashing 4"

RIDGE FLASHING - CONCEALED

Flashing is attached with screws and neoprene washers

4" min.

RIDGE FLASHING - EXPOSED

Formed metal ridge vent with weather baffle

RIDGE VENT

Roofing membrane

4" min.

4" min.

Cap flashing is restrained by a continuous cleat

shingle roofing

FLAT TO SLOPING ROOF

4" min.

Continuous cleat

Metal roofing

FLAT TO SLOPING ROOF

½" edge crimp

5" min.

Crimp 1" to form splash diverter

8" min. for wood shingles; 11" min. for shakes and other shingles

EXPOSED VALLEY

Lap at least 4"

6" min.

4" min.

TOP OF SHED @ WALL

Eave flashing for cold climates - double layer of underlayment extending to a point 24" inside interior wall line; on low slopes, extend 36" and cement layers.

Project wood shingles and shakes 1" to 1½" to form drip.

3"

Use a metal drip edge with other roofing shingles.

ROOF EAVE

All dimensions are minimum. Weather conditions and roof slope may dictate greater overlaps.

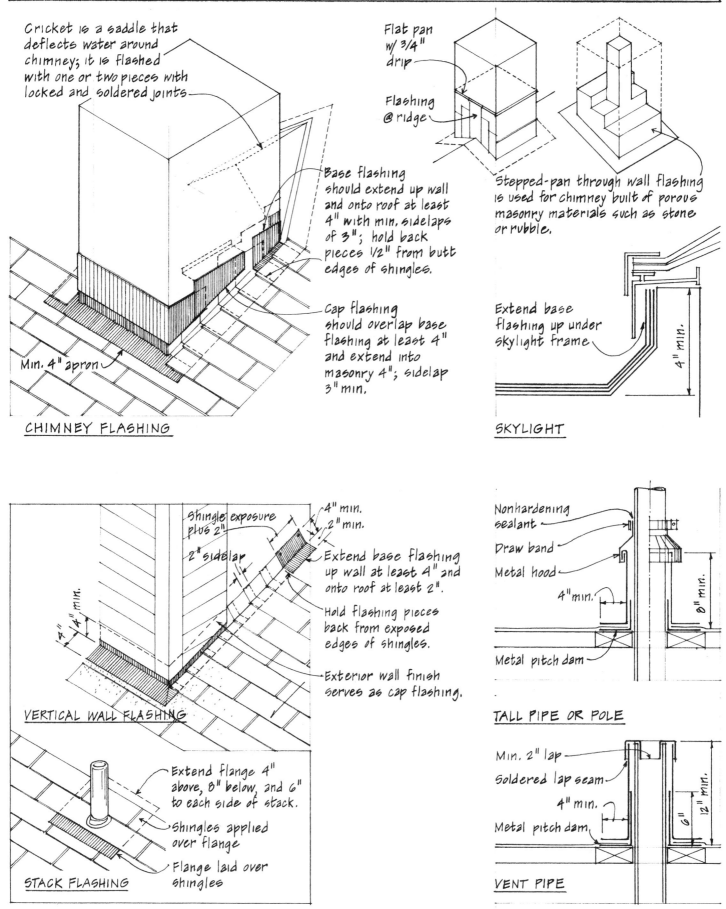

Cricket is a saddle that deflects water around chimney; it is flashed with one or two pieces with locked and soldered joints

Base flashing should extend up wall and onto roof at least 4" with min. sidelaps of 3"; hold back pieces ½" from butt edges of shingles.

Cap flashing should overlap base flashing at least 4" and extend into masonry 4"; sidelap 3" min.

Min. 4" apron

CHIMNEY FLASHING

Flat pan w/ ¾" drip

Flashing @ ridge

Stepped-pan through wall flashing is used for chimney built of porous masonry materials such as stone or rubble.

Extend base flashing up under skylight frame

4" min.

SKYLIGHT

Shingle exposure plus 2"

4" min.
2" min.

2" sidelap

4" min.

Extend base flashing up wall at least 4" and onto roof at least 2".

Hold flashing pieces back from exposed edges of shingles.

Exterior wall finish serves as cap flashing.

VERTICAL WALL FLASHING

Extend flange 4" above, 8" below, and 6" to each side of stack.

Shingles applied over flange

Flange laid over shingles

STACK FLASHING

Nonhardening sealant

Draw band

Metal hood

4" min.

8" min.

Metal pitch dam

TALL PIPE OR POLE

Min. 2" lap

Soldered lap seam

4" min.

6"

12" min.

Metal pitch dam

VENT PIPE

Wall flashing is installed to collect any moisture that may penetrate a wall and divert it to the outside through weep holes. The drawings on this page illustrate where wall flashing is usually required.

Masonry walls are especially susceptible to water penetration. Rain penetration can be controlled by properly tooling mortar joints, sealing joints such as those around window and door openings, sloping the horizontal surfaces of sills and copings, and coating the wall with a silicone-based sealer. Cavity walls are also effective in resisting water penetration.

Flashing in masonry walls require weep holes which are formed in the head joints directly above the flashing at 2' o.c.

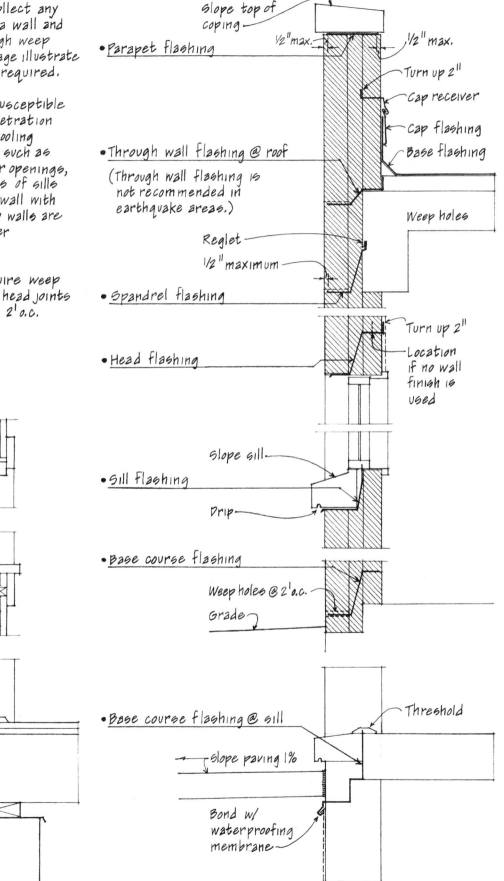

• Head flashing

Turn up 2"

• Sill flashing

Threshold

Slope paving 1%

• Base course flashing

Slope top of coping

• Parapet flashing   ½" max.   ½" max.

Turn up 2"

Cap receiver

Cap flashing

Base flashing

• Through wall flashing @ roof

(Through wall flashing is not recommended in earthquake areas.)

Weep holes

Reglet

½" maximum

• Spandrel flashing

Turn up 2"

Location if no wall finish is used

• Head flashing

Slope sill

• Sill flashing

Drip

• Base course flashing

Weep holes @ 2' o.c.

Grade

• Base course flashing @ sill

Threshold

Slope paving 1%

Bond w/ waterproofing membrane

A foundation system should be waterproofed to prevent ground water, under hydrostatic pressure or through capillary action, from penetrating the substructure. Waterproofing requires a continuous water-resistant membrane that is capable of sealing off those parts of a foundation which come into contact with the earth.

If subsoil conditions do not cause water to build up under hydrostatic pressure, the foundation wall can simply be parged to control moisture penetration due to capillarity. Parging consists of two ¼" coats of Type M mortar from the footing to 6" above grade. A coal tar or asphaltic coating can be applied over the parging for increased moisture resistance.

Water-resistant membranes for basement walls and slabs may also consist of:

- Butyl rubber or polyvinyl chloride (PVC) sheets with laps sealed with adhesive or cement
- Cementitious plaster coatings
- Bentonite clay which swells when wetted to become impervious; sprayed on or applied in sheet form.

Water-resistant membranes require a rigid, stable, and level substrate and protection while backfilling.

Gravel or a drainage membrane with filter fabric is used to allow water to flow down to the footing drains.

Equally as important as waterproofing is a drainage system that can help to relieve any buildup of hydrostatic pressure against the basement wall. It usually consists of perforated pipe or tile, 4" in diameter. These footing drains should be sloped to lead water to a storm sewer system, a sump, or to daylight when on a slope.

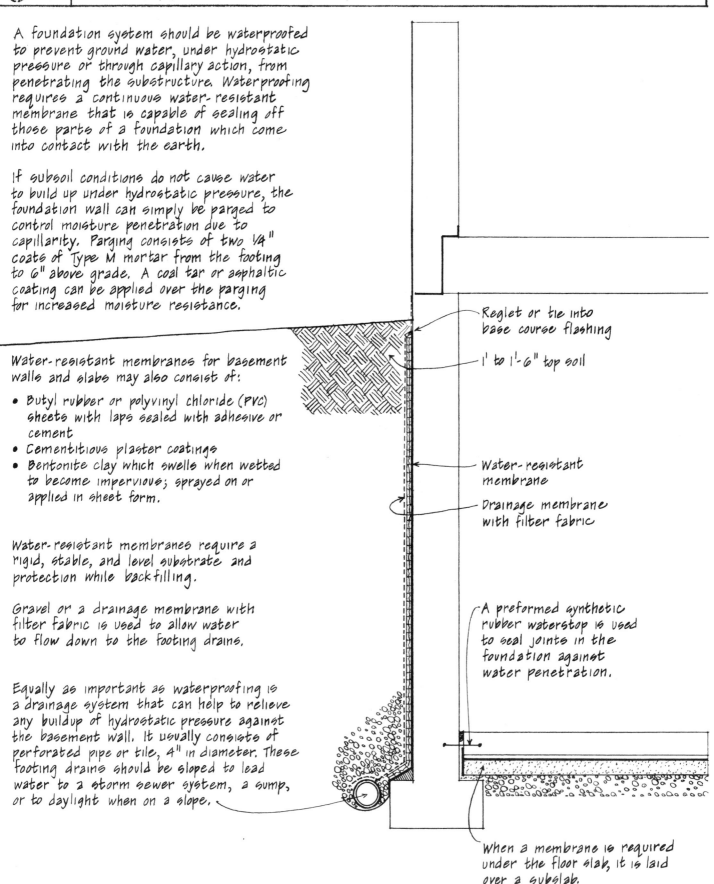

Reglet or tie into base course flashing

1' to 1'-6" top soil

Water-resistant membrane

Drainage membrane with filter fabric

A preformed synthetic rubber waterstop is used to seal joints in the foundation against water penetration.

When a membrane is required under the floor slab, it is laid over a subslab.

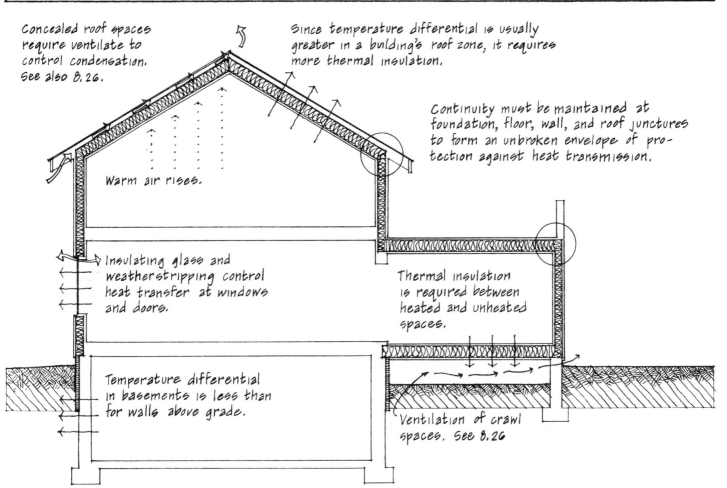

Concealed roof spaces require ventilate to control condensation. See also 8.26.

Since temperature differential is usually greater in a building's roof zone, it requires more thermal insulation.

Warm air rises.

Continuity must be maintained at foundation, floor, wall, and roof junctures to form an unbroken envelope of protection against heat transmission.

Insulating glass and weatherstripping control heat transfer at windows and doors.

Thermal insulation is required between heated and unheated spaces.

Temperature differential in basements is less than for walls above grade.

Ventilation of crawl spaces. See 8.26

RECOMMENDED MINIMUM THERMAL RESISTANCES (R) OF BUILDING INSULATION *

Zone	Ceiling or roof	Exterior wall	Floor over unheated space
Minimum recommended	19	11	11
Southern zone	26	13	11
Temperate zone	30	19	13
Northern zone	38	19	22

* These R-values are only general recommendations. Check the local or state energy code for specific recommendations.

The primary purpose of a building's thermal insulation is to control heat transfer through its exterior assemblies and thereby prevent excessive heat loss in cold seasons and heat gain in hot weather. This control can effectively reduce the amount of energy required by the building's heating and cooling equipment to maintain conditions for human comfort.

• For further discussion of the factors that affect human comfort, see 11.2-11.3.

• For building siting factors that also affect a building's potential heat loss or gain, see Chapter 1.

Material		1/k	1/C
WOOD	Hardwoods	0.91	
	Softwoods	1.25	
	Plywood	1.25	
	Particleboard, 5/8"		0.82
	Wood fiberboard	2.00	
MASONRY UNITS	Common brick	0.20	
	Face brick	0.11	
	Concrete block, 8",		
	Sand & gravel aggregate		1.11
	Lightweight aggregate		2.00
	Granite and marble	0.05	
	Sandstone	0.08	
CONCRETE & MASONRY MATERIALS	Concrete,		
	Sand & gravel aggregate	0.08	
	Lightweight aggregate	0.60	
	Cement mortar	0.20	
	Stucco	0.20	
ROOFING	Built-up roofing		0.33
	Fiberglass shingles		0.44
	Slate roofing		0.05
	Wood shingles		0.94
SIDING	Aluminum siding		0.61
	Wood shingles		0.87
	Wood bevel siding		0.81
	Vinyl siding		1.00
BUILDING PAPER	Vapor-permeable felt		0.06
	Polyethylene film		-0-
DOORS	Steel, polystyrene core		2.13
	Steel, urethane core		5.56
	Wood hollow core, 1¾"		2.04
	Wood solid core, 1¾"		3.13
PLASTER & GYPSUM	Cement plaster,		
	Sand aggregate	0.20	
	Gypsum plaster,		
	Lightweight aggregate	0.67	
	Gypsum board, ½"		0.45
FLOORING	Carpet & pad		1.50
	Hardwood, 25/32"		0.71
	Terrazzo		0.08
	Vinyl tile		0.05

Material		1/k	1/C
METAL	Aluminum	.0007	
	Brass	.0010	
	Copper	.0004	
	Lead	.0041	
	Steel	.0032	
GLASS	Single, clear, ¼"		0.88
	Double, clear, 3/16" space		1.61
	¼" space		1.72
	½" space		2.04
	Double, blue/clear		2.25
	gray/clear		2.40
	green/clear		2.50
	Double, clear, with		
	low emittance coating		3.23
	Triple, clear		2.56
	Glass block, 4"		1.79
AIR SPACE	¾", nonreflective		1.01
	¾", reflective		3.48

1/k = (R) per inch of thickness
1/C = (R) for the thickness indicated

(R) is a measure of a material's resistance to heat flow. It is expressed as the temperature difference required to cause heat to flow through a unit area of material at the rate of one heat unit per hour. (F°/Btu/hr · ft²)

(R_T) is the total thermal resistance for a construction assembly, and is simply the sum of the individual R-values of assembly's component materials.

(U) is the overall heat transfer coefficient, and expresses the rate of heat transfer through a unit area of a building component caused by a difference of one degree between the air temperatures on the two sides of the component. The U-value for a component or assembly is the reciprocal of its R-value. ($U = 1/R_T$)

(Q) is the rate of heat flow through a construction assembly and is equal to:

$U \times A \times (t_i - t_o)$, where

U = overall coefficient of assembly
A = exposed area of assembly
($t_i - t_o$) is the difference between the inside and outside air temperatures.

The table above can be used to estimate the thermal resistance of a construction assembly. For specific R-values of materials and building components such as windows, consult the manufacturer.

Form	Material	R-value per inch of thickness	
BATT OR BLANKET	Fiberglass . . . . 3.3 Rock wool 3.3		Installed between studs, joists, rafters, or furring; considered incombustible except for paper facing.
RIGID BOARDS	Cellular glass . . . . 2.5 Polystyrene, molded . . . . . 3.6 Polystyrene, extruded . . . 5.0 Polyurethane, expanded . . 6.2 Polyisocyanurate . . . . 7.2 Perlite, expanded 2.6		Boards may be applied over a roof deck, over wall framing as sheathing, in cavity walls, or beneath an interior finish material; the plastics are combustible and give off toxic fumes when burned; extruded polystyrene can be used in contact with the earth but any exposed surfaces should be protected.
FOAMED IN PLACE	Polyurethane 6.2		Used to insulate irregularly shaped spaces.
LOOSE FILL	Cellulose . . . . 3.7 Perlite . . . . 2.7 Vermiculite 2.1		Used to insulate attic floors and wall cavities; cellulose can be combined with adhesives for sprayed application; cellulose should be treated and UL listed for fire resistance.
CAST	Insulating concrete 1.1		Used primarily as an insulating layer under membrane roofing; insulating values depends on its density.

Almost all building materials offer some resistance to heat flow. To achieve the desired R_T value, however, wall, floor and roof assemblies usually require the addition of an insulating material. The table above outlines the basic forms and materials used to insulate a building's component assemblies.

The steady state method for calculating heat loss or gain (see previous page) takes into account primarily the thermal resistance (R_T) of the construction assembly and the air temperature differential. Other factors that affect heat loss or gain are:

- The surface color and reflectivity of the materials used
- The mass of the assembly, which affects the time lag or delay before any stored heat is released by the structure; time lag becomes a significant factor with thick, dense materials.
- The orientation of the building's exterior surfaces, which affects solar heat gain as well as exposure to wind and the attendant potential for air infiltration.
- Latent heat sources and heat gain from a building's occupants, lighting, and equipment.
- Proper installation of thermal insulation and vapor barriers.

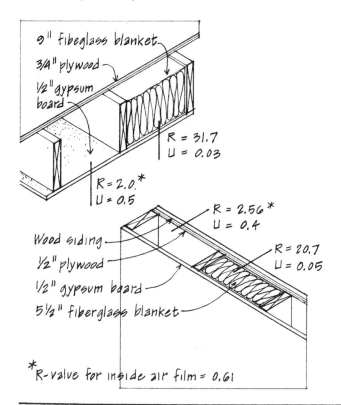

9" fiberglass blanket
3/4" plywood
1/2" gypsum board
R = 31.7
U = 0.03
R = 2.0 *
U = 0.5
R = 2.56 *
U = 0.4
Wood siding
1/2" plywood
1/2" gypsum board
5½" fiberglass blanket
R = 20.7
U = 0.05

* R-value for inside air film = 0.61

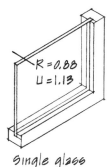

R = 0.88
U = 1.13

Single glass

R = 1.61
U = 0.62

Double glass w/ 3/16" air space

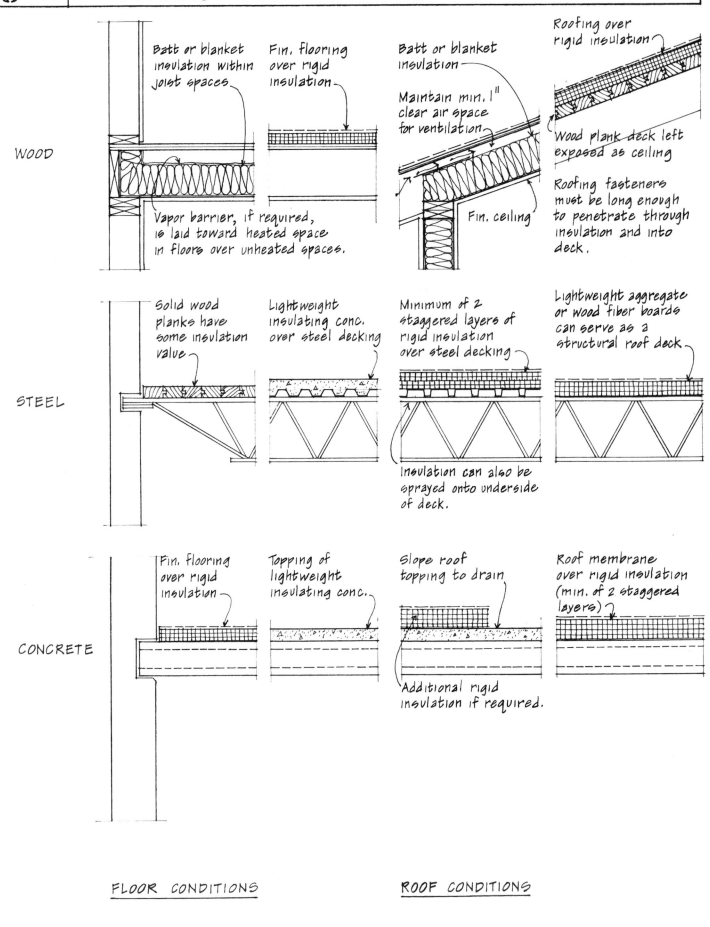

WOOD

Batt or blanket insulation within joist spaces

Fin. flooring over rigid insulation

Vapor barrier, if required, is laid toward heated space in floors over unheated spaces.

Batt or blanket insulation

Maintain min. 1" clear air space for ventilation

Fin. ceiling

Roofing over rigid insulation

Wood plank deck left exposed as ceiling

Roofing fasteners must be long enough to penetrate through insulation and into deck.

STEEL

Solid wood planks have some insulation value

Lightweight insulating conc. over steel decking

Minimum of 2 staggered layers of rigid insulation over steel decking

Insulation can also be sprayed onto underside of deck.

Lightweight aggregate or wood fiber boards can serve as a structural roof deck

CONCRETE

Fin. flooring over rigid insulation

Topping of lightweight insulating conc.

Slope roof topping to drain

Additional rigid insulation if required.

Roof membrane over rigid insulation (min. of 2 staggered layers)

FLOOR CONDITIONS   ROOF CONDITIONS

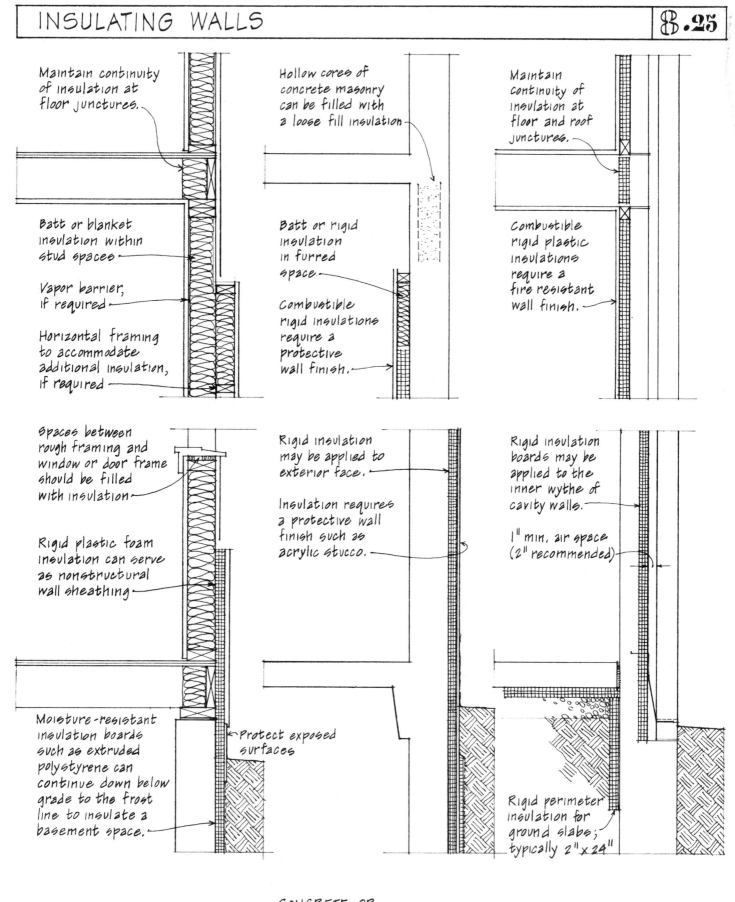

Maintain continuity of insulation at floor junctures.

Batt or blanket insulation within stud spaces.

Vapor barrier, if required

Horizontal framing to accommodate additional insulation, if required

Spaces between rough framing and window or door frame should be filled with insulation

Rigid plastic foam insulation can serve as nonstructural wall sheathing

Moisture-resistant insulation boards such as extruded polystyrene can continue down below grade to the frost line to insulate a basement space.

Hollow cores of concrete masonry can be filled with a loose fill insulation

Batt or rigid insulation in furred space.

Combustible rigid insulations require a protective wall finish.

Rigid insulation may be applied to exterior face.

Insulation requires a protective wall finish such as acrylic stucco.

Protect exposed surfaces

Maintain continuity of insulation at floor and roof junctures.

Combustible rigid plastic insulations require a fire resistant wall finish.

Rigid insulation boards may be applied to the inner wythe of cavity walls.

1" min. air space (2" recommended)

Rigid perimeter insulation for ground slabs; typically 2" x 24"

FRAME WALLS

CONCRETE OR
SOLID MASONRY WALLS

MASONRY CAVITY WALLS

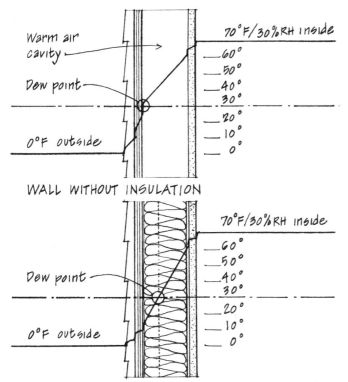

Warm air cavity

70°F/30%RH inside

— 60°
— 50°
— 40°
— 30°
— 20°
— 10°
— 0°

Dew point

0°F outside

WALL WITHOUT INSULATION

70°F/30%RH inside

— 60°
— 50°
— 40°
— 30°
— 20°
— 10°
— 0°

Dew point

0°F outside

WALL WITH INSULATION
requires a vapor barrier to prevent water vapor from condensing within the layer of insulation. A vapor barrier becomes more important as the level of thermal insulation increases.

PERMEABILITY OF SOME BUILDING MATERIALS	
Material	Permeance (Perm)
Brick, 4"	0.8
Concrete, 1"	3.2
Concrete block, 8"	2.4
Gypsum board, 3/8"	50.0
Plaster, 3/4"	15.0
Plywood, 1/4", exterior glue	0.7
Built-up roofing	0.0
Aluminum foil, 1 mil	0.0
Polyethylene, 4 mil	0.08
Polyethylene, 6 mil	0.06
Duplex sheet, asphalt + foil	0.002
Asphalt saturated + coated paper	0.2
Kraft paper, foil-faced	0.5
Blanket insulation, faced	0.4
Cellular glass	0.0
Polystyrene, molded	2.0
Polystyrene, extruded	1.2
Paint, 2 coats, exterior	0.9

Moisture is normally present in the air as water vapor. Evaporation from a building's occupants and equipment can raise the air's humidity. This moisture vapor will transform itself into a liquid state (condense) when the air in which it exists becomes completely saturated with all the vapor it can hold and reaches its dew point temperature. Warm air is capable of holding more moisture vapor and has a higher dew point than cooler air.

Since it is a gas, moisture vapor always moves from high to lower pressure areas. This normally means it tends to diffuse from the higher humidity levels of a building's interior toward the lower humidity levels outside. This flow is reversed when hot, humid conditions exist outdoors and a building's interior spaces are cool. Most building materials offer little resistance to this passage of moisture vapor. If the moisture vapor comes into contact with a cool surface whose temperature coincides with the air's dew point, it will condense.

Condensation can lessen the effectiveness of thermal insulation, be absorbed by a building's materials, and deteriorate finishes. Moisture vapor, therefore, must be:

① prevented by <u>vapor barriers</u> from penetrating the enclosed spaces of exterior construction, and/or

② allowed to escape, by means of ventilation, before it can condense into a liquid.

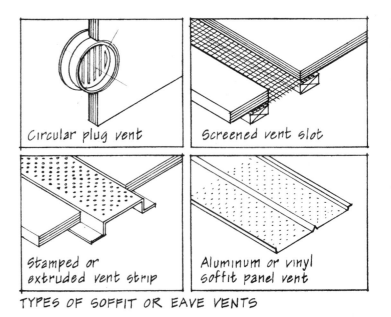

Circular plug vent

Screened vent slot

Stamped or extruded vent strip

Aluminum or vinyl soffit panel vent

TYPES OF SOFFIT OR EAVE VENTS

Ridge ventilation may be provided by a continuous ridge vent, or louvers in the gable end walls

• ROOF AND ATTIC VENTILATION is provided by eave vents and, on sloping roofs, by vents close to the ridge. The total net free ventilating area should be at least 1/300 th of the area of the space being ventilated, with 50% of the required area being at or along the ridge. Openings should be protected against the entrance of rain, snow, and insects.

Vent holes and stacks

A vapor barrier for flat roof assemblies is recommended only when the average outdoor January temperature is below 40°F and interior relative humidity is 45% or greater.

When a vapor barrier is used, the insulation layer may have to be vented. Consult roofing manufacturer for recommendations.

• VAPOR BARRIERS are normally placed on the warm (in winter) side of insulated construction.

In warm, humid climates, the vapor barrier may have to be placed on the outer face of the construction.

1" min. clearance for ventilation

Eave or soffit vent should be continuous or consist of evenly distributed openings.

Some rigid insulation boards have inherent vapor resistance, while other insulating materials have a vapor retarding facing. A vapor barrier is most effective, however, when it is applied as a separate layer with no breaks and with all seams lapped and sealed.

Surface condensation on windows can be controlled by raising the surface temperature with a warm air supply or by using double or triple glazing.

Over unheated spaces, the vapor barrier is placed on the warm side of the insulated floor.

Exterior sheathing, building paper, and siding should be permeable to allow any vapor in the wall to escape to the outside.

Wire mesh

• CRAWL SPACES require a vapor barrier to control ground moisture. Unheated crawl spaces also require ventilation. The openings should be located on opposite sides of the crawl space and near corners to encourage cross ventilation.

Openings should have a net area of at least 1½ S.F. for each 25 lineal feet of wall.

Air-tight construction may require a forced ventilating system with an air-to-air heat exchanger to rid interior spaces of moisture, odors, and pollutants.

Building materials expand and contract in response to normal changes in temperature. Expansion joints allow for this thermal movement in order to prevent distortion, cracks, or breaks in the building materials. Expansion joints should provide a complete separation of material and allow free movement while, at the same time, maintain the weathertightness of the structure.

The width of an expansion joint depends on the building materials and the temperature range involved. It varies from 1/4" to 1"or more, and should be calculated for each specific situation.

- For surfaces with severe solar exposure, expansion joints should be provided at more frequent intervals.

- Parapet walls require expansion joints near corners to prevent their displacement.

- Additional expansion joints are required in the exterior wythe of masonry cavity walls ; exterior wythe must be secured to backup masonry with flexible anchors.

- Horizontal expansion joints are required at steel shelf angles in masonry walls, and above masonry walls that abut a structural frame.

- Nonbearing masonry partitions require an expansion joint when they abut a roof or floor structure that might deflect.

- Long, linear building elements, such as handrails, fascias, gravel stops, and window or curtain wall framing also require expansion joints.

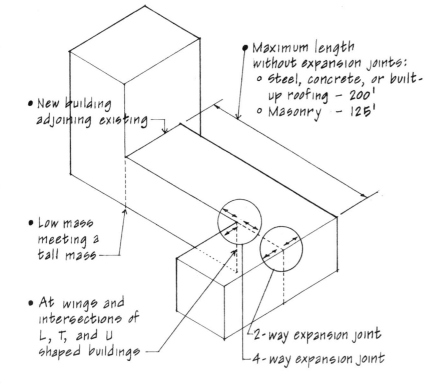

- New building adjoining existing

- Low mass meeting a tall mass

- At wings and intersections of L, T, and U shaped buildings

- Maximum length without expansion joints:
  - Steel, concrete, or built-up roofing – 200'
  - Masonry – 125'

2-way expansion joint

4-way expansion joint

COEFFICIENT OF LINEAR EXPANSION per unit length per one degree change in temperature (F°)					
	$\times 10^{-7}$		$\times 10^{-7}$		$\times 10^{-7}$
Aluminum	128	Parallel to wood grain:		Brick masonry	34
Brass	104	Fir	21	Portland cement	70
Bronze	101	Maple	36	Concrete	55
Copper	93	Oak	27	Granite	44
Iron, cast	59	Pine	54	Limestone	42
Iron, wrought	67	Perpendicular to grain:		Marble	45
Lead	159	Fir	320	Plaster	92
Nickel	70	Maple	270	Rubble masonry	35
Steel, mild	65	Oak	300	Slate	44
Steel, stainless	99	Pine	190	Glass	47

Coefficient of surface expansion is approximately twice the linear coefficient.
Coefficient of volume expansion is approximately three times the linear coefficient.

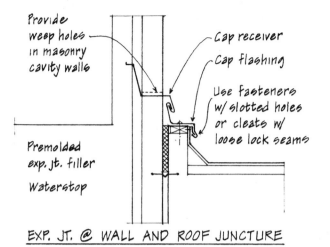

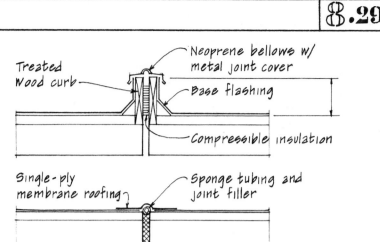

Provide weep holes in masonry cavity walls

Cap receiver

Cap flashing

Use fasteners w/ slotted holes or cleats w/ loose lock seams

Premolded exp. jt. filler

Waterstop

EXP. JT. @ WALL AND ROOF JUNCTURE

Treated wood curb

Neoprene bellows w/ metal joint cover

Base flashing

Compressible insulation

Single-ply membrane roofing

Sponge tubing and joint filler

FLAT ROOF EXPANSION JOINTS

These expansion joint details, although general in nature, have the following elements in common:

- A joint . . . . A complete break through the structure which is usually filled with a compressible material.

- A weatherstop which may be in the form of:

  - An elastic joint sealant (see 8.30)
  - A flexible waterstop embedded within the construction
  - A flexible membrane over flat roof joints.

(See 5.23 for more masonry expansion joints.)

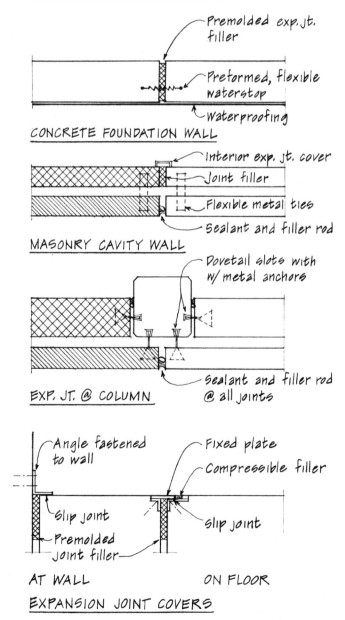

Premolded exp. jt. filler

Preformed, flexible waterstop

Waterproofing

CONCRETE FOUNDATION WALL

Interior exp. jt. cover

Joint filler

Flexible metal ties

Sealant and filler rod

MASONRY CAVITY WALL

Dovetail slots with w/ metal anchors

Sealant and filler rod @ all joints

EXP. JT. @ COLUMN

Expansion joint covers are used to conceal joints in interior floor, wall, and ceiling surfaces. They usually consist of a rigid plate fixed to one side of the joint with an overlapping slip joint on the other.

Angle fastened to wall

Fixed plate

Compressible filler

Slip joint

Premolded joint filler

Slip joint

AT WALL   ON FLOOR

EXPANSION JOINT COVERS

Compressed   As installed   Elongated

To provide an effective seal against the passage of water and air, a joint sealant must be durable, resilient, and have both cohesive and adhesive strength.

Sealants can be classified according to the amount of extension and compression they can withstand before failure.

- **Low range sealants**
  ○ Movement capability of ± 5%
  ○ Oil-based or acrylic compounds
  ○ Referred to as caulking and used for small joints where little movements is expected.

- **Medium range sealants**
  ○ Movement capability of ± 5% to ± 10%
  ○ Butyl rubber, acrylic or neoprene compounds
  ○ Used for nonworking, mechanically fastened joints.

- **High range sealants**
  ○ Movement capability of ± 12% to ± 25%
  ○ Polymercaptans, polysulfides, polyurethanes, and silicones
  ○ Used for working joints subject to a significant amount of movement, such as those in curtain walls.

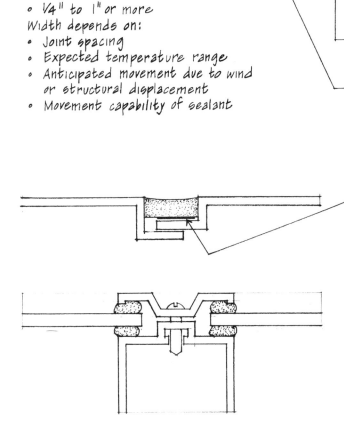

Joints should be tooled to ensure full contact with and adhesion to substrate

Sealant joint depth

Full contact depth

Sealant depth
○ ¼" min. for ¼" joints
○ equal to joint width for joints up to ½"
○ half of joint width for joints ½" or wider, but not more than ½"

Joint width = sealant width
○ ¼" to 1" or more
Width depends on:
- Joint spacing
- Expected temperature range
- Anticipated movement due to wind or structural displacement
- Movement capability of sealant

The substrate must be clean, dry, and compatible with the sealant material.

A primer may be required to improve the adhesion of a sealant to the substrate.

The joint filler controls the depth of the sealant contact with the joining parts. It should be compressible and be compatible with but not adhere to the sealant. It may be in the form of a rod or tubing of polyethylene foam, polyurethane foam, neoprene, or butyl rubber.

When there is insufficient depth for a compressible filler, a bond breaker, such as polyethylene tape, is required to prevent adhesion between the sealant and the bottom of the joint recess.

Most sealants are viscous liquids which cure after being applied with a hand operated or power gun. These are referred to as gunnable sealants. Some lap joints, however, are difficult to seal with gunnable sealants. These joints may require instead a preformed solid tape sealant (polybutene or polyisobutylene) that is held in place under compression.

SPECIAL CONSTRUCTION

9

This chapter discusses those elements of a building which have unique characteristics and which therefore should be considered as separate entities. While not always affecting the exterior form of a building, they do influence the internal organization of spaces, the pattern of the structural system, and in some cases, the layout of heating, plumbing, and electrical systems.

Stairs provide means for vertical movement between stories of a building and are, therefore, important links in a building's overall circulation scheme. Whether punctuating a two-story volume of space or rising through a narrow shaft of space, a stairway takes up a significant amount of space. A stair's landings should be logically integrated with a building's structural system to avoid overly complicated framing conditions. Safety and ease of travel are, in the end, probably the most important considerations in the design and placement of stairs.

A fireplace is a source of heat and a visual point of interest for any interior space. The placement and size of a fireplace in a room should be related to the scale and use of the space. Whether it is an integral part of a wall or a freestanding element within a space, a fireplace must be constructed to draft properly. The damper and flue sizes should correspond to the size and proportions of the fireplace and precautions should be taken against fire hazards and heat loss.

Kitchens and bathrooms are unique areas of a building that demand the careful integration of plumbing, electrical, and heating/ventilating systems with the functional and aesthetic requirements of the spaces. These areas also require special fixtures and equipment, as well as durable, easy to maintain, and sanitary surfaces and finishes.

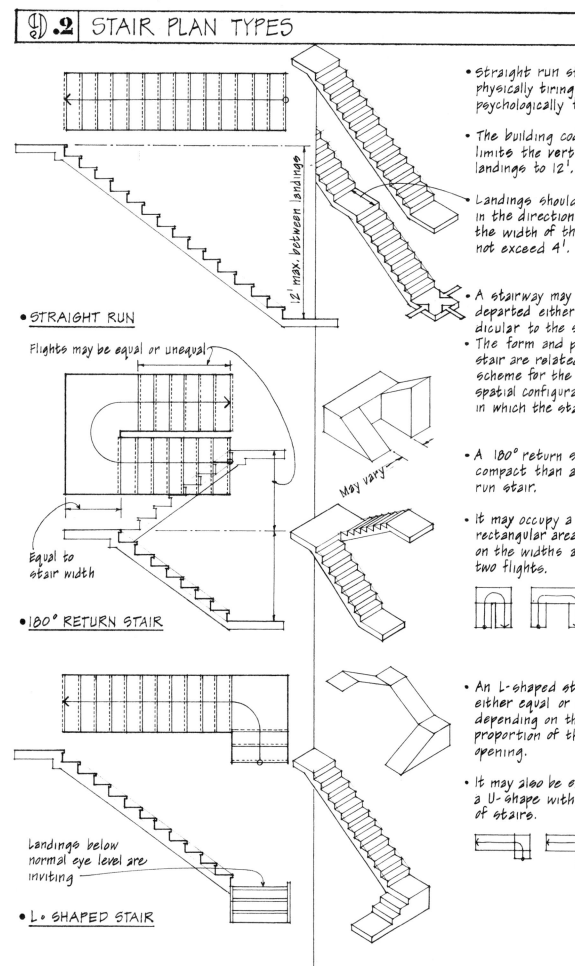

- STRAIGHT RUN

Flights may be equal or unequal

Equal to stair width

- 180° RETURN STAIR

Landings below normal eye level are inviting

- L-SHAPED STAIR

12' max. between landings

May vary

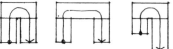

- Straight run stairs can be physically tiring as well as psychologically forbidding

- The building code generally limits the vertical rise between landings to 12'.

- Landings should have a dimension in the direction of travel equal to the width of the stair, but it need not exceed 4'.

- A stairway may be approached and departed either axially or perpendicular to the stair run.

- The form and placement of a stair are related to the circulation scheme for the building and the spatial configuration of the area in which the stair is located.

- A 180° return stair is more compact than a single straight run stair.

- It may occupy a square or rectangular area in plan depending on the widths and runs of its two flights.

- An L-shaped stair may have either equal or unequal flights, depending on the desired proportion of the stairway opening.

- It may also be extended into a U-shape with three flights of stairs.

- Winders refer to the triangular treads which are used to conserve space when a stairway changes direction.

- Winders can be hazardous since they offer little foothold at their interior corners.

- The building code generally restricts the use of winders to certain residential occupancies and specifies the minimum tread run.

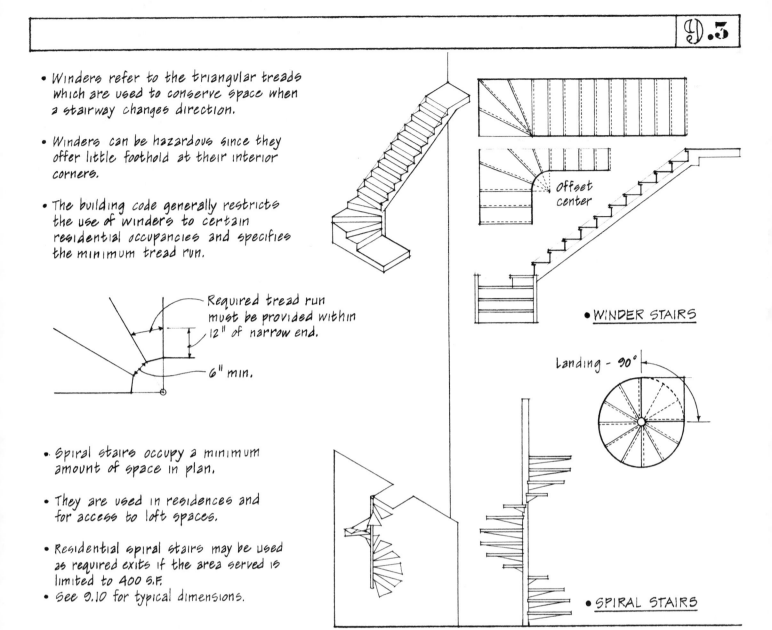

Required tread run must be provided within 12" of narrow end.

6" min.

Offset center

• WINDER STAIRS

Landing - 90°

- Spiral stairs occupy a minimum amount of space in plan.

- They are used in residences and for access to loft spaces.

- Residential spiral stairs may be used as required exits if the area served is limited to 400 S.F.
- See 9.10 for typical dimensions.

• SPIRAL STAIRS

• RAMPS

Ramps provide smooth transitions between the floor levels of a building. To have comfortably low slopes, they require relatively long runs. They are typically used to provide

Access for the handicapped
Access for wheeled equipment
Smooth, continuous movement through or around a tall space.

Short, straight ramps act as beams and may be constructed as wood, steel, or concrete floor systems. Long or curvilinear ramps are usually of steel or reinforced concrete.

Ramps should have nonslip surfaces, especially when exposed to the weather.

1:12 max. slope for handicapped access and when ramp is used as an emergency exit

1:8 max. for other ramps

5' min.

6' min.

Landings are required at the top and bottom, and for each 5' of rise.

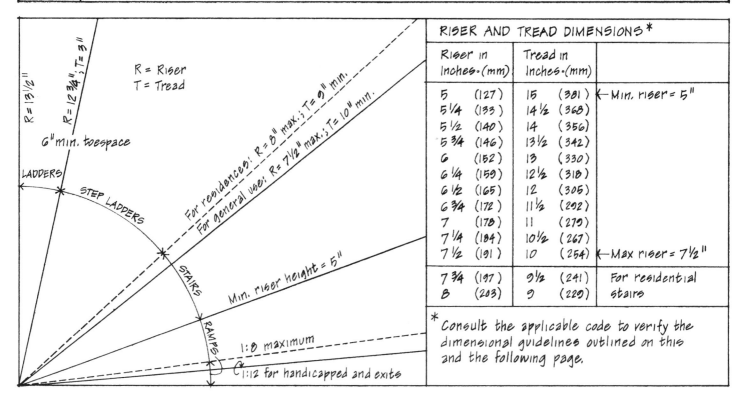

RISER AND TREAD DIMENSIONS*		
Riser in Inches·(mm)	Tread in Inches·(mm)	
5 (127)	15 (381)	← Min. riser = 5"
5 1/4 (133)	14 1/2 (368)	
5 1/2 (140)	14 (356)	
5 3/4 (146)	13 1/2 (342)	
6 (152)	13 (330)	
6 1/4 (159)	12 1/2 (318)	
6 1/2 (165)	12 (305)	
6 3/4 (172)	11 1/2 (292)	
7 (178)	11 (279)	
7 1/4 (184)	10 1/2 (267)	
7 1/2 (191)	10 (254)	← Max riser = 7 1/2"
7 3/4 (197)	9 1/2 (241)	For residential stairs
8 (203)	9 (229)	

* Consult the applicable code to verify the dimensional guidelines outlined on this and the following page.

The dimensions of a stair's risers and treads should be proportioned to accommodate our body movement. Their pitch, if steep, can make ascent physically tiring as well as psychologically forbidding, and can make descent precarious. If a stair's pitch is shallow, its treads should be deep enough to fit our stride.

Building codes regulate the minimum and maximum dimensions of risers and treads. Some codes specify a maximum riser dimension of 7 1/2" and a minimum tread of 10"; others limit a riser to 7" and require a tread of at least 11". Residential stairs are usually allowed to have 8" risers and 9" treads.

For comfort, the riser and tread dimensions can be proportioned according to the following formula:

- (2x riser) + tread = 24 to 25 (inches) ←

Exterior stairs are generally not as steep as interior stairs, especially where dangerous conditions such as snow and ice exist. The proportioning formula can therefore be adjusted to yield a sum of 26.

For safety, all risers in a flight of stairs should be the same height and all treads should have the same run. Building codes limit the allowable variation in riser height or tread run to 3/16."

The actual riser and tread dimensions for a set of stairs are determined by dividing the total rise (the floor-to-floor height) by the desired riser height. The result is rounded off to arrive at a whole number of risers. The total rise is then redivided by this whole number to arrive at the actual riser height.

This riser height must be checked against the maximum riser height allowed by the building code. If necessary, the number of risers can be increased by one and the actual riser height recalculated.

Once the actual riser height is fixed, the tread run can be determined by using the riser: tread proportioning formula.

Since in any flight of stairs, there is always one less tread than the number of risers, the total number of treads and the total run can easily be determined.

STAIR TERMINOGY

Handrail

Floor level

2'-6" to 2'-10"

6'-8" min. headroom

6'-6" for residences

Riser

Tread

Total rise

Rise of Flight B

Run of Flight B

Stair width

Rise of Flight A

Landing

Floor level

1½" min. clearance

Handgrip section 1¼" to 2" wide

2'-6" to 2'-10"

1½" max.

Run (tread)

Rise (riser)

A minimum of 3 risers per flight is recommended

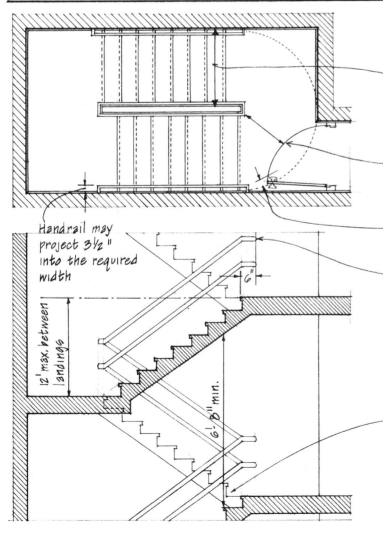

Handrail may project 3½" into the required width

12' max. between landings

6'-8" min.

6"

Building codes base the required width of a stair on the type of occupancy and the occupant load served.

Min. width	Occupant load (OL)
2'-8"	Private stairway; OL < 10
3'-0	OL ≤ 50
3'-8"	OL > 50

Door should swing in direction of exit. Door swing must not reduce the landing width to less than one half of its required width.

When fully open, the door must not intrude into required width by more than 3½".

Except for residential stairways and stairways less than 3'-8" in width, handrails are required on both sides of the stair. At least one handrail should extend beyond the top and bottom risers at least 6." The ends should return to a wall or terminate in a newel post.

Offsetting the risers at a landing can enable the handrail to turn without a pronounced vertical drop.

A wood stair is constructed of the following elements:

- <u>Carriages</u>, or rough stringers, are the main framing members that support the stair treads and risers.

- <u>Stringers</u> are the sloping side boards against which the risers and treads terminate; they are usually finish members although some are housed to serve as a carriage and support the risers and treads.

- <u>Treads</u> are the footways that span the distance between the carriages.

- <u>Risers</u> are vertical boards that close off the stair space and help make the construction rigid; some stairs have no risers.

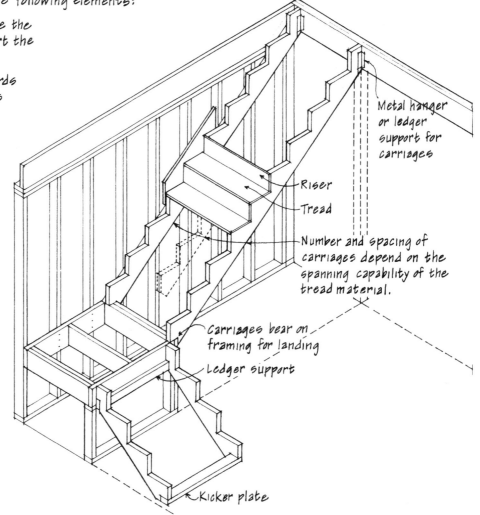

Metal hanger or ledger support for carriages

Riser

Tread

Number and spacing of carriages depend on the spanning capability of the tread material.

Carriages bear on framing for landing

Ledger support

Kicker plate

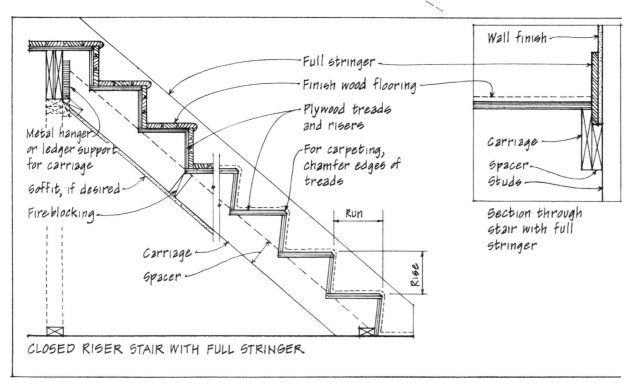

Full stringer

Finish wood flooring

Plywood treads and risers

For carpeting, chamfer edges of treads

Metal hanger or ledger support for carriage

Soffit, if desired

Fireblocking

Carriage

Spacer

Run

Rise

CLOSED RISER STAIR WITH FULL STRINGER

Wall finish

Carriage

Spacer

Studs

Section through stair with full stringer

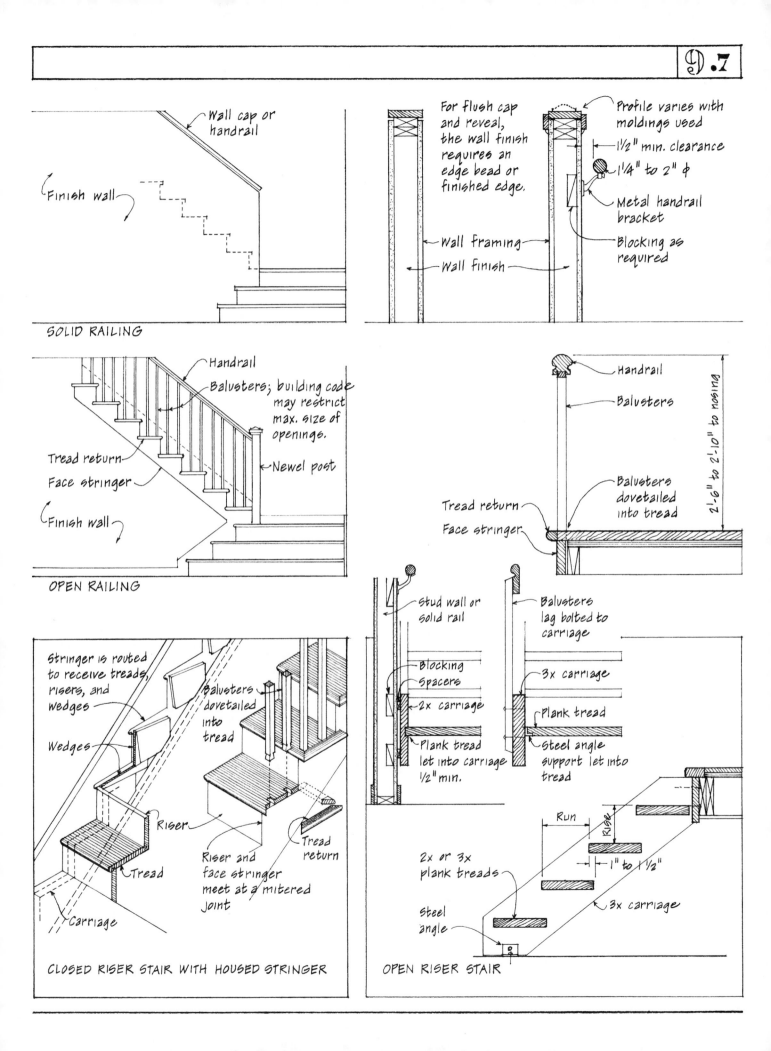

SOLID RAILING

Wall cap or handrail

Finish wall

For flush cap and reveal, the wall finish requires an edge bead or finished edge.

Wall framing

Wall finish

Profile varies with moldings used

1½" min. clearance

1¼" to 2" ∅

Metal handrail bracket

Blocking as required

OPEN RAILING

Handrail

Balusters; building code may restrict max. size of openings.

Tread return

Face stringer

Finish wall

Newel post

Handrail

Balusters

Balusters dovetailed into tread

Tread return

Face stringer

2'-6" to 2'-10" to nosing

CLOSED RISER STAIR WITH HOUSED STRINGER

Stringer is routed to receive treads, risers, and wedges

Balusters dovetailed into tread

Wedges

Riser

Riser and face stringer meet at a mitered joint

Tread return

Tread

Carriage

OPEN RISER STAIR

Stud wall or solid rail

Balusters lag bolted to carriage

Blocking spacers

3x carriage

2x carriage

Plank tread

Plank tread let into carriage ½" min.

Steel angle support let into tread

2x or 3x plank treads

steel angle

Run

Rise

1" to 1½"

3x carriage

Steel stairs are analogous in form to wood stairs.

- Steel channel sections serve as the stringers

- The stair treads span the distance between the stringers; they are usually in the form of steel pans filled with concrete.

- Steel treads may also consist of bar grating or flat plates with a textured top surface; these tread types are used in utility stairs.

- Pre-engineered and prefabricated steel stairs are available.

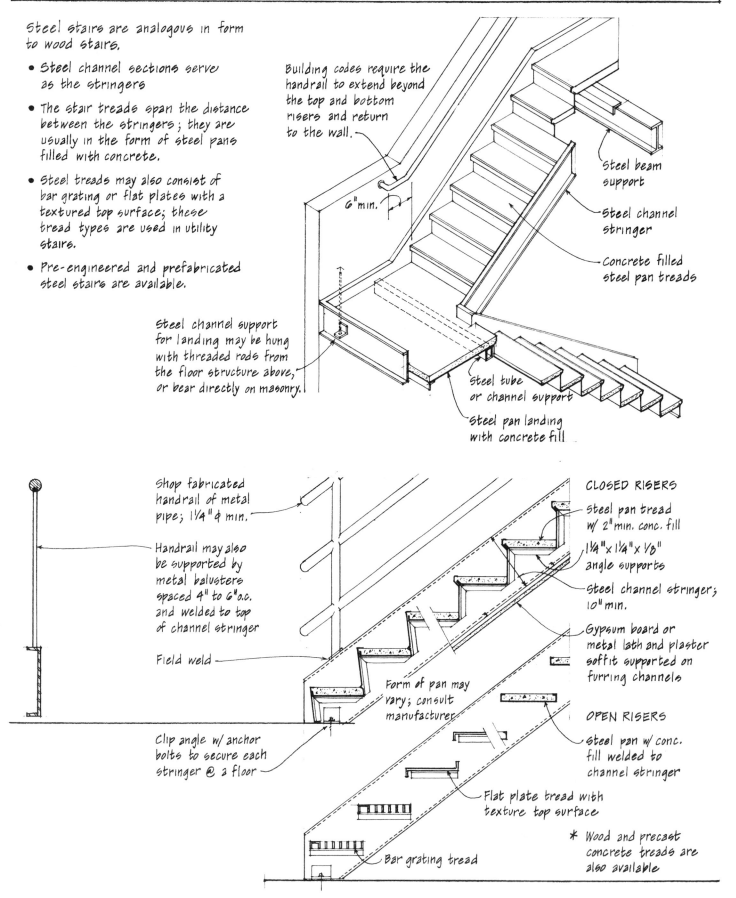

Building codes require the handrail to extend beyond the top and bottom risers and return to the wall.

6" min.

Steel beam support

Steel channel stringer

Concrete filled steel pan treads

Steel channel support for landing may be hung with threaded rods from the floor structure above, or bear directly on masonry.

Steel tube or channel support

Steel pan landing with concrete fill

Shop fabricated handrail of metal pipe; 1¼"∅ min.

Handrail may also be supported by metal balusters spaced 4" to 6" o.c. and welded to top of channel stringer

Field weld

Clip angle w/ anchor bolts to secure each stringer @ a floor

Form of pan may vary; consult manufacturer

CLOSED RISERS

steel pan tread w/ 2" min. conc. fill

1¼" x 1¼" x ⅛" angle supports

Steel channel stringer; 10" min.

Gypsum board or metal lath and plaster soffit supported on furring channels

OPEN RISERS

steel pan w/ conc. fill welded to channel stringer

Flat plate tread with texture top surface

Bar grating tread

* Wood and precast concrete treads are also available

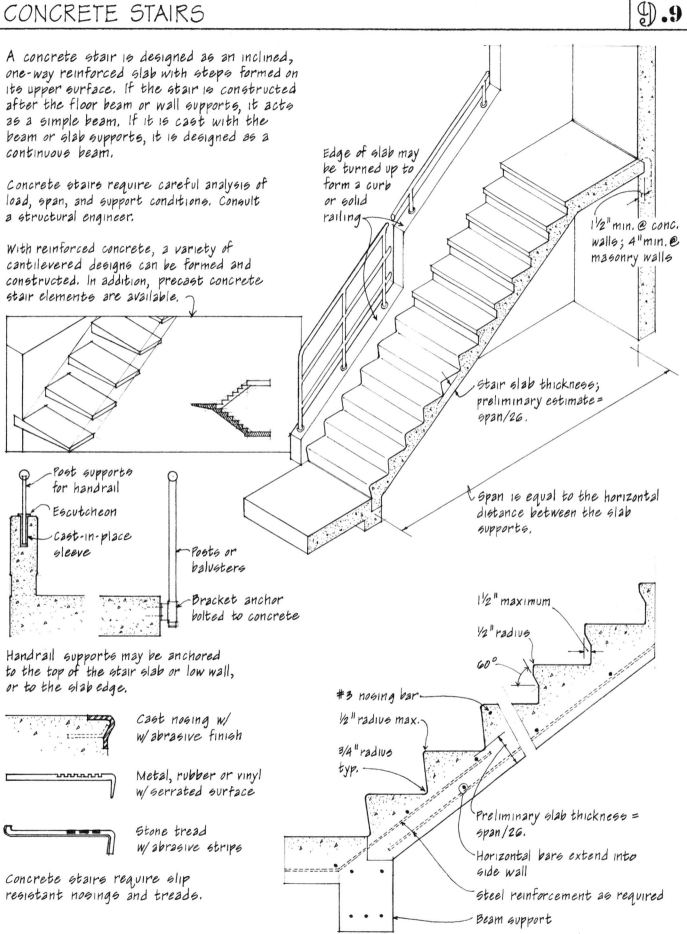

A concrete stair is designed as an inclined, one-way reinforced slab with steps formed on its upper surface. If the stair is constructed after the floor beam or wall supports, it acts as a simple beam. If it is cast with the beam or slab supports, it is designed as a continuous beam.

Concrete stairs require careful analysis of load, span, and support conditions. Consult a structural engineer.

With reinforced concrete, a variety of cantilevered designs can be formed and constructed. In addition, precast concrete stair elements are available.

Edge of slab may be turned up to form a curb or solid railing

1½" min. @ conc. walls; 4" min. @ masonry walls

Stair slab thickness; preliminary estimate = span/26.

Span is equal to the horizontal distance between the slab supports.

Post supports for handrail

Escutcheon

Cast-in-place sleeve

Posts or balusters

Bracket anchor bolted to concrete

Handrail supports may be anchored to the top of the stair slab or low wall, or to the slab edge.

Cast nosing w/ w/ abrasive finish

Metal, rubber or vinyl w/ serrated surface

Stone tread w/ abrasive strips

Concrete stairs require slip resistant nosings and treads.

1½" maximum

½" radius

60°

#3 nosing bar

½" radius max.

¾" radius typ.

Preliminary slab thickness = span/26.

Horizontal bars extend into side wall

Steel reinforcement as required

Beam support

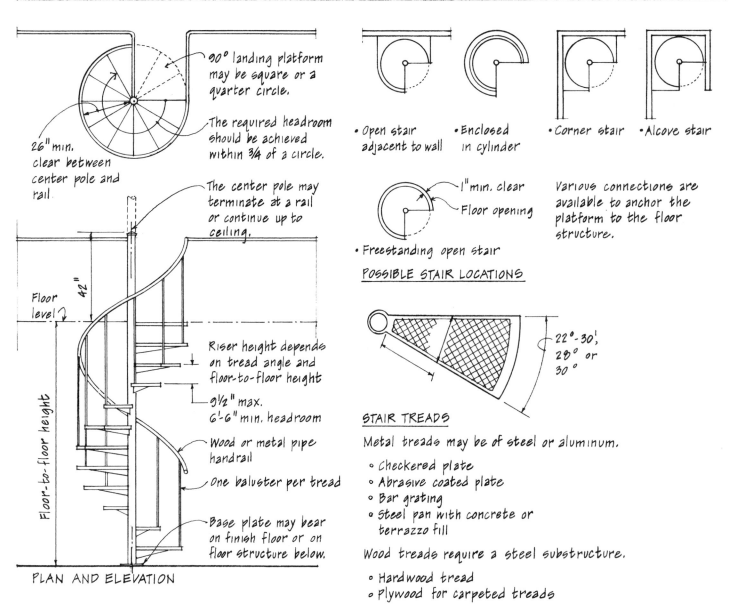

90° landing platform may be square or a quarter circle.

The required headroom should be achieved within ¾ of a circle.

26" min. clear between center pole and rail.

The center pole may terminate at a rail or continue up to ceiling.

42"

Floor level

Floor-to-floor height

Riser height depends on tread angle and floor-to-floor height

9½" max.
6'-6" min. headroom

Wood or metal pipe handrail

One baluster per tread

Base plate may bear on finish floor or on floor structure below.

PLAN AND ELEVATION

• Open stair adjacent to wall   • Enclosed in cylinder   • Corner stair   • Alcove stair

1" min. clear
Floor opening

Various connections are available to anchor the platform to the floor structure.

• Freestanding open stair

POSSIBLE STAIR LOCATIONS

22°-30',
28° or
30°

STAIR TREADS

Metal treads may be of steel or aluminum.

○ Checkered plate
○ Abrasive coated plate
○ Bar grating
○ Steel pan with concrete or terrazzo fill

Wood treads require a steel substructure.

○ Hardwood tread
○ Plywood for carpeted treads

REPRESENTATIVE SIZES AND DIMENSIONS OF SPIRAL STAIRS *

Tread angle	Nº of treads in a circle	Riser height	Headroom
22°-30'	16	7"	7'-0"
28°	12 - 13	7½"-7¾"	6'-9"
30°	12	8½"-9"	6'-9"

*
Consult manufacturer's literature to confirm the dimensional guidelines contained in these tables.

Stair diameter	Well opening	Platform size	Width: Pole to rail	Center pole/ base plate diameter
60"	64"	31"	26"	4" - 12"
66"	70"	34"	29"	4" - 12"
72"	76"	37"	31½"	4" - 12"
78"	82"	40"	34½"	4" - 12"
84"	88"	43"	37½"	6" - 12"
90"	94"	46"	40½"	6" - 12"
96"	100"	49"	43½"	6" - 12"

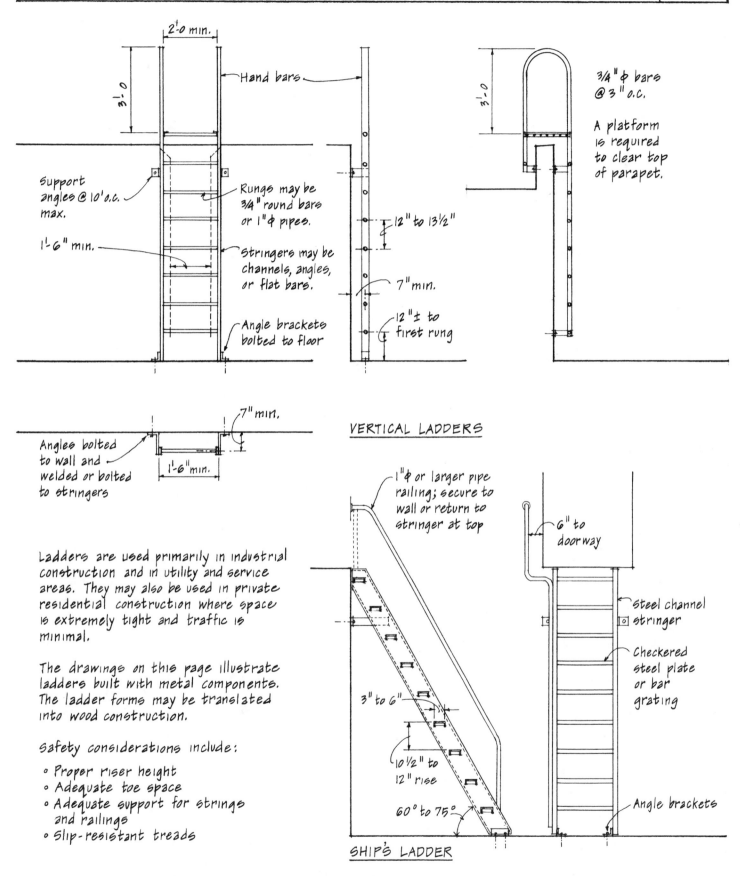

2'-0 min.

3'-0

Hand bars

3/4" ⌀ bars @ 3" o.c.

A platform is required to clear top of parapet.

3'-0

Support angles @ 10' o.c. max.

Rungs may be 3/4" round bars or 1" ⌀ pipes.

1'-6" min.

Stringers may be channels, angles, or flat bars.

12" to 13½"

7" min.

Angle brackets bolted to floor

12" ± to first rung

7" min.

Angles bolted to wall and welded or bolted to stringers

1'-6" min.

VERTICAL LADDERS

Ladders are used primarily in industrial construction and in utility and service areas. They may also be used in private residential construction where space is extremely tight and traffic is minimal.

The drawings on this page illustrate ladders built with metal components. The ladder forms may be translated into wood construction.

Safety considerations include:

o Proper riser height
o Adequate toe space
o Adequate support for strings and railings
o Slip-resistant treads

1" ⌀ or larger pipe railing; secure to wall or return to stringer at top

3" to 6"

10½" to 12" rise

60° to 75°

SHIP'S LADDER

6" to doorway

Steel channel stringer

Checkered steel plate or bar grating

Angle brackets

Elevators are means of direct, vertical travel for a building's occupants, equipment, and supplies. The type, size, number, and arrangement of elevators required are determined by:

- Type of occupancy
- Amount and tempo of traffic to be carried
- Total vertical travel distance
- Average round-trip time and elevator speed desired.

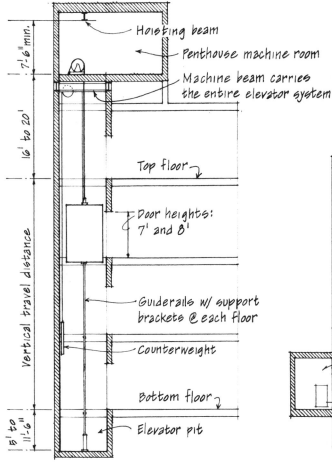

Hoisting beam

Penthouse machine room

Machine beam carries the entire elevator system

Top floor

Door heights: 7' and 8'

Guiderails w/ support brackets @ each floor

Counterweight

Bottom floor

Elevator pit

7'-6" min.

16' to 20'

Vertical travel distance

5' to 11'-6"

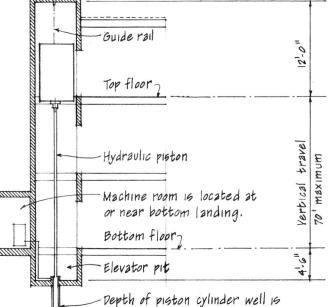

Guide rail

Top floor

Hydraulic piston

Machine room is located at or near bottom landing.

Bottom floor

Elevator pit

12'-0"

Vertical travel 70' maximum

4'-6"

Depth of piston cylinder well is equal to height of elevator travel.

ELECTRIC ELEVATORS

Electric-powered elevators require a penthouse to accommodate hoisting and control equipment. Geared traction elevators are capable of speeds up to 350 fpm and are suitable for medium-rise buildings. Gearless traction elevators are available with speeds up to 1200 fpm and typically serve highrise buildings.

HYDRAULIC ELEVATORS

A hydraulic elevator uses a hydraulic piston to raise and lower the elevator cab. It does not require a penthouse but its lower speed and piston length limit its use to buildings up to six stories in height.

- These guidelines are for preliminary planning only. Consult the local code and the elevator manufacturer for size and structural requirements as well as shaftway requirements for fire separation, ventilation, and soundproofing.

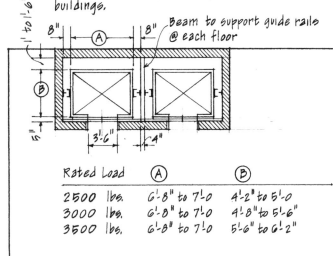

1' to 1'-6"

8" | 8"

Ⓐ

Ⓑ

5"

3'-6" | 4"

Beam to support guide rails @ each floor

Rated Load	Ⓐ	Ⓑ
2500 lbs.	6'-8" to 7'-0	4'-2" to 5'-0
3000 lbs.	6'-8" to 7'-0	4'-8" to 5'-6"
3500 lbs.	6'-8" to 7'-0	5'-6" to 6'-2"

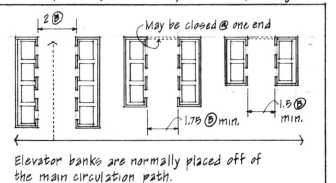

2 Ⓑ

May be closed @ one end

1.75 Ⓑ min.

1.5 Ⓑ min.

Elevator banks are normally placed off of the main circulation path.

Escalators can move a large number of people efficiently and comfortably among a limited number of floors. Six floors are a practical limit. Because escalators move at a constant speed, there is practically no waiting period, but there should be adequate queuing space at each loading and discharge point. Escalators cannot be used as required exits.

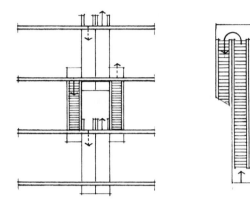

PARALLEL ARRANGEMENT

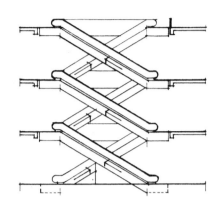

CRISSCROSS ARRANGEMENT

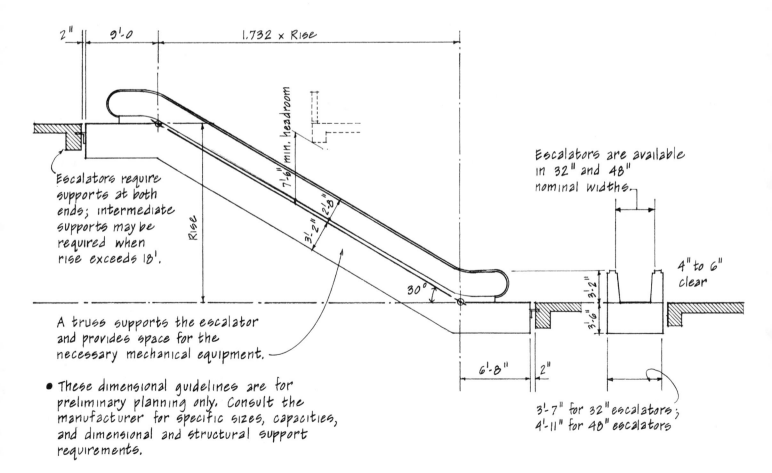

2"   9'-0   1.732 x Rise

7'-6" min. headroom

Rise

3'-2"   2'-8"

30°

Escalators require supports at both ends; intermediate supports may be required when rise exceeds 18'.

A truss supports the escalator and provides space for the necessary mechanical equipment.

Escalators are available in 32" and 48" nominal widths.

4" to 6" clear

3'-2"

3'-6"

6'-8"   2"

3'-7" for 32" escalators;
4'-11" for 48" escalators

• These dimensional guidelines are for preliminary planning only. Consult the manufacturer for specific sizes, capacities, and dimensional and structural support requirements.

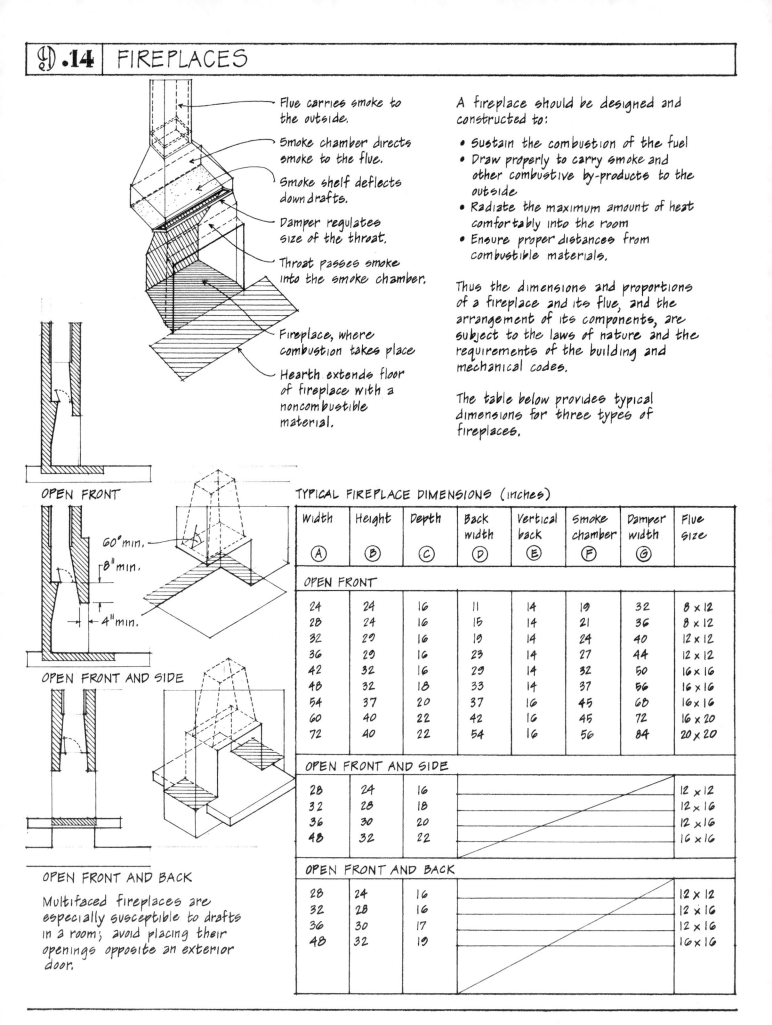

Flue carries smoke to the outside.

Smoke chamber directs smoke to the flue.

Smoke shelf deflects down drafts.

Damper regulates size of the throat.

Throat passes smoke into the smoke chamber.

Fireplace, where combustion takes place

Hearth extends floor of fireplace with a noncombustible material.

A fireplace should be designed and constructed to:

- Sustain the combustion of the fuel
- Draw properly to carry smoke and other combustive by-products to the outside
- Radiate the maximum amount of heat comfortably into the room
- Ensure proper distances from combustible materials.

Thus the dimensions and proportions of a fireplace and its flue, and the arrangement of its components, are subject to the laws of nature and the requirements of the building and mechanical codes.

The table below provides typical dimensions for three types of fireplaces.

OPEN FRONT

60° min.

8" min.

4" min.

OPEN FRONT AND SIDE

OPEN FRONT AND BACK

Multifaced fireplaces are especially susceptible to drafts in a room; avoid placing their openings opposite an exterior door.

TYPICAL FIREPLACE DIMENSIONS (inches)

Width ⓐ	Height ⓑ	Depth ⓒ	Back width ⓓ	Vertical back ⓔ	Smoke chamber ⓕ	Damper width ⓖ	Flue size
OPEN FRONT							
24	24	16	11	14	19	32	8 × 12
28	24	16	15	14	21	36	8 × 12
32	29	16	19	14	24	40	12 × 12
36	29	16	23	14	27	44	12 × 12
42	32	16	29	14	32	50	16 × 16
48	32	18	33	14	37	56	16 × 16
54	37	20	37	16	45	68	16 × 16
60	40	22	42	16	45	72	16 × 20
72	40	22	54	16	56	84	20 × 20
OPEN FRONT AND SIDE							
28	24	16					12 × 12
32	28	18					12 × 16
36	30	20					12 × 16
48	32	22					16 × 16
OPEN FRONT AND BACK							
28	24	16					12 × 12
32	28	16					12 × 16
36	30	17					12 × 16
48	32	19					16 × 16

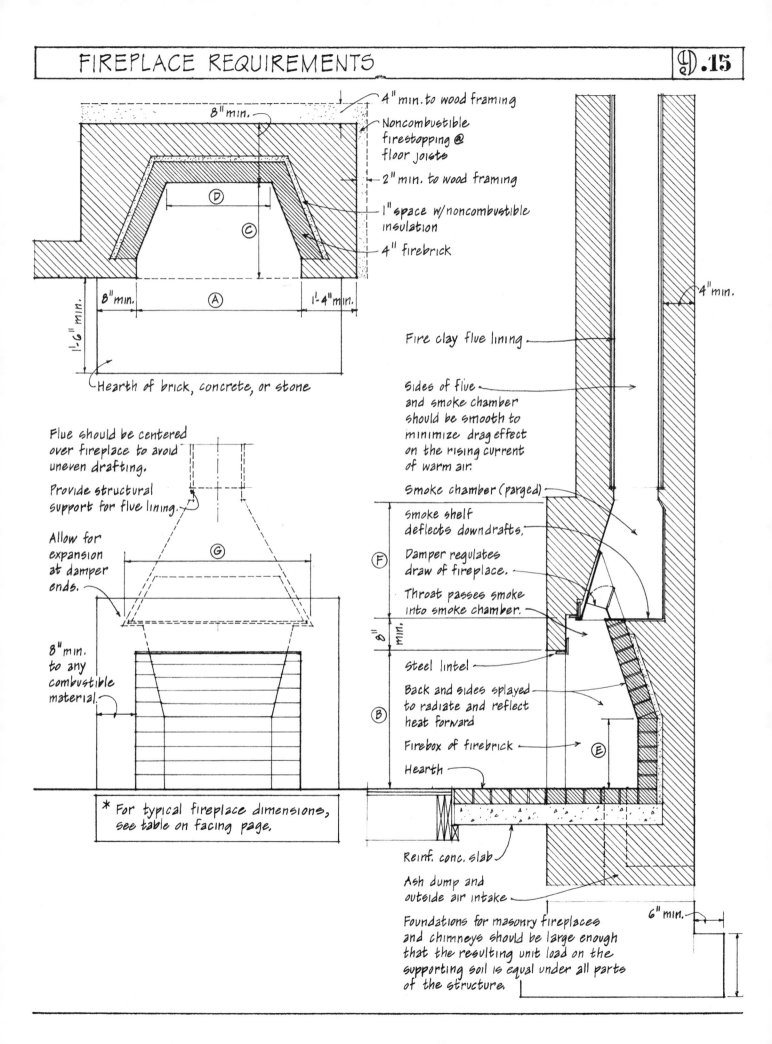

8" min.

4" min. to wood framing

Noncombustible firestopping @ floor joists

2" min. to wood framing

1" space w/noncombustible insulation

4" firebrick

Ⓓ

Ⓒ

Ⓐ

8" min.

1'-4" min.

1'-6" min.

Hearth of brick, concrete, or stone

4" min.

Fire clay flue lining

Sides of flue and smoke chamber should be smooth to minimize drag effect on the rising current of warm air.

Flue should be centered over fireplace to avoid uneven drafting.

Provide structural support for flue lining.

Allow for expansion at damper ends.

Ⓖ

8" min. to any combustible material.

Smoke chamber (parged)

smoke shelf deflects downdrafts.

Ⓕ

Damper regulates draw of fireplace.

Throat passes smoke into smoke chamber.

8" min.

Steel lintel

Back and sides splayed to radiate and reflect heat forward

Ⓑ

Firebox of firebrick

Ⓔ

Hearth

* For typical fireplace dimensions, see table on facing page.

Reinf. conc. slab

Ash dump and outside air intake

Foundations for masonry fireplaces and chimneys should be large enough that the resulting unit load on the supporting soil is equal under all parts of the structure.

6" min.

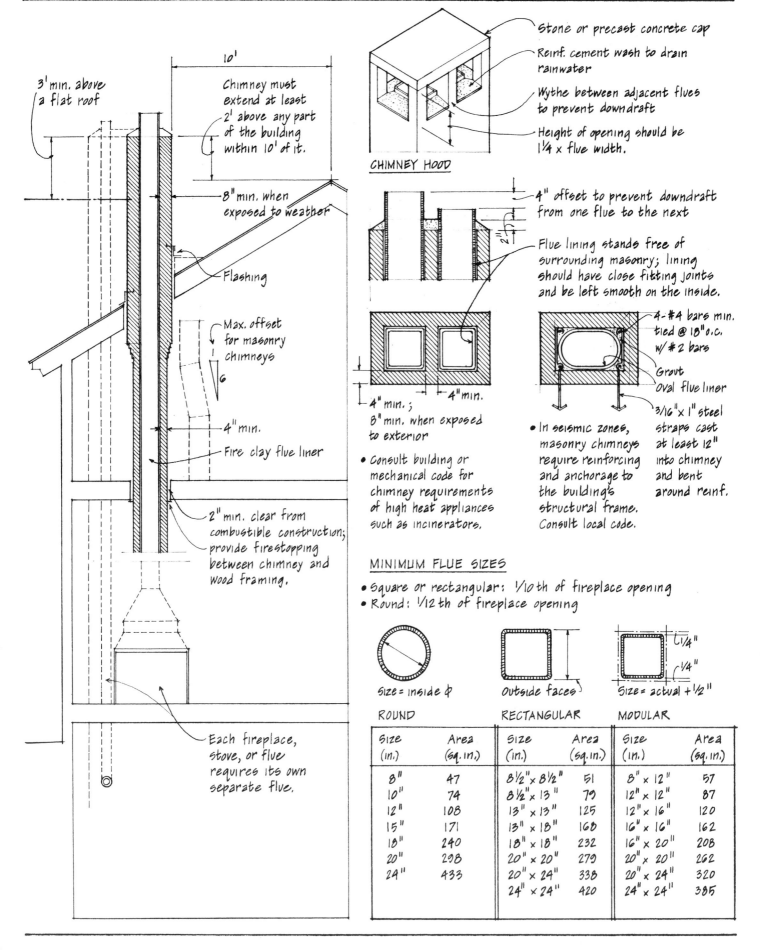

3' min. above a flat roof

10'

Chimney must extend at least 2' above any part of the building within 10' of it.

Stone or precast concrete cap

Reinf. cement wash to drain rainwater

Wythe between adjacent flues to prevent downdraft

Height of opening should be 1¼ x flue width.

CHIMNEY HOOD

8" min. when exposed to weather

Flashing

Max. offset for masonry chimneys

6

4" min.

Fire clay flue liner

2" min. clear from combustible construction; provide firestopping between chimney and wood framing.

4" offset to prevent downdraft from one flue to the next

2"

Flue lining stands free of surrounding masonry; lining should have close fitting joints and be left smooth on the inside.

4" min.; 8" min. when exposed to exterior

4" min.

4-#4 bars min. tied @ 18"o.c. w/ #2 bars

Grout

Oval flue liner

3/16"x 1" steel straps cast at least 12" into chimney and bent around reinf.

• Consult building or mechanical code for chimney requirements of high heat appliances such as incinerators.

• In seismic zones, masonry chimneys require reinforcing and anchorage to the building's structural frame. Consult local code.

Each fireplace, stove, or flue requires its own separate flue.

MINIMUM FLUE SIZES

• Square or rectangular: 1/10th of fireplace opening
• Round: 1/12th of fireplace opening

Size = inside ⌀

Outside faces

¼"

¼"

Size = actual + ½"

ROUND		RECTANGULAR		MODULAR	
Size (in.)	Area (sq. in.)	Size (in.)	Area (sq. in.)	Size (in.)	Area (sq. in.)
8"	47	8½" x 8½"	51	8" x 12"	57
10"	74	8½" x 13"	79	12" x 12"	87
12"	108	13" x 13"	125	12" x 16"	120
15"	171	13" x 18"	168	16" x 16"	162
18"	240	18" x 18"	232	16" x 20"	208
20"	298	20" x 20"	279	20" x 20"	262
24"	433	20" x 24"	338	20" x 24"	320
		24" x 24"	420	24" x 24"	385

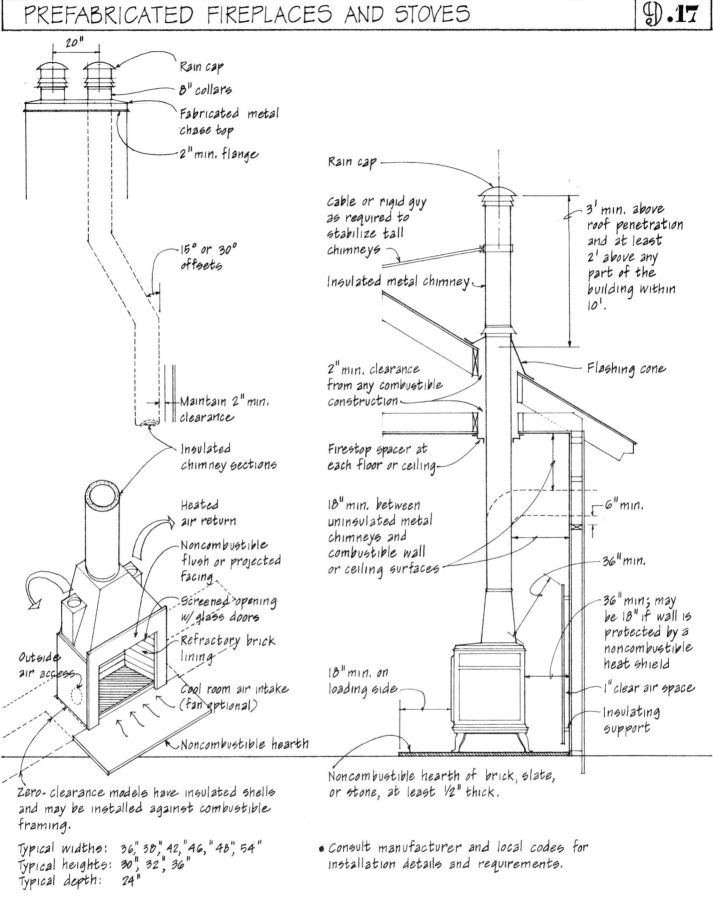

20"

Rain cap

8" collars

Fabricated metal chase top

2" min. flange

15° or 30° offsets

Maintain 2" min. clearance

Insulated chimney sections

Heated air return

Noncombustible flush or projected facing

Screened opening w/ glass doors

Refractory brick lining

Outside air access

Cool room air intake (fan optional)

Noncombustible hearth

Zero-clearance models have insulated shells and may be installed against combustible framing.

Typical widths: 36", 30", 42," 46," 48", 54"
Typical heights: 30", 32", 36"
Typical depth: 24"

Rain cap

Cable or rigid guy as required to stabilize tall chimneys

Insulated metal chimney

3' min. above roof penetration and at least 2' above any part of the building within 10'.

Flashing cone

2" min. clearance from any combustible construction

Firestop spacer at each floor or ceiling

18" min. between uninsulated metal chimneys and combustible wall or ceiling surfaces

6" min.

36" min.

36" min; may be 18" if wall is protected by a noncombustible heat shield

1" clear air space

Insulating support

18" min. on loading side

Noncombustible hearth of brick, slate, or stone, at least ½" thick.

• Consult manufacturer and local codes for installation details and requirements.

PREFABRICATED FIREPLACES

WOODBURNING STOVES

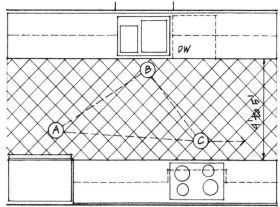

PARALLEL WALL

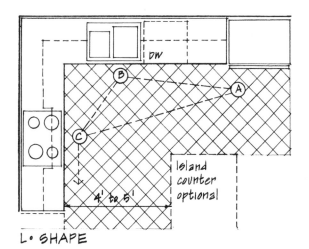

L• SHAPE

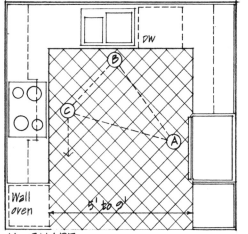

Wall oven

U• SHAPE

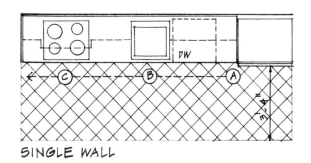

SINGLE WALL

These plans illustrate the basic types of kitchen layouts. These plans can be readily adapted to various structural or spatial situations, but they are all based on a work triangle that connects the three major kitchen centers:

Ⓐ Refrigerator center for receiving and food preparation;
Ⓑ Sink center for food preparation and clean-up;
Ⓒ Range center for cooking and serving.

The sum of the sides of the triangle should not be more than 22' nor less than 12'.

Additional factors to consider in laying out a kitchen space include:

• The type and size of fixtures and appliances to be used
• The amount of work surfaces and storage required
• The degree of enclosure envisioned for the space
• Requirements for natural light, views, and ventilation
• The type and degree of access desired
• The integration of electrical, plumbing, and mechanical systems

HANDICAPPED ACCESS

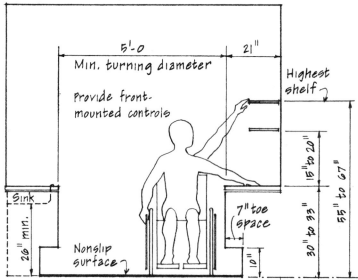

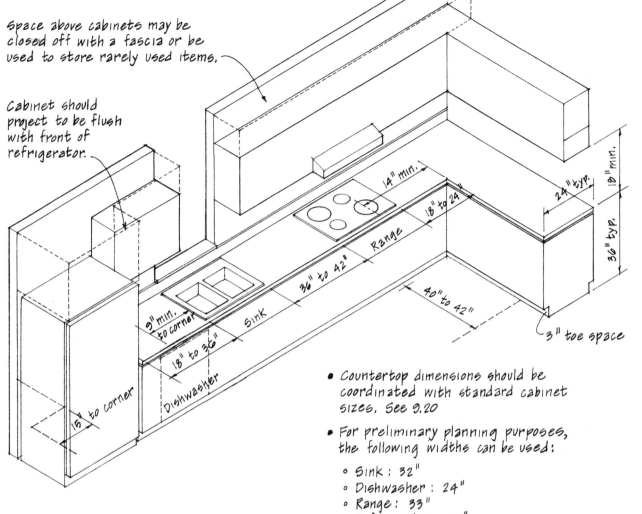

Space above cabinets may be closed off with a fascia or be used to store rarely used items.

Cabinet should project to be flush with front of refrigerator.

14" min.

18" to 24"

24" typ.

18" min.

36" typ.

3" toe space

40" to 42"

36" to 42"

Range

18" to 24"

Sink

9" min. to corner

18" to 36"

Dishwasher

15" to corner

- Countertop dimensions should be coordinated with standard cabinet sizes. See 9.20

- For preliminary planning purposes, the following widths can be used:
  - Sink: 32"
  - Dishwasher: 24"
  - Range: 33"
  - Refrigerator: 32"

- Under counter and overhead storage requirements will influence the layout and work center dimensions.

KITCHEN HEIGHTS AND CLEARANCES

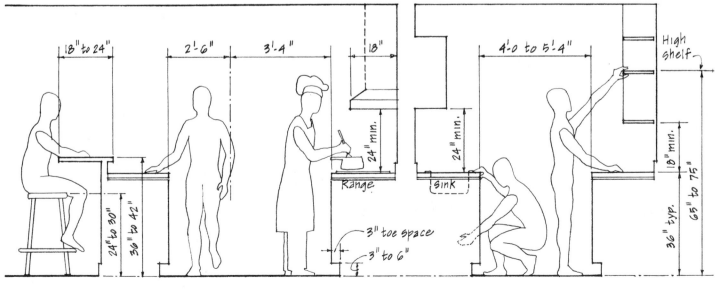

18" to 24"

2'-6"

3'-4"

18"

4'-0 to 5'-4"

High shelf

24" min.

Range

24" min.

Sink

18" min.

36" typ.

65" to 75"

24" to 30"

36" to 42"

3" toe space

3" to 6"

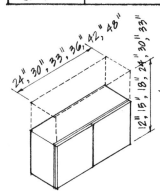
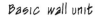

Basic wall unit

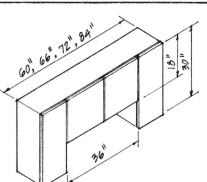
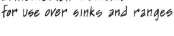

Combination wall unit
for use over sinks and ranges

Kitchen cabinets may be made of enameled steel or of wood. Wood cabinets are usually of particle board or plywood with hardwood frames, and may have plastic laminate, hardwood veneer, or lacquer finishes.

Stock kitchen cabinets are manufactured in 3" modules and should conform to standards established by the National Kitchen Cabinet Association (NKCA). There are three basic types of units: base units, wall units, and special units. Consult manufacturer for available sizes, finishes, hardware, and accessories.

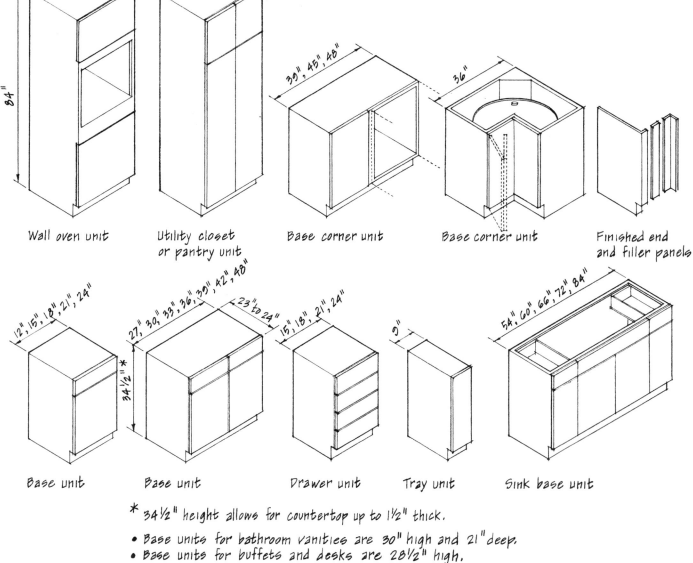

Wall oven unit

Utility closet or pantry unit

Base corner unit

Base corner unit

Finished end and filler panels

Base unit

Base unit

Drawer unit

Tray unit

Sink base unit

* 34½" height allows for countertop up to 1½" thick.

• Base units for bathroom vanities are 30" high and 21" deep.
• Base units for buffets and desks are 28½" high.

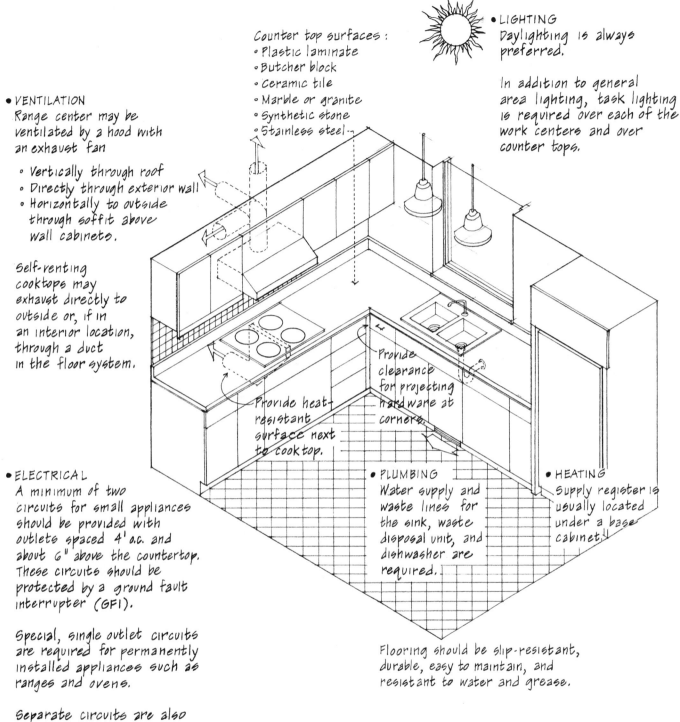

Counter top surfaces:
- Plastic laminate
- Butcher block
- Ceramic tile
- Marble or granite
- Synthetic stone
- Stainless steel

• LIGHTING
Daylighting is always preferred.

In addition to general area lighting, task lighting is required over each of the work centers and over counter tops.

• VENTILATION
Range center may be ventilated by a hood with an exhaust fan

- Vertically through roof
- Directly through exterior wall
- Horizontally to outside through soffit above wall cabinets.

Self-venting cooktops may exhaust directly to outside or, if in an interior location, through a duct in the floor system.

Provide heat-resistant surface next to cooktop.

Provide clearance for projecting hardware at corners.

• ELECTRICAL
A minimum of two circuits for small appliances should be provided with outlets spaced 4' o.c. and about 6" above the countertop. These circuits should be protected by a ground fault interrupter (GFI).

Special, single outlet circuits are required for permanently installed appliances such as ranges and ovens.

Separate circuits are also required for appliances such as the refrigerator, dishwasher, garbage disposal unit, and microwave oven.

• GAS
Gas appliances require their separate fuel supply lines.

• PLUMBING
Water supply and waste lines for the sink, waste disposal unit, and dishwasher are required.

• HEATING
Supply register is usually located under a base cabinet.

Flooring should be slip-resistant, durable, easy to maintain, and resistant to water and grease.

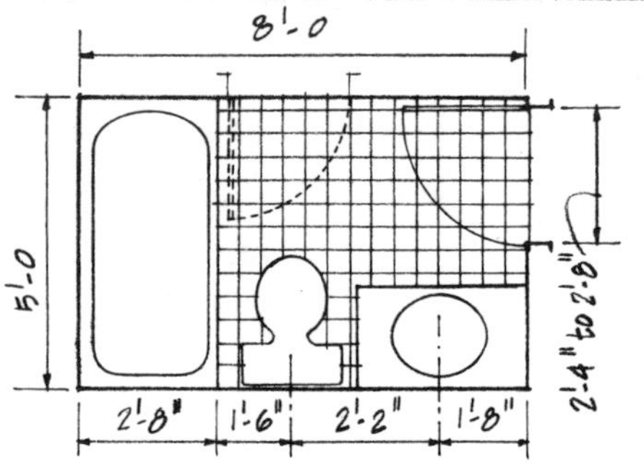

These bathroom plans illustrate basic layouts and relationships which can be adjusted to suit specific situations. Fixture spacing and clearances are important for safe and comfortable movement within a bathroom space. Recommended dimensions can be perceived through the study of these plans and the drawings on the facing page. The overall dimensions of a bathroom may vary according to the actual sizes of the fixtures used.

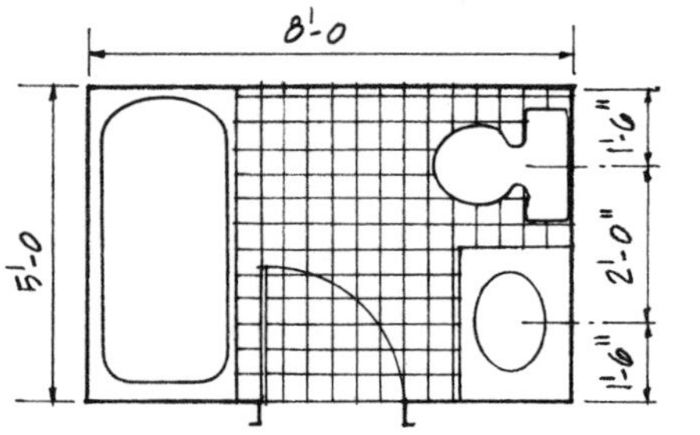

The layout of bathrooms and other restroom facilities should also take into account:

- the space for and locations of accessories such as towel bars, mirrors, and medicine cabinets
- the number of plumbing walls required and the location of stacks, vents, and horizontal runs.

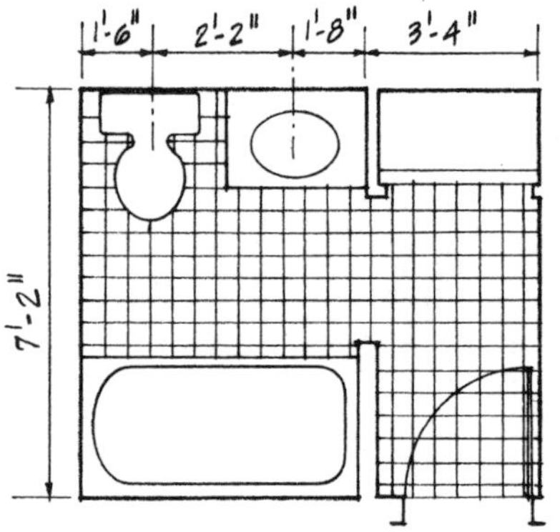

WHEELCHAIR ACCESS

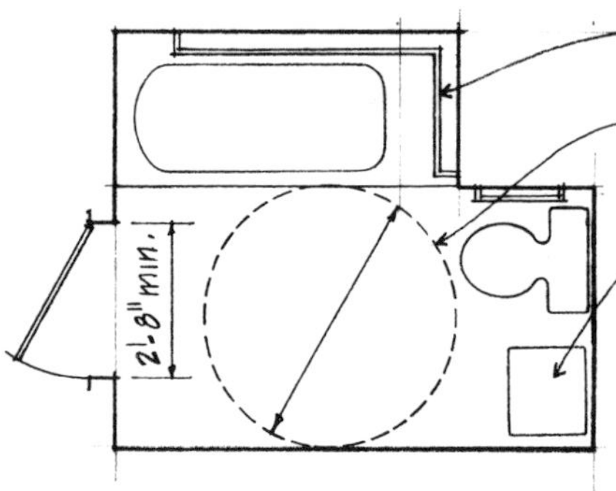

- Provide grab bars around tub and water closet.
- Provide a min. 5' diameter space for turning around.
- Provide knee space 26" high under sink.

- Provide oversized stalls in public restrooms.

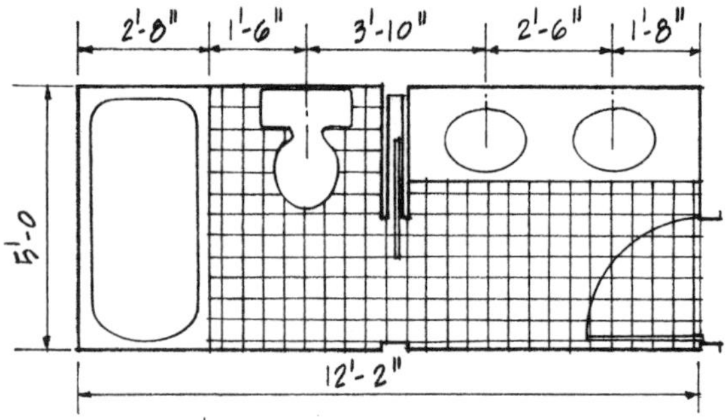

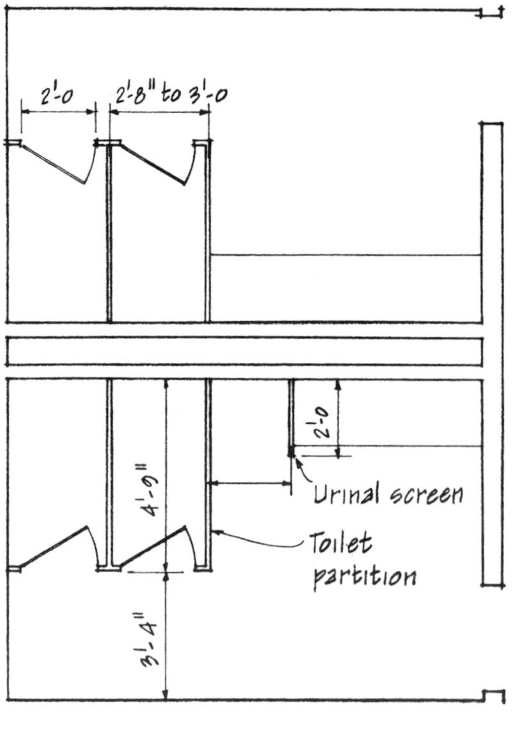

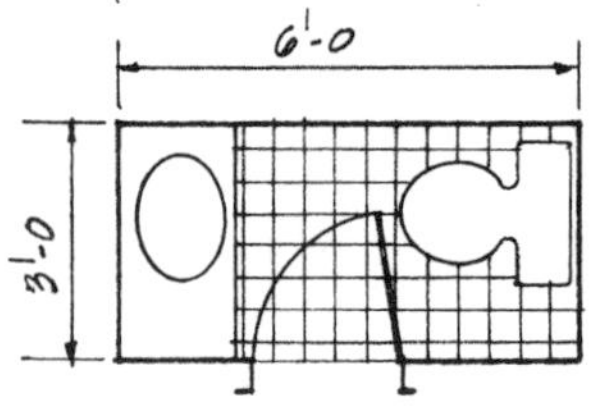

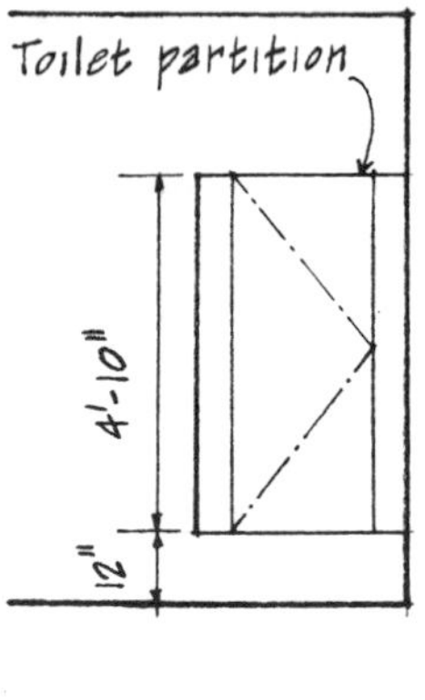

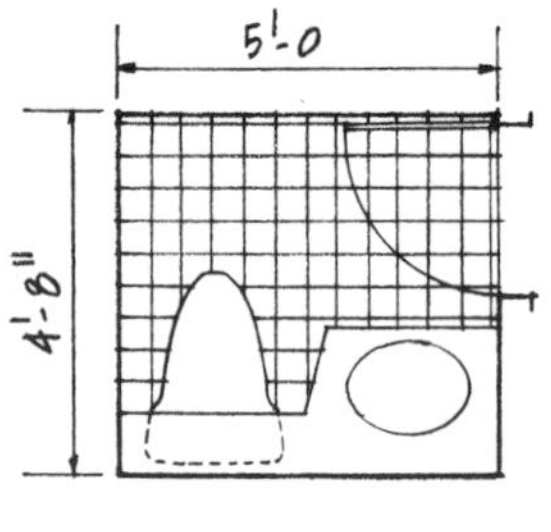

Urinal screen

Toilet partition

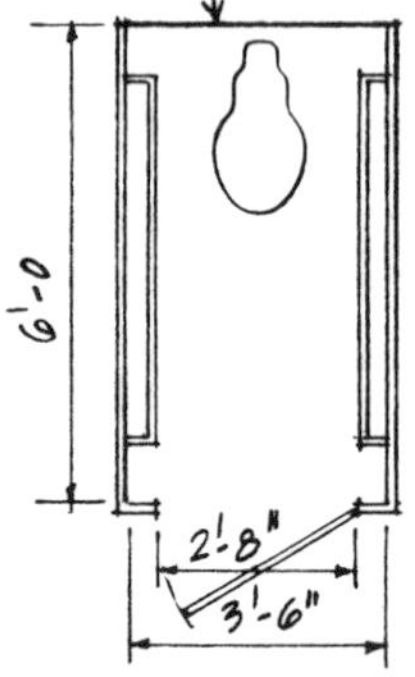

Toilet partition

	Water closet	Lavatory	Lavatory	Bathtub	Shower
Width:	20" to 24" (seat 14")	30" to 36"	18" to 24"	3'-6" to 6'-0	2'-6" to 3'-6"
Depth:	22" to 29"	21"	16" to 21"	2'-6" to 2'-8"	2'-6" to 3'-6"
Height:	20" to 28" (seat 15")	31"	31" rim to floor	12" to 20"	6'-2" to 6'-8"

May be surface mounted, semi-recessed, or fully recessed.

	Urinal	Bidet	Square bathtub	Water cooler
Width:	18"	14"	3'-8" to 4'-2"	10" to 18"
Depth:	12" to 24"	30"	3'-8" to 4'-2"	10" to 14"
Height:	24" rim to floor	14"	12" to 16"	15" to 30"

	Utility sink	Single bowl sink	Double bowl	Double bowl with drainboards
Width:	22" to 48"	12" to 33"	28" to 46"	54" to 84"
Depth:	18" to 22"	13" to 21"	16" to 21"	21" to 25"
Height:	27" to 29" rim to floor	8" to 12"	8" to 10"	8"

The range of fixture dimensions shown above is for preliminary planning. Consult manufacturer for actual dimensions of specific models.

FIXTURE MATERIALS

- Water closets, urinals, and bidets: Vitreous china
- Lavatories, bathtubs, and utility sinks: . . . . . . Vitreous china
  Enameled cast iron
  Enameled steel
- Shower receptors: . . . . Terrazzo
  Enameled steel
- Shower enclosures: . . . . Enameled steel
  Stainless steel
  Ceramic tile
  Fiberglass
- Kitchen sinks: . . . . Enameled cast iron
  Enameled steel
  Stainless steel

FIXTURE CLEARANCES

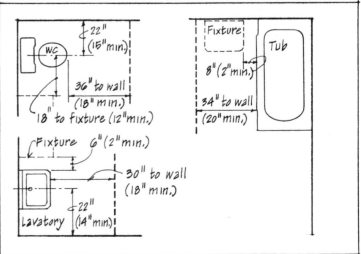

Bathrooms require natural or mechanical ventilation.

- Operable windows or skylights provide natural ventilation.
- Exhaust fan (which may be combined with a light fixture, fan forced heater, or a radiant heat lamp) should be located close to the shower or high on an exterior wall opposite the bathroom door.
- The light fixture over the tub or shower should be resistant to water vapor.

Backing for the tub or shower enclosure should be moisture resistant.

All finishes should be durable, sanitary, and easy to clean, and flooring should have a nonslip surface.

Daylighting is always desirable.

A single overhead light fixture is usually not acceptable. Auxiliary lighting is required over the tub or shower, over the lavatory and vanity counter, and over any compartmentalized toilet spaces.

Plumbing walls should have sufficient depth to accommodate the required water supply and waste lines and vents.

Electrical switches and convenience outlets should not be accessible from tub or shower. All convenience outlets should be protected by a ground fault interrupter (GFI).

Space is required for accessories such as a medicine cabinet, mirror, towel bars, toilet paper holder, and soap dish.

Storage space is required for towels, linen, and supplies.

FINISH WORK | 10

This chapter illustrates the major materials and methods used to finish a building's exterior and interior surfaces. Exterior wall surfaces should be durable and weather-resistant. Interior walls should be wear-resistant and cleanable; floors should be durable and safe to walk on; ceilings should be relatively maintenance-free.

Rigid finish materials capable of spanning short distances may be applied to a supporting grid of linear members. More flexible finish materials, on the other hand, require a solid, rigid backing. Additional technical factors to consider include a finish material's acoustic qualities, fire resistance, and thermal insulation value.

Surface finishes have a critical influence on the aesthetic qualities of a space. In the selection and use of a finish material, we should carefully consider color, texture, pattern, and the way it meets and joins with other materials. If a finish material has modular characteristics, then its unit dimensions can be used to regulate the dimensions of a wall, floor, or ceiling surface.

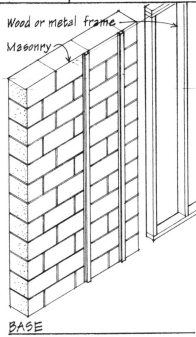

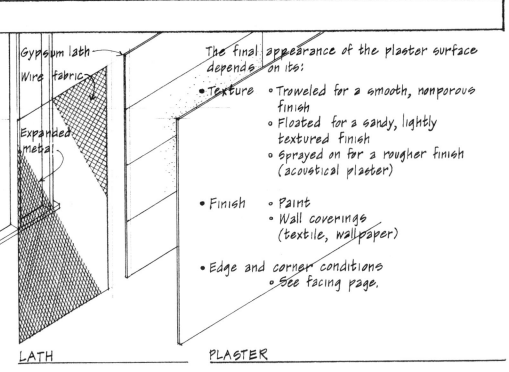

Wood or metal frame

Masonry

Gypsum lath

Wire fabric

Expanded metal

The final appearance of the plaster surface depends on its:

- Texture
  - Troweled for a smooth, nonporous finish
  - Floated for a sandy, lightly textured finish
  - Sprayed on for a rougher finish (acoustical plaster)

- Finish
  - Paint
  - Wall coverings (textile, wallpaper)

- Edge and corner conditions
  - See facing page.

BASE

LATH

PLASTER

BASE

Masonry Walls:

- Plaster may be applied directly to masonry or concrete surfaces.
- These surfaces must be sufficiently rough and porous to allow for a good bond, and free of oil and other parting materials.
- Bonding agents are used when applying plaster directly to dense, nonporous surfaces such as concrete.
- Where there is a possibility of moisture or condensation getting into the wall, plaster should be applied over lath and furring.

Wood or Metal Framing:

- The framing supports the metal or gypsum lath to which the plaster is applied.
- The frame must be sturdy, rigid, plane, and level.
- Deflection should be limited to 1/360 th of the framing's span.

LATH

Metal Lath:

- Metal lath consists of expanded sheet metal or wire fabric.
- The metal is usually a steel alloy which is galvanized or coated with a rust-inhibiting paint.
- The weight and strength of the metal lath used is related to the spacing and rigidity of its supports.
- Paper-backed metal lath is used as a base for ceramic tile and exterior stucco walls.

Gypsum Lath:

- Gypsum lath consists of sheets of hardened gypsum plaster faced with a fibrous paper to which plaster adheres.
- Perforated gypsum lath has 3/4"⌀ holes @ 4"o.c. to improve the plaster bond under fire exposure.
- Insulating (foil-backed) and fire-resistant (Type X) laths are available.

PLASTER

Gypsum Plaster:

Plaster is a cementitious material that sets and hardens to form a finish wall or ceiling surface. Gypsum plaster may be used for any interior wall or ceiling surface that is not subject to severe moisture conditions. Stucco is a portland cement plaster which is used primarily as an exterior cladding material. (See 10.8 for more on stucco.)

Gypsum plaster consists of calcined gypsum, water, and an aggregate, such as fine sand. Organic fibers may be added to basecoat plaster to help form mechanical keys with metal lath. Wood fiber or perlite is used to decrease the plaster's weight and to increase its fire resistance. Lime is used to improve a plaster's workability. Keene's cement is used in finish coat plasters when a dense, smooth surface is desired.

Plaster is applied in layers, the number of which depends on the type and strength of the base used.

1. Scratch coat must adhere firmly to the lath and be raked to provide a keyed foundation for the following coats.
2. Brown coat is brought up to the grounds and provides a level base for the finish coat.
3. Finish coat is the final thin layer of plaster.

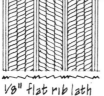

Diamond mesh | 1/8" flat rib lath | 3/8" rib lath | woven wire (for stucco only)

METAL LATHS

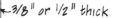

3/8" or 1/2" thick

16" wide x 48" long
(24" widths and lengths to 12'
are available.)

Metal lath type	Weight lbs./S.F.	Support spacing (inches o.c.)	
		Vertical	Horizontal
Diamond mesh	0.27	16	12
Diamond mesh	0.38	16	16
1/8" flat rib lath	0.31	16	12
1/8" flat rib lath	0.38	24	19
3/8" rib lath	0.38	24	24
Welded or woven wire	0.19	16	16
Wire fabric w/ paper backing	0.19	16	16

GYPSUM LATH

- 16" spacing for both horizontal and vertical applications
- Available with a foil backing which serves as a vapor barrier and a reflective insulator
- Type X lath has glass fibers and other additives to improve its fire resistance.

ACCESSORIES

Metal Trim Shapes:

Various metal accessories are used to trim the edges and corners of plaster surfaces. These trim accessories also serve as grounds which help the plasterer level the finish coat and bring it up to the proper thickness. For this reason, all grounds should be securely fastened to their supports and installed straight, level, and plumb.

Wood grounds may be used where a nailable base is required for the addition of wood trim.

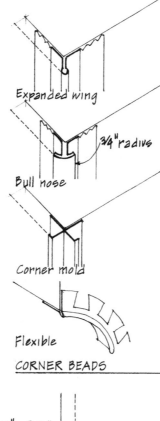

Expanded wing

3/4" radius

Bull nose

Corner mold

Corner mold

Flexible

CORNER BEADS

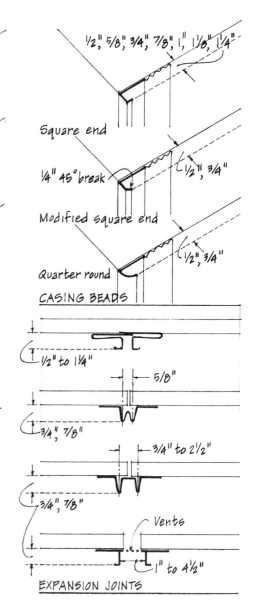

1/2", 5/8", 3/4", 7/8", 1", 1 1/8", 1 1/4"

Square end

1/4" 45° break / 1/2", 3/4"

Modified square end / 1/2", 3/4"

Quarter round / 1/2", 3/4"

CASING BEADS

1/2" to 1 1/4"

5/8"

3/4", 7/8"

3/4" to 2 1/2"

3/4", 7/8"

Vents

1" to 4 1/2"

EXPANSION JOINTS

1/2"

3/4"

2 1/16"

1/8"

PICTURE MOLDS

3/4" reveal

Plaster face

3/4"

F. REVEAL MOLD

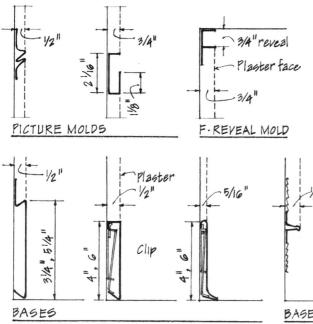

1/2"

3/4", 5 1/4"

4", 6"

Plaster 1/2"

Clip

4", 6"

5/16"

4", 6"

BASES

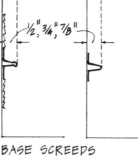

1/2", 3/4", 7/8"

BASE SCREEDS

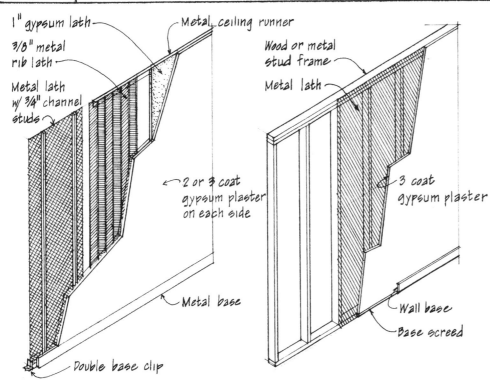

1" gypsum lath

3/8" metal rib lath

Metal lath w/ 3/4" channel studs

Metal ceiling runner

2 or 3 coat gypsum plaster on each side

Metal base

Double base clip

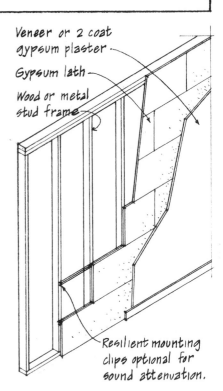

Wood or metal stud frame

Metal lath

3 coat gypsum plaster

Wall base

Base screed

Veneer or 2 coat gypsum plaster

Gypsum lath

Wood or metal stud frame

Resilient mounting clips optional for sound attenuation.

SOLID PLASTER PARTITION

- 2" total thickness of partition conserves floor space.

- 3 coat plaster is applied to both sides of metal or gypsum lath.

- Proprietary ceiling runners and floor runners or base clips are required to stabilize the partition.

- 3/4" channels are used to reinforce the partition around wall openings.

PLASTER OVER METAL LATH

- 3 coat plaster with a total thickness of 5/8" to 3/4" is applied over metal lath.

- The wood or metal studs are spaced 16" or 24" o.c., depending on the weight of metal lath used. See table on 10.3.

- The long dimension of the lath is laid across the supports; rib lath laid with the ribs across the supports.

- Lath is lapped 1/2" on the sides, 1" at the ends, and 3" at internal corners; use corner beads at external corners.

PLASTER OVER GYPSUM LATH

- 2 coat plaster is normally used over gypsum lath.

- Veneer plaster is a high strength plaster that can be applied as a very thin (1/16" to 1/8") 1 or 2 coat finish over a special gypsum board base.

- Supports are spaced 16" o.c. for 3/8" lath, and 24" o.c. for 1/2" lath.

- The long dimension of the lath is laid across the supports; ends of lath should bear on a support or be supported by sheet metal clips.

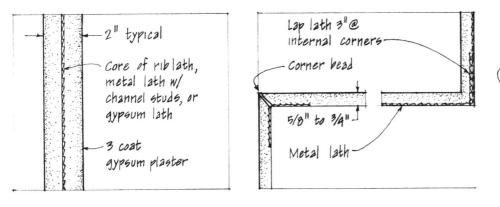

2" typical

Core of rib lath, metal lath w/ channel studs, or gypsum lath

3 coat gypsum plaster

Lap lath 3" @ internal corners

Corner bead

5/8" to 3/4"

Metal lath

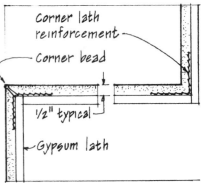

Corner lath reinforcement

Corner bead

1/2" typical

Gypsum lath

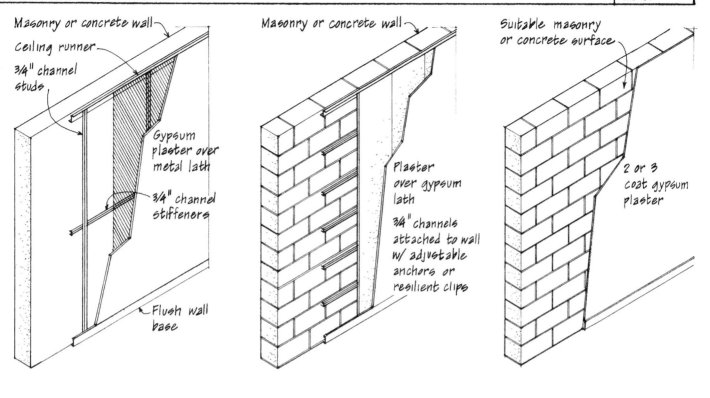

Masonry or concrete wall
Ceiling runner
3/4" channel studs
Gypsum plaster over metal lath
3/4" channel stiffeners
Flush wall base

Masonry or concrete wall
Plaster over gypsum lath
3/4" channels attached to wall w/ adjustable anchors or resilient clips

Suitable masonry or concrete surface
2 or 3 coat gypsum plaster

PLASTER OVER FURRING   PLASTER OVER FURRING   DIRECT APPLICATION

- Plaster should be applied over lath and furring when:
  - The masonry surface is not suitable for direct application.
  - The possibility exists that moisture or condensation might penetrate the wall.
  - Additional air space or space for insulating material is required.
  - A resilient wall surface is desired for acoustical treatment of the space.
- Plaster requires either metal or gypsum lath over the furring; the application and support spacing are similar to the examples shown on the preceding page.
- Wood or metal furring may be applied vertically or horizontally.
- Horizontal stiffeners may be required for vertical furring that is installed away from the wall.
- Furring may be attached to the wall with resilient clips for acoustical treatment and independent movement between the plaster and masonry.
- Wall anchors are available that adjust to various furring depths.

- 2 coat plaster, 5/8" thick, is normally used when applied directly over masonry.
- Plaster may be applied directly to brick, clay tile, or concrete masonry if the surface is sufficiently rough and porous to allow for a good bond.
- A bonding agent is required when applying plaster directly to dense, nonporous surfaces such as concrete.

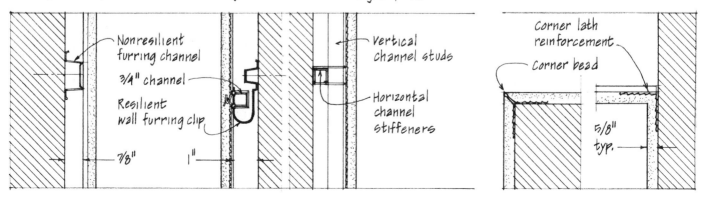

Nonresilient furring channel
3/4" channel
Resilient wall furring clip
7/8"
1"

Vertical channel studs
Horizontal channel stiffeners

Corner lath reinforcement
Corner bead
5/8" typ.

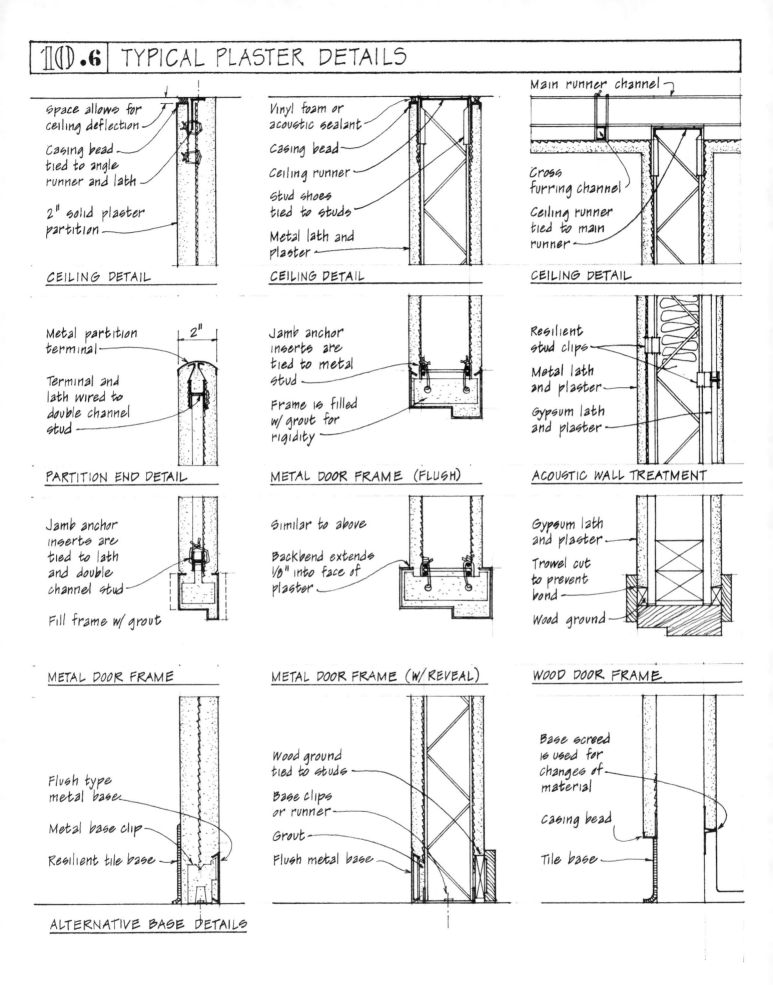

space allows for ceiling deflection

Casing bead tied to angle runner and lath

2" solid plaster partition

CEILING DETAIL

Vinyl foam or acoustic sealant

Casing bead

Ceiling runner

Stud shoes tied to studs

Metal lath and plaster

CEILING DETAIL

Main runner channel

Cross furring channel

Ceiling runner tied to main runner

CEILING DETAIL

Metal partition terminal

Terminal and lath wired to double channel stud

2"

PARTITION END DETAIL

Jamb anchor inserts are tied to metal stud

Frame is filled w/ grout for rigidity

METAL DOOR FRAME (FLUSH)

Resilient stud clips

Metal lath and plaster

Gypsum lath and plaster

ACOUSTIC WALL TREATMENT

Jamb anchor inserts are tied to lath and double channel stud

Fill frame w/ grout

METAL DOOR FRAME

Similar to above

Backbend extends ⅛" into face of plaster

METAL DOOR FRAME (W/ REVEAL)

Gypsum lath and plaster

Trowel cut to prevent bond

Wood ground

WOOD DOOR FRAME

Flush type metal base

Metal base clip

Resilient tile base

ALTERNATIVE BASE DETAILS

Wood ground tied to studs

Base clips or runner

Grout

Flush metal base

Base screed is used for changes of material

Casing bead

Tile base

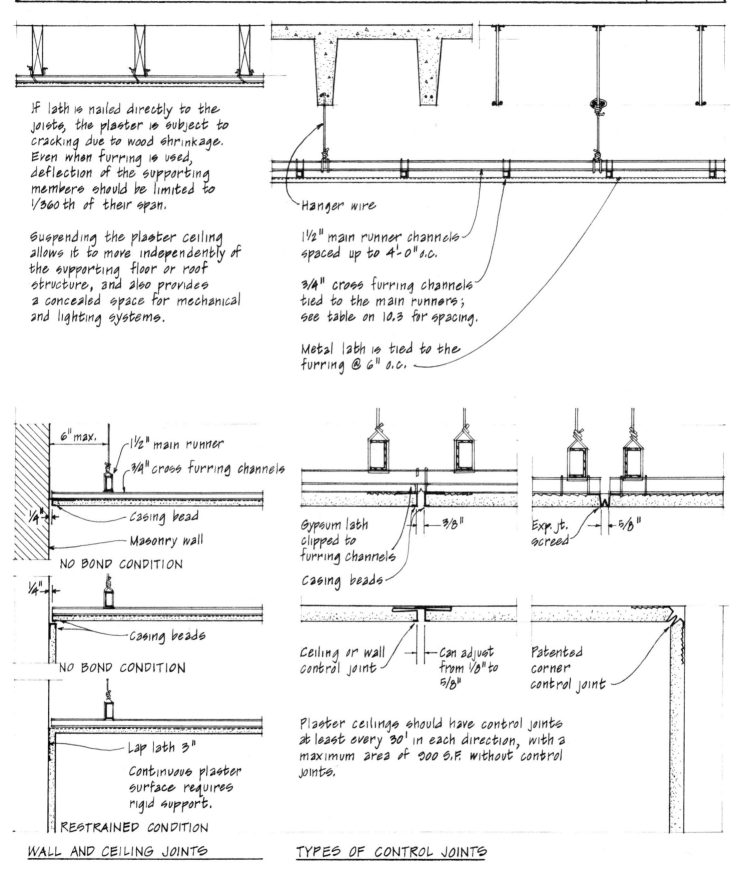

If lath is nailed directly to the joists, the plaster is subject to cracking due to wood shrinkage. Even when furring is used, deflection of the supporting members should be limited to 1/360th of their span.

Suspending the plaster ceiling allows it to move independently of the supporting floor or roof structure, and also provides a concealed space for mechanical and lighting systems.

Hanger wire

1½" main runner channels spaced up to 4'-0" o.c.

3/4" cross furring channels tied to the main runners; see table on 10.3 for spacing.

Metal lath is tied to the furring @ 6" o.c.

6" max.

1½" main runner

3/4" cross furring channels

Casing bead

Masonry wall

¼"

NO BOND CONDITION

¼"

Casing beads

NO BOND CONDITION

Lap lath 3"

Continuous plaster surface requires rigid support.

RESTRAINED CONDITION

WALL AND CEILING JOINTS

Gypsum lath clipped to furring channels

Casing beads

3/8"

Exp. jt. screed

5/8"

Ceiling or wall control joint

Can adjust from 1/8" to 5/8"

Patented corner control joint

Plaster ceilings should have control joints at least every 30' in each direction, with a maximum area of 900 S.F. without control joints.

TYPES OF CONTROL JOINTS

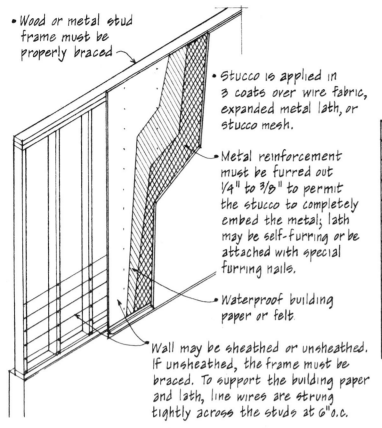

• Wood or metal stud frame must be properly braced

• Stucco is applied in 3 coats over wire fabric, expanded metal lath, or stucco mesh.

• Metal reinforcement must be furred out 1/4" to 3/8" to permit the stucco to completely embed the metal; lath may be self-furring or be attached with special furring nails.

• Waterproof building paper or felt.

• Wall may be sheathed or unsheathed. If unsheathed, the frame must be braced. To support the building paper and lath, line wires are strung tightly across the studs at 6" o.c.

STUCCO OVER FRAME CONSTRUCTION

• Masonry wall with joints struck flush

• Stucco is applied in 2 coats to a suitable masonry or concrete surface.

• The masonry or concrete wall should be structurally sound and its surface should be free of dust, grease, or other contaminants that would prevent good suction or chemical bond. In addition, the surface should be rough and porous enough to ensure a good mechanical bond.

• If a good bond is doubtful, use metal reinforcement, a dash coat of portland cement and sand, or a bonding agent.

STUCCO OVER MASONRY WALLS

Thickness of portland cement stucco

Base	Minimum finished thickness from face of base
Expanded metal lath or wire fabric	7/8" (exterior) 5/8" (interior)
Masonry walls	1/2"
Concrete walls	7/8" maximum
Concrete ceilings	3/8" maximum

The finish coat may have a float, stippled, combed, or pebbled texture. The finish may be natural or be integrally colored through the use of pigment, colored sand, or stone chips.

Stucco or exterior plaster is normally used for exterior walls and soffits. It can also be used for interior walls and ceilings that are subject to direct wetting or high moisture conditions.

Stucco is similar to gypsum plaster in its formulation and application, but portland cement is used instead of gypsum to produce a surface that is both weather- and fire-resistant.

Like gypsum plaster, stucco is a relatively thin, hard, brittle material that requires reinforcement or a sturdy, rigid, unyielding base. Unlike gypsum plaster, which expands slightly as it hardens, portland cement stucco shrinks as it cures. This shrinkage, along with the stresses caused by structural movement of the base support and variations in temperature and humidity, can cause the stucco to crack. Control and relief joints are required to eliminate or minimize any cracking.

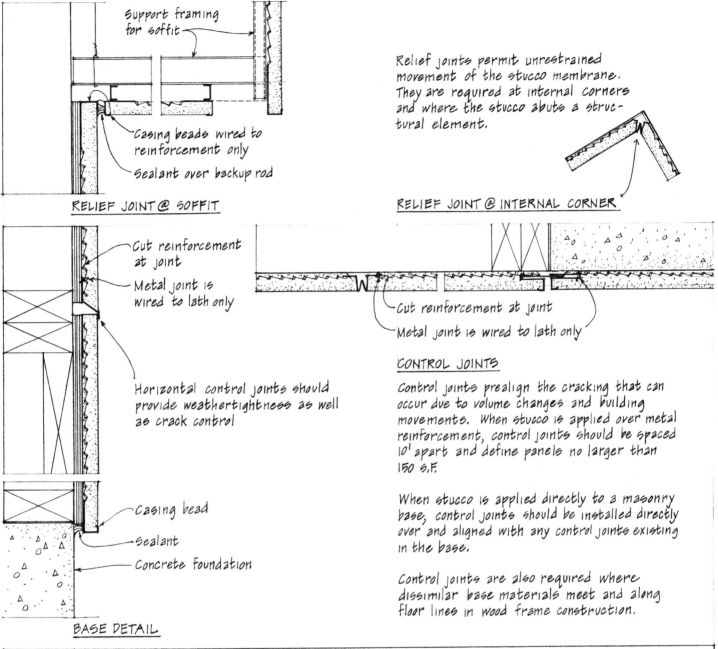

Support framing for soffit

Casing beads wired to reinforcement only

Sealant over backup rod

RELIEF JOINT @ SOFFIT

Relief joints permit unrestrained movement of the stucco membrane. They are required at internal corners and where the stucco abuts a structural element.

RELIEF JOINT @ INTERNAL CORNER

Cut reinforcement at joint

Metal joint is wired to lath only

Horizontal control joints should provide weathertightness as well as crack control

Casing bead

Sealant

Concrete foundation

BASE DETAIL

Cut reinforcement at joint

Metal joint is wired to lath only

CONTROL JOINTS

Control joints prealign the cracking that can occur due to volume changes and building movements. When stucco is applied over metal reinforcement, control joints should be spaced 10' apart and define panels no larger than 150 S.F.

When stucco is applied directly to a masonry base, control joints should be installed directly over and aligned with any control joints existing in the base.

Control joints are also required where dissimilar base materials meet and along floor lines in wood frame construction.

Rigid insulation board 1" to 4" thick, secured to gypsum sheathing or a suitable masonry surface with adhesive.

Prime coat reinforced with glass fiber mesh to prevent surface cracks

Finish coat in any of several textures and integral colors

Total thickness of prime and finish coats = 1/4" ±

Acrylic-based stucco systems are available for cladding the exteriors of buildings. The system consists of a thin layer of acrylic polymer stucco, reinforced with glass fiber mesh and applied over a layer of rigid plastic foam insulation. The rigid insulation can be secured with adhesive to either masonry or sheathed frame walls. To improve the system's impact resistance, the acrylic stucco can be reinforced with heavy-duty mesh. Consult manufacturer for details.

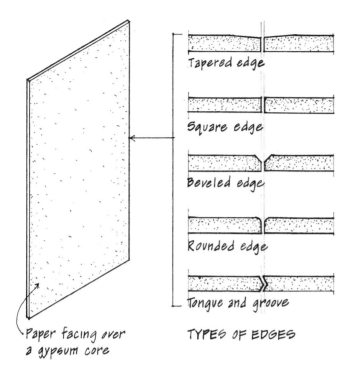

Paper facing over
a gypsum core

TYPES OF EDGES

Tapered edge

Square edge

Beveled edge

Rounded edge

Tongue and groove

Gypsum board consists of a gypsum core surfaced and edged to satisfy specific performance, location, application, and appearance requirements. It has good fire resistance and dimensional stability. In addition, its relatively large sheet size makes it an economical material to install. Gypsum wallboard is often referred to as drywall because of its low moisture content and little or no water is used in its application to interior walls or ceilings.

Gypsum board may have different edge conditions. Base or intermediate boards in multilayer construction may have square or tongue-and-groove edges. Prefinished boards may have square or beveled edges. Most commonly, however, gypsum board has a tapered edge. The tapered edge allows the joints to be taped and filled to produce strong, invisible seams. Gypsum board thus can form smooth surfaces which are monolithic in appearance and which can be finished by painting or applying a paper, vinyl, or fabric wall covering.

TYPE AND EDGE	THICKNESS	SIZE	USE OR DESCRIPTION
Regular wallboard; Tapered edge	1/4", 3/8", 1/2", 5/8"	4' wide; 8' to 16' long	1/4" board is used as the base layer in sound control walls; 3/8" board is used in multilayer construction, and for remodeling projects; 1/2" and 5/8" boards are for single layer construction.
Coreboard; Square or t&g edge	1"	2' wide 4' to 16'	Used to enclose elevator shafts, stairways, and mechanical chases, and for solid gypsum partitions.
Foil-backed board; Square or tapered edge	3/8", 1/2", 5/8"	4' wide; 8' to 16' long	Aluminum foil backing serves as a vapor barrier and, if facing a min. 3/4" dead air space, as reflective insulation.
Water-resistant board; Tapered edge	1/2", 5/8"	4' wide; 8' to 12' long	Used as a base for ceramic or other nonabsorbent tile in high moisture areas.
Type X board; Tapered or rounded edge	1/2", 5/8"	4' wide; 8' to 16' long	Core has glass fibers and other additives to increase its fire resistance; available with foil backing.
Prefinished board; Square edge	5/16"	4' wide; 8' long	Vinyl or paper surfaced in various colors, patterns, and textures.
Backing board; Square or t&g edge	3/8", 1/2", 5/8"	4' wide; 8' long	Used as the base in multilayer systems; available with regular or Type X cores, or with foil backing.
Sheathing Square or t&g edge	1/2", 5/8"	2' or 4' wide; 8' to 10' long	Used as sheathing for exterior wood or metal stud walls; available with regular or Type X cores.

Gypsum board may be applied to above grade masonry or concrete walls whose surfaces are dry, smooth, plane, and free of oil or other parting materials.

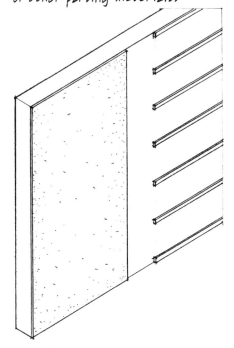

Vertical application: Board length parallel to framing

Horizontal application: Board length perpendicular to framing

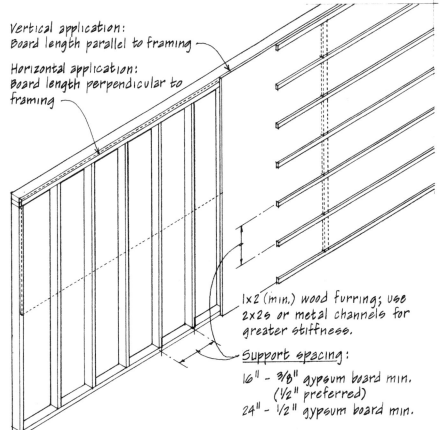

1x2 (min.) wood furring; use 2x2s or metal channels for greater stiffness.

Support spacing:

16" - 3/8" gypsum board min. (1/2" preferred)
24" - 1/2" gypsum board min.

Exterior and below grade masonry or concrete walls require furring before the application of gypsum board to eliminate the capillary transfer of water and to minimize condensation on interior wall surfaces.

Gypsum board may be fastened directly to wood or metal stud framing that is structurally sound and rigid enough to prevent buckling or cracking of the gypsum board. The face of the frame should form a flat and level plane.

Horizontal application is preferred for greater stiffness if it results in fewer joints. Butt end joints, which should be kept to a minimum, must fall over a support.

Wood or metal furring is required when:

• The frame or masonry base is not sufficiently flat.
• The primary supports are spaced too far apart.
• Additional space for thermal or acoustic insulation is desired.
• The use of resilient furring channels is needed to improve the acoustic performance of the assembly.

Gypsum board can be curved. The maximum bending radius is as follows.

Board thickness:	Lengthwise:	By width:
1/4"	5'-0	15'-0
3/8"	7'-6"	25'-0
1/2"	20'-0	

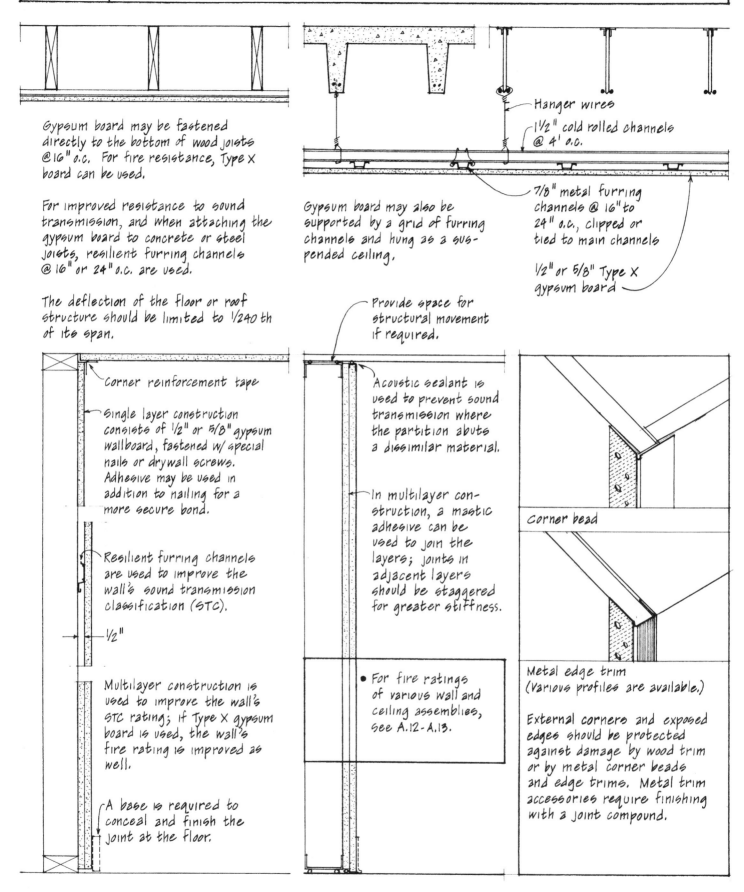

Gypsum board may be fastened directly to the bottom of wood joists @ 16" o.c. For fire resistance, Type X board can be used.

For improved resistance to sound transmission, and when attaching the gypsum board to concrete or steel joists, resilient furring channels @ 16" or 24" o.c. are used.

The deflection of the floor or roof structure should be limited to 1/240 th of its span.

Gypsum board may also be supported by a grid of furring channels and hung as a suspended ceiling.

Hanger wires

1 1/2" cold rolled channels @ 4' o.c.

7/8" metal furring channels @ 16" to 24" o.c., clipped or tied to main channels

1/2" or 5/8" Type X gypsum board

Corner reinforcement tape

Single layer construction consists of 1/2" or 5/8" gypsum wallboard, fastened w/ special nails or drywall screws. Adhesive may be used in addition to nailing for a more secure bond.

Resilient furring channels are used to improve the wall's sound transmission classification (STC).

1/2"

Multilayer construction is used to improve the wall's STC rating; if Type X gypsum board is used, the wall's fire rating is improved as well.

A base is required to conceal and finish the joint at the floor.

Provide space for structural movement if required.

Acoustic sealant is used to prevent sound transmission where the partition abuts a dissimilar material.

In multilayer construction, a mastic adhesive can be used to join the layers; joints in adjacent layers should be staggered for greater stiffness.

• For fire ratings of various wall and ceiling assemblies, see A.12-A.13.

Corner bead

Metal edge trim
(Various profiles are available.)

External corners and exposed edges should be protected against damage by wood trim or by metal corner beads and edge trims. Metal trim accessories require finishing with a joint compound.

Ceramic tiles are relatively small, modular surfacing units made of clay or other ceramic material. The tiles are fired in a kiln at very high temperatures. The result is a durable, tough, dense material that is water-resistant, difficult to stain, and easy to clean, and its colors generally do not fade.

Ceramic tile is available glazed or unglazed. Glazed tile has a face of ceramic material fused into the body of the tile, and may have glossy, matte, or crystalline finishes in a wide range of colors. Unglazed tiles are hard and dense, and derive their color from the body of the material. These colors tend to be more muted.

Ceramic tile may be applied as individual pieces or in sheet form. Ceramic mosaic tiles may be faced with paper or backed with mesh to form 1'x 1' or 1'x 2' sections with the proper tile spacing. Both glazed wall and ceramic mosaic tiles are also available in large sheets pregrouted with flexible, silicone grout.

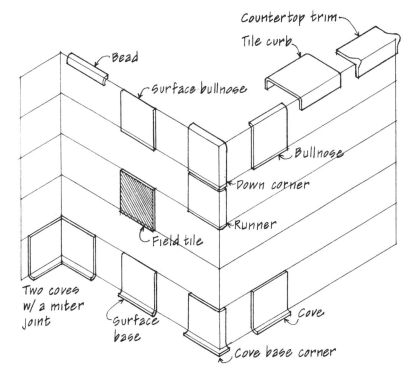

TYPES OF TILE TRIM SHAPES

TYPES AND TYPICAL SIZES OF CERAMIC TILE

Consult manufacturer for exact sizes, shapes, colors, and glazes.

GLAZED WALL TILE   (5/16" thick)

Interior tiles are used for interior walls. Exterior tiles are weatherproof and frostproof, and can be used for both exterior and interior walls. With a crystalline glaze, they can be used for light duty floors.

CERAMIC MOSAIC TILE   (1/4" thick)

Ceramic mosaic tile is usually unglazed. The porcelain type is resistant to freezing and abrasion, and may be used for floors and walls. Porcelain tiles have bright colors, while the natural clay tiles have more muted colors.

QUARRY AND PAVER TILES   (3/8", 1/2", 3/4" thick)

Quarry tile is unglazed floor tile of natural clay or porcelain. The tiles are impervious to dirt, moisture and stains, and resistant to freezing and abrasion. Pavers are similar to ceramic mosaic tiles but larger. They are weatherproof and can be used on floors subject to heavy duty use.

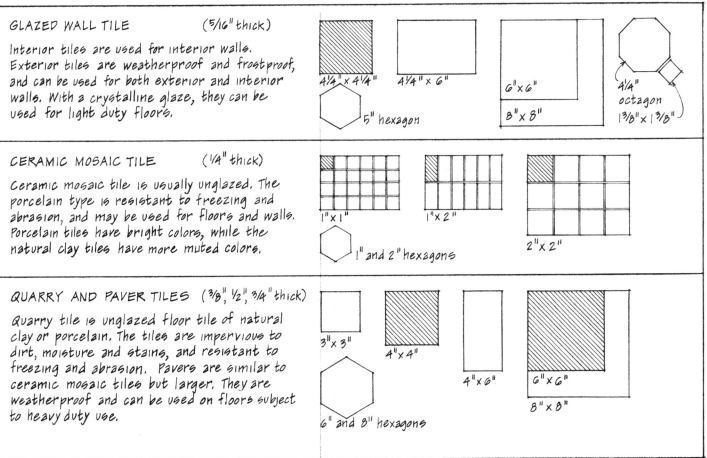

THINSET APPLICATION ON WALLS with dry-set mortar, latex-portland cement mortar, or organic adhesive over a solid backing of:

- Gypsum board - Use water-resistant backer board in tub and shower areas.
- Gypsum plaster - 2 or 3 coat thickness; not used in wet areas.
- Plywood - Exterior grade at least 3/8" thick; not used in wet areas.
- Concrete/glass fiber-reinforced board - 1/2" thick; for use in wet areas; use only w/ dry-set or latex-portland cement mortars.

Wall surfaces should be structurally sound, plumb, and true. When dry-set or latex-portland cement mortar is used on a masonry or concrete wall, the surface should be roughened to ensure a good bond.

THICKBED INSTALLATION ON WALLS AND FLOORS

- A relatively thick (3/4" to 1" on walls and 3/4" to 1 1/4" on floors) portland cement mortar bed is used as a setting or leveling bed.
- Tiles are laid with a bond coat of neat portland cement, latex-portland cement, or dry-set mortar.
- A cleavage membrane is used to isolate the mortar bed from damaged or unstable backings and to allow some independent movement of the supporting construction.
- The mortar bed should be reinforced with metal lath or mesh whenever it is backed by a membrane.
- Mortar bed installations can be used over open framing or a solid backing of masonry, concrete, gypsum board or plaster, plywood, or concrete/glass fiber-reinforced backer board.

THINSET APPLICATION ON FLOORS:

- Maximum deflection of the floor under full load should be limited to 1/360th of the span.
- The concrete slab should be smooth, level, and properly reinforced and cured; a leveling topping can be used if required.
- A double wood floor is required, consisting of a 5/8" min. plywood subfloor and an underlayment of 1/2" or 5/8" exterior-grade plywood. A 1/4" space should be provided between the underlayment and vertical surfaces.

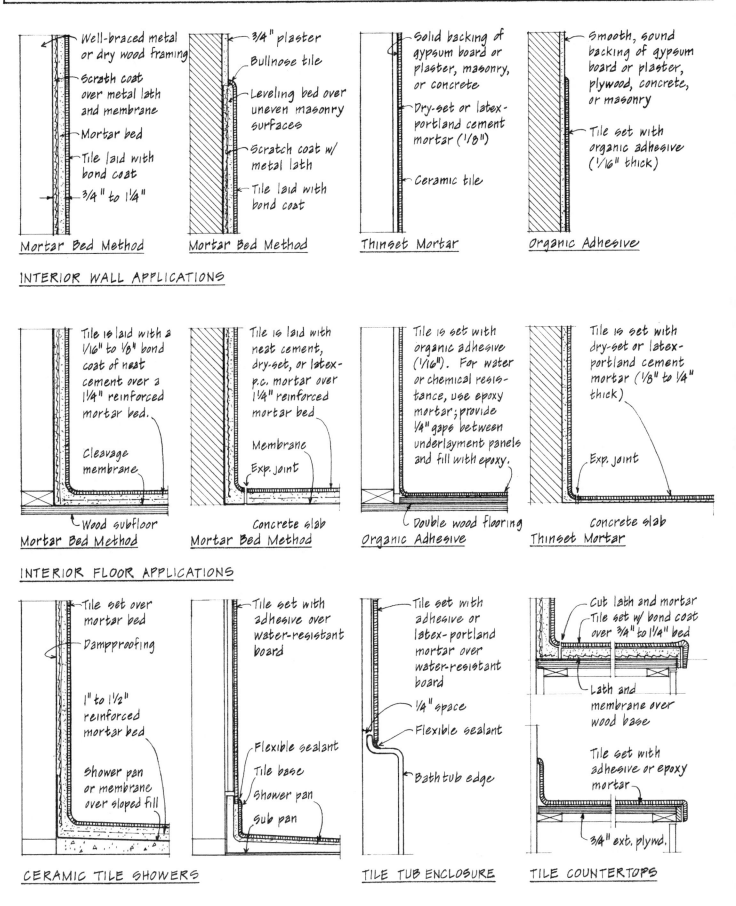

INTERIOR WALL APPLICATIONS

Mortar Bed Method
- Well-braced metal or dry wood framing
- Scrath coat over metal lath and membrane
- Mortar bed
- Tile laid with bond coat
- 3/4" to 1 1/4"

Mortar Bed Method
- 3/4" plaster
- Bullnose tile
- Leveling bed over uneven masonry surfaces
- Scratch coat w/ metal lath
- Tile laid with bond coat

Thinset Mortar
- Solid backing of gypsum board or plaster, masonry, or concrete
- Dry-set or latex-portland cement mortar (1/8")
- Ceramic tile

Organic Adhesive
- Smooth, sound backing of gypsum board or plaster, plywood, concrete, or masonry
- Tile set with organic adhesive (1/16" thick)

INTERIOR FLOOR APPLICATIONS

Mortar Bed Method
- Tile is laid with a 1/16" to 1/8" bond coat of neat cement over a 1 1/4" reinforced mortar bed.
- Cleavage membrane
- Wood subfloor

Mortar Bed Method
- Tile is laid with neat cement, dry-set, or latex-p.c. mortar over 1 1/4" reinforced mortar bed
- Membrane
- Exp. joint
- Concrete slab

Organic Adhesive
- Tile is set with organic adhesive (1/16"). For water or chemical resistance, use epoxy mortar; provide 1/4" gaps between underlayment panels and fill with epoxy.
- Double wood flooring

Thinset Mortar
- Tile is set with dry-set or latex-portland cement mortar (1/8" to 1/4" thick)
- Exp. joint
- Concrete slab

CERAMIC TILE SHOWERS
- Tile set over mortar bed
- Dampproofing
- 1" to 1 1/2" reinforced mortar bed
- Shower pan or membrane over sloped fill

- Tile set with adhesive over water-resistant board
- Flexible sealant
- Tile base
- Shower pan
- Sub pan

TILE TUB ENCLOSURE
- Tile set with adhesive or latex-portland mortar over water-resistant board
- 1/4" space
- Flexible sealant
- Bathtub edge

TILE COUNTERTOPS
- Cut lath and mortar
- Tile set w/ bond coat over 3/4" to 1 1/4" bed
- Lath and membrane over wood base
- Tile set with adhesive or epoxy mortar
- 3/4" ext. plywd.

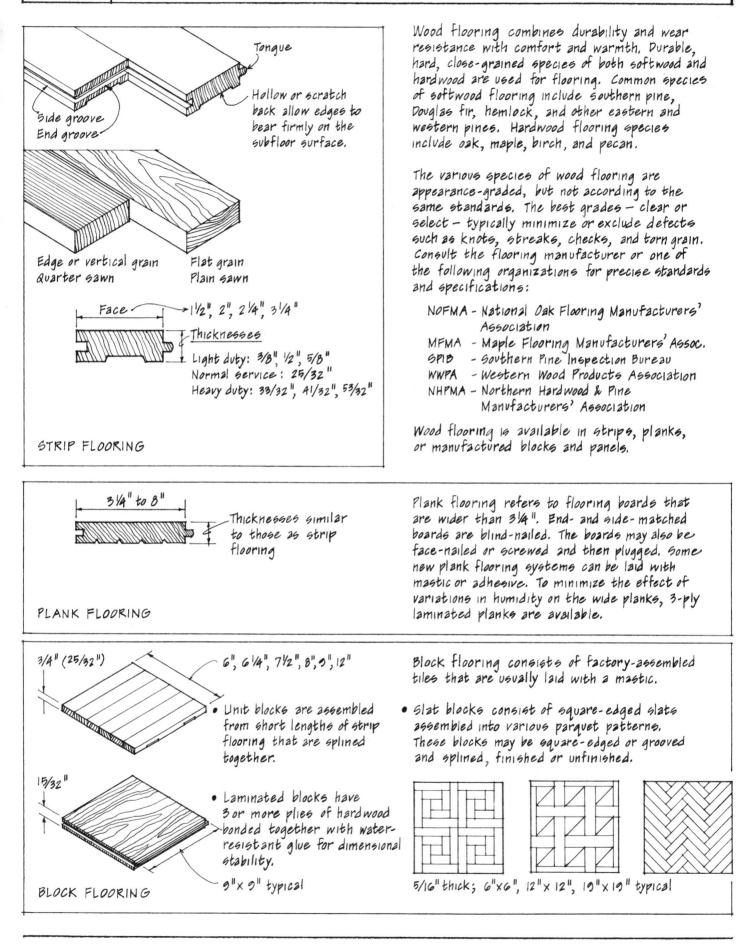

Tongue

Hollow or scratch back allow edges to bear firmly on the subfloor surface.

Side groove
End groove

Edge or vertical grain
Quarter sawn

Flat grain
Plain sawn

Face → 1½", 2", 2¼", 3¼"

Thicknesses

Light duty: 3/8", ½", 5/8"
Normal service: 25/32"
Heavy duty: 33/32", 41/32", 53/32"

STRIP FLOORING

Wood flooring combines durability and wear resistance with comfort and warmth. Durable, hard, close-grained species of both softwood and hardwood are used for flooring. Common species of softwood flooring include southern pine, Douglas fir, hemlock, and other eastern and western pines. Hardwood flooring species include oak, maple, birch, and pecan.

The various species of wood flooring are appearance-graded, but not according to the same standards. The best grades — clear or select — typically minimize or exclude defects such as knots, streaks, checks, and torn grain. Consult the flooring manufacturer or one of the following organizations for precise standards and specifications:

NOFMA – National Oak Flooring Manufacturers' Association
MFMA – Maple Flooring Manufacturers' Assoc.
SPIB – Southern Pine Inspection Bureau
WWPA – Western Wood Products Association
NHPMA – Northern Hardwood & Pine Manufacturers' Association

Wood flooring is available in strips, planks, or manufactured blocks and panels.

3¼" to 8"

Thicknesses similar to those as strip flooring

PLANK FLOORING

Plank flooring refers to flooring boards that are wider than 3¼". End- and side-matched boards are blind-nailed. The boards may also be face-nailed or screwed and then plugged. Some new plank flooring systems can be laid with mastic or adhesive. To minimize the effect of variations in humidity on the wide planks, 3-ply laminated planks are available.

3/4" (25/32")

6", 6¼", 7½", 8", 9", 12"

• Unit blocks are assembled from short lengths of strip flooring that are splined together.

15/32"

• Laminated blocks have 3 or more plies of hardwood bonded together with water-resistant glue for dimensional stability.

9" x 9" typical

BLOCK FLOORING

Block flooring consists of factory-assembled tiles that are usually laid with a mastic.

• Slat blocks consist of square-edged slats assembled into various parquet patterns. These blocks may be square-edged or grooved and splined, finished or unfinished.

5/16" thick; 6"x6", 12" x 12", 19"x19" typical

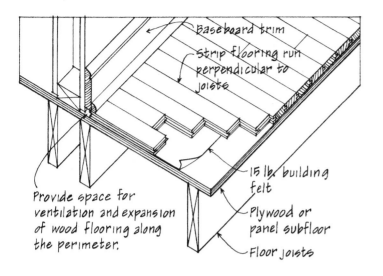

- Baseboard trim
- Strip flooring run perpendicular to joists
- Provide space for ventilation and expansion of wood flooring along the perimeter.
- 15 lb. building felt
- Plywood or panel subfloor
- Floor joists

STRIP FLOORING OVER SUBFLOOR AND JOISTS

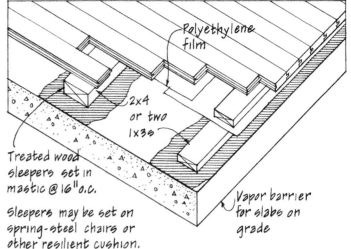

- Polyethylene film
- 2x4 or two 1x3s
- Treated wood sleepers set in mastic @ 16" o.c.
- Sleepers may be set on spring-steel chairs or other resilient cushion.
- Vapor barrier for slabs on grade

STRIP FLOORING OVER CONCRETE SLAB

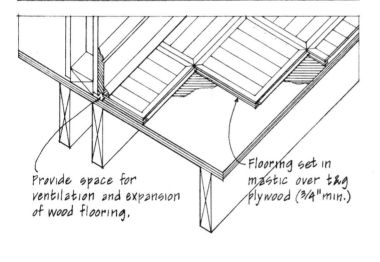

- Provide space for ventilation and expansion of wood flooring.
- Flooring set in mastic over t&g plywood (3/4" min.)

BLOCK FLOORING OVER SUBFLOOR

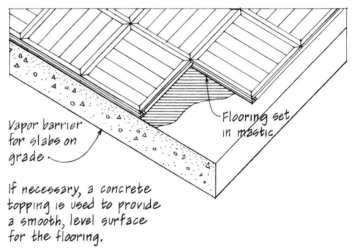

- Vapor barrier for slabs on grade
- Flooring set in mastic
- If necessary, a concrete topping is used to provide a smooth, level surface for the flooring.

BLOCK FLOORING OVER CONCRETE SLAB

Wood strip and plank flooring requires a wood subfloor or spaced wood sleepers as a base. Plywood or panel subfloors, integral parts of a wood joist floor system, may be laid over other floor systems as well to receive the wood flooring. Treated wood sleepers are usually required over concrete slabs to receive a wood subfloor or the finish wood flooring. This is especially important to protect the flooring from dampness when it is installed on slabs on or below grade.

Wood block flooring requires a clean, dry, smooth, flat surface such as a plywood subfloor or underlayment. While block tiles can be applied to the surface of a dry concrete slab, it is best, especially in basements, to lay the flooring over a plywood subfloor and a vapor barrier set on treated wood sleepers.

Wood flooring will shrink and swell as its moisture content changes with variations in atmospheric humidity. It should not be installed until the building is enclosed, permanent lighting and the heating plant are installed, and all building materials are dry. The wood flooring should be stored for several days in the spaces where it will be installed to allow the flooring to become acclimated to the interior conditions. As the flooring is installed, space should be provided along the floor's perimeter for ventilation and expansion of the flooring.

TYPE	COMPONENTS	THICKNESS	SIZES	PERMISSIBLE LOCATION
Vinyl sheet	Vinyl resins w/ fiber back	.065" to .160"	6' to 15' wide	B·O·S
Vinyl tile (homogeneous)	Vinyl resins	1/16" to 1/8"	9"x 9" 12" x 12"	B·O·S
Vinyl tile (composition)	Vinyl resins w/ fillers	.050" to .095"	9"x9" 12" x 12"	B·O·S
Cork tile	Raw cork and resins	1/8" to 1/4"	6"x6" 9"x9"	S
Cork tile w/ vinyl coating	Raw cork w/ vinyl resins	1/8", 3/16"	9"x9" 12"x12"	S
Rubber tile	Rubber compound	3/32" to 3/16"	9"x9" 12"x12"	B·O·S

(S) suspended

(O) on grade

(B) below grade

Surface must be clean, dry, firm, and smooth.

Double layer wood floor: Panel underlayment of hardboard (1/4"min.) or sanded plywood (3/8" min.) or particleboard (3/8" min.)

Single layer wood floor: Combination subfloor/ underlayment panels (5/8"min.) See 4.11.

WOOD SUBFLOORS

Surface must be clean, dry, dense, and smooth.

2" to 3" reinforced concrete topping over precast slabs

1" concrete topping over lightweight concrete slabs

Provide a vapor barrier and a gravel base under slabs on grade.

For slabs below grade, provide a waterproof membrane and a 2" subslab.

CONCRETE SUBFLOORS

2½", 4", 6"

Resilient flooring	Carpet	Any flooring	
Butt cove	Straight	Set on cove	Cove and cap strips

Various resilient flooring accessories are available for use as wall bases, stair nosings and treads, and thresholds.

Resilient flooring materials provide an economical, relatively dense, nonabsorbent flooring surface that is durable and easy to maintain. Their degree of resilience enables them to resist permanent indentation and contributes to their quietness and comfort underfoot. How comfortable a resilient floor covering is, however, depends not only on its resilience but also on its backing and the hardness of the supporting substrate.

None of the resilient flooring types is superior in all respects. Listed below are the types that perform well in specific areas.

Resilience and quietness: cork tile, rubber tile, foam-cushioned vinyl sheet and tile.

Resistance to indentation: Solid vinyl tile, foam-cushioned vinyl sheet and tile.

Stain resistance: Vinyl cork tile, vinyl sheet and tile.

Alkali resistance: Vinyl sheet and tile.

Grease resistance: Vinyl sheet and tile, vinyl cork tile.

Durability: Vinyl sheet and tile

Ease of maintenance: Vinyl cork tile, foam-cushioned vinyl sheet.

Metal or plastic-tipped divider strips are used to:
- localize shrinkage cracking
- serve as construction joints
- separate the different colors of a floor pattern
- act as decorative elements.

Expansion joints are required over isolation or expansion joints in the subfloor. They consist of a pair of divider strips separated by a resilient material such as neoprene.

Terrazzo is a ground and polished concrete topping consisting of marble chips or other colored coarse aggregate in a portland cement or resinous binder. It provides a dense, extremely durable, smooth flooring surface whose mottled coloring is controlled by the size and colors of the aggregate and the color of the binder.

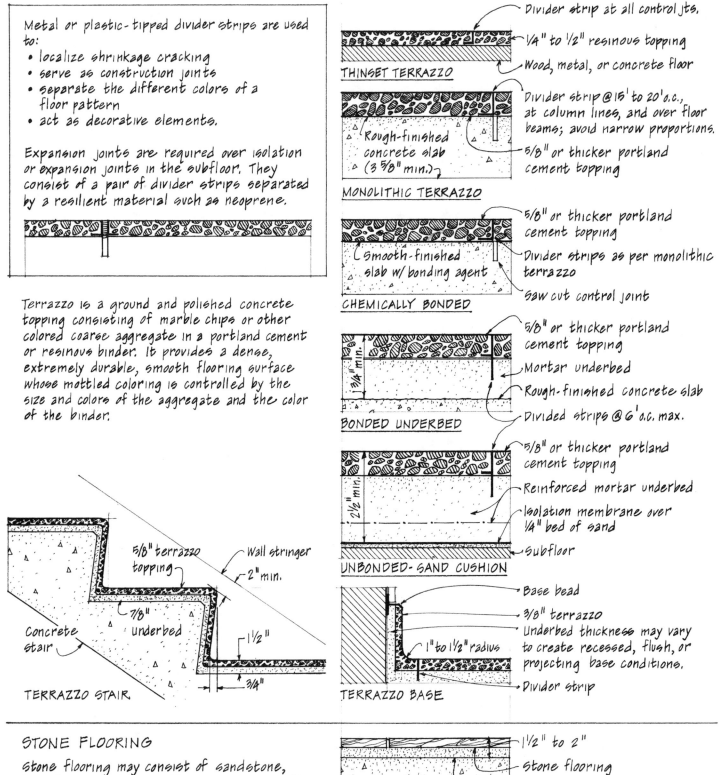

THINSET TERRAZZO
- Divider strip at all control jts.
- 1/4" to 1/2" resinous topping
- Wood, metal, or concrete floor

MONOLITHIC TERRAZZO
- Rough-finished concrete slab (3 5/8" min.)
- Divider strip @15' to 20' o.c., at column lines, and over floor beams; avoid narrow proportions.
- 5/8" or thicker portland cement topping

CHEMICALLY BONDED
- 5/8" or thicker portland cement topping
- Smooth-finished slab w/ bonding agent
- Divider strips as per monolithic terrazzo
- Saw cut control joint

BONDED UNDERBED
- 5/8" or thicker portland cement topping
- 3/4" min.
- Mortar underbed
- Rough-finished concrete slab
- Divided strips @ 6' o.c. max.

UNBONDED - SAND CUSHION
- 5/8" or thicker portland cement topping
- 2 1/2" min.
- Reinforced mortar underbed
- Isolation membrane over 1/4" bed of sand
- Subfloor

TERRAZZO STAIR
- 5/8" terrazzo topping
- Wall stringer
- 2" min.
- 7/8" underbed
- Concrete stair
- 1 1/2"
- 3/4"

TERRAZZO BASE
- Base bead
- 3/8" terrazzo
- Underbed thickness may vary to create recessed, flush, or projecting base conditions.
- 1" to 1 1/2" radius
- Divider strip

STONE FLOORING

Stone flooring may consist of sandstone, limestone, polished marble or granite, or split face slate. The tiles or slabs may be laid in regular or irregular patterns. Consideration should be given to the stone's weight and the dead load it will impose on the floor structure.

- 1 1/2" to 2"
- Stone flooring
- 3/4" mortar bed

- Thin slate may be set with thinset mortar or adhesive.

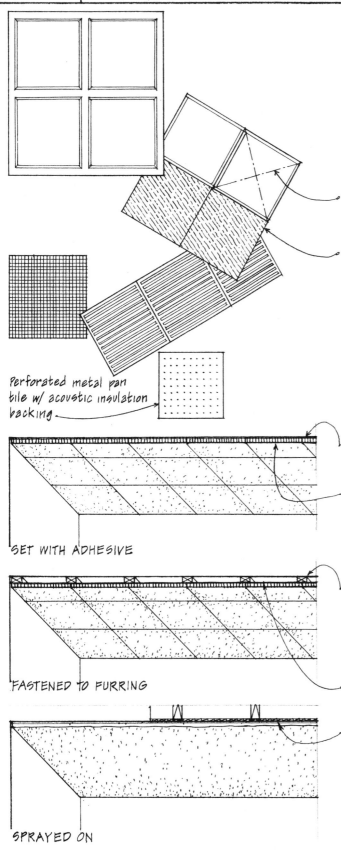

Perforated metal pan tile w/ acoustic insulation backing.

Acoustical ceiling tiles are usually of incombustible glass or mineral fiber. These modular units have perforated, patterned, textured, or fissured faces which allow sound to penetrate into the fiber voids. Because of their light weight and low density, the tiles can be easily damaged. To improve their resistance to humidity, impact, and abrasion, the tiles may be factory-painted or have a ceramic, plastic, or aluminum facing.

Acoustical ceiling tiles are manufactured in 12"x 12", 24"x 24", and 24"x 48" modules. Tiles based on 20", 30", 48", and 60" are also available.

Typical tile thicknesses: 1/2", 5/8", 3/4". Tiles may have square, beveled, rabbeted, or tongue-and-groove edges.

Consult the ceiling tile manufacturer for:
• Sizes, patterns, and finishes
• Noise reduction coefficient (NRC)
• Fire rating
• Light reflectance value
• Suspension system details.

A solid backing such as concrete, plaster, or gypsum board is required.

Tiles are set with a special adhesive that allows a true, flat plane to be maintained even though there may be slight irregularities in the base surface.

SET WITH ADHESIVE

1x3 furring strips @ 12" o.c. are used when the base surface is not flat enough or is otherwise unsuitable for the adhesive application of the ceiling tiles. Cross furring and shims may also be required to establish a flat, level base.

FASTENED TO FURRING

Tiles should be backed with building paper to provide a draft-tight ceiling surface.

Acoustical material of mineral or cellulose fibers mixed with a special binder may be sprayed directly onto hard surfaces such as concrete or gypsum board. The material can also be sprayed onto metal lath, which provides better sound absorption and permits curved or irregular ceiling shapes to be formed.

SPRAYED ON

DIRECTION APPLICATION OF ACOUSTICAL CEILINGS

Acoustical ceiling tiles can be suspended to provide a concealed space for mechanical ductwork, electrical conduit, and plumbing lines. Light fixtures, sprinkler heads, fire detection devices, and sound systems can be recessed into the ceiling plane. The ceiling membrane can be fire rated and provide fire protection for the supporting floor and roof structure. Thus, the ceiling system is able to integrate the functions of lighting, air distribution, acoustical control, and fire protection.

Although the suspension systems of each manufacturer may vary in their details, they all consist of a grid of main channels or runners, cross tees, and splines. This grid, which is hung from the supporting floor or roof structure, may be exposed, semi-concealed, or fully concealed. In most suspension systems, the acoustical tiles are removable for replacement or for access into the ceiling space.

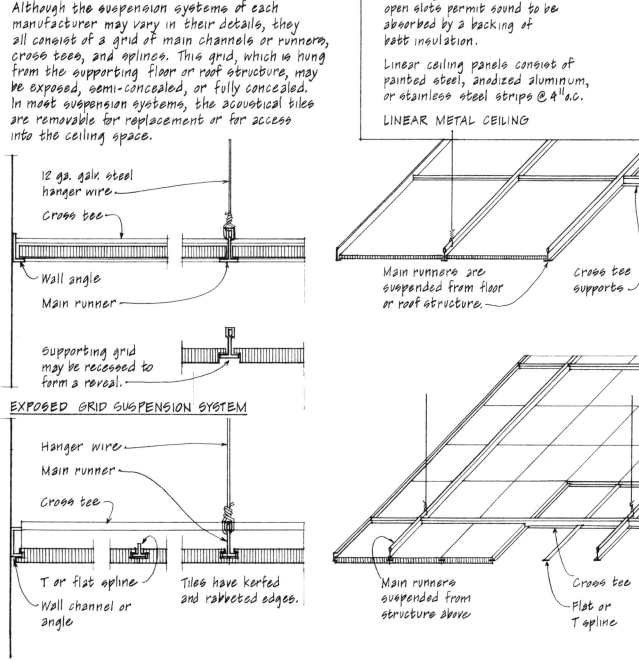

Carrier

Integrated light fixture

Slots may be open or closed; open slots permit sound to be absorbed by a backing of batt insulation.

Linear ceiling panels consist of painted steel, anodized aluminum, or stainless steel strips @ 4" o.c.

LINEAR METAL CEILING

Main runners are suspended from floor or roof structure.

Cross tee supports

12 ga. galv. steel hanger wire

Cross tee

Wall angle

Main runner

Supporting grid may be recessed to form a reveal.

EXPOSED GRID SUSPENSION SYSTEM

Hanger wire

Main runner

Cross tee

T or flat spline

Wall channel or angle

Tiles have kerfed and rabbeted edges.

CONCEALED GRID SUSPENSION SYSTEM

Main runners suspended from structure above

Cross tee

Flat or T spline

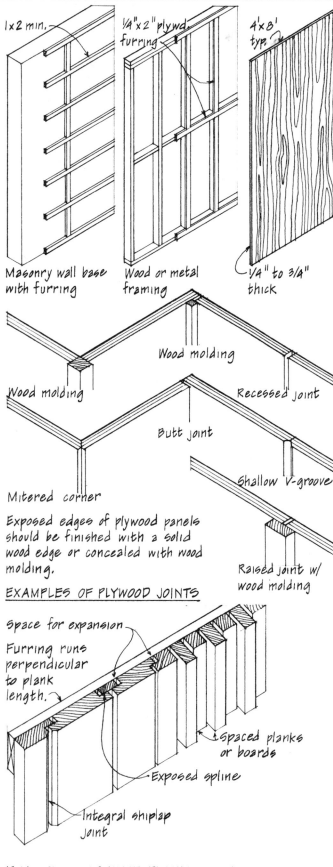

1x2 min.

1/4" x 2" plywd. furring

4' x 8' typ.

1/4" to 3/4" thick

Masonry wall base with furring

Wood or metal framing

Interior wood paneling may consist of plywood panels or solid wood planks. Plywood panels may be applied directly to wood or metal framing or furring. Furring is required over masonry or concrete walls. Furring may also be used over frame walls when improved thermal insulation properties, greater acoustical isolation, or additional wall depth is desired. The panels are normally fastened with nails or screws although adhesives can be used for greater rigidity. The final appearance of the paneled wall will depend on the treatment of the joints and the panels' grain or figure.

Solid wood planks may also be used for interior paneling. The planks may have square cut, tongue and groove, or shiplap edges. The resulting wall pattern and texture will depend on the plank width, orientation, spacing, and joint details.

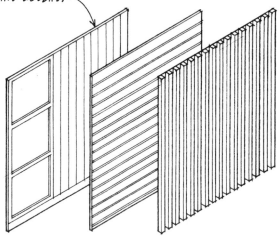

Wood molding

Wood molding

Recessed joint

Butt joint

Mitered corner

Shallow V-groove

Exposed edges of plywood panels should be finished with a solid wood edge or concealed with wood molding.

Raised joint w/ wood molding

EXAMPLES OF PLYWOOD JOINTS

Space for expansion

Furring runs perpendicular to plank length.

Spaced planks or boards

Exposed spline

Integral shiplap joint

EXAMPLES OF WOOD PLANK JOINTS
Space should be provided for expansion of wood.

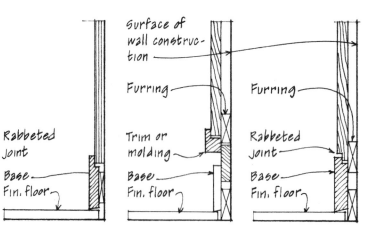

Surface of wall construction

Furring

Furring

Rabbeted Joint

Trim or molding

Rabbeted Joint

Base

Base

Base

Fin. floor

Fin. floor

Fin. floor

EXAMPLES OF BASE DETAILS
Details at ceiling and horizontal rails are similar.

Rotary

Flat slicing

Quarter slicing

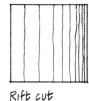
Half round slicing

Rift cut

Back cut

WOOD GRAIN FIGURES

Different wood grain figures may be produced by varying the way in which the wood veneer is cut from a log.

The appearance of naturally finished plywood paneling depends on the species of wood used for the face veneer, its grain figure, and the pattern developed by the way in which the panels are matched or arranged.

VENEER GRADES FOR PLYWOOD

N - Select, smooth surface for natural finishes

A - Smooth face suitable for painting

B - Solid surface utility panel

HARDWOOD VENEER GRADES

Premium grade	High quality veneer with only slight imperfections; multipiece faces must be matched.
Good grade	Suitable for natural finishes; matching of veneer faces is not required, but no sharp contrasts in color are allowed.
Sound grade (#2)	Sound, smooth surface suitable for painting.
Utility grade (#3)	May have open defects, but these are limited in size.

Book

Slip

V pattern

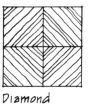
Diamond

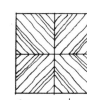
Reverse diamond

Box

Herringbone

Center

Reverse box

Vertical butt Horizontal book

Balance

Random

VENEER MATCHING PATTERNS

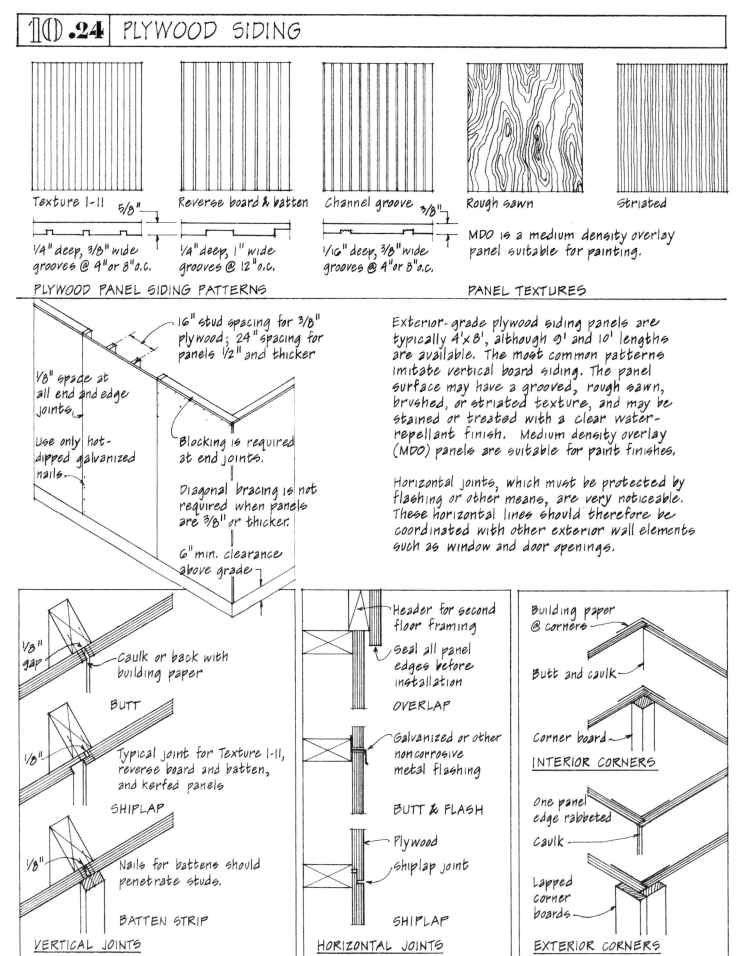

Texture 1-11   5/8"

1/4" deep, 3/8" wide
grooves @ 4" or 8" o.c.

Reverse board & batten

1/4" deep, 1" wide
grooves @ 12" o.c.

Channel groove   3/8"

1/16" deep, 3/8" wide
grooves @ 4" or 8" o.c.

Rough sawn

Striated

MDO is a medium density overlay
panel suitable for painting.

PLYWOOD PANEL SIDING PATTERNS
        PANEL TEXTURES

16" stud spacing for 3/8"
plywood; 24" spacing for
panels 1/2" and thicker

1/8" space at
all end and edge
joints.

Use only hot-
dipped galvanized
nails.

Blocking is required
at end joints.

Diagonal bracing is not
required when panels
are 3/8" or thicker.

6" min. clearance
above grade

Exterior-grade plywood siding panels are
typically 4'x8', although 9' and 10' lengths
are available. The most common patterns
imitate vertical board siding. The panel
surface may have a grooved, rough sawn,
brushed, or striated texture, and may be
stained or treated with a clear water-
repellant finish. Medium density overlay
(MDO) panels are suitable for paint finishes.

Horizontal joints, which must be protected by
flashing or other means, are very noticeable.
These horizontal lines should therefore be
coordinated with other exterior wall elements
such as window and door openings.

1/8" gap

Caulk or back with
building paper

BUTT

Typical joint for Texture 1-11,
reverse board and batten,
and kerfed panels

1/8"

SHIPLAP

1/8"

Nails for battens should
penetrate studs.

BATTEN STRIP

VERTICAL JOINTS

Header for second
floor framing

Seal all panel
edges before
installation

OVERLAP

Galvanized or other
noncorrosive
metal flashing

BUTT & FLASH

Plywood

shiplap joint

SHIPLAP

HORIZONTAL JOINTS

Building paper
@ corners

Butt and caulk

Corner board

INTERIOR CORNERS

One panel
edge rabbeted

Caulk

Lapped
corner
boards

EXTERIOR CORNERS

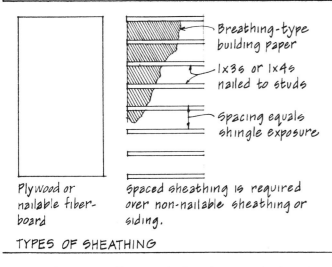

Plywood or nailable fiber-board

Spaced sheathing is required over non-nailable sheathing or siding.

- Breathing-type building paper
- 1x3s or 1x4s nailed to studs
- Spacing equals shingle exposure

TYPES OF SHEATHING

On exterior walls, wood shingles are laid in uniform courses that resemble lap siding. As with lap siding, the courses should be adjusted to meet the heads and sills of window openings and other horizontal bands neatly. The shingles may be stained or painted. Premium-grade shingles can be left unpainted to weather naturally.

Wood shingle siding may be applied in single or double coursing, with the following exposures:

SHINGLE LENGTH	SINGLE COURSING	DOUBLE COURSING
° 16"	6" to 7½"	8" to 12"
° 18"	6" to 8½"	9" to 14"
° 24"	8" to 11½"	12" to 20"

Dimension and fancy butt shingles are cut to uniform widths and shapes. They are used on walls to create certain effects such as scalloped or fishscale textures.

Square   Arrow   Diamond   Round   Octagonal   Half cove   Hexagonal   Fishscale

SINGLE COURSING APPLICATION

- Nº 2 red label shingles
- ¼" joints
- Nail 2" above beltline of succeeding course
- 1¼" min. offset between joints
- Exposure (see table)
- Double starting course; lap foundation 1"

DOUBLE COURSING APPLICATION

- Nº 1 blue label shingles
- Nº 3 undercourse
- Outer course is ½" lower than under-course
- Exposure (see table)
- Triple starting course; lap foundation 1"

At corners, alternating courses are lapped over the adjacent corner shingles on the other side. Exposed edges should be treated. Corner boards can also be used to receive the shingles at both interior and exterior corners. Building paper should be used to flash corners and wherever the shingles abut wood trim.

CORNERS

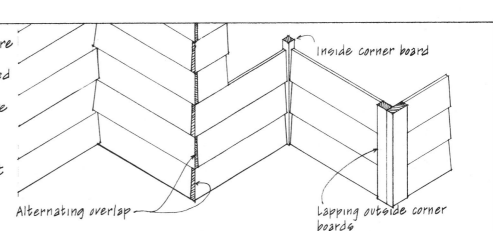

Inside corner board

Alternating overlap

Lapping outside corner boards

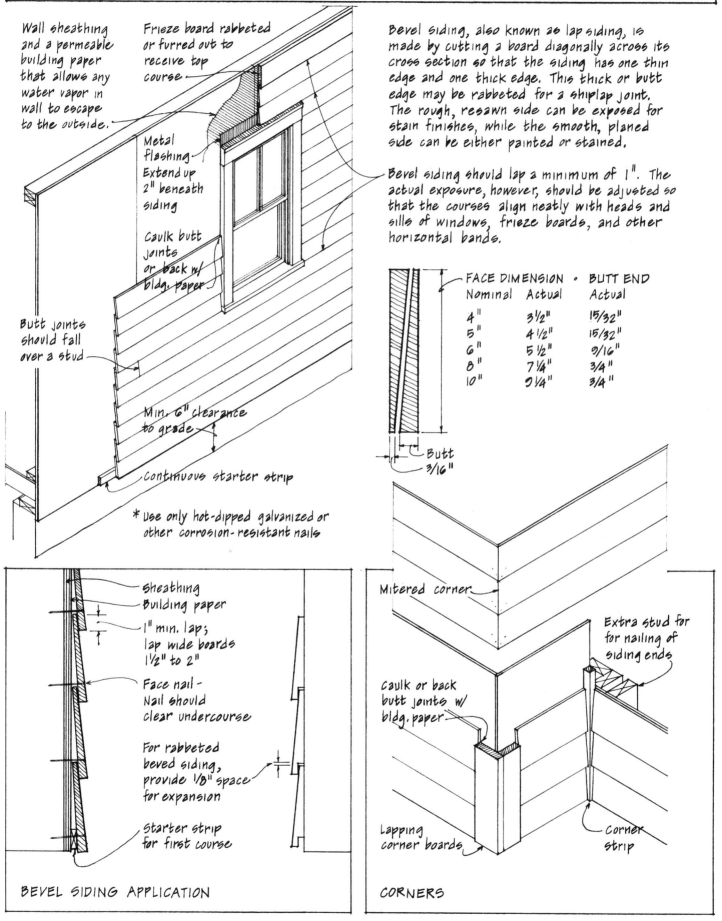

Wall sheathing and a permeable building paper that allows any water vapor in wall to escape to the outside.

Frieze board rabbeted or furred out to receive top course.

Metal Flashing- Extend up 2" beneath siding

Caulk butt joints or back w/ bldg. paper

Butt joints should fall over a stud

Min. 6" clearance to grade

Continuous starter strip

* Use only hot-dipped galvanized or other corrosion-resistant nails

Bevel siding, also known as lap siding, is made by cutting a board diagonally across its cross section so that the siding has one thin edge and one thick edge. This thick or butt edge may be rabbeted for a shiplap joint. The rough, resawn side can be exposed for stain finishes, while the smooth, planed side can be either painted or stained.

Bevel siding should lap a minimum of 1". The actual exposure, however, should be adjusted so that the courses align neatly with heads and sills of windows, frieze boards, and other horizontal bands.

FACE DIMENSION		BUTT END
Nominal	Actual	Actual
4"	3½"	15/32"
5"	4½"	15/32"
6"	5½"	9/16"
8"	7¼"	3/4"
10"	9¼"	3/4"

Butt 3/16"

Mitered corner

Caulk or back butt joints w/ bldg. paper

Lapping corner boards

Extra stud for for nailing of siding ends

Corner strip

sheathing
Building paper

1" min. lap; lap wide boards 1½" to 2"

Face nail - Nail should clear undercourse

For rabbeted bevel siding, provide 1/8" space for expansion

Starter strip for first course

BEVEL SIDING APPLICATION

CORNERS

Vertical siding can be laid in various patterns. Matched boards that interlap or interlock can have flush, V-groove, or beaded joints. Square-edged boards can be used with other boards or battens to protect their vertical joints and form board-and-board or board-and-batten patterns.

While horizontal siding is nailed directly to the wall studs, vertical siding requires solid blocking at 24"o.c., or plywood sheathing at least 5/8" or 3/4" thicker. Over thinner sheathing, 1x4 furring can be used at 24"o.c. A permeable building paper that allows water vapor to escape to the outside is used under the siding.

As with other siding materials, only hot-dipped galvanized or other corrosion-resistant nails should be used. Treat ends and edges of siding, and the backs of batten strips, with a preservative.

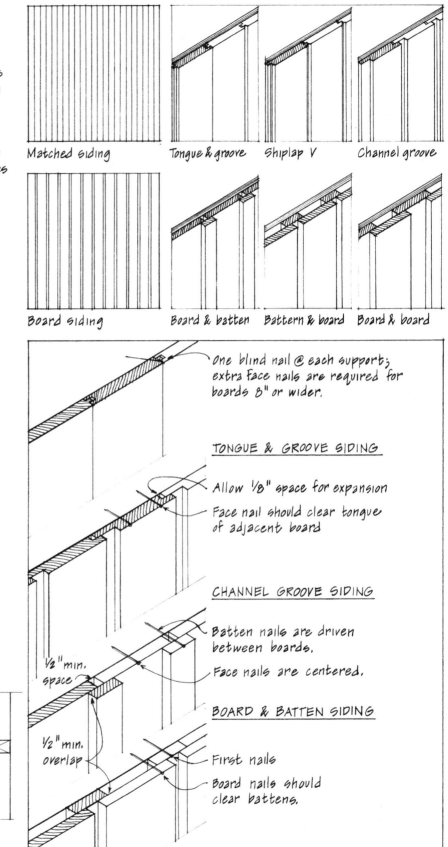

Matched siding   Tongue & groove   Shiplap V   Channel groove

Board siding   Board & batten   Battern & board   Board & board

Building paper

Corner boards are lapped for matched siding.

Undercut (bevel) to form drip at bottom

Building paper

Batten strips lap each other at corners.

End joints should be beveled and sealed during installation.

CORNERS

One blind nail @ each support; extra face nails are required for boards 8" or wider.

TONGUE & GROOVE SIDING

Allow 1/8" space for expansion

Face nail should clear tongue of adjacent board

CHANNEL GROOVE SIDING

Batten nails are driven between boards.

Face nails are centered.

BOARD & BATTEN SIDING

1/2" min. space

First nails

1/2" min. overlap

Board nails should clear battens.

BATTERN & BOARD SIDING

Dowel

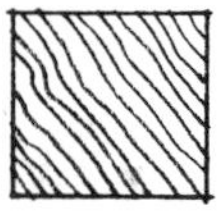

Half-round

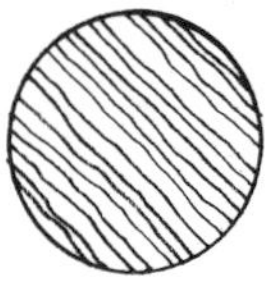

Use to conceal vertical and horizontal joints.

Shoe

Quarter-round

Use to finish inside corners; base shoe finishes base trim at the floor line.

Square

For use as trim, a variety of stock wood moldings are available at millwork shops. They vary in section, length, and species of wood. They can be used singly or be combined to form more complex sections. In addition to these stock sections, wood moldings can be milled to custom specifications.

The type of wood used for trim depends on the type of finish to be applied to the woodwork. For painted finishes, the wood should be close-grained, smooth, and free of pitch streaks or other imperfections. If the woodwork is to receive a transparent or natural finish, the wood should have a uniform color, an attractive grain figure, and a degree of hardness.

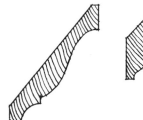   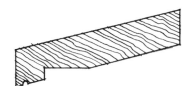 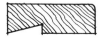

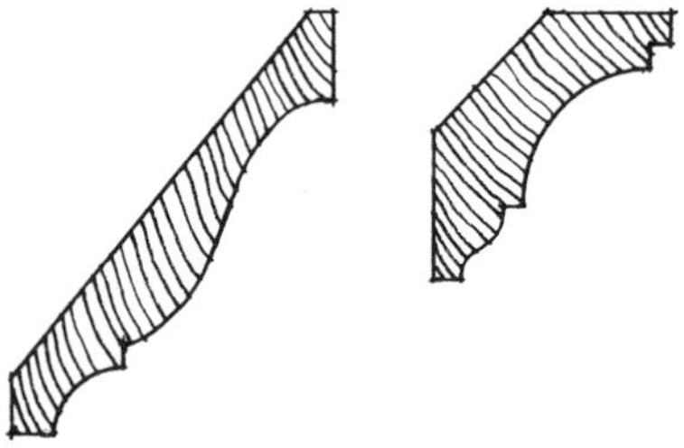

Crowns

Use at the meeting of wall and ceiling surfaces, and at mantels.

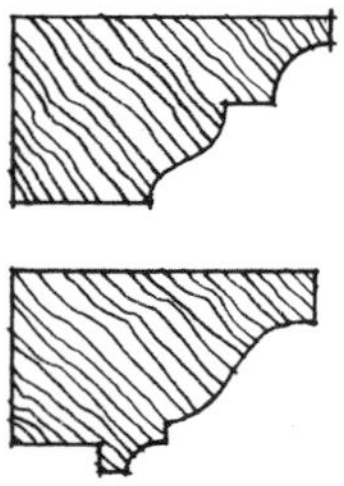

Caps

Use over windows, doors, and at the tops of wainscots.

Sill

The bottom trim of window and door openings.

Stool

The interior trim at the bottom of windows.

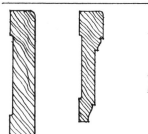 

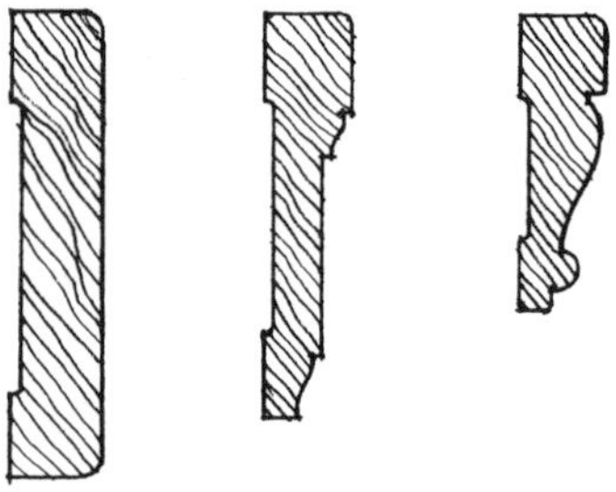

Casings

Use to trim head and side jambs of windows and doors.

Chair rails

Use to protect a wall surface from chair backs.

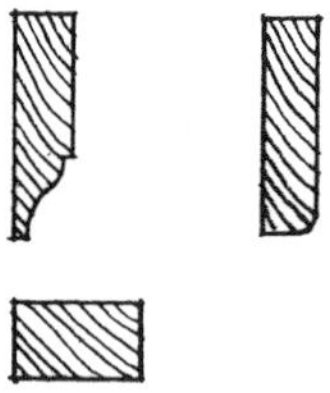

Stops

Use at jambs to guide windows and stop doors.

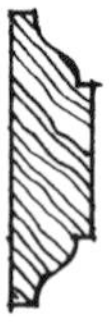

Panel strip

Use to conceal joints in paneling.

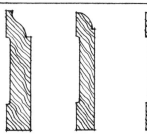 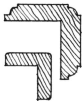

Bases

Use where sidewalls meet the floor, and as window and door casings.

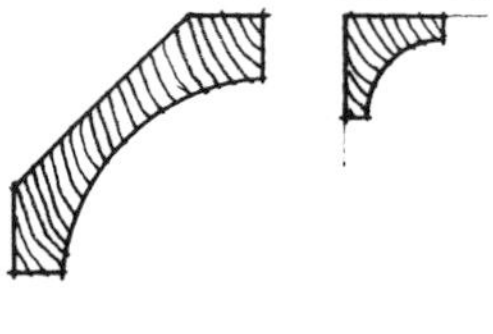

Coves

Use where surfaces meet at 90°.

Corner

Use at exterior corners.

Screen

Use to finish the screening on windows and doors.

Interior trim is normally applied after the finish walls, ceiling, and flooring are in place. Although decorative in nature, interior trim also serves to conceal, finish, and perfect the joints between interior materials. Common types of interior trim include:

CORNICES

Cornices are used to finish the joint between ceilings and walls, especially when they are of different materials.

DOOR AND WINDOW TRIM

Head and side jamb casings conceal and finish the joint or gap between door and window frames and the surrounding wall surface. Stools and aprons are used to finish the joint between window sills and interior walls.

BASEBOARDS

Baseboards and base shoes conceal and finish the joint between interior walls and the flooring.

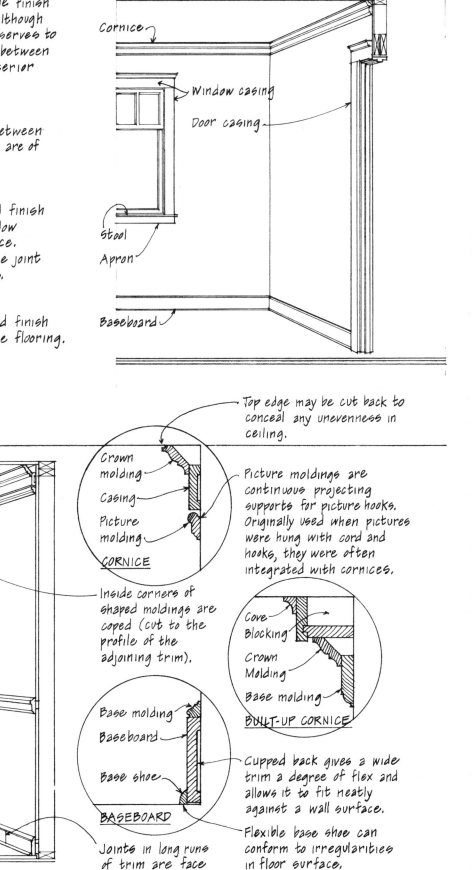

Cornice

Window casing

Door casing

Stool

Apron

Baseboard

Cornice

Chair rails and dado caps are used to cap the top of wood panel wainscots.

Baseboard

Top edge may be cut back to conceal any unevenness in ceiling.

Crown molding

Casing

Picture molding

CORNICE

Picture moldings are continuous projecting supports for picture hooks. Originally used when pictures were hung with cord and hooks, they were often integrated with cornices.

Cove Blocking

Crown Molding

Base molding

BUILT-UP CORNICE

Inside corners of shaped moldings are coped (cut to the profile of the adjoining trim).

Base molding

Baseboard

Base shoe

BASEBOARD

Cupped back gives a wide trim a degree of flex and allows it to fit neatly against a wall surface.

Flexible base shoe can conform to irregularities in floor surface.

Joints in long runs of trim are face mitered.

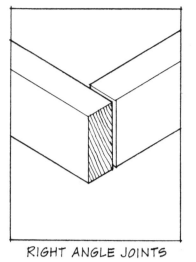

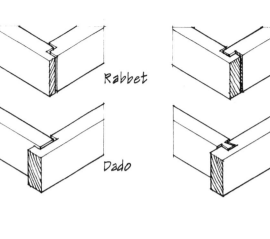

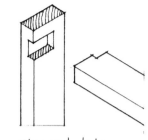

Rabbet

Dado

Dado & rabbet

Dovetail dado

Stopped dado

RIGHT ANGLE JOINTS

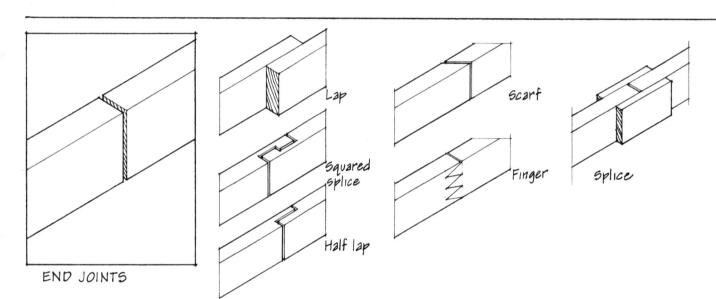

Lap

Squared splice

Half lap

Scarf

Finger

Splice

END JOINTS

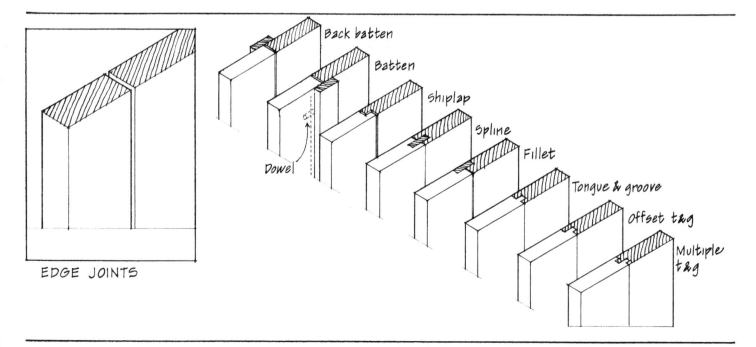

Back batten

Batten

Shiplap

Dowel

Spline

Fillet

Tongue & groove

Offset t&g

Multiple t&g

EDGE JOINTS

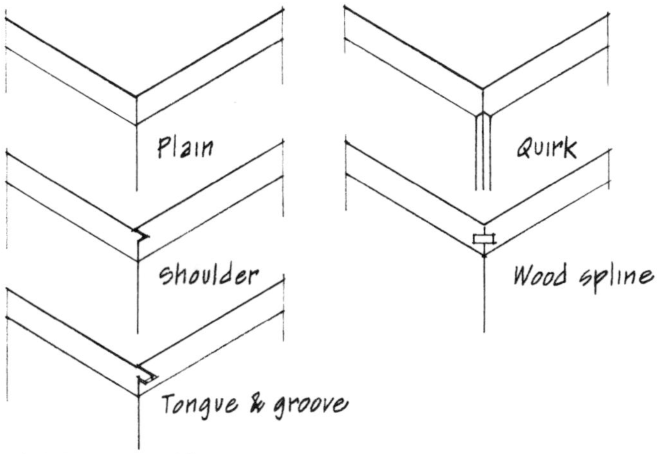

MITER JOINTS

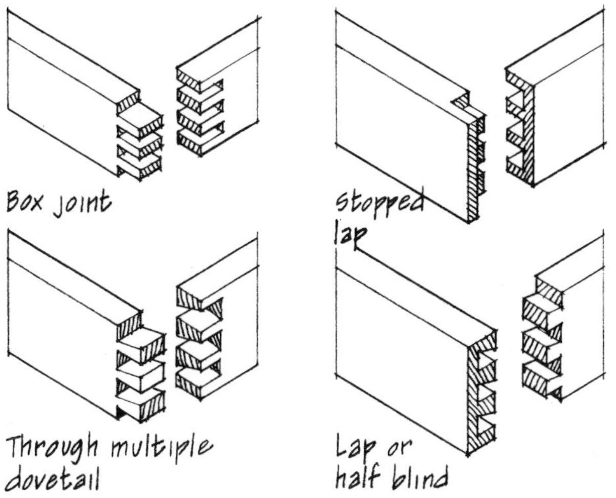

Plain

Quirk

Shoulder

Wood spline

Tongue & groove

Box joint

Stopped lap

Through multiple dovetail

Lap or half blind

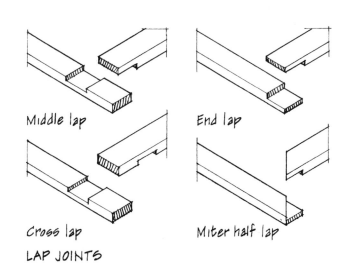

LAP JOINTS

Middle lap

End lap

Cross lap

Miter half lap

The strength and rigidity of ordinary wood framing are more important than its appearance since it is normally covered with a finish surface. In finish trim, cabinetry, and furniture work, however, a wood joint's appearance becomes just as important as its strength. Small scale work requires more sophisticated and refined joints which present a clean appearance.

Wood joints can express the manner in which the members are connected, or they can be relatively inconspicuous. In either case, they must remain tight. If they open due to the wood's shrinkage or structural movement, they become both weaker and more noticeable.

In designing and constructing a wood joint, it is important to understand the basic nature of the forces (compressive, tensile, shear) acting on the joint, and to comprehend their relationship to the wood grain's direction. (See 12.2.)

MORTISE AND TENON JOINTS

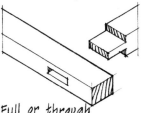

Ship

Pinned blind

Half blind

Haunch blind

Full or through

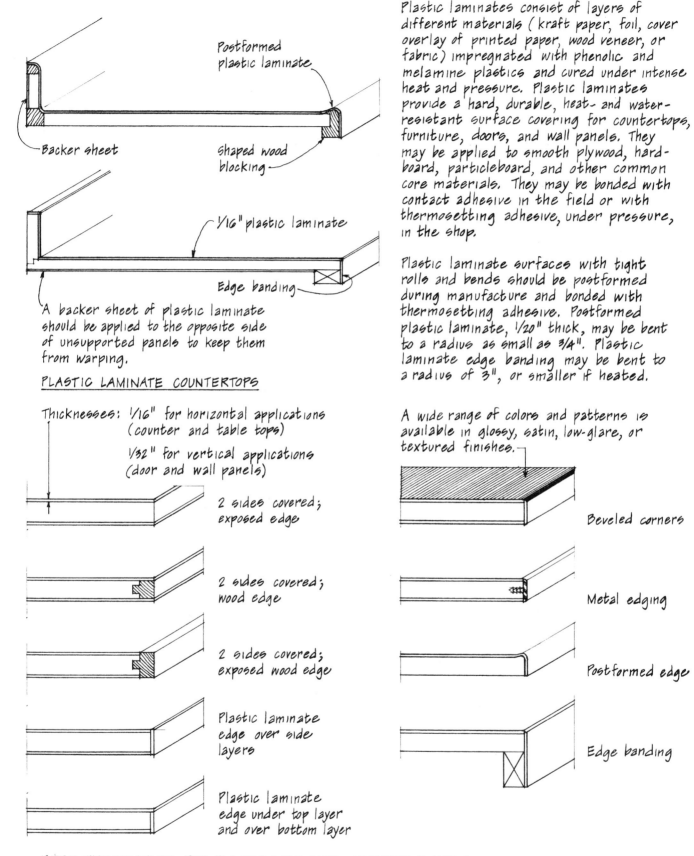

Postformed plastic laminate

Backer sheet

Shaped wood blocking

1/16" plastic laminate

Edge banding

A backer sheet of plastic laminate should be applied to the opposite side of unsupported panels to keep them from warping.

PLASTIC LAMINATE COUNTERTOPS

Thicknesses: 1/16" for horizontal applications (counter and table tops)

1/32" for vertical applications (door and wall panels)

2 sides covered; exposed edge

2 sides covered; wood edge

2 sides covered; exposed wood edge

Plastic laminate edge over side layers

Plastic laminate edge under top layer and over bottom layer

Plastic laminates consist of layers of different materials (kraft paper, foil, cover overlay of printed paper, wood veneer, or fabric) impregnated with phenolic and melamine plastics and cured under intense heat and pressure. Plastic laminates provide a hard, durable, heat- and water-resistant surface covering for countertops, furniture, doors, and wall panels. They may be applied to smooth plywood, hardboard, particleboard, and other common core materials. They may be bonded with contact adhesive in the field or with thermosetting adhesive, under pressure, in the shop.

Plastic laminate surfaces with tight rolls and bends should be postformed during manufacture and bonded with thermosetting adhesive. Postformed plastic laminate, 1/20" thick, may be bent to a radius as small as 3/4". Plastic laminate edge banding may be bent to a radius of 3", or smaller if heated.

A wide range of colors and patterns is available in glossy, satin, low-glare, or textured finishes.

Beveled corners

Metal edging

Postformed edge

Edge banding

EDGE TREATMENTS FOR PLASTIC LAMINATE COVERED PANELS

MECHANICAL & ELECTRICAL SYSTEMS 11

This chapter discusses the mechanical and electrical systems which are required to maintain the necessary conditions of environmental comfort, health, and safety for a building's occupants. The intent is not to provide a complete design manual but to outline those factors which should be considered for the successful operation of these systems and their integration with a building's other systems.

Heating, ventilating, and air-conditioning systems condition the interior spaces of a building for the environmental comfort of the occupants. A potable water supply is essential for human consumption and sanitation. The efficient disposal of fluid waste and organic matter is necessary in order to maintain sanitary conditions within a building and in the surrounding area. Electrical systems furnish light and heat for a building's occupants, and power to run its machines.

These systems require a significant amount of space. Because much of these systems' hardware is normally hidden from view—within concealed construction spaces or special rooms—the layout of these systems should be carefully integrated with each other as well as with a building's structural and enclosure systems.

① Temperature of the surrounding air

② Mean radiant temperature of the surrounding surfaces

③ Relative humidity of the air

④ Air motion

⑤ Dust

⑥ Odors

The mechanical system of a building includes the heating, cooling, ventilating, and air-conditioning equipment used to control the environmental comfort factors listed to the left. The first four factors are of primary importance in determining thermal comfort, and may also be controlled by a building's siting, materials, and construction assemblies.

Balancing heat loss and heat gain to arrive at a comfortable temperature is the first step in achieving thermal comfort. The human body can lose heat by radiation, convection, conduction, or evaporation.

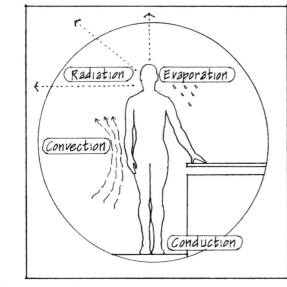

RADIATION: The transmission of heat energy through the air from a warm surface to cooler surfaces.

• Light colors reflect while dark colors absorb heat; poor reflectors make good radiators.
• Radiant heat cannot go around corners and is not affected by air motion.

CONVECTION: The transmission of heat from a warm surface to the surrounding air.

• Large temperature differentials and increased air motion induce more heat transmission by convection.

CONDUCTION: The transmission of heat from a warm body directly to a cooler body.

• Conduction has little effect on actual heat loss.

EVAPORATION: The transmission of heat through the evaporative process of moisture turning into water vapor.

• Evaporation is an important factor when high temperatures, humidity, and activity levels exist.
• Heat loss by evaporation increases with air motion.

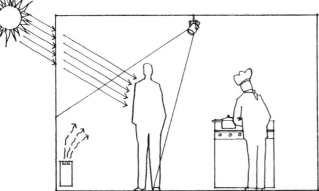

Source of heat within a building include:

o Solar radiation through a building's wall and roof assemblies.

o Building equipment such as heaters, light fixtures, and ranges.

o Human activity.

The objective of an air-conditioning system is to adjust the thermal comfort factors according to outdoor and indoor conditions and the level of human activity so that comfort-zone conditions exist within a space.

The following relationships between the four primary thermal comfort factors can be used to describe recommended comfort zones.

- Air temperature is controlled by the supply of warm or cool air to a space through various media: air, water, or electricity.

- Mean radiant temperature of surfaces is controlled by using radiant heat panels (hot water or electrical resistance heating) or by washing surfaces with warm air.

- Relative humidity is controlled by the introduction of water vapor, or its removal, by ventilation.

- Air motion is controlled by mechanical ventilation.

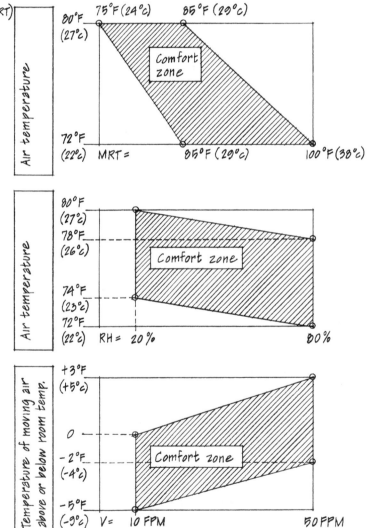

AIR TEMPERATURE AND MEAN RADIANT TEMPERATURE (MRT)

- The higher the mean radiant temperature of the surrounding surfaces, the cooler the air temperature should be.
- MRT has about 40% more effect on comfort than air temperature.
- In cold weather, the MRT of the interior surfaces of exterior walls should not be more than 5°F (3°C) below the indoor air temperature.

AIR TEMPERATURE AND RELATIVE HUMIDITY (RH)

- The higher the relative humidity of a space, the lower the air temperature should be.
- RH is more critical at high temperatures than within the normal temperature range.
- Low humidity (<20%) can have undesirable effects such as the buildup of static electricity and the drying out of wood; high humidity can cause condensation problems.

AIR TEMPERATURE AND AIR MOTION (V)

- The cooler the moving air stream is, relative to the room air temperature, the less velocity it should have.
- Air velocity should range between 10 and 50 feet per minute (FPM).
- Higher velocities can cause drafty conditions.
- Air motion is especially helpful for cooling by evaporation in hot, humid weather.

Air temperature requirements are also affected by the age group of the building's occupants, the weight and color of the clothing they wear, and the level of their activity.

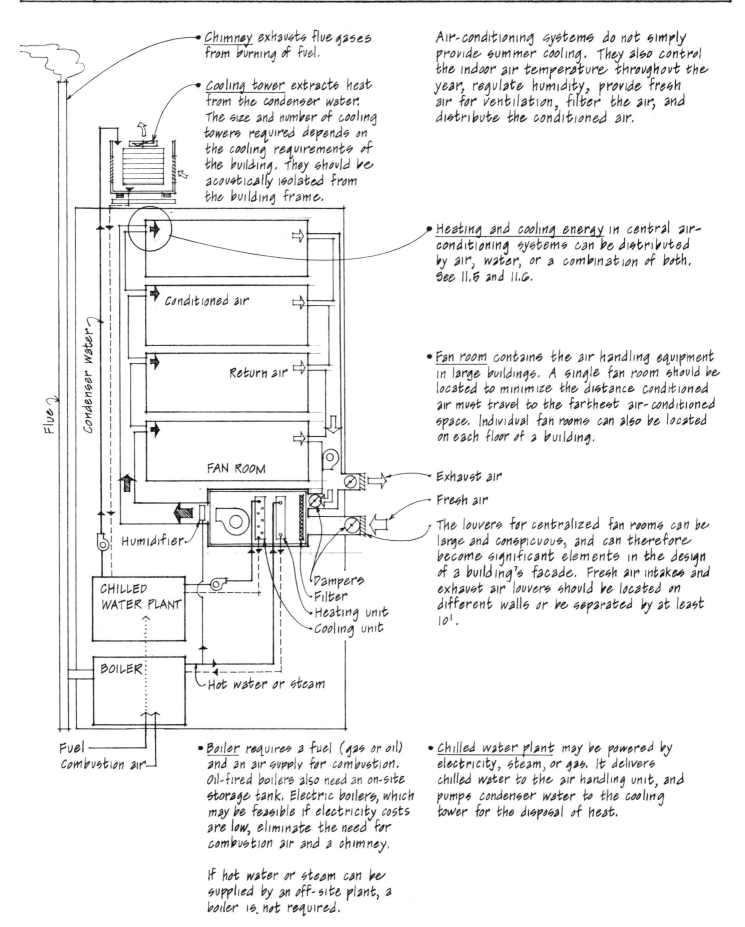

• Chimney exhausts flue gases from burning of fuel.

• Cooling tower extracts heat from the condenser water. The size and number of cooling towers required depends on the cooling requirements of the building. They should be acoustically isolated from the building frame.

Air-conditioning systems do not simply provide summer cooling. They also control the indoor air temperature throughout the year, regulate humidity, provide fresh air for ventilation, filter the air, and distribute the conditioned air.

• Heating and cooling energy in central air-conditioning systems can be distributed by air, water, or a combination of both. See 11.5 and 11.6.

• Fan room contains the air handling equipment in large buildings. A single fan room should be located to minimize the distance conditioned air must travel to the farthest air-conditioned space. Individual fan rooms can also be located on each floor of a building.

Flue

Condenser water

Conditioned air

Return air

FAN ROOM

Humidifier

Exhaust air

Fresh air

The louvers for centralized fan rooms can be large and conspicuous, and can therefore become significant elements in the design of a building's facade. Fresh air intakes and exhaust air louvers should be located on different walls or be separated by at least 10'.

Dampers
Filter
Heating unit
Cooling unit

CHILLED WATER PLANT

BOILER

Hot water or steam

Fuel
Combustion air

• Boiler requires a fuel (gas or oil) and an air supply for combustion. Oil-fired boilers also need an on-site storage tank. Electric boilers, which may be feasible if electricity costs are low, eliminate the need for combustion air and a chimney.

If hot water or steam can be supplied by an off-site plant, a boiler is not required.

• Chilled water plant may be powered by electricity, steam, or gas. It delivers chilled water to the air handling unit, and pumps condenser water to the cooling tower for the disposal of heat.

Factors to consider in the selection, design, and installation of an air-conditioning system include:

- Performance, efficiency, and both the initial and life costs of the system.
- Fuel and power sources required and the means for their delivery and storage.
- Flexibility of the system to service different zones of a building, which may have different demands because of use or site orientation.
- Noise and vibration controls required.
- Space requirements for the mechanical equipment and the distribution system.

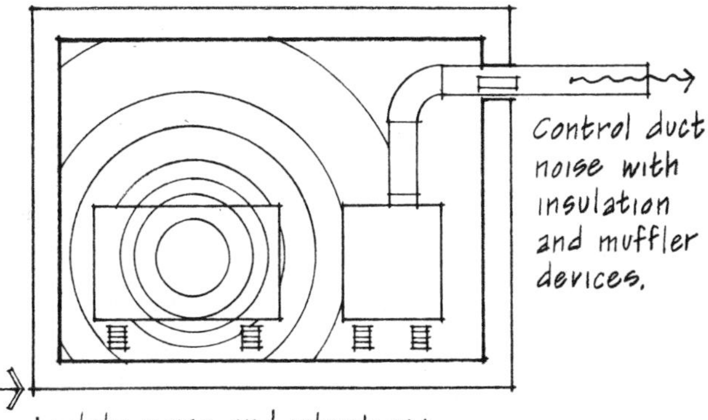

Control duct noise with insulation and muffler devices.

Isolate noise and vibration:

- By distance (location)
- With mass (enclosure)
- By using vibration control devices (installation)

In small buildings, heating energy may be supplied by forced air, hot water, or electric heating systems.

Cooling may be provided in a forced air system by an outdoor compressor and condensing unit. This unit supplies cold refrigerant to evaporator coils in the main supply ductwork.

A forced air system can also incorporate filtering, humidifying, and dehumidifying devices into the installation.

Fresh air ventilation is usually provided by natural means.

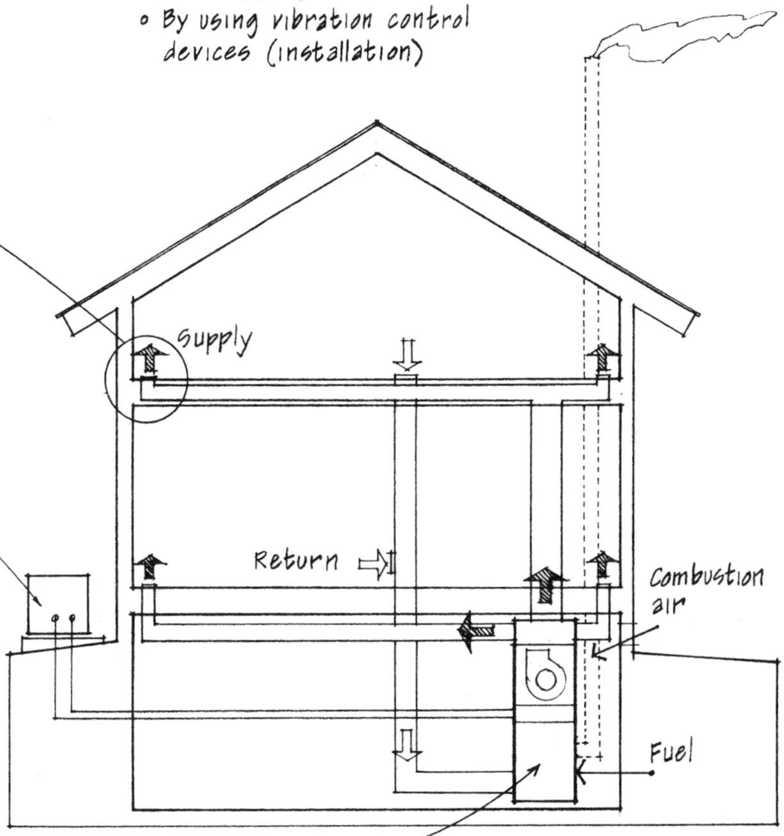

Supply

Return

Combustion air

Fuel

Furnace or boiler may be powered by gas, oil, or electricity. Oil furnaces require a fuel storage tank. Electric furnaces do not require combustion air or a chimney.

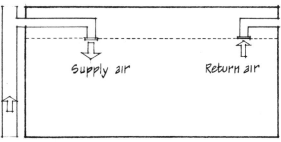

SINGLE ZONE SYSTEM

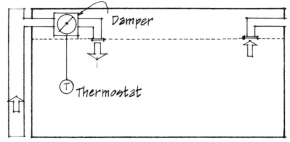

VARIABLE AIR FLOW SYSTEM

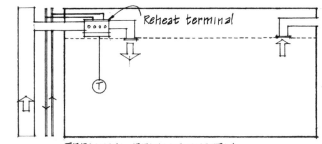

TERMINAL REHEAT SYSTEM

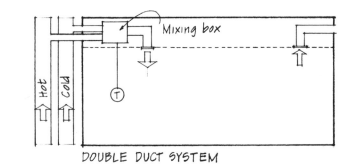

DOUBLE DUCT SYSTEM

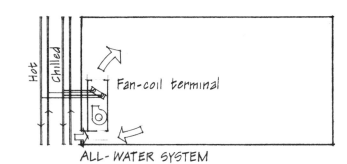

ALL-WATER SYSTEM

ALL-AIR SYSTEMS

Single duct systems:

In a single zone system, conditioned air is delivered at a constant temperature through a low velocity duct system to the served spaces.

The variable air flow system uses dampers at the terminal outlets to control the air flow according to the requirements of each space.

The terminal reheat system is more flexible since it supplies air at about 55°F (12°c) to terminals equipped with hot water reheat coils to compensate for changing space requirements.

Double duct systems:

Separate duct systems deliver warm air and cool air to terminal mixing units which contain thermostatically controlled dampers. The mixing units may serve individual spaces or a number of zones.
This is usually a high-velocity system to reduce duct sizes and installation space.

ALL-WATER SYSTEMS

Pipes, which require less installation space than air ducts, deliver hot and/or chilled water to fan-coil units in the served spaces.
The fan-coil units draw a mixture of outdoor and room air over the coils of heated or chilled water and then back into the space.

In a 2-pipe system, one pipe supplies either hot or chilled water to each fan-coil unit and the other returns it.
In a 4-pipe system, two separate piping circuits — one for hot water and one for chilled water — are used to provide simultaneous heating and cooling to different zones of a building.

Ventilation is provided through wall openings, by infiltration, or by a separate duct system.

AIR AND WATER SYSTEMS

High velocity ducts deliver conditioned primary air to induction units in the served spaces. The primary air induces room air to mix with it and pass over coils that are heated or cooled by a secondary water system.

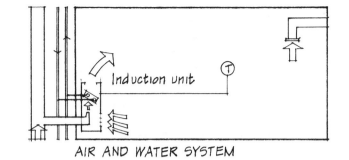

AIR AND WATER SYSTEM

PACKAGED AIR-CONDITIONING UNITS

Packaged air-conditioning units are self-contained systems which can serve either single- or multizone configurations.
They may be located on the roof or on a pad alongside the building.
Small units can be installed in window or wall openings.
Cooling is provided by condensing units which require an outdoor location.
Heating is provided by a gas or oil furnace, electric resistance heaters, or a heat pump.

Heat pumps are electrically powered heating and cooling units. For cooling, the normal refrigeration cycle is used to absorb and transfer excess heat to the outdoors. For heating, heat energy is drawn from the outdoor air by reversing the cooling cycle and switching the heat exchange functions of the condenser and evaporator.
Heat pumps are most efficient in moderate climates where heating and cooling loads are almost equal. In freezing temperatures, a heat pump requires an electric resistance heater to keep the outdoor coils from freezing.

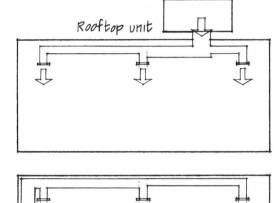

Rooftop unit

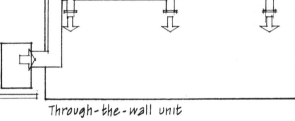

Through-the-wall unit

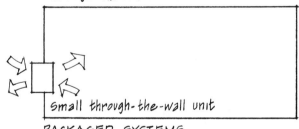

Small through-the-wall unit

PACKAGED SYSTEMS

ELECTRIC HEATING

Electric resistance heating elements may be incorporated into baseboard convection units or into fan-forced unit heaters. These small unit heaters may be recessed in the floor or wall, be suspended from the ceiling, or be located under a cabinet.

Electric resistance heating cables can also be embedded in ceiling panels or floor slabs to provide radiant heating. See 11.12.

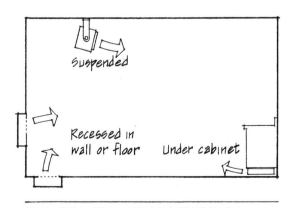

Suspended

Recessed in wall or floor   Under cabinet

ELECTRIC RESISTANCE HEATERS

Factors to consider in the location of heating, cooling, and air-conditioning equipment include:

- Power, fuel, air, and water requirements; some equipment requires direct access to the outdoors.
- Access required for service and maintenance.
- Construction requirements for the enclosure of the mechanical plant, for fire resistance, and for noise and vibration control.
- Structural requirements imposed by the weight of the equipment.
- Type and layout of the distribution system used for the heating and cooling media.
- Type of installation – concealed within the building's construction or exposed to view.

A building's mechanical equipment can occupy a significant amount of space within the building volume. Some pieces of equipment also require space or a domain for access, service, and maintenance. If this machinery takes up 10% to 15% of a building's area, as is often the case, then it becomes necessary to consider the implications of the equipment's placement within the building.

A building's machinery and equipment may be located:

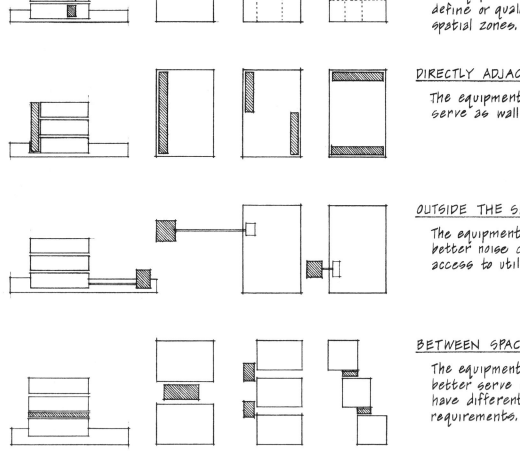

WITHIN A SPACE

Central locations are ideal for short runs and efficient distribution patterns. The equipment enclosure may serve to define or qualify a number of related spatial zones.

DIRECTLY ADJACENT TO A SPACE

The equipment enclosures may serve as wall or barrier elements.

OUTSIDE THE SPACE

The equipment may be isolated for better noise control or for easier access to utilities and service.

BETWEEN SPACES

The equipment may be dispersed to better serve spaces or zones that have different demands and load requirements.

Note that the above relationships also apply to the location of plumbing and electrical equipment.

The air-conditioning equipment may be central-ized in one location or dispersed throughout a building. Some equipment requires both indoor and outdoor components; others may be self-contained units which can be located on the roof or on exterior walls. The distribution pattern of the ducts or piping used to deliver the heating or cooling medium to the served spaces is determined by:

○ The locations of the heating, cooling, and air-conditioning equipment
○ The arrangement of the served spaces.

Air duct systems require more space than either pipes carrying hot or chilled water or wiring for electric resistance heating. For this reason, ductwork must be carefully laid out to be integrated with a building's struc-ture and spaces, as well as with its plumbing and electrical systems. If the ductwork is to be left exposed, it becomes even more important that the layout have a visually coherent order and be coordinated with the physical elements of the space (e.g., structural elements, lighting fixtures, surface patterns).

Vertical duct runs are housed in mechanical shafts while horizontal runs may be under ground slabs, in basement or crawl spaces, or within floor or roof construction assemblies.

Horizontal distribution patterns may be classified as radial, perimeter, or lateral in nature.

● Radial patterns minimize the length of horizontal runs. They can be used in clear spaces which are free of obstacles.

● Perimeter loop patterns are effective against heat losses and gains that occur along the perimeter of a building. They are used in conjunction with concrete ground slabs.

● Lateral patterns require the longest horizontal runs, but offer a wide, uniform, and flexible system of distribution. Exposed ductwork systems usually utilize a lateral pattern layout.

To minimize friction loss, ductwork should have short, direct runs with a minimum of turns and offsets. In addition, ducts should be insulated against heat loss or gain and sound transmission.

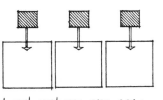
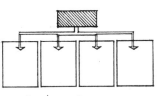

Local systems are eco-nomical to install, require short distribution runs, and allow spaces to have individual temperature control.

Central systems are generally more energy-efficient, easier to service, and offer better control of air quality.

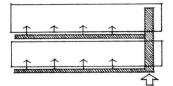

Floor

Ductwork

Ceiling
Lighting fixture

Careful integration of structural, mechanical, and electrical systems can conserve space.

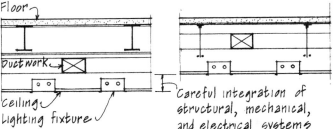

Main vertical feeder uses less floor area but increases building height.

Main horizontal feeder uses more floor area but decreases building height.

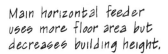
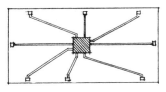
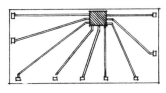

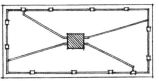
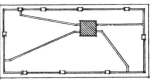

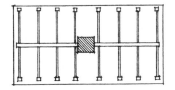
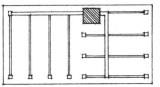

The location of heating and cooling outlets depends on the size and proportions of the space, the areas of heat loss or gain, the wall, floor and ceiling construction, and the occupants' acitivity patterns. The type of outlet used depends on its placement within the space, it heating or cooling capacity, and its dimensions and appearance. Below are illustrated various types of outlets according to location and the heating or cooling medium used.

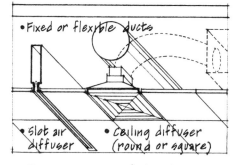
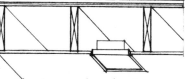
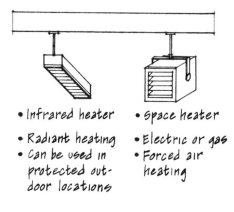

- Fixed or flexible ducts
- Slot air diffuser
- Ceiling diffuser (round or square)
- Require a suspended ceiling
- Supplied by low-velocity ductwork
- May be a part of an integrated, modular ceiling system

- Electric ceiling heater
- Convection or forced air heating
- May be combined with a light fixture and/or an exhaust fan
- See 11.12 for radiant ceiling panels.

- Infrared heater
- Radiant heating
- Can be used in protected out-door locations

- Space heater
- Electric or gas
- Forced air heating

CEILING LOCATIONS

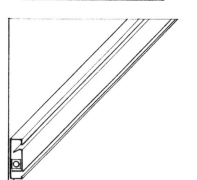

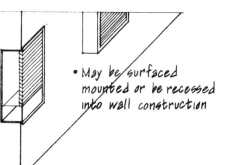

- Baseboard unit
- Fin tube or fan coil unit, or electric resistance heater

- May be used on a window wall, as a window sill, or be built into a wall cabinet.
- Mullion or wall-mounted unit
- Fin tube or fan coil unit, or electric resistance heater

- May be surfaced mounted or be recessed into wall construction
- Electric wall heaters
- Heat by radiation, convection, or forced air

WALL LOCATIONS (See facing page for air grilles and diffusers.)

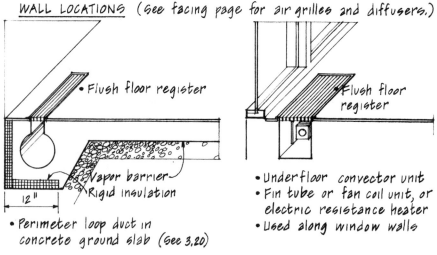
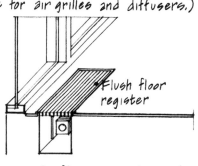
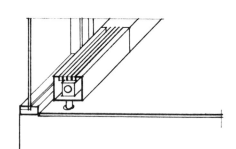

- Flush floor register
- 12"
- Vapor barrier
- Rigid insulation
- Perimeter loop duct in concrete ground slab (See 3.20)

- Flush floor register
- Underfloor convector unit
- Fin tube or fan coil unit, or electric resistance heater
- Used along window walls

- Freestanding fin tube unit
- Low profile units may be used along window walls

FLOOR LOCATIONS

Air for heating, cooling, and ventilating is supplied through grilles, registers, and diffusers. They should be evaluated in terms of their air flow capacity and velocity, pressure drop, noise factor, and appearance.

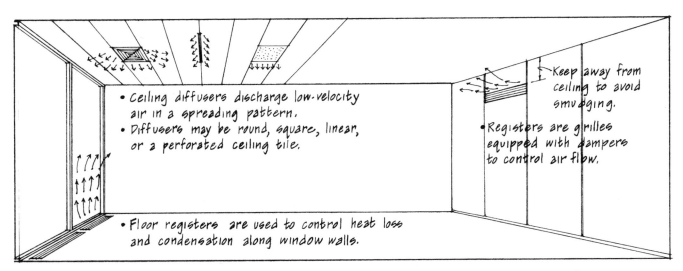

- Ceiling diffusers discharge low-velocity air in a spreading pattern.
- Diffusers may be round, square, linear, or a perforated ceiling tile.
- Floor registers are used to control heat loss and condensation along window walls.

Keep away from ceiling to avoid smudging.

- Registers are grilles equipped with dampers to control air flow.

Air supply outlets should be located to distribute warm or cool air to the occupied areas of a space comfortably, without noticeable drafts, and without stratification. The throw distance and spread or diffusion pattern of the supply outlet should be carefully considered along with any obstructions that might interfere with the air distribution.

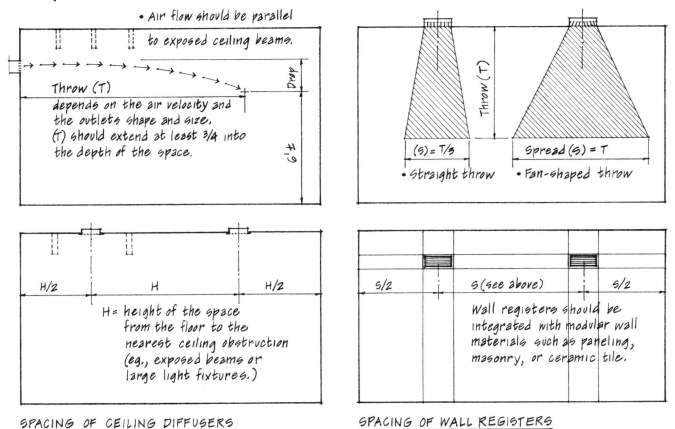

- Air flow should be parallel to exposed ceiling beams.

Throw (T) depends on the air velocity and the outlets shape and size. (T) should extend at least 3/4 into the depth of the space.

- Straight throw $(S) = T/3$
- Fan-shaped throw   Spread $(S) = T$

H/2   H   H/2

H = height of the space from the floor to the nearest ceiling obstruction (eg., exposed beams or large light fixtures.)

S/2   S(see above)   S/2

Wall registers should be integrated with modular wall materials such as paneling, masonry, or ceramic tile.

SPACING OF CEILING DIFFUSERS

SPACING OF WALL REGISTERS

Radiant panel heating systems utilize heated ceilings, floors, and sometimes walls, as radiating surfaces. The heat source may be pipes carrying hot water or electric resistance heating cables embedded within the ceiling, floor, or wall construction.

Radiant heat travels in a direct path.

- It cannot go around corners and may therefore be obstructed by physical elements within the space such as furniture.
- It cannot counteract cold downdrafts along exterior glass areas.
- It is not affected by air motion.

Because radiant panel heating systems cannot respond quickly to changing temperature demands, they may be supplemented with perimeter convector units. For complete air-conditioning, separate ventilating, humidity control, and cooling systems are required.

Floor installations are effective warming concrete slabs. In general, however, ceiling installations are preferred because the ceiling construction has less thermal capacity and thus faster heat response. Ceiling panels can also be heated to a higher surface temperature than floor slabs.

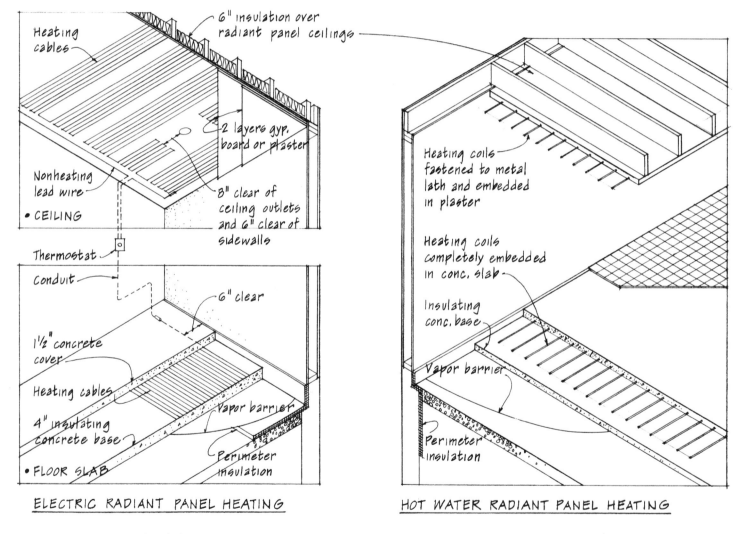

ELECTRIC RADIANT PANEL HEATING

HOT WATER RADIANT PANEL HEATING

Preassembled radiant heating panels are commercially available. They may be used with modular, suspended ceiling systems or to heat specific areas of a space.

In both electric and hot water systems, the installations are completely concealed except for thermostats or balancing valves.

Water is utilized in a building in the following ways:

○ Consumed by drinking, cooking, washing etc. . . .(must be potable)
○ Circulated by heating and cooling systems. . . . . .(should be soft or neutral)
○ Stored by fire protection systems . . . .(no special requirements)
○ Controlled to maintain desirable humidity levels

Water must be supplied to a building in the correct quantity, and at the proper flow rate, pressure and temperature, to satisfy the above requirements. For human consumption, water must be palatable and free of harmful bacteria. To avoid the clogging or corrosion of pipes and equipment, water may have to be treated for hardness or excessive acidity.

If water is supplied by a municipal or public system, there can be no direct control over the quantity or quality of water supplied until it reaches the building site. If a public water system is not available, then either rainwater storage tanks or drilled wells are required.

Well water, if the source is deep enough, is usually pure, cool, and free of discoloration and taste or odor problems. Factors to consider in the selection of a well location include:

• Quality of the water to be supplied; should be checked by the local health department.
• Amount of water that can be supplied by the source.
• Required depth and cost of the well.
• Proximity of the well to areas containing pollutants.

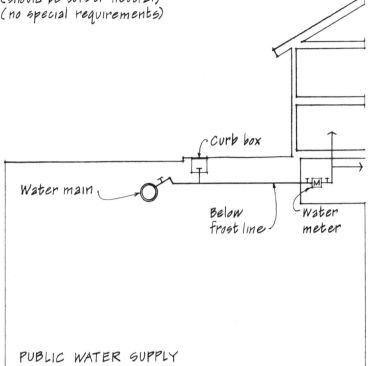

Curb box

Water main

Below frost line

Water meter

PUBLIC WATER SUPPLY

Water supply systems operate under pressure. The service pressure of a water supply system must be great enough to absorb pressure losses due to vertical travel and friction as the water flows through pipes and fittings, and still satisfy the pressure requirement of each plumbing fixture. Public water systems usually supply water at about 50 psi. This pressure is the approximate upper limit for most private well systems.

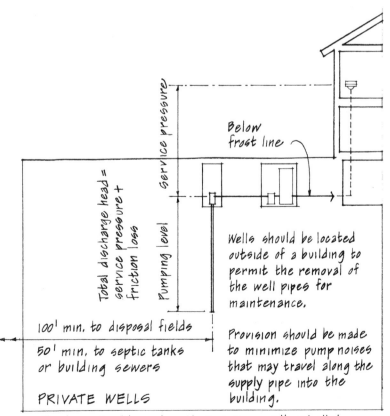

Total discharge head = service pressure + friction loss

Pumping level

Service pressure

Below frost line

Wells should be located outside of a building to permit the removal of the well pipes for maintenance.

Provision should be made to minimize pump noises that may travel along the supply pipe into the building.

100' min. to disposal fields

50' min. to septic tanks or building sewers

PRIVATE WELLS

Check applicable codes that govern well installations.

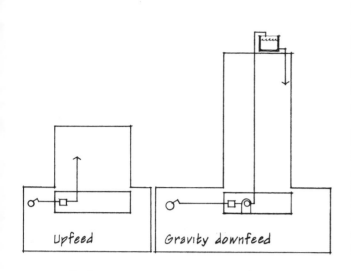

Upfeed | Gravity downfeed

+ Fixture pressure requirements
+ Pressure loss due to vertical lift
+ Pressure loss due to friction in pipe runs
_____
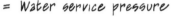
= Water service pressure

Larger pipes cause less pressure loss.

Every pipe fitting causes fricture loss.

2' capped air chambers @ fixture branches

Expansion joint of pipe and fittings

1/2" to 1" glass fiber or rock wool insulation

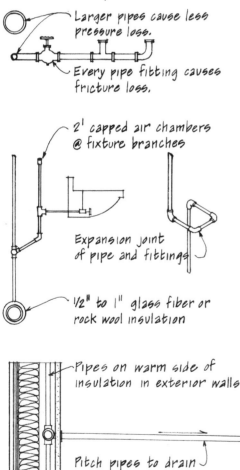

Pipes on warm side of insulation in exterior walls

Pitch pipes to drain

If water is supplied at 50 psi, upfeed distribution is feasible for lowrise buildings up to 6 stories in height. For taller buildings, or where the water service pressure is insufficient to maintain adequate fixture service, water is pumped up to an elevated or rooftop storage tank for gravity downfeed. Part of this water is often used as a reserve system for fire protection systems.

Hot water is supplied by gas-fired or electric heaters and circulated in tall buildings by the natural rising action of hot water. In long, low buildings, pumps are required for hot water circulation and distribution. Hot water storage tanks may be required for large installations and widespread fixture groupings. For safety, pressure relief valves are required for all water heaters.

There must be sufficient pressure at each fixture to ensure their satisfactory operation. Fixture pressure requirements vary from 5 to 30 psi. Too much pressure is as undesirable as insufficient pressure. Water supply pipes are therefore sized to use up the differential between the service pressure (allowing for the pressure loss due to vertical lift) and the pressure requirement for each fixture.

The amount of pressure loss due to friction depends on the size of the supply pipe, the actual distance of the water flow, and the number of fittings (valves, tees, elbows) through which the water passes.

Pipe supports should be spaced to carry the weight of the pipe as well as the water being distributed through it. • Vertically, at least every story
     • Horizontally, every 6' to 10'
Adjustable hangers can be used to ensure proper pitch along horizontal runs for drainage purposes.

Water hammer is a noise that can occur when water is shut off abruptly. To absorb this shock, air chambers or manufactured shock absorbers are used at fixture branches. In tall buildings, special joints are required to allow for the expansion of long pipe runs carrying hot water.

Cold water pipes should be insulated and covered with a vapor barrier to prevent surface condensation and heat flow into the water from the warmer surrounding air. Hot water pipes should be insulated against heat loss and should be no closer than 6" to parallel cold water pipes.

In very cold climates, water pipes in exterior walls and unheated buildings can freeze and rupture. Provision should be made for their drainage to a low point in the system where a drainage faucet is located.

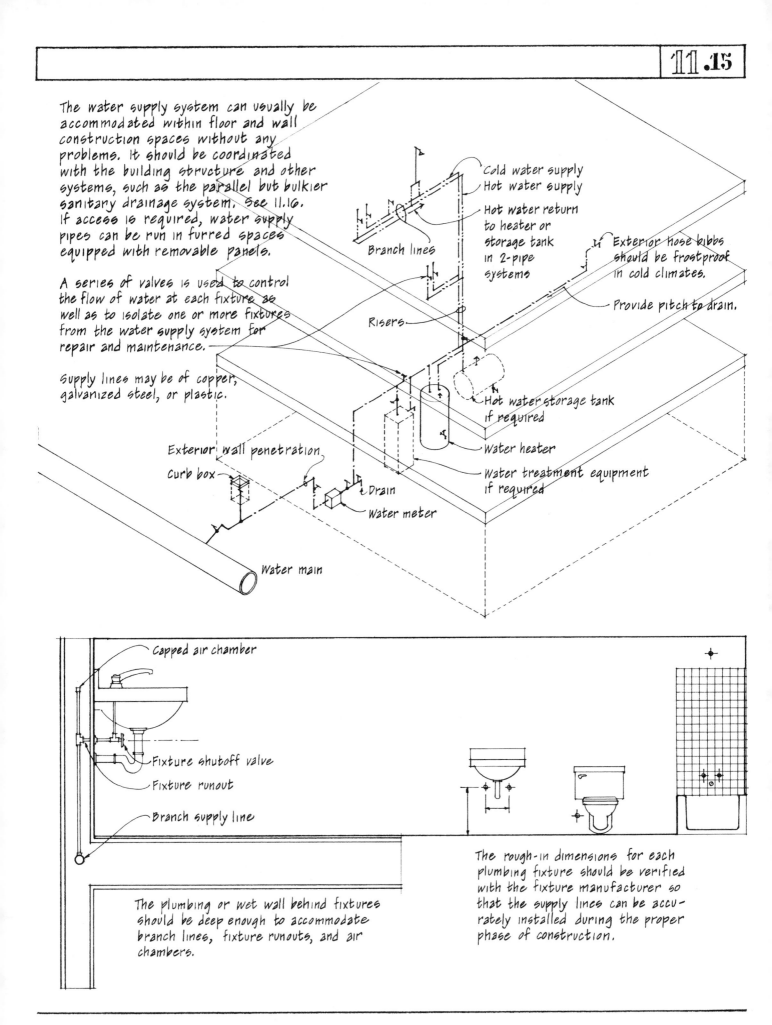

The water supply system can usually be accommodated within floor and wall construction spaces without any problems. It should be coordinated with the building structure and other systems, such as the parallel but bulkier sanitary drainage system. See 11.16. If access is required, water supply pipes can be run in furred spaces equipped with removable panels.

A series of valves is used to control the flow of water at each fixture as well as to isolate one or more fixtures from the water supply system for repair and maintenance.

Supply lines may be of copper, galvanized steel, or plastic.

Cold water supply
Hot water supply

Hot water return to heater or storage tank in 2-pipe systems

Branch lines

Exterior hose bibbs should be frostproof in cold climates.

Provide pitch to drain.

Risers

Hot water storage tank if required

Exterior wall penetration

Curb box

Drain

Water meter

Water heater

Water treatment equipment if required

Water main

Capped air chamber

Fixture shutoff valve

Fixture runout

Branch supply line

The plumbing or wet wall behind fixtures should be deep enough to accommodate branch lines, fixture runouts, and air chambers.

The rough-in dimensions for each plumbing fixture should be verified with the fixture manufacturer so that the supply lines can be accurately installed during the proper phase of construction.

The water supply system terminates at each plumbing fixture. After water has been drawn and used, it enters the sanitary drainage system. The primary objective of this drainage system is to dispose of fluid waste and organic matter as quickly as possible.

Since a sanitary drainage system relies on gravity for its discharge, its pipes are much larger than the water supply lines, which are under pressure. Drainage lines are sized according to their location in the system and the total number and type of fixtures served. Alway consult the local plumbing code for pipe sizing, pipe materials, and restrictions on the length and slope of horizontal runs and on the types and number of turns allowed.

A sump pump is required for fixtures located below the street sewer.

Building sewer line

Sanitary street sewer

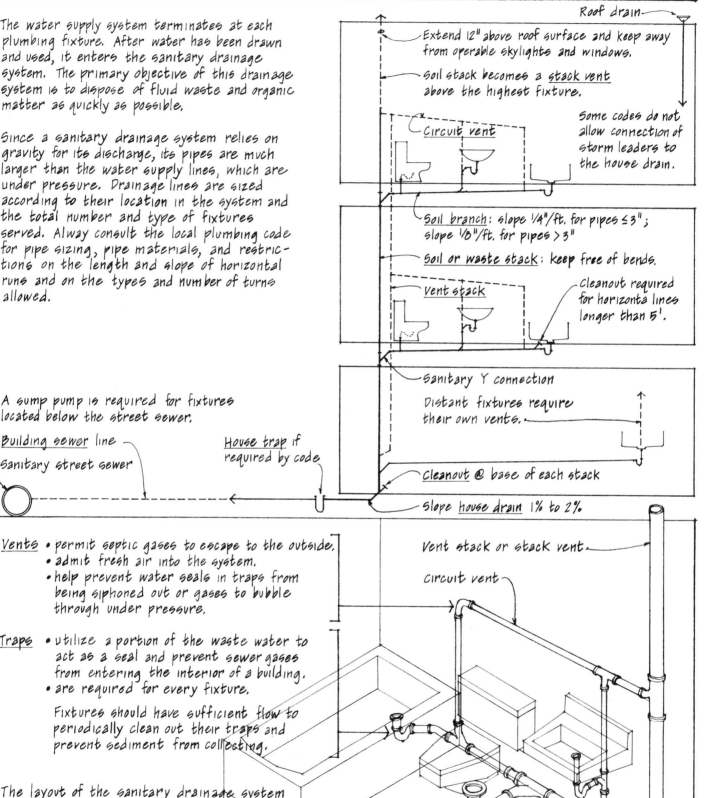

Roof drain

Extend 12" above roof surface and keep away from operable skylights and windows.

Soil stack becomes a stack vent above the highest fixture.

Some codes do not allow connection of storm leaders to the house drain.

Circuit vent

Soil branch: slope 1/4"/ft. for pipes ≤3"; slope 1/8"/ft. for pipes >3"

Soil or waste stack: keep free of bends.

Vent stack

Cleanout required for horizontal lines longer than 5'.

Sanitary Y connection

Distant fixtures require their own vents.

Cleanout @ base of each stack

House trap if required by code

Slope house drain 1% to 2%

Vents
- permit septic gases to escape to the outside.
- admit fresh air into the system.
- help prevent water seals in traps from being siphoned out or gases to bubble through under pressure.

Traps
- utilize a portion of the waste water to act as a seal and prevent sewer gases from entering the interior of a building.
- are required for every fixture.

  Fixtures should have sufficient flow to periodically clean out their traps and prevent sediment from collecting.

The layout of the sanitary drainage system should be as direct and straightforward as possible to prevent the deposit of solids and clogging. Cleanouts should be located to allow pipes to easily cleaned if they do clog.

Vent stack or stack vent

Circuit vent

Soil branch

Soil stack

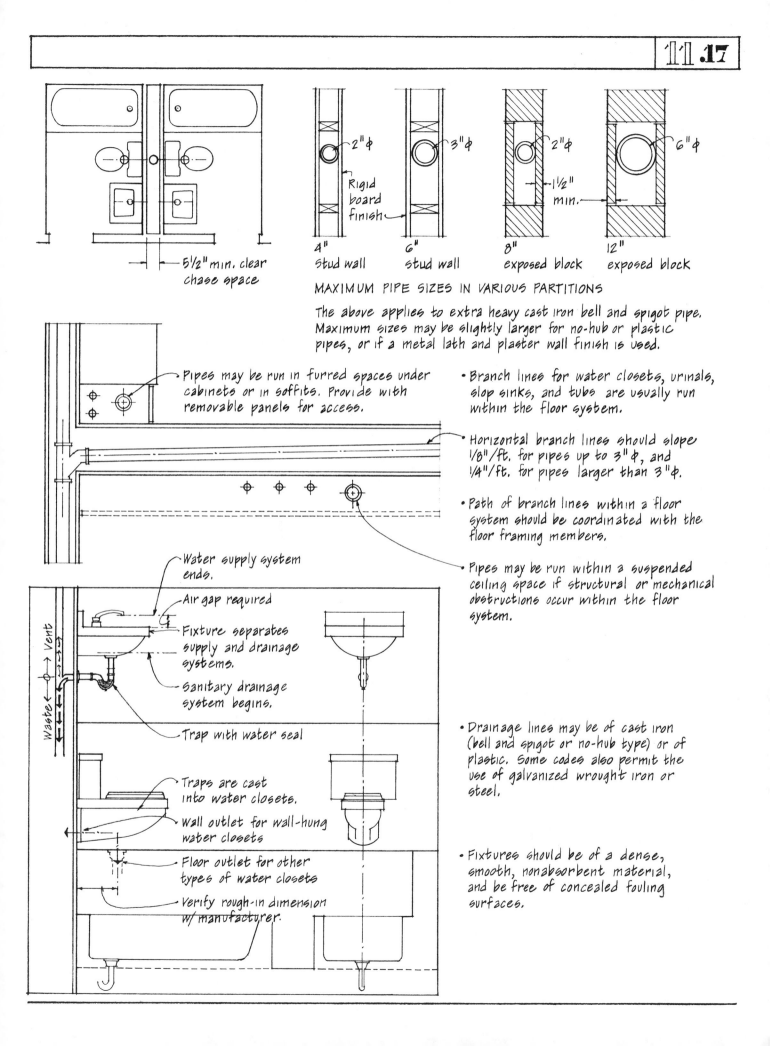

5½" min. clear chase space

2"φ — Rigid board finish
4" stud wall

3"φ
6" stud wall

2"φ — 1½" min.
8" exposed block

6"φ
12" exposed block

MAXIMUM PIPE SIZES IN VARIOUS PARTITIONS

The above applies to extra heavy cast iron bell and spigot pipe. Maximum sizes may be slightly larger for no-hub or plastic pipes, or if a metal lath and plaster wall finish is used.

• Pipes may be run in furred spaces under cabinets or in soffits. Provide with removable panels for access.

• Branch lines for water closets, urinals, slop sinks, and tubs are usually run within the floor system.

• Horizontal branch lines should slope 1/8"/ft. for pipes up to 3"φ, and 1/4"/ft. for pipes larger than 3"φ.

• Path of branch lines within a floor system should be coordinated with the floor framing members.

• Pipes may be run within a suspended ceiling space if structural or mechanical obstructions occur within the floor system.

Water supply system ends.

Air gap required

Fixture separates supply and drainage systems.

Sanitary drainage system begins.

Trap with water seal

Vent → Waste ← Waste →

Traps are cast into water closets.

Wall outlet for wall-hung water closets

Floor outlet for other types of water closets

Verify rough-in dimension w/ manufacturer.

• Drainage lines may be of cast iron (bell and spigot or no-hub type) or of plastic. Some codes also permit the use of galvanized wrought iron or steel.

• Fixtures should be of a dense, smooth, nonabsorbent material, and be free of concealed fouling surfaces.

A building's sewage wastes are usually deposited into a public sewage system for treatment and disposal. When this is not possible, a private sewage disposal system is required. Its type and size depends on the following:

- Number of people served
- Type and permeability of the soil
- Site topography
- Elevation of the ground water table
- Proximity to wells and streams.

A private sewage disposal system always requires a septic tank.

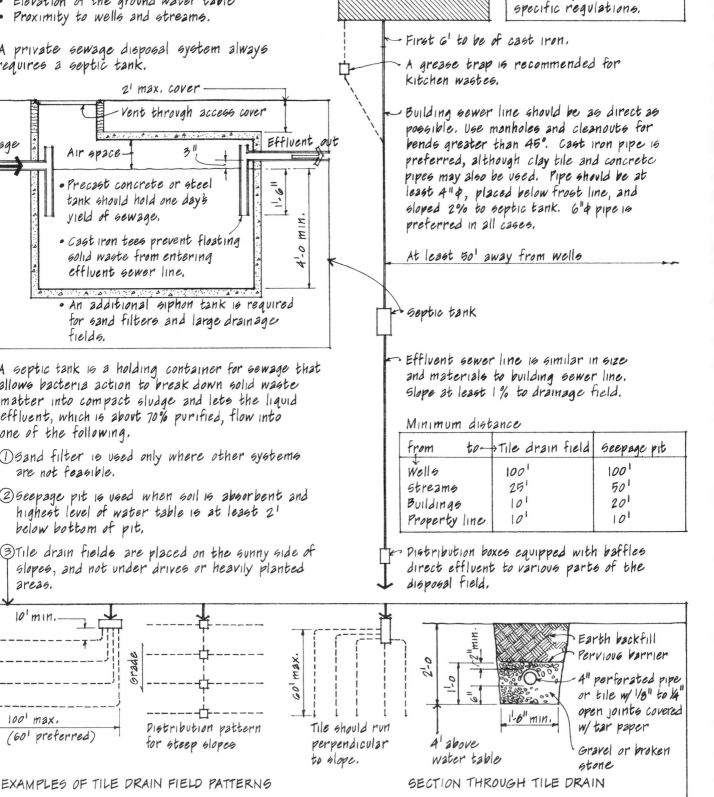

Consult local codes and health regulations for specific regulations.

- First 6' to be of cast iron.

- A grease trap is recommended for kitchen wastes.

- Building sewer line should be as direct as possible. Use manholes and cleanouts for bends greater than 45°. Cast iron pipe is preferred, although clay tile and concrete pipes may also be used. Pipe should be at least 4"⌀, placed below frost line, and sloped 2% to septic tank. 6"⌀ pipe is preferred in all cases.

At least 50' away from wells

- Septic tank

- Precast concrete or steel tank should hold one day's yield of sewage.

- Cast iron tees prevent floating solid waste from entering effluent sewer line.

- An additional siphon tank is required for sand filters and large drainage fields.

A septic tank is a holding container for sewage that allows bacteria action to break down solid waste matter into compact sludge and lets the liquid effluent, which is about 70% purified, flow into one of the following.

① Sand filter is used only where other systems are not feasible.

② Seepage pit is used when soil is absorbent and highest level of water table is at least 2' below bottom of pit.

③ Tile drain fields are placed on the sunny side of slopes, and not under drives or heavily planted areas.

- Effluent sewer line is similar in size and materials to building sewer line. Slope at least 1% to drainage field.

Minimum distance

From to→	Tile drain field	Seepage pit
Wells	100'	100'
Streams	25'	50'
Buildings	10'	20'
Property line	10'	10'

- Distribution boxes equipped with baffles direct effluent to various parts of the disposal field.

EXAMPLES OF TILE DRAIN FIELD PATTERNS

SECTION THROUGH TILE DRAIN

The electrical system of a building supplies power for lighting, heating, and the operation of electrical equipment and appliances. This system must be installed according to code to operate safely, reliably, and efficiently.

Electrical energy flows through a conductor because of a difference in electrical charge between two points in a circuit. This potential energy is measured in <u>volts</u>. The actual amount of energy flow or current is measured in <u>amperes</u>. The power required to an electric current flowing is measured in <u>watts</u>. Power in watts equals the current in amperes times the pressure in volts. ($W = A \times V$)

Just as pressure is lost due to friction as water flows through pipes, the flow of electrical current is impeded by resistance, measured in <u>ohms</u>, as it travels through a conductor.

Power is supplied to a building by the electric utility company. The schematic diagram below illustrates several voltage systems that may be furnished by the public utility according to a building's load requirements. A large installation may use its own <u>transformer</u> to switch from a more economical, higher supply voltage to the service voltage.

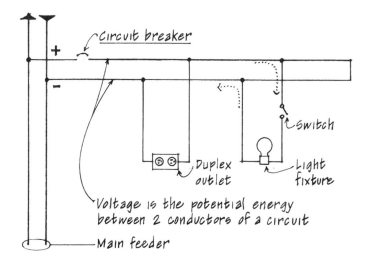

Voltage is the potential energy between 2 conductors of a circuit

SCHEMATIC OF A BRANCH CIRCUIT

For electric current to flow, a circuit must be complete. <u>Switches</u> control flow by introducing breaks in the circuit until power is required.

All electrical equipment should meet the Underwriters' Laboratories (UL) standards. Consult local applicable codes for specific requirements in the design and installation of an electrical system.

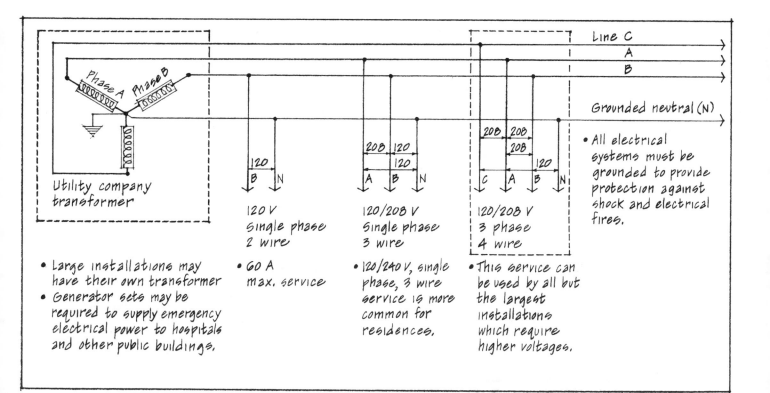

• All electrical systems must be grounded to provide protection against shock and electrical fires.

120 V
single phase
2 wire

120/208 V
single phase
3 wire

120/208 V
3 phase
4 wire

• Large installations may have their own transformer
• Generator sets may be required to supply emergency electrical power to hospitals and other public buildings.

• 60 A max. service

• 120/240 V, single phase, 3 wire service is more common for residences.

• This service can be used by all but the largest installations which require higher voltages.

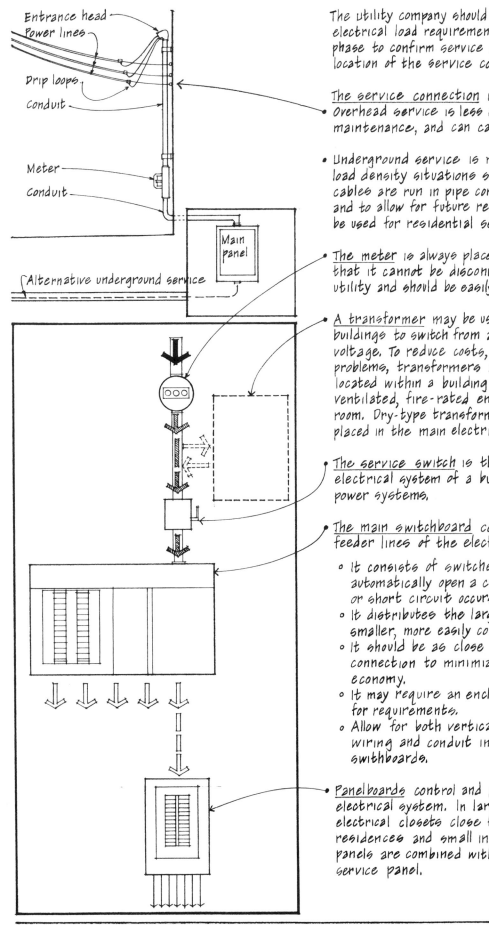

Entrance head
Power lines
Drip loops
Conduit
Meter
Conduit
Alternative underground service
Main panel

The utility company should be notified of the estimated total electrical load requirements for a building during the planning phase to confirm service availability and to coordinate the location of the service connection and meter.

The service connection may be overhead or underground. Overhead service is less expensive, easily accessible for maintenance, and can carry high voltages over long runs.

• Underground service is more expensive but is used in high load density situations such as urban areas. The service cables are run in pipe conduit or raceways for protection and to allow for future replacement. Direct burial cable may be used for residential service connections.

The meter is always placed ahead of the service switch so that it cannot be disconnected. It is supplied by the public utility and should be easily accessible.

• A transformer may be used by medium-sized and large buildings to switch from a high supply voltage to the service voltage. To reduce costs, maintenance, and noise and heat problems, transformers are usually placed outdoors. If located within a building, large transformers require a ventilated, fire-rated enclosure adjacent to the switchgear room. Dry-type transformers in small buildings may be placed in the main electric room.

The service switch is the main disconnect for the entire electrical system of a building, except for any emergency power systems.

The main switchboard controls and protects the main feeder lines of the electrical system.

  ○ It consists of switches and circuit breakers which automatically open a circuit when an overload condition or short circuit occurs.
  ○ It distributes the large incoming power supply into smaller, more easily controlled parcels.
  ○ It should be as close as possible to the service connection to minimize voltage drop and for wiring economy.
  ○ It may require an enclosure; check the applicable codes for requirements.
  ○ Allow for both vertical and horizontal distribution of wiring and conduit in the construction around switchboards.

Panelboards control and protect the branch circuits of an electrical system. In large buildings, they are located in electrical closets close to the load ends of circuits. In residences and small installations, the distribution panels are combined with the switchboard to form a service panel.

Once the electrical power requirements for the various areas of a building are determined, wiring circuits must be laid out to distribute the power to the points of utilization. Panelboards, fed by the main switchboard, distribute the power supply into branch circuits. These panels may serve similar types of circuits (eg., lighting circuits) or specific areas of a building.

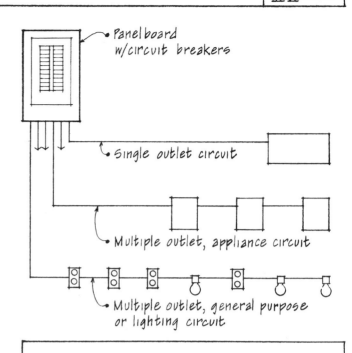

Panelboard w/circuit breakers

Single outlet circuit

Multiple outlet, appliance circuit

Multiple outlet, general purpose or lighting circuit

- Branch circuits contain the final distribution points of the electrical system. Each branch circuit is sized according to the amount of load it must carry. About 20% of its capacity is reserved for flexibility, expansion, and safety. To avoid an excessive drop in voltage, a branch circuit should not exceed 100 feet in length. There are three types of branch circuits:

  ○ Single outlet circuits are designed to serve a specific appliance or piece of equipment.
  ○ Multiple outlet, appliance circuits are designed to serve a number of small appliances.
  ○ Multiple outlet, general purpose circuits supply power for lighting and receptacles.

Receptacles in wet locations, such as in bathrooms, should be protected by a ground fault interrupter (GFI). A GFI device trips or breaks the circuit almost instantaneously when any leakage of current occurs. This protection may provided by a GFI receptacle or by a GFI breaker at the service panel.

- Low voltage switching is used when a central control point is desired from which all switching may take place. The low voltage switches control relays which do the actual switching at the service outlets. Low voltage systems allow branch circuits to be shortened and their wiring can be run without conduit.

- Separate wiring circuits are required for the sound and signal equipment of telephone, cable TV, intercom, and security or fire alarm systems.

- Telephone systems should have their outlets located and wired during construction. Large installations also require a service connection, terminal enclosures, riser spaces, etc., similar to electrical systems. Large systems are usually designed, furnished, and installed by the telecommunications company.

- Cable television systems may receive their signals from an outdoor antenna or satellite dish, a cable company, or a closed circuit system. If several outlets are required, a 120V outlet is supplied to serve an amplifier. Coaxial cables in a nonmetallic conduit or raceway transmit the amplified signal to the various outlets.

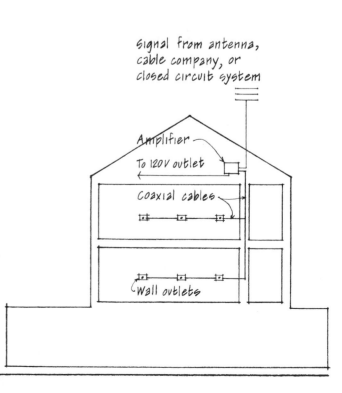

Signal from antenna, cable company, or closed circuit system

Amplifier

To 120V outlet

Coaxial cables

Wall outlets

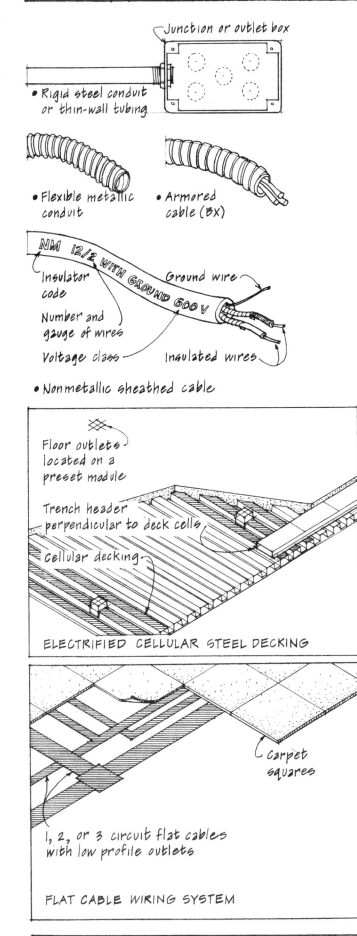

Junction or outlet box

• Rigid steel conduit or thin-wall tubing

• Flexible metallic conduit

• Armored cable (BX)

NM 12/2 WITH GROUND 600 V

Insulator code
Number and gauge of wires
Voltage class
Ground wire
Insulated wires

• Nonmetallic sheathed cable

Floor outlets located on a preset module

Trench header perpendicular to deck cells

Cellular decking

ELECTRIFIED CELLULAR STEEL DECKING

Carpet squares

1, 2, or 3 circuit flat cables with low profile outlets

FLAT CABLE WIRING SYSTEM

Metals, offering little resistance to the flow of electric current, make good conductors. Copper is most often used. The various forms of conductors — wire, cable, and bus bars — are sized according to their safe current carrying capacity and the maximum operating temperature of their insulation. They are identified according to:

• Number and size of conductors
• Voltage class
• Type of insulation.

A conductor is covered with insulation to prevent its contact with other conductors or metal, and to protect it against heat, moisture, and corrosion. Materials with a high resistance to the flow of electric current, such as rubber, porcelain, glass, and some synthetics, are commonly used to insulate electrical wiring and connections.

Conduit provides support for wires and cables, protects them against physical damage and corrosion, and protects the surrounding area against fire hazards. Metal conduit also provides a continuous grounded enclosure for the wiring. For fireproof construction, rigid steel conduit, thin-wall metallic tubing, or flexible metallic conduit can be used. For frame construction, armored or nonmetallic sheathed cable is used. Plastic tubing and conduit is most commonly used for underground wiring.

Being relatively small, conduit can be easily accommodated in most construction systems. Conduit should be adequately supported and laid out as directly as possible. Codes generally restrict the radius and number of bends a run of conduit may have between junction or outlet boxes. Coordination with the building's mechanical and plumbing systems is required to avoid conflicting paths.

Electrical conductors may also be run within cellular steel decking or cellular raceways cast into the topping of concrete slabs. Flat wiring systems are also available for installation directly under carpeting.

For exposed installations, special conduit, raceways, troughs, and fittings are available. As with exposed mechanical systems, the layout should be visually coordinated with the physical elements of the space.

Light fixtures, wall switches, and receptacle outlets are the most visible parts of an electrical system. Switches and receptacle outlets should be located for convenient access, and coordinated with visible surface patterns. Wall plates for these devices may be of metal, plastic, or glass, and are available in a variety of colors and finishes.

A receptacle outlet designed to serve a specific type of appliance will have a specific configuration so that only attachments from that of appliance will fit the receptacle. Outdoor receptacles should have a waterproof cover, and in all wet locations, receptacles should be protected by a ground fault interrupter.

Load requirements for light fixtures and electrically powered appliances and equipment are specified by their manufacturer. The design load for a general purpose circuit, however, depends on the number of receptacles served by the circuit and how they used. Consult the applicable local code for the required number and spacing of receptacle outlets. The following can be used as a guide.

- Residences:
  1 outlet every 12' along walls in living areas
  1 outlet every 4' along countertops in kitchens
  1 GFI-protected outlet in bathrooms.

- Offices:
  1 outlet every 10' along walls, or
  1 outlet for every 40 SF of floor area for the first 10 and
  1 outlet for every 100 SF thereafter.

Plan symbols

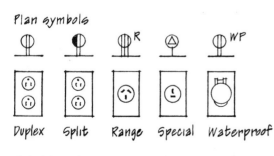

Duplex   Split   Range   Special   Waterproof

EXAMPLES OF RECEPTACLE OUTLETS

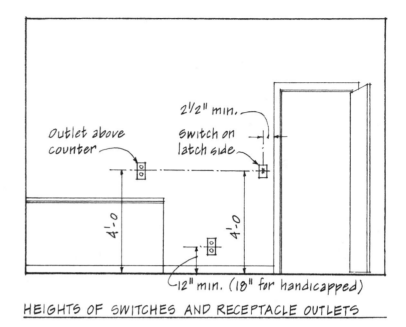

HEIGHTS OF SWITCHES AND RECEPTACLE OUTLETS

▬▬ Panelboard, recessed	⊡▭ Fluorescent fixture
══ Panelboard, surface	○ Ceiling incandescent
▬ Lighting panel	⊢○ Wall incandescent
▨ Power panel	▢▢▢ Track light
T Transformer	Ⓡ Recessed light
Ⓖ Generator	Ⓧ Exit light outlet
Ⓜ Motor	△ Special purpose outlet
⊡ Disconnect switch	▢ Television outlet
S Single pole switch	CH Chime
S₃ 3-way switch	▢ Pushbutton
⊢○ₛ Switch/receptacle	Ⓕ Fan receptacle
S_DM Dimmer switch	Ⓙ Junction box
⊢○ Duplex outlet	▤ Underfloor J-box
⊟ Floor duplex outlet	Ⓣ Thermostat
◁ Telephone outlet	◀ Computer data

EXAMPLES OF ELECTRICAL PLAN SYMBOLS

Task Difficulty		Footcandle (Fc) Level
Casual	(dining)	20
Ordinary	(reading)	50
Moderate	(drafting)	100
Difficult	(sewing)	200
Severe	(surgery)	>400

1 Footcandle
= 1 lumen/SF
= 10.76 lux

RECOMMENDED ILLUMINATION LEVELS

CONTRAST

The primary purpose of a lighting system is to provide sufficient illumination for the performance of visual tasks. As a reference, recommended illumination levels for various categories of tasks are listed to the left. These illumination levels specify only the quantity of light to be supplied. How this light is supplied affects how a space is perceived or how an object is seen, and is just as important as the lighting level. The quality of a lighting system varies according to the brightness ratios in the space, the light's diffusion, and its color.

Contrast between the object viewed and its background is required for its form, shape, and texture to be seen. As the brightness level increases, the need for contrast decreases. When the contrast in brightness becomes excessive, glare can result and cause discomfort for the viewer. Excessive brightness ratios can occur between a light source and its background or between adjacent surfaces in a space.

The surrounding area Ⓒ should range from 1/5 to 5 times the brightness of the visual task area Ⓐ.

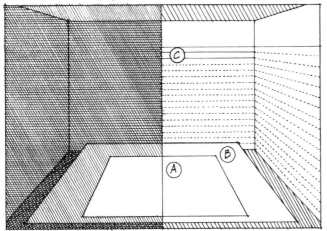

3:1 is the maximum recommended brightness ratio between the visual task area Ⓐ and its immediate background Ⓑ.

BRIGHTNESS RATIOS

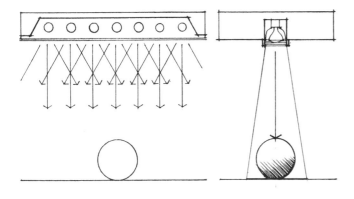

① Reduce the brightness ratio between light source and background. ② Use shielded luminaires to minimize a direct view of lamps. ③ Locate fixtures out of the direct glare zone.

POSSIBLE SOLUTIONS TO DIRECT GLARE

Diffused light emanates from broad or multiple light sources and reflecting surfaces. It produces fairly uniform illumination with few shadows. Directional light, on the other hand, produces brightness variations and shadows which are necessary for the perception of shape, form, and texture. A mix of diffused and directional lighting is often desirable and beneficial, especially when a variety of tasks are to be performed in a room.

The perceived color of a surface is the result of its ability to reflect or absorb the color of the light falling on it. The spectral distribution of a light source is important because if certain wavelengths of color are missing, then those colors cannot be reflected and will appear to be missing in any surface illuminated by that light.

Artificial light is natural light that is produced by manufactured elements. The quantity and quality of light produced differ according to the type of lamp used. The light is further modified by the housing that holds and energizes the lamp.

There are three major types of artificial light sources, incandescent, fluorescent, and high intensity discharge (HID) lamps. For accurate, current data on lamp sizes, wattages, lumen output, and average life, consult the lamp manufacturers' catalogs.

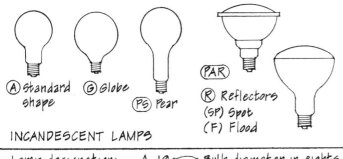

Ⓐ Standard shape Ⓖ Globe ⒫Ⓢ Pear Ⓡ Reflectors (SP) Spot (F) Flood (PAR)

INCANDESCENT LAMPS

- Lampholder holds and energizes the lamp.
- Lamp
- Reflectors control how light is distributed.
- Diffusers alter the quality of light.

The term <u>luminaire</u> refers to the entire lighting unit, consisting of the lamp or lamps, the connection to the power supply, the mounting mechanism, and elements that shield, reflect, or diffuse the light.

- Lamp designation: A-19 ← Bulb diameter in eights of an inch ← Bulb shape
- Point light source
- Low efficacy (12%)
- Good color rendition
- Easy to dim w/ rheostats

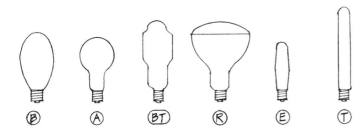

Ⓑ Ⓐ ⒷⓉ Ⓡ Ⓔ Ⓣ

<u>HID LAMPS</u> Mercury vapor, high pressure sodium, and metal halide lamps combine the form of an incandescent lamp with the efficiency of a fluorescent.

Ⓣ Shape lamp length: 18" - 15 W

24" - 20 W
36" - 30 W
48" - 40 W
96" - 75 W

8¼" - 22W
12" - 32W
16" - 40W

9W

22½" - 40W

<u>FLUORESCENT LAMPS</u>
- Linear light source
- Color rendition varies
- 50 to 80 lumens/watt

The S/MH guideline specifies the ratio of maximum luminaire spacing to mounting height that is necessary to achieve an acceptable uniformity of illumination. S/MH ratios are calculated and supplied by the luminaire manufacturer.

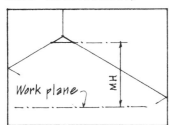

Work plane

Direct lighting of the visual task surface

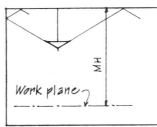

Work plane

Indirect lighting, using the ceiling as a reflector

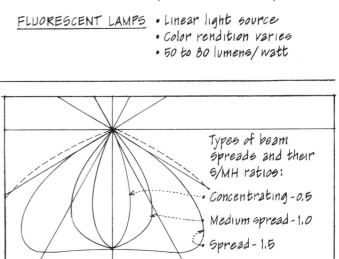

Types of beam spreads and their S/MH ratios:
- Concentrating - 0.5
- Medium spread - 1.0
- Spread - 1.5
- Wide spread > 1.5

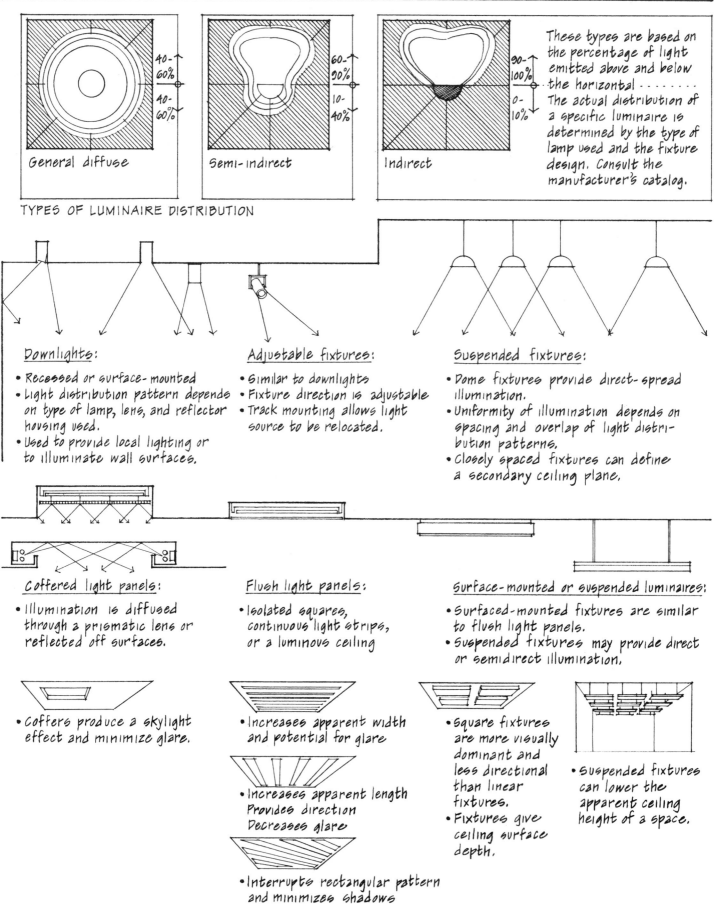

TYPES OF LUMINAIRE DISTRIBUTION

General diffuse   40-60% / 40-60%

Semi-indirect   60-90% / 10-40%

Indirect   90-100% / 0-10%

These types are based on the percentage of light emitted above and below the horizontal . . . . The actual distribution of a specific luminaire is determined by the type of lamp used and the fixture design. Consult the manufacturer's catalog.

Downlights:

- Recessed or surface-mounted
- Light distribution pattern depends on type of lamp, lens, and reflector housing used.
- Used to provide local lighting or to illuminate wall surfaces.

Adjustable fixtures:

- Similar to downlights
- Fixture direction is adjustable
- Track mounting allows light source to be relocated.

Suspended fixtures:

- Dome fixtures provide direct-spread illumination.
- Uniformity of illumination depends on spacing and overlap of light distribution patterns.
- Closely spaced fixtures can define a secondary ceiling plane.

Coffered light panels:

- Illumination is diffused through a prismatic lens or reflected off surfaces.

- Coffers produce a skylight effect and minimize glare.

Flush light panels:

- Isolated squares, continuous light strips, or a luminous ceiling

- Increases apparent width and potential for glare

- Increases apparent length
  Provides direction
  Decreases glare

- Interrupts rectangular pattern and minimizes shadows

Surface-mounted or suspended luminaires:

- Surfaced-mounted fixtures are similar to flush light panels.
- Suspended fixtures may provide direct or semidirect illumination.

- Square fixtures are more visually dominant and less directional than linear fixtures.
- Fixtures give ceiling surface depth.

- Suspended fixtures can lower the apparent ceiling height of a space.

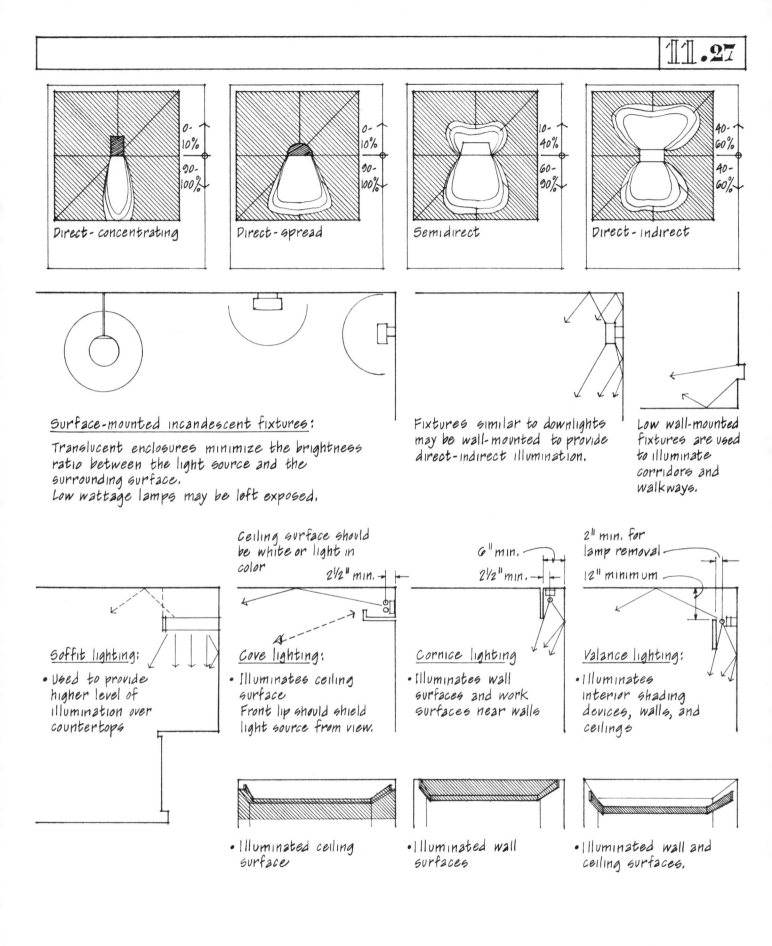

Direct - concentrating

0-10%
90-100%

Direct - spread

0-10%
90-100%

Semidirect

10-40%
60-90%

Direct - indirect

40-60%
40-60%

Surface-mounted incandescent fixtures:

Translucent enclosures minimize the brightness ratio between the light source and the surrounding surface.
Low wattage lamps may be left exposed.

Fixtures similar to downlights may be wall-mounted to provide direct-indirect illumination.

Low wall-mounted fixtures are used to illuminate corridors and walkways.

Ceiling surface should be white or light in color

2½" min.

6" min.

2½" min.

2" min. for lamp removal
12" minimum

Soffit lighting:
• Used to provide higher level of illumination over countertops

Cove lighting:
• Illuminates ceiling surface
Front lip should shield light source from view.

Cornice lighting
• Illuminates wall surfaces and work surfaces near walls

Valance lighting:
• Illuminates interior shading devices, walls, and ceilings

• Illuminated ceiling surface

• Illuminated wall surfaces

• Illuminated wall and ceiling surfaces.

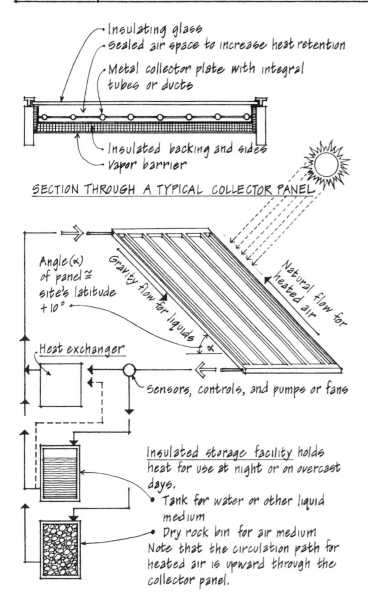

- Insulating glass
- Sealed air space to increase heat retention
- Metal collector plate with integral tubes or ducts
- Insulated backing and sides
- Vapor barrier

SECTION THROUGH A TYPICAL COLLECTOR PANEL

Angle (α) of panel ≅ site's latitude + 10°

Gravity flow for liquids

Natural flow for heated air

Heat exchanger

Sensors, controls, and pumps or fans

Insulated storage facility holds heat for use at night or on overcast days.
- Tank for water or other liquid medium
- Dry rock bin for air medium

Note that the circulation path for heated air is upward through the collector panel.

The heating and cooling components of the solar energy system are similar to those of conventional systems.
- For heating: Air-water or all-air system
- For cooling: A heat pump or absorption cooling unit is required.
- A backup heating system is recommended.

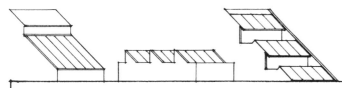

Active solar energy systems absorb, transfer, and store energy from solar radiation for building heating and cooling. They normally consist of the following components:

- Solar collector panels
- Circulation and distribution system for the heat transfer medium
- Heat exchanger and storage facility

The solar collector panels are the system's prime components. They should be oriented within 20° of true south and not be shaded by nearby structures, terrain, or trees. The required collector surface area depends on the heat exchange efficiency of the collector and heat transfer medium, and the building's heating and cooling load. Current recommendations range from 1/3 to 1/2 of the building's net floor area.

The heat transfer medium (air, water, or other liquid) carries the collected heat energy from the solar panels to the heat utilization equipment or to a storage utility for later use.

Liquid medium:
- Piping is used for circulation and distribution.
- An antifreeze solution provides freeze protection.
- A corrosion-retarding additive is required for aluminum pipes.

Air medium:
- Ductwork for air collectors requires more installation space.
- Larger collector surfaces are also required since heat transfer coeffient for air is less than that of liquids.
- Panel construction is simpler and not subject to problems of freezing, leakage, and corrosion.

For an active solar energy system to be efficient, the building itself must be thermally efficient and well insulated. Its siting, orientation, and window openings should take advantage of the sun's summer and winter solar radiation. See 1.12 for passive solar design.

- Collector panels may form a single plane or a series of parallel planes.
- Locating the panels away from the building requires a longer and less efficient distribution run for the heat transfer medium.

Solar collector panels are normally integral parts of a building's roof or wall systems. Their large surface area therefore has a strong influence on a building's exterior form and image.

NOTES ON MATERIALS

This chapter describes the major types of building materials, their physical properties, and their uses in building construction.

Each building material has distinct properties of strength, elasticity and stiffness, density or hardness, resistance to wear, fire-resistance, and thermal conductivity. The most effective structural materials are those which combine elasticity with stiffness. Elasticity is the ability of a material to deform under stress—bend, stretch, or compress—and return to its original shape when the applied stress is removed. Every material has its elastic limit beyond which it will permanently deform or break. Materials which undergo plastic deformation before actually breaking are termed ductile. Brittle materials, on the other hand, have low elastic limits and rupture under loads with little visible deformation. Because brittle materials have less reserve strength than ductile materials, they are not as suitable for structural purposes.

Stiffness is a measure of the force required to push or pull a material to its elastic limit. A material's stiffness, along with the stiffness of its cross-sectional shape, are important factors when considering the relationship between span and deflection under loading.

Many building materials are manufactured in standard shapes and sizes. These stock dimensions, however, may vary slightly between manufacturers. They should be verified in the planning and design phases of a building so that unnecessary cutting or wasting of material can be minimized during construction.

Following the discussion of building materials is an outline of the various materials and methods used to fasten and finish materials.

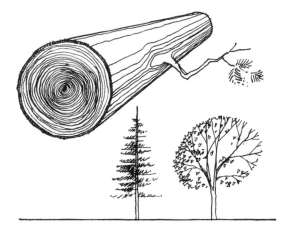

As a construction material, wood is strong, durable, light in weight, and easy to work. In addition, it offers natural beauty and warmth to sight and touch. Although it has become necessary to employ conservation measures to ensure a continued supply, wood is still used in construction in many and varied forms.

Their are two major classes of wood: softwood and hardwood. These terms do not indicate the relative hardness, softness, or strength of a wood. Softwoods are the evergreens, and are used for general construction. Hardwoods come from deciduous or broadleaf trees, and are typically used for flooring, stairs, paneling, furniture, and interior trim.

The manner in which a tree grows affects its strength, its susceptibility to expansion and contraction, and its effectiveness as an insulator. Tree growth also affects how pieces of sawn wood (lumber) may be joined to form structure and enclosure.

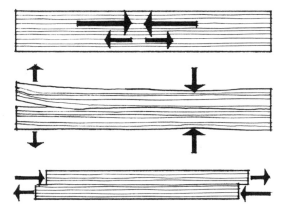

Grain direction is the major determining factor in the use of wood as a structural material. Tensile and compressive forces are best handled by wood in a direction parallel to its grain. Typically, a given piece of wood will withstand ⅓ more force in compression than in tension parallel to its grain. The allowable compressive force perpendicular to its grain is only about ⅕ to ½ of the allowable compressive force parallel to the grain. Tensile forces perpendicular to the grain will cause the wood to split.

Wood's shear strength is greater across its grain than parallel to the grain. It is therefore more susceptible to horizontal shear than to vertical shear.

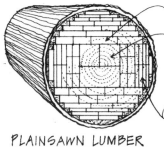

Dimension lumber
Timbers and beams
Flat grain lumber

PLAINSAWN LUMBER

The manner in which lumber is cut from a log affects its strength as well as its appearance.

Plainsawn lumber:
• may have a variety of noticeable grain patterns
• tends to twist and cup, and wears unevenly
• tends to have raised grain
• shrinks and swells less in thickness, more in width.

Vertical grain lumber

QUARTERSAWN LUMBER

Quartersawn lumber:
• has more even grain patterns
• wears more evenly with less raised grain and warping
• shrinks and swells less in width, more in thickness
• is less affected by surface checks
• is more expensive and results in more waste in cutting.

To increase its strength, stability, and resistance to fungi, decay and insects, wood is seasoned by air-drying (a lengthy process) or through the use of kilns. It is impossible to completely seal a piece of wood to prevent changes in its moisture content. Below a moisture content of about 30%, wood expands as it absorbs moisture and shrinks as it loses moisture. This possibility of shrinkage and swelling must always be taken into account when detailing and constructing wood joints, both in small and large scale work.

Shrinkage tangential to the wood grain is usually twice as much as radial shrinkage. Vertical grain lumber shrinks uniformly while plainsawn cuts near a log's perimeter will cup away from the center.

The thermal expansion of wood is generally much less than volume changes due to changes in moisture content. Moisture content is therefore the controlling factor.

Wood defects affect the grading, appearance, and use of the wood. They may also affect the wood's strength, depending on their number, size, and location. Defects include the natural characteristics of wood, such as knots, shakes, and pitch pockets, as well as manufacturing characteristics, such as splits, checking, and warp.

Wood is decay-resistant when its moisture content is under 20%. If installed and maintained below this moisture content level, wood will not rot.

Species that are naturally resistant to decay-causing fungi include redwood, cedar, bald cypress, black locust, and black walnut. Insect-resistant species include redwood, eastern red cedar, and bald cypress.

Preservative treatments are available to further protect wood from decay and insect attack. Of these, pressure treatment is the most effective, especially when the wood is in contact with the ground. There are three types of preservatives.

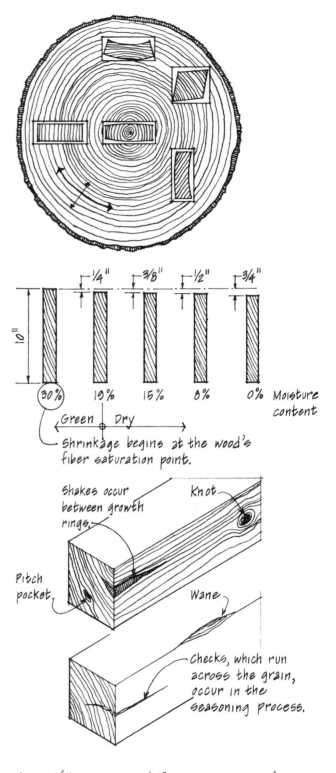

Shrinkage begins at the wood's fiber saturation point.

Shakes occur between growth rings. Knot

Pitch pocket

Wane

Checks, which run across the grain, occur in the seasoning process.

- Water-borne preservatives leave the wood clean, odorless, and readily paintable; preservatives do not leach out when exposed to weather. ⟶ AWPB (American Wood Preservers Bureau) LP-2 (LP-22 for ground contact)
- Oil-borne preservatives may color the wood, but treated wood is paintable; pentechlorophenol is highly toxic. ⟶ AWPB LP-3 (LP-33 for ground contact)
- Creosote treatment leaves wood with colored, oily surfaces; odor remains for a long period; used especially in marine and salt water installations. ⟶ AWPB LP-5 (LP-55 for ground contact)

Nominal thickness or width	Minimum dressed size of dry lumber; moisture content <19%	Note: Lumber is measured in board-feet; 1 board-foot = 1"x 12"x 1 foot of length (nominal)
1"	3/4"	Lumber is specified according to its nominal dimensions. The nominal size is the lumber's rough, unfinished size. The dressed, actual size is smaller due to the seasoning and surfacing of the lumber before use.
2"	1½"	
3"	2½"	
4"	3½"	
5"	4½"	The face dimension is the finished width of a piece that is exposed to view after installation.
6"	5½"	
8"	7¼"	
10"	9¼"	Lumber is commonly available in lengths from 6' to 24', in multiples of 2'.
12"	11¼"	
14"	13¼"	

Because of the diversity of its applications and its use for remanufacturing purposes, hardwood is graded according to the amount of clear, usable lumber in a piece that may be cut into smaller pieces of a certain grade and size. Softwood is classified in the following manner.

YARD LUMBER

- **Boards**
  - 1" to 1½" thick; 2" and wider
  - Graded for appearance rather than strength
  - Used as siding, subflooring, interior trim

- **Dimension lumber**
  - 2" to 4" thick; 2" and wider
  - Graded for strength (stress-graded) rather than appearance
  - Used for general construction

  - Light framing   2" to 4" wide
  - Joists and planks   6" and wider
  - Decking   4" and wider (Select and Commercial grades)

- **Timbers**
  - 5" x 5" and larger
  - Graded for strength and serviceability
  - Often stocked in green, undressed condition
  - May be classified as structural lumber along with joists and planks

FACTORY AND SHOP LUMBER   Used primarily for remanufacturing purposes (doors, windows, millwork)

Lumber may be structurally graded as follows (in descending order, according to stress grade).

- Light framing: construction, standard, utility grades
- Structural light framing, joists and planks: Select structural, Nº 1, 2, and 3 grades; some species may also have an appearance grade for exposed work.
- Timber: Select structural and Nº 1 grades

Lumber may be appearance graded as follows.

- Select: A, B, or B and better, used for natural finishes.
            C, D, for painted finishes
- Common: for general construction

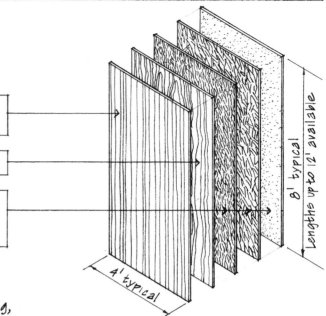

Wood panel products are less susceptible to shrinking or swelling, require less labor to install, and make more efficient use of wood resources than solid wood products. The major types of wood panel products are:

- Plywood is a laminated panel of wood veneers laid with their grain direction at right angles to one another.

- Composite panels consist of 2 face veneers bonded to wood fiber cores.

- Nonveneer panels consist of wood strands, flakes, or particles which are compressed and bonded together under pressure (e.g., oriented strand board, waferboard, particleboard).

Engineered panel grades have relatively high shear strength for loads perpendicular to the panel face. They are therefore used for wall and roof sheathing, subflooring, and underlayment. Most structural panels have a grade-stamp on their back with the following information.

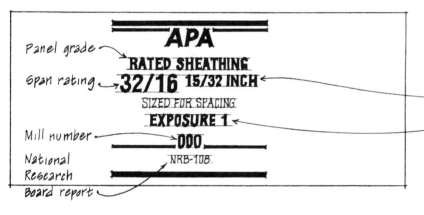

Panel grade
Span rating
Mill number
National Research Board report

APA
RATED SHEATHING
32/16 15/32 INCH
SIZED FOR SPACING
EXPOSURE 1
000
NRB-108

TYPICAL APA (American Plywood Association)
PERFORMANCE-RATED PANEL REGISTERED
TRADEMARK.

Veneer grades:

N Smooth, "natural finish" veneer
A Smooth, paint-grade
B Smooth, with plugs and tight knots
C Sheathing grade
D Limited to interior panels

Thicknesses: 1/4" to 1 1/8"

Exposure classifications:

Exterior - 100% waterproof glueline for permanent exposure to weather

Exposure 1 - Bonded with exterior glue to resist moisture during construction

Exposure 2 - Bonded with intermediate glue for moderate exposure to moisture

Laminated timbers are engineered, stress-rated structural members. They are built up of several layers of wood which are securely bonded with waterproof or water-resistant glue. The grain of the laminations are approximately parallel and run longitudinally. Several grades of lumber may be used — the higher grades in areas of highest stress, the lower grades in areas of lower stress.

For large structural members, laminated timber is preferable to solid timber in terms of appearance, weather resistance, controlled moisture content, and available sizes. Being factory-made, laminated timbers are consistent in size, appearance and strength, and more dimensionally stable than solid timber.

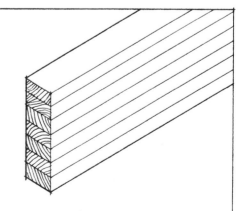

* See 4.15 for typical sizes and spans.

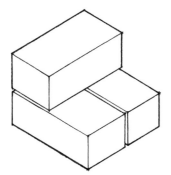

Masonry refers to building blocks which are formed and hardened into modular units. This modular aspect (i.e., uniform size and proportional relationships) distinguishes masonry from most of the other construction materials discussed in this chapter.

Masonry units are formed from shapeless material and hardened in one of two ways.

① <u>Through heat:</u>
   Brick
   Structural clay tile   } Made from various types of clay
   Terra cotta

② <u>Through chemical action:</u>
   Concrete block
   Concrete brick   } Made from a mixture of cement or gypsum, aggregate, and water
   Gypsum block

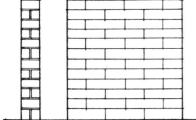

Compared to wood, steel and concrete, masonry units and the mortar used to bond them together are relatively weak. Masonry units should therefore be laid up in such a way that the entire masonry mass acts an entity. See 5.19 to 5.21 for structural requirements and types of masonry walls.

Masonry is structurally most effective in compression. The following are minimum compressive strength values for various types of masonry units.

BRICK	2500 psi	Type SW	(severe weather) for use below grade and where exposed to freezing
	2200 psi	Type MW	(Medium weather) for walls above grade
	1250 psi	Type NW	(No weather) for interior use

It should be noted that the allowable compressive stresses in unreinforced masonry walls are much less than the values given here since the quality of the masonry units, mortar, and workmanship may vary. See table on 5.19 for these values.

CONCRETE MASONRY UNITS	800 psi 600 psi	Type N S	Hollow loadbearing units	Type S units are limited to walls not exposed to the weather.
	1500 psi 1000 psi	Type N S	Solid loadbearing units	
	3000 psi 2000 psi	Type N S	Concrete brick units	

Mortar consists of:

- Portland and/or masonry cements
- Clean, well-graded sand
- Water
- Lime used in portland cement-lime mortars to enhance workability, water retention, and flexibility.

The mortar used to bond the masonry units together can also be graded according to compressive strength and use.

MORTAR	2500 psi	Type M	For basements, foundations, and reinforced masonry
	1800 psi	Type S	For exterior walls and interior loadbearing walls
	750 psi	Type N	For interior walls and solid masonry veneers

(See also table on 5.19.)

BRICK SIZES

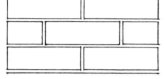

Brick unit type	Nominal dimensions (inches) T	H	L	Modular coursing (inches)
Standard modular	4	2 2/3	8	3C = 8
Engineer	4	3 1/5	8	5C = 16
Economy	4	4	8	1C = 4
Double	4	5 1/3	8	3C = 16
Roman	4	2	12	2C = 4
Norman	4	2 2/3	12	3C = 8
Norwegian	4	3 1/5	12	5C = 16
Utility	4	4	12	1C = 4
Triple	4	5 1/3	12	3C = 16
SCR brick	6	2 2/3	12	3C = 8
6" Norwegian	6	3 1/5	12	5C = 16
6" Jumbo	6	4	12	1C = 4
8" Jumbo	8	4	12	1C = 4
8" Square	4	8	8	1C = 8

See 5.29 for bonding patterns

The actual dimensions of brick units vary due to shrinkage during the manufacturing process. The nominal dimensions given above include the thickness of the mortar joints, which may vary from 1/4" to 1/2".

CONCRETE MASONRY UNITS

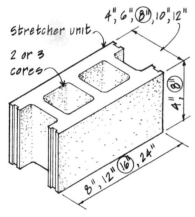

Stretcher unit

2 or 3 cores

4", 6", 8", 10", 12"

8", 12", 16", 24"

Nominal dimensions, including thickness of mortar joints

Concrete brick

The basic unit of concrete masonry is the concrete block. There are three types of concrete block.

- Solid loadbearing units (75% or more net area)
- Hollow loadbearing units
- Hollow nonloadbearing units

Aggregates, which constitute about 90% of the block by weight, affect the strength and other properties of the finished unit. There are two types of aggregate used.

- **Normal weight** — Sand and gravel; 40 lbs. per block unit
  Compressive strength: 1200 to 1800 psi
  Density: 130 to 145 lbs./cu.ft.
  Low absorption

- **Lightweight** — Expanded shale, expanded slag, cinders, or pumice; 22 to 28 lbs. per block unit
  Compressive strength: 700 to 1500 psi
  Density: 75 to 105 lbs./cu.ft.

Concrete masonry units are manufactured in many shapes to satisfy various construction conditions. Their availability varies with locality and manufacturer.

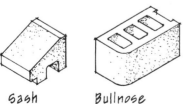
Sash

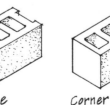
Bullnose

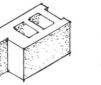
Corner

Jamb

Lintel

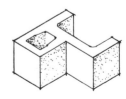
Pilaster

Units may have scored, fluted, ribbed, or split faces. See 5.31 for bonding patterns.

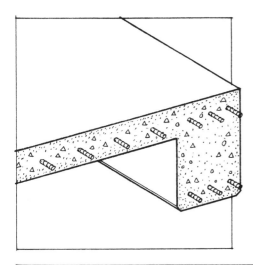

Concrete is widely used in construction because it combines many of the advantages of wood, steel, and masonry. It is inherently strong in compression. To handle tensile and shear stresses, it can encase and bond with steel reinforcement. It is capable of being formed into almost any shape with a variety of surface finishes, textures, and patterns. (See 5.47) In addition, concrete structures are relatively low in cost and inherently fire resistant.

Concrete's liabilities include its weight (150 lbs./cu.ft. for normal reinforced concrete) and the forming or molding process that is required before it can be placed to set and cure.

Concrete consists of two parts, cement paste and aggregate, which are mixed from four ingredients.

CEMENT PASTE

① Portland cement

Type I . . . . Normal – a general purpose cement
Type II . . . . Moderate – for moderate resistance to sulfate attack
Type III . . . High early strength – used when a high strength is desired within a short curing period (3 to 7 days)
Type IV . . . Low-heat – used to minimize the heat of hydration in large concrete masses, such as dams
Type V . . . . Sulfate-resisting – for construction exposed to severe sulfate attack

Types IA, IIA, and IIIA correspond to types I, II, and III, but contain air-entraining materials which make the concrete more workable and more resistant to severe frost action.

② Water . . . . Should be clean, free of organic mateial, alkali, sulfates, oil; a general criterion is that the water should be drinkable

AGGREGATE

③ Fine aggregate . . . . Well-graded sand up to 1/4"
④ Coarse aggregate . . . . Gravel or crushed rock from 1/4" to 1 1/2"

Aggregrate should be clean, durable, and free of organic matter.

Lightweight aggregate . . . . Expanded shale, slate and slag are used to reduce the weight of structural concrete while retaining most of its strength. Vermiculite and perlite are used to produce low density, insulating concrete.

ADMIXTURES

Air-entraining agents . . . . Added to improve workability and resistance of concrete to severe frost action and the effects of salts applied for snow and ice removal.
Accelerators . . . . Added to increase the rate of curing and early strength development.
Retarders . . . . Added to retard the set of the concrete in hot weather or when more time to work the wet concrete is desired; retarders also act as water-reducing agents.
Plasticizers . . . . Added to make the concrete easier to place in forms.
Coloring dyes and pigments . . . . Added for coloration.

The quality of a concrete product depends on the characteristics of its ingredients, the proportions of the mix, and the manner in which it is placed, finished, and cured.

The potential strength of concrete is determined primarily by its water-cement ratio. Theoretically, the strength of concrete will increase as the amount of water used per unit weight of cement decreases. If too much water is used, the concrete mix will be weak and porous after curing. If too little water is used, however, the mix will be dense but difficult to place and work. For most applications, the water-cement ratio should range from 0.45 to 0.60 (weight of water = 45% to 60% of the weight of the cement). The actual water-cement ratio used should be appropriate for the desired strength, workability, durability, and watertightness of the concrete.

The most economical mix occurs when the fine and coarse aggregates are evenly graded so that a minimum amount of cement paste is required to surround all of the aggregate and fill the spaces in between. The proportion of fine to coarse aggregate, and the maximum size of coarse aggregate that may be used, depend on the method of placement, the steel reinforcement of the concrete section, and the finishing requirements.

Steel is used to resist the tensile stresses in reinforced concrete, and to resist the cracking that may occur because of curing shrinkage or thermal expansion and contraction. Concrete columns and beams sometimes require steel to handle some of their compressive stresses as well.

Reinforcing steel must be protected from fire and corrosion by a covering thickness of concrete. ⟹

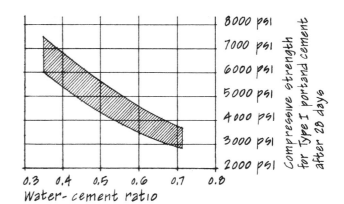

Water-cement ratio

Compressive strength for Type I portland cement after 28 days

Concrete is normally specified according to the compressive strength it will develop within 28 days after placement (7 days for high-early-strength concrete).

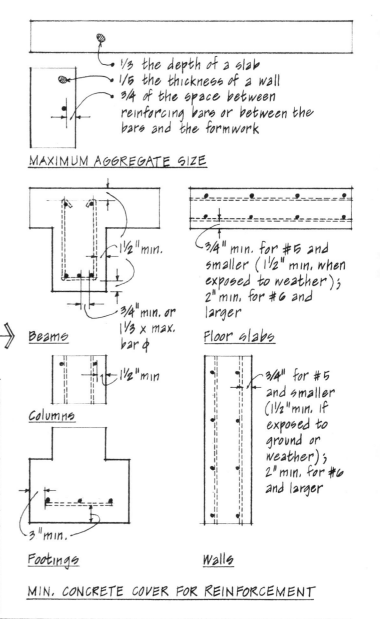

1/3 the depth of a slab
1/5 the thickness of a wall
3/4 of the space between reinforcing bars or between the bars and the formwork

MAXIMUM AGGREGATE SIZE

1½" min.

3/4" min. or 1⅓ x max. bar ⌀

Beams

3/4" min. for #5 and smaller (1½" min. when exposed to weather); 2" min. for #6 and larger

Floor slabs

1½" min

Columns

3/4" for #5 and smaller (1½" min. if exposed to ground or weather); 2" min. for #6 and larger

3" min.

Footings

Walls

MIN. CONCRETE COVER FOR REINFORCEMENT

ASTM STANDARD REINFORCING BARS			
Bar size	Nominal dimensions:		
	Diameter (inches)	Cross-sectional area (inches²)	Weight per linear feet (lbs.)
# 3	.375	.11	.376
# 4	.500	.20	.668
# 5	.625	.31	1.043
# 6	.750	.44	1.502
# 7	.875	.60	2.044
# 8	1.000	.79	2.670
# 9	1.128	1.00	3.400
# 10	1.270	1.27	4.303

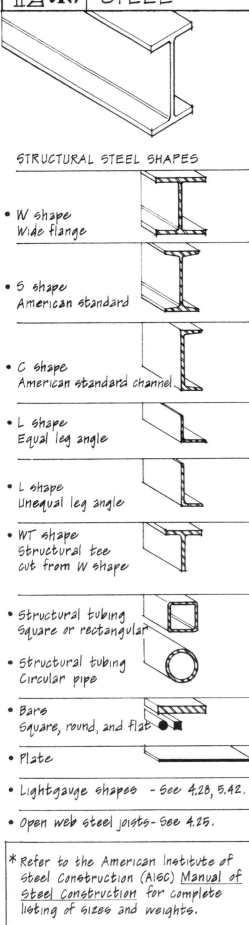

STRUCTURAL STEEL SHAPES

- W shape
  Wide flange

- S shape
  American standard

- C shape
  American standard channel

- L shape
  Equal leg angle

- L shape
  Unequal leg angle

- WT shape
  Structural tee
  cut from W shape

- Structural tubing
  Square or rectangular

- Structural tubing
  Circular pipe

- Bars
  Square, round, and flat

- Plate

- Lightgauge shapes - See 4.28, 5.42.

- Open web steel joists- See 4.25.

* Refer to the American Institute of Steel Construction (AISC) <u>Manual of Steel Construction</u> for complete listing of sizes and weights.

<u>STEEL</u> is used for light and heavy structural framing as well as a wide range of building products such as windows, doors, hardware, and fastenings. As a structural material, steel combines high strength and stiffness with elasticity. Measured in terms of weight to volume, it is probably the strongest low-cost material available.

Although classified as an incombustible material, steel becomes ductile and loses its strength under high-heat conditions (over 1000°F). When used in buildings that require fire-resistant construction, structural steel must be coated, covered, or enclosed with fire-resistant materials. (See A.12) Since it is normally subject to corrosion, steel must be painted, galvanized, or chemically treated for protection against oxidation.

Most structural steel is medium carbon grade steel, which is available in plate and bar forms, and in the structural shapes illustrated on the left. These shapes may be fastened by welding or mechanical means.

- <u>Carbon steel</u> • ASTM A36 is the most common strength grade
  • Yield point = 36,000 psi

- <u>High strength, low alloy steel</u>
  • ASTM A572 most commonly used
  • Yield point = 50,000 psi
  • ASTM A242 and A588 weathering steels have superior corrosion resistance due to a tight oxide coating they form on their surfaces; they may be left exposed.

Steel may be heat-treated or altered with additives to form alloys during its manufacture. Below are some of these alloy elements and the steel properties they modify.

- Aluminum......Improves surface hardening.
- Chromium.....Increases corrosion resistance and hardness.
- Copper........Increases strength and corrosion resistance.
- Manganese....Promotes hardness and wear resistance.
- Molybdenum...Increases corrosion resistance and strength.
- Nickel........Increases tensile strength and corrosion resistance.
- Tungsten......Improves strength retention at high temperatures.

Other ferrous metals used in building construction include:

- <u>Cast iron</u> • High carbon content
  • Brittle but strong in compression
  • Used for piping, grates, and ornamental work

- <u>Wrought iron</u> • Extremely low carbon content
  • Corrosion resistant
  • Soft, malleable, and tough
  • Used for grilles, hardware, and ornamental work

Nonferrous metals contain no iron. Aluminum, copper, and lead are nonferrous metals commonly used in building construction.

ALUMINUM is a relatively soft yet strong, lightweight, and workable metal. Its corrosion resistance is due to the transparent film of natural oxide it forms on its surface. This oxide coating can be thickened to increase the aluminum's corrosion resistance by an electrical and chemical process known as anodizing. During the anodizing process, aluminum's naturally light, reflective surface can be dyed a number of warm, bright colors. Enamel or lacquer finishes may also be applied to aluminum.

Aluminum is widely used in extruded and sheet forms for secondary building elements such as windows, doors, roofing, flashing, trim, and hardware. For use in structural framing, high strength aluminum alloys are available in shapes similar to those of structural steel. Aluminum sections may be welded, bonded with adhesives, or mechanically fastened.

Care must be taken to insulate aluminum from contact with other metals to prevent galvanic action. It should also be isolated from alkaline materials such as wet concrete, mortar, and plaster.

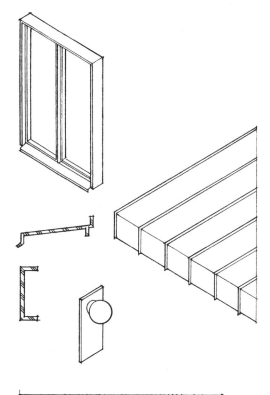

COPPER is used in construction where corrosion resistance, impact resistance, ductility, or high electrical and thermal conductivity is required. Its color and resistance to atmospheric and saltwater corrosion make it an excellent outdoor material. Copper is most commonly used in sheet form for roofing and flashing.

Copper will corrode aluminum, steel, stainless steel, and zinc. It should be fastened, attached, or supported only with copper or carefully selected brass fittings. Contact with red cedar in the presence of moisture (as in wood shingle roofing) will cause premature deterioration of the copper.

BRASS is an alloy of copper and zinc that is used for doors, windows, hardware, and fastenings. It is often termed bronze, as in architectural or statuary bronze.

LEAD is a soft, malleable, corrosion resistant material used for flashing, sound isolation, and radiation shielding. Although lead is the heaviest of the common metals, its pliability makes it desirable for application over uneven surfaces. Lead dust or vapors are toxic.

GALVANIC ACTION can occur between two dissimilar metals when enough moisture is present for electric current to flow. This electric current will tend to corrode one metal while plating the other. The severity of the galvanic action depends on how far apart the two metals are on the galvanic series table.

GALVANIC SERIES

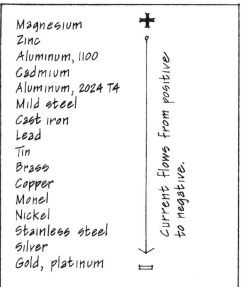

Magnesium   +
Zinc
Aluminum, 1100
Cadmium
Aluminum, 2024 T4
Mild steel
Cast iron
Lead
Tin   Current flows from positive
Brass   to negative.
Copper
Monel
Nickel
Stainless steel
Silver
Gold, platinum   –

The metal that is higher in the table is sacrificial and corrodes.

Glass is a chemically inert, transparent, hard, brittle material. It is used in building construction in various forms. Foamed or cellular glass is used as rigid, vaporproof thermal insulation. Glass fibers are used in textiles and for material reinforcement. In spun form, glass fibers form glass wool which is used for acoustical and thermal insulation. Glass block is used to control light transmission, glare, and solar radiation. Glass, however, is used most commonly to glaze a building's window, sash, and skylight openings.

The three basic types of flat glass are:

SHEET GLASS.................... ① Molten glass is drawn horizontally or vertically and then annealed. Inherent wave distortion is most noticeable in the larger sizes and thicker sheets; to minimize this distortion, glass should be glazed with the wave running horizontally.

FLOAT GLASS................... ② Glass is floated on a bed of molten tin and then annealed slowly. Flat, parallel surfaces minimize distortion and eliminate the need for grinding and polishing.
Float glass is the most widely used type of flat glass.

PLATE GLASS.................. ③ Glass is rolled, then ground and polished.
Plate glass provides virtually clear, undistorted vision.

Variations of the three basic types of glass include:

Pattern glass.................... ● Translucent glass with linear or geometric patterns embossed on one or both sides; similar to plate glass but not ground and polished.

Wire glass...................... ● Wire mesh or parallel wires are inserted into rolled glass during manufacture; wires hold glass together when cracked by impact or heat; qualifies as a safety glazing material and may be used as a fire resistant material to glaze fire doors and windows.

Heat-absorbing or tinted glass...... ● Tinted glass absorbs solar radiation, reduces heat buildup in a building, and controls glare; tint may be bronze, gray, or blue-green; tint also reduces light transmission.

Reflective coated glass.......... ● Transparent metal coating applied to the glass surface reduces the solar energy transmitted into a building; coating may be applied to one surface of single glazing, in between the plies of laminated glass, or to the exterior or interior surfaces of insulating glass.

Tempered glass................. ● Glass is heat-strengthened for increased resistance to impact and thermal stresses; 3 to 5 times stronger than annealed glass; pulverizes into pebble-sized pieces when broken.

Laminated glass................. ● A thin sheet of tough, transparent plastic is laminated between two layers of glass; when broken, glass particles tend to adhere to the plastic sheet; qualifies as a safety glazing material; special types are available that are burglar resistant, bullet resisting, or soundproofing.

Insulating glass................. ● Two layers of glass are separated by a hermetically sealed air space to provide thermal insulation and restrict condensation; glass edge units have a 3/16" air space; metal edge units have a 1/4" or 1/2" air space.

GLASS PRODUCT	TYPE	NOMINAL THICKNESS	MAXIMUM AREA	WEIGHT (lbs./S.F.)	
Window or sheet glass	AA, A, B	SS 3/32"	60" x 60"	1.22	• Verify maximum sizes with glass manufacturer.
		DS 1/8"	60" x 80"	1.63	
Float or plate	Mirror	1/4"	75 S.F.	3.28	• Any glass 1/8" or thicker can be tempered, except for patterned or wire glass; tempered glass can also be incorporated into insulating or laminated glass units.
	Glazing	1/8"	74" x 120"	1.64	
		1/4"	128" x 204"	3.28	
Heavy float or plate	Glazing	5/16"	124" x 200"	4.10	
		3/8"	124" x 200"	4.92	
		1/2"	120" x 200"	6.54	• Reflective coatings may be applied to float, plate, tempered, laminated, or insulating glass.
		5/8"	120" x 200"	8.17	
		3/4"	115" x 200"	9.18	
		7/8"	115" x 200"	11.45	
Patterned glass	Various patterns	1/8"	60" x 132"	1.60	
		7/32"	60" x 132"	2.40	
Wire glass	Polished-mesh	1/4"	60" x 144"	3.50	
	Patterned-mesh	1/4"	60" x 144"	3.50	
	Parallel wires	7/32"	54" x 120"	2.82	
		1/4"	60" x 144"	3.50	
		3/8"	60" x 144"	4.45	
Tinted glass	Bronze	1/8"	35 S.F.	1.64	• Solar energy transmission reduced 35% to 75%.
		3/16"	120" x 144"	2.45	
		1/4"	128" x 204"	3.27	
		3/8"	124" x 200"	4.90	• Visible light transmission reduced 32% to 72%.
		1/2"	120" x 200"	6.54	
	Gray	1/8"	35 S.F.	1.64	
		3/16"	120" x 144"	2.45	
		1/4"	128" x 204"	3.27	
		3/8"	124" x 200"	4.90	
		1/2"	120" x 200"	6.54	
Laminated glass	2 - 1/8" float	1/4"	72" x 120"	3.30	
	Heavy float	3/8"	72" x 120"	4.80	
		1/2"	72" x 120"	6.35	
		5/8"	72" x 120"	8.00	
Insulating glass	Glass edge:				
2 - 3/32" sheets.....	3/16" air space	3/8"	10 S.F.	2.40	• R-value = 1.61
2 - 1/8" sheets.....	3/16" air space	7/16"	24 S.F.	3.20	• R-value = 1.61
	Metal edge:				
2 - 1/8" DS sheet,	1/4" air space	1/2"	22 S.F.	3.27	• R-value = 1.72
plate, or float......	1/2" air space	3/4"	22 S.F.	3.27	• R-value = 2.04
2 - 3/16" plate or	1/4" air space	5/8"	34 S.F.	4.90	• R-values for units with 1/2" air space and low emittance coating:
float............	1/2" air space	7/8"	42 S.F.	4.90	
2 - 1/4" plate or	1/4" air space	3/4"	50 S.F.	6.54	$e = 0.20$, R = 3.13
float............	1/2" air space	1"	70 S.F.	6.54	$e = 0.40$, R = 2.63
					$e = 0.60$, R = 2.33

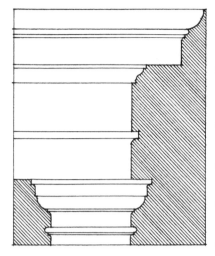

Stone is an aggregate or combination of minerals, each of which is composed of inorganic chemical substances. To qualify as a construction material, stone should have the following qualities:

- Strength — Most types of stone have more than adequate compressive strength. A stone's shear strength, however, is usually about 1/10 of its compressive strength.

- Hardness — Hardness is important when stone is used for flooring, paving, or stairs.

- Durability — Resistance to the weathering effects of rain, wind, heat, and frost action is necessary for exterior stonework.

- Workability — A stone's hardness and grain texture must allow it to be quarried, cut, and shaped.

- Density — A stone's porosity affects its ability to withstand frost action and staining.

- Appearance — Appearance factors include color, grain, and texture.

Stone may be classified according to geological origin into the following types:

- Igneous........Cooled molten rock (granite)
- Sedimentary....Deposited by glacial action (limestone)
- Metamorphic....Formed under intense pressure and heat (marble, slate)

As a loadbearing wall material, stone is similar to modular unit masonry. Although stone masonry is not necessarily uniform in size, it is laid up with mortar and used in compression. Almost all stone is adversely affected by sudden changes in temperature and should not be used where a high degree of fire resistance is required.

Stone is used in construction in the following forms:

- Rubble — Used primarily as a wall material.
- Dimension — Cut stone is the most widely used form and has many applications, from wall panels and cornices to flooring.
- Flagstone — Flat slabs are used for flooring and horizontal surfacing.
- Crushed rock — Used as aggregate in concrete products.

Types of stonework include:

- Rubble — Rough, uncut stonework
- Ashlar — Cut or split stone masonry patterns
- Trim — Cut stone for copings, cornices, sills, and lintels

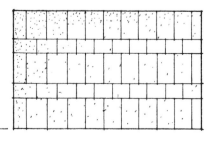
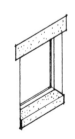
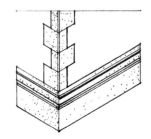

Plastics are synthetic, high polymer materials that are tough, resilient, lightweight, and resistant to corrosion and moisture. Most importantly, they can be formed or molded into a variety of complex shapes. While there are many types of plastics with a wide range of characteristics, they can be divided into two basic categories.

THERMOSETTING plastics go through a pliable stage, but once they are set or cured, they remain rigid and cannot be softened again by reheating.

THERMOPLASTIC materials hold their shape at normal temperatures, but at a higher temperature, known as the softening point, they can be molded into a new shape.

In the table below are listed the plastics that are commonly used in construction and their primary uses.

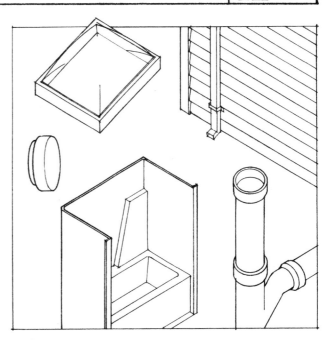

THERMOSETS (Abbreviation)	USES
Epoxies (EP)	Adhesives; coating compounds
Melamines (MF)	High-pressure laminates; adhesives
Phenolics (PF)	Electrical parts; laminates; foamed insulation
Polyesters	Fiberglass-reinforced plastics; bathroom fixtures; window frames
Polyurethanes (UP)	Rigid foam insulation
Silicones (SI)	Brick and masonry waterproofing
THERMOPLASTICS (Abbreviation)	**USES**
Acrylonitrile-butadiene-styrene (ABS)	Pipe and pipe fittings; door hardware
Acrylics (Polymethyl methacrylate - PMMA)	Glazing; lighting fixtures; roofing; latex paints
Cellulosics (Cellulose acetate-butyrate - CAB)	Pipe and pipe fittings; adhesives
Nylons (Polyamides - PA)	Synthetic fibers and filaments; locks, latches, rollers
Polycarbonates (PC)	Safety glazing; lighting fixtures
Polyethylene (PE)	Vapor barriers; pipe; electrical insulation
Polypropylene (PP)	Pipe and pipe fittings; carpeting fiber
Polystyrene (PS)	Lighting fixtures; foamed insulation
Vinyls (Polyvinyl chloride - PVC)	Flooring; siding; gutters; window frames; facings

A nail consists of a metal shaft, pointed at one end, and formed into a head at the other.

Material:
- Nails are usually of mild steel, but may also be of aluminum, copper, brass, zinc, or stainless steel.
- Nails may be coated with zinc, copper, or brass.
- Tempered, high carbon steel nails are used for greater strength in masonry applications.
- The type of metal used should be compatible with the materials being secured to avoid loss of holding power and prevent staining of the materials' surfaces.

Length and diameter of the shank:
- Nail lengths are designated by the term penny (d).
- Nails range in length from 2d (about 1") to 60d (about 6").
- Nails longer than 20d may be referred to as spikes.
- Rule of thumb: Nail length = 3 x thickness of the material being secured.
- Large diameter nails are used for heavy work while lighter nails are used for finish work.
- Thinner nails are used for hardwood than for softwood.

Form of the shank:
- For greater gripping strength, nail shafts may be serrated, barbed, threaded, fluted, or twisted.
- Nail shafts may cement-coated for greater resistance to withdrawal, or be zinc-coated for corrosion resistance.

Nail heads:
- Flat heads provide the largest amount of contact area and are used when exposure of the heads is acceptable.
- The heads of finish nails are only slightly larger than the shaft and may be tapered or cupped.
- Double-headed nails are used for easy removal in temporary construction (eg., concrete formwork).

Nail points:
- Most nails have diamond-shaped points.
- Sharp-pointed nails have greater holding strength but may tend to split some woods.
- Blunt points should be used for easily split woods.
- Nails may also have needle, truncated, or chisel points.

Power-driven fasteners:
- Pneumatic nailers and staplers, driven by a compressor, are capable of fastening materials to wood, steel, or concrete.
- Powder-driven fasteners use gunpowder charges to drive a variety of studs into concrete or steel.
- Consult the manufacturer for types of fastenings available and applications.

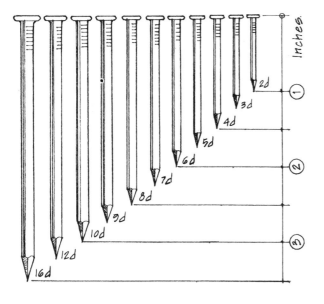

Inches.

- 2d — 1
- 3d
- 4d
- 5d
- 6d — 2
- 7d
- 8d
- 9d
- 10d — 3
- 12d
- 16d

Common nails • For general construction (2d-60d)

Box nails • For light construction (2d-40d)

Casing nails • For interior trim (2d-40d)

Finishing nails • For cabinetry (2d-20d)

Wire brads • For light work (3/16"-3")

Cut nails • For wood flooring (2d-20d)

Double-headed nails • For temporary construction

Masonry nails • For concrete and masonry

Drywall nails • For gypsum board

Roofing nails • For roofing; may have washers to seal nail holes.

Power-driven studs • For fastening into concrete or steel

Because of their threaded shafts, screws have greater holding power than nails and are more easily removable. The more threads they have per inch, the greater their gripping strength. Screws are classified by:

- Use......... Wood, machine, sheet metal, drywall, set screws
- Type of head .. Flat, round, oval, or pan; slotted, Phillips, or hex socket
- Finish....... Steel, brass, aluminum, bronze, stainless steel
- Lengths ..... 1/2" to 6"
- Diameters.... Up to 24 gauge

A wood screw's length should be about 1/8" less than the combined thickness of the boards being joined, with 1/2 to 2/3 of the screw's length penetrating the base material. Fine-threaded screws are generally used for hardwoods while coarse-threaded ones are used for softwoods.

Holes for screws should be predrilled and be equal to the base diameter of the threads. Some screws, such as drywall screws, are self-drilling.

Bolts are round sections of metal, headed at one end and threaded at the other. They are normally used for structural wood or metal connections. Special types are available to anchor plates to masonry or concrete.

- Lengths..... 3/4" to 30"
- Diameters.... 1/4" to 1 1/4"
- Head types... Flat, round, oval; square or hexagonal
- Nuts........ Drilled and threaded to receive threaded end of bolt.
- Washers..... Used to increase the force-exerting contact area between the head or nut and the material being fastened.
  - May also be used to provide seals, insulate incompatible metals from each other, and act as spacing devices.

- Lag bolts or screws are used when only one end of the bolt is accessible.

- Toggle bolts are used to fasten materials to plaster, gypsum board, and other thin wall materials.

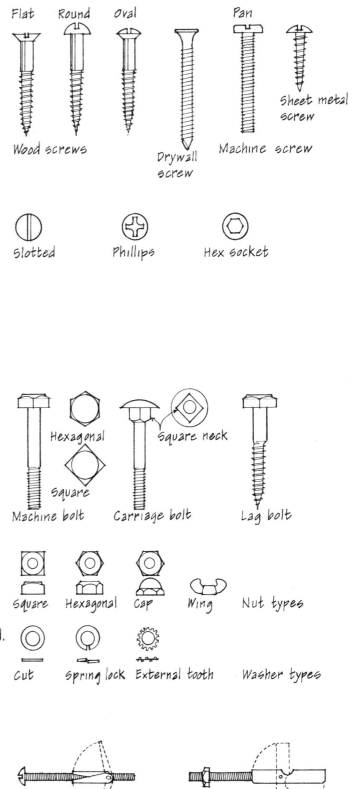

Flat Round Oval Pan

Wood screws Drywall screw Machine screw Sheet metal screw

Slotted Phillips Hex socket

Hexagonal Square neck
Square
Machine bolt Carriage bolt Lag bolt

Square Hexagonal Cap Wing Nut types

Cut Spring lock External tooth Washer types

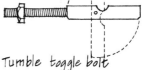

Spring wing toggle bolt Tumble toggle bolt

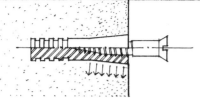

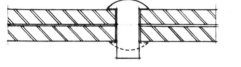

Expansion shields and anchors
- Used to secure materials to plaster, gypsum board, masonry, or concrete bases.
- Upon the insertion and turning of a screw or bolt, the shield expands in size and exerts pressure on the base material.

Metal framing connectors
- Used to connect wood framing members to each other or to masonry or concrete supports.
- Typical types include post bases and caps, joist and beam hangers, framing anchors, tension ties, and holdowns.

Timber connectors
- Used to distribute a load over a larger area of the timber in heavy frame construction and trusswork.
- Split ring connectors are used for wood-to-wood connections and shear plates for steel-to-wood connections.

Rivets
- Used to permanently join structural steel members.
- Have been largely superseded by less labor-intensive techniques of bolting or welding.

Adhesives are used to secure the surfaces of two materials together. Numerous types of adhesives are available, many of them being tailor-made for use with specific materials and under specified conditions. They may be supplied in the form of a solid, liquid, powder, or film; some require a catalyst to activate their adhesive properties. Always follow the manufacturer's recommendations in the use of an adhesive. Important considerations in the selection of an adhesive include:

- Strength . . . . Adhesives are usually strongest in resisting tensile and shear stresses and weakest in resisting cleavage or splitting stresses.
- Curing or setting time . . . . Ranges from immediate bonding to curing times of up to several days.
- Setting temperature range . . . . . Some adhesives will set at room temperature while others require baking at elevated temperatures.
- Method of bonding . . . . Some adhesives bond on contact while others require clamping or higher pressures.
- Characteristics . . . . Adhesives vary in their resistance to water, heat, sunlight, chemicals, as well as their aging properties.

Common types of adhesives include:

- Animal or fish glues . . . . Primarily for indoor use where temperature and humidity do not vary greatly; may be weakened by exposure to heat or moisture.
- White glue . . . . Polyvinyl glue; sets quickly and does not stain; slightly resilient.
- Epoxy resin . . . . Extremely strong; may be used to secure both porous and nonporous materials; may dissolve some plastics; unlike other adhesives, epoxy glues will set at low temperatures and under wet conditions.
- Resorcin resin . . . . Strong, waterproof, and durable for outdoor use; flammable; dark color may show through paint.
- Contact cement . . . . Forms a bond on contact; does not require clamps; generally used to secure large sheet materials such as plastic laminate.

The purpose of a coating is to protect, preserve, or visually enhance the surface to which it is applied. The main types of coatings are paints, varnishes, and stains.

PAINTS are opaque film-forming materials that consist of pigments, binders, and solvents.

VARNISHES contain no pigments and form clear or transparent coatings.

STAINS penetrate and impart color to wood surfaces without obscuring the natural wood grain; some are pigmented and approach paint's film-forming properties.

Considerations in the selection of a coating include:
• Compatibility of the coating with the surface to which it is applied.
• The surface preparation and priming required.
• The method of application and drying time required.
• Conditions of use and the required resistance to water, heat, sunlight, temperature variations, mildew, chemicals, and physical abrasion.

The table below lists the basic types of paints and coatings according to surface material and finish. The listing is adapted from recommendations of the National Paint and Coatings Association. Always follow the manufacturer's recommendations in the application of a paint or other protective coating.

PRIMERS AND SEALERS

Interior surfaces

Walls
• Latex
• Alkyd
• Oil base
• Alkali resistant

Wood
• Enamel undercoats
• Clear wood sealers
• Paste wood fillers

Masonry
• Block fillers
• Cement grout

Exterior surfaces

Wood
• Oil base
• Oleoresinous

Metal
• Oil base
  ○ Red lead *
  ○ Zinc chromate
• Alkyd base
  ○ Red lead *
  ○ Zinc chromate
• Zinc oxide
• Latex inhibitive
• Wash primers
• Portland cement paints

* Lead is toxic and its use is restricted to nonresidential applications.

FINISH COATS

Interior surfaces

Gloss finishes
• Wall paints
• Enamels
• Floor enamels
  ○ Alkyd
  ○ Epoxy
  ○ Urethane
• Clear finishes
  ○ Floor and trim varnishes
  ○ Shellac

Semi-gloss finishes
• Wall paints
• Enamels
• Latex paints
• Clear finishes
  ○ Flat varnishes
  ○ Penetrating sealers

Flat finishes
• Alkyd wall paints
• Latex wall paints
• Fire-retardant paints

Miscellaneous finishes
• Pigmented stains
• Dye-type stains

Exterior surfaces

Oil base finishes
• Gloss house paints
• Barn paints
• Shingle stains

Oleoresinous finishes
• Trim enamels
• Metal paints

Alkyd enamels
• Trim enamels
• Masonry paints

Latex finishes
• Latex house paints
• Masonry paints

Miscellaneous coatings
• Zone-marking paints
• Aluminum paints
  ○ Heat-resistant paint
  ○ Roof coatings
• Clear wood finishes
• Alkali resistant finishes
• Roof coatings
  ○ Bituminous
  ○ Latex
• Portland cement
• powder paints

All materials to receive paint or other coating must be properly prepared and primed to ensure adhesion of the coating to their surfaces and to maximize the life of the coating. In general, surfaces should be dry and free of contaminants, such as dirt, grease, moisture, and mildew. The following are recommendations for various materials.

- **Aluminum** .... Any corrosion should be removed by wire brushing.
  Any oil or other foreign matter should be removed with solvents or by steam cleaning.
  Unweathered aluminum may require a surface-etching treatment before painting.
  Prime with a zinc chromate coating.

- **Brick** .... Dirt, loose mortar, efflorescence, or other foreign matter should be removed by wire brushing, air pressure, or steam cleaning.
  Brick should weather for a month before finishing.
  Brick may be sealed with a latex primer or a clear silicone water-repellent.

- **Concrete** .... Surface should be free of dirt, excess mortar, form oils, or curing compounds.
  Concrete should weather for a month before coating.
  Porous surfaces may require a block filler or cement grout primer.
  Grouted or chalky surfaces may require an alkali-resistant primer.
  Concrete may also be sealed with a clear silicone water-repellent.

- **Concrete block** ...... Block should be free of dirt, loose or excess mortar, and be thoroughly dry.
  Porous surfaces may require a block filler or cement grout primer if the acoustical value of a rough surface is not important.

- **Concrete floors** ..... Floor should be free of dirt, wax, grease and oils, and should be etched with a muriatic acid solution to improve adhesion of the coating.
  Prime with an alkali-resistant coating.

- **Galvanized iron** ...... All grease, residue, and corrosion should be removed with solvent or chemical washes.
  Surface may be primed with a zinc oxide or portland cement paint.
  If weathered, galvanized iron should be treated as a ferrous metal.

- **Gypsum board** .... Surface should be clean and dry.
  Use a latex primer-sealer to avoid raising the fibers of the paper surface.

- **Old paint surfaces** .... Surface should be clean, dry, and roughened by sanding or washing with a detergent solution.

- **Plaster and stucco** .... Plaster and stucco should be allowed to dry thoroughly and be completely cured.
  Soft surfaces should be treated to provide a hard, paintable surface.
  Fresh plaster should be primed with an alkali-resistant coating.

- **Steel** .... Surface should be free of rust, metal burrs, and foreign matter.
  Surface may be cleaned with solvents or by wire brushing, sandblasting, flame cleaning, or pickling with acids.

- **Wood** .... Wood should be clean, dry, well-seasoned lumber.
  Knots and pitch stains should be sanded and sealed before priming.
  Surfaces to be painted should be primed or sealed to stabilize the moisture content of the wood and prevent the absorption of succeeding coats; stains and some paints may be self-priming.
  All nail holes, cracks, and other small holes should be filled after the full prime coat.

APPENDIX

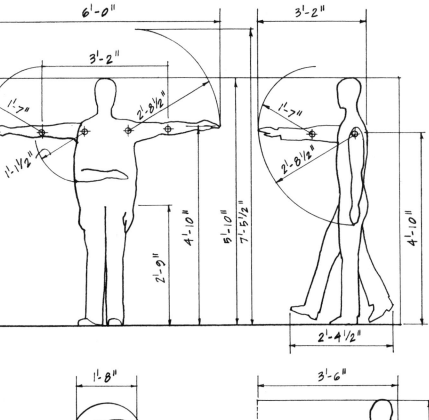

Caution should always be exercised when using a set of dimensional tables or illustrations such as these. These are based on average measurements which may have to be adjusted to satisfy specific user needs. Variations from the norm will always exist due to the differences between men and women, among various age and racial groups, and from one individual to the next.

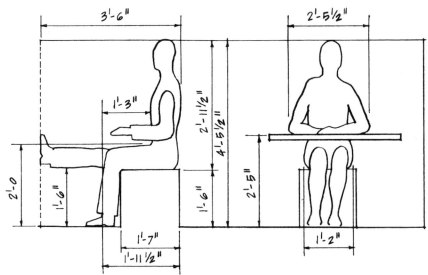

Our body dimensions, and the way we move through and perceive space, are prime determinants of a building's scale, proportions, and spatial layout. It should be noted that there is a difference between the structural dimensions of our bodies and those dimensional requirements that result from how we reach for something on a shelf, sit down at a table, walk down a stairway, or interact with other people. These functional dimensions will vary according to the nature of our activity and the social situation.

Planning for the handicapped involves the design of facilities that are:

- Accessible to those confined to a wheelchair and the ambulatory:
  - Avoid changes in level and the use of stairs.
  - Use ramps only where necessary

- Identifiable to the blind:
  - Use raised lettering, audible warning signals, and textured surfaces to indicate stairs or hazardous openings.

- Usable:
  - Circulation spaces should be adequate for comfortable movement.
  - All public facilities should have fixtures designed for use by the handicapped.

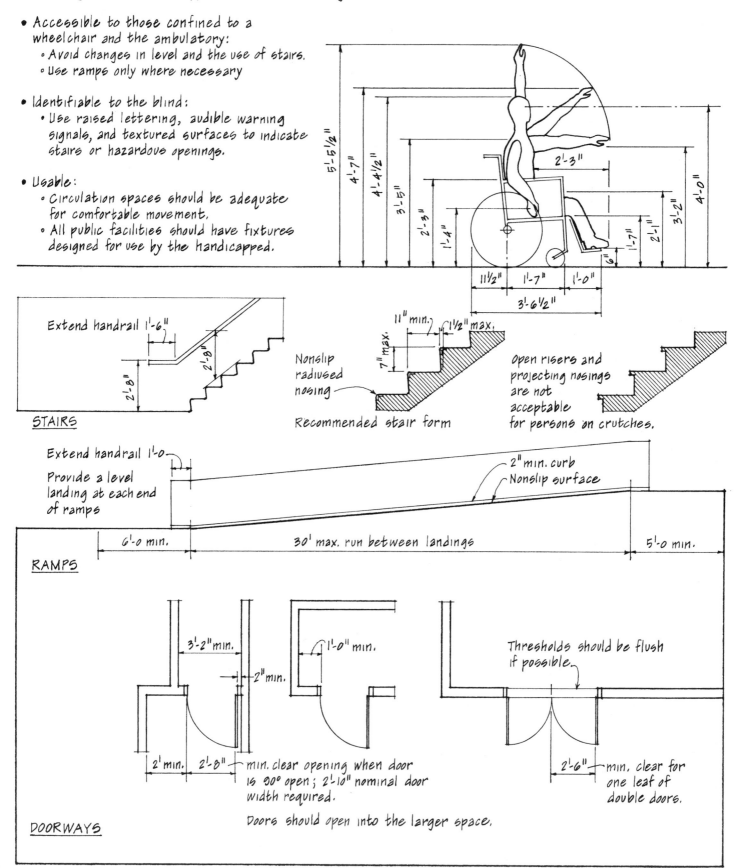

STAIRS

Extend handrail 1'-6"

Nonslip radiused nosing

Recommended stair form

Open risers and projecting nosings are not acceptable for persons on crutches.

RAMPS

Extend handrail 1'-0"

Provide a level landing at each end of ramps

2" min. curb
Nonslip surface

6'-0 min.   30' max. run between landings   5'-0 min.

DOORWAYS

3'-2" min.
2" min.
2' min.   2'-8"   min. clear opening when door is 90° open; 2'-10" nominal door width required.

1'-0" min.

Thresholds should be flush if possible.

2'-6"   min. clear for one leaf of double doors.

Doors should open into the larger space.

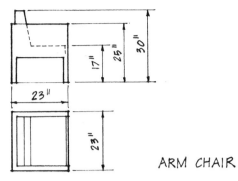

ARM CHAIR

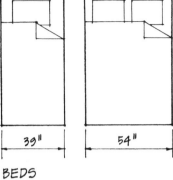

BEDS

Queen: 60"
King: 72", 76"

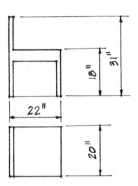

SIDE CHAIR

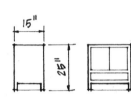

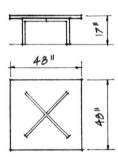

NIGHT TABLE

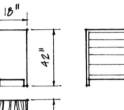

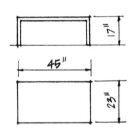

HIGH CHEST

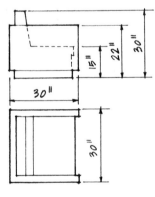

LOUNGE CHAIR

LOW TABLES

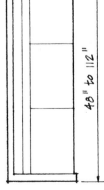

SOFA

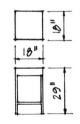
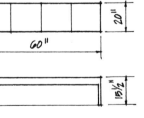

STOOL   BENCH

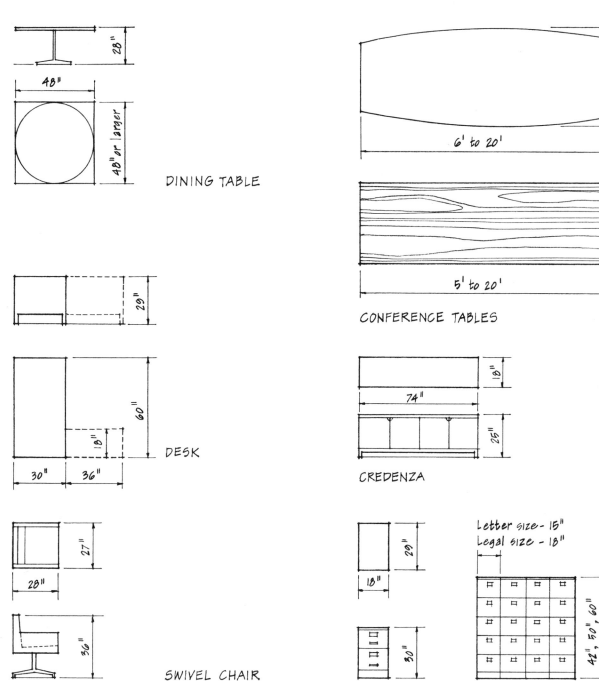

DINING TABLE

CONFERENCE TABLES

DESK

CREDENZA

SWIVEL CHAIR

FILE CABINETS

All dimensions are typical. Verify with manufacturer.

Furniture may • Serve as space-defining elements
            • Define circulation paths
            • Be built-in or set as objects in space.

Selection factors include function, comfort, scale, color, and style.

MINIMUM UNIFORMLY DISTRIBUTED LIVE LOADS (lbs./S.F.)

ASSEMBLY FACILITIES
Theaters with fixed seats 60
Auditoriums and gyms w/ movable seats 100
Corridors and lobbies 100
Stages 150

LIBRARIES
Reading rooms 60
Book stacks .150

MANUFACTURING FACILITIES 125

OFFICES
Office spaces 80
Lobbies 100

RESIDENTIAL FACILITIES
Private dwellings, apartment units,
and hotel rooms 40
Public rooms 100
Corridors 60

SCHOOLS
Classrooms 40
Corridors 100

SIDEWALKS AND VEHICULAR DRIVES 250

STAIRS, FIRE ESCAPES, EXITWAYS 100

STORAGE WAREHOUSES
Light 125
Heavy 250

STORES
Retail: first floor 100
             upper floors 75
Wholesale .125

ROOF LOADS
Minimum, not including wind or
seismic loads 20
Roof gardens 100

In the design of a building, the assumed live loads should be the maximum expected to be produced by the intended use or expectancy. In some instances, such as with parking garages, concentrated loads will take precedence.

Always verify the live load requirements with the local building code.

AVERAGE WEIGHTS OF MATERIALS (lbs./C.F.)

SOIL, SAND AND GRAVEL
Cinder 45
Clay, damp 110
Clay, dry 63
Earth, dry and loose 76
Earth, moist and packed 96
Sand and gravel, dry and loose 105
Sand and gravel, wet 120

WOOD
Cedar 22
Douglas fir 32
Hemlock 29
Maple 42
Oak, red 41
Oak, white 46
Pine, southern 29
Redwood 26
Spruce 27

METAL
Aluminum 165
Brass, red 546
Bronze, statuary 509
Copper 556
Iron, cast 450
Iron, wrought 485
Lead .710
Nickel 565
Stainless steel 510
Steel, rolled 490
Tin 459
Zinc .440

CONCRETE
Stone, plain 144
Stone, reinforced 150
Cinder 100
Lightweight: Expanded shale 105
                    Perlite 35-50

STONE
Granite 175
Limestone 165
Marble 165
Sandstone 147
Slate .175

Water
Maximum density @ 4°C 62
Ice 56
Snow 8

AVERAGE WEIGHTS OF MATERIALS (lbs./S.F.)

FLOOR AND ROOF CONSTRUCTION
Concrete, reinforced, per inch
- Stone 12.5
- Lightweight 6-10

Concrete, plain, per inch
- Stone 12
- Lightweight 3-9

Concrete, precast
- 6" hollow core, stone 40
- 6" hollow core, lightweight 30
- 2" cinder concrete plank 15
- 2" gypsum plank 12

Steel deck 2-4

FLOOR FINISHES
- Cement finish, 1" 12
- Marble 30
- Terrazzo, 1" 13
- Wood, Hardwood 25/32" 4
- Softwood 3/4" 2.5
- Wood block 3" 15
- Vinyl tile 1.33

CEILINGS
- Acoustical tile, 3/4" 1
- Acoustic plaster on gypsum lath 10
- Channel suspended system 1

ROOFING
- Built-up, 5-ply felt and gravel 6
- Copper or tin 2
- Corrugated iron 2
- Corrugated fiberglass 0.5
- Monel metal 1.5
- Shingles, Fiberglass 3
- Slate 10
- Wood 2
- Tile, Concrete 16
- Clay 14

WALLS AND PARTITIONS
Brick, per 4" of thickness 35

Concrete masonry units
- Stone or gravel aggregate, 4" . . . 34
- 6" . . . 50
- 8" . . . 58
- 12" . . . 90
- Lightweight aggregate, 4" . . . 22
- 6" . . . 31
- 8" . . . 38
- 12" . . . 55

- Glass block, 4" 18
- Gypsum board, 1/2" 2
- Metal lath 0.5
- Metal studs with gypsum board 6
- Plaster, 1"
  - Cement 10
  - Gypsum 5
- Plywood, 1/2" 1.5
- Stone, Granite, 4" 59
- Limestone, 6" 55
- Marble, 1" 13
- Sandstone, 4" 49
- Slate, 1" 14
- Tile, Ceramic 2.5
- Glazed wall tile 3
- Tile, Structural clay, 4" 18
- 6" 28
- 8" 34
- Wood studs, 2x4, with Gypsum board both sides 8

INSULATION
- Batt or blanket, per inch 0.3
- Fiberboard 2
- Foamed board, per inch 0.2
- Loose 0.5
- Poured in place 2
- Rigid 0.8

GLASS
- Insulating glass, 1/8" plate 3.25
- Polished plate, 1/4" 3.30
- Sheet, DS 1/8" 1.60
- HS 1/4" 3.25
- Wire glass, 1/4" 3.50

Inch / Foot

Decimal equivalents

Cm / Inches

1 cm = 0.3937 inch
1 inch = 2.54 cm = 25.4 mm

Meters / Feet

1 meter = 3.281 feet
1 foot = 0.3048 meter = 304.8 mm

FACTOR		MULTIPLES • SUBMULTIPLES • PREFIXES • SYMBOLS	
Thousand million	10^9	Giga	G
One million	10^6	Mega	M
One thousand	10^3	Kilo	k
One hundred	10^2	Hecto	h
Ten	10^1	Deca	da
One-tenth	10^{-1}	Deci	d
One-hundredth	10^{-2}	Centi	c
One-thousandth	10^{-3}	Milli	m
One-millionth	10^{-6}	Micro	u

MEASUREMENT TYPE	IMPERIAL UNIT	METRIC UNIT	SYMBOL	CONVERSION FACTOR
LENGTH	mile	kilometer	km	1 mile = 1.609 km
	yard	meter	m	1 yard = 0.9144 m = 914.4 mm
	foot	meter	m	1 foot = 0.3048 m
		millimeter	mm	= 304.8 mm
	inch	millimeter	mm	1 inch = 25.4 mm
AREA	square mile	sq. kilometer	km^2	$1 \text{ mile}^2 = 2.590 \text{ km}^2$
		hectare	ha	$= 259.0 \text{ ha}$ $(1 \text{ ha} = 10,000 \text{ m}^2)$
	acre	hectare	ha	1 acre = 0.4047 ha
		square meter	m^2	$= 4046.9 \text{ m}^2$
	square yard	square meter	m^2	$1 \text{ yard}^2 = 0.8361 \text{ m}^2$
	square foot	square meter	m^2	$1 \text{ foot}^2 = 0.0929 \text{ m}^2$
		sq. centimeter	cm^2	$= 929.03 \text{ cm}^2$
	square inch	sq. centimeter	cm^2	$1 \text{ inch}^2 = 6.452 \text{ cm}^2 = 645.2 \text{ mm}^2$
VOLUME	cubic yard	cubic meter	m^3	$1 \text{ yard}^3 = 0.7646 \text{ m}^3$
	cubic foot	cubic meter	m^3	$1 \text{ foot}^3 = 0.02832 \text{ m}^3$
		liter	liter	$= 28.32 \text{ liters}$ $(1000 \text{ liters} = 1 \text{ m}^3)$
		cubic decimeter	dm^3	$= 28.32 \text{ dm}^3$ $(1 \text{ liter} = 1 \text{ dm}^3)$
	cubic inch	cubic millimeter	mm^3	$1 \text{ inch}^3 = 16390 \text{ mm}^3$
		cubic centimeter	cm^3	$= 16.39 \text{ cm}^3$
		milliliter	ml	$= 16.39 \text{ ml}$
		liter	liter	$= 0.01639 \text{ liter}$

MEASURMENT TYPE	IMPERIAL UNIT	METRIC UNIT	SYMBOL	CONVERSION FACTOR
MASS	ton	kilogram	kg	1 ton = 1016.05 kg
	kip (1000 lbs.)	kilogram	kg	1 kip = 453.59 kg
	pound	kilogram	kg	1 lb. = 0.4536 kg
	ounce	gram	g	1 oz. = 28.35 g
CAPACITY	quart	liter	liter	1 qt. = 1.137 liter
	pint	liter	liter	1 pt. = 0.568 liter
	fluid ounce	cubic centimeter	cm³	1 fl. oz. = 28.413 cm³
MASS PER UNIT AREA	pound/sq. ft.	kilogram/square meter	kg/m²	1 psf = 4.882 kg/m²
	pound/sq. in.	kilogram/square meter	kg/m²	1 psi = 703.07 kg/m²
	ounce/sq. ft.	gram/square meter	g/m²	1 oz./ft² = 305.15 g/m²
DENSITY	pound/cubic foot	kilogram/cubic meter	kg/m³	1 lb./ft.³ = 16.02 kg/m³
	pound/cubic inch	gram/cubic centimeter	g/cm³	1 lb./in.³ = 27.68 g/cm³
		megagram/cubic meter	Mg/m³	27.68 Mg/m³
VOLUME RATE OF FLOW	cu. ft./minute	liter/second	liter/s	1 ft.³/min. = 0.4731 liter/s
	cu. ft./second	cubic meter/second	m³/s	1 ft.³/sec. = 0.02832 m³/s
	cu. in./second	milliliter/second	ml/s	1 in.³/sec. = 16.39 ml/s
	gallon/hour	liter/hour	liter/h	1 gal./hr. = 4.5461 liter/h
	gallon/minute	liter/second	liter/s	1 gal./min. = 0.07577 liter/s
	gallon/second	liter/second	liter/s	1 gal./sec. = 4.5461 liter/s
FUEL CAPACITY	gallon/mile	liter/kilometer	liter/km	1 gpm = 2.825 liter/km
	miles/mile	kilometers/liter	km/liter	1 mpg = 0.354 km/liter
VELOCITY	miles/hour	kilometer/hour	km/h	1 mph = 1.609 km/h
	feet/minute	meter/minute	m/min	1 fpm = 0.3048 m/min.
	feet/second	meter/second	m/s	1 fps = 0.3048 m/s
	inch/second	millimeter/second	mm/s	1 in./sec. = 25.4 mm/s
TEMPERATURE	°Fahrenheit	degree Celsius	°C	$t°C = 0.5556 (t°F - 32)$ $= 5/9 (t°F - 32)$
○ Temperature interval	°Fahrenheit	degree Celsius	°C	1 degree F = 0.5556 degree C
HEAT	British thermal unit (Btu)	joule	J	1 Btu = 1055 J
		kilojoule	kJ	1 Btu = 1.055 kJ
● Heat flow rate	Btu/hour	watt	W	1 Btu/hr. = 0.2931 W
		kilowatt	kW	1 Btu/hr. = 0.0002931 W
● Density of heat flow rate	Btu/ft².hour	watt/square meter	W/m²	1 Btu/ft².hr = 3.155 W/m²
● Thermal conductivity	Btu.inch/ ft².hour.deg F	watt/meter.deg C	W/m °C	1 Btu.in/ft².hr. °F = 0.1442 W/m °C
● Thermal conductance	Btu/ft².hr.deg F	watt/meter².deg C	W/m² °C	1 Btu/ft².hr. °F = 5.678 W/m² °C
● Refrigeration	ton	watt	W	1 ton = 3519 W
POWER	horsepower	watt	W	1 hp = 745.7 W
		kilowatt	kW	= 0.7457 kW
LIGHTING	footcandle	lux	lux	1 ft. candle = 10.76 lux (1 lux = 1 lumen/ft.²)
	lumen/sq. foot	lux	lux	1 lumen/ft.² = 10.76 lux

Building codes specify:

- The required means of egress for a building's occupants in case of a fire.
- The fire-resistance ratings of materials and construction required for a building depending on its:
  - location (fire district)
  - use and occupancy
  - size (height and area per floor)
- The fire alarm, sprinkler, and other protection systems required for certain uses and occupancies.

These requirements are intended to control the spread of fire and to allow sufficient time for the occupants of a burning building to exit safely before the structure weakens to the extent that it becomes dangerous. The following outlines the principles involved in fire protection. <u>Consult the local applicable code in force for specific requirements.</u>

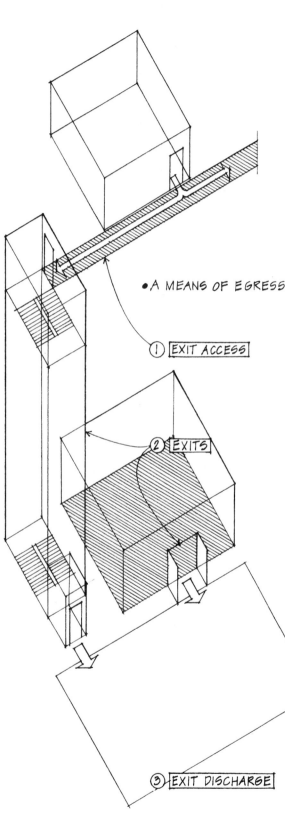

① EXIT ACCESS

② EXITS

③ EXIT DISCHARGE

- A MEANS OF EGRESS must provide safe and adequate access to protected exits leading to a place of refuge. Thus, there are three components to an egress system:

- The path or passageway leading to an exit should be as direct as possible, be unobstructed with projections such as open doors, and be well lit; emergency power for lights and exit signs may be required.
- Exits and exit paths should be clearly marked.

- An exit must provide a protected means of evacuation from an exit access to a safe discharge point.
- Exit passageways and stairways must be of 2-hour construction with self-closing doors that are rated at 1½ hours.
- For most occupancies, a minimum of two exits is required to provide a margin of safety in case one exit is blocked.
- Exits should be located as remote from each other as possible without creating dead-end passageways.
- The maximum travel distance from the most remote on a floor to the nearest exit is specified by code according to a building's use, occupancy, and degree of fire hazard.
- The required width of an exit is based on a building's use and occupant load. It is usually specified as the number of persons allowed per unit of width (usually 22"). Examples:
  - Places of assembly 100
  - Offices, schools, stores . . . 60
  - Residential buildings 45
- See 9.5 for stairway dimensions and requirements.
- In tall buildings, one or more of the exit stairways may be required to be placed in a smokeproof enclosure.

- All exits must discharge to a safe place of refuge outside of the building at ground level.
- In some cases, a protected passageway or foyer may connect an exit stairway to the outside.

Building codes classify buildings into types of construction which represent varying degrees of resistance to fire. (See table below.) A building's maximum height and area per floor will be limited by its construction type as well as its use, occupancy, and location. In some cases, this size limitation may be exceeded if the building is equipped with a fire sprinkler system, or if it is divided with fire walls into areas not exceeding the size limitation.

Fire walls must have a fire rating of 2 to 4 hours and extend from the building's foundation through the roof to a parapet or to the underside of a noncombustible roof. Openings in fire walls are restricted in size and must be protected by self-closing fire doors, fire-rated window assemblies, or ducts equipped with fire dampers.

The table below outlines the required fire-resistive ratings of building elements for the various types of construction. Consult the local applicable code to confirm these requirements and the building use groups listed on the right. On the following two pages are illustrated representative construction assemblies and their fire ratings.

EXAMPLES OF BUILDING USE GROUPS

(A) Assembly
Auditoriums, theaters, stadiums

(B) Business
Offices, retail shops, restaurants

(E) Educational
Schools, day-care facilities

(F) Factories
Manufacturing plants, mills

(H) Hazardous uses
Facilities handling flammable or explosive materials

(I) Institutional
Hospitals, nursing homes, reformatories

(R) Residential
Homes, apartment buildings, hotels

(S) Storage
Warehousing facilities

FIRE-RESISTIVE REQUIREMENTS (in hours)

| BUILDING ELEMENT | NONCOMBUSTIBLE | | | | COMBUSTIBLE | | | |
| | Type I | Type II | | | Type III | Type IV | Type V | |
	Fire-resistive	Fire-resistive	1-hour	No requirement	1-hour	Heavy timber	1-hour	No requirement
Structural frame	3 - 4	2	1	None	1	1 or H.T.	1	None
Floors	2	2	1	None	1	H.T.	1	None
Interior bearing walls	3 - 4	2	1	None	1	1	1	None
Exterior walls, windows, doors	Varies with distance from property line and adjacent structures							
Roofs	0-2	0-1	0-1	None	1	H.T.	1	None
Permanent partitions	1	1	1	None	1	1 or H.T.	1	None
Fire walls	2-4	2-4	2-4	2-4	2-4	2-4	2-4	2-4
Exit and stairway enclosures	2	2	2	2	2	2	2	2
Shaft enclosures	2	2	1	1	1	1	1	0-1

Fire-resistant construction is rated according to the length of time a material or assembly can be exposed to fire without sustaining significant damage. Fire-resistant construction therefore involves both reducing a material's flammability and controlling the spread of fire.

On this and the facing page is a sampling of fire-resistance ratings for various construction assemblies. For more detailed specifications, consult the Underwriters' Laboratories, Inc. Materials List, or the governing building code.

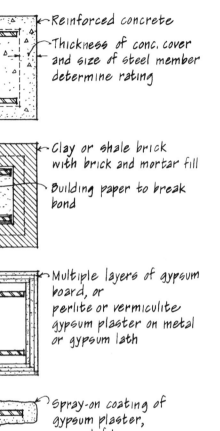

- Reinforced concrete
- Thickness of conc. cover and size of steel member determine rating

- Clay or shale brick with brick and mortar fill
- Building paper to break bond

- Multiple layers of gypsum board, or
- perlite or vermiculite gypsum plaster on metal or gypsum lath

- Spray-on coating of gypsum plaster, mineral fibers, or magnesium oxychloride cement

- water-filled column connected to water main or storage tank

Because structural steel can be weakened by the high temperatures of a fire, it requires protection to qualify for certain types of construction.

FIRE PROTECTION FOR STRUCTURAL STEEL

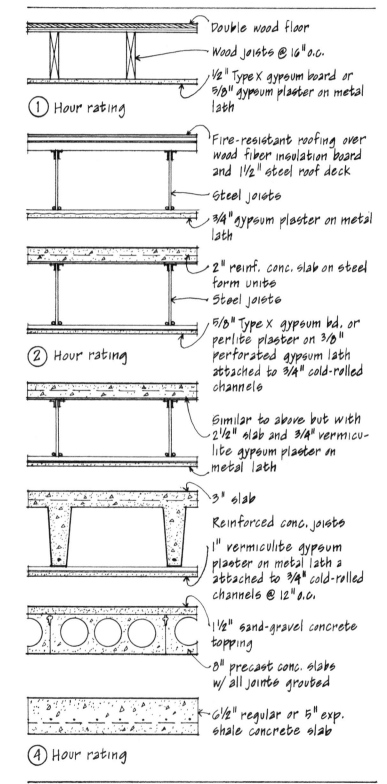

- Double wood floor
- Wood joists @ 16" o.c.
- 1/2" Type X gypsum board or 5/8" gypsum plaster on metal lath

(1) Hour rating

- Fire-resistant roofing over wood fiber insulation board and 1 1/2" steel roof deck
- Steel joists
- 3/4" gypsum plaster on metal lath

- 2" reinf. conc. slab on steel form units
- Steel joists
- 5/8" Type X gypsum bd. or perlite plaster on 3/8" perforated gypsum lath attached to 3/4" cold-rolled channels

(2) Hour rating

- Similar to above but with 2 1/2" slab and 3/4" vermiculite gypsum plaster on metal lath

- 3" slab
- Reinforced conc. joists
- 1" vermiculite gypsum plaster on metal lath a attached to 3/4" cold-rolled channels @ 12" o.c.

- 1 1/2" sand-gravel concrete topping
- 8" precast conc. slabs w/ all joints grouted

- 6 1/2" regular or 5" exp. shale concrete slab

(4) Hour rating

FLOOR AND ROOF PROTECTION

Materials used to provide fire protection for a building's elements must be inflammable and be able to withstand very high temperatures without disintegrating. They should also be low conductors of heat to insulate the protected materials from the heat generated by a fire.

Materials commonly used for fire protection include concrete (often with lightweight aggregate), gypsum or vermiclute plaster, gypsum wallboard, and mineral fiber products. Wood may be chemically treated to reduce its flammability.

2x4 studs @ 16" o.c.

5/8" gyp. plaster on metal lath, or 2 layers 1/2" regular gyp. bd. or 5/8" Type X gyp. bd. on each side

2½" steel studs @ 16"o.c.

5/8" gypsum plaster on metal lath, or 5/8" Type X gyp. bd. on each side

2" solid gypsum plaster on 3/4" channels and 3/8" gypsum lath

① Hour rating

2x4 studs @ 16" o.c.

7/8" neat wood fibered gypsum plaster on metal lath, or 2 layers 5/8" Type X gyp. bd. on each side

Steel studs @ 16" or 24" o.c.

3/4" perlite gypsum plaster on 3/8" perforated gypsum lath, or 2 layers 1/2" Type X gyp. bd. on each side

2" solid gypsum plaster

1/2" Type X gyp. bd. on each side of 1" gypsum coreboard

② Hour rating

1" t&g flooring or 1/2" plywood over wood planks at least 3" thick

6x10 min. for floor beams; 4x6 min. for roof beams and truss members

8x8 min. for columns supporting floor loads; 6x6 min. for columns supporting only roof loads

HEAVY TIMBER CONSTRUCTION

Solid reinforced concrete

6½" - 4 hour rating
6" - 3 hour rating
5" - 2 hour rating
3½" - 1 hour rating

Solid brick masonry w

8" - 4 hour rating
6" - 2 hour rating
4" - 1 hour rating

Brick cavity wall

10" - 4 hour rating

Concrete masonry wall

8" - 2 to 4 hour rating
6" - 1½ hour rating
4" - 1 hour rating

Ratings of all masonry walls may be increased with a coating of portland cement or gypsum plaster.

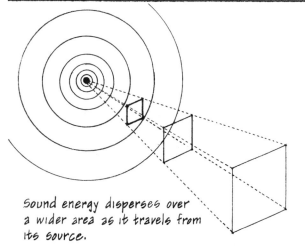

Sound energy disperses over a wider area as it travels from its source.

Acoustics may be defined as the science of sound, including its production and transmission, and the control of its effects. Sound requires a source for its production, a path for its transmission, and a receiver. It may be defined by the frequency, velocity, and magnitude of its energy waves. Sound waves generated by a vibrating object radiate outward from the source equally in all directions until they reach a surface that either reflects or absorbs them.

The acoustical design of spaces involves the reinforcement of desirable sounds and the control of undesirable noise. A room's acoustics is dependent on its shape, form, volume, and the nature of its surfaces.

Room form

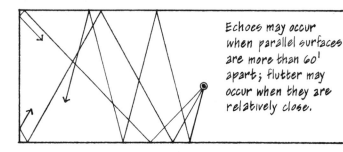

Echoes may occur when parallel surfaces are more than 60' apart; flutter may occur when they are relatively close.

- Parallel surfaces reflect sound back and forth across a space.
- Parallel surfaces may cause excessive reverberation and undesirable echoes or flutter.

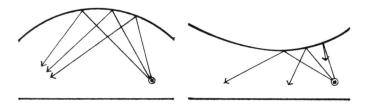

- Concave surfaces focus sound.
- Concave surfaces can create undesirable hot spots of sound.

- Convex surfaces diffuse sound.
- Diffused sound is desirable in listening areas.

- High cubical and long, narrowly proportioned spaces may require splayed surfaces to diffuse reflected sounds and absorbent surfaces to control reverberation.

Nature of the surfaces

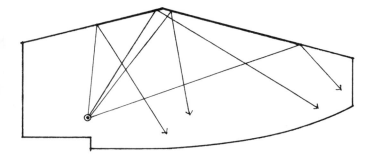

- Hard surfaces reflect sound while soft, porous surfaces tend to absorb sound energy.
- The level of sound, reverberation time, and resonance desired for the intended use of a space will determine the area and disposition of hard and soft surfaces within the space.

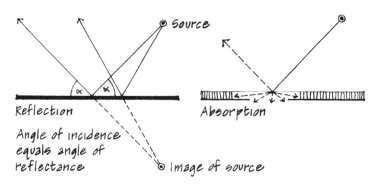

Reflection   Absorption

Angle of incidence equals angle of reflectance

Undesirable noise should be controlled at its source. Noise sources within a building include:

Mechanical equipment and supply systems

- Select quiet equipment.
- Use resilient mountings and flexible bellows to isolate equipment vibrations from the building structure and supply systems.
- Control noise transmission through ductwork by:
  - Lining the ducts internally with glass fiber
  - Installing sound attenuating mufflers
  - Using smooth duct turns.
- Minimize cross talk through ducts by maximizing the distance between diffusers in adjacent spaces.

Water supply and drainage systems

- Use expansion valves and flexible loop connections to prevent pipe rattling and noise transmission along the pipes.
- Seal pipe penetrations through walls and floors with flexible packing.

When control of a noise source does not reduce the undesirable sound to an acceptable level, then its transmission through the air or a building's structure must be controlled by sound absorption or isolation.

Sound absorption is achieved through the use of fibrous materials or panel resonators.

Fibrous materials

- The acoustic efficiency of a fibrous material depends on its thickness, density, porosity, exposure, and the method used to mount it.

Panel resonators

- A panel resonator consists of a thin membrane material such as plywood mounted in front of a sealed air space. Panel resonators are effective absorbers of low frequency sounds.

Many sound-absorbing products are commercially available, such as acoustical ceiling tile. Other materials and products that are effective sound absorbers include carpeting, heavy drapes, and upholstered furnishings.

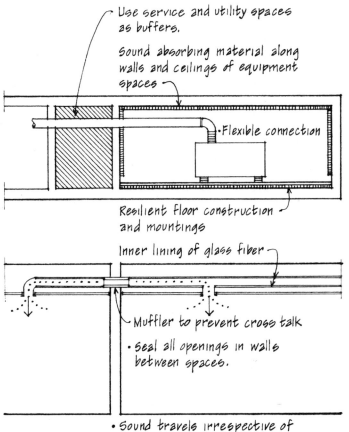

Use service and utility spaces as buffers.

Sound absorbing material along walls and ceilings of equipment spaces

Flexible connection

Resilient floor construction and mountings

Inner lining of glass fiber

Muffler to prevent cross talk

- Seal all openings in walls between spaces.

- Sound travels irrespective of airflow direction.

A screen of spaced wood strips or cellular masonry can be used for appearance; these elements will, however, decrease the exposure of the sound absorbing material.

Loose weave fabric, open-back carpet, or perforated metal screen

Glass fiber acoustical insulation

Deep air space increases low frequency sound absorption.

Sound isolation involves increasing a path's resistance to both air-borne and structure-borne sound.

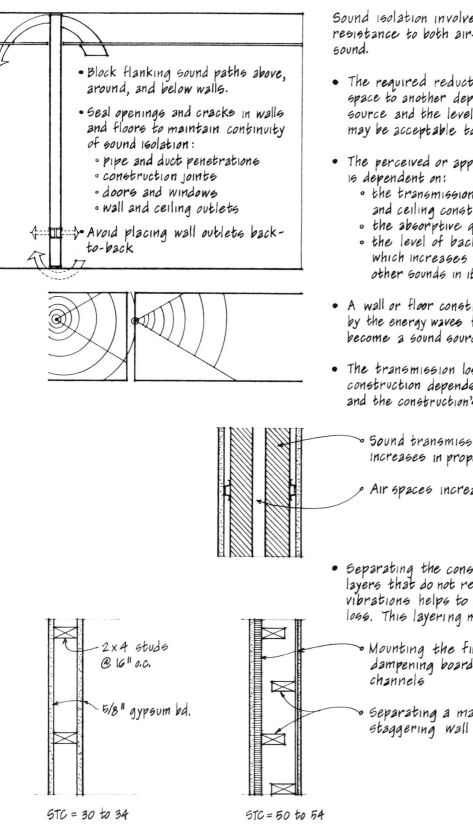

- Block flanking sound paths above, around, and below walls.

- Seal openings and cracks in walls and floors to maintain continuity of sound isolation:
  - pipe and duct penetrations
  - construction joints
  - doors and windows
  - wall and ceiling outlets

- Avoid placing wall outlets back-to-back

- The required reduction in noise level from one space to another depends on the level of the sound source and the level of the sound's intrusion that may be acceptable to the listener.

- The perceived or apparent sound level in a space is dependent on:
  - the transmission loss through the wall, floor, and ceiling construction
  - the absorptive qualities of the receiving space
  - the level of background or masking sound, which increases the threshold of audibility for other sounds in its presence.

- A wall or floor construction that is vibrated by the energy waves from a sound source will itself become a sound source.

- The transmission loss through a wall or floor construction depends on the frequency of the sound and the construction's mass, resilience, and area.

- Sound transmission loss through a material increases in proportion to its mass.

- Air spaces increase transmission loss

- Separating the construction into independent layers that do not readily transmit sound energy vibrations helps to increase transmission loss. This layering may be achieved by:

  - Mounting the finish material over sound dampening boards or resilient furring channels

  - Separating a masonry wall into wythes or staggering wall studs.

2 x 4 studs @ 16" o.c.

5/8" gypsum bd.

STC = 30 to 34   STC = 50 to 54

- STC (Sound transmission class) is an index of a partition's resistance to the passage of sound.

The Construction Specifications Institute (CSI) has established Masterformat, a standard outline for construction specifications. This format is also used to organize the technical literature published by trade associations and manufacturers.

Masterformat has sixteen primary divisions.

Division 1 • General Requirements
Division 2 • Sitework
Division 3 • Concrete
Division 4 • Masonry
Division 5 • Metals
Division 6 • Wood and Plastics
Division 7 • Thermal and Moisture Protection
Division 8 • Doors and Windows
Division 9 • Finishes
Division 10 • Specialties
Division 11 • Equipment
Division 12 • Furnishings
Division 13 • Special construction
Division 14 • Conveying systems
Division 15 • Mechanical
Division 16 • Electrical

Each division is subdivided into specific categories, each of which is assigned a five-digit number. To the right and on the following pages, major subdivisions are listed. For a complete list, write to the Construction Specifications Institute.

DIVISION 1 • GENERAL REQUIREMENTS

01010	Summary of work
01020	Allowances
01025	Measurement and payment
01030	Alternates/alternatives
01035	Modification procedures
01040	Coordination
01050	Field engineering
01060	Regulatory requirements
01070	Identification systems
01090	References
01100	Special project procedures
01200	Project meetings
01300	Submittals
01400	Quality control
01500	Construction facilities
01600	Material and equipment
01650	Facility startup/commissioning
01700	Contract closeout
01800	Maintenance

DIVISION 2 • SITEWORK

02010	Subsurface investigation
02050	Demolition
02100	Site preparation
02140	Dewatering
02150	Shoring and underpinning
02160	Excavation support systems
02170	Cofferdams
02200	Earthwork
02300	Tunneling
02350	Piles and caissons
02480	Marine work
02500	Paving and surfacing
02600	Utility piping materials
02660	Water distribution
02680	Fuel and steam distribution
02700	Sewerage and drainage
02760	Restoration of underground pipe
02770	Ponds and reservoirs
02780	Power and communications
02800	Site improvements
02900	Landscaping

DIVISION 3 • CONCRETE

03100	Concrete formwork
03200	Concrete reinforcement
03250	Concrete accessories
03300	Cast-in-place concrete
03370	Concrete curing
03400	Precast concrete
03500	Cementitious decks and toppings
03600	Grout
03700	Concrete restoration and cleaning
03800	Mass concrete

DIVISION 4 • MASONRY

04100	Mortar and masonry grout
04150	Masonry accessories
04200	Unit masonry
04400	Stone
04500	Masonry restoration and cleaning
04600	Corrosion resistant masonry
04700	Simulated masonry

DIVISION 5 • METALS

05010	Metal materials
05030	Metal coatings
05050	Metal fastenings
05100	Structural metal framing
05200	Metal joists
05300	Metal decking
05400	Cold formed metal framing
05500	Metal fabrications
05580	Sheet metal fabrications
05700	Ornamental
05800	Expansion control
05900	Hydraulic structures

DIVISION 6 • WOOD AND PLASTICS

06050	Fasteners and adhesives
06100	Rough carpentry
06130	Heavy timber construction
06150	Wood and metal systems
06170	Prefabricated structural wood
06200	Finish carpentry
06300	Wood treatment
06400	Architectural woodwork
06500	Structural plastics
06600	Plastic fabrications
06650	Solid polymer fabrications

DIVISION 7 • THERMAL AND MOISURE PROTECTION

07100	Waterproofing
07150	Dampproofing
07180	Water repellants
07190	Vapor retarders
07195	Air barriers
07200	Insulation
07240	Exterior insulation and finish systems
07250	Fireproofing
07270	Firestopping
07300	Shingles and roofing tiles
07400	Manufactured roofing and siding
07480	Exterior wall assemblies
07500	Membrane roofing
07600	Flashing and sheet metal
07700	Roof specialties and accessories
07800	Skylights
07900	Joint sealers

DIVISION 8 • DOORS AND WINDOWS

08100	Metal doors and frames
08200	Wood and plastic doors
08250	Door opening assemblies
08300	Special doors
08400	Entrances and storefronts
08500	Metal windows
08600	Wood and plastic windows
08650	Special windows
08700	Hardware
08800	Glazing
08900	Glazed curtain walls

DIVISION 9 • FINISHES

09100	Metal support systems
09200	Lath and plaster
09250	Gypsum board
09300	Tile
09400	Terrazzo
09450	Stone facing
09500	Acoustical treatment
09540	Special wall surfaces
09545	Special ceiling surfaces
09550	Wood flooring
09600	Stone flooring
09630	Unit masonry flooring
09650	Resilient flooring
09680	Carpet
09700	Special flooring
09780	Floor treatment
09800	Special coatings
09900	Painting
09950	Wall coverings

DIVISION 10 • SPECIALTIES

10100	Visual display boards
10150	Compartments and cubicles
10200	Louvers and vents
10270	Access flooring
10300	Fireplaces and stoves
10350	Flagpoles
10400	Identifying devices
10500	Lockers
10520	Fire protection specialties
10600	Partitions
10650	Operable partitions
10670	Storage shelving
10700	Exterior protection devices for openings
10750	Telephone specialties
10800	Toilet and bath accessories

DIVISION 11 • EQUIPMENT

11010	Maintenance equipment
11020	Security and vault equipment
11040	Ecclesiastical equipment
11050	Library equipment
11060	Theater and stage equipment
11100	Mercantile equipment
11130	Audio-visual equipment
11150	Parking control equipment
11160	Loading dock equipment
11170	Solid waste handling equipment
11190	Detention equipment
11200	Water supply and treatment equipment
11300	Fluid waste treatment and disposal
11400	Food service equipment
11450	Residential equipment
11460	Unit kitchens
11470	Darkroom equipment
11480	Athletic and recreational equipment
11600	Laboratory equipment
11680	Office equipment
11700	Medical equipment
11870	Agricultural equipment

DIVISION 12 • FURNISHINGS

12050	Fabrics
12100	Artwork
12300	Manufactured casework
12500	Window treatment
12600	Furniture and accessories
12670	Rugs and mats
12700	Multiple seating
12800	Interior plants and planters

DIVISION 13 • SPECIAL CONSTRUCTION

13010	Air supported structures
13020	Integrated assemblies
13030	Special purpose rooms
13080	Sound, vibration, and seismic control
13090	Radiation protection
13120	Pre-engineered structures
13150	Aquatic facilities
13300	Utility control systems
13500	Recording instrumentation
13600	Solar energy systems
13700	Wind energy systems
13750	Cogeneration systems
13800	Building automation systems
13900	Fire suppression systems
13950	Special security construction

DIVISION 14 • CONVEYING SYSTEMS

14100	Dumbwaiters
14200	Elevators
14300	Escalators and moving walks
14400	Lifts
14500	Material handling systems
14600	Hoists and cranes
14800	Scaffolding
14900	Transportation systems

DIVISION 15 • MECHANICAL

15050	Mechanical materials and methods
15250	Mechanical insulation
15300	Fire protection
15400	Plumbing
15500	Heating, ventilating, and air conditioning
15550	Heat generation
15650	Refrigeration
15750	Heat transfer
15850	Air handling
15880	Air distribution
15950	Controls
15990	Testing, adjusting, and balancing

DIVISION 16 • ELECTRICAL

16050	Electrical materials and methods
16200	Power generation systems
16300	Medium voltage distribution
16400	Service and distribution
16500	Lighting
16600	Special systems
16700	Communications
16850	Electric resistance heating
16900	Controls
16950	Testing

Trade associations are valuable sources of product information and construction standards.

Adhesives Manufacturers Association • 111 E. Wacker Dr., Chicago, IL 60601
Air-Conditioning and Refrigeration Institute • 1501 Wilson Blvd., Arlington, VA 22209
Aluminum Association • 900 19th St. NW, Suite 300, Washington, DC 20006
American Architectural Manufacturers Association • 2700 River Rd., Suite 118, Des Plaines, IL 60018
American Concrete Institute • P.O. Box 19150, Redford Station, Detroit, MI 48219
American Concrete Pipe Association • 8320 Old Courthouse Rd., Vienna, VA 22180
American Forest Council • 1250 Connecticut Ave. NW, Washington, DC 20006
American Gas Association • 1515 Wilson Blvd., Arlington, VA 22209
American Hardboard Association • 520 N. Hicks Rd., Palatine, IL 60067
American Hardware Manufacturers Association • 931 N. Plum Grove Rd., Schaumburg, IL 60173
American Home Lighting Institute • 230 N. Michigan Ave., Chicago, IL 60601
American Institute of Architects • 1735 New York Ave. NW, Washington, DC 20006
American Institute of Steel Construction, Inc. • 400 N. Michigan Ave., Chicago, IL 60611
American Institute of Timber Construction • 11818 E. Mill Plain Blvd., Vancouver, WA 98684
American Insurance Association • 85 John St., New York, NY 10038
American National Standards Institute, Inc. • 1430 Broadway, New York, NY 10018
American Paper Institute • 260 Madison Ave., New York, NY 10016
American Plywood Association • 7011 S. 19th St., Tacoma, WA 98411
American Society for Testing and Materials • 1916 Race St., Philadelphia, PA 19103
American Society of Civil Engineers • 345 E. 47th St., New York, NY 10017
American Society of Heating, Refrigeration, and Air-Conditioning Engineers • 1791 Tullie Circle NE, Atlanta, GA 30329
American Society of Landscape Architects • 4401 Connecticut Ave. NW, Washington, DC 20006
American Society of Mechanical Engineers • 345 E. 47th St., New York, NY 10017
American Society of Sanitary Engineering • P.O. Box 40362, Bay Village, OH 44140
American Wood Preservers Institute • 1945 Galws Rd., Vienna, VA 22180
Architectural Woodwork Institute • 2310 S. Walter Reed Dr., Arlington, VA 22206
Asphalt Roofing Manufacturers Association • 6288 Montrose Rd., Rockville, MD 20852
Associated General Contractors of America, Inc. • 1957 E St. NW, Washington, DC 20006
Batelle Memorial Institute • 505 King Ave., Columbus, OH 43201
Brick Institute of America • 11490 Commerce Park Dr., Reston, VA 22091
Building Officials and Code Administrators International Inc. • 4051 Flossmoor Rd., Country Club Hills, IL 60477
Building Research Advisory Board • 2101 Constitution Ave., Washington, DC 20418
California Redwood Association • 405 Enfrente Dr., Novato, CA 94949
Carpet and Rug Institute • 310 Holiday Dr., Dalton, GA 30720
Cast Iron Soil Pipe Institute • 5959 Shallowford Rd., Chattanooga, TN 37421
Cedar Shake and Shingle Bureau • 515 116th Ave. NE, Bellevue, WA 98004
Concrete Reinforcing Steel Institute • 933 N. Plum Grove Rd., Schaumburg, IL 60173
Construction Specifications Institute • 601 Madison St., Alexandria, VA 22314
Copper Development Association, Inc. • 405 Lexington Ave., New York, NY 10017
Council of American Building Officials • 2233 Wisconsin Ave. NW, Washington, DC 20007
Door and Hardware Institute • 7711 Old Springhouse Rd., McLean, VA 22102
Ductile Iron Pipe Research Association • 245 Riverchase Parkway E., Birmingham, AL 35244
Electrification Council • 1111 19th St. NW, Washington, DC 20036
Expanded Shale, Clay and Slate Institute • 6218 Montrose Rd., Rockville, MD 20852
Facing Tile Institute • Box 8880, Canton, OH 44711
Fine Hardwoods- American Walnut Association • 5603 W. Raymond St., Indianapolis, IN 46241
Flat Glass Marketing Association • 3310 Harrison, Topeka, KS 66611
Forest Products Laboratory • U.S. Dept. of Agriculture, P.O. Box 5130, Madison, WI 53705
Gypsum Association • 1603 Orrington Ave., Evanston, IL 60201
Hardwood Manufacturers Association • 2831 Airways Blvd., Memphis, TN 38132
Hardwood Plywood Manufacturers Association • 1825 Michael Faraday Dr., Reston, VA 22090
Home Ventilating Institute • 30 W. University Dr., Arlington Hts., IL 60004
IIT Research Institute • 10 W. 35th St., Chicago, IL 60616

Illuminating Engineering Society of North America • 345 E. 47th St., New York, NY 10017
Indiana Limestone Institute of America, Inc. • Suite 400, Stone City Bank Bldg., Bedford, IN 47421
International Conference of Building Officials • 5360 S. Workman Mill Rd., Whittier, CA 90601
Maple Flooring Manufacturers Association • 60 Revere Dr., Northbrook, IL 60062
Marble Institute of America • 33505 State St., Farmington, MI 48024
Metal Lath/Steel Framing Association • 600 S. Federal St., Chicago, IL 60605
Mineral Insulation Manufacturers Association • 1420 King St., Alexandria, VA 22314
NAHB Research Foundation, Inc. • P.O. Box 1627, Rockville, MD 20850
National Bureau of Standards • Center for Building Technology, Washington, DC 20234
National Concrete Masonry Association • 2302 Horse Pen Rd., Herndon, VA 22070
National Electrical Manufacturers Association • 2101 L St. NW, Washington, DC 20037
National Fire Protection Association • 1800 M St. NW, Washington, DC 20036
National Forest Products Association • 1250 Connecticut Ave. NW, Washington, DC 20006
National Hardwood Lumber Association • P.O. Box 34518, Memphis, TN 38184
National Kitchen Cabinet Association • P.O. Box 6830, Falls Church, VA 22046
National Oak Flooring Manufacturers Association • P.O. Box 3009, Memphis, TN 38173
National Paint and Coatings Association • 1500 Rhode Island Ave. NW, Washington, DC 20005
National Particleboard Association • 18928 Premiere Ct., Gaithersburg, MD 20879
National Precast Concrete Association • 825 E. 64th St., Indianapolis, IN 46220
National Research Council of Canada • Ottawa, Canada, KIA 0R6
National Safety Council • 444 N. Michigan Ave., Chicago, IL 60611
National Society of Professional Engineers • 1420 King St., Alexandria, VA 22314
National Terrazzo and Mosaic Association • 3166 Des Plaines Ave., Des Plaines, IL 60018
National Wood Window and Door Association • 1400 E. Touhy Ave., Des Plaines, IL 60018
Northeastern Lumber Manufacturers Association • 4 Fundy Rd., Falmouth, ME 04105
Perlite Institute, Inc. • 600 S. Federal St., Chicago, IL 60605
Plastic Pipe Institute • 355 Lexington Ave., New York, NY 10017
Plywood Research Foundation • P.O. Box 11700, Tacoma, WA 98411
Porcelain Enamel Institute • 1101 Connecticut Ave. NW, Washington, DC 20036
Portland Cement Association • 5420 Old Orchard Rd., Skokie, IL 60076
Resilient Floor Covering Institute • 966 Hungerford Dr., Rockville, MD 20805
Society of American Registered Architects • 1245 S. Highland Ave., Lombard, IL 60148
Society of American Wood Preservers, Inc. • 7297 Lee Hwy., Falls Church, VA 22042
Society of Plastics Industries, Inc. • 1275 K St. NW, Washington, DC 20005
Southern Building Code Congress International • 900 Montclair Rd., Birmingham, AL 35213
Southern Cypress Manufacturers Association • 2831 Airways Blvd., Memphis, TN 38132
Southern Forest Products Association • P.O. Box 52468, New Orleans, LA 70152
Stanford Research Institute • 333 Ravenswood Ave., Menlo Park, CA 94025
Steel Deck Institute • P.O. Box 3812, St. Louis, MO 63122
Steel Door Institute • 14600 Detroit Ave., Cleveland, OH 44107
Steel Joist Institute • 1205 48th Ave. N., Myrtle Beach, SC 29577
Steel Manufacturers Association • 815 Connecticut Ave. NW, Washington, DC 20006
Steel Window Institute • 1230 Keith Bldg, Cleveland, OH 44115
Stucco Manufacturers Association • 14006 Ventura Blvd., Sherman Oaks, CA 91423
Superintendent of Documents • U.S. Government Printing Office, Washington, DC 20402
Tile Council of America • P.O. Box 326, Princeton, NJ 08542
Underwriters' Laboratories, Inc. • 333 Pfingsten Rd., Northbrook, IL 60062
Urban Land Institute • 1090 Vermont Ave. NW, Washington, DC 20005
U.S. Dept. of Housing and Urban Development • 451 Seventh St. SW, Washington, DC 20411
U.S. League of Savings Institutions • 1709 New York Ave. NW, Washington, DC 20006
Vermiculite Association • 600 S. Federal St., Chicago, IL 60605
Western Red Cedar Lumber Association • 1500 Yeon Bldg., Portland, OR 97204
Western Wood Products Association • 1500 Yeon Bldg., Portland, OR 97204
Wire Reinforcement Institute • 8316-A Greensboro Dr., McLean, VA 22102

A.22 GRAPHIC MATERIAL SYMBOLS

These symbols are some of the abstract conventions commonly used in architectural drawings.

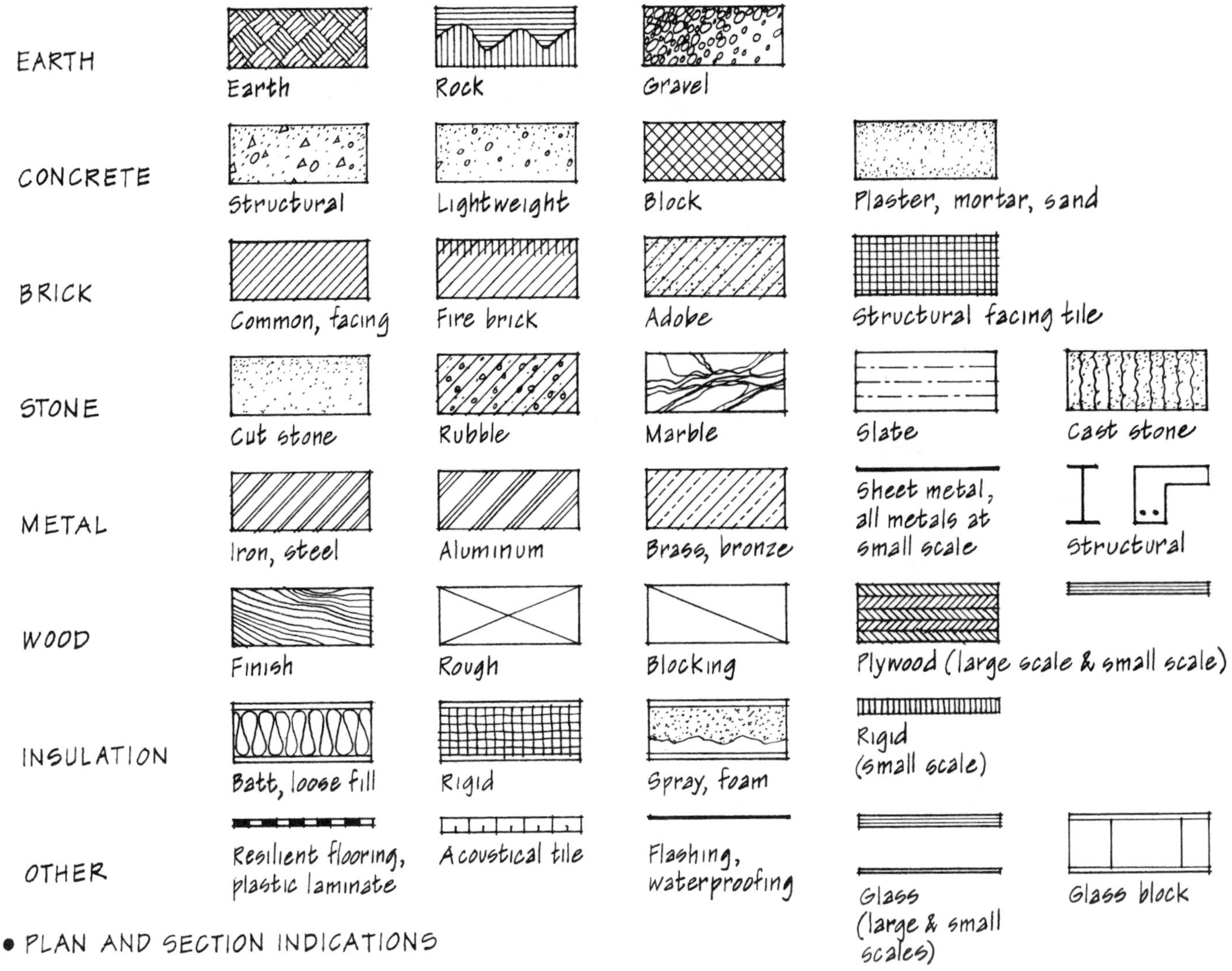

EARTH
Earth
Rock
Gravel
CONCRETE
Structural
Lightweight
Block
Plaster, mortar, sand
BRICK
Common, facing
Fire brick
Adobe
Structural facing tile
STONE
Cut stone
Rubble
Marble
Slate
Cast stone
METAL
Iron, steel
Aluminum
Brass, bronze
Sheet metal, all metals at small scale
Structural
WOOD
Finish
Rough
Blocking
Plywood (large scale & small scale)
INSULATION
Batt, loose fill
Rigid
Spray, foam
Rigid (small scale)
OTHER
Resilient flooring, plastic laminate
Acoustical tile
Flashing, waterproofing
Glass (large & small scales)
Glass block

• PLAN AND SECTION INDICATIONS

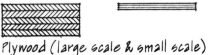

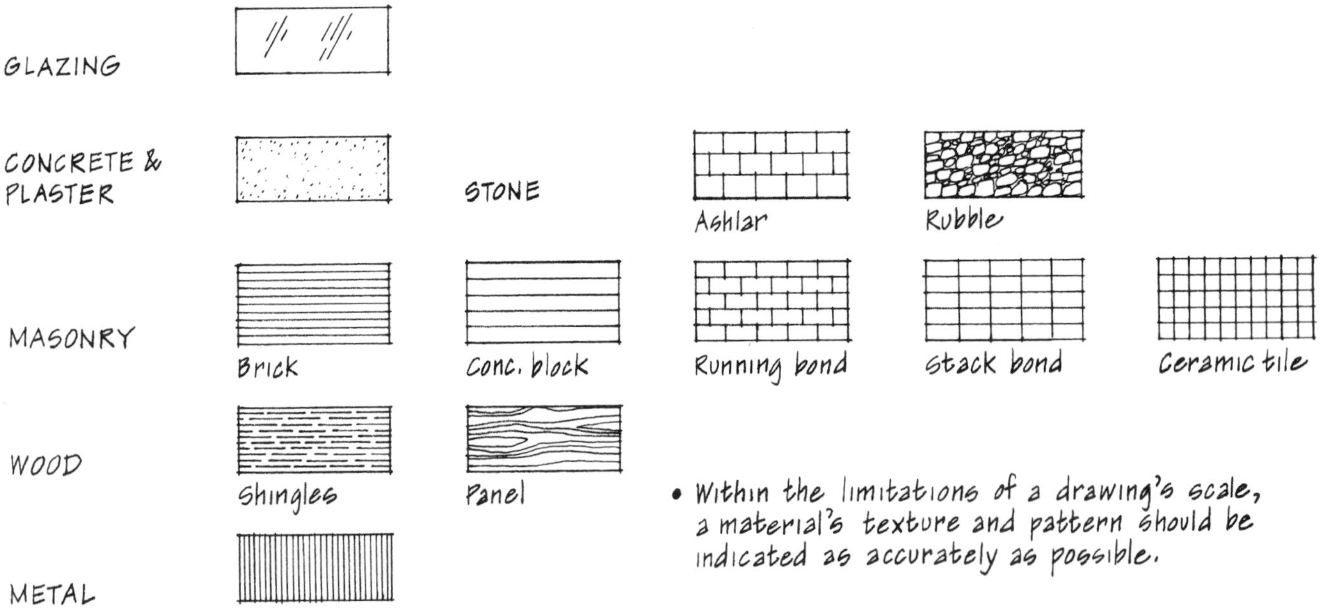

GLAZING
CONCRETE & PLASTER
STONE
Ashlar
Rubble
MASONRY
Brick
Conc. block
Running bond
Stack bond
Ceramic tile
WOOD
Shingles
Panel
METAL

• Within the limitations of a drawing's scale, a material's texture and pattern should be indicated as accurately as possible.

• ELEVATION INDICATIONS

BIBLIOGRAPHY

Allen, Edward. _The Professional Handbook of Building Construction_. Wiley, 1985.

Allen, Edward, and Joseph Iano. _The Architect's Studio Companion_. Wiley, 1989.

Dietz, Albert. _Dwelling House Construction_, 4th Ed. MIT Press, 1974.

Egan, M. David. _Concepts in Architectural Acoustics_. McGraw-Hill, 1972.

Egan, M. David. _Concepts in Thermal Comfort_. Prentice-Hall, 1975.

Friedmann, Arnold, and John Pile, Forrest Wilson. _Interior Design, An Introduction to Architectural Interiors_, 3rd Ed. Elsevier, 1982.

Goetz, Karl-Heinz, and Dieter Hoor, Karl Mohler, Julius Natterer. _Timber Design and Construction Sourcebook_. McGraw-Hill, 1989.

Hart, Henn and Sontag. _Multi-Storey Buildings in Steel_. Granada Publishing, 1978.

Horbostel, Hornung. _Materials and Methods of Contemporary Construction_. 2nd Ed. Prentice-Hall, 1982.

Kauffman, John, and Jack Christensen, eds. _IES Lighting Handbook_. Illuminating Engineering Society, 1972.

Liebing, Ralph, and Mimi Ford Paul. _Architectural Working Drawings_. Wiley, 1977.

McGuinness, William, and Benjamin Stein. _Building Technology: Mechanical and Electrical Equipment for Buildings_. Wiley, 1977.

Olin, Harold B., and John Schmidt, Walter Lewis. _Construction: Principles, Materials and Methods_, 3rd Ed. U.S. League of Savings Institutions, 1983.

Olgyay, Victor. _Design with Climate_. Princeton University Press, 1963.

Parker, Harry, and James Ambrose. _Simplified Design of Reinforced Concrete_, 5th Ed. Wiley, 1984.

Parker, Harry, and James Ambrose. _Simplified Design of Structural Steel_, 5th Ed. Wiley, 1983.

Parker, Harry, and James Ambrose. _Simplified Design of Structural Wood_, 4th Ed. Wiley, 1988.

Ramsey and Sleeper. _Architectural Graphic Standards_, 8th Ed. Wiley, 1988.

Salvadori, Mario, and Robert Heller. _Structure in Architecture, The Building of Buildings_, 3rd Ed. Prentice-Hall, 1986.

Schodek, Daniel. _Structures_. Prentice-Hall, 1980.

MODEL CODES, STANDARDS, AND SPONSORING ORGANIZATIONS

ASTM Standards and Specifications
    American Society for Testing and Materials

Basic Building Code

Basic Fire Prevention Code

Basic Plumbing Code
    Building Officials and Code Administrators International, Inc.

Fire Prevention Code

National Building Code
    American Insurance Association

Life Safety Code

National Electric Code
    National Fire Protection Association

National Plumbing Code
    American Society of Mechanical Engineers

Southern Standard Building Code
    Southern Building Code Congress

Underwriters' Laboratories, Inc. Building Materials List
    Underwriters' Laboratories, Inc.

Uniform Building Code
    International Conference of Building Officials

Uniform Plumbing Code
    International Association of Plumbing and Mechanical Officials

INDEX

Best Selling Backlist By Ching

Drawing
A Creative Process

By Francis D.K. Ching,
Ching Design Associates

Drawing, A Creative Process demonstrates the intriguing interplay among seeing, visualization, and expression through drawing. Ching shows how to unlock the imagination in rendering to tap new powers of creativity. Ching reveals how to convey an idea, action, process, or relationship; alter an observed image to match what one wants to see; and communicate complex subjects with a simple drawing or series of drawings.

210 pages, paper, more than 400 illustrations, ISBN 0-442-31818-9 (1989) $23.95

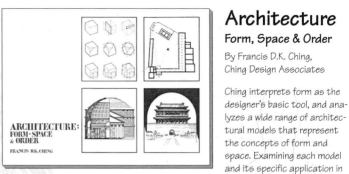

Architecture
Form, Space & Order

By Francis D.K. Ching,
Ching Design Associates

Ching interprets form as the designer's basic tool, and analyzes a wide range of architectural models that represent the concepts of form and space. Examining each model and its specific application in history, the author demonstrates the timelessness of basic architectural elements and principles. Crystal-clear illustrations and in-depth discussions cover point, line, plane, volume, proportion, scale circulation, and the interdependence of form and space.

350 pages, paper, Illustrations, ISBN 0-442-21535-5 (1979) $27.95

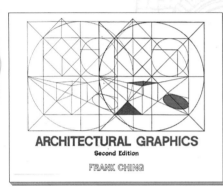

Architectural Graphics
Second Edition

By Francis D.K. Ching,
Ching Design Associates

In this book, Ching emphasizes the development of better mental and manual skills to enhance your approach to graphic communication. He explains more precise ways of using line weight variation and tonal values to show depth; paraline drawings to show cutaway views of building interiors; sloping lines to offer perspective and include reflections in interior spaces, and a host of other practical illustration and composition skills. A large selection of line drawing demonstrates each method presented.

192 pages, paper, 200 line drawings, ISBN 0-442-21864-8 (1985) $23.95

Home Renovation

By Francis D.K. Ching,
Ching Design Associates,
and Dale E. Miller

This detailed yet accessible book fully explains and illustrates how to transform any home into a more functional, comfortable, and pleasing environment. Practical steps are given for documenting the condition of a home and evaluating current and future needs. You will find out how to improve existing space through the use of light, color, door and window modifications, wall rearrangements, and furnishings. Also covered is how to convert attics, basements, and garages.

338 pages, paper, numerous illustrations, ISBN 0-442-21592-4 (1983) $27.95

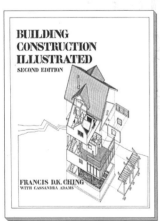

Building Construction Illustrated
Second Edition

By Francis D.K. Ching,
Ching Design Associates, and
Cassandra Adams, Research Consultant

The volume's organization follows the typical design process—from selection of the building site to finish work and beyond—and coverage of systems and technology no longer commonly used has been streamlined.

400 pages, paper, 380 line drawings,
ISBN 0-442-23498-8 (1991) $25.95

Interior Design Illustrated

By Francis D.K. Ching,
Ching Design Associates

In this beautifully illustrated work, Ching explores how basic structural elements and systems combine to form our interior environments, and considers the factors that affect their design, formation, and use. Discussions on windows, stairs and doors, and environmental systems such as HVAC, acoustics, water and electricity are included, Also examined are principles concerning the use of color, texture, and light, and illustrates a full range of modern furniture styles.

320 pages, paper, 300 line drawings, ISBN 0-442-21537-1 (1987) $27.95